W 59.

D1263955

EZRA POUND: THE CRITICAL HERITAGE

THE CRITICAL HERITAGE SERIES

GENERAL EDITOR: B. C. SOUTHAM, M.A., B.LITT. (OXON.)
Formerly Department of English, Westfield College, University of London

For a list of books in the series see the back end paper

*PS 3531
082
2647*

EZRA POUND

THE CRITICAL HERITAGE

Edited by
ERIC HOMBERGER
School of English and American Studies
University of East Anglia

MAR – 2 1979

ROUTLEDGE & KEGAN PAUL: LONDON AND BOSTON

205921

First published 1972
by Routledge & Kegan Paul Ltd
Broadway House, 68–74 Carter Lane,
London EC4V 5EL and
9 Park Street,
Boston, Mass. 02108, U.S.A.
© *Eric Homberger 1972*
No part of this book may be reproduced in
any form without permission from the
publisher, except for the quotation of brief
passages in criticism
ISBN 0 7100 7260 0

Printed in Great Britain
by W & J Mackay Limited, Chatham

FOR JUDY

General Editor's Preface

The reception given to a writer by his contemporaries and near-contemporaries is evidence of considerable value to the student of literature. On one side we learn a great deal about the state of criticism at large and in particular about the development of critical attitudes towards a single writer; at the same time, through private comments in letters, journals or marginalia, we gain an insight upon the tastes and literary thought of individual readers of the period. Evidence of this kind helps us to understand the writer's historical situation, the nature of his immediate reading-public, and his response to these pressures.

The separate volumes in the *Critical Heritage Series* present a record of this early criticism. Clearly, for many of the highly productive and lengthily reviewed nineteenth- and twentieth-century writers, there exists an enormous body of material; and in these cases the volume editors have made a selection of the most important views, significant for their intrinsic critical worth or for their representative quality—perhaps even registering incomprehension!

For earlier writers, notably pre-eighteenth century, the materials are much scarcer and the historical period has been extended, sometimes far beyond the writer's lifetime, in order to show the inception and growth of critical views which were initially slow to appear.

In each volume the documents are headed by an Introduction, discussing the material assembled and relating the early stages of the author's reception to what we have come to identify as the critical tradition. The volumes will make available much material which would otherwise be difficult of access and it is hoped that the modern reader will be thereby helped towards an informed understanding of the ways in which literature has been read and judged.

B.C.S.

Contents

ACKNOWLEDGMENTS   *page* xvii
ABBREVIATIONS   xix
INTRODUCTION   I
NOTE ON THE TEXT   34

Meeting Ezra Pound

1 WILLIAM CARLOS WILLIAMS, March 1904   35
2 EDWARD THOMAS, May, June, December 1909   36
3 D. H. LAWRENCE, November 1909   38
4 W. B. YEATS, December 1909   39
5 T. S. ELIOT, 1909–10   40
6 HARRIET MONROE, 1910   41

A Lume Spento (June 1908)

7 Unsigned notice, *Book News Monthly*, May 1909   42

Personae (April 1909)

8 Unsigned review, *Evening Standard and St. James's Gazette*,
   April 1909   43
9 W. L. COURTNEY, unsigned review, *Daily Telegraph*, April
   1909   44
10 F. S. FLINT, review, *New Age*, May 1909   46
11 EDWARD THOMAS, 'A New Note in Verse', *Daily
   Chronicle*, June 1909   48
12 EDWARD THOMAS, from 'Two Poets', *English Review*,
   June 1909   50
13 Unsigned review, *Observer*, June 1909   53
14 Unsigned review, *Bookman* (London), July 1909   54
15 Unsigned review, 'Heresy and Some Poetry', *Nation*
   (London), August 1909   55
16 RUPERT BROOKE, review, *Cambridge Review*, December
   1909   58

17 A new poet makes his debut; unsigned notice, *Bookman*
(London), July 1909   60

Exultations (October 1909)

18 EDWARD THOMAS, 'The Newest Poet', *Daily Chronicle*,
November 1909   61
19 Unsigned review, *Spectator*, December 1909   62
20 Unsigned review, *Observer*, December 1909   63
21 F. S. FLINT, 'Verse', *New Age*, January 1910   64
22 Unsigned review, *Nation* (London), March 1910   66

The Spirit of Romance (June 1910)

23 Unsigned notice, *Nation* (New York), March 1910   67
24 EDWARD THOMAS, review, *Morning Post*, August 1910   68

Provença (November 1910)

25 FLOYD DELL, review, *Chicago Evening Post*, January 1911   70
26 H. L. MENCKEN, review, *Smart Set*, April 1911   73
27 Reverberations in America, December 1910   75
28 J. B. YEATS to his son, February 1911   76

Canzoni (July 1911)

29 CHARLES GRANVILLE, 'Modern Poetry', *Eye-Witness*,
August 1911   77
30 Unsigned review, *Westminster Gazette*, August 1911   80
31 G. D. H. COLE, initialled review, *Isis*, November 1911   82
32 J. C. SQUIRE, review, *New Age*, December 1911   83
33 F. S. FLINT, review, *Poetry Review*, January 1912   84

Sonnets and Ballate of Guido Cavalcanti (April 1912)

34 ARUNDEL DEL RE, review, *Poetry Review*, July 1912   86
35 JOHN BAILEY, unsigned review, *The Times Literary
Supplement*, November 1912   89

Ripostes (October 1912)

36 HAROLD CHILD, unsigned review, *The Times Literary
Supplement*, December 1912   94
37 F. S. FLINT, review, *Poetry and Drama*, March 1913   95

CONTENTS

38 Ezra Pound in Chicago, September 1912–April 1913   98

39 Pound and *Poetry*: a letter to *Nation* (New York), April
    1913   100

40 Pound and *Poetry*: WALLACE RICE in *Dial*, May 1913   101

41 Pound and *Poetry*: HARRIET MONROE replies, May 1913   106

Cathay (April 1915)

42 FORD MADOX HUEFFER, 'From China to Peru', *Outlook*,
    June 1915   108

43 A. R. ORAGE on the thought and form of *Cathay*, 1915   110

44 CARL SANDBURG, 'The Work of Ezra Pound', *Poetry*,
    February 1916   112

45 WILLIAM MARION REEDY on the position of Pound,
    February and July 1916   117

Gaudier Brzeska: A Memoir (April 1916)

46 Unsigned review, *Dial*, August 1916   119

Lustra (October 1916)

47 The problem of getting published, 1: a postcard from Elkin
    Mathews's reader, 1916   121

48 The problem of getting published, 2: the memorandum of
    agreement, 1916   123

49 KATE BUSS, 'Ezra Pound . . . his Rare Chinese Quality',
    Boston Evening Transcript, December 1916   124

50 A poet in rebellion against emotion, December 1917   126

51 LOUIS UNTERMEYER on a poet in pantomime, December
    1920   128

52 BABETTE DEUTSCH, 'Ezra Pound, Vorticist', *Reedy's Mirror*,
    December 1917   131

53 MAXWELL BODENHEIM, 'A Poet's Opinion', *Little Review*,
    June 1917   137

54 J. B. YEATS to John Quinn, November 1917   139

55 JOSEPH CONRAD to John Quinn, February 1918   139

56 A. R. ORAGE on *Ezra Pound: His Metric and Poetry*, July 1918   140

Pavannes and Divisions (June 1918)

57 LOUIS UNTERMEYER, 'Ezra Pound—Proseur', *New
    Republic*, August 1918   142

58 CONRAD AIKEN, 'A Pointless Pointillist', *Dial*, October 1918   145

59 EMANUEL CARNEVALI, 'Irritation', *Poetry*, January 1920   148

60 W. G. HALE on Pound's failings as a Latinist, April 1919   155

Quia Pauper Amavi (October 1919)

61 A. R. ORAGE on Pound, Propertius and 'decadence', *Readers and Writers (1917–1921)*, 1922   158

62 Grumbles about the 'Homage', *New Age*, November 1919   160

63 Pound's defence of the 'Homage', December 1919   163

64 ROBERT NICHOLS, 'Poetry and Mr. Pound', *Observer*, January 1920   165

65 A reply from WYNDHAM LEWIS, January 1920   168

66 Pound defends the 'Homage' again, January 1920   169

67 JOHN GOULD FLETCHER on the decline and fall of an expatriate, May 1920   171

68 HAROLD MONRO, from *Some Contemporary Poets*, 1920   174

69 MAY SINCLAIR, 'The Reputation of Ezra Pound', *North American Review*, May 1920   177

Instigations (April 1920)

70 VAN WYCK BROOKS on Pound as expatriate, June 1920   186

71 H. L. MENCKEN, notice, *Smart Set*, August 1920   190

72 'W. C. BLUM' [Dr James Sibley Watson], 'Super School-master', *Dial*, October 1920   191

Hugh Selwyn Mauberley (June 1920)

73 Unsigned review, *The Times Literary Supplement*, July 1920   194

74 EDWIN MUIR, review, *New Age*, October 1922   194

Umbra: The Early Poems of Ezra Pound (June 1920)

75 EDWIN MUIR, review, *New Age*, July 1920   196

76 A. R. ORAGE on Pound's departure from London, January 1921   199

Poems 1918–21 (December 1921)

77 MAXWELL BODENHEIM, 'The Isolation of Carved Metal', *Dial*, January 1922   203

78 JOHN PEALE BISHOP, 'The Intelligence of Poets', *Vanity Fair*, January 1922   207

79 BRIAN HOWARD on Pound's 'clean, white spirit of
   disinfection', March 1922   209
80 HARRIET MONROE, a retrospective view, May 1925   211

A Draft of XVI Cantos (January 1925)

81 GLENWAY WESCOTT, review, *Dial*, December 1925   215

Personae: The Collected Poems of Ezra Pound (December 1926)

82 FORD MADOX FORD: 'Ezra', *New York Herald Tribune
   Books*, January 1927   218
83 WILLIAM CARLOS WILLIAMS on Pound's exile, February
   1927   224
84 R. P. BLACKMUR on Pound's 'Variety of Masks', April 1927   227

Selected Poems (November 1928)

85 JOHN GOULD FLETCHER, the neglected assessment, April
   1929   229
86 HENRY BAMFORD PARKES on the theories and influence of
   Pound, December 1932   239
87 A supervision with Dr Leavis on 'Mauberley', 1933   243

A Draft of XXX Cantos (August 1930)

88 DUDLEY FITTS, 'Music Fit for the Odes', *Hound and Horn*,
   Winter 1931   246
89 EDA LOU WALTON on some types of obscurity, April 1933   256
90 GEOFFREY GRIGSON, 'The Methodism of Ezra Pound', *New
   Verse*, October 1933   259
91 D. G. BRIDSON, review, *New English Weekly*, October 1933   264
92 MARIANNE MOORE, review, *Criterion*, April 1934   269

Guido Cavalcanti Rime (January 1932)

93 ETIENNE GILSON, review, *Criterion*, October 1932   273
94 JOHN SPARROW, doubts about Pound and 'Mauberley', 1934   280

Make It New (September 1934)

95 G. M. YOUNG, review, *Observer*, October 1934   285
96 G. K. CHESTERTON, review, *Listener*, November 1934   287
97 BONAMY DOBRÉE, review, *Criterion*, April 1935   288

Eleven New Cantos XXXI–XLI (October 1934)

98 PHILIP BLAIR RICE, 'The Education of Ezra Pound', *Nation* (New York), November 1934   292

99 JOHN CROWE RANSOM, 'Pound and the Broken Tradition', review, *Saturday Review of Literature*, January 1935   294

100 GEORGE BARKER, review, *Criterion*, July 1935   297

Homage to Sextus Propertius
(November 1934)

101 STEPHEN SPENDER, review, *Spectator*, December 1934   300

102 JOHN SPEIRS, 'Mr. Pound's Propertius', *Scrutiny*, March 1935   302

The Fifth Decad of Cantos (June 1937)

103 STEPHEN SPENDER, notice, *Left Review*, July 1937   309

104 EDWIN MUIR, review, *Criterion*, October 1937   309

105 DELMORE SCHWARTZ, 'Ezra Pound's Very Useful Labors', *Poetry*, March 1938   311

106 JAMES LAUGHLIN IV, 'Ezra Pound's Propertius', *Sewanee Review*, October–December 1938   320

107 ARCHIBALD MACLEISH on Pound's revolutionary modernism, *Atlantic Monthly*, June 1939   330

Guide to Kulchur (July 1938)

108 PHILIP MAIRET, review, *Criterion*, January 1939   332

109 DUDLEY FITTS on a bad boy strutting and shocking, *Saturday Review*, May 1939   335

110 WILLIAM CARLOS WILLIAMS on Pound's great risk, *New Republic*, June 1939   336

Cantos LII–LXXI (January 1940)

111 'H. H.' [JAMES LAUGHLIN IV] and 'S. D.' [DELMORE SCHWARTZ], *Notes on Ezra Pound's Cantos: Structure and Metric* 1940   338

112 EDWIN MUIR on the Cantos as a political poem, July–December 1940   347

113 RANDALL JARRELL on the deterioration of Pound, December 1940   348

114 ROBERT FITZGERALD, 'Mr. Pound's Good Governors', *Accent*, Winter 1941   351
115 PAUL ROSENFELD, 'The Case of Ezra Pound', *American Mercury*, January 1944   353

The Pisan Cantos (July 1948)

116 ROBERT FITZGERALD, ' "What thou Lovest Well Remains" ', *New Republic*, August 1948   359
117 LOUIS L. MARTZ, review, *Yale Review*, Autumn 1948   364
118 REED WHITTEMORE, review, *Poetry*, November 1948   369
119 WILLIAM CARLOS WILLIAMS, from a review, *Imagi*, spring 1949   371
120 C. M. BOWRA, 'More Cantos from Ezra Pound', *New Statesman and Nation*, September 1949   373
121 RICHARD EBERHART on the character of Pound's work, *Quarterly Review of Literature*, 1949   375
122 JOHN BERRYMAN, 'The Poetry of Ezra Pound', *Partisan Review*, April 1949   388
123 MALCOLM COWLEY, 'The Battle over Ezra Pound', *New Republic*, October 1949   405
124 KATHLEEN RAINE on Pound's Confucius and modern poetry, *New Republic*, March 1952   412
125 RONALD BOTTRALL, 'The Achievement of Ezra Pound', *Adelphi*, May 1952   415

Literary Essays (January 1954)

126 CHARLES TOMLINSON, review, *Spectator*, February 1954   422
127 DONALD DAVIE, 'Instigations to Procedures', *New Statesman and Nation*, March 1954   425
128 W. W. ROBSON, review, *Blackfriars*, April 1954   428
129 ROY FULLER, review, *London Magazine*, May 1954   430

Section: Rock-Drill (March 1956)

130 NOEL STOCK, review, *Meanjin*, March 1956   435
131 RANDALL JARRELL on the extraordinary misuse of extraordinary powers, *Yale Review*, September 1956   438
132 A. ALVAREZ, review, *Observer*, March 1957   441
133 DONALD DAVIE, 'Bed-Rock', *New Statesman and Nation*, March 1957   443

134 PHILIP LARKIN, notice, *Manchester Guardian*, March 1957   444

135 YVOR WINTERS on the Cantos 1956   445

Thrones
96–109 de los Cantares (December 1959)

136 DELMORE SCHWARTZ, 'Ezra Pound and History', *New Republic*, February 1960   447

137 JOHN WAIN, 'The Shadow of an Epic', *Spectator*, March 1960   453

138 DONALD HALL, 'The Cantos in England', *New Statesman and Nation*, March 1960   457

139 W. D. SNODGRASS, review, *Hudson Review*, Spring 1960   461

140 JOHN HOLLOWAY, review, *London Magazine*, June 1960   463

141 LOUIS SIMPSON, 'A Swift Kick in the Rhetoric', *Book Week*, January 1966   465

A Lume Spento and Other Early Poems
(October 1965)

142 PETER LEVI, S. J. on the earliest Pound, *Jubilee*, February 1966   469

143 COLIN FALCK, review, *Encounter*, August 1966   471

144 HAYDEN CARRUTH, 'On a Picture of Ezra Pound', *Poetry*, May 1967   472

Drafts and Fragments of Cantos CX–CXVII
(December 1968)

145 HERBERT LEIBOWITZ, from 'The Muse and the News', *Hudson Review*, Autumn 1969   475

148 DERWENT MAY, review, *Observer*, March 1970   476

APPENDIX: THE PRINTING OF POUND'S WORKS 1908–60   478

BIBLIOGRAPHY   481

INDEX   488

Acknowledgments

I have often been grateful for the conversation and advice of Dr Patrick Parrinder of King's College, Cambridge, and Dr Michael Egan of the University of Lancaster.

Much profitable time during the preparation of this book was spent in the offices of Pound's publishers, Faber & Faber and New Directions. In particular, Mrs Else Lorch, Miss Bonnie Armstrong and Mrs Sarah Gleadell have been very helpful.

For permission to reprint, and for answering queries, acknowledgment is due to Mr Conrad Aiken; Mr A. Alvarez and Curtis Brown Ltd; Professor A. J. Ayer; Mr George Barker; Mr John Berryman and *Partisan Review*, © 1949 *Partisan Review*; Mr Ronald Bottrall; Mr D. G. Bridson; Sir Geoffrey Keynes for Rupert Brooke; Mr Hayden Carruth and *Poetry: A Magazine of Verse*; A. P. Watt & Son for G. K. Chesterton; Mr Leslie Clarke of the University of California Library, Berkeley; Mrs Margaret Cole for G. D. H. Cole; Mr Malcolm Cowley from *New Republic*, 3 October 1949 © 1949 Editorial Publications, reprinted by permission of the magazine and author; Professor Arundel del Re; Professor Donald Davie; Miss Babette Deutsch; Professor Bonamy Dobrée; David Higham Associates Ltd for Mr Ronald Duncan; Mr Richard Eberhart and *Quarterly Review of Literature*; Mr J. A. Edwards of the University of Reading Library; Mr Colin Falck and *Encounter*; Mrs Dudley Fitts, Professor Norman Holmes Pearson and the Estate of Dudley Fitts for Dudley Fitts; Mr Robert Fitzgerald; Mrs Charlie May Fletcher for J. G. Fletcher; Mrs Ianthe Price for F. S. Flint; Professor Roy Fuller; Professor Donald Gallup; Professor Etienne Gilson; Professor D. H. Greene of New York University; Mr Geoffrey Grigson; Mr Thom Gunn; Dr John Holloway and *London Magazine*; Mrs Mary Jarrell for Randall Jarrell; Professor Nicholas Joost; Dr J. T. Boulton and Nottingham University Press for D. H. Lawrence; Mr Philip Larkin; Mr Herbert Leibowitz and *Hudson Review* © 1969 by The Hudson Review, Inc.; Peter Levi, S. J. and John Johnson; Mr Robert Lowell; Professor R. M. Ludwig; Mr Archibald MacLiesh; Philippa MacLiesh of the Society of Authors; Mr Philip Mairet; Professor Louis L. Martz and *Yale Review*; Fr Gervase Mathew; Miss Nest C. Elkin

Mathews for Elkin Mathews; Mr Derwent May; Miss Ann Melsom, Librarian of the *Observer*; Cornell University Press for Mencken's review in *Smart Set* © 1968 by Cornell University; Mr Arthur Miller of the Newberry Library; Mrs Willa Muir and the Hogarth Press for Edwin Muir; *Nation*; *New Republic*; Mr D. S. Dyerson and *New Statesman and Nation*; *New York Times* © 1933 by the New York Times Company, reprinted by permission; *Observer*; Artemis Press and Mrs A. R. Orage for A. R. Orage; Professor H. B. Parkes; *Poetry*; Princess Mary de Rachewiltz; Miss Kathleen Raine and *New Republic*; Mrs Kathryn C. Rice and *Nation* for Philip Blair Rice; Professor W. W. Robson; Otterburg, Steindler, Houston & Rosen, Inc. and the Estate of Edna Bryner Schwab for Paul Rosenfeld; Mrs Lilian Steichen Sandburg for Carl Sandburg; *Saturday Review*; Professor Louis Simpson; Mr W. D. Snodgrass and *Hudson Review*; Warden John Sparrow; *Spectator*; Mr John Speirs and Cambridge University Press; Mr Stephen Spender; Mr Noel Stock; Mrs W. T. Symons; Miss Myfanwy Thomas for Edward Thomas; Professor R. G. Thomas; *The Times Literary Supplement*; Mr Louis Untermeyer and *New Republic*; Mr Rayner Unwin; Mr John Wain and *Spectator*; Dr James Sibley Watson; Mr Glenway Wescott and Harold Ober Associates; Mr Reed Whittemore; William Carlos Williams: uncollected materials. All rights reserved. Reprinted by permission of New Directions Publishing Corp., Inc., agents for Mrs W. C. Williams; Van Wyck Brooks: from *Freeman*, 16 June 1920, reprinted by permission of E. P. Dutton & Co., Inc.; Christy & Moore, Ltd for J. B. Yeats; Mrs Janet Lewis Winters for Yvor Winters; Guardian Newspapers Ltd.

Previously uncollected and/or unpublished material by Ezra Pound: copyright © 1971 by Ezra Pound. Reprinted by permission of Dorothy Pound, Committee for Ezra Pound, New Directions Publishing Corporation, New York, agent.

It has proved difficult in certain cases to locate the proprietors of copyright material. However all possible care has been taken to trace ownership of the selections included and to make full acknowledgment for their use.

Abbreviations

ALS	*A Lume Spento and Other Early Poems.* London, 1965.
Bibliography	Donald Gallup, *A Bibliography of Ezra Pound,* second impression, corrected. London, 1969.
Cantos	*The Cantos of Ezra Pound.* New collected edition. London, 1964. Contains Cantos 1–109.
CSP	*Collected Shorter Poems.* Second edition. London, 1968. A 'slightly enlarged' edition of *Personae.* London, 1952.
Kulchur	*Guide to Kulchur.* Norfolk, Connecticut, [1938].
Letters	*The Letters of Ezra Pound 1907–1941,* edited by D. D. Paige. London, 1951.
Life	Noel Stock, *The Life of Ezra Pound.* London, Routledge & Kegan Paul, 1970.
LE	*Literary Essays of Ezra Pound,* edited with an introduction by T. S. Eliot. London, 1954.
Pound/Joyce	*Pound/Joyce: The Letters of Ezra Pound to James Joyce, with Pound's Essays on Joyce,* edited with a commentary by Forrest Read. New York, [1967].
Translations	*The Translations of Ezra Pound,* edited with an introduction by Hugh Kenner. London, 1953.
YL	Unpublished letters by Pound in the Yale University Library. These were collected and transcribed by D. D. Paige. Each sheet of the typescript is numbered.

Introduction

A volume in this series about a living writer requires a word of explanation. Ezra Pound's great longevity makes it possible to think in terms of a 'tradition' or 'heritage' of critical thought having developed during the long course of his literary career. Our own perspective on this material is inevitably distorted: possibly some of the criticism of Pound which seems hopelessly irrelevant today may at some future time be a stimulant to further thought. With this in mind, this anthology has been compiled with the intention of representing the variety of comment on Pound's work. Material from newspapers and periodicals has been preferred to passages or chapters from books: the inaccessibility and ephemeral nature of the publications, the less formal quality of the writing, seemed to argue for this emphasis. On occasion, assumptions and tones appear which either have not been adequately represented in books or have not been preserved elsewhere.

The quantity of potential material was, of course, very great, and the selections have nearly all been taken from English and American sources. Pound made a considerable impression in Europe (he lived in Paris and then Rapallo after 1921), and there is a body of criticism on his work in French, Italian and German. This material is discussed briefly in the Bibliography: it seemed better served by a study or an anthology in its own right. Not all of the best or most influential essays could be included: a number are currently in print and widely available (see Bibliography); some amusing, indeed foolish things have elbowed their way among what is, hopefully, more august company.

Though born in Idaho, Pound was raised and educated in a suburb of Philadelphia. By most standards he was a sophisticated, well-travelled (spending the summers of 1890 and 1902 touring Europe), well-educated young man when he took his Ph.B. in Romance literature at Hamilton College in June 1905. He toyed briefly with the idea of a career in the United States Consular Service, or of studying law—possibly with a little encouragement from his genteel mother—but in the end he did an M.A. in Romance literature at the University of Pennsylvania. Pound had a brief, inglorious taste of academic life in the autumn and winter of 1907–8, when he lectured at Wabash College in Crawfordsville, Indiana.

By 8 February, after being fired for 'Bohemian' behaviour, he was once again bound for Europe.

He had begun to assemble a maiden book of verse while still in Indiana. None of the established American magazines, such as *Scribner's* or the *Century*, would publish the poems he submitted (a source of great annoyance which eventually resulted in his oft-repeated anger at American editors and magazines: *'Phasellus Ille'* is an early gloss), nor could a commercial publisher be persuaded to do a first book by an unknown poet. Since there was, however, the possibility that a commercial publisher would do a reprint—if favourable notices of a private edition were put before them—Pound had printed at his own expense in Venice in June 1908 *A Lume Spento* in an edition of a hundred copies. He sent several home to his father in Philadelphia with suggestions about possible reviewers. Review copies of his pamphlet were sent to newspapers and magazines in London, where Pound himself planned to travel after leaving Venice. His reception was planned with characteristic persistence, as though Pound knew that the path to Parnassus lay through the right clubs in London.

One brief notice appeared in a London newspaper, the *Evening Standard and St. James's Gazette*, in which *A Lume Spento* was described as[1]

Wild and haunting stuff, absolutely poetic, original, imaginative, passionate, and spiritual. Those who do not consider it crazy may well consider it inspired. Coming after the trite and decorous verse of most of our decorous poets, this poet seems like a minstrel of Provence at a Suburban musical evening . . . The unseizable magic of poetry is in the queer paper volume, and words are no good in describing it.

A review appeared in New York by Ella Wheeler Wilcox (1850–1919), a popular, sentimental rhymester who had been a friend of Pound's father:

A LUME SPENTO ('With Tapers Quenched') is the title of a slender little booklet of verse which came to me from Venice, Italy, the other day. This is the dedication: 'This book is dedicated to such as love the same beauty that I love, somewhat after my own fashion: and In Memoriam of William Brooke Smith, Painter and Dreamer of Dreams'.

The name of the poet is 'Ezra Pound' and when I realize that this poet is grown to the age of manhood it makes my own youth seem far and far away; for somewhere among my souvenirs of a Springtime of life there is a little tintype picture of several youths and maidens: and the father of this poet is among the number and so am I.

And when I stop and remember that my own wee son, who tarried so short a time on earth, would be also mangrown were he here: and he too might be writing verses, even as the son of my friend of long ago.

And so, with more than the interest of an older writer in a younger singer, I give these strange, and weird, and new songlets a setting here, that 'those who love what he loves after his fashion' [sic] may read . . . .

She then quotes thirty-four lines of verse from 'La Fraisne', 'Ballad for Gloom' and 'Threnos', and ends: 'Success to you, young singer in Venice! Success to "With Tapers Quenched".'[2] There was no joy to be had from this sort of recognition, and Pound was annoyed, though perhaps as much by the inaccurate quotation of a poem as by her tone. It was at least a little publicity ,'for which I should be glad if I made patent medicine instead of poetry' (Stock, *Life*, p. 55).

LONDON: THE FIRST CAREER 1908–9

When Pound arrived in London in September 1908 Swinburne and Meredith, survivors of another age, were still alive. Hardy had renounced fiction for poetry. Yeats now looked back upon *The Wind Among the Reeds* (1899) as signifying an age, a phase in the growth of his style, which was now past. It is better for a poet today ('Adam's Curse') to

> go down upon your marrow bones
> And scrub a kitchen pavement, or break stones
> For an old pauper, in all kinds of weather;
> For to articulate sweet sounds together
> Is to work harder than all these. . . .

Yeats, then, was leaving the nineties behind. But when Pound came to the shop of Elkin Mathews, bookseller and publisher, he was himself a disciple, albeit an extremely talented one, of the poets of the 'tragic generation'. Mathews (1851–1921), at once impressed by Pound's work, had a minor, but interesting, place in the history of the nineties. Initially in partnership with John Lane, and then as an independent publisher, Mathews had published *The Book of the Rhymers' Club* (1892), *The Yellow Book* (1894–7), and titles by Arthur Symons, Carman and Hovey (whose *Vagabondia* was a favourite of Pound), Selwyn Image, Lionel Johnson and Ernest Dowson. He had used Aubrey Beardsley as an illustrator. On the recommendation of Symons he had published James Joyce's *Chamber Music* in 1907, and he was the publisher of Yeats. John Quinn, a wealthy American lawyer and art patron, came to London in

1904 to learn from Mathews the details of Lionel Johnson's death. His taste seems to have been strongly though narrowly developed, and in the Aesthetes he found poetry which he understood and enjoyed to the extent that he felt ill at ease with anything which departed strongly from it. *A Lume Spento*, with its rich sense of tradition and manifest respect for the Aesthetes much in evidence, caught his fancy, and within a few months Mathews became Pound's publisher.

His relations with Pound during the rest of his life were a paradigm, in a sense, of Pound's relations with Edwardian literary taste. He published eight titles by Pound, but was frequently at a loss over what to make of him. It was the Jesuits, Pound confided to Kate Buss in 1916, who had prevented his *Catholic Anthology*, containing five poems by T. S. Eliot, from being reviewed. Mathews couldn't understand why Pound insisted on the title: 'Why, why will you needlessly irritate people?' (*Letters*, p. 121). In May 1916 he and Pound waged a bitter battle over *Lustra*. D. H. Lawrence's *The Rainbow* had been prosecuted in 1915, and Harriet Shaw Weaver had gone from one publisher to another in the winter and spring of 1916 with the manuscript of Joyce's *A Portrait of the Artist as a Young Man*. Under English law the printer as well as the publisher was liable, and Elkin Mathews was convinced that ruinous prosecution would follow if the whole of Pound's manuscript was published. He saw no alternative but to ask for a number of phrases, lines and whole poems to be deleted. Pound, never the most politic of men (though he knew well enough what had happened to Lawrence, and of Joyce's difficulty), felt Mathews was being bloody minded and said so—to anyone who would listen. In the end their disagreement was settled, grudgingly, when Mathews went ahead with a trade and an unexpurgated edition of *Lustra* at his own expense (Nos 47–8).

A further breach occurred in 1917 when Mathews found several excuses not to publish T. S. Eliot's first collection of poetry, *Prufrock and Other Observations*. Mathews had, on Pound's recommendation, published W. C. Williams's *The Tempers* in 1913; but genuinely advanced literature was more than he could take. In 1919 Pound offered Mathews the manuscript of *Quia Pauper Amavi*, but when he suggested the deletion of the 'Homage to Sextus Propertius' and 'Moeurs Contemporaines', Pound refused and went to Harriet Shaw Weaver. With her agreement, and the financial backing of John Quinn, *Quia Pauper Amavi* appeared with the imprint of the Egoist Press. Pound's connection with Mathews ended in June 1920 on the publication of

Umbra, a selection from his early work. With Mathews's death a year later his ties with commercial publishers in London were suddenly at an end. It was not until T. S. Eliot joined the staff of Faber & Gwyer that he was once again published in England. At the outset of his career, Mathews was of great usefulness to Pound; but as he outgrew his earlier verse Mathews became less and less sympathetic—and of course less and less useful. But Mathews remained, even well into the war, a focus of aspirations for young poets: 'All I knew about Mr. Mathews', wrote Herbert Read, 'was that he had been publishing the kind of poetry I was interested in'.[3]

Mathews played an early and crucial role in promoting Pound's reputation. He took the young poet to a meeting of the Poets Club on 23 February 1909, at which Pound listened to Bernard Shaw and Hilaire Belloc hold forth and generally thought the evening a 'bore'. Mathews introduced him to a wide variety of writers, such as Laurence Binyon, the poet who was also a keeper at the British Museum where Pound was working every day. He was also introduced to Maurice Hewlett, the novelist, and to May Sinclair, who in turn introduced Pound to Ford Madox Hueffer (later Ford), the novelist, poet, and editor of the *English Review*. Within a few months of arriving in London he had also met Ernest Rhys, who made possible the publication of *The Spirit of Romance* in 1910; T. Sturge Moore, a minor poet, critic, book designer and friend of Yeats; and the art critic P. G. Konody.

Pound gave copies of *A Quinzaine for This Yule* to many of his new acquaintances, and was soon able to write home that it was 'getting into the right hands'. Edward Dowden and Henry Newbolt wrote to him appreciatively about the small pamphlet. When *Personae* appeared in mid-April Pound was not 'unknown' and the reviews were extremely promising. W. L. Courtney, an influential bookman and editor, praised the 'thread of true beauty' of *Personae* in the *Daily Telegraph* of 23 April (No. 9). Pound's 'freshness of inspiration' was noted in the *Bookman* of July (No. 14). Rupert Brooke, who was then twenty-two, pointed to Pound's potential greatness in the *Cambridge Review* of 2 December. (No. 16), but he also complained about 'the dangerous influence of Whitman' and others noticed Pound's uneven style, his fondness for archaisms and strange verse forms. There was much about *Personae* which smelled of the lamp. The one serious attack on it, in the *Nation* of 28 August (No. 15), was too pompous and blimpish to be taken seriously; Pound wrote home that it was useful for publicity (YL, 115). The emphasis of one early reviewer stands out: F. S. Flint writing in the *New Age* of 27 May (No. 10) was alone in his praise of Pound for 'showing sufficient craft and artistry'. Few critics in 1908 talked in terms of craft or artistry, or thought of poetry as something consciously made, whose procedures should be subject to careful scrutiny: critics were looking for 'sentiment', 'spirit', 'vision', 'sincerity', and 'taste' (as in the mouth). The most important review was that by Edward Thomas in the *English Review* in June (No. 12). Thomas, then thirty-one and a freelance essayist and critic, praised *Personae* with enthusiasm. Approval in the journal which printed Hardy, James, Conrad, Galsworthy, W. H. Hudson, and Wells was approval at an exalted level indeed. It was this review which 'made' Pound's debut in London. A paragraph in the issue of *Punch* for 23 June testifies to his ascending star:[4]

Mr. Welkin Mark [Elkin Mathews] (exactly opposite Long Jane's [John Lane]) begs to announce that he has secured for the English market the palpitating works of the new Montana (U.S.A.) poet, Mr. Ezekiel Ton, who is the most remarkable thing in poetry since Robert Browning. Mr. Ton, who has left America to reside for a while in London and impress his personality on English editors, publishers and readers, is by far the newest poet going, whatever other advertisements may say. He has succeeded, where all others have failed, in evolving a blend of the imagery of the unfettered West, the vocabulary of Wardour Street, and the sinister abandon of Borgiac Italy.

That Pound was romantically handsome and photogenic did not hinder his progress. Gossip-column material appeared in the *Bookman* in July (No. 17), illustrated by a photograph of the young poet in a high collar, his square jaw setting off a great mound of curly hair and piercing eyes. The American literary press was not slow to follow. 'An American Poet Discovered in England' announced the *Literary Digest* of 27 November 1909 above an article which quoted extensively from Thomas's review and from *Punch*.

Mathews was quick to follow up the success of *Personae* with a second collection, *Exultations*, on 25 October 1909. Perhaps one should say *critical* success: despite the splendid reviews, *Personae* had not shown a profit by 9 September (YL, 118). Edward Thomas picked up the note of Pound's fashionableness in a review titled 'The Newest Poet' in the *Daily Chronicle* of 23 November (No. 18). He could now only report an emptiness, a 'turbulent opacity', where before he felt Pound had been struggling to express something individual. Thomas concluded that Pound was 'so pestered with possible ways of saying a thing that at present we must be content to pronounce his condition still interesting— perhaps promising—certainly distressing'. A reviewer in the Birmingham

Daily Post experienced a similar difficulty: 'we can find nothing but evidence of a highly interesting personality unable to express itself' (Stock, *Life*, p. 75). What had seemed charming and unusual in *Personae* was, on second glance, merely annoying. One poem at least was a notable success with the reviewers: the 'Ballad of the Goodly Fere'. Edward Marsh wanted to include it in *Georgian Poetry*.[5] T. E. Lawrence thought 'the "Goodly Fere" is by far his best thing'.[6] A reviewer of *Canzoni* in *Granta*, an undergraduate magazine at Cambridge, commented 'Perhaps there is, in this book, nothing so fine as the splendid "Ballad of the Goodly Fire[sic]", which to our mind, besides being Mr. Pound's masterpiece, stands among the very best of modern religious poems' (14 October 1911). W. B. Yeats told an audience in Chicago that the poem was of 'permanent value'.[7] With this poem Pound became a *popular* poet.

AMERICA 1910

In November 1909 R. B. Cunninghame Graham, the Scottish writer, linked Pound's name with Conrad, Hudson, Galsworthy, James and George Moore as being among 'our best writers'.[8] He was widely regarded as one of the most promising younger writers. While in London Pound had lectured at the Regent Street Polytechnic on mediaeval and Romance literature, and on the suggestion of Ernest Rhys some of his lecture materials were published as *The Spirit of Romance* in London and New York in 1910. Thus Pound was introduced to the American reading public initially as a scholar. 'A charming piece of appreciative criticism' remarked the *Independent* (17 November 1910), but for the reviewer in the New York version of the *Nation* the bits of 'really good comment' hardly seemed worth hunting for (No. 23). The *English Review*, no longer edited by Hueffer, complained in a brief note that 'Mr. Pound retains the stupid little affectations that mar much of his poetry' (July 1910).

The *Spirit of Romance* was followed by *Provença*, published in Boston in November 1910. 'Mr. Pound is a very new kind of poet,' wrote Floyd Dell in the 'Friday Literary Review' of the *Chicago Evening Post* of 6 January 1911 (No. 25):[9]

Thinking of the art exhibition just held in London, one might, for want of a better figure, call him a Neo-Impressionist poet. Like the Neo-Impressionist painters, like the Impressionists in their day, Mr. Pound is open to misunderstanding, and even to ridicule. . . . But though these poems have often an unconventional form, bizarre phraseology, catalectic or involved sentence structure and recondite meanings, yet it is always apparent that the poet knows what he is doing. . . . Ezra Pound is a true poet; his singing has distinctive spiritual and stylistic qualities which command the most respectful attention; and to those who approach his work in some humility of spirit it is capable of giving a deep aesthetic satisfaction.

H. L. Mencken, writing in the *Smart Set* in April 1911 (No. 26), was equally enthusiastic: 'considered as a whole, this collection of verses is one of the most striking that has come from the press in late years. Here we have a poet with something to say and with the skill to say it in a new way, eloquently, sonorously and sometimes almost magnificently.' A reviewer in the *Bookman* in New York (April 1912) drew this picture of his character: 'he makes one feel . . . that he is a big personality, one who is both lover and thinker, a rude dominant man, almost burly, hewing out his own proper effects in a strikingly original manner.' Pound's reception in America was easily as promising as that in England. But without the attention of the weighty, prestigious quarterlies, it was not until the controversy surrounding *Poetry* in late 1912 and 1913 that he began to be widely known.

THE DECLINE 1911–16

Canzoni, his next collection of verse, appeared in London in July 1911. Obviously a sequel to his work on Romance literature, it confirmed the impression that Pound was bookish and a little pedantic. 'We shut up the book', explained a reviewer in the *Westminster Gazette* in August 1911 (No. 30), 'as we might turn away from a shelf of bizarre but not very valuable curios in an old window.' His personality, his 'fierce individuality', was all that could be offered in balance. J. C. Squire, clearly in advance of contemporary opinion, directed attention to Pound's craftsmanship, artistry, and diligence (No. 32). This was the most perceptive and useful approach which a critic of *Canzoni* could take. The complaints about Pound's bookishness (a review in the *Cambridge Review* of 25 January 1912 described the effect as of 'a voice of beauty stifled and crying to be let free') were not wrong, but they dwelt on the obvious. Squire had the collection in clear focus:

He is a genuine artist with eyes of his own and brains of his own, who will manage to express something strong and living. . . . The more one reads them the more one perceives how excellent is Mr. Pound's artistry within limits he has imposed on himself and how much hard thinking (though very little emotion) has gone to the making of the poems.

A new and distinguished form of recognition came in 1912. Arthur Quiller-Couch included two poems from *Provença* ('Portrait' and 'Ballad for Gloom') in *The Oxford Book of Victorian Verse*. 'This is no small honour,' Pound wrote to Harriet Monroe, 'at least I should count it a recognition. Nevertheless he had hit on two poems which I had marked "to be omitted" from the next edition of my work' (*Letters*, p. 47). His next volume, *Ripostes*, which appeared in October 1912, made explicit what had been latent in *Canzoni*: that Pound was attempting to find a new tone, less bookish, more conversational, natural, and contemporary. As with Quiller-Couch, Pound had already begun to go beyond what his readers expected, or were prepared to accept. Nearly to a man, the reviewers of *Ripostes* were dissatisfied with the change in Pound's verse. The humourlessness of critics like Harold Child in *The Times Literary Supplement* (No. 36), and the general failure to detect the force of 'The Seafarer', suggest a widespread absence of sympathy or even comprehension. *Ripostes* was a more interesting collection than *Canzoni*, more varied, experimental and personal. Its poor reception intensified Pound's fear that editors, critics, the press generally, and in the end the whole of society, were locked into a deadening stiffness, a resistance to anything that was genuinely new. This became the foundation for his social criticism—with the addition of Confucian ethics and Douglasite economics—and indicates the moment when the 'mature' and 'modern' Pound begins to emerge, when he began to look at the world through the tinted lenses of alienation. He explained the significance of the reception of *Ripostes* some years later to Malcolm Cowley:[10]

He had lost many of his English readers when he published *Ripostes* in 1912. The public doesn't like to be surprised and the new poems had been surprising, even a little shocking; they had proved that Pound wasn't merely an author of masculine ballads or a new Browning who brought medieval characters to life in medieval phrases.

Pound became foreign correspondent for Harriet Monroe's *Poetry* in October 1912. Though his first contributions attracted some attention, it was not until the first major instalment of the 'Contemporania' poems in April 1913 that he became a *cause célèbre*. These were the poems in which he announced his rejection of the 'mediaeval', and his discovery of a new subject with its conscious commitment to the stance of social critic. The transformation from his work as recent as *Provença* and

Canzoni was manifest. The occasion of his notoriety was a bitter conservative attack on the 'new' poetry, and on the magazine which had been most sympathetic to it, Harriet Monroe's *Poetry*. Angry letters appeared in the *Nation* and the *Dial* (Nos 39–41) quoting Pound's verse as the most exaggerated, disruptive, unpleasant and indecent tendency in modern art. Even Yeats, who was to make Pound his private secretary at the end of 1913, and who had acknowledged Pound's help 'to get back to the definite and concrete away from modern abstractions', admitted certain reservations: 'Yet in his own work he is very uncertain, often very bad though very interesting sometimes. He spoils himself by too many experiments and has more sound principles than taste.'[11] Nevertheless, later in the year Yeats wrote to Harriet Monroe:[12]

Although I do not really like with my whole soul the metrical experiments he has made for you, [yet] I think those experiments show a vigorous creative mind. He is certainly a creative personality of some sort, though it is too soon yet to say of what sort. His experiments are perhaps errors, I am not certain; but I would always sooner give the laurel to vigorous errors than to any orthodoxy not inspired.

He was still an object of amusement to some. A couplet in *Punch* in January 1913 suggested a laughable identification:[13]

> The bays that formerly old Dante crowned
> Are worn to-day by Ezra Loomis Pound.

Will Lawrence, brother of T. E. Lawrence and a friend of Pound's, made a manful effort to take him seriously: 'Ezra wrote to me too, a wonderful letter, and with it sent a lot of strange new poems. Awful rot many of them, and meant to be so, just skits and satires. When he is serious he is very good for me.'[14] The tone of the 'Contemporania' poems, and his contribution to *Blast* in 1914, seemed to many a bitter declaration of independence from Edwardian literary taste. Richard Aldington, a young poet whom Pound had encouraged, was not alone in expressing boredom at his pose of 'enormous arrogance and petulance' (*Egoist*, July 1914). In the 'Salutation' poems from this period, and in 'Epilogue', Pound explicitly rejected the 'stale' and 'depleted' manner of his early work and the audience which it pleased (*CSP*, p. 94):

> You were praised, my books,
> > because I had just come from the country;
> I was twenty years behind the times
> > so you found an audience ready.

His next work, *Cathay*, was published by Mathews in April 1915. The poems in *Cathay* were based on the transcriptions of classical Chinese verse by the American orientalist Ernest Fenollosa. Pound had used Chinese material in *Des Imagistes*, Edward Thomas noting in a review that Pound had 'seldom done better than here under the restraint imposed by Chinese originals or models'.[15] Reviewers of *Cathay* were quick to praise the dignity and restraint of this work, perhaps with the violence and satire of the 'Contemporania' poems in mind. Clutton Brock praised his diction in *The Times Literary Supplement* of 29 April 1915 as being 'simple and sharp and precise'. Hueffer declared that it was Pound's best work to date. Orage, editor of the *New Age*, agreed, but registered a pointed criticism: 'the thoughts contained in the Chinese poems are of a very simple character. The imaginary persons are without subtlety, one might say, without mind. But it cannot be the case that only simple natures can be subjects of poetry; or that "naturalness" belongs to them alone' (No. 43).

'Contemporania' had achieved a degree of notoriety, despite the approval which greeted *Cathay*, that may have scared Mathews when, in May 1916, Pound proposed to collect the series together with the title *Lustra*. With the war on, with pacifists and conscientious objectors repressed savagely under the Defence of the Realm Act (DORA), it is no surprise that the praise he received from an American editor for his struggle for 'stark seeing and saying of things' (No. 45) was unlikely to be echoed in London. Lawrence's *The Rainbow*, with its forthright sensuality and Lesbian love scene, was effectively suppressed by a nervous publisher after a magistrates' hearing. A reader for Mathews suggested that *Lustra* was 'more fitted for the Waste Paper Basket than the literary public' (No. 47). When the printers refused to set the whole of the manuscript, Mathews was pushed into a confrontation with Pound. In the end reviewers of the 'trade' edition were more puzzled than outraged by Pound's proclaimed effort to write with the freedom and energy of the best prose (by which he meant Stendhal, de Maupassant, Flaubert, and Joyce). The very shrillness of his nervously asserted independence led some critics to wonder if behind it lay a 'hidden timidity' or a restless 'peacock over-consciousness'. It was suspected that the advocates of the 'new poetry', pre-eminently Pound himself, had had to work the whole thing up, that their 'newness' was a product more of will than anything else: they were simply possessed of a morbid passion to be *different*. The complacency behind such suspicions is clear in this comment from the *Atlantic Monthly* in April 1916:[16]

That egoistic self-consciousness is a primary motive in the new movement [in poetry] appears sufficiently in the demand on the part of Mr. Ezra Pound, the self-appointed high priest of the coterie, that poets be endowed so that they may escape the need of writing to please the public.

Pound's motives were questioned, and his 'revolt' was widely assumed to be nothing more than an insincere and arrogant gesture on the part of a weak man. By 1916 he was an isolated figure, writing to Joyce (*Pound-Joyce*, pp. 61–2):

I have absolutely no connections in England that are any use. There is no editor whom I wouldn't cheerfully fry in oil and none who wouldn't cheerfully do the same. The English review tried to cheat me in 1912. Since then I have printed no where in England save a few poems printed in Monro's magazine, but he has stopped printing until the end of the war. The New Age don't pay for poetry.

The war, the absence of allies (such as Wyndham Lewis and Ford Madox Hueffer), the death of others (Gaudier Brzeska, T. E. Hulme), and the decline of Pound's standing in London combined to emphasize his isolation. His most consuming work during 1916 and 1917 was the preparation of *Certain Noble Plays of Japan* for the Cuala Press, and '*Noh*' *or Accomplishment* for Macmillan. He also collected his translations from Fontenelle in October 1917 as *Dialogues of Fontenelle*. All three books represented little more than busy-work. Editing the letters of Yeats *père*, John Butler Yeats, for the Cuala Press in May 1917 was probably his most pleasing work during this time.

T. S. ELIOT AS A CRITIC OF POUND 1917–18

In August 1917 T. S. Eliot, then twenty-nine years old, wrote the first of many pieces of criticism on Pound. It was a review of '*Noh*' *or Accomplishment* in the *Egoist* (see Bibliography). The review of '*Noh*' is more interesting for what it reveals about Eliot's high valuation of translation for the practice of poetry than for anything he says about Pound. His second piece was a substantial essay entitled *Ezra Pound: His Metric and Poetry* published as an anonymous pamphlet in New York in November 1917. John Quinn had arranged for Alfred A. Knopf in New York to publish *Lustra*, and had the happy idea that a brochure might usefully introduce Pound's recent work to a wider audience. Pound nominated Eliot to write the essay, and superintended its composition. He also insisted that it be published anonymously: 'I want to boom Eliot', he explained to Quinn, 'and one can't have too obvious a ping-pong match at that sort of thing.'[17] Eliot made it clear at the outset of his essay that it was being written for *l'homme moyen sensuel*, 'for the admirer of a poem [of Pound's] here or there, whose appreciation is capable of yielding him a larger return.' But what he was trying to convince such a reader was that Pound's importance lay in his 'intensive study of metre' and not, particularly, in 'sentiment', 'spirit', 'vision', or 'sincerity'. In other words, Eliot was attempting to shift the grounds of taste in contemporary thought about poetry. The effort is, perhaps, better known through his biting remarks on Georgian poetry, and his attitude towards the Victorians. An adequate response to Pound's work, he argues, requires some sense of its development: if the reader will only follow the stages of his poetry, even the most advanced will not prove inaccessible; 'when anyone has studied Mr. Pound's poems in *chronological* order, and has mastered *Lustra* and *Cathay*, he is prepared for the *Cantos*—but not till then. If the reader fails to like them, he has probably omitted some step in his progress, and had better go back and retrace the journey.' Certain aspects of Eliot's approach to Pound, particularly the emphasis on technique, were hinted at in the criticism of F. S. Flint and J. C. Squire. But Eliot's position is made much more forceful by the pressure of larger issues, particularly the relationship of the 'individual talent' to 'tradition', as well as his gift for memorable phrasing.

He returned to Pound's work with 'A Note on Ezra Pound' in *To-day* in September 1918. 'The point', he maintains, 'is to come to conclusions respecting the place of his work as a whole in contemporary literature.' Part of Pound's importance lay in actual achievement, in having 'made masterpieces, some of translation, some of re-creation'; more generally, it was his historical sense, his perception of 'what *they* have that *we* want', which made Pound's work so important for contemporary poetry. The problem, as Eliot saw it, concerned the ways the poet may bring the past to bear upon the present, and he was to give it classic formulation in 'Tradition and the Individual Talent' in the *Egoist* (September–December 1919). He scored a neat blow against some of Pound's critics in 'A Note on Ezra Pound' by arguing that Pound's erudition and sensitivity to 'the emotions of literary stimulus' (i.e. bookishness) were among the most traditional aspects of his work. The significance of Eliot's comment is best seen against the background of the bland and complacent 'great traditions' invoked by Charles Granville (No. 29). The Cantos began to appear, fragmentarily, in *Future* (February, March, April 1918), and Eliot offered a new suggestion about their meaning (*To-day*, September 1918):

In appearance, it is a rag-bag of Mr. Pound's reading in various languages, from which one fragment after another is dragged to light, and illuminated by the beauty of his phrase. . . . And yet the thing has, after one has read it once or twice, a positive coherence; it is an objective and reticent autobiography.

But perhaps the appropriate reference here is to *The Waste Land*, rather than to the poem which Pound was attempting to write.

POUND IN POST-WAR ENGLAND AND AMERICA 1918–21

Despite the narrowness of his interests, and the elegant evasiveness of his style, Eliot possessed a coherent and sympathetic understanding of Pound's work. In this he was virtually alone when *Quia Pauper Amavi*, containing 'Homage to Sextus Propertius', 'Moeurs Contemporaines', 'Langue d'Oc', and 'Three Cantos', appeared in 1919. Parts of the 'Homage' were published in *Poetry* in March 1919, and a Professor of Classics at the University of Chicago, W. G. Hale, severely censured Pound for his inadequacy as a translator.[18] Critics in England were just as quick to attack the 'Homage' as a laughably inadequate attempt at a translation. Robert Nichols savaged Pound in the *Observer* (No. 64), agreeing with Rascoe that on the basis of the 'Homage' Pound's claim to be a poet, far less a translator, should not be taken too seriously: 'In himself Mr. Pound is not, never has been and almost, I might hazard, never will be, a poet.'

Pound insisted that the poem was not a translation, writing to A. R. Orage (who was about to serialize it in the *New Age*) that 'my job was to bring a dead man to life, to present a living figure' (*Letters*, pp. 211–13). Orage's reviewer argued that the poem 'ventures rather too near the original to be taken simply as a free fantasia on Roman themes' (No. 62). The 'Homage' has become a major stumbling block for critics inclined to disapprove of Pound or what he stands for; and an ability to read Latin virtually disqualifies certain critics from understanding what Pound was actually doing. From Hale and Nichols to Robert Conquest, traditionally-minded critics have seized upon the 'Homage' as ultimate proof of Pound's insincerity. But it is, in itself, a passionate and beautiful poem, as intensely felt as anything in the canon.

Eliot responded to the hostile attacks upon the poem in his review of *Quia Pauper Amavi* in the *Athenaeum* (24 October 1919). His main point, which has dominated the best comment on the poem by J. P. Sullivan and Hugh Kenner, is that the 'Homage' is a new *persona*, a creation of a new character, recreating Propertius in himself, and himself in Propertius. It is probably a truer interpretation of that man of letters than Professor Mackail's; but to regard it as a 'translation' is to consider its author's work in that piecemeal fashion which is to be deprecated.

When he came to edit a selection of Pound's poems in 1928 Eliot omitted the 'Homage', writing that he was

doubtful of its effect upon the uninstructed reader, even with my instructions. If the uninstructed reader is not a classical scholar, he will make nothing of it; if he be a classical scholar, he will wonder why this does not conform to his notions of what translation should be. It is not a translation, it is a paraphrase, or still more truly (for the instructed) a *persona*.

The decision was probably a mistake, but one which he and his firm, Faber & Faber, tried to set right with their publication of the 'Homage' as a separate volume in 1934, which was the occasion of a fine essay-review by John Speirs (No. 102). The Cantos remained a puzzle to Eliot: 'the casual or lazy reader will find in these Cantos only a succession of bright images, and a collection of obscure literary allusions. . . . Only those who have studied Mr. Pound's method from his other work will find any continuity or meaning.' 'Eliot has done a dull but, I think, valuable puff in *The Athenaeum*,' Pound wrote to John Quinn on 25 October 1919, 'granite wreaths, leaden laurels, no sign of exhileration; but I daresay it is what is best in that quarter' (*Letters*, p. 213).

In the immediate post-war period Pound's work reached a small, discriminating audience in America. His reputation was mainly due to two collections of his prose which appeared in New York between 1918 and 1920. The first, *Pavannes and Divisions*, was published by Knopf at the end of June 1918. It was a book with little of the moral earnestness of Van Wyck Brooks, or the social idealism of Randolph Bourne or Max Eastman. Pound characteristically began the volume with his satirical pieces from the *Little Review*. Reviewers hardly got past these to the weightier essays on de Gourmont, Ford, Crabbe, Joyce, Elizabethan classicists, and 'The Serious Artist' before raising an almighty howl. 'But here is the unbelievable', complained Louis Untermeyer in the *New Republic* (No. 57), 'a carefully enshrined series of trivialities, translations, annotated excerpts, beauty submerged in banalities, criticism smothered in a mixture of snobbery and bad temper.' Conrad Aiken speculated in the *Dial* (No. 58) about how seriously Pound meant his journalism to be taken.

A second collection, *Instigations*, was published by Boni & Liveright in April 1920. Though it was more diffuse than *Pavannes and Divisions* (including essays on James, a commentary on French poetry, and Fenol-losa's essay on the Chinese written character) it generally received better reviews. Mencken praised it in the *Smart Set* (No. 71) and described Pound as 'the most extraordinary man that American literature has seen in our time'. Van Wyck Brooks was equally enthusiastic about Pound: 'in his atmosphere literature becomes a high, difficult and austere pur-suit' (No. 70). But even praise of this order was insufficient to create a substantial reading public for Pound. By 31 December 1930, a decade after publication, *Instigations* had only sold 591 copies.[19] Even though people weren't buying his books, Pound was enough of a public figure to be picked up by *Vanity Fair*. In the issue of February 1920 a handsome photograph of Pound by Malcolm Arbuthnot appeared, announcing that he was, along with Shaw, George Moore, Kipling, Barrie, and Hardy, one of the 'Living Masters of English Prose Style'. Pound is described as 'a modernist prose writer, and an adept in *vers libre*' and 'an excellent critic of the new and untrammeled order'.

Pound's major work of this period, 'Hugh Selwyn Mauberley', appeared in an elegant and immaculately produced limited edition of two hundred copies from the Ovid Press in June 1920. 'Mauberley' was collected for the first time in *Poems 1918–21*, but was not widely avail-able in England until 1928. By then it came with T. S. Eliot's assurance that it was a great poem, though at first it had not been recognized as a modern classic. Edwin Muir wrote one of the few notices of the poem, remarking on its difficulty: 'Mr. Pound's H. S. Mauberley is cryptic, one feels, out of pride, and out of courtesy for the few who will listen to him—a courtesy which takes the form, almost unique in our time, of not assuming that the listener is such a dunce that *everything* needs to be explained to him' (No. 74). This owes something to Eliot, though he was far from alone in noticing Pound's tense apprehension at the adequacy of his readers. Whether there were any readers of Pound's work remained uncertain: *Hugh Selwyn Mauberley* appeared in a small edition, and *Umbra* had been ignored. T. S. Eliot saw Pound's position with great clarity:[20]

The fact is that there is now no organ of any importance in which [Pound] . . . can express himself, and he is becoming forgotten. It is not enough for him simply to publish a volume of verse once a year—or no matter how often—for it will simply not be reviewed, and will be killed by silence.

As I consider that Pound and Lewis are the only writers in London whose work is worth pushing, this worries me. I know that Pound's lack of tact has done him great harm. But I am worried as to what is to become of him.

Pound did not publish another book in England for eight years, during which time Eliot established himself as the most influential poet and critic of his time. They remained close personal friends, but were occasionally compared, at Pound's expense, by reviewers. The severest judgment was made by Edmund Wilson in the *New Republic* (19 April 1922), reviewing Pound's *Poems 1918–21*:

In the 'Hugh Selwyn Mauberley' poems . . . we have one of his most furious attempts to conceal his fundamentally simple reactions in formidable and complicated riddles. His failure is particularly flagrant because he here copies T. S. Eliot—in one case quite slavishly parodies 'Burbank with a Baedeker'—and hence challenges comparison with him. The comparison goes all against Pound. Where Eliot in one knotty stanza will open a vivid window on the past and convey a sharp emotion about it, Pound merely paraphrases statements of obvious fact in tortured pedantic jargon.

Wilson returned to this damaging comparison in a review of *The Waste Land* in the *Dial* (December 1922), describing the Cantos then available as 'a bewildering mosaic with no central emotion to provide a key'.[21] Eliot, displeased by the comparison, wrote to the managing editor of the *Dial*, Gilbert Seldes, on 27 December 1922:[22]

While I wish to express my appreciation of Mr. Wilson's praise, as well as your own, there is one point in Mr. Wilson's article to which I must strongly take exception. I do very much object to be made use of by anyone for the purpose of disparaging the work of Ezra Pound. I am infinitely in his debt as a poet, as well as a personal friend, and I do resent being praised at his expense.

(Wilson was not, in any event, discouraged by Eliot's admonition, extending the comparison in 'T. S. Eliot', a long article in the *New Republic* of 13 November 1929, which was incorporated in *Axel's Castle* in 1931.) Though he was a critic deeply sympathetic towards the modernist movement, Wilson's misgivings about Pound are of representative significance. Despite Eliot's attempts to explain the Cantos, what was clearly to be Pound's major *opus* confused the critics. Vergil Geddes expressed in *Poetry* (November 1921) what was a widely shared attitude:

They contain, in parts, some excellent passages, but as a whole their verbosity is too cryptic. They give, adequately enough, the consensus of Pound's mental manoeuverings, and they give his vagrancies in erudition and his antiquarian journeys; but they do not sustain the mental affiliations which I find in the other poems.

THE FORGOTTEN YEARS 1922–6

In 1925 Harriet Monroe, in a memoir of Pound, looked back some fifteen years to the time when she first came across his work (No. 80). It was no exaggeration to say that he was, as he once said of Yeats, 'already a sort of dim figure with its associations set in the past' (*Letters*, p. 58). During the period when he lived in Paris (1921–4), and in the years which followed in Rapallo, Pound was not, to be sure, absolutely forgotten. He was nominated to the *Vanity Fair* 'Hall of Fame', along with the Russian operatic singer Chaliapin, in March 1922. The composer Aaron Copland set his 'An Immorality' and chanted it 'in a high, cold and passionate voice' at Paul Rosenfeld's salon in New York.[23] Rosenfeld was one of the many young writers who met Pound in Paris in the early twenties, and writing about him in 1944 (No. 115), when a great deal had changed, he remembered that Pound had seemed to him a remarkably gifted figure, but not a great poet nor even an important one. But expatriate Americans such as Ernest Hemingway were grateful for his help, and Ernest Walsh honoured Pound's work and example in his periodical *This Quarter* in January 1925. Hemingway contributed a pugnacious 'Homage to Ezra'.

Pound was aware that his position in England and America was not, by most standards, very high, as he remarked to R. P. Blackmur in November 1924 (*Letters*, p. 261):

My American publishers do not exist. It becomes more and more evident that the American publisher must be left out of one's calculations. Likewise English and henglish publishers. There may some day be a cheaper continental edition [of XVI Cantos]. . . . I do not, personally, intend to devote much energy to it; and as I see things at present, I shall never again take any steps whatever to arrange publication for any of my work in either England or America. *Tant pis pour les indigènes* [So much the worse for the natives].

Within two years he once again felt the need to descend from Parnassus. He put out a feeler, which came to nothing, to Mencken about the possibility of contributing regularly to the *American Mercury* (YL, 828). Gallup lists only three contributions to periodicals in 1926, two being letters to the editor. In the same year he wrote to Carl Sandburg that 'time has again worked round to point where I ought again to try to cause a little liveliness, as I perhaps managed to do a decade ago, when we were all so much younger and wiser.'[24] Pound's sole venture as an editor got under way in 1927, but the *Exile*, as Pound called it, suffered from his isolation in Rapallo. Though he did obtain poems from Yeats, and from the Objectivists in New York (Carl Rakosi, Louis Zukofsky), the contributions lacked a rootedness and sense of purpose which, whatever its other failings, had always characterized Eliot's *Criterion*. The *Exile* lasted through four numbers.

Personae AND RE-DISCOVERY 1926–30

Personae: The Collected Poems of Ezra Pound was published by Boni & Liveright in New York at the end of December 1926. A reviewer in *Poetry* (July 1927) reported that 'I found no curiosity about him among young people who read or write poetry. Only here and there one runs across some vague knowledge of him' which had resulted in 'a general neglect of his art and an abatement of his influence'. With *Personae* Pound was rediscovered by a new generation of writers and readers, as Robert Fitzgerald writes in *Encounter* (July 1956):

> The first of Ezra Pound's verses that I remember seeing were in the volume *Personae*, borrowed when I was in school. In appearance this book had a style very distinct and rich. . . . A short poem called 'Doria' seemed unforgettable to me. . . . The 'Ballad of the Goodly Fere' moved me. . . . I thought nothing could be finer than some of the poems in *Cathay*.

The work thus newly admired, as Fitzgerald indicates, was the body of Pound's poetry written before 1920. With its re-publication he began a new life as a poet: there developed an admiration of his early work, and a suspiciousness and incomprehension of the Cantos, which had every appearance of repeating the history of his earlier reputation.

Prominent reviews of *Personae* were written by old friends: Ford Madox Ford in the *New York Herald Tribune Books* (No. 82), W. C. Williams in the *New York Evening Post Literary Review* (No. 83), and Richard Aldington in *The Times Literary Supplement* (5 January 1928). Eliot's review in the *Dial* (January 1928), titled 'Isolated Superiority', expressed again his view that Pound was of the greatest technical importance for the young poets:

> I cannot think of any one writing verse, of our generation and the next, whose verse (if any good) has not been improved by the study of Pound's. His poetry is an inexhaustible reference book of verse form. There is, in fact, no one else to study.

R. P. Blackmur, then a twenty-three year old freelance critic, described Pound's achievement as 'a triumph of style varying from a hard radiance to the most limpid image', and defended Pound along lines suggested by Eliot: 'the ultimate value of his poetry should be in the adequacy of his methods and the freshness of his ways of feeling, rather than the novelty or truth of his substance' (No. 84).

Eliot was, apparently, dissatisfied with Pound's choice of poems in *Personae*, or he may have felt there was a stronger need to introduce his work in England: in any event the *Selected Poems*, edited with an introduction by him, appeared in December 1928. Eliot's introduction, a trenchant and influential essay, explained Pound's 'originality' in terms of his 'archeological' or 'historical' sense: his great work lay in the discovery of Chinese poetry, and the revivification of Provençal verse. The Cantos 'are the only "poem of some length" by any of my contemporaries that I can read with enjoyment and admiration'. 'Hugh Selwyn Mauberley' was manifestly a great poem: 'the versification is more accomplished than that of any other of the poems in this book, and more varied'. T. Earle Welby (1881–1933) was correct to conclude, in a review in the *Saturday Review* (22 December 1928), that Eliot's introduction was 'in effect a plea for accepting Mr. Pound whole and without grimace'. The emphasis on 'Mauberley', particularly when argued by Dr Leavis in Cambridge (No. 87), was decisive in establishing this one poem at least in the canon of Pound's permanent work. The poem figured centrally in Dr Leavis's *New Bearings in English Poetry* (1932), though the direction of the argument was respectfully but firmly opposed to Eliot's emphasis on the technical importance of Pound's work. His praise of 'Mauberley' came at the expense of any interest in Pound's development (which had been a major direction of Eliot's criticism) and was accompanied by a dismissal of the Cantos as 'little more than a game—a game serious with the seriousness of pedantry'. (Leavis became a forceful critic of Pound's thinking about literature: he published a reply to Pound's *How to Read* entitled *How to Teach Reading: A Primer for Ezra Pound* (1932), in which he attacked Pound's notion of technique as resulting in 'a more or less elegantly pedantic dilettantism'.)[25]

A Draft of XXX Cantos 1930–3

In August 1930 *A Draft of XXX Cantos* appeared in a beautifully produced edition of just over 200 copies from the Hours Press in Paris. Publication followed in New York and London three years later. The problems of interpreting the *XXX Cantos* were formidable. Pound's own explanation of their form, as Yeats recorded in *A Packet for Ezra Pound* (1928), quoted by Geoffrey Grigson at the beginning of No. 90,

was difficult and far from self-evident. Dudley Fitts in the *Hound &
Horn* in 1931 (No. 88) suggested the usefulness of an analogy with music.
But most of the other reviewers were at a loss to explain the poem. A
critic in *The Times Literary Supplement* (28 December 1933) insisted that
'the necessity of his design should make itself felt'. Geoffrey Grigson,
editor of the influential little magazine *New Verse*, complained that the
Cantos lacked 'cellular inevitability' (No. 90). Eliot commissioned a
young disciple of Pound, Louis Zukofsky, to review *XXX Cantos* in the
Criterion (April 1931), but his emphasis on Pound's objectivity ('He has
not obtruded personally, never found it worth his while to discover an
interesting subjective self to please people') was ignored. Of course
there was room to leaven the perplexity and seriousness of the critics,
and Edith Sitwell offered herself for the role of jester: the Cantos, she
wrote in the *Morning Post* of 6 March 1934, 'make me feel as if I had been
condemned to Life Imprisonment in the Gentleman's Third Class Cloak-
room at Victoria, an unsuitable place for me'.

Ford, who was living in Toulon in the summer of 1932, proposed to
the American publishers of *XXX Cantos*, Farrar & Rinehart, that a
pamphlet of testimonials might usefully be compiled[26]

because Ezra is not half as much recognized as he ought to be in his own
country. . . . American reviewers as a rule do not take Ezra half seriously
enough and he has managed to offend a great number of them. But if you could
quote some good English notices—and I would see that there were some—that
might have an effect of brow beating people that don't like him.

*The Cantos of Ezra Pound: Some Testimonials by Ernest Hemingway, Ford
Madox Ford, T. S. Eliot, Hugh Walpole, Archibald MacLeish, James Joyce
and Others*, edited by D[aniel]. C[haucer]. (i.e., Ford), a twenty-two
page pamphlet, was tucked into review copies of *A Draft of XXX Cantos*
when it was finally published on 15 March 1933. Allen Tate's contribution suggested that Ford's efforts on Pound's behalf were needed:

The appearance of the Cantos in America will be, for the public, Pound's first
book. Liveright's edition of the *Collected Poems*, four or five years ago found so
scandalously few buyers that it hardly counts. . . . The influence of such a
poet is always incalculable but we do know that Pound's influence on his younger
contemporaries has been enormous. Not through his disciples, who invariably
falsify the master with exaggeration but by his scattered and remote followers
who are able to learn, to transform and, in themselves, to create, the great poet's
influence must be measured long after his time.

This is a salutary reminder of the size of Pound's audience. The American edition of *XXX Cantos* appeared in an edition of 1,000 copies, 1,500 in England. There was a first-printing order of 4,080 in America for Eliot's *Poems 1909–1925* in 1932, and for editions of 3,000 and 3,700 for his *Selected Essays* in England and America in the same year. (See the Appendix on the printing of Pound's works.) Even when compared to Eliot, who was hardly a popular writer, Pound's appeal only extended to a tiny, elite audience.

The American reception of *XXX Cantos* was led by two reviews by important young critics, Allen Tate and R. P. Blackmur. Writing in the *Nation* (10 June 1931), Tate made the paradoxical proposition that the Cantos 'are not about anything. But they are distinguished verse.' Blackmur's 'The Masks of Ezra Pound' appeared in *Hound & Horn* (January–March 1934). There were two Pounds for Blackmur, the first was the author of the 'Homage', the poet who learnt the use of the 'mask' and whose translations achieved a wholeness and 'tough elegance' (this was echoing Eliot, who praised the 'tough reasonableness' of the Caroline poets in *Homage to John Dryden* in 1924). The other Pound was more obviously original, writing without the aid of the mask or of translation, but was manifestly less successful, less interesting.

POUND IN THE 1930S

Subsequent volumes of the Cantos appeared in 1934, 1937 and 1940. Among the younger generation of critics and poets who wrote about Pound during this period, perhaps the most interesting was Delmore Schwartz (1914–66). A New York Jewish socialist, deeply influenced by Eliot, Schwartz was in a sense an ideal vehicle to illustrate the contradictions of the critical heritage. He had a clear insight into the ethical and didactic basis of Pound's Cantos but could not come to terms with their content (No. 105). To praise his technical importance, genuflecting towards Eliot, while at the same time suggesting that we might just as happily read 'capital' for 'usury' in Canto XLI, is an unsatisfactory compromise. The distinction which Eliot had proposed between the technical importance of Pound and the meaning of the Cantos could in the end lead only to doublethink. The poem was becoming *more* political,[27] and Pound meant it as such: even sympathetic readers began to think again. Allen Tate, with less reason to disagree with Pound's politics than Schwartz, confessed in *Partisan Review* (May–June 1941) that *Cantos LII–LXXI* 'leave me very, very cold':

In the first thirty we were able to attribute structure to the verse because we felt a certain historical unity in the material: there is for us something like a direct line from Homeric Greece through the Italian Renaissance to modern Europe; but between John Adams and the agrarian emperors of China there is only a community of economic abstraction, which Major Douglas alone understands today, and of high courtesy, which Mr. Pound evidently despairs of reviving.

The name of Major C. H. Douglas continually appears in reviews of Pound's work in this period. Rayner Heppenstall defined a large body of feeling when he wrote in the *Adelphi* (January 1935): 'What wrong Major Douglas did him! And what a grand lyric poet was lost, in the author of *Cathay*, when he decided that "some economic awareness is advisable".' Douglas, the proponent of an economic and financial policy called Social Credit, was a latterday Henry George. Orage, always an heterodox socialist, abandoned Guild Socialism in favour of Social Credit, and in 1918 or 1919 introduced Pound to Douglas. Orage had been swept quite off his feet by the cogency of Douglas's arguments that the power to create credit (that is, to create new money) should not remain in the hands of a small body of individuals—'usurers'—to whom even the state must turn. Remove this power from the usurers, Douglas argued, and put it under some form of state control, not necessarily state ownership, and the pernicious problem of usury will have been dealt with.

Ideas about the 'just price', usury, and public control of credit haunt Pound's work in the twenties and thirties, when both Fascists and Communists joined hands in the belief that financiers and armaments merchants caused the war and profited from it. Pound believed, and his reading in Brooks Adams's passionate and monomaniacal *The Law of Civilization and Decay* (1895) supported the view that the study of history could provide examples of societies which prospered or declined according to the banking system adopted.[28] Great stretches of the Cantos, his minute investigations into the economic, financial, and cultural structures of dynastic China, Renaissance Italy, and Federal America, are meant to document his case.

But to talk of 'usury' is, in simple truth, usually to talk about *Jewish* usury and Jewish financiers. Pound's anti-Semitism has been explained away by the argument that he really meant 'usurer' when he wrote or broadcast 'kike'; perhaps he believed this himself.[29] But this is not a defence, it is merely a semantic quibble. As Benda would have understood it, Pound's *trahison* was in not seeing the consequences of this hateful 'idea' when it was turned 'into action'. We should remember that his Fascism was in effect Mussolini-worship, and not a commitment to National Socialism.[30] When he wrote to Harriet Monroe on 30 November 1926 that 'I personally think extremely well of Mussolini' (*Letters*, p. 279), for what the distinction is worth, he was praising a man and an ideology less racist than the *NSDAP*.[31] It was not until the Italian racial laws of September and November 1938 that Jews were banned from teaching in schools and universities, and from working in corporations, banking, and insurance. Eichmann arrived to take charge of the deportation of the Italian Jews in March 1944. Pound continued his propaganda broadcasts for Mussolini until the regime collapsed in September 1943, at which point he transferred his propaganda work to the press and publishing houses of the German puppet-state, the Salò Republic.

Men like poor Gorham Munson in America, leader of the Social Credit movement and editor of *New Democracy*, saw his radical, democratic cause usurped by racists, Fascists, and demagogues—and got out. People wondered what excuses could be offered for Pound.

'SHOULD EZRA POUND BE SHOT?' 1945–8

In 1941 W. C. Williams denounced Pound's broadcasts over Rome Radio in an article whose title alluded to the English traitor Lord Haw-Haw (William Joyce). Eunice Tietjens attacked him in the pages of *Poetry* (April 1942). In 1944 Paul Rosenfeld wrote of Pound as a 'case' to be explained (No. 115). When he was finally arrested by units of the United States Army on 6 May 1945, and, after a period in a prison camp in Pisa, was returned to Washington in November 1945 to testify before a District of Columbia Grand Jury, Pound stood before the American public as the most prominent embodiment of 'modern' literature, and the most prominent American pro-Fascist 'traitor'. The conjunction of modernism in literature and political treason was catnip for the burgeoning philistinism of the McCarthyite right wing. If he had time for such things, Pound might have thought back to the review of *Personae* in the *Nation* of 28 August 1909 (No. 15) in which he was accused of being a traitor to the world of letters, a disturbing irony which was echoed in the pressure of opinion anxious to make Pound an example as much for the irresponsibility of his poetry as for his political activities.

His supporters began to rally round: the New York liberal paper *PM* published excerpts from his broadcasts on 25 November 1945. On 11

December statements appeared from Charles Norman (a future biographer of Pound), E. E. Cummings, W. C. Williams, Conrad Aiken, Karl Shapiro, and F. O. Matthiessen in defence of the accused poet. The most characteristic liberal line, which prevailed in the end, was that Pound was insane, and of diminished responsibility (and that the broadcasts were wholly ineffectual anyway). The Communist literary left was substantially more vengeful: Isidor Schneider attacked Pound in the New Masses on 11 December 1945.[32] Two weeks later (29 December 1945) an article entitled 'Should Ezra Pound be Shot?' appeared in the same paper, with comments from Lion Feuchtwanger, Albert Maltz, Eda Lou Walton (author of No. 89), Norman Rosten, F. O. Matthiessen, and Arthur Miller. Support for those after Pound's head came from the editor of the Saturday Review, Henry Seidel Canby, in an editorial on 15 December. The debate was in the end cut short by psychiatric testimony which prevented Pound from coming to trial. He was judged mentally unfit to answer the charges against him, and was committed for an indefinite period to St Elizabeth's, a Federal Hospital in Washington. It was very much in doubt whether Pound would ever again be taken seriously as a poet.

The Pisan Cantos AND THE BOLLINGEN PRIZE 1948–9

At the end of July 1948 the publicity department of James Laughlin's New Directions Publishing Corporation issued a press release about The Pisan Cantos, consisting of comments from Allen Tate, T. S. Eliot, Conrad Aiken, John Crowe Ransom, W. C. Williams, Delmore Schwartz, Richard Eberhart, Robert Lowell, Theodore Spencer, and Horace Gregory. There was an obvious need to assert the existence of the 'poetic' value of the Cantos, and to oppose its confusion with the immediate political issues of Pound's past. The distinction was not uncongenial to the age which cut its teeth on The Sacred Wood, Principles of Literary Criticism, Seven Types of Ambiguity, The Double Agent, The World's Body and Reactionary Essays, and provided the basic argument for the award of the Bollingen Prize for poetry to The Pisan Cantos in 1949. In retrospect, it is the personal, virtually confessional quality of these Cantos which distinguishes them as a new turning point in the whole poem, a point emphasized by Robert Lowell:[33]

The last Cantos are in the open: they are Pound, such as he is, and will be. As I have been re-reading them, a certain wonder has come on me, and I have thought of Brunetto Latini, running—not as one who has lost, but as one who is winning.

(Lowell returned to Pound's work in 1960, remarking in a brief note to James Laughlin that 'I've just read the *Pisan Cantos* again, and feel that no poetry since Thomas Hardy so moves the heart. Our best long poem, and as remarkable an advance over the earlier Cantos as "Mauberley" was over the earlier *Personae*')[34]

Reviewers of *The Pisan Cantos* quickly picked up this theme. Robert Fitzgerald, a young poet and translator, called attention to a new personal interest, 'a personal desolation and a kind of repentance, that is enormously moving' (No. 116). Another poet, Francis Golffing, made a substantial claim for the Cantos, one which was clearly post-Eliot: 'while the spirit of the Cantos is Alexandrine in the sense of drawing indifferently on a wealth of traditional motifs, it is at the same time covertly normative, presenting as it does a *summa* of the relevant past to the contemporary reader' (*Furioso*, winter 1949). Old friends, such as W. C. Williams, wrote with a growing sense that Pound desperately needed defending (No. 119).

On 20 February 1949 the Library of Congress announced the award of the Bollingen Prize for 'the highest achievement of American poetry' to *The Pisan Cantos*. The members of the advisory jury, appointed by the Librarian of Congress, were Conrad Aiken, W. H. Auden, Louise Bogan, Katherine Garrison Chapin, T. S. Eliot, Paul Green, Robert Lowell, Katherine Anne Porter, Karl Shapiro, Allen Tate, Willard Thorp, Leonie Adams, and Theodore Spencer. Once again controversy swirled about Pound. The enemies of modern poetry needed just a little paranoia to draw conclusions from the membership of the jury, and conclusions flowed freely. Within a week letters appeared in the *New York Times*. Robert Hillyer, no admirer of Pound or of modern poetry, mounted the most wide-ranging, prominent attack in two articles, 'Treason's Strange Fruit: The Case of Ezra Pound' and 'Poetry's New Priesthood' in the *Saturday Review of Literature* of 11 and 18 June 1949. It was widely recognized that Hillyer's target was the 'establishment', as represented by the advisory jury, which may seem more securely copper-bottomed today than in 1949. The statement accompanying the award was uncompromising: 'To permit other considerations than that of poetic achievement to sway the decision would destroy the significance of the award and would in principle deny the validity of that objective perception of value on which civilized society must rest.' But

Hillyer, and other critics of the award saw, instead of 'that objective perception of value', a contradictory situation by which one branch of the government was honouring an accused traitor, still under indictment. The implications of the award raised many difficult questions. William Barrett wondered in *Partisan Review* (April 1949) whether it was possible, in a lyric poem, 'for technical embellishments to transform vicious and ugly matter into beautiful poetry?' Clement Greenburg revealed widely-felt liberal uneasiness in a reply to Barrett in *Partisan Review* (May 1949):

I do not quarrel here with the Fellows' aesthetic verdict, but I question its primacy in the affair at hand, a primacy that hints at an absolute acceptance of the autonomy not only of art but of every separate field of human activity.

The debate about the award of the Bollingen Prize to Pound is one of the infrequent literary debates whose implication reverberates through the whole of American culture. The *Zeitgeist* of New Criticism is strongly present in the argument; but underlying that is the more serious problem of totalitarian and extremist art in a secular, pluralist democracy. Pound's work challenges an open society where it is most vulnerable. Ironically enough, the terms of the Bollingen award constitute the strongest rejection of Pound's historical, political, and ethical meaning. By praising 'poetic achievement' the advisory jury in effect tamed *The Pisan Cantos*, and made the whole poem safe for democracy.

POUND IN THE FIFTIES AND AFTER

While he was in St Elizabeth's, a Federal mental hospital in Washington, Pound's reputation was restored. In part this was due to the distinction of his friends (Hemingway, Eliot, Cummings); his publishers played a significant role in making his literary (as opposed to economic or political) work widely available. The steady flow of material (*Literary Essays, Translations, Letters*, the *Seventy Cantos*, and the reissued *Personae*) kept his name before the public. The strangest irony is that the young poets, in their reaction against the modernist legacy, were uninterested in Pound and abused his work with the contemptuous tones of W. G. Hale and Robert Nichols. Philip Larkin dismissed *Section: Rock-Drill* in a paragraph (No. 134). Thom Gunn described *Thrones* as 'a jumble of nonconsecutive and usually extremely obscure allusions in many languages, including Chinese. There is of course no apparent organization' (*Yale Review*, June 1960). The *Literary Essays* were kicked about by

Charles Tomlinson (No. 126) and W. W. Robson (No. 128). The shift of opinion in Pound's favour in the past few years is clearly seen here: on re-reading their reviews a decade and a half later, both Tomlinson and Robson insisted that postscripts repudiating their earlier hostility to Pound be included. In a letter to the editor (May 1969) Thom Gunn flatly refused permission to reprint his review of *Thrones*:

Rereading the review I find it nasty and unfair. I do not take *Thrones* in its context of all the Cantos, for one thing. I do not honor the man who is probably the greatest poet we have had in this century. And I do not like the complacent and uncharitable tone of the whole of my piece. It is that of a dwarf sneering at a giant.

It was left to an American poet and editor, Donald Hall, to snap at this species of 'little Englandism' in the reviews of Pound, and to argue that 'In a better world, literary men would queue all night to get their copies of *Thrones*' (No. 138).

During the fifties Pound became an acceptable 'research' subject in the universities, though this is only intermittently correct about America. Academic work on Pound was unknown in English universities until the sixties. Led by John Hamilton Edwards, there was a sustained effort to make the study of Pound academically respectable. Edwards had written a sympathetic critical biography of Pound as a doctoral thesis at the University of California, Berkeley, in 1952. He edited, also from Berkeley, the *Pound Newsletter* from 1954 to 1956. In collaboration with William W. Vasse, Edwards was responsible for the *Annotated Index to the Cantos of Ezra Pound* (1959).

Criticism of Pound in the academy has been dominated by two people: Hugh Kenner and Donald Davie. Kenner, Professor of English at the University of California, Santa Barbara, is the author of critical studies of Chesterton, Eliot, Wyndham Lewis, and James Joyce. He is the staunchest defender of modernism in the American academic community, and his *The Poetry of Ezra Pound* (1951) has exerted considerable influence. Kenner has made it inevitable that the defence of modernism passes into the hands of the conservative, even reactionary, fringe of critics. He interprets Pound's political thought as a radical-conservative, which inevitably causes serious distortions, for Pound's thought contains elements of traditional liberalism and progressivism. But this is not to say that Kenner is an unreliable guide to Pound's techniques and intentions: merely that his partisanship requires more than usual scepticism on the part of his readers. Davie, on the other hand, is much less easily described. His own poetry has strong affinities with the 'Movement', and virtually no contact whatsoever with Pound's. Davie's *Ezra Pound: Poet as Sculptor* (1964), an elegant but not particularly convincing book, is a sustained and occasionally bitter attack upon the intention behind the Cantos. Davie attacks the absurd, insane presumption behind the plan of the poem; he dismisses the Chinese Cantos as 'pathological and sterile'; he rebukes Pound's wasteful and arbitrary method of dealing with history: in other words, the Cantos are a failure which should warn us against trying anything like it again.

I think Pound made the essential point, with regard to Davie, at the end of 'The Serious Artist': 'The stupid or provincial judgment of art bases itself on the belief that great art must be like the art that it has been reared to respect.' The Cantos are a revolutionary poem, making fewer concessions to the reader than *The Waste Land* or *Paterson* or *The Maximus Poem*. It is appropriate here, at the end of a survey of the critical heritage of Pound's work, to insist that we are just beginning to understand the Cantos. That seems to me a healthy state of affairs. As for Pound's ultimate stature as a poet, it is as puzzling a question as the meaning and form of his work.

NOTES

1 Quoted by T. S. Eliot in *Ezra Pound: His Metric and Poetry* (1917); reprinted in *To Criticize the Critic and other Writings* (London, 1965), pp. 163–4.

2 This review has proved difficult to locate. A clipping of it is in one of Homer Pound's scrapbooks. Noel Stock (*Life*, p. 55) identifies it as appearing in the *New York American-Journal Examiner* of 14 December 1908. After a search no newspaper of this name could be found in the New York Public Library. Professor Donald Gallup, who kindly supplied me with his transcription of the clipping, said in a letter that it definitely did not appear in the magazine section of the *New York Sunday American* of 13 December 1908.

3 Herbert Read, *The Contrary Experience: Autobiographies* (London, 1963), p. 163.

4 'Publishers' Announcements. Mr. Welkin Mark's New Poet', *Punch* (23 June 1909), cxxxvi, 449. Quoted by Eliot in *Ezra Pound: His Metric and Poetry*.

5 Christopher Hassall, *Edward Marsh, A Patron of the Arts: A Biography* (London, 1959), p. 193.

6 *The Home Letters of T. E. Lawrence and His Brothers* (London, 1954), p. 249.

7 'Poetry's Banquet', *Poetry* (April 1914), iv, p. 27.

8 R. B. Cunninghame Graham, 'The Short Story' (a letter), *Saturday Review* (27 November 1909), cviii, 662.

9 Pound was pleased with Dell's review, and said so, writing to Dell from Philadelphia (letters quoted by G. Thomas Tanselle, 'Two Early Letters of Ezra Pound', *American Literature* (March 1962), xxxiv, 114–19).

10 Malcolm Cowley, *Exile's Return: A Literary Odyssey of the 1920's* (London, 1961), p. 122.

11 W. B. Yeats to Lady Gregory, 3 January 1913, quoted in A. N. Jeffares, *W. B. Yeats: Man and Poet* (Routledge & Kegan Paul and New Haven, 1949), p. 167.

12 W. B. Yeats to Harriet Monroe, ? December 1913, *The Letters of W. B. Yeats,* edited by Allan Wade (London, 1954), p. 585.

13 'English Bards and American Reviewers', *Punch* (22 January 1913), cxliv, 58.

14 W. G. Lawrence, letter of 28 January 1914, *The Home Letters of T. E. Lawrence and His Brothers*, p. 496.

15 Edward Thomas, 'Exotic Verse', *New Weekly* (9 May 1914), i, 249. In a letter to Gordon Bottomley of 22 May 1914 Thomas commented 'What imbeciles the Imagistes are', a view doubtless widely shared (*Letters from Edward Thomas to Gordon Bottomley*, edited by R. George Thomas (London, 1968), p. 233).

16 Lewis Worthington Smith, 'The New Naiveté', *Atlantic Monthly* (April 1916), cxvii, 492.

17 B. L. Reid, *The Man From New York: John Quinn and His Friends* (New York, 1968), p. 280. Reid gives an excellent account of the history of the pamphlet. See also Daniel H. Woodward, 'John Quinn and T. S. Eliot's First Book of Criticism', *Papers of the Bibliographical Society of America* (second quarter 1962), lvi, 259–65.

18 Burton Rascoe (1892–1957), an American critic and editor, took Hale's charges as final confirmation that Pound was 'utterly and incomprehensibly ignorant', and that he was an 'ignorant fraud': 'Never has a man with less talent and more charlatanry . . . succeeded in wielding so wide and pernicious an influence . . .', *Chicago Tribune,* March 1918, quoted by Martin Gilkes, *A Key to Modern English Poetry* (London 1937), ch. 7.

19 Walker Gilmer, *Horace Liveright: Publisher of the Twenties* (New York 1970), p. 244.

20 T. S. Eliot to John Quinn, January 1920, quoted in Donald Gallup, 'T. S. Eliot and Ezra Pound: Collaborators in Letters', *Poetry Australia* (February 1970), No. 32, 66. See also Reid, *The Man From New York*, p. 434. Quinn was able to come to Pound's help, negotiating for him the position of Paris correspondent of *Dial*.

21 Edmund Wilson, 'The Poetry of Drought', *Dial* (December 1922), lxxiii, 616.

22 Eliot to Seldes, quoted by Daniel H. Woodward, 'Notes on the Publishing History and Text of "The Waste Land" ', *Papers of the Bibliographical Society of America* (third quarter 1964), lviii, 258.

23 Edmund Wilson, 'Paul Rosenfeld: Three Phases', *The Commentary Reader*, edited by Norman Podhoretz (New York, 1966), p. 549.

24 Quoted in *The Letters of Carl Sandburg*, edited by Herbert Mitgang (New York, 1968), p. 242.

25 The only other important reply to Pound, other than Ford Madox Ford's in the *New Review* (Spring 1932), was Allen Tate, 'Laundry Bills', *Poetry* (November 1932), xli, 107–12.

26 *The Letters of Ford Madox Ford*, edited by Richard M. Ludwig (Princeton, 1965), pp. 212–13. See also pp. 213–16 for his letters to Eliot, Walpole, Williams, and Ernest Hemingway.

27 Robert Lowell's comment deserves greater currency: 'Pound's social credit, his Fascism, all these various things, were a tremendous gain to him; he'd be a very Parnassian poet without them. Even if they're bad beliefs—and some were bad, some weren't, and some were just terrible, of course—they made him more human and more to do with life, more to do with the times. They served him. Taking what interested him in these things gave a kind of realism and life to his poetry that it wouldn't have had otherwise'. *Writers at Work: The 'Paris Review' Interviews*, second series, introduced by Van Wyck Brooks (New York, 1965), p. 354.

28 Pound reviewed Douglas's *Economic Democracy* in the *Athenaeum* (2 April 1920): 'It is extremely difficult to find a flaw in this doctrine on the basis of ethics or equity.' But Pound has never shown any great familiarity with the enormous body of writings on Douglas and 'money economics'. I am thinking of F. P. Ramsey, 'The Douglas Proposals', *Cambridge Magazine* (1922), xi, 74–5; J. M. Keynes, 'The Problem of the Management of Money', *A Treatise on Money*, vol. 2 (London, 1930); and John Lewis, *Douglas Fallacies: A Critique of Social Credit* (London, 1935). Pound's hostility towards Keynes was in evidence not long after the publication of *The Economic Consequences of the Peace* (London, 1919), and remains a curious problem. See Earle Davis, *Vision Fugitive: Ezra Pound and Economics* (Lawrence, Kans., 1968). There is an alleged meeting between Douglas and Keynes (as 'Mr. Bukos') in Canto XXII, which is also mentioned in a letter to H. G. Wells of 3 February 1940 (*Letters*, p. 435).

29 Pound's anti-Semitism and fascism has usually been met, in the past two decades, with a knee-jerk dismissal. It seems to me that we are at this date able to move away from this situation. I am myself unable to think of Pound's political commitments, and racial ideas, with anything but the deepest loathing; but this is no reason to dismiss the subject from consideration.

30 For the evolution of Pound's attitude towards Mussolini see *Letters*, pp. 279 (1926), 320 (1932); *Jefferson and/or Mussolini* (1936; written in 1933); 'Murder by Capital', *Criterion* (July 1933), xii, 589; *Kulchur* (1938), p. 105; Canto LXXIV. There are many other references. There is a chapter on Pound's

politics in John R. Harrison, *The Reactionaries* (London, 1966), but the analysis is misleading and inaccurate, ignoring the crucial point that Pound's attitudes evolved, and that the Fascism he found attractive in 1926 had substantially changed in the years before the war. There is an acute comment on Pound's politics in Denis Donoghue, *The Ordinary Universe: Soundings in Modern Literature* (London, 1968), p. 294.

31 There is an incisive comparison of the racial theories of National Socialism and Fascism in A. James Gregor, *The Ideology of Fascism: The Rationale of Totalitarianism* (London and New York, 1969), pp. 241–82. Gregor also prints the text of the 'Manifesto of Fascist Racism' of 15 July 1938, pp. 383–6.

32 Isidor Schneider, 'Traitor or Holy Idiot?', *New Masses* (11 December 1945), lvii, 13. Schneider identifies the issue of *PM* and summarizes the views of the contributors, but I have not been able to locate it after a search. It must be said that the quality of literary comment in *New Masses*, and its successors, has been very primitive and literalist. For another example of the inadequacy of this material, see Samuel Sillen, 'A Prize for Ezra Pound', *Masses and Mainstream* (April 1949), ii, 3–6.

33 Dante meets Brunetto Latini in the *Inferno*, xv, 26–110 (Binyon's translation):

> 'O my son', said he, 'of this herd, who'er
> One instant stops, an hundred years must lie
> Helpless against the fire a hand to stir. . . .'.

34 Manuscript note of 20 November 1960 in *The Pisan Cantos* file in the New Directions office in New York. In giving permission to quote this note Mr Lowell requested that the 'casual free ungravely critical occasion of my statement' be indicated.

Save for numerous silent corrections, there being little point in faithfully reproducing hundreds of niggling spelling errors and simple errors of fact, the texts are printed verbatim. Deletions are marked by the use of ellipsis or indicated with square brackets. Numbered notes are those added by the editor.

MEETING EZRA POUND

1. William Carlos Williams

30 March 1904

Letter from Williams to his mother, *The Selected Letters of William Carlos Williams*, edited with an introduction by John C. Thirlwall (New York: McDowell, Obolensky, 1957), p. 6.

Williams (1883–1963), American poet, met Pound during the academic year 1902–3 when he was a student in the department of dentistry (he subsequently changed to medicine, which he practised in Rutherford, New Jersey) in the University of Pennsylvania. For the rest of his life he and Pound were (sometimes touchy) friends. Williams's *Autobiography* (1951) describes their relationship. (See also Emily Mitchell Wallace, 'Pound and Williams at the University of Pennsylvania', *Pennsylvania Review* (spring 1967), i, 41–53.) Williams reviewed *Personae* (No. 83), *A Draft of XXX Cantos* (see Bibliography), and *Guide to Kulchur* (No. 110).

Dear Mama: The reason I didn't write last Sunday was because I was out of town. My friend Pound invited me to spend Saturday and Sunday with him, so on Friday I wrote to you and then set off on my trip. . . . His parents are very nice people and have always been exceptionally kind to me. Mrs. Pound had prepared a fine meal. . . . After supper Pound and I went to his room where we had a long talk on subjects that I love yet have not time to study and which he is making a life work of. That is literature, and the drama and the classics, also a little philosophy. He, Pound, is a fine fellow; he is the essence of optimism and has a cast-iron faith that is something to admire. If he ever does get blue nobody knows it, so he is just the man for me. But not one person in a thousand likes him, and a great many people detest him and why? Because he is so darned full of conceits and affectation. He is really a brilliant talker and thinker but delights in making himself just exactly what he is not: a laughing boor. His friends must be all patience in order to find him out and even then you must not let him know it, for he will immediately put on some artificial mood and be really unbelievable. It is too bad, for he loves to be liked, yet there is some quality in him which makes him too proud to try to please people. I am sure his only fault is an exaggeration of a trait that in itself is good and in every way admirable. He is afraid of being taken in if he trusts his really tender heart to the mercies of a cruel crowd and so keeps it hidden and trusts no one. . . .

2. Edward Thomas

May, June, December 1909

Extracts from *Letters from Edward Thomas to Gordon Bottomley*, edited and introduced by R. George Thomas (London: Oxford University Press, 1968), pp. 185, 187, 197.

Thomas (1878–1917), English poet, was an early admirer of Pound's work. His enthusiastic opinion of *Personae* (Nos 11 and 12; see Introduction, p. 6) was considerably modulated in his review of *Exultations* (No. 18), as the comment below of 14 December suggests. Bottomley (1874–1948), a minor Georgian poet and playwright, had been Thomas's intimate friend and correspondent since 1904. Bottomley's 'King Lear's Wife', a verse play, appeared in *Georgian Poetry 1913–1915*.

1 May 1909: Here is Ezra Pound & I think he has very great things in him & the love poems & the 'Famam Librosque'—in fact nearly all— are extraordinary achievements. I know nothing about him but have an idea he has come from America.

12 June 1909: Oh I do humble myself over Ezra Pound. He is not &

cannot ever be very good. Certainly he is not what I mesmerized my-self—out of pure love of praising the new poetry!—into saying he was & I am very much ashamed & only hope I shall never meet the man. My greatest humiliation is due to regret for cheapening praise & using the same words about such a man as about, say, Sturge Moore, though of course I did indicate the chaos of the work.

14 December 1909: Ezra Pound's second book was a miserable thing & I was guilty of a savage recantation after meeting the man at dinner. It was very treacherous & my severity was due to self-contempt as much as dislike of his work.

3. D. H. Lawrence

November 1909

Extract from *Lawrence in Love: Letters to Louie Burrows*, edited by James T. Boulton (University of Nottingham Press, 1968), pp. 46–7.

Lawrence (1885–1930), English novelist and poet, had just been 'discovered' by Ford Madox Ford, editor of the *English Review*, when he met Pound. Violet Hunt was a London hostess, a minor novelist, and Ford's mistress. Pound was a frequent visitor to her home, 'South Lodge'. Douglas Goldring has written a memoir of the 'South Lodge' circle (see Bibliography) which contains a chatty glimpse of Pound's early London life. Witter Bynner has quoted a later, more jaundiced, comment by Lawrence on Pound: ' "In the old London days, Pound wasn't so literary as he is now. He was more of a mountebank then. He practiced more than he preached, for he had no audience. He was always amusing" ' (*Journey with Genius: Recollections and Reflections Concerning the D. H. Lawrences* (London: Peter Nevill, 1953), p. 145).

---

20 November 1909: I went on Tuesday to Violet Hunt's 'at home' at the Reform Club in Adelphi Terrace, on the Embankment. It was very jolly. Elizabeth Martindale & Ellaline Terris and Mary Cholmondeley were there—and Ezra Pound. He is a well-known American poet—a good one. He is 24, like me, but his god is beauty, mine life. He is jolly nice: took me to supper at Pagani's, and afterwards we went down to his room at Kensington. He lives in an attic, like a traditional poet—but the attic is a comfortable well furnished one. He is an American Master of Arts & a Professor of the Provençal group of languages, & he lectures once a week on the minstrels [at] the London Polytechnic. He is rather remarkable—a good bit of a genius, & with not the least self-consciousness.

This afternoon I am going up to tea with him & we are going out after to some friends who will not demand evening dress of us. He knows W. B. Yeats & all the Swells.

4. W. B. Yeats

10 December 1909

From a letter to Lady Gregory, *The Letters of W. B. Yeats*, edited by Allan Wade (London: Rupert Hart-Davis, 1954), p. 543.

Mrs Emery, the married name of Florence Farr, was an actress whose work with the psaltery and ideas about spoken verse interested Yeats. See his 'Speaking to the Psaltery' in *Essays and Introductions* (1961), and Florence Farr's *The Music of Speech* (1909).

This queer creature Ezra Pound . . . has become really a great authority on the troubadours, has I think got closer to the right sort of music for poetry than Mrs. Emery—it is more definitely music with strongly marked time and yet it is effective speech. However he can't sing as he has no voice. It is like something on a very bad phonograph.

5. T. S. Eliot

1909–10

Extract from an interview with Eliot in *Writers at Work: The 'Paris Review' Interviews*, second series, introduced by Van Wyck Brooks (New York: The Viking Press, 1965), p. 95.

Eliot (1885–1965), American poet, was educated at Harvard and Oxford. He met Pound after the outbreak of war in 1914, and Pound was instrumental in getting Eliot's early poetry into print. They remained life-long friends. Eliot was Pound's most influential interpreter (see Introduction, pp. 1–32), and Pound was a peppery critic of Eliot's work, as in his review of *After Strange Gods* in the *New English Weekly* (March 1934).

Pound's verse was first shown me by an editor of the *Harvard Advocate*, W. G. Tinckom-Fernandez, who was a crony of mine and Conrad Aiken's and the other Signet [a Harvard literary club] poets of the period. He showed me those little things of Elkin Mathews, *Exultations* and *Personae*. He said, 'This up your street; you ought to like this'. Well, I didn't really. It seemed to me rather fancy old-fashioned romantic stuff, cloak-and-dagger kind of stuff. I wasn't very impressed by it. When I went to see Pound I was not particularly an admirer of his work, and though I now regard the work I saw then as very accomplished, I am certain that in his later work is to be found the grand stuff.

6. Harriet Monroe

1910

Extract from 'Ezra Pound', *Poetry* (May 1925), xxvi, 90–1. The rest of this article is No. 80.

Harriet Monroe (1860–1936), a minor American poet, was the founder and editor of *Poetry: A Magazine of Verse*. Pound became her foreign editor, and a frequent contributor. Their relationship was eventually strained by the outspokenness of Pound's satires, particularly over the subject of sex. She was prepared to defend him in 1913 (No. 41).

The name evokes memories. First of being in London in 1910 on my way around the world to Peking; and of hearing about this young American from Elkin Mathews, his first publisher; and of carrying *Personae* away with me, and breathing the book's perfume on the long Siberian journey. . . .

At the time of the Siberian reading of *Personae* and *Exultations* I knew nothing of Mr. Pound's dynamic personality; so the impassioned beauty of his poems—their strange new insinuating rhythms, their half-interval cadences, their Debussy-like under-tones and over-tones—seemed to come out of the air, from some presence disembodied, impassioned, tense and sure.

> As bright white drops upon a leaden sea,
> Grant so my songs to this grey folk may be!

said the poet in his opening 'Grace Before Song'; and the poems that followed had the crystal clarity and iridescent gleam of dew-drops in the morning sun. As Mr. Mathews had said, they were 'pure poetry', with no dusty alloy of baser motive than the sheer command of the muse.

A LUME SPENTO

Venice, June 1908

---

7. Unsigned notice, *Book News Monthly*

May 1909, xxvii, 719

Pound was an occasional contributor to *Book News Monthly*.

Mr. Pound is talented, but he is very young. The academician bristles
all over his work. French phrases and scraps of Latin and Greek punc-
tuate his poetry and prose, and the carelessness that attends the swift
birth of an idea marks his every line. He affects obscurity and loves the
abstruse; he has apparently been influenced by Whitman. This small
volume of poems, entitled *With Tapers Quenched*, contains some strange
specimens of verse, though a certain underlying force gives promise of
simplicity to come—when Mr. Pound has learned that simplicity and
greatness are synonymous.

PERSONAE

London, 16 April 1909

8. Unsigned review, *Evening Standard and St. James's Gazette*

21 April 1909, 5

Various influences are manifest in this daintily produced volume of verse. The Old French singers and Browning—contrasts indeed!—are the most prominent. Mr. Pound has any amount of affectations, and sometimes is incoherent in order to seem original, but, in spite of draw-backs, he manages to suggest his essential sincerity. It is a queer little book which will irritate many readers. We dislike its faults, and confess to being puzzled here and there. And yet—and yet we are attracted occasionally by lines which are almost, if not quite, nonsense. Our con-clusion is that Mr. Pound is a poet, though a fantastic one.

9. W. L. Courtney, unsigned review, *Daily Telegraph*

23 April 1909, 6

Courtney (1850–1928) read classics at University College, Oxford, and was elected a Fellow in philosophy at New College. In 1890 he joined the *Daily Telegraph* and became literary editor. He became editor of the *Fortnightly Review* in 1894, and subsequently chairman of the London publishing house, Chapman & Hall. He published verse by Pound in the *Fortnightly* as well as essays on Tagore (1 March 1913), Vorticism (1 September 1914), and Rémy de Gourmont (1 December 1915).

Most people are more or less the victims of that convention which made Byron ridicule the idea of a man named as Amos Cottle ('Phoebus, what a name!') winning fame as a poet, and so they may be expected to smile on taking up a volume of poems the author of which is Mr. Ezra Pound. They may begin by smiling, they will end with admiration, not un-mixed with irritation, for here is a poet with individuality and with sufficient disregarding for the conventional to express that individuality in the way that likes him best rather than in the way which more accom-modating talents would have chosen. He limits himself just so far as he chooses to measures which those who run may read; he indulges in rhyme when he likes; runs off into mere assonance, or uses lines which need the most careful reading if we would beat their music out. Yet, for the most part, there is through all a thread of true beauty, which gives the book something of a haunting charm. It lifts it out of the ruck of those many volumes the writers of which toe the line of poetic conven-tions and please us for more than a single reading in that they have mastered the knack of saying certain things in certain fashions. 'Most can grow the flower now, for all have got the seed,' said the late Laureate. Mr. Pound is of the few who have gone forth into life and found something of a new seed, and his 'flower' is one that is unques-tionably beautiful, though it will scarcely please many of those who

44

prefer rather new varieties of the old favourites than Hesperidean novelties. It is true that Mr. Pound shows himself a keen reader of Browning; indeed, his lines on Browning's 'And a cat's in the water-butt,' form a triumphant piece of parody.

[quotes 'Mesmerism', *CSP*, p. 27.]

Mr. Pound is much moved by the spirit of the troubadours; to them he turns again and again for theme, and gives us verses instinct with beauty, even when the outline is blurred. A few simple lines in one of his poems might be given as a test. Those readers who are touched by them will find much to delight in this little book, those who are unmoved will have little difficulty in finding metal more attractive:

> For I am homesick after mine own kind
> And ordinary people touch me not.
> > And I am homesick
> After mine own kind that know, and feel
> And have some breath for beauty and the arts.

From one of his irregular but forceful pieces, 'Revolt Against the Crepuscular Spirit in Modern Poetry', we give a fuller taste of Mr. Pound's quality:

[quotes 'Revolt: Against the Crepuscular Spirit in Modern Poetry', *Personae*, p. 53 'I would shake off' to 'its masters, but shadow!']

It is more or less inevitable that we should on being touched by a new writer, seek to 'place' him by comparison with the old. Mr. Ezra Pound then suggests such incompatibilities as a troubadour of old Provence and—Walt Whitman. He has much of the sense of beauty of things and of words ('little red elf words', 'little green leaf words') of the one, much of the vigorous individuality of the other.

10. F. S. Flint, review, *New Age*

27 May 1909, v, 101–2

Pound sent a clipping of this review to his father, remarking that although it was not especially well written, it served as advertising (YL, 108).

Flint (1885–1960) was a self-educated man whose verse, though derivative, and essays secure him an important place in the history of Imagism. After the First World War he entered the Civil Service, eventually becoming chief of the overseas section of the statistics division in the Ministry of Labour.

'Make strong old dreams lest this our world lose heart'
—Epigraph to *Personae*

Mr. Pound is a poet with a distinct personality. Essentially, he is a rebel against all conventions except sanity; there is something robustly impish and elfish about him. He writes with fresh beauty and vigour; and revolting against the crepuscular spirit in modern poetry, he cries:

[quotes the first eleven lines of 'Revolt: Against the Crepuscular Spirit in Modern Poetry', *Personae* (1909), p. 53.]

And the songs and histories of the old Provençal poets being at his command, the bitter-sweet vision of Dante part of his emotional existence, to them he turns for the personae of his dreams. Whoever has read anything at all of the Troubadours cannot but admire the colour and intense energy of their lives; battle and love and song succeeding each other, entered into with the same ardour and passion, the hot meridional sun beating itself into all. Bertran of Born—strange, wild figure of songs and war, that troubled the peace of an English Henry. Arnaud of Marvoil—son of a serf and poet, admitted to court the Countess of Beziers, banished when too importunate. Piere Vidal—who ran as a wolf because his lady's name was Louve, brought back fainting, all fanged by the hounds—masochism before the man. They move in Mr. Pound's dreams; but whether his strengthening and beautifying of them with English verse will give us heart, I do not know—or, rather, I fear we shall lose heart in watching them; for, it seems, the world is in the grip of a dragon against which, so far, has appeared no effectual Saint George.

Let us once and for all acknowledge what Mr. Pound owes to Browning, his mediaeval poets, mystics and thinkers, and perhaps a little to Mr. Yeats and Thompson; and take his poems as poetry, without reference to sources of raw material. I think there is sufficient craft and artistry, originality and imagination in *Personae* to warrant one in giving them high praise. Mr. Pound writes in a free form of verse that will not, I hope, lead him into the wastes. He is working towards a form that other English poets might study. . . .

This book is as tufted with beauty as the bole of an old elm tree with green shoots. . . . One must read 'Na Audiart', 'Praise of Ysolt', a fine piece of work, 'An Idyll for Glaucus', to appreciate Mr. Pound's quality. Perhaps he was himself among those whom he saw coursing and crying:

> 'Tis the white stag, Fame, we're a-hunting,
> Bid the world's hounds come to horn.

The wind swept round the earth to make that last image; it has the matinal gusto Keats heard in Kean's delivery of

> Be rising with the lark to-morrow, gentle Norfolk.

I do not like the forms evan'scent, 'thout, 'cause, and

'DAEMON',

'Quasi KALOUN' S.T. says

has no right in a poem.

11. Edward Thomas, 'A New Note in Verse'
Daily Chronicle

7 June 1909, 3

This initialled review was written in the first flush of Thomas's enthusiasm over Pound (see No. 2): within a week he regretted 'cheapening praise'.

Carelessness of sweet sound and of all the old tricks makes Mr. Pound's book rather prickly to handle at first. It was practically nothing but this prickliness that incited us to read his book through a second time. We read it a third time—because it was good the second, and, nevertheless, still held back other good things. But we know from experience that it is impossible to show in a bit of a column that a new writer is good and in a new way. Nor will we trust him in the form of extracts to anyone's tender mercies, but give simply the one poem short enough for quotation. It is called 'The White Stag':

[quotes 'The White Stag', *CSP*, p. 39.]

That will at least give you some idea of the way Mr. Pound's work bursts upon the mind. All his poems are like this, from beginning to end, and in every way, his own, and in a world of his own. For brusque intensity of effect we can hardly compare them with any other work. Of course, this is due partly to his faults and to his pride in revolt, to his lack of all mere amiability, to his austerity, to his abruptness as of a swift beetle that suddenly strikes your cheek and falls stunned with its own force, to his use of a number of archaisms in the midst of a chaste and simple vocabulary.

But these faults have the same origin as his virtues, and are doubtless at present inseparable from them. He is so possessed by his own strong conception, that he not only cannot think of wrapping them up in a conventional form, but he must ever show his disdain for it a little; one of his poems is, in so many words, a revolt against the crepuscular spirit in modern poetry. But the disdain is the other side of a powerful love for something else, and it is usually either implicit or entirely concealed. Yet, when we consider it, there is singularly little crudity and practically no extravagance. It is mostly hard, naked, and grim.

Well, and what is this new thing? somebody is asking. It is only the very old, felt and said anew; the love of a mind for the wild wood, for women, for his own songs, for his friend, for life. And in half at least the poet chooses to let men long dead utter his words—a troubadour of the Middle Ages, a companion of Villon's, an 'unknown writer' of the eighteenth century, a Saxon of the eighth, a Crusader, a poet in Nineveh!

Yet as we read we forget that it has been done before; we share something of the spirit of love that has entered him, and see all things anew. And, setting aside the archaisms, which do not count one way or the other, the method is so simple. No remarkable melody; no golden words shot with meaning; a temperate use of images, and now far-fetched; no flattering of modern fashions, in descriptions of Nature, for example; no apostrophe, no rhetoric, nothing 'Celtic'. It is the old miracle that cannot be defined, nothing more than a subtle entanglement of words, so that they rise out of their graves and sing. And part of our pleasure in reading the book has been the belief, in which we are confident, that the writer is only just getting under sail, that he will reach we know not where; nor does he, but somewhere far away in the unexplored.

12. Edward Thomas, from 'Two Poets', *English Review*

June 1909, ii, 627–32

The other poet under review is Maurice Hewlett.

It is easier to enjoy than to praise Mr. Pound, easier to find fault with him, easiest to ridicule. His *Personae*, probably a first book, is strewn with signs of two battles not yet over, the battle with the world of a fresh soul who feels himself strong but alone, and the battle with words, the beautiful, the soiled, the rare, the antique words. It is not wonderful then that one coming up from the outside should be tempted for a moment to turn away from the battlefield with a promise to come back and see who and what is left. And yet such tumults are fascinating for themselves, especially if we know that sometimes when they are over, nothing, from the spectator's point of view, is left. In Mr. Pound's case we feel sure there will be a great soul left. Also, in the meantime, the book is well worth having for itself and regardless of its vague large promise.

Let us straightway acknowledge the faults; the signs of conflict; the old and foreign words and old spellings that stand doubtless for much that the ordinary reader is not privileged to detect; the tricky use of inverted commas; the rhythms at one time so free as not to be distinguishable at first from prose, at another time so stiff that 'evanescent' becomes evan'scent; the gobbets of Browningesque; and one piece of construction at the foot of p. 39 which we cannot unravel and are inclined to put down as not the only case of imperfect correction of proofs.

To say what this poet has not is not difficult; it will help to define him. He has no obvious grace, no sweetness, hardly any of the superficial good qualities of modern versifiers; not the smooth regularity of the Tennysonian tradition, nor the wavering, uncertain languor of the new, though there is more in his rhythms than is apparent at first through his carelessness of ordinary effects. He has not the current melancholy or resignation or unwillingness to live; nor the kind of feeling for nature that runs to minute description and decorative metaphor. He cannot be usefully compared with any living writers, though he has read Mr. Yeats. Browning and Whitman he respects, and he could easily burlesque Browning if he liked. He knows mediaeval poetry in the popular tongues, and Villon, and Ossian. He is equally fond of strict stanzas of many rhymes, of blank verse with many unfinished lines, of rhymeless or almost rhymeless lyrics, of Pindarics with or without rhyme. But these forms are not striking in themselves, since all are subdued to his spirit; in each he is true in his strength and weakness to himself, full of personality and with such power to express it that from the first to the last lines of most of his poems he holds us steadily in his own pure, grave, passionate world.

It will appear paradoxical to say after this that the chief part of his power is directness and simplicity. A characteristic opening is this, put in the mouth of an Italian poet—'Italian Campagna, 1309, The Open Road':

> Bah! I have sung women in three cities,
> But it is all the same;
> And I will sing of the sun. . . .

or this, from 'A Villonaud: Ballad of the Gibbet; or the Song of the Sixth Companion of Villon':

> Drink ye a skoal for the gallows tree!
> François and Margot and thee and me,
> Drink we the comrades merrily
> That said us, 'Till then' for the gallows tree!

In the poem 'In Tempore Senectutis' the old man says to his old love:

> Red spears bore the warrior dawn
>   Of old.
> Strange! Love, hast thou forgotten
> The red spears of the dawn,
> The pennants of the morning?

The finest of his pieces are the love-poems. In 'Scriptor Ignotus: Ferrara, 1715,' he astonishes us by using again the poet's claim, Ronsard's and Shakespeare's, to give immortality to a mistress by words, by 'A new thing as hath not heretofore been writ.' But it is not a playing upon an old theme as, *e.g.*, Locker-Lampson played on it. It is a piece of strong tender passion that happens to lean upon the old theme and to honour it. 'In Praise of Ysolt' is equally beautiful in an entirely different way, showing that the writer does not depend upon a single mood or experience. The beauty of it is the beauty of passion, sincerity and intensity, not of beautiful words and images and suggestions; on the contrary, the expression is as austere as Biblical prose. The thought dominates the words and is greater than they are.

It opens:

> In vain have I striven to teach my heart to bow;
> In vain have I said to him
> 'There be many singers greater than thou'.

> But his answer cometh, as winds and as lutany,
> As a vague crying upon the night
> That leaveth me no rest, saying ever,
>   'Song, a song.'

In the 'Idyl for Glaucus' a woman hovers by the sea in search of Glaucus, who has tasted 'the grass that made him sea-fellow with the other gods.' Here the effect is full of human passion and natural magic, without any of the phrases which a reader of modern verse would expect in the treatment of such a subject. In 'From Syria' and 'From the Saddle' the thought is not new but it is made his own by genuineness, weakened only by allowing such a line as

> So if my line disclose distress.

'And thus in Nineveh' we venture to quote in its entirety, not as the best but as the shortest of these love-poems, with this warning that, like the two last, it does not reveal Mr. Pound neat, though we are confident that it will give conviction to our praise of his style:

[quotes 'And Thus in Nineveh', *CSP*, p. 38.]

And on the same page is this wonderful little thing that builds itself so abruptly, swiftly, clearly into the air:

> I ha' seen them mid the clouds on the heather.
> Lo! they pause not for love nor for sorrow,
> Yet their eyes are as the eyes of a maid to her lover,
> When the white hart breaks his cover
> And the white wind breaks the morn.
>   *'Tis the white stag, Fame, we're a-hunting,*
>   *Bid the world's hounds come to horn!*

In taking leave of this admirable poet we should like to mention other poems we have particularly enjoyed, 'La Fraisne', 'Famam Librosque Cano' (a prophetic sketch, of the kind of reader he will one day have), 'Ballad for Gloom,' 'For E. McC.' (these two last very brilliant and noble), 'Occidit,' and 'Revolt against the Crepuscular Spirit in Modern Poetry'; and to apologise to him for our own shortcomings and to any other readers for that insecurity of modern criticism of which we feel ourselves at once a victim and a humble cause.

13. Unsigned review, *Observer*

20 June 1909, 5

Mr. Ezra Pound has lost none of his magic since the coming of the queer little paper book from Italy that was his first message to 'this grey folk' of England. There are in *Personae* some of the poems that delighted us in *A Lume Spento*. There is 'La Fraisne,' the story of the man in the Ash Wood of Malvern, whom men call mad because he has 'put aside all folly and all grief,' and finds his bride, the dog-wood tree, and the pool of the wood 'sweeter than the love of women' which has driven him mad. This poem has a haunting atmosphere of beauty. 'Cino,' again, is extraordinarily full of charm. Its metre sings, and the suggestion of every word, placed as only a poet can place it, goes far beyond the thing said. The cadences sing of 'melodies unheard,' musical though they are in themselves. It is something, after all, intangible and indescribable that makes the real poetry. Criticism and praise alike give no idea of it. Everyone who pretends to know it when he sees it should read and keep this book. Its spirit is the High Romance, and it is never sickly and never monotonous, but the real work of a real 'Poet that doth drink of life, As lesser men drink wine.'

14. Unsigned review, *Bookman* (London)

July 1909, xxxvi, 188–9

This review may be by Edward Thomas. Professor R. George Thomas of University College, Cardiff, editor of Thomas's correspondence with Gordon Bottomley and of Thomas's poems, suggests the attribution because Thomas frequently reviewed new poetry for the *Bookman*, because he on occasion reviewed the same book several times, and, finally, because the substance of this review points towards his authorship.

No one who has any feeling for what is poetry can read through *Personae* without feeling that Mr. Pound has the root of the matter in him. Faults his book has in plenty, but they are the faults of youth, faults of an eager, adventurous spirit who will not keep tamely to the beaten track, and seeking ways of his own, must needs go often astray before he finds them. He disdains the fetters of regular rhyme; his metrical harmonies are frequently unfamiliar, and at times seem crude and harsh, perhaps because our ears are unused to them; he conjures largely with assonance and alliteration. Again and again his verse strikes you as too artificial, too tricky; the frequent use of old words and eccentricities of phrasing give it an affectation; yet again, also, you come upon some lyric that is beautifully simple in form and utterance, that orbs itself easily and naturally as thus, with 'In Tempore Senectutis'. . . . Or turn to 'In Durance' and you will have Mr. Pound almost at his best and almost at his worst. . . .

No eccentricities go to the making of great poetry; when Browning rose to his highest he was neither eccentric nor obscure. There is real imaginative power and breath of originality about such things as 'An Idyl for Glaucus', the 'Ballad for Gloom', 'And Thus in Nineveh', 'Praise for Ysolt', and certain other of his poems, which give you confidence that Mr. Pound will outgrow the influence of Browning's perversities and conquer his own; in the meantime, *Personae* is a profoundly interesting achievement; no new book of poems for years past has had such a freshness of inspiration, such a strongly individual note, or been more alive with undoubtable promise.

15. Unsigned review, 'Heresy, and Some Poetry', *Nation* (London)

28 August 1909, v, 789–91

Pound was not upset by this review. He sent a copy of it to his mother early in September 1909, remarking that this sort of attack caused quite an 'ado' which was at least good for the sake of publicity (YL, 115).

From time to time one hears of artistic malcontents who would have poetry do what music is doing nowadays, which is, altering its mode of expression. Of course, music is changing its expression because the content of music is, in some sort, changing; but what these malcontents do not see is that the boundaries of poetic content were long ago extended to such spacious width that it is not humanly possible to extend the *imperium* of poesy, and consequently, that the mode of proper poetic expression is also, within broad limits, practically fixed. We may liken the two arts to states, and the expression of the arts to government. Poetry is a very ancient state, its antique frontiers thrown out as far as ages of experience show may be congruous to good government; and the mode of government (that is, the art's expression) has long ago adapted itself to the administration and control of all the various peoples and climates within the state. It is unlikely that anything will occur within the borders of the poetic state with which the established poetic government will not be able to cope. But music is a new and upstart state. It is continually throwing out new and more ambitious frontiers; and therefore the state government (the expression of music) has to be continually altered to meet the requirements of the new provinces that are from time to time absorbed. Strauss and Debussy, for instance, are not insurgents against the constitution; rather they are viceroys ruling, with provisional powers, recent additions to the empire of music. But we may justly accuse a poet of mere rebellion and treason if, while abiding within the old boundaries, he defies the constituted, but extremely elastic, government of his state. Not such were Browning and Whitman; they were rather eccentric, but quite law-abiding citizens. Such, however, is Mr. Ezra Pound. He has mistaken insurgence for strength, treason for originality. Not having anything particularly new to say (it is none the worse for that), he yet seeks to be unusual through a strange method of expression. By this we do not only mean queer tricks of metre and diction; poetry easily allows such eccentricities. Mr. Ezra Pound gives us plenty of them; some are successful and pleasant, others irritating and foolish. One may tolerate such Chaucerian words in modern verse as 'swevyn' for 'dream', and 'everychone' for 'everyone.' But 'ellum' for 'elm,' in a poem written not in dialect, and 'mine fashion' for 'my fashion,' are merely silly; and to address Phoebus Apollo as ''Pollo Phoibee, old tin pan, you,' is not humorous, but ludicrous. Such matters some modern critical opinion holds to be insignificant, though they are greatly important really; but they are not Mr. Pound's gravest offences. And we could forgive his habit of beginning a poem in the middle, and his uses of German, French, and Italian words. The grave error that Mr. Pound commits lies in the initial shaping and conduct of his thought. From the beginning he will not, or cannot, manage his thought according to the high and nameless, but rigorous, logic of poetry. Poetry does not consist in a fine clothing of words; the words must clothe, not only a spirit, but a spiritual shape. A mere gusty wind of spirit will not do for poetry; it must be a spirit with formed lineaments and stature, a spirit with at least the shape of divinity. Except in a few cases where he is following Romance models, one finds no such spirit wearing Mr. Pound's words; they are but carried on unruly tempests of thought or emotion. We dare say Mr. Pound finds these poems of his full of subtleties and allurement, for he knows, no doubt, what meaning runs through them. But for most others many of them will seem, we fear, only abrupt, discontinuous and meaningless exclamations, rather trying to patience. One sometimes detects vigorous poetic phrasing in his work, and the ring of heroic thought, as in the 'Ballad for Gloom':—

> I have loved my God as a child at heart
> That seeketh deep bosoms for rest,

> I have loved my God as maid to man
> But, lo, this thing is best:
> To love your God as a gallant foe that plays behind the veil,
> To meet your God as the night winds meet beyond Arcturus' pale.

Mr. Pound very properly objects to the 'crepuscular spirit in modern poetry,' and would be the cock that 'scatters the rear of darkness thin,' as he says, rather finely:—

> Great God, if we be damn'd to be not men, but only dreams,
> Then let us be such dreams the world will tremble at.

Certainly, Mr. Pound makes a lively din; and it is because it is lively, and not mechanical, that we have criticised it at some length. There are admirable qualities in his work, but not the supreme quality; like the cock's, Mr. Pound's din lacks measure. Were that present, he would be one of the most notable poets of our time.

There are no doubt those who would commend Mr. Pound for breaking away from the 'holy habit' of poetic thought; in these free days, they will think, it is a hardship that the manner of poetic expression should be fixed and determinate, even though the bounds of that manner be so large that for those who understand its necessary limitings its service is perfect freedom. Such persons might do a good deal worse than read Mr. Darrell Figgis's *Vision of Life*. Mr. Figgis's poetry is not at all conventional, or even orthodox; it is new and original. Yet it is quite good poetry, implicitly obeying the code of poetic law. . . .

16. Rupert Brooke, review, *Cambridge Review*

2 December 1909, xxxi, 166–7

Brooke (1887–1915), the golden boy of Edwardian letters, repented his early enthusiasm for Pound and their relationship remained awkward. Brooke attacked Pound in the *Poetry Review* (November 1912) for a less than enthusiastic reference to Lascelles Abercrombie, a minor Georgian poet. Pound referred to this attack in a letter to Harriet Monroe of 22 October 1912 (*Letters*, p. 46), and announced his determination to 'stand alone'. Brooke's review is collected in *The Prose of Rupert Brooke*, edited by Christopher Hassall (London: Sidgwick & Jackson, 1956).

Mr. Ezra Pound's work was 'discovered' recently by certain London papers, and, a little timorously, acclaimed as valuable and inspiring. He is—do not his name and his verse betray it?—a young American; and he writes *vers libre*. His virtues and faults are both obvious. He is blatant, full of foolish archaisms, obscure through awkward language not subtle thought, and formless; he tastes experience keenly, has an individual outlook, flashes into brilliance, occasionally, and expresses roughly a good deal of joy in life. The dedication of the book is very pleasant, and oddly expressive of the author's character. 'This book is for Mary Moore of Trenton, if she wants it'. The abandon, the suggestion of jolly power, and the slight posing of that, are typical of his character. When Mr. Pound writes notes, and in some of his poems, the posing, the unnecessary assumption of a twisted Browningesque personality, it is exceedingly tiresome. But when inspiration cleans him a little of that, and when he writes in metre, the result is quite good. He writes a 'Ballad of the Gibbet', in which his 'persona' is the sixth of the companions of Villon on a famous occasion.

[quotes 'A Villonaud: Ballad of the Gibbet', ll. 17–28, *CSP*, pp. 25–6.]

There, in spite of the affectation of 'disdeign', one cannot but feel a note of exultation that is rare enough in modern poetry, whether written by the young or by the middle-aged. But though in this, and in other metrical poems, Mr. Pound shows he is a poet, he has fallen, it appears, under the dangerous influence of Whitman, and writes many poems in unmetrical sprawling lengths that, in his hands, have nothing to commend them. In these forms he generally, not always, fails to express much beauty. He rather wantonly adopts them, no doubt, in youthful protest against the flood of metrical minor verse of today. A little quiet reasoning is all he needs. For the truth of the matter is very clear. There are certain extremely valuable 'aesthetic' feelings to be got through literature. These can be got, it is empirically certain, sometimes through prose, of the ordinary and of the Whitmanic kind, often and more intensely through poetry, in which the three elements of thought, words, and metre are employed. That is the beginning and end of the whole affair. The only especial note to be made in the case of Mr. Pound is that he sometimes uses a poetical variety of prose which is metrical in so far as it is composed entirely of iambic feet, but not in so far as it pays no attention to lines. The lengths are chopped off anyhow. It is certain now (thanks in part to Mr. Saintsbury), as it has long been obvious, that the foot is immensely important in English prosody. It is still more certain that the line is. Otherwise *Lorna Doone* and much of Dickens would be pure verse.

Mr. Pound has great talents. When he has passed through stammering to speech, and when he has more clearly recognized the nature of poetry, he may be a great poet. It is important to remember his name; and we shall be made to recognize it when he turns from prose, admirable prose as it sometimes is, to confine himself to the form in which he wrote 'Camraderie':

[quotes 'Camraderie', *Selected Poems*, ed. T. S. Eliot, p. 192.]

17. A new poet makes his debut

July 1909

An unsigned item from 'News Notes', *Bookman* (London) July 1909, xxxvi, 154–5.

This sort of publicity eased Pound's entry into Edwardian literary society. A handsome photo of Pound in profile by Elliott & Fry accompanied this note.

Mr. Ezra Pound, whose new book of poems, *Personae*, has met with an unusually appreciative reception, is a young American of English descent, his forbears having been among those early settlers who went out to the New World in the seventeenth century. On his mother's side he is distantly related to Longfellow, whose poetry he does not admire; he is a Fellow of the University of Pennsylvania; has travelled much in Spain; lived for some while in Venice; and is now making his home in England with no particular desire to depart from us, though he has a very much greater liking for the English people than for their climate. He has two other small books of verse to his name, *A Lume Spento* and *A Quinzaine for this Yule*, which were printed in limited editions for private circulation. The smallness of his output does not indicate barrenness or indolence, but that he has a faculty of self-criticism: he has written and burned two novels and three hundred sonnets; last spring he delivered at the Polytechnic here an introductory course of six lectures on 'The Development of Literature in Southern Europe', and he has prepared a long course of lectures on 'Romance Literature' which he is to deliver at the Polytechnic this autumn; moreover, he is still only twenty-three. He has lately completed a new book, a prose and verse sequence, which he is calling *The Dawn*.

EXULTATIONS

London, 25 October 1909

18. Edward Thomas, 'The Newest Poet', *Daily Chronicle*

23 November 1909, 3

Mr. Pound's verses look so extraordinary, dappled with French, Provençal, Spanish, Italian, Latin and Old English, with proper names that we shirk pronouncing, with crudity, violence and obscurity, with stiff rhythms and no rhythms at all, that we are tempted to think that they are the expression or at least the mask of an extraordinary man. It is a relief to us to turn from all but meaningless suavity and skill to something that appears to be individual. And doubtless no ordinary man could or would write like Mr. Pound. But having allowed the turbulent opacity of his peculiarities to sink down we believe that we see very nearly nothing at all. Thus in a poem on Piere Vidal, the fool who 'ran mad as a wolf because of his love . . . and how men hunted him with dogs', we find nothing which we cannot ourselves feel with the help of the introductory note in prose. The verses show us only such things as the writer's effort to imagine what it would be like to be a wolf:

> God! how the swiftest hind's blood spurted hot
> Over the sharpened teeth and purpling lips.

In some of his poems he produces no effect at all, and we are at leisure to note the peculiar taste of the writer with astonishment, as, for example, the Irish turns in this verse:

> Though I am hungry for their lips
>   When I see them a-hiding
> And a-passing out and in through the shadows
> —and it is white they are—

> But if one should look at me with the old
>   hunger in her eyes,
> How will I be answering her eyes?
> For I have followed the white folk of the forest.

Here it may be that there was something to be expressed which failed to be, because it was difficult. But in the poem addressed to the beautiful women of London:

> I am aweary with the utter and beautiful weariness
> And with the ultimate wisdom and with things terrene;
> I am aweary with your smiles and your laughter
> And the sun, and the wind's again
> Reclaim their booty and the heart o' me—

the thought is simple and plain enough, and interesting as a human fact, but it can hardly be claimed that it is expressed in a beautiful way or in any way which gives it an individual value as a cry from the heart. When Mr. Pound has a subject, as in the 'Glaucus' of his first volume, he can treat it in a manner deserving attention, not always, but now and then. When he writes in the first person he is so obscure as to give some excuse for finding him incapable of self-expression. And both in personal and detached poems he is, as a rule, so pestered with possible ways of saying a thing that at present we must be content to pronounce his condition still interesting—perhaps promising—certainly distressing. If he is not careful he will take to meaning what he says instead of saying what he means.

19. Unsigned review, *Spectator*

11 December 1909, ciii, 1000–1

Mr. Ezra Pound is that rare thing among modern poets, a scholar. He is not only cultivated, but learned. Many modern influences are patent in his verse—Whitman, Rossetti, Browning, Mr. Yeats—but the dominant ones are mediaeval, the romances of the troubadours and old monkish legends. We feel that this writer has in him the capacity for remarkable poetic achievement, but we also feel that at present he is somewhat weighted by his learning. His virility and passion are immense, but somehow we seem to know their origins. He strikes us as a little too bookish and literary, even when he is most untrammelled by metrical conventions. It is ungracious to carp at work which in itself is so fine, but we think it right to hint at the danger. For the rest, Mr. Pound's merits are singularly clear. The 'Ballad of the Goodly Fere' a wonderful presentation of Christ, haunts our memory, as does the savage sestina which contains the reflections of Bertran de Born. Admirable, too, is the strange soliloquy of 'Piere Vidal Old'. Mr. Pound has flute-notes as well, as can be seen from the 'Portrait' on p. 25, and the lovely 'Night Litany'. If he has defects, he has at any rate the true and brimming inspiration. Mr. Flint's *In the Net of the Stars* has something of the same manner, but the writer has not Mr. Pound's richness or strength of thought.

20. Unsigned review, *Observer*

26 December 1909, 3

In a letter to his father in December 1909 (YL, 142), Pound mentioned this review as being colourless.

One is glad to welcome another tiny volume of most delicate verse from Mr. Ezra Pound, whose *Personae* had a charm of fancy and of finish that has carried it to a high degree of success. It is quite safe to say that few new poets have so quickly become known to literary London. *Exultations* has some lines in every poem that one wants to quote. There is the speech of Piere Vidal, who tells of the gloriously fierce Loba, for love of whom he ran as a wolf and was hunted by dogs.

> God curse the years that turn such women grey!

and many lines equally haunting. There is the imaginative idea in

'Histrion,' which most of us have felt but none of us have written, though Emerson said something like it once. Above all, there is the daring but beautiful 'Ballad of the Goodly Fere,' in which we could wish the alteration of one line only, the rest being a magnificent picture of an often neglected side of the Christ-ideal. Mr. Ezra Pound is no poetaster. He must guard his 'sorrowful great gift,' but not withhold it.

21. F. S. Flint, 'Verse', *New Age*

6 January, 1910 vi, 233–4

Flint's last paragraph announces the campaign for *vers libre*.

Mr. Pound exults through the souls of great men. He says:

[quotes 'Histrion' ll. 1–10, *ALS*, p. 108.]

But though he would have it that 'the Masters of the Soul' speak through him, it seems truer to say that he himself speaks through the glamour which their names cast over him. That is why, for instance, Sandalphon, the angel of prayer according to the Talmud, breaks out with a *forsitan*! Why, too, the poem 'Night Litany' has a refrain:

> O Dieu, purifiez nos coeurs!
> purifiez nos coeurs!

and the 'Sestina: Altaforte' is introduced thus:

> Loquitur: *En* Bertrans de Born.
> Dante Alighieri put this man in hell for that he was a
> stirrer-up of strife.
> Eccovi!
> Judge ye!
> Have I dug him up again?

The first lines are:

Damn it all! all this our South stinks peace.
You whoreson dog, Papiols, come! Let's to music.

Why, too, Simon Zelotes, speaking somewhile after the Crucifixion, in the 'Ballad of the Goodly Fere', or Christ, uses a jargon which, I believe, is supposed to be Old English. It consists mainly in the clipping of words; but still it is a jargon. Why, too, Mr. Pound entitles his poems in different languages: 'Nel Biancheggiar', 'Planh', 'Laudantes Decem . . .', 'Aux Belles de Londres'. For Mr. Pound is an American, and a hotchpotch of picturesqueness, made up of divers elements—in literature, words from divers tongues—is the American idea of beauty. Thank heaven that Mr. Pound is a poet also, and that this picturesqueness is only sauce to the dish. Still, one sees no reason why the refrain quoted above should not be:

O God, make clean our hearts!
make clean our hearts!

Except that the French makes the poem picturesque, and, therefore, from an American point of view, more beautiful. But that 'Eccovi! Judge ye!' and the funny 'Have I dug him up again?' I am afraid not; for the 'Sestina: Altaforte' is rant.

But with all these reservations one must agree that there is in Mr. Pound's new book a rift of real, though vague, beauty, impalpable gold, as in the 'Laudantes Decem . . .' and 'Planh'; and in the sonnet 'Plotinus' he lifts himself suddenly out of the picturesqueness and the subtle into six lines of bare, wrought beauty:

But I was lonely as a lonely child.
I cried amid the void and heard no cry,
And then for utter loneliness, made I
New thoughts as crescent images of *me*.
And with them was my essence reconciled
While fear went forth from mine eternity.

It is when Mr. Pound is speaking for himself that he achieves most, I think, and certainly not in impersonations which depend on expletives —'damns!' and 'Gods!'—to galvanise them into life. If Mr. Pound could only forget his literature he would exult to more purpose.

One thing is proved by these two little books of his, *Personae* and *Exultations*, and that is that the old devices of regular metrical beat and regular rhyming are worn out; the sonnet and the three-quatrain poem will probably always live; but for the larger music verse must be free from all the restraints of a regular return and a squared-up frame; the poet must forge his rhythm according to the impulse of the creative emotion working through him. . . .

22. Unsigned review, *Nation* (London)

19 March 1910, vi, 973–4

Mr. Ezra Pound would, no doubt, scorn to be thought a poet who polishes his crystals; but it does seem to us that in his *Exultations* he is beginning to allow some outward form to his verses. It was indeed, remarkable that such a passionate lover of Dante, Villon, and the poets of Provence, should have been content with a savage and often ludicrous crudity of expression. He seemed to trust entirely to the formative powers inherent in his ideas; but these ideas were neither very potent nor very interesting as poetic substance. In these *Exultations* of his he is less derivative in matter, his thoughts are often his own, and they are more intense, and, though not free from absurdity, the book contains much that is externally, as well as internally, captivating, as thus:

> Pale hair that the moon has shaken
> Down over the dark breast of the sea,
> O magic her beauty has shaken
> About the heart of me.

If Mr. Pound will go on with the development in method in this latest volume of his, he will add to English poetry something which is unusual riches, and not merely a set of curios. Two poems, at least, in *Exultations* give warrant for this; 'Histrion', by virtue of its idea, and the 'Ballad of the Goodly Fere', by virtue of its execution.

After Mr. Pound's somewhat feverish eccentricities, *The Mountainy Singer* of Mr. Seosamh MacCathmhaoil (the brutal Saxon calls him Mr. Joseph Campbell) seems a book of serene orthodoxy. . . .

THE SPIRIT OF ROMANCE

London, 20 June 1910
New York, July 1910

---

23. Unsigned notice, *Nation* (New York)

2 March 1910, xlii, 221

Ezra Pound, having 'floundered somewhat ineffectually through the slough of philology' and read with enthusiasm a considerable amount of the poetry of the Latin countries, records his likings in *The Spirit of Romance*. The book consists of a series of translations, some borrowed, some original, together with a few bits of information and some appreciative comment. The original translations, in prose arranged as verse, are intended to be 'merely exegetic.' Their success may be judged from

> Yea, he betrays our faith who creeds not her,

as a rendering for the line,

> E fa 'l di nostra fè se non la crede,

in which Guinizelli is claiming for his lady the power to convert a heretic by her mere greeting. It is to Guinizelli that Mr. Pound attributes the invention of the sonnet. The few bits of really good comment are too rare to be worth hunting for. The book purports to be 'an attempt to define somewhat the charm of the pre-Renaissance literature of Latin Europe,' but does not bear a trace of synthetic criticism of any sort; and the spirit of romance appears only in the title, unless it is responsible for the statement in the 'praefatio ad lectorem electum' that the 'Grundriss von Grüber' 'consists of 21,000 folio pages.' But much may be forgiven Mr. Pound, in view of the definition enshrined in this same preface: 'Art is a fluid moving above or over the minds of men.'

24. Edward Thomas, review, *Morning Post*

1 August 1910

Mr. Ezra Pound's *Spirit of Romance* deals with the poetry of the Latin races, roughly speaking, from the Provençals to Villon, Camões, and Lope de Vega. It does not pretend to be exhaustive, but to express the opinions of Mr. Pound upon certain representative poets. He is 'interested in poetry', both as a scholar and as a human being, and he writes probably for those who have more humanity than scholarship. His aim is to instruct, his ambition 'to instruct painlessly', and he confines himself to 'such medieval works as still possess an interest other than archaeological for the contemporary reader who is not a specialist'. His quotations are long and numerous; as they are often from little known or difficult writers they are valuable. Whatever may be thought of his opinions and his way of expressing them, there can be no doubt that his translations are in the main admirable, having the two qualities of intelligibility and suggesting the superiority of the original. He says himself that his criticism has 'consisted in selection rather than in presentation of the opinion'. If that were so we should have nothing but praise for the book, but it is not. It is restlessly opinionated. He has, or desires to have, an opinion upon everything; and if he has not then his eccentric speech makes it appear that he has. He relies, in fact, as much upon his personality as upon his learning. We are delighted to agree with him far more often than we disagree. On the subject of classic and romantic, for example, he says a number of true things, though he must admit that he is just as far as ever from the truth, even if he did not confound everything by saying: 'Certain qualities and certain furnishings are germane to all fine poetry; there is no need to call them either classic or romantic'.

He might have given more space than he does to proving that certain lines of Ovid are 'as haunted as anything in Ossian'. All he does is to show that the substance of these lines is very much like the substance of some 'Celtic' writer. This is not enough, and he seems to admit as much himself, when he speaks of Ovid's 'polished verse' and his demand for 'the definite'. Apuleius is far nearer to Ossian, and in him Mr. Pound rightly perceives a different 'atmosphere' and the 'indefiniteness' of later writers, 'who speaks of "the Duke Joshua" and "that good Knight Alexander of Macedon" '. It is altogether a question of atmosphere and style, and Mr. Pound should not have plunged so heavily into disagreement without more circumspection. The same is true of his assertion that the 'Oedipus Coloneus' has 'all the paraphernalia of the "Romantic" school'. It is just conceivable that he is right, but his bare assertion of the contrary to received opinion is not enough to raise the question. The fact is that he is too much bent upon being interesting, upon being something more than a scholar. He is thus lured into digressions which could only be sustained by a strong personality. There is no reason why a writer of strong personality should not turn aside to abuse Whitman in a chapter upon 'Montcorbier, *alias* Villon'; but Mr. Pound is not such a one. His personality is negative, and rises to the appearance of being positive only by contradiction. His aim at being better than dryasdust by allowing his personality free play is therefore not so successful as it is laudable. At one moment he is a scholar writing in a way which is over the head of the unlearned, and at another he is the free, courageous man wearing his learning lightly like a daisy. He cannot combine the scholar and the man. We regret to say this, because a point has been reached where men refuse to take works of learned dullness, and of this the learned are aware and they are considering their ways.

Mr. Pound has considered his ways, but on the whole we had rather he confined himself to translation and the severest exposition. If he does so he will do extremely well, for already in this volume he has almost done what nobody else has done—given an account of the Provençal writers which to some extent accounts for Dante's admiration and their surviving repute.

PROVENÇA

Boston, 22 November 1910

25. Floyd Dell, review, *Chicago Evening Post*

6 January 1911, 5

Dell (1887–1969) was, in 1911, an associate editor of the 'Friday Literary Review' of the *Evening Post*. He subsequently became a leading radical journalist, editor of the *Masses* and the *Liberator*, and a novelist. Pound was quite pleased with this notice. His letters to Dell are published by G. Thomas Tanselle, 'Two Early Letters of Ezra Pound', *American Literature* (March 1962), xxxiv, 114–19. In 1913 Dell saluted the appearance of 'Contemporania' (No. 38).

Though Mr. Pound is an American, he has already received his critical accolade in England. One may have noted, among the very impressive praises that the poet has received in the English press, an occasional note of bewilderment. And a reader, though he have no intention of challenging these praises, may find the bewilderment altogether pardonable. For Mr. Pound is a very new kind of poet. Thinking of the art exhibition just held in London, one might, for want of a better figure, call him a Neo-Impressionist poet. Like the Neo-Impressionist painters, like the Impressionists in their day, Mr. Pound is open to misunderstanding, and even to ridicule. People are saying that one of the Neo-Impressionist pictures was secured by tying a paint brush to a donkey's tail and backing the animal up to the canvas. A jocose little story like that might be invented to explain one of Mr. Pound's poems.

But though these poems have often an unconventional form, bizarre phraseology, catalectic or involved sentence structure and recondite meanings, yet it is always apparent that the poet knows what he is doing. This sense—the sense that effects which are beyond one's immediate power of comprehension have been exquisitely designed and exactly

70

carried out—is at the base of the pleasure afforded by all art of a high order. It is enough for people of taste to have this feeling (so much more chastened than the patronizing enjoyment they are wont to take in beauty of an accidental sort), to realize that they are in the presence of good art. In this spirit it is that so many critics have given Mr. Pound's work the stamp of their approval, even while admitting that they have not discovered the standards to which it conforms. And it is in this spirit that one more reviewer introduces it to the public.

It may be complained that this is a confession of critical short-coming. It is hardly less, indeed. Yet one may be somewhat expert in artistic criticism, and fail to understand Whistler when he first appears. One may sincerely admire Monet, and yet be entirely unable to explain to a skeptic why haystacks should be painted lavender. And one may have acquired, in regard to poetry, that critical vocabulary and manner which add conviction to an otherwise bald and uninteresting confession of admiration—and yet not be able to bring it to bear on Ezra Pound.

The only thing which can justify Ezra Pound is Ezra Pound. Indeed, one regrets having stood so long with vague and vain explanatory gestures before such a poem as the one which begins thus:

[quotes 'Cino', ll. 1–10, *CSP*, p. 20.]

And in this 'Night Litany' there is a style so direct that it would require a daring or an obtuse mind to pronounce the use of foreign phrase an affectation or the peculiar arrangement of the lines a vagary:

[quotes 'Night Litany', ll. 1–13, *CSP*, p. 40.]

But no presentation of this poet would be just which did not include suggestions of the tremendous, the shocking vigour of which he is capable. One stanza will be enough—a stanza from the poem in which there speaks one Bertrans de Born. In a little note at the head of the poem Mr. Pound says: 'Dante Alighieri put this man in hell for that he was a stirrer up of strife. Eccovi! Judge ye! Have I dug him up again?'

[quotes 'Sestina: Altaforte', stanza 1, *CSP*, p. 42.]

The poet gives expression to the spirit which makes possible such a poem, in another entitled 'Revolt Against the Crepuscular Spirit in Modern Poetry'. It begins:

> I would shake off the lethargy of this our time, and give
> For shadows—shapes of power,
> For dreams men.

71

And it ends:

> High God, if men are grown but pale, such phantoms
> That must live only in these mists and tempered lights
> And tremble for dim hours that knock o'er loud
> Or tread too violent in passing them;
> Great God, if these thy sons are grown such thin ephemera,
> I bid Thee grapple chaos and beget
> Some new Titanic spawn to pile the hills and stir
> This earth again.

Much more might be quoted to show the poet in his moods of tenderness. And one might regret that this volume of selections does not include a stirring ballad entitled 'The Goodly Fere', which is at the same time a remarkable reworking of the vein of the Christ-mythus (to use a convenient term with entire respect) in the fashion of Browning's 'Epistle of Karshish'.[1]

That there is in these poems an indebtedness to Browning, also to Walt Whitman, and perhaps to Henley, as well as to the Provençal poetry from which the poet's inspiration is so largely derived—these things are obvious enough. It is a matter of keen regret that something more truly illuminating cannot be said. But, if the extracts from poems do not at once settle the matter, the word of the reviewer must be given for what it may be found to be worth. Ezra Pound is a true poet; his singing has distinctive spiritual and stylistic qualities which command the most respectful attention; and to those who approach his work in some humility of spirit it is capable of giving a deep aesthetic satisfaction.

---

[1] The 'Ballad of the Goodly Fere' was, in fact, included in *Provença*, as Pound wrote to Dell, 'if your copy does not contain "The Goodly Fere" it is defective'.

26. H. L. Mencken, review, *Smart Set*

April 1911, xxxiii, 166–7

Mencken (1880–1956), American journalist and critic, was, as co-editor of *Smart Set* with George Jean Nathan from 1914 to 1924, an influential literary figure. He and Pound were correspondents. This review is collected in *H. L. Mencken's 'Smart Set' Criticism*, edited by William H. Nolte (Cornell University Press, 1969), pp. 76–8.

Ezra Pound, author of *Provença*, tells us frankly that his chief aim is to sound a revolt against the puerile kittenishness which marks so much of latter day English poetry. Nine-tenths of our living makers and singers it would seem are women, and fully two-thirds of these women are ladies. The result is a boudoir tinkle in the tumult of the lyre. Our poets are afraid of passion; the realities of life alarm them; the good red sun sends them scurrying. Instead of celebrating with their wind music 'great deeds, strong men, hearts hot, thoughts mighty,' they

> dream pale flowers,
> Slow moving pageantry of hours that languidly
> Drop as o'erripened fruit from sallow trees.

Such is Mr. Pound's complaint against the bards of our decadence. In his little book he attacks them, not only with precept, but also with example. That is to say, he himself writes in the clangorous, passionate manner that he advocates—and it must be said for him in all honesty that his stanzas often attain to an arresting and amazing vigor. The pale thing we commonly call beauty is seldom in them. They are rough, uncouth, hairy, barbarous, wild. But once the galloping swing of them is mastered, a sort of stark, heathenish music emerges from the noise. One hears the thumping of a tom-tom. Dionysos and his rogues are at their profane prancing. It is once more the springtime of the world.

Naturally enough, Mr. Pound finds poets—and heroes—to his liking in the Middle Ages—those spacious days of feasting, fighting and hard loving. A ballad of the gibbet, in the manner of Villon and with good

73

François himself the gibbet bird, is one of the best things in the book. Again we have a fine song of the open road, credited to some Wanderer of the Campagna in 1309. Yet again there is the last song of Arnaut of Marvoil, troubadour to the Countess of Beziers in the twelfth century. From the Provençal of Bertrans de Born comes a lament upon the death of Prince Henry Plantagenet, elder brother to the Lion Heart; from Lopé de Vega comes a song to the Virgin Mother; from Jaufre Rudel and Arnaut Daniel certain fantastic canzon forms. Bertrans bawls vociferously in a battle song:

[quotes the third stanza of 'Sestina: Altaforte', *CSP*, p. 42.]

'The Ballad of the Goodly Fere' (*i.e.*, mate, companion) is Mr. Pound's only venture into the old English ballad form, but here he achieves a remarkable imitation, not only of the form, but also of the naif spirit of the early tales in rhyme. It is Simon the Apostle that speaks, 'some while after the crucifixion.' A few stanzas follow:

[quotes stanzas ix, x, xi, xii of 'Ballad of the Goodly Fere', *CSP*, p. 48.]

Mr. Pound is an American, but he had to go to England to gain recognition. The present volume, I believe, is the first book from his hand to be printed in this country. It has defects a-plenty. More than once the very earnestness of the poet destroys the effect he essays to produce. His violence at times grows almost comic. One recalls the early profanities of Kipling. But, considered as a whole, this little collection of verses is one of the most striking that has come from the press in late years. Here we have a poet with something to say and with the skill to say it in a new way, eloquently, sonorously and sometimes almost magnificently.

27. Reverberations in America

December 1910

William Stanley Braithwaite, from 'Magazines and Poets', *Boston Evening Transcript* (7 December 1910), p. 21, and from a review of *Provença* in the issue of 9 December 1910, quoted in Stock, *Life*, p. 92.

Braithwaite (1878–1962) was an influential reviewer and anthologist in Boston. He edited an *Anthology of Magazine Verse* from 1913 to 1939.

What I do dare prophesy is that England has had little or nothing to do with the younger generation of our poets, now that she has come through her Celtic and imperialistic singers to the end of her afterglow of the Victorian era. . . .

Two indications have pointed to this recently: Miss May Sinclair, the English novelist, who in visiting this country a few years ago, voiced practically this hope in her study of three American poets, Moody, Torrence and Robinson,[1] and in the acclamation of the English critics over the work of Mr. Ezra Pound. It is the duty of the American people, something more than a national duty, a spiritual obligation of each individual whose aspirations, ideals and hopes these poets interpret and express, giving speech and realization to the deepest instincts of their natures, to foster and nourish these prophets and artists, who will not only make them singly more perfect men and women but collectively a greater and finer nation.

We began the examination of this book of poems [*Provença*] with great expectations and we lay it down with considerable contempt for the bulk of English criticism that has pretended to discover in these erratic utterances the voice of a poet. . . . The great faults in Mr. Pound are the hopes by which he may yet achieve and justify what has been

[1] May Sinclair, 'Three American Poets of To-day', *Atlantic Monthly* (September 1906), xcviii, pp. 325–35.

prematurely awarded him by his English sponsors. . . . Mr. Pound may, as he declares, have no deep regard for Longfellow, who, it seems, is related to him on his mother's side, but he can learn a great deal from the Cambridge poet what would be profitable to his art when he attempts to embody his ideas and feelings into poetry.

28. J. B. Yeats to his son

11 February 1911

Extract from J. B. Yeats, *Letters to His Son W. B. Yeats and Others 1869–1922*, edited with a memoir by Joseph Hone (New York: E. P. Dutton; London: Faber & Faber, 1946), pp. 133–4.

Yeats (1839–1922), Irish portrait-painter and conversationalist, was educated at Trinity College, Dublin. Pound first met Yeats *père* during the summer of 1910 when he and John Quinn went on a picnic. W. B. Yeats asked Pound to edit *Passages from the Letters of John Butler Yeats* for the Cuala Press (1917).

Have you met Ezra Pound? Carlton Glidden, an artist of talent who has a lot to learn, but who is a very nice fellow indeed, told me to-day that Ezra Pound was at his studio a few days ago and talked a lot about you, quoting quantities of your verse, which he had by heart, placing you very high, and as the best poet for the last century and more. I tell you this as he is going in a few days to Europe to stay in Paris, &c. Quinn met him and liked him very much. The Americans, young literary men, whom I know found him surly, supercilious and grumpy. I liked him myself very much, that is, I liked his look and air, and the few things he said, for tho' I was a good while in his company he said very little. As I have just heard this I thought I would let you know in case you met him in transit through London. . . .

CANZONI

London, July 1911

29. Charles Granville, 'Modern Poetry', *Eye-Witness*

10 August 1911, i, 247-8

Granville, a bookman and publisher was, briefly, proprietor of Dora Marsden's *Freewoman*, and his firm, Stephen Swift, published Pound's Cavalcanti translations and *Ripostes* (see Stock, *Life*, p. 112 and Jane Lidderdale and Mary Nicholson, *Dear Miss Weaver: Harriet Shaw Weaver 1876–1961* (London: Faber 1970), pp. 48, 49, 55).

For a decade or so confusion has reigned in the minds of poets and critics on the subject of poetry. At first sight it may appear presumptuous to say that a poet is 'all at sea' in his enjoyment of his own particular medium of expression. And yet this has often been the case of late years.

No master-work of British poetry has appeared within the period I have named; yet British poets are not wanting. There are even potential giants in our midst. The cant talk of unknowing or undiscriminating persons that the age of giants is past is the merest twaddle.[1] The age of giants is ever with us; as long as the human race continues the age of giants will persist. Each age produces a different kind of giant: nay, one age may produce even a variety of giants, each distinct from all that have gone before.

But a giant does not easily emerge when floundering in an age that is sceptical towards everything. A poet today cannot place his name upon the great roll of British poets if he is indifferent to what has gone before, or regards it with sceptical eyes. He must not take up the attitude towards our poetical literature shown by the crowd. He cannot lisp in numbers about airmen where he has read of the aerial feats of Iris. In short, he must not think himself capable of standing alone, cutting himself off from the great traditions.

1 Cf. Ford Madox Hueffer, *The Critical Attitude* (London, 1911), 173-4.

An attempt to do this has been made by Mr. Ezra Pound. The result is lamentable failure.

Unfortunately, he has been encouraged by the critics to repeat the attempt. If critics really understood the subject-matter of their criticisms it would be better for art. If a critic of poetry, for example, understood poetry we should not be burdened with the idiotic reviews of 'Recent Verse' printed periodically by the daily press. These are mostly written by the caretaker, the typist, or the office-boy. There is plenty of internal evidence to prove the statement. The result is that when a poet appears, bearing upon his work ever so few marks of the true artist, the reviewer bows and scrapes, neglecting entirely the duty of criticism. Many reviewers regard modern verse much in the same way as a certain Cornishwoman regarded her son's preaching. 'My son do preach be-yeautiful sermons', she declared, adding by way of proof: 'Why, nubbody do understand "em".' Now the beautiful sermons preached by the modern poet have such a lack of perspicuity that no reader can understand them. And perspicuity is of the essence of good poetry.

The work of Mr. Ezra Pound is an excellent case in point. Critics praised his two earlier volumes: and as a result we now have a third possessing the same qualities as the others. Of these qualities the bad almost totally eclipse the good. The volume ought never to have been printed. If critics had taken Mr. Pound to task for his previous foolish eccentricities, we might have been spared the unpleasant duty of dealing with him here. However, Mr. Pound is a poet, though as yet he has produced little but balderdash. One or two things redeem him, and therefore he has to be dealt with.

We need not attempt the very difficult task of defining poetry; but we can at least enunciate two or three qualities whose presence is necessary in all poetic compositions.

(1) Poetry is born of the emotions. A true poet is capable of imposing his own emotion upon hearer and reader.

(2) The expression of the poet's emotion must be in rhythmic and beautiful language.

(3) The language must be characterised by perspicuity, for the sole reason that the emotion is not conveyable to reader or hearer unless it be clearly expressed.

Now, without going further into the essentials of poetry, let us examine Mr. Pound's *Canzoni* in the light of these three necessary qualities. I have read this book from beginning to end with a very genuine desire to discover emotion. I have found none. It is all the result of mere reading; an iteration and reiteration in eccentric forms, or eccentric no-forms, of the emotions of others. The personal touch is entirely wanting; and without the personal touch there is no poetry, not even in its dramatic form.

With regard to the second necessary quality, I find that there is an utter carelessness as to rhythm. This, although admissible to some extent in the master-work of a giant, is not to be tolerated in such a book as that before us. As for beauty, there are here and there to be found very beautiful lines. It is just for this reason that Mr. Pound is worth looking at; for this reason too is there hope for his future. But it would be an immense advantage if he would remember that his bid is for a place in English literature. The jargon and jingle of his titles and of some of his lines rather suggest his desire to write in a dozen languages at once. Unless he gives up this bad habit he will never get a British niche. He will want a place somewhere under the sea, where all peoples meet and understand each other as a matter of course. Whilst on the subject of Mr. Pound's manifest love of Babel melodies, I would point out that he had better avoid German. The translations of poems by Heine in this book are execrable to the last degree. They serve nothing, and are not to be understood at all unless placed side by side with the German. That is a grave accusation to make against any translator. He has neither literally translated nor conveyed the spirit of the original. If he has attempted to do the latter at the expense of exactness, he has failed, and murdered Heine in the attempt. It is an immoral act to have thrust Heine, or any part of him, upon English readers in this guise. In justification of what I say I will cite one example (there are worse):

HEINE
Doch die Kastraten klagten,
Als ich meine Stimm' erhob;
Sie klagten und sie sagten,
Ich sänge viel zu grob.

Und lieblich erhoben sie Alle
Die kleinen Stimmelein,
Die Trillerchen, wie Krystalle,
Sie klangen so fein und rein.

Sie sangen von Liebessehnen,
Von Liebe und Liebeserguss;
Die, Damen schwammen in Thränen
Bei solchern Künstgenuss.

[quotes poem v from 'Translations and Adaptations from Heine', *CSP*, pp. 59–60.]

And yet Mr. Pound can write:

> O Harry Heine, curses be
> I live too late to sup with thee!

I would assure Mr. Pound that Heine would not have enjoyed a meal with him in the present stage of his poetical evolution.

Passing to the third quality, that of perspicuity, I take a passage from Mr. Pound, which I suppose is meant to express an emotion:

> Because my soul cried out, and only the long ways
> Grown weary gave me answer, and
> Because she answered when the very ways were dumb
> With all their hoarse, dry speech grown faint and chill.

This is a fair sample of Mr. Pound's methods. No! Chinese word-puzzles do not convey emotion!

As I have said, Mr. Pound has the poet in him; but he will never do anything worth preserving till he abandons his eccentricities. A genius should not covet the brain-twists, and their productions, of the lunatic!

30. Unsigned review, *Westminster Gazette*

19 August 1911, 12

Precious stones and rich colours and ivory and rose and gold, richly embroidered phrases, tags of Latin and Italian and French are scattered profusely over the pages of Mr. Ezra Pound's new volume of verse. This kind of prodigality, together with his exotic metrical forms, tend to set his reader's mind on his ingenuity in weaving intricate show-pieces rather than on the faculties he may possess necessary to the writing of poetry. Canzon, Ballata, Ballatetta, Madrigale, Mr. Pound heads his verses; 'Era Mea,' 'De Ægypto,' 'Li Bel Chasteus,' 'Erat Hora,' he entitles them. He translates from Propertius, Heine, Leopardi, Du Bellay —almost from himself at times—and he intends to parody 'The Shropshire Lad' with a piece of doggerel headed 'Song in the Manner of Housman'.

All this has a look of affectation combined with pedantry. We shut up the book as we might turn away from a shelf of bizarre but not very valuable curios in an old window. It is difficult to see why a man with anything very pressing to say, any haunting dream to tell, with any irrepressible fountain of music leaping and echoing in his mind should take such elaborate pains to be elaborate. Mr. Pound decks up and cumbers his Pegasus to such an extent with this jingling and antique saddlery that it is only very rarely we can see the steed for its harness.

Yet it is obvious that Mr. Pound, when he forgets to pose and frees himself from a kind of superciliousness, is a poet as well as a curious experimenter. But even as a poet he is singularly unequal and as a versifier often careless. We do not often hear simply his own voice. He ends his book with a series of poems that recall, one after another, Browning and Meredith and Whitman and the Troubadours. A very tenuous shade of Swinburne is not long absent from his shoulder. He can be simple and direct in one line, meretricious and grotesque in the next. We realise that he has seen things in a vivid and original fashion and felt things that might be the stuff of poetry, and no less realise that he seldom manages to make us feel or see them. There is too much parade in his work:

> If on the tally-board of wasted days
> They daily write me for proud idleness,
> Let high Hell summons me, and I confess,
> No overt act the preferred charge allays. . . .

What a medley of pretension that is! Mr. Pound's work is too egotistic and not individual enough. By much the greater part of his volume is at least one remove from reality—from his own reality. And if there is one thing on earth and in man that is of the very essence of reality— that strange alliance between soul and sense—it is poetry.

31. G. D. H. Cole, initialled review, *Isis*

4 November 1911, no. 467, 52–3

Cole (1889–1959), English socialist, labour historian, lecturer, author and journalist, was Professor of Political Theory at Oxford. Cole was the leading writer and propagandist of Guild Socialism, and was president of the British Fabian Society from 1952 until his death. He was co-editor of *Oxford Poetry 1914*.

Canzoni is a strange medley of influences; but it is no bad sense imitative. Mr. Pound nearly always chooses to model his work on somebody else's, or rather on some school; but what he has to say is always individual and his own. It is especially interesting to see a modern poet affected by the same influences as moulded the form and temper of the Elizabethan lyric. Mr. Pound often reminds us of the Elizabethans, not so much directly, as in catching from Ronsard and DuBellay something of what the Elizabethans found, and modifying it to his purpose with other and more modern influences. He is in some sense Euphuistic; he has a vocabulary and a style of his own, and takes a delight in them for their own sakes; but he knows also how to vary them for expressions of such different kinds as in his best Canzon 'The Spear' and the 'Victorian Eclogues'. On the whole we like Mr. Pound's short pieces best; for in them he seems to attain to a more perfect unity of feeling, a greater clarity and distinctness of expression. It is hard to particularize among so many good things, but we cannot forbear to mention 'Paracelsus in Excelsus', and 'Blandula, Tenulla, Vagula', without feeling at all sure that we have named the best. Of the longer poems, 'Excuses', the first of the 'Victorian Eclogues' and the two Canzoni, 'The Spear' and 'The Yearly Slain' now strike us as best. The last especially gains at every reading. But this applies to all Mr. Pound's work: we can never know him well enough to judge him properly till it is too late to review him. *Personae*, *Exultations* and *Canzoni* have all been books which grow in value as we keep them, and we do not doubt that Mr. Pound will yet do better than any. Each of his books so far has given us a part of his genius; some day we hope he will give us all at once.

32. J. C. Squire, review, *New Age*

21 December 1911, x, 183

Squire (1884–1958) was a Cambridge-educated journalist, critic and minor poet who, as the editor of *London Mercury*, was a conservative force in literary politics. Writing to W. C. Williams in 1920 Pound referred to 'the wet dung of the London Murkury' (*Letters*, p. 222). See Introduction, p. 8.

People have differed—and, if I may say so, rightly—about the merits of Mr. Ezra Pound's previous books of verse. But nobody could deny that he was certainly himself in them. In this volume, too, he contrives to be himself; but with rather more difficulty. The plupart of the poemata in this opus (one falls insensibly into polyglottery after reading Mr. Pound) are essays in Early Italian and kindred forms. These forms lend themselves to decorative effect, to subtly-woven harmonies of phrase and rhythm and rhyme. Their rigid elaborateness, however, induces, or at any rate, favours, at worst a frigidity, and at best a trivially and sentimentally titillating content. But Mr. Pound has a very strong back. His vigour is such that he bears always with credit, and sometimes with ease, not only this burden of alien and archaic forms, but also those other self-imposed burdens of Latin, Provençal, and Italian tags and mediaeval bric-a-brac vocabulary and properties. The reason that he comes out of it so well is that instead of being like an incompetent modern eccentric who should revert to the methods and materials of Cimabue because he could not attract attention in any other way, he is a genuine artist with eyes of his own and brains of his own, who will manage to express something strong and living whatever materials he uses, but who would gain and not lose if he could forget all about the poets of Dante's day, their roses and their flames, their gold and their falcons, and their literary amorousness, and walk out of the library into the fresh air.

The Canzoni at first reading irritate or bore one. They flow well, and one recognises the craft at work, but the heavy incrustations of verbiage are very tiring. But the more one reads them the more one perceives how excellent is Mr. Pound's artistry within the limits that he has imposed on himself and how much hard thinking (though very little emotion) has gone to the making of the poems. The more one finds in them the more one regrets that Mr. Pound cannot get rid of his linguistic fancy dress. . . .

Of the miscellaneous poems in the volume, 'Psyche of Eros,' 'Paracelsus in Excelsis,' 'Li Bel Chasteus,' and 'Threnos' are the most admirable. The last-named, a lament over Tristram and Iseult, with its opening:—

> No more for us the little sighing
> No more the winds at twilight trouble us,

and its refrain like a muffled bell,

> Lo, the fair dead,

has a mournful music that echoes in one's ears when one has shut the book.

Mr. Pound once breaks forth into burlesque. Even those of us who carry about our copies of 'A Shropshire Lad' with our pipes and bunches of keys, must confess that the following lines of Mr. Pound's get home on Mr. A. E. Housman's matter if not on his manner:

[quotes 'Mr. Housman's Message', *CSP*, pp. 57–8.]

33. F. S. Flint, review, *Poetry Review*

January 1912, i, 28–9

Let it be conceded at once, without cavil, that the authentic note of poetry sounds throughout this last book of Mr. Ezra Pound's. But is he the instrument, or is he the wind in the instrument? So much of his inspiration seems bookish, so much of his attraction lies in the vivid picturesqueness of his romance-besprinkled page. Look at his variegated record: In 1908 he published *A Lume Spento*, in the same year *A Quinzaine for this Yule*, then followed his *Personae*, his *Exultations*, largely reprints of the two preceding books, and now come his *Canzoni*. Then, if you run your eye over the pages of his books, you meet Latin and Mediaeval Latin, the 'langue d'oc' and the 'langue d'oil,' Dante's Italian and modern Italian, Spanish, French, German, quaint (or queynt!) forgotten English; and, lastly, English. Yes, *lastly* English. So it is in this volume of *Canzoni*. If Mr Pound can find a foreign title to a poem, he will do so. Queer exotic hybridity! It would almost be true to say, also, that if Mr Pound can translate a poem, he will do so, rather than make one. He translates from Heine, Propertius, Dante, Pico della Mirandola, Joachim du Bellay, Leopardi; the bulk of the work in this book is not ostensibly translated, but it reads as though it were. Therefore, again, is Mr Pound the instrument, trumpeting the authentic note, or is he the wind in the instrument? You can state it both ways: either Mr Pound is the instrument, accredited with the keys, and attuned for the wind of the old songs and the old dreams, or his is the breath that, once more, gives to songs and dreams their ancient fullness. Whichever way you look at it, the note is the same, the true note of poetry, not as it is understood by the sixpenny dullness of weekly journalism, or in the literary dysentery of halfpenny newspapers—in neither can there be understanding, but as it is *heard* by the poet who takes the stars for his guide and the fairness of the earth to wife. The point to settle—though not here—is, has the singer of the Canzoni married . . . by proxy? Of course, criticism could not answer, crudely, yes or no. The question is much more complex than that.

Mr Pound will not have added much to his reputation with these Canzoni; but he will have strengthened it a great deal. Incidentally, he will have shown carpers at his form and rhythmical experiments that he, too, can, if he choose, write prettily in the regular metres. The important thing to say now, in this short review, is, that those who have the grace to and can spend money on modern poetry should buy this book. A wide experience of modern verse is behind that advice.

SONNETS AND BALLATE OF
GUIDO CAVALCANTI

Boston, 27 April 1912
London, May 1912

34. Arundel del Re, review, *Poetry Review*

July 1912, i, 324–5

Del Re (b. 1892), Professor of Italian Literature, has lectured at
Oxford, the Tokyo Imperial University and the University of
Wellington, New Zealand. He was sub-editor of the *Poetry Review*
in 1912.

It is difficult to justify the appearance of this new translation of Guido
Cavalcanti's lyrics. A work of love as it evidently is, arising out of a
desire to express and to 'embody in English some trace of that power
which implies the man' should, one would think, at least be free from
slovenliness and inaccuracy. Accuracy and care has never been harmful
to true art, and Mr Pound himself knows it quite well.

The original idea of 'printing only the poems and an unrhymed
gloze,' while obviating much pedestrian verse and bad translation, would
scarcely have proved an adequate or reliable comment. Either Mr Pound
knows very little about the Italian language, or he is totally lacking in
that critical judgment necessary to the translator.

The text used, to which, by the way, he never refers, is not only
obsolete and untrustworthy, but also betrays ignorance of some of the
commonest rules of syntax, grammar and metrics. I do not mean by
this, that Mr Pound should have followed any given edition, but to
justify a departure from the generally accepted ones, he should have
taken care that his text was more correct and nearer to the spirit of the
original. Not only does he omit to quote even the most important

variants, but he continually disproves the judiciousness of his choice. Taking as an instance sonnet No. XVIII, let us compare it with the text of Ercole or Arnone. I have put in italics the principal variants of the latter from Mr Pound's edition, the two readings in each case immediately following the one on the other.

> Beltà di donna, e di saccente core,
>   E cavalieri armati, che sian genti,
> Cantar d'augelli, e ragionar d'amore,
>   Adorni legni in mar, forti e correnti:
>   [Verse one, lines 1 to 4.]
> Beltà di donna e di *piagente* core,
>   e cavalier armati molto genti,
> cantar d'augelli e ragionar d'amore,
>   adorni leg*n'* in mar *forte* correnti,

> Ciò che può la beltade e la valenza,
> De la mia Donna in suo gentil coraggio,
> Par, che rassembre vile a chi ciò guarda;
>   [Verse three, lines 1 to 3.]
> *passa la gran* bel*tate* e la *piagenza*
> de la mia *donna e il* suo gentil coraggio,
> sí cherassembra vile a chi ciò guarda.

> E tanto ha più d'ogni altra conoscenza
>   [Verse four, line 1.]
> E tant'*è* più d'*ogn'* altra conoscenza,

The difference between the two is, at least, startling, and as far as I can perceive, none of the amendments introduced by the translator have any sound critical or poetic basis.

Mr Pound enounces in the introduction some of his theories on rhythm and the poetic correspondence between word and emotion: these are not entirely underived from other theorists on the subject. It is not possible to discuss here the rendering of such words as *gentile, virtute, valore,* nor yet his interpretation of the episode of Oderisi in the Purgatorio and Cavalcante in the Paradiso. Referring to the passages mentioned I can see no reason for considering the one as modifying the other and still less for admitting that Dante meant to place his poetry above that of his great friend. In the latter, Dante's answer to Cavalcante

> Da me stesso non vegno:
> Colui che attende là, per qui mi mena

is merely an explanation of how, not for any intrinsic poetic merit of his own, but by the will of Beatrice, he (Dante), has come to undertake this journey without Guido. Even here Mr Pound's carelessness is nothing short of extraordinary. He contrives to misspell or to allow such misprints as Cherci for Cerchi, Bundelmonti for Buondelmonti, Oderesi for Oderisi,—and with Dante before him—Cristofore Landiano for Cristoforo Landino. Even in a quotation of such importance as that of Carducci's variant of the famous verse which he attacks

E fa di claritate tremar l'a're

he spells *l'are*, the altars, instead of *l'a're*, and again, he writes 'Donna mi pregna' for 'Donna mi prega'. Without giving these slips an overdue importance, they are sufficient to condemn him as a serious student.

The translation of the 'Sonnets and Ballate'—why not Sonetti e Ballate or Sonnets and Ballads?—show the author to be earnestly striving after a vital idea of which one sometimes catches a glimpse amidst the general tangle and disorder. I do not know if Mr Pound has more to learn than to unlearn. Notwithstanding its almost overpowering defects this is a sincere if slip-shod attempt to translate into English the 'accompaniment' and 'the mental content of what the contemporaries of Guido Cavalcante drew forth from certain forms of thought and speech.' He has not succeeded but there is always room for such an attempt. Herein I think may be sought a justification for this book.

35. John Bailey, unsigned review, *The Times Literary Supplement*

21 November 1912, no. 567, 527

'The Poems of Cavalcanti'. The other book under review is Rossetti's *Poems and Translations*. Pound's reply, in the issue of 5 December, follows.

Bailey (1864–1931), an English barrister and bookman, was on the staff of the *Quarterly Review* and was a frequent contributor to *The Times Literary Supplement*. Bailey's essays are collected in *Poets and Poetry* (1911).

Dr. Arnold once said something to the effect that we should feel far less strange if we found ourselves set down in Roman society of the age of Caesar than we should in that of our own medieval ancestors. Any one who should happen to have been reading Cicero's letters and the poems of Guido Cavalcanti within a few days of each other will appreciate the full truth of that remark. Except for religion (and in how many people of our time is religion, however real, an openly expressed part of their life and conversation?) Cicero's letters breathe exactly the same atmosphere as those of any rich and public-spirited statesman of intellectual tastes to-day. The poetry of such a man as Cavalcanti, on the other hand, transports us into a world in which at first sight everything appears to us fantastic, artificial, and even absurd. Horace Walpole thought the *Divina Commedia* was like the ravings of a Methodist parson in Bedlam. But the *Divina Commedia* is a piece of pure rationality compared with the love poetry of its author and his contemporaries. The Comedy is to a very large extent a picture, even a realistic picture, of historical and biographical fact, things Dante had seen and people whom he had known; and its central purpose, the setting forth of the way from earth to heaven, is still for thousands of men and women the one supremely interesting subject in the world. But nothing could seem more remote from our lives and interests than this love poetry of lovers who often scarcely knew their mistresses by sight and yet went on dying of love's

89

wounds and darts and fires through interminable sequences of sonnets. And not only is the love itself, from our point of view, strangely unreal, but where it is real the method of expressing it almost robs it of its reality. The medieval poet of love starts for his subject from such an immense distance and interposes between himself and it, such an immense array of allegory and artificiality that we are apt to think that he never arrives at his goal at all. Many religious people to-day can express their religion in terms of the *Divine Comedy*; few lovers can express their love in the language of the Sonnets, Ballate, and Canzoni. They soon grow weary of the Court of Love and its wounded lovers, and turn away to Burns and Mary Morison.

Yet this curious poetry, though not belonging to the high universal order, has a peculiar charm of its own. It can never be, like Homer or Catullus, the poetry of all the world, for the world has no time to cut paths through tangles of artificiality. But for those who have time and the necessary culture and imagination, there is a rare fascination in so absolute an escape from all that is contemporary or even actual into this *hortus inclusus* of art. Mr. Ezra Pound is evidently one of these. He says, in his interesting though perhaps rather arrogant Introduction, that he has 'lived with these sonnets and ballate daily, month in and month out, and has been drawn daily deeper into them, and daily into contemplation of things that are not of an hour.' Lovers of old Italian poetry will be grateful to him for his attempt to make the study of Cavalcanti easier for them. He has here translated as much of Cavalcanti as any Englishman who needs the help of translations is likely to study, and he has placed the original Italian opposite his versions, which adds greatly to the interest of his book. On the other hand, he gives no index of first lines, and no table of contents detailed enough to enable his readers to find any particular poem.

What is to be said of Mr. Pound's translations? Not, we are afraid, that they will supersede or rival those of Rossetti. Mr. Pound has, indeed, surpassed Rossetti in one respect—that of quantity. Rossetti translated nineteen sonnets, six ballate, one madrigal, as well as four canzoni which are not now attributed to Cavalcanti. Mr. Pound gives us thirty-five sonnets, one madrigal, and fourteen ballate. This is a substantial gain. But where we have Rossetti no one will wish to substitute Mr. Pound for him, though the English student of Cavalcanti may be glad to have both. A great deal of work has been done on Cavalcanti and the poets of his day since Rossetti's time, and Mr. Pound, of course, has the advantage of it and is able to set Rossetti right more than once. But

Rossetti was a great poet, and perhaps a still greater translator; and, besides, he was the son of an Italian poet and scholar. These are advantages with which Mr. Pound cannot compete. He is sometimes clumsy, and often obscure, and has no fine tact about language, using such words and phrases as 'Ballatet,' 'ridded,' 'to whomso runs,' and others of dubious or unhappy formation. A more serious fault still is that he frequently absolves himself altogether from the duty of rhyming, and if an English blank verse sonnet were ever an endurable thing it would not be when it pretends to represent an Italian original. Then, though he says high and true things about rhythm in his Introduction, he seems in practice to have forgotten that not only primitive but medieval verse had much more of the quality of a dance in it than modern poetry commonly has. The very word ballata or ballad originally meant a song which was danced as well as sung; and the lyrics of Dante and his contemporaries are audibly rich in this gracious dancing quality. But who could think of dancing to such lines as these:—

> And I can cry for Grief so heavily
> As hath man never,
> For Grief drags to my heart, a heart so sore
> With wandering speech of her, who cruelly
> Outwearieth me ever. . . .

But this is not one of the most beautiful ballads even in the original. Let us take instead that other which Mr. Pound justly calls 'matchless and poignant.' And let us take the opportunity given us by the recent reprint of Rossetti's versions in Everyman's Library to compare the two translators. Here, first of all, is the lovely Italian:—

> Perch' io non spero di tornar già mai,
> Ballatetta, in Toscana,
> Va tu leggiera e piana
> Dritta a la donna mia,
> Che per sua cortesia
> Ti farà motto onore.

Now here is Mr. Pound:—

> Because no hope is left me, Ballatetta,
> Of return to Tuscany,
> Lightfoot go then some fleet way
> Unto my Lady straightway,
> And out of her courtesy
> Great honour will she do thee.

It is very literal; but was ever anything less musical? And in these things, as Mr. Pound knows, the music is the meaning. The third stanza is happier:—

[quotes 'Ballata XI', stanza 4, *Translations*, ed. Hugh Kenner, pp. 121–2.]

But hear Rossetti:—

> Because I think not ever to return
>   Ballad, to Tuscany,—
>   Go therefore thou for me
>   Straight to my Lady's face
>   Who of her noble grace
>   Shall show thee courtesy.

> Ah! ballad, unto thy dear offices
>   I do commend my soul, thus trembling:
>   That thou mayst lead it, for pure piteousness,
>   Even to that lady's presence whom I sing.
>   Ah! ballad, say then to her, sorrowing,
>   Whereso thou meet her then:—
>   'This thy poor handmaiden
>   Is come, nor will be gone,
>   Being parted now from one
>   Who served Love painfully.'

How much more of the original rhyme and movement Rossetti preserves, especially in the little prelude! And how, like a poet, he feels the urgency of that repetition of 'Deh, Ballatetta,' in the first and fifth lines of the stanza; and how free he is from dull padding like 'thy words in sum.'

But it is no disgrace to have fallen below Rossetti, though a reviewer is bound to warn readers that where Rossetti exists the lover of poetry must not accept the substitute of Mr. Pound. But Rossetti, as we have seen, does not cover all the ground; and if Mr. Pound's renderings are not fine poetry, they are at least useful helps towards the study of the original, which is not always easy. And those who know how lovely that original is when the strangeness, which is at first so daunting, has come to be another element in that mingled charm of musical words and gracious thoughts and fancies will not refuse their gratitude to any one who has laboured to bring it nearer to them.

Pound's reply:

Sir,—I have to thank your critic for his courteous review of my *Sonnets and Ballate of Guido Cavalcanti*; but he seems to have misunderstood the aim of my work. I thought I had made clear in my preface that my endeavour was not to display skill in versification but to present the vivid personality of Guido Cavalcanti. . . . There being one melodious translation with orderly rhymes there was little need of another. Guido cared more for sense than for music, and I saw fit to emphasize this essential aspect of his work. The music is easily available for anyone who will learn Italian pronunciation. The meaning is more than once in doubt even after long study. I thought I served my audience best by setting forth the meaning.

Surely Rossetti's preface and mine should show the reader that there could be no possible clash or contention between the aesthetic method and my scholastic one; he was as avowedly intent on making beautiful verses as I am on presenting an individual.

RIPOSTES

London, October 1912

36. Harold Child, unsigned review, *The Times Literary Supplement*

12 December 1912, no. 570, 568

Child (1869–1945), English literary critic and journalist, was educated at Brasenose College, Oxford. He was a contributor to *The Times Literary Supplement* for many years, and wrote drama criticism for *The Times*. S. C. Roberts edited Child's *Essays and Reflections* in 1948.

Mr. Ezra Pound's originality is of a different kind. He begins with a challenge—

> When I behold how black, immortal ink
>   Drips from my deathless pen—ah, well-away!
> Why should we stop at all for what I think?
>   There is enough in what I chance to say.

Do you bite your thumb—or, rather, do you cock your hat—at me, Sir? He ends with a poem headed 'From a thing by Schumann.' They are fine, careless fellows, those poets. And in between come brilliant examples of cleverness, magical use of words, proofs of sound learning, metrical triumphs—mixed up with more cocking of the hat, 'things' that remind us of nothing so much as the defiant gestures of retreating small boys, and essays in what we will call by the gentle name of wilfulness. At the Post-Impressionist exhibition some spectators may be seen dancing with fury, others quaking with laughter, others indiscriminately worshipping and a few using their brains coolly. Mr. Ezra Pound's book will have the same effect, no doubt, upon its readers. Now and then it is hard not to join the first group. Perhaps on reading 'From a thing by Schumann,' it is safer to pass by, as one might pass by a bust in its third stage by Matisse, with the polite reflection that we do not understand its aim and therefore cannot see the art or the beauty of it. There is enough, we understand, in what Mr. Pound chances to say; but why should a poet have chanced to say this 'thing,' when he can write such 'things' as the poem to Swinburne, 'Salve Pontifex,' or the fine, harsh 'Seafarer,' or the exquisite 'Thou keep'st thy rose-leaf'— each of which has its little bursts of wilfulness to give flavour to beauty, but is it not the cocking of a hat, not a vulgar gesture of defiance? We should like to commend earnestly to Mr. Pound's consideration a passage from the recently translated lectures by John Keble. The young men, he says, think they have indeed written something great if by lucky chance they have stitched in, here and there, some striking and clever patches. . . . I should like, once for all, to warn them that it is just the jejune poet who, hopeless of better, sticks to what first comes into his mind; that he has a frigid spirit who, troubling little as to the subject, is readily pleased with his own productions; but that it is the great and earnest soul which tries every possible means, which selects only the best, which spares neither labour nor learning if only he may thus produce an adequate and beautiful representation of that in which his heart delights.

37. F. S. Flint, review, *Poetry and Drama*

March 1913, i, 60–2

The *Ripostes* of Mr. Pound is the fourth book of his own verse that has come to me for review, and it seems to me an opportune moment to say a few words about Mr Pound's art, as a whole. *La versification,* said Marmontel, *est une mosaïque dont il faut remplir le dessin.*[1] It is a common error in England to suppose that poetry is versification, thus defined. Mr Pound's work is a vehement protest against this stupidity; he has sought to prove by example that poetry is, what its name implies, creation, and not the kindergarten art Marmontel thought it to be.

[1] Versification is a mosaic whose design must be filled in.

Moreover, from the *Personae* to the *Ripostes*, there is evidence of a determination towards a mastery of his medium; he is one of the few people in this country who do care for poetry as an art, and not merely as an accident, or the lazy pleasure of expressing one's twopenny-halfpenny personality in the easiest possible manner. Mr Pound has served a long apprenticeship in the technics of his craft, and with the sapphics of 'Apparuit,' the 'free' rhythm of 'The Return' and 'Δώρια' (all in *Ripostes*), he has attained a skill in handling words that is astonishing to those who understand. The sapphics of 'Apparuit' and the alliterative verse translation from the Anglo-Saxon of the 'Seafarer' (also in *Ripostes*) complete his analysis of the development of the poetic art from the Middle Ages to the present which was begun in the *Spirit of Romance*, a prose work, and continued in the experiments in polyphonic rhyme of the *Canzoni* and in the translations from Arnaut Daniel, not yet published in book form. The book *Canzoni* (which, by the way, is a masterpiece of quiet, patient irony) contains five poems in forms never before attempted in English, the rhyme schemes of which had been considered too difficult for the language and incompatible with its genius. Nor must it be supposed that all this is a formal accomplishment merely; one does not get poetry into the shape of 'Δώρια,' for instance, or of 'The Return,' without the genuine impulse; no amount of clever shamming, or borrowed ornament, or mosaïcism will produce the effect of a rhythm of this kind. Mr Pound has earned the right to put his poetry into any form he pleases; he has given his *vers libre* a solid basis in tradition, and may laugh at the critics. The laugh has all along been on his side. The *vers libre* was not, after all, invented by Whitman, nor even by Gustave Kahn.

The three best poems in *Ripostes*—'Apparuit,' 'Δώρια,' and 'The Return'—admit of no cavil. They stand, I think, as Mr Pound's finest work: 'Δώρια' as a perfect translation of pure emotion, 'Apparuit' and 'The Return' as transcripts of emotional vision. Next to them, I like best 'The Tomb at Akr Çaar,' wherein the soul addresses its mummy. In 'Salve Pontifex' Mr Pound admires what was great in Swinburne, the Swinburne of 'The Triumph of Time,' of 'The Ballad of Life,' and of 'The Last Oracle.' This poem will please those of Victorian taste, and as rhythmic form it still holds good. 'Portrait d'une Femme,' 'Sub Mare,' 'Plunge,' and the two poems entitled 'Effects of Music upon a Company of People' are attempts at precise rendering of exact psychology, the same kind of exact psychology, no doubt, which attracted Mr Pound to Guido Cavalcanti, and which caused him to take up the ungrateful task of translating that poet without rhetoric and without such music as would obscure the sense. The last-named poems are a curious statement of Mr Pound's visual perception of a group emotion. There are other poems in the book that are a pleasure to read, a poem addressed to New York, for instance; but you will find these for yourselves, I hope.

'For good fellowship, for good custom, a custom out of Tuscany and Provence,' Mr Pound has printed with his *Ripostes* the 'Complete Poetical Works' of T. E. Hulme, *videlicet*, five poems, thirty-three lines —and 'for good memory,' too, 'seeing that they recall certain evenings and meetings of two years gone, dull enough at the time, but rather pleasant to look back upon.' It is a pity that Mr Pound's preface says nothing more of these evenings, at which the part of organising secretary and of Cerberus, to bark away undesirable comers, was played by Mr Hulme, who, having created the Poets' Club and, like Frankenstein, been rended by it, started these Thursday evening meetings in a Soho restaurant as a solace and an amusement. They were not dull always: there were generally some six or seven of us—T. E. Hulme, Ezra Pound, Edward Storer, T. D. FitzGerald, myself, Miss Florence Farr, F. W. Tancred; at times the sculptor Epstein would come; Mr Pound himself did not join us until the third evening, and he may have forgotten or have been unaware of the excitement with which the diners on the other side of our screen heard him declaim the 'Sestina: Altaforte,' now in *Exultations*; how the table shook and the decanters and cutlery vibrated in resonance with his voice! I do not think that that evening was dull. However, the outcome of those meetings was three or four books of verse and Mr. Hulme's 'Complete Poetical Works.' We all had a hand in the editing of those Poetical Works; but here is one which we used to call 'The Red-faced Farmer,' and which is, I believe, entirely as Mr Hulme first wrote it, *editio princeps* (as, indeed, are all the others, which somehow managed to stray back to their original form—an obstinate fellow, their author!):

AUTUMN

A touch of cold in the autumn night—
I walked abroad,
And saw the ruddy moon lean over a hedge
Like a red-faced farmer.
I did not stop to speak, but nodded,
And round about were the wistful stars
With white faces like town children.

For good reason, we were hugely pleased with this, and we were satisfied with it as Mr Hulme's standing contribution to the feast, until, one
day, to our enormous astonishment, he produced four more short pieces,
the 'Complete Poetical Works.' It is a good joke, with sufficient in the
material to make one regret that Mr Hulme ever learned German, and
read philosophy, and abandoned the making of little Japanese pictures
in verses. The group lived vigorously for some months, then slow dis-
integration. I think we lasted a year or more.

38. Ezra Pound in Chicago

1912–13

Selections quoted by Harriet Monroe in *A Poet's Life*: *Seventy
Years in a Changing World* (New York: Macmillan, 1938).

(a) Comment, *Chicago Evening Post* (September 1912):
   We have an idea that the new magazine *Poetry* will be read almost
entirely by men. Not that the contents of the first number are challeng-
ingly masculine, but merely that women do not read poetry. Milady
will not like very much 'To Whistler—American' [by Ezra Pound]
because its oratorical simplicity will deceive her into thinking that it is
prose. 'Middle Aged' [also by Pound], however, will do much to reconcile her to the idea that Ezra Pound is a real poet. [Both poems by Pound
appeared in the first issue of *Poetry* in 1912.]

(b) Floyd Dell, 'To a Poet', *Chicago Evening Post Literary Review* (4
April 1913), 4 (On Dell see No. 25):
   Ezra Pound, we salute you!
   You are the most enchanting poet alive.
   Your poems in the April *Poetry* are so mockingly, so delicately, so
unblushingly beautiful that you seem to have brought back into the

world a grace which (probably) never existed, but which we discover by an imaginative process in Horatius and Catullus.

But here there is no possibility of a mistake. Professors have never annotated you, Ezra Pound, and silly old bibliophiles have never collected you in first editions and fine bindings. Nobody admires you whose admiration should cause us to suspect you.

There is no mistake about you, Ezra Pound. You are a creator of beauty in a world where only by a divinely creative process does beauty exist. (Quarrelsome poet, do not stop to discuss the matter now; besides, your prose is not convincing, anyway.) The point is that you are a Poet.

Salve!

(c) B.L.T. [Bert Lester Taylor], parody of 'Tenzone', *Chicago Tribune* (1913):

'Spring in State Street'

> Will people accept them?
>   (i.e. these bargains).
> O dainty colorings and range of prices!
> Gowns of charmeuse in all
>   the colours of the season;
> Blouse skirts of Russian cloth,
>   tucked belt of softest satin,
> And only at $37.50.

Get it straight. Ezra Pound is a poet, and much of his stuff contrasts refreshingly with the conventional oompa-oompa. Formal rimes and rhythms are not necessary to poetry.
['Tenzone' appeared in the April 1913 issue of *Poetry*.]

(d) Another contributor to the *Chicago Tribune* parodied 'Salutation':
> O degenerates in the art of writing,
>   and fallen ones,
> I have seen Cubists splattering their prints. . . .
> You are far worse than nothing;
> And they are much worse than nothing;
> And the nude descending the staircase,
>   and does not even own clothing. . . .

39. Pound and *Poetry*: a letter to *Nation* (New York)

April 1913

Raymond Macdonald Alden, from 'The New Poetry', *Nation* (17 April 1913), xcvi, 386–7.

Alden (1873–1924) was an American educator and author of several books of criticism.

Harriet Monroe and Alice Corbin Henderson, the editors of *Poetry*, replied to Alden in the issue of 1 May 1913. The passages quoted here are from Pound's 'Tenzone' and 'Salutation the Second', both appearing in the April 1913 issue of *Poetry*.

In order that we may be in no doubt as to what the editor of *Poetry* welcomes . . . the same number gives more than half its pages to a collection of what may safely be called futurist verses. They open thus:

> Will people accept them? (i.e., these songs);

they refer with elaborate indecorousness to the reporters, and pretty ladies who will *not* accept them; they flaunt occasional indecencies which are at once harmless and inexcusable, because unconnected with passion; they are guiltless of form, as form is known to masters or students of the art of poetry—in short, they exhibit with wanton richness all the signs of what I have called the morbid hypertrophy of romanticism. . . .

When Mr. Noyes was lately here, his Elizabethan ballads and Victorian lyrics were received with really notable enthusiasm—not because he is a great poet (whether he is or no is not implied), but because he speaks the language, metrical, emotional, and ethical, of our race. If the contributor to *Poetry* were to appear among us, urging his songs to

> Dance and make people blush,

without the riot of advertising which preceded the paintings of the kindred school, his work would also attract two classes of admirers, but two classes which are fortunately small in number—the frankly lascivious and the devotees of *art nouveau*.

40. Pound and *Poetry*: Wallace Rice in *Dial*

May 1913

Wallace Rice, 'Mr. Ezra Pound and *Poetry*', a letter, *Dial* (1 May 1913), liv, 370–1.

Rice (1859–1939) was a prolific Chicago journalist, popular historian and anthologist.

Our national aphorism, 'Some things can be done as well as others,' may be, as Mr. John A. Hobson has pointed out, a great asset in material affairs, but when it is acted upon in matters of art its value grows doubtful. We have dramatic enthusiasts ignorant of the art of acting, amateur stage managers unable to manage, compilers of verse without judgment, editors who have never before edited, all seeking to uplift masses eager to learn, yet all placing stumbling-blocks, through their own lack of standards, in the way of those earnestly aspiring to the heights.

Though no one can quarrel with literature in its highest form, nor with any periodical devoted to such a cause, one must regret that *Poetry* is being turned into a thing for laughter. No one need offer any particular criticism of the earlier work of Mr. Ezra Pound; it is as he prefers it. But with the practical identification of *Poetry* and Mr. Pound one may pick a very pretty quarrel, since it involves not only a lowering of standards, but a defense of the thesis, unusual in 'A Magazine of Verse,' that poor prose must be good poetry. Take this from the April number:

[quotes 'The Condolence', *CSP*, pp. 91–2, printed as prose.]

Is this anything but prose? and dull prose? Is it interesting, except to psychopathologists and students of barbaric survivals in the twentieth century? Does it reveal a personality, or hint at work one would like to know better? 'But,' some of Mr. Pound's admirers have answered, 'it has subtle rhythm.' To which the obvious reply is that English poetry has no subtle rhythm, nor can it have until its ictus, the strongest and most insistent in the history of speech, becomes subtle. The technical problem of English verse is largely the variance of rhythm, but the variances, again, are seldom subtle. The subtler rhythms in English literature are in its prose; and, it may be added, if subtlety implies difficulty of immediate discernment, the worse the prose the more subtle its rhythm.

Take an instance from another source:

> When Narcissus died,
> The pool of his pleasure changed
> From a cup of sweet waters
> Into a cup of salt tears,
> And the Oreads came weeping
> Through the woodland
> That they might sing to the pool
> And give it comfort.
> And when they saw that the pool had changed
> From a cup of sweet waters
> Into a cup of salt tears,
> They loosened the green tresses of their hair,
> And cried to the pool,
> And said:
> 'We do not wonder that you should mourn
> In this manner for Narcissus,
> So beautiful was he.'
> 'But was Narcissus beautiful?'
> Said the pool.
> 'Who should know better than you?'
> Answered the Oreads,
> 'Us did he ever pass by,
> But you he sought for,
> And would lie down on your banks
> And look down at you,
> And in the mirror of your waters
> He would mirror his own beauty.'
> And the pool answered:
> 'But I loved Narcissus

Because as he lay on my banks
And looked down at me,
In the mirror of his eyes
I saw my own beauty
Mirrored.'

This is not an unusually beautiful example of *vers libre*. On the contrary, it is Oscar Wilde's 'The Disciple,' which its author called a 'poem in prose.' And it *is* prose—poetic prose assuredly, but prose. Wilde did not write it as it is written here, in what might be called Jerked English, any more than Mr. Pound wrote the previous specimen with the lines run together. Wilde knew his to be prose and wrote it accordingly; Mr. Pound believed his to be poetry and so wrote it. Certainly 'The Disciple' is the more poetic of the two.

But whether a given literary composition is poetry or not, does not depend upon the manner in which the type is arranged on the printed page. If this were so, the printer would be the poet, not the writer. When Mr. Pound's various examples of what he considers poetry are printed as prose, they are prose. In contrast with Wilde's in any form, they are prosy prose.

Mr. Pound's admirers insist, however, upon the essential originality of his recent writings, and say that in destroying the conventions of rhyme and rhythm he is expanding the province of poetry. It is possible that, following the manner of Whitman, he is aiding in the fixation of a third form of literary expression, prose in form, poetic in content. But surely, after Macpherson and Whitman, that is no claim to originality.

One of Mr. Pound's defenders has said in words what *Poetry* has been teaching by implication, that 'formal rhythm is not necessary to poetry.' Such a statement involves complete confusion between two significations of the word poetry. We speak with propriety of a sermon, an essay, an oration, a novel, a prose drama, indeed of any work of art, as 'poetic,' meaning thereby that it arouses in us emotions similar to those excited by poetry.

But poetry, like every other Art or art, is concerned with form as well as substance. It is the metrical arrangement of words to express beauty, Poe's 'Music plus Idea,' and formal rhythm is as essential to it as to its sisters by birth, Music and the Dance. To deny that is to deny poetry, alone among the Arts and arts, the possession of a technic, reducing it forthwith below the level of literary prose, which unquestionably has technic; it will be recalled that Walter Pater refused through life to write poetry because it confused this. And it is to deny the technic of ascertained metre unchallenged through thirty centuries. In this sense alone Mr. Pound's work is original.

The attitude of *Poetry* toward poetry is that of Mrs. Mary Baker G. Eddy toward Medical Science. Yet, if poetry have no technic and, left formless thereby, is at one with illiterary prose, why devote a magazine to it? Every newspaper, programme, advertisement contains similar English—and English quite without false pretence. As has been pointed out, technic *qua* technic possesses charm for the cultivated mind. It is hardly too much to say that nothing atechnical has survived in any Art. Reduced to its simplest terms technic is knowing how—the experience of the ages manifesting itself in practice. Moreover, within the canons of the art there is perfect freedom; without, the baldest enslavement to every passing fad and fancy—as here.

Remember that youth essaying his first poetic flights draws strength for his wings largely from the greater poets who precede him and leave him heir to their powers. Every beginner imitates, and one familiar with his predecessors has little trouble in naming the sources from which he chooses his forms of expression, if not his thoughts. It is not until he has outgrown this period of unconscious assimilation and attained his own manner that he is worthy the name of poet. For, as Mr. Pound has observed, 'Any donkey can imitate a man's manner.'

In the April number of *Poetry* there are a dozen examples of Mr. Pound's work. Much the larger part of them are prose, like the one cited. The origins of all are evident. Whitman at his prosiest accounts for much, and in one Mr. Pound insists that he and the older bard have one sap and one root. There are touches here and there of MM. Maeterlinck and Albert Mockel, and something of Mr. W. B. Yeats. Nor should Stephen Crane be forgotten. The last instance is Japanese in content, though without the beautiful definition of the Japanese form. In other words, Mr. Pound's lines are derivations, experiments in the manner of a novice, searchings after individual expression without attainment. His roots are far back in the traditional past, inevitably.

If one searches for originality of thought, it is not here. Whitman had something to say and said it; Mr. Pound is still occupied with youthful Bohemianism and impudence. His intense egoism, too intense to carry self-confidence with it, is apparent. The power of self-criticism implied in a sense of humor is lacking. A care for syntax has gone the way of other traditions. One of his efforts has the ring of Mr. Roosevelt before a vice commission. Feeling for words and for form is slight. Imagination is in abeyance. The Song of Solomon fathers the most poetic of his work in style and substance. Thought is everywhere tenuous and capable of compression in statement, and the philosophy is uncertain. Some of the lines seem written for indecency's sake, which is more than those contending for 'art for art's sake' ask for. Most objectionable is the familiar attitude of the charlatan, announcing that his is the only cure, and that those disagreeing with him are the real quacks.

But Mr. Pound may be left to the court of appeal the years will hale him before, if he survive. Many young men write verses, or wish to, and are impatient at the restraints which lack of technic imposes. If one of them lives to attain full poethood, the verses of his artistic adolescence meet with one of three fates: they are suppressed, they are completely rewritten, or they appear in his published works as *juvenilia* —itself an apology for their survival.

The case is different with the magazine which has chosen to employ and exploit this young man. It has been able to do this consistently only by a supercilious dismissal of the great tradition of English poetry, using 'traditional' as a term of contempt. And there is so much for it to do by a maintenance of the standards. We have seen the tradition expanded by men dead only yesterday—Swinburne and William Vaughn Moody. Mr. Yeats has enlarged its boundaries by a little. The modern social feeling, the growing solidarity of women, the wonders of science are clamoring for poetic expression. Though there be no great poets among us, John Churton Collins has pointed out that from their lesser brethren 'it is in some respects but a step to the work of the great poets of the next age.'[1] The editors of the usual magazines have their own standards, and many of the singers of the day know their best work to be at variance with these standards. It was hoped that *Poetry* would search out these poets and such poems, many of them of much significance and beauty.

So far there has been little done in these directions. The quest has seemingly been for the bizarre, for the astonishing, for the novelty for novelty's sake, even for the shocking. The paper of the magazine has been poor, the type that of the newspapers, the cover and form inadequate to the dignity of the cause, the proof-reading heedless. The editor too seldom allows a number to go out without containing her own verses, though these show a steady retrogression from a once high

[1] Collins (1848–1908), Professor of English Literature at Birmingham from 1904, had wide experience as a university extension lecturer. Pound filled the vacancy on the staff of the Regent Street Polytechnic caused by his death.

standard. Her own sense of self-criticism in abeyance, Mr. Pound was bound to occur.

Chicago, April 22, 1913.

41. Pound and *Poetry*: Harriet Monroe replies

May 1913

Harriet Monroe, 'In Defense of *Poetry*', a letter, *Dial* (16 May 1913), liv, 409.

William Vaughn Moody (1869–1910), John Reed (1887–1920), Vachel Lindsay (1879–1931), Yeats and Tagore were all contributors to *Poetry*.

Your correspondent's sweeping indictment of *Poetry* and all its works, in your last issue, almost leaves me no ground to stand on. However, I still find room enough to question Mr. Wallace Rice's right to the tripod.

'The editors who have never before edited' are less to be dreaded than those who have edited too much. Mr. Rice has edited so many anthologies—among them, *The Little Book of Brides, The Little Book of Kisses, The Little Book of Sports*—that the keen edge of his judgment as an authority on poetry is somewhat worn. 'English poetry has no subtle rhythm,' he drones, apparently quite unconscious that this statement is a declaration of ineligibility to the office of critic of poetry. It is as if some critic of painting, congenitally color-blind, should announce that there is no difference between green and blue.

Mr. Rice then gets on safer ground. Poetry, like every other Art or art, he solemnly asserts, is concerned with form as well as substance; it is the metrical arrangement of words to express beauty. To deny this is to deny poetry the possession of a technic, to deny the technic of ascertained metre unchallenged through thirty centuries. No, we don't deny that 'poetry is concerned with form as well as substance'—all that we deny is Mr. Rice's competence to discern form. We don't 'deny poetry the possession of a technic,' though we are compelled to deny his narrow conception of poetic technic. We hardly know what he may mean by 'the technic of ascertained metre unchallenged through thirty centuries,' as he can hardly be familiar with all the languages of the earth since ancient Egypt, or with the vast history of human quarrels on the subject of poetic technic since first the devil said, 'Is it Art?' Indeed, we doubt if he knows as much on the subject as Mr. Pound, who has devoted some years to an exhaustive study of metrical forms and variations on the poetry of eleven languages.

We have no intention of defending Mr. Pound's poetry. Quite competently it defends itself; as Mr. Rice says, he 'may be left to the court of appeal the years will hale him before, if he survives.' Meantime, as the years are long in coming, *Poetry* will not be able, either in his case or those of other adventurously modern poets, to sit on the fence of tradition until the verdict of time is pronounced. That would be the safe course, doubtless; we commend it to those who always think that the last word has been said.

'And there is so much for it [that is, the magazine] to do by a maintenance of the standards!' Mr. Rice wails. 'The modern social feeling, the growing solidarity of women, the wonders of science, are clamoring for poetic expression.' Quite true; if Mr. Rice will review the first seven numbers of *Poetry*, he may get some light on these subjects through Moody's 'I Am the Woman,' John Reed's 'Sangar,' Lindsay's 'General Booth,' Towne's 'Beyond the Stars,' Yeats's allegory of his fate, Rabindra Nath Tagore's lyrics, and Ezra Pound's 'Contemporania.'

HARRIET MONROE,
Editor of *Poetry*.

Chicago, May 9, 1913.

CATHAY

London, 6 April 1915

42. Ford Madox Hueffer, 'From China to Peru', *Outlook*

19 June 1915, xxxv, 800–1

Hueffer (i.e. Ford) (1873–1939), English novelist and editor, played an important role in the recognition of Pound's talent (see Introduction, pp. 5,21). Pound's important essay 'The Prose Tradition in Verse' was written about Ford's poetry.

The poems in *Cathay* are things of a supreme beauty. What poetry should be, that they are. And if a new breath of imagery and of handling can do anything for our poetry, that new breath these poems bring.

In a sense they only back up a theory and practice of poetry that is already old—the theory that poetry consists in so rendering concrete objects that the emotions produced by the objects shall arise in the reader. What could be better poetry than the first verse of 'The Beautiful Toilet'?

> Blue, blue is the grass about the river
> And the willows have overflowed the close garden.
> And within, the mistress, in the midmost of her youth,
> White, white of face, hesitates, passing the door:
> Slender, she puts forth a slender hand.

Or what could better render the feelings of protracted war than the 'Song of the Bowmen of Shu'?

[quotes 'Song of the Bowmen of Shu', *CSP*, p. 137.]

Or where have you had better rendered, or more permanently beautiful a rendering of the feelings of one of those lonely watchers in the outposts of progress, whether it be Ovid in Hyrcania, a Roman sentinel upon the Great Wall of this country, or merely ourselves in the lonely recesses of our minds, than the 'Lament of the Frontier Guard'?

[quotes 'Lament of the Frontier Guard', *CSP*, p. 143.]

Yet the first two of these poems are over two thousand years old and the last more than a thousand.

And Mr. Pound's little volume is like a door in a wall, opening suddenly upon fields of an extreme beauty, and upon a landscape made real by the intensity of human emotions. We are accustomed to think of the Chinese as arbitrary or uniform in sentiment, but these poems reveal [them] as being just ourselves. I do not know that that matters much; but what does matter to us is the lesson in the handling of words and in the framing of emotions. . . . Beauty is a very valuable thing; perhaps it is the most valuable thing in life; but the power to express emotion so that it shall communicate itself intact and exactly is almost more valuable. Of both of these qualities Mr. Pound's book is very full. Therefore I think we may say that this is much the best work he has yet done, for, however closely he may have followed his originals—and of that most of us have no means whatever of judging—there is certainly a good deal of Mr. Pound in this little volume.

43. A. R. Orage on the thought and form of *Cathay*

1915

A. R. Orage, *The Art of Reading* (New York: Farrar & Rinehart, 1930), pp. 143–5.

Orage (1873–1934), English journalist, editor of the *New Age,* advocate of Guild Socialism and Social Credit, disciple of Gurdjieff, and editor of the *New English Weekly,* was a forceful critic of modern literature. His columns in the *New Age* under the pseudonym 'R.H.C' have been collected in *Readers and Writers* (1922) and *The Art of Reading*. Pound's obituary article on Orage appeared in the *Criterion,* April 1935.

If I were to say that *Cathay* contains the best and only good work Mr. Ezra Pound has yet done, my judgment might be defended. The volume contains, among other poems, a reprint of 'The Seafarer', Mr. Pound's masterly translation from the original Anglo-Saxon. This poem is without doubt one of the finest literary works of art produced in England during recent years. For this poem alone, *Cathay* is worth its weight in gold. But there are others to whose pleasure I almost as readily succumb. In a note Mr. Pound tells us that they are accurate translations from the Chinese, made in the first instance by Fenollosa and only in the second by Mr. Pound himself. Some of them date back to the Fifth Century B.C., others are as recent as the Eighth Century A.D. I can only say that they delight and astonish me. In character they are not dissimilar to the Anglo-Saxon poem referred to. Mr. Pound's taste in including the 'Seafarer' with them is, in fact, impeccable. But it would be a very pretty work of criticism to distinguish the individual qualities proper to each. In my judgment the Anglo-Saxon is a little less perfect; it has not the pure simplicity of its Chinese exemplars. On the other hand, it is as we should expect, a little more manly in its sentiment.

[quotes 'Song of the Bowmen of Shu' and 'The River-Merchant's Wife: A Letter', *CSP*, pp. 137, 140.]

I would make two further observations. As in the 'Seafarer', the thoughts contained in the Chinese poems are of a very simple character. The imaginary persons are without subtlety, one might say, without mind. But it cannot be the case that only simple natures can be subjects of poetry; or that 'naturalness' belongs to them alone. I have noted in the *vers librists* a tendency to confine themselves to the elementary emotions of elementary people; as if the possession of a cultivated mind excluded its owner from poetry. But Browning was quite as simple, straightforward and 'natural' in, say, 'Bishop Blougram's Apology' as Rihaku was in his 'Merchant's Wife's Letter'. The difference is that Browning was 'perfecting' the expression of a powerful and subtle mind, while Rihaku was perfecting the mind relatively of a child. The extension of the directness and simplicity, the veracity and the actuality aimed at by *vers librists,* into subtler regions than the commonplace is advisable if they are not to keep in the nursery of art.

My other observation is on the subject of the form. I have not denied being 'pleased' with the poems, though their form is that of free-rhythm. Nobody can fail indeed to derive some pleasure from them. But, all the same, the pleasure is much less than I should derive from the same contents in an orderly form. Content is not everything in poetry, as everybody knows. As well as the content the form itself is an integral and, in great poetry, an indistinguishable element of the pleasure. The form and the content are at once one and two. In these poems however, as in all free-rhythm, the form is not a positive source of pleasure, though I admit there is not a subtraction from the pleasure. It is simply absent. But given a content as pure (that is, as perfectly natural) and a form equally *perfectly* natural—that is, delicately regularized, selected, artistic—the total pleasure must obviously be more intense. From an unaccompanied melody we should rise to a symphony. Modern *vers libre* is only an imperfect form of art. It is, in fact, a transitional form between no poetry at all or a pedantic poetry, and perfect poetry. As a phenomenon of our time it is, in part, due to writers who simply have no poetry in them, and, in part, to writers genuinely reacting against the school of Tennyson; the revolutionaries and the charlatans once more mingling, as in every reform movement. To which of these component parties in the school of free-rhythm Mr. Pound belongs there is no doubt. And hence I wish him speedily out of it.

44. Carl Sandburg, 'The Work of Ezra Pound', *Poetry*

February 1916, vii, 249–57

Sandburg (1878–1967), American poet, journalist, and biographer of Abraham Lincoln, was a leading figure in the Chicago renaissance. His *Chicago Poems* appeared in 1916.

Pound mentioned this essay in a letter to Alice Corbin Henderson in March 1917 as 'altogether the most lengthy treatment I have yet had from any critic' (*Letters*, p. 162).

If I were driven to name one individual who, in the English language, by means of his own examples of creative art in poetry, has done most of living men to incite new impulses in poetry, the chances are I would name Ezra Pound.

This statement is made reservedly, out of knowing the work of Pound and being somewhat close to it three years or so. I hope that no luck of war or peace will ever back me into a corner where, by force and duress, I must lie shackled and hungry in a donjon keep until I name the world's champion poet. If, however, as a friendly stranger in a smoking compartment, you should casually ask me for an offhand opinion as to who is the best man writing poetry today, I should probably answer, 'Ezra Pound.'

All talk on modern poetry, by people who know, ends with dragging in Ezra Pound somewhere. He may be named only to be cursed as wanton and mocker, poseur, trifler and vagrant. Or he may be classed as filling a niche today like that of Keats in a preceding epoch. The point is, he will be mentioned.

One must know how to spell his name, and have heard rumors of where he hangs his hat when he eats, and one must have at least passing acquaintance with his solemn denunciadoes and his blurted quiddities, in order to debate on modern poetry, and in such debate zigzag a course of progress.

When Nicodemus wanted to know more about the real Jesus of Nazareth, he had the justice to make a night call and ask Jesus some questions.

Let some of those thrusting spears and ink pots at Ezra Pound try to be fair enough to read him.

In the early regulations of the University of Paris, this oath was required of professors: 'I swear to read and to finish reading, within the time set by the statutes, the books and parts of books assigned for my lectures.' Some like form should be insisted on for reviewers and commentators who in this push-button and dumb-waiter age rush into type with two-minute judgments on twenty-year accomplishments.

Though a Fabre spends ninety years watching spiders and writing a book, any ordinary book reviewer or critic nowadays will type haphazard a column of words on the work of a lifetime, and assume without humility or prayer to say this is good and that is bad.

Though an Ezra Pound toil ten years at one aim and coin high joy and red life into a commanding book of poetry, there are plenty of offhand scholars who assume that he means nothing to anybody because he means nothing to them.

The opposition to Pound divides roughly into two groups: first, the mumbo-jumbo school who assert with grave faces that this sort of poetry has never before been written, and therefore it is not poetry; and second, the pish-tush school whose risibilities are tickled with turning the poems upside down, inside out, or backwards and forwards.

In the cool and purple meantime, Pound goes ahead producing new poems having the slogan, 'Guts and Efficiency,' emblazoned above his daily program of work. His genius runs to various schools and styles. He acquires traits and then throws them away. One characteristic is that he has no characteristics. He is a new roamer of the beautiful, a new fetcher of wild shapes, in each new handful of writings offered us.

Maybe it is a psalm of his glory in certain old roads 'where the hills part in three ways,' where also he has 'seen the copper come down tingeing the mountains,' and sunset 'torch flames painting the front of that church.' Maybe it is a London girl combing her hair, and he watches her across the street from his room, and wonders pleasantly about her till she sings and her voice sends him running from the rasp of its falsetto. The old, old things that are always lovely haunt him, whether they move on the faces of women, petals of flowers, waves of moonlight, or the waters of Venice by night, which he gives in murmurous lines like these:

[quotes 'Night Litany', *CSP*, p. 40, 'And the beauty' to 'the time of its coming?'.]

From these soft waters and this gentle blurred nocturne, he may turn to this picture and its hard movement:

> Gray cliffs,
>   and beneath them
> A sea
> Harsher than granite,
>   unstill, never ceasing.

Or his translation of Bertrans de Born's ballad of the lover of war, wherein the master speaks to his jongleur, Papiol, in this wise:

> And I watch his spears through the dark clash,
> And it fills all my heart with rejoicing
> And pries wide my mouth with fast music.
> The man who fears war and squats opposing
> My words for stour, hath no blood of crimson,
> But is fit only to rot in womanish peace.
> Papiol, Papiol, to the music:
> May God damn forever all who cry, 'Peace!'

Though the Vorticist school now claims Pound and he endorses the claim, he is also an ancient of the ancients. His translations from the Chinese are vivid in feeling and keen in sympathy. One realizes the closeness of the Chinese soul as a next-door human neighbor, fellow-traveler on an old, old planet, after reading *Cathay*.

Drawing a style of writing from hitherto obscure Romance literature and the troubadours, from the Chinese and the Egyptian, from modern science, Nietzsche and syndicalism, the technique of Pound baffles any accurate analysis in a single paper. His own statements of his theories do not get at the gist of the matter, and he passes his warmest inspirations to others through poems in the actual instead of theoretic.

As well should one reduce to chemical formula the crimson of a Kentucky redbird's wing as dissect the inner human elements that give poetic craft to this heart song from 'Planh':

> But if one should look at me with the old hunger in her eyes,
> How will I be answering her eyes?
>
> For I have followed the white folk of the forest,

Aye! It's a long hunting,
And it's a deep hunger I have when I see them a-gliding
And a-flickering there where the trees stand apart.

But oh, it is sorrow and sorrow,
When love dies down in the heart.

He has prowled in streets, taprooms, libraries and lexicons. Out of a
mixed lore gathered among hooligans, bookmen and beautiful women,
he projects such films as these:

[quotes 'Francesca', 'On His Own Face in a Glass', 'Li Po' and 'Ancient
Wisdom, Rather Cosmic', *CSP*, pp. 50, 49, 129.]

Out of thousands of Christ poems, there are not a dozen that live
on shining with the luminous power of the Christ life. Judges like
William Butler Yeats say Pound's 'Ballad of the Goodly Fere' will last.
These are two of its fourteen verses:

I ha' seen him cow a thousand men
On the hills o' Gallilee,
They whined as he walked out calm between,
Wi' his eyes like the gray o' the sea.

Like the sea that brooks no voyaging
With the winds unleashed and free,
Like the sea that he cowed at Genseret
Wi' twey words spoke suddenly.

On the fly-leaf of a book of Italian translations Ezra Pound wrote:

The reader must bear in mind that these poems were written one by one. It is
impossible to read the book 'straight through' with any pleasure. It is unfair to
Guido to attempt it. The poem of the close school is a subject for meditation. It
is best to read one at a time. Four or five together are all that should ever be
tried.

The same counsel goes for those who take up the collected works of
Ezra Pound. These are not in the same class with reading matter farmers
buy from mail-order houses to while away long winter nights and the
rainy season. . . .

His way of working, his art and craftsmanship, is more conscious
and deliberate, more clear-cut in purpose and design, than might be
thought from first glance at the careless surface of one of his free-
running poems. While he is an ignorant barbarian on the sources of his

inspiration and the power by which he works out his inward flashes, once the urge and blaze is on him he works by rules, measurements, formulae and data as strict and definite as any worker who uses exact science, and employs fractions of inches, and drills in steel by thousandths of millimeters. These two sentences may offer clues to the intuitions that guide him:

Poetry is a sort of inspired mathematics, which gives us equations, not for abstract figures, triangles, spheres and the like, but equations for the human emotions. If one have a mind which inclines to magic rather than science, one will prefer to speak of these equations as spells or incantations; it sounds more arcane, mysterious, recondite.

Since he wrote the foregoing in *The Spirit of Romance* some years ago, he has been joined with the Imagists and from them passed on to the Vorticists. Wyndham Lewis in *Blast* starts with the Red Indian, and then cites Poe, Whistler, Henry James, and Walt Whitman, ending with Ezra Pound as the high points of American art. These are Lewis' notes on Pound:

Demon pantechnicon driver, busy with removal of old world into new quarters. In his steel net of impeccable technique he has lately caught Li Po. Energy of a discriminating element.

People write poetry because they want to. It functions in them as air in the nostrils of an athlete in a sprint. Moods, thoughts, emotions, surge over writers as they do over inventors and politicians. It is a dark stuff of life that comes and goes.

There are those who play safe and sane in poetry, as in mechanics and politics. To each realm its own gay madmen. Some win their public while they live. Others must mould a very small public while alive, and be content with a larger one after death. Still others need no public at all, and in the rôle of by-standers they get more enjoyment and knowledge of life than as performers.

In a world with so high a proportion of fools, it is neither disgrace nor honor when people say of a finished work, 'I can't understand it.' The last word on the merits of it will be spoken by the future. And sometimes the future decides that a work is beautiful and worth treasuring, and then ironically destroys it and leaves behind no word of explanation nor apology.

I like the pages of Ezra Pound. He stains darkly and touches softly. The flair of great loneliness is there. He is utter as a prairie horseman, a biplane in the azure, a Norse crag, or any symbol of the isolate, contemplative spirit of man unafraid and searching. He is worth having.

45. William Marion Reedy on the position of Pound

February and July 1916

Extract from an editorial in the issue of 11 February 1916 in *Reedy's Mirror*, on the occasion of Harriet Monroe delivering a talk in St Louis on 'The New Poetry', and an extract from 'What I've Been Reading', *Reedy's Mirror* 14 July 1916, xxv, 462–3.

Reedy (1862–1920) was a Missouri journalist who turned the St Louis *Sunday Mirror* into a weekly political and literary magazine which he ran as *Reedy's Mirror* from 1913 to 1920. Pound replied to Reedy, correcting numerous errors of fact, in the issue of 18 August 1916; the reply was reprinted as an appendix in *Pavannes and Divisions* (1918).

The works of Ezra Pound had fallen dead-born in England, but when his bare, esurient, rhymeless and almost rhythmless writings appeared in *Poetry,* he found an audience that understood. His own countrymen, seeing with the eyes of Miss Monroe, discovered him, and their discovery reacted upon England with happy results for Mr. Pound.

Most pungent and pugnacious of personalities is Ezra Pound, head of the Vorticist movement in England, poet, critic and polemical pest to the unregenerate followers of convention. He was born in Utah, I believe, but that is immaterial. He writes poetry of a skeletal sort. He was the first of the imagists. He brought to the consideration of poetry the Chinese concept, as Whistler brought to painting the Japanese. He rendered into English some thirteenth century Italian poets, with a singular absence of that *morbidezza* which is generally associated with Italian expression. I don't 'get' Ezra Pound's poetry, but I do 'get' a strong impression of his value in a good fight he is making for stark seeing and saying of things. He is the foe of literary language, of *clichés*, of saying things in the phrases of poets gone before. He did a brave thing when he championed *Spoon River Anthology* in England, for its innocence of the sin of adhering to what we may call 'poetical diction.' Altogether, Mr. Pound is a true radical in his devotion to veritism, in his regard for the anatomy of poetry and his contempt for mere verbal upholstery. Now he's gone beyond imagism and has become a vorticist. I'm not sure I know what vorticism is—even after Mr. Pound has explained it. I have read the organ of Vorticism—*Blast*, and emerged from it with a vertigo as a result of the whirl of the vortex. So, when I read his *Gaudier-Brzeska* (pronounced Jaerschke) . . . it was with a strong sense of the loyal enthusiasm of Pound and the fine ecstasy of Gaudier-Brzeska for an art or concept exasperatingly obnubilated. . . .

The more Mr. Pound or Gaudier-Brzeska himself explains, the more the art becomes unintelligible. In a way, I seem to see that Gaudier went farther back for the impression of emergence than does Rodin, as Rodin went farther back than the Della Robbias. This new art is one of 'masses defined by planes,' but it seems to me that this is talking to us in a new language, known only to the sculptor. It's like the speech of one with 'the gift of tongues' I heard recently at a 'Holiness meeting'. The vorticist in sculpture tries probably to put over to us in planes his emotions, as a musician conveys us his emotions in tones. The idea is to get everything over as directly as possible, without interposition of symbols, without ornament, without proposition or form. This is the equivalent of imagism, but it is to me meaningless—what is a formless form, and how can there be expression without some mutually agreed upon symbols for thoughts or feelings? Those who care for art should read this book for it will put every one of their accepted theories to the test implied in a sweeping repudiation. Vorticism throws all the old art concepts into a hopper and crushes them and runs them out into something like what comes out of a cement mixer. . . . But the man, Gaudier-Brzeska, is worth while. His letters to friends, descriptive of life in the trenches, with flashes of art criticism, are most attractive. And besides, it's stimulating—almost affrighting—to read Ezra Pound's tremendous pontifications.

GAUDIER BRZESKA: A MEMOIR

London, April 1916

46. Unsigned review, *Dial*

15 August 1916, lxi, 112

It is to be feared that not many people in America will have the courage or even the curiosity to open Mr. Pound's *Gaudier-Brzeska: A Memoir* after a glance at the cover. On this cover is reproduced the photograph of a young sculptor with long hair and an unpleasant leer, in front of whom is a work entitled 'Bird Swallowing a Fish', executed in what is roughly (often very roughly) called the Cubist style. There is no use in attempting to recommend this volume by concealing the fact that it is written by an extremely modern poet about an extremely modern sculptor.

And yet to those who are not already discouraged it may be said that the memoir has a three-fold interest. In the first place it presents an unusual personality and a 'romantic' career. Henri Gaudier was an eccentric and brilliant young Frenchman who lived and wandered about in England and Germany in typical Bohemian fashion, finally settling in London. Here he first began sculpture and allied himself to the 'vorticist' group, a number of writers, painters and sculptors whose official organ is a magazine called *Blast*. At the outbreak of the war Gaudier, who had arbitrarily added to his name the hyphen Brzeska (pronounced Breshkah) returned to France to enlist. But as he had 'skipped' his military service, he was arrested and threatened with 'ten years in Africa.' That night he climbed from the window of his temporary prison, escaped to England, explained his case to the French Embassy, and returned with better credentials to serve in the trenches, where he was killed in June, 1915. His letters from the trenches to Pound and others are the most vivid impressions of the war which the present reviewer has seen. Brzeska describes the whole thing as a 'bloody bath of idealism.' With a barbaric pride which is very characteristic he takes no pains to conceal his delight in killing. But he also writes of the larks and nightingales, 'The shells do not disturb the songsters. . . . They solemnly proclaim man's foolery and sacrilege of nature. I respect their disdain.' The life of such a man is surely worth a glance, especially as it was ended at the age of twenty-three. Of his sculpture anyone may judge from the excellent reproductions of the plates, but not at a glance. The present reviewer had the opportunity of knowing the sculptor and seeing his work in the summer of 1914, and though he was by no means converted, he was convinced on examination that Brzeska was a fine craftsman in the new style and that he often succeeded in expressing emotion by means of his 'arrangement of planes' and 'balance of masses.' There was, however, a good deal of malicious trickery in all his work. The third field of interest in Mr. Pound's book is—Mr. Pound; his humor, his rhetoric against the Philistine, and especially the theories of art held by the 'vorticist' group. Under this last heading Mr. Pound assumes, not without a certain right, the mantle of Whistler. Mr. Pound has gained much in sanity and in clearness of expression; he is now not only amusing, he is stimulating. He brings out Brzeska's preference for the barbaric emotion of Egyptian and Assyrian sculpture as opposed to the alleged effeminacy of the Greek. The keystone of vorticism is the direct interpretation of feeling. As to sculpture this ideal is best stated by a quotation from Mr. Binyon's *Flight of the Dragon*: 'It is not essential that the subject-matter should represent or be like anything in nature; only it must be alive with a rhythmic vitality of its own'.[1] This is at least worth thinking over, and the book contains much else that is equally suggestive.

[1] Laurence Binyon's *The Flight of the Dragon: An Essay in the Theory and Practice of Art in China and Japan* appeared in the 'Wisdom of the East Series' in 1911.

LUSTRA

London, October 1916
New York, 16 October 1917

---

47. The problem of getting published, 1
A postcard from Elkin Mathews's reader

Pound submitted *Lustra* to Mathews early in 1916. It was apparently sent to the printers, Clowes, who refused to set several of the poems. This postcard, from Mathews's (unknown) reader, is among the documents held in the Ezra Pound collection at the University of California, Berkeley.

---

pages
9 & 10   Sorry stuff to begin with
15   An impudent piece
19   D⁰ ['Commission']
20   Poor Walt Whitman   ['A Pact']
        Let's hope he will survive it
28   Silly nonsense
29   Better keep his *baser passions* to himself. No one else
        wants them   ['Further Instructions']
35   Personal   not funny   ['The New Cake of Soap']
36   We shall get ourselves rather disliked
        (This is quite true)   ['Salvationists']
38   *Beastly*   ['The Temperaments']
39   Meditation certainly *curious*   ['Meditatio']
44   What words of wisdom!   ['Phyllidula' and/or 'The
        Patterns']
45   Smelly like its subject   ['The Seeing Eye']
54   Coitus   [in ink]   What a simile!   ['Coitus']
57   Papyrus.   How truly beautiful!

58   Delicious lasciviousness
61   Foolish   Zuutians would be better title
65   Pitiful Parody of beautiful verse   ['Ancient Music']
The only poems worth reading are the translations.

      splendid   See page 39
    The⟨ self conceit⟨ of the author.

Pact! (save the mask!) is the only redeeming feature of most of the others, which with a few exceptions are more fitted for the Waste Paper Basket than the literary public.

48. The problem of getting published, 2
The memorandum of agreement

These are the detailed emendations and deletions which Elkin Mathews proposed to Pound for the publication of *Lustra*. On the verso of the contract there is a note that the printers, Clowes, agree to print a private edition for the author—with the exception of 'The Temperaments', 'Ancient Music' and 'The Lake Isle' 'which they decline to print in any form whatever'. Pound was furious and attempted to enlist Yeats, the literary agent J. B. Pinker, and Augustine Birrell, Liberal M.P. and Irish Secretary, in his fight against Mathews's attempt to censor his work. (An important selection of Pound's letters on this are reprinted in *Pound/Joyce*.) *Lustra* eventually appeared in an 'emasculated' edition of 800 copes, and an edition for private circulation of 200.

Mathews (1851–1921) was an English publisher and bookseller (see Introduction, pp. 3–5).

Page 16—Salutation the Second—you must omit 11.6 to end
  ,, 19—Commission—If included must be revised—delete two last lines on this page, and the lines 'Go to the adolescent' to the end of p. 20
  ,, 29 Further Instruction. On the last line but ~~three two~~ two the word 'Christ' must be omitted—as it won't affect the sense its retention would only give needless offense.
  ,, 35 The New Cake of Soap—This must be deleted
  ,, 37 Epitaph—Delete because the meaning is dubious
  ,, 38 The Temperaments—This must be deleted
  ,, 41 Meditatio—This must be deleted—very nasty
  ,, 44 Phyllidula
  ,, ,,   The Patterns   ,,   ,,   .
  ,, 45 The Seeing Eye—Must be deleted—very nasty—

Page 54   Coitus—the Gk word Phallos means penis—*simply* and the
           latin word Phallus is merely derived from it—in any case the
           title *must* be changed—

„   58   The poem to Atthis—anything but 'delicate'—must be
           omitted

„   65   Ancient Music—Blasted blasphemy ⎫   ~~delete~~
                            & a damned parody ⎬   must be
                                                   omitted

„   66   Substitute 'Jupiter' for God in the two places where the word
           occurs

     —   Cabaret Dancers—some of the very 'delicate' allusions might
           with advantage be toned down—

„   123   is it necessary to describe that *particular* intaglio?

49. Kate Buss, 'Ezra Pound: Some Evidence of his Rare Chinese Quality'

Boston Evening Transcript, 6 December 1916, section 3, 5

Kate Buss was an early American admirer of Pound's work and
carried on a lengthy correspondence with him. She sent a copy of
this initialled review to Pound in London. In his reply (*Letters*,
p. 154) he carefully corrects the point she makes about 'Albatre'
and emphasizes that the *Lustra* poems generally preceded those in
Cathay, despite their dates of publication.

There are probably few translators who have been able more definitely
to separate the spirits of Chinese and Japanese poetry in translation than
Mr. Pound. *Cathay*, and a longer *Cathay*, printed in his newest collection of poems named *Lustra* are eloquent tribute to his perceptions. Perhaps this separation is more definitely felt because one senses Mr. Pound's
own Chinese quality. It is the only classification I dare hold to, as my

mind jumps about each new book that he writes into the ardors of new shapes and newer roamings. I still feel pleasantly certain that he would not have written such a poem as 'Albatre' . . . if he had not mused over and understood and arranged 'The Beautiful Toilet', written by Mei Sheng one hundred and fifty years before the time of Christ:

[quotes 'The Beautiful Toilet', *CSP*, p. 138.]

Mr. Pound, whose affiliations with America are thin ice on spring rivers, and who pleases himself in his chosen business of being a poet, incidentally hopes to find favour with four people who comprise his tribune. . . . One is tempted to guess the quartet the gauntlet is so straightly flung. . . .

[quotes 'Causa', *CSP*, p. 97.]

Mr. Pound once wrote me that life was too complicated to be treated coherently in hurried writing, and one might say that about his poems. They are too complicated for hasty judgment. One must read—and read again a week later. They are ironical, jeering and intolerant, they are lonely, contemplative, searching, carefully formed and firmly living. Perhaps you hate Ezra Pound. He says many of us have the manner. Perhaps you like him, but whatever else you do you cannot ignore him. He has an individual fashion of saying things and he is without fear. Also it seems to me that if he, like Li Po, sometimes tries to embrace the moon in a yellow river, at another time he writes a poem like 'The Return', which by its own chill intensity is forced into the anthology that beauty alone compiles.

50. A poet in rebellion against emotion

December 1917

G. W. Cronin, 'Classic Free Verse', *New York Call Magazine* 23 December 1917, 18.

The quotation from Carl Sandburg is from No. 44. Giovanitti, an Italian immigrant to America, published a prose poem against imprisonment, *Arrows in the Gale*, in 1914. The *Call* was a socialist daily newspaper.

In the poetry of Ezra Pound free verse reaches its classical stage. No longer, as in Whitman, an instinct, an iconoclasm, it has learned, by way of the French symbolists, to do remarkable stunts, acquired a technique and a system all its own, and become deliberate, exquisite, self-assured and positive. One of those rare periods we designate auriferously. The Golden Age. The Golden Age of Vers Libre!

Lustra makes me think of other golden ages, of Horace, for instance, and the meticulous gentlemen of Queen Anne. Perhaps it is the tone of the book, which is rather satiric, and detached, than lyrical and personal. This almost excessive air of detachment about Ezra Pound's work gives an impression of coldness, of almost bitter aloofness from the common run. His rebelliousness is purely aesthetic and intellectual, however, against stupidity, banality—one suspects—against simplicity itself. He is determined to accept no emotion at its face value—and accepts none. Without emotion, he does not move one. The natural metier of such an attitude is the epigram. Ezra Pound's epigrams scintillate a cold, clear sparkle, sharp and mordant. His sayings about women are always or nearly always, brilliant, cynical and heartless: they are, to him

> Flawless as Aphrodite
> Thoroughly beautiful
> Brainless.

In his cognizance of the other sex, the fatal and destructive allurement, the vicious and cruel enslavement, which characterized many of

126

the love poems of the preceding French school and earned them the un-welcome name of 'decadents', has quite finished. Ezra Pound seems entirely master of his own weapon against passion: it is the critical sense, tempered by indifference.

> The faint odour of your patchouli—
> Faint, almost, as the line of cruelty
> about your chin—
> Assails me, and concerns me almost as little.

These elegent stabbing lines recall Augustan phrases of polished Roman wits . . .:

[quotes 'Arides', *CSP*, p. 109.]

In such passages as these Ezra Pound seems to be the literary god-father of Edgar Lee Masters; but whereas the former achieves only a sort of malicious persiflage, the latter, by the force of a psychic penetration, strikes out lines of poignant—sometimes ghastly—splendour, like conflagrations, catastrophically human.

Many literary currents meet and mingle in the *Lustra*—Greek, Latin, French, Italian, German, the Renaissance and Modern painting—futurism, post-impressionism. Ezra Pound is classic, without being in the least pagan; he has, apparently, no real joy in anything, because, I think, his sensations are secondary, aesthetic, not pure, primary and direct.

Golden ages occur at moments of over-civilization, when life seems to reach an impasse, devoid of first thoughts. Then come wars and catastrophes. The *Lustra* is bookish instead of revealing further heights or depths of existence, it bears the echoes of dead literatures. Ezra Pound chose the newer (and more ancient) form; but his spirit is with the men of a just-past generation, which Arthur Symons has so nobly evaluated. Carl Sandburg has said 'If I were driven to name one individual who, in the English language by means of his own examples of creative art in poetry, has done most of living men to incite new impulses in poetry, the chances are I would name Ezra Pound'. That may be true; frequently it is the lesser poets—the Beaumonts and Fletchers—who are most loudly acclaimed and imitated by their contemporaries rather than the big figures.

Personally I would rather have one of Arturo Giovanitti's things, such as 'The Last Nickel' or 'The Walker' or one of Carl Sandburg's Chicago poems than the whole volume called *Lustra*, in spite of the Cathay translations contained therein.

Intellectual fantasies! This 'New York' of Ezra Pound is as detached from its actuality as William Blake's 'London'—the sounding of a name, a word and a mirage.

[quotes 'N.Y.', *CSP*, p. 74.]

Compare this to the robustious Manhattan of Walt! Or the Chicago of Sandburg. 'Hog-Butcher to the World!' Pound's finest moods are delicately chiselled and Greekish, for he says, characteristically:

[quotes 'Ité', *CSP*, p. 104.]

The Lustra is full of hard light—and wounds.

51. Louis Untermeyer on a poet in pantomime

December 1920

From 'China, Provence and Points Adjacent', *Dial* (December 1920), lxiii, 634–5.

Untermeyer (b. 1885), American poet and critic, edited *Modern American Poetry* (1919, frequently revised). J. A. Robbins has edited *EP to LU: Letters Written to Louis Untermeyer by Ezra Pound* (1963). See also Jean Starr Untermeyer, 'Ezra Pound: The Mosaic of a Mandarin', *Private Collection* (New York: Alfred A. Knopf, 1965), pp. 208–17.

Ezra Pound's volume is a far more puzzling affair. Its range and variety are its most outstanding quality and its chief defect. The volume seems a catch-all for Pound's slightest utterance. Poems in the imagist manner, lugubrious Cantos in a Sordello form, arrangements in the vorticist vein, epigrams from the Greek, Lalage and other ladies from the Latin, paraphrases from the German, scraps from the Spanish, idioms from the Italian, water-colors from the Chinese, echoes from Provence— one gets nothing so much as a confused jumble and smattering of erudition. The effect is less that of the man of the world than the man about literature. All is carefully noted, collected, tagged, and set down. Nothing is too inconsequential or unworthy of inclusion. It is all here; even the absurd apostrophe to Swinburne ('Salve Pontifex') and the inane, schoolboy burlesque of 'Summer is icumen in'. What makes this lust for print the more puzzling is the fact that Mr. Pound has not only a critical but a selective gift. In fact the latter concentrative quality (as is proved by the transcriptions of Fenollosa's notes, *Cathay*) is his most salient trait. What then will even his youngest disciple say to the awkward and malformed versions of eight Heine poems that read like so many humorless parodies, the paper-motto silliness of such a couplet as

[quotes, 'The New Cake of Soap', *CSP*, p. 108.]

and 'Papyrus' which I quote in its entirety:

[quotes 'Papyrus', *CSP*, p. 122.]

White paper is evidently not so precious as the publishers would have us believe.

This overmastering desire to exhibit every triviality, to let not one bad joke blush unseen, spoils many a bright page and most of the volume. Pound chatters on, and his wandering loquacity dulls the edge of a really keen irony. . . . The patient reader will find and delight in such sharp performances as ' "Phasellus Ille" ', 'N.Y.', 'Arides', 'Portrait D'Une Femme', 'The Social Order', 'Salutation', and 'Commission', where cold irony gives way to hot anger. I quote the first few lines:

[quotes 'Commission', ll. 1–8, *CSP*, p. 97.]

Any lover of aesthetics will also find much to admire in the subtleties of light, shadow, movement and what is naïvely called 'atmosphere' in such brief pictures as 'Albatre', 'Fish and the Shadow', 'The Encounter', the 'Fan-Piece for Her Imperial Lord' (and excellent example of condensation from an original many times as long), 'The Coming of War' and this—

[quotes 'In a Station of the Metro', *CSP*, p. 119.]

But *Lustra* is something more than a haphazard and too inclusive collection; it is the record of a retreat, a gradual withdrawal from life. In the early days when Pound first moved his physical lar and his aesthetic penates to London, he gave promise of achieving a personal utterance to match a decided personality. In many of the early poems, such as 'Piere Vidal Old', 'Ballad of Gloom', and the exquisite 'Greek Epigram' (all originally in *Personae* and *Exultations*), the influence of Browning and Bertran de Born was unmistakable. But it was not overmastering, and it was confidently expected that a few years would bring Pound to a more striking and less scholastic habit of mind. The first part of this expectation was fulfilled, but, strangely enough, it only placed an emphasis on his inverted scholasticism. Pound, it became evident, was no pioneer, no intrepid traveller; he was always an exponent of 'movements,' a schoolman, alternating between an incurably romantic veneration of the past and an even more cloistral aversion to the crowd. Now it is classicism that he embraces, now imagism, now a furtive effort to look at the violence of life in the terms of vorticism—always the contact with the actual world is feared. More and more he shrinks back into literature. And so in *Lustra*, we find him established. He has become a connoisseur of the curious; a haunter of old bookstalls; a formalist arguing in a musty and deserted classroom. The library is his ivory tower, and he has locked himself in. Once in a while he opens a window and hears people laughing and brawling in the street. But he listens only for a moment. The window is slammed, the curtains are drawn, the perfumed candles lit—and he is back again, picking his way through literatures, amassing technicalities and dreaming of himself in his favorite rôle—the pedagogue in power, the pundit on parade. The sum total of all this is staggering, the net result infinitesimal.

Pound has gone on, collecting cultures, and all they have yielded him is an accent, an attitude. He poses before the mirror of his art and drapes himself in a coat of many colors that he has taken, patch by patch, from other and more authentic designers. He has really little to say, but he says it in a manner that gives his words a superficial significance. It is not so much the phrase as the gesture that accompanies it that is distinguished and arresting. It is this gesture that explains and identifies Pound. Some of his followers who are not so well known have surpassed him in his own *métiers*: the Aldingtons are far more Hellenic and chiseled than he; T. S. Eliot has a much lighter touch in recording the ironies and overtones of conversation; John Gould Fletcher is a more successful experimenter in the clash of colors; Maxwell Bodenheim has a more delicate and dextrous imagination and a far greater feeling for words—but Pound triumphs in the gesture. He puts up his hard, his fingers become nimble, his eyebrows go up and what, when spoken, is tawdry and trivial, becomes glamorous with a possible mystery. This is his power. The escape into literature is complete; the poetry is mostly dumb show, but he can still simulate life. He is Gordon Craig's super-marionette and his art is poetry in pantomime.

52. Babette Deutsch, 'Ezra Pound, Vorticist' *Reedy's Mirror*

21 December 1917, xxvi, 860–1

Miss Deutsch (b. 1895) is an American poet and critic. Her *This Modern Poetry* (1935) was an early American appraisal of the modern movement. In a letter to the editor she writes of first reading Pound: 'he was not only greatly gifted but . . . he was unique and naturally attracted the attention of his juniors. I no longer recall where I first read him. It may have been in the *Little Review* or, unlikely as that seems, in the *Smart Set,* or in *Poetry.* I must have seen scattered poems before reading any of his books. What I recall chiefly is the delight and the excitement that his work afforded.'

In an earlier edition of *Who's Who*, the poet might have dubbed himself romanticist. Certainly his history would entitle him to that name. He got his fellowship in Romantics in a small American college, and at twenty he was wandering through the romance countries: Italy, Spain, and Provence, studying as he fared. He seems at this period of his youth to have been bathing all his sensibilities in a kind of golden other age. What lured and held him then was not so different, however, from the things that hold and lure him now. His contempt for the mob was somewhat sharpened and strengthened as he has been forced into closer grips with it, but he can still win back, or forward, to an aloofness from the angry factory-ridden world in which he willy-nilly dwells. It should be noted, though, that Pound does not in any sense believe, or lead those who know his work to believe, that he was born too late. He is a modern of the moderns, whose credo it is that a study of comparative literatures of many epochs and races is essential to that keen critical faculty which is part of an artist's equipment. 'We do not avoid comparison with the past,' he says of the group of rebellious painters, sculptors, and writers, of which he is a very vocal member. 'We prefer that the comparison be made by some intelligent person whose idea of "the tradition" is not limited by the conventional taste of four or five centuries and one continent.'

But completely soaked as he himself was in the romantic tradition, it was natural that his first attempts at self-expression were by way of translation or paraphrase in some sort of the songs and ballads of the Romance poets. Throughout even his more recent work there are traces of his personal passion for certain heroic figures, certain dim but glamorous tales. Especially does he recur to that Piere Vidal of Provence, who 'ran mad, as a wolf, because of his love for Loba of Penautier,' and who was hunted through the forest with hounds; and to the bold En Bertrans de Born, who, being dismissed from his lady, asked of every beauty in the neighborhood her unique charm: from one her two hands and throat, from another her free-running speech, from a third her stature, from 'Audiart'

> Though she with a full heart
> Wish me ill,
> . . . .
> . . . .
> Her straight fresh body,
> She is so supple and young,
> Her robes can but do her wrong.

These *Personae*, *Exultations*, and 'Canzoniere' were reprinted under the title *Provença* at the same time that Pound published his first prose volume, a book of literary history called *The Spirit of Romance*. This latter is somewhat disappointing. While it shows the intensive study and fervid appreciation of the period which his verse reveals, the sanguine glow is lacking. As for the poems, 'Histrion' is eloquent of what he strove for in these reincarnations of dead singers:

[quotes 'Histrion', *ALS*, p. 108.]

This is clear metaphysics, if poor poetry, and probably for the latter reason, has been omitted from his recent inclusive volume. That concludes with 'three cantos of a poem of some length', so rich in allusion that Pound's informing spirit seems indeed to cease from all being. But the same central thought apparently radiates through it, however different its refractions: 'Worlds we have, how many worlds we have.'

The fond labor of translating the sonnets and ballate of Guido Cavalcanti seems to have been necessary to Pound's release from the spells which bound him to the ancient world. In *Ripostes*, published in 1912, he appears to be no longer dwelling in dead men's dreams. Instead of sinking himself in another personality, he begins to view his own moods and reactions with the objectivity which this study had made possible to him. And with his renunciation of the old themes he substitutes for the old forms the cadences of the imagist. 'The perception of the intellect is given in the word,' he declares, 'that of the emotions in the cadence. It is only, then, in perfect rhythm joined to the perfect word that the two-fold vision can be recorded.' Imagism has been succinctly defined as 'that which presents an intellectual and emotional complex in an instant of time.' Pound defines it in the vocabulary of his insurgent fellow-artists as 'a vortex from which and through which and into which ideas are constantly rushing.' An acceptance of these definitions as complementary gives in a word the intention of the vorticist group, and that expression of it which the poets nominate imagism. One of the most important poems of this period is the one which Pound calls 'The Return.' He records it as 'an objective reality,' which 'has a complicated significance.' Certain it is that whatever it may represent in the poet's consciousness, the delicate incision of its wording and the flow and pause of its rhythms are strongly suggestive:

[quotes 'The Return', *CSP*, p. 85.]

While Pound was exploring these fresh fields he was examining with the same ardor the culture and the literature of other ages and races. Now he turned his face to the east, and perhaps the most significant work he has given us is in the translations from the Chinese which were the fruit of these journeyings. His first book, based on Ernest Fenollosa's notes, was a group of poems, for the most part those of Rihaku, who 'flourished in the eighth century of our era.' Not merely his translations give evidence of Pound's sense of words, and of the beauty and pain and restlessness which they body forth, but there is the evidence of the two lines which he is too much the poet to paraphrase, because he recognizes the perfection of their idiomatic brevity:

> Drawing sword, cut water, water again flow:
> Raise cup, quench sorrow, sorrow again sorry.

For the most part these poems deal with those familiar things which never cease to stir the heart of man: battle, and love, and the fear of death, 'Wet Spring in the Garden,' and the loneliness of living. The Exile's letter is so beautiful that it is a pity to quote only a part. It speaks, at the close, of the festival his friend had made for him, of 'Red jade cups, food well set on a blue jewelled table,'

[quotes 'Exile's Letter', *CSP*, pp. 144–6, 'With the willow' to 'about sunset', 'And the girls' to 'white headed', and 'What is the' to 'thinking'.]

Since the publication of *Cathay*, Pound has given us three books which are each significant of a phase of his development and expressive of his theory of art. The first is the large jade-green volume of memoirs of his friend, Gaudier-Brzeska. In giving his profound appreciation of this young insurgent sculptor Pound states clearly and emphatically his own credo and his own rebellion. The book is invaluable as a succinct and powerful presentment of the spirit informing the modern revolution in the arts. A year later, as literary executor of the famous scholar, Ernest Fenollosa, Pound transmitted an enriched inheritance to his beneficiaries. To the Chinese poems he added translations, based on Professor Fenollosa's notes, of the 'Noh' plays of Japan, which are interesting not merely as the lyrical rendering of an ancient and esoteric art, but because these dance-dramas are used by their translator as examples of long Imagist poems. Finally comes *Lustra*, the first book of Pound's poems to appear in this country in five years, containing both those representative of his progress in that period and the finest examples of his earlier work. His envoy is characteristic:

[quotes 'Tenzone', *CSP*, p. 91.]

Pound was so early irritated by America's genial disregard of art that he fled some years ago to England, where he has lived, in isolated disgust, ever since. But though the English mob is perhaps less chafing than its trans-Atlantic cousin, he can neither abide it nor withdraw himself from it. He is like a figure of a man who leans out to the crowd holding the fingers of one hand to his nose, and lifting with the other a gleaming ambrosial cup. To his derisive hatred for mediocrity is joined a kind of marble calm.

> Come my songs, let us speak of perfection—
> We shall get ourselves rather disliked.

It is for the sake of perfection that he is so roused. He has no great care for profundities. But he rejoices in the terse evocation of a mood:

[quotes 'In a Station of the Metro', *CSP*, p. 119.]

He defines the following poem as 'a state of consciousness,' careless if it is anyone's but his own:

[quotes 'Heather', *CSP*, p. 119.]

But seldom as he may dilute his precious purple, he is clear about his intention. He wishes to express the fusion of perception and emotion for his own satisfaction. It follows that he will call forth a sympathetic response from those who have known the same thing, but they will be limited in proportion as his poem is intensely personal and refined. These are, moreover, largely the qualities of his work. He is the Zeno of the twentieth century, demanding that 'nudity should resume its classic decency.' There is a curious likeness between this artist of delicate perceptions and his elder and more raucous compatriot, Walt Whitman. His own feeling about his predecessor is given in no veiled terms in 'A Pact':

[quotes 'A Pact', *CSP*, p. 98.]

But the stupidities and cruelties which Whitman embraced with love and good-humor divert the more sensitive artist as a red scarf distracts a bull. He is taken from the pursuit of his art by his vain efforts to gore the mob that ignores it. Nothing could be further from Whitman's humanity than Pound's 'Ité':

[quotes 'Ité', *CSP*, p. 104.]

But he sounds a more compassionate note when he denounces the 'vegetable bondage of the blood'; when he declares to those 'of finer sense'

> Take thought:
> I have weathered the storm,
> I have beaten out my exile.

It is Pound's too engrossing sense of intelligence crushed by over-whelming mediocrity which wrenches him from the contemplation of beauty to vituperative attack upon vulgar modesty, perverts his worship of perfection to an esoteric artificiality, and stings him to humor that tastes of gall. This is the secret of his 'Ancora,' as of other less lovely ebullitions. It may be this oppressive perception of the unequal struggle between the scattered few, reasonable in their generation, and the enormous mass which they have never leavened, which has made Pound so excellent a translator of Fontenelle's *Dialogues Des Morts*. These little discourses between Socrates and Montaigne, Agnes Sorel and Roxelane, Bombastes Paracelsus and Molière, are rich in the bitter wit and ironic wisdom which their translator frequently utters in cadenced rhymes.

Pound may be remembered for many things, for the solitude whence he hurls his scornful mirth and furious invective; for the scholarly sympathy with which he has wrought the thoughts of other men, of times and places alien to our own; for his own fastidious and beautiful poems. He is now thirty-two years old, and, by his own count, a man of middle age. What we shall have from him hereafter will be the work of one no longer glowing with the resurgent vitality of youth. But he is yet a rebel thinker; a romantic, who looks forward with harsh joy to being slain by his 'unnamable children'; a vorticist, to paraphrase his own definition, 'from whom and through whom and into whom ideas are constantly rushing.'

53. Maxwell Bodenheim, 'A Poet's Opinion', *Little Review*

June 1917, iv, 28

Pound's editorial of acceptance on becoming foreign editor of the *Little Review* (May 1917) announced his hope that the magazine would supplement the work of the *Egoist* in publishing Rémy de Gourmont, Joyce, Wyndham Lewis, and T. S. Eliot. Bodenheim felt that some reply was called for (by 1917 Eliot's verse had only appeared in Pound's *Catholic Anthology*, and in *Poetry* and *Others*). Margaret Anderson defended Pound in the same issue, arguing that his 'autocracy of opinion' was justified because his brain 'functions aesthetically rather than emotionally', and that Pound's way of seeing things derived strength from seeing things in black and white.

Bodenheim (1893–1954), American poet and novelist, was a Greenwich Village character. He is the author of *My Life and Loves in Greenwich Village* (1954).

Ezra Pound writes in his editorial which headed your last number that 'the two novels by Joyce and Lewis, and Mr. Eliot's poems, are not only the most important contributions to English literature of the past three years, but are practically the only works of the time in which the creative element is present, which in any way show invention, or a progress beyond precedent work'.

It is easy to make statements of this kind, but, having made them, a critic should tell us on what he bases his dictum. The trouble with criticism of art today is that it isn't criticism. The critic writes statements of untempered liking or disliking, and does not trouble to support them with detailed reasons. We are simply supposed to take the critic's word for the matter. I haven't sufficient belief in the infallibility of Ezra Pound's mind to require no substantiation of his statements. I have several faults to find with his methods of criticising poetry. He's a bit too easily swayed by his personal emotions, in that regard. I happen to know that in an article of his which appeared in *Poetry* some time ago he omitted the name of a very good modern American poet from the 'American-team' he was mentioning, merely because he has a personal dislike for that poet.

He has, also, too great a longing to separate poets into arbitrary teams of best and worst. Poets are either black or white to him—never grey.

In speaking of Harriet Monroe he says that she has conducted her magazine in a spirited manner, considering the fact that she is faced with the practical problem of circulating a magazine in a certain peculiar milieu. But he does not add that those are not the colours in which Miss Monroe herself comes forth. If she admitted that she was a practical woman, trying to print as much good poetry as she can, and still gain readers, there would only be the question of whether one believed that compromise is always the only method of assuring the existence of a magazine. But she refuses to admit that she is a serious compromiser. She stands upon a pedestal of utter idealism. Mr. Pound did not mention this aspect.

His claim that Eliot is the only really creative poet brought forth during recent times is absurd, H. D., Fletcher, Marianne Moore, Williams, Michelson at his best, Carl Sandburg, and Wallace Stevens are certainly not inevitably below Eliot in quality of work. Eliot's work is utterly original, attains moments of delicate satire, and digs into the tangled inner dishonesties of men. But many of the poets I have mentioned are as good in their own way as Eliot is in his, in addition to their being just as original as he. I have not Mr. Pound's fondness for making lists, so I'm afraid I may have omitted the names of some American poets entitled to mention, even from my own limited view point. But I will say that at least the number of poets I have mentioned are fully the equals of Mr. Pound's nominee for supreme honors—T. S. Eliot.

54. J. B. Yeats to John Quinn

19 November 1917

From B. L. Reid, *The Man From New York: John Quinn and his Friends* (New York: Oxford University Press, 1968), p. 314.

He is a powerful stringent. . . . It is his deliberate intention to inflict pain. And one does not mind, for it is salutary. . . . It is wonderful how people hate him. But hatred is the harvest he wants to gather— great sheaves of it, beneath a sky of disastrous moonlight. . . . He is a hair shirt to be worn next the skin.

55. Joseph Conrad to John Quinn

6 February 1918

From B. L. Reid, *The Man From New York: John Quinn and his Friends*, p. 340.

Conrad (1857–1924), English novelist, received a copy of *Lustra* as a present from Quinn.

E. P. is certainly a poet but I am afraid I am too old and too wooden-headed to appreciate him as he deserves. The critics here consider him harmless; but as he has, I believe, a very good opinion of himself I don't suppose he worries his head about the critics very much. Besides, he has many women at his feet; which must be immensely comforting.

56. A. R. Orage on *Ezra Pound: His Metric and Poetry*

July 1918

'R.H.C.' [A. R. Orage], 'Readers and Writers', *New Age* (25 July 1918), xxiii, p. 201.

Ezra Pound: His Metric and Poetry was a brochure, written anonymously by T. S. Eliot, distributed with copies of the American edition of *Lustra*. See Introduction pp. 12–13.

Under the title of *Ezra Pound: His Metric and Poetry*, a whole book—really, however, only an essay—has been devoted to the work of our well-known contributor and sometime pièce de resistance. For this honour, if honour it be, I think that Mr. Pound is indebted more to what he has preached than to what he has practised; for on his actual achievement, considerable though it is, I doubt whether even in America anybody could have been found to write a book about his work. Mr. Pound, however, will not deny that he is an American in this respect, if in none other, that he always likes to hitch his waggon to a star. He has always a ton of precept for a pound of example. And in America, more than in any other country save, perhaps, Germany, it appears to be required of a man that there shall be 'significance', intention, aim, theory—anything you like expressive of direction—in everything he does. As I have before pointed out, there does not appear to me to be anything *very* original in the creation of poetic images, or even in the employment of irregular metric; neither of them can be said to constitute a new departure in poetic technique. Yet, as we have seen, Mr. Pound has elevated each of them to be the star of a cult, with the consequence that we now have professed 'schools' of poetry calling themselves Imagist or Verslibrist respectively. These are examples of what I mean in saying that Mr. Pound loves to hitch his waggon to a star.

It must be admitted, however, that this habit of Mr. Pound has its good as well as its somewhat absurd side; there is only a step, you know, from the ridiculous to the sublime. It must also be affirmed, however it may reflect upon our English critics, that it is precisely the good side of Mr. Pound's technique which they usually condemn. For the good side consists in this, that all the poets who can claim to belong to the school of Mr. Pound must display in addition to the above-mentioned defects, the certain and positive merits of study of their art, and deliberate craftsmanship. No poet, I think, dare claim to be a pupil of Mr. Pound who cannot prove that he has been to school to poetry and submitted himself to a craft-apprenticeship; and no poet will long command Mr. Pound's approval who is not always learning and experimenting. Now this, which I call the good side in Mr. Pound's doctrine, is disliked in England, where it has for years been the habit of critics to pretend that poetry grows on bushes or in parsley-beds. That poetry should be the practice of 'a learned, self-conscious craft' to be carried on by a 'guild of adepts' appears to Mr. Archer, for example, to be a heresy of the first order. How much of the best poetry, he exclaims, has been written with 'little technical study behind it'; and how little necessary, therefore, any previous learning is. To the dogs with Mr. Pound's doctrine! Let the motto over the gates of the Temple of Poetry be: 'No previous experience required.' It will be seen, of course, how the confusion in Mr. Archer's mind has arisen. Because it is a fact that the 'best' poetry *looks* effortless, he has fallen into the spectator's error of concluding that it *is* effortless. And because, again, a considerable part of the work of the 'learned, self-conscious craftsmen' is pedantic and artificial, he has been confirmed in his error. The truth of the matter, however, is with Mr. Pound. Dangerous as it may be to require that a poet shall be learned in his profession, it is much more dangerous to deprecate his learning. By a happy fluke, it may be, a perfect poem may occasionally be written 'without previous study'; from too much previous study there may also occasionally result only verse smelling of the lamp; but in the long run and for the cultivation of poetry as an art there is no doubt that the most fruitful way is the way of the craftsman and the adept.

57. Louis Untermeyer, 'Ezra Pound— Proseur', *New Republic*

17 August 1918, xvi, 83–4

Mencken, writing to Untermeyer on 20 May 1918, approved: 'Your piece on Pound is capital. I have a feeling that you are right about him. . . .' On August 30 he mentioned this review again: 'I feel you are right about Pound. He has gone the Dreiser route. Puritan pressure has him into a mere bellower. There is a lesson in this for all of us' (*Letters of H. L. Mencken*, edited by Guy J. Forgue (New York: Alfred A. Knopf, 1961), pp. 123, 127). For Mencken's fears about Dreiser, see his essay 'The Dreiser Bugaboo' in the *Seven Arts* (August 1917).

It seems an incredible thing that the poet who wrote *Provença* sometime about 1911 is also the studio oracle that in 1918 has put his excursions and false alarums into such permanent type. But here is the unbelievable; a carefully enshrined series of trivialities, translations, annotated excerpts, beauty submerged in banalities, criticism smothered in a mixture of snobbery and bad temper. Yet it is something more than a jumble of mannered prose and ostentatious finalities. It is the record of a creative talent grown sterile, of a disorderly retreat into the mazes of technique and pedantry. No living American poet started with a more vigorous determination than Ezra Pound. He began by blazing his own path through a trampled poetic forest. Then he started wandering whenever he saw a by-road, followed every curious twist and turn, pursued the will-o'-the-wisps of the bizarre, until finally he has lost himself in the backwoods and marshes of literature. Equipped with a restless athleticism and a freshness of personality, he did something to words that, even though it speedily degenerated into an idiom as tight as the clichés from which it reacted, was an impetus and influence to a small regiment of writers. He was one of the most pitiless antagonists of the mawkish and treacle-dripping verse that was being manufactured and retailed under the gaudy label of poetry; it was under his leadership that the Imagists became not only a group, but a fighting protest.

It is scarcely fair to argue, as has been attempted, that England changed the eager, experimental boy into a cynical litterateur. One may become as completely immersed in the pedantry of culture in the Philadelphia which Pound left as in the Bohemia of London which he now inhabits. There was undoubtedly something of the scholiast and a little of the antiquarian in his nonage; even his first book, for all its intensity, throbs with a passion that is, at bottom, a literary passion.

Provença, in spite of its echoes of Browning and Bertran de Born, was a highly personal and distinctive collection. In it Pound achieved a half defiant, half disdainful independence. It made the publication of *Lustra*, his most recent volume of poems, doubly disappointing. *Lustra* was not so much a collection of poems as a catch-all for Pound's slightest gibes and gesticulations. And *Pavannes and Divisions* seems to serve the same purpose for Pound's prose dicta. Here are the scrapped experiments, introductions to a catalogue of vortographs, malformed models, filings and tailings from the craftsman's workshop, a list of exceptions filed with the editor of *Reedy's Mirror* in 1916, an extract from a letter to the *Dial* circa 1913—all the old, petty irritations and amiable heresies are carefully collected, tagged and set down for the edification of the cognoscenti, the delicately attuned, the nuance worshippers. Possibly the final criticism of the book is that of its publisher, Mr. Knopf, who in an advertisement couples it with Wyndham Lewis's *Tarr* and labels them both 'For the Intelligentsia.'

It remains to be seen how much the intransigents and aestheticians will appreciate this collection of out of date manifestoes and poorly disguised platitudes. The intelligentsia will doubtless be startled to learn that 'Poetry is a composition of words set to music,' that 'Our only measure of truth is our own perception of truth,' that it is not advisable when writing a symmetrical poem to 'put in what you want to say and then fill up the remaining vacuums with slush.' The intelligentsia will be still more uplifted by finding in this volume 'L'Homme Moyen Sensuel,' a long piece of doggerel, in which Pound says, in pointless and mostly false rhyme, what H. L. Mencken has been saying in pointed prose for the last dozen years.

But Pound compensates for such bland repetitions and truisms. Frequently he gives us criticism which is as penetrating and graceful, as 'Shelley's "Sensitive Plant" is one of the rottennest poems ever written,' or 'Milton is the most unpleasant of English poets. . . . His popularity has been largely due to his bigotry.' Browning usually commands his admiration, but 'Crabbe will perhaps keep better than Browning.' Wordsworth is recognized as 'a silly old sheep with a genius for Imagism—and this talent, or the fruits of this talent, he buried in a desert of bleatings.' ('Don't,' says Pound in A Few Don'ts to Poets, 'use such an expression as "dim lands of peace." ' Such a mixture is sloppy and unnatural; it 'dulls the image.') Education is characterized as 'an onanism of the soul.' And the speech of the Sanatogen school reinforces his style when Pound, in an energetic effort to define beauty, says: 'You feel bucked up when you come on a swift moving thought in Plato or a fine line in a statue.' In fact, these scattered essays with their enthusiasm for Arnold Dolmetsch, for certain neglected Elizabethans and for the twelfth century troubadours (by far the most careful, as it is the least self-conscious of the chapters) reveal Pound less as a pioneer than as a press agent. But his is a publicity strictly for the intelligentsia. Pound never lets one forget his scorn of America and his antagonism to the crowd. His unconcealed dislike of Demos, half contempt, half fear, together with his patrician attitudes, make him seem something of an anachronism, a hyperaesthetic pedant, a disgruntled aristogogue.

This dissatisfaction with his age and his inability to command its attention accounts for most of Pound's splenetic outbursts. The nimble arrogance of Whistler has been a bad example for him. For where Whistler carried off his impertinences with a light and dazzling dexterity, Pound, a far heavier-handed controversialist, begins by being truculent and ends by being tiresome. He is best in his least original moments, when he is estimating the richness of Rémy de Gourmont, interpreting the exuberant artifice of the Provençal poets or translating the twelve dialogues of Fontenelle that are so strange a contrast, in spite of their classical similarity, to Landor's *Imaginary Conversations*. These essays do much to offset the vacuity of 'Stark Realism' or the sexual preoccupations in 'Jodindranath Mawhwor's Occupation,' which masks as a general irony but is actually a satire on itself.

And so the reckless poet of 1910 develops into the sophisticated proseur; he declines into querulous dogmatizing; he becomes the scholiast gone to seed. Even more than in *Lustra*, one senses the decadence which appraises the values in life chiefly as aesthetic values and which expresses its superiority in petulance instead of assurance, in a flash of erudition rather than the light of wisdom. It is a queer, out of tune collection; queerer than ever this year, 1918.

58. Conrad Aiken, 'A Pointless Pointillist', *Dial*

October 1918, lxv, 306–7

Aiken (b. 1889), a contemporary of Eliot's at Harvard, is an American poet, novelist and critic. His criticism collected in *A Reviewer's ABC*, edited by Rufus Blanshard (1961), contains reviews of *Personae* (1926) and *Active Anthology*.

If one might conceive, in the heliotrope future, any Ph. Demon so inspired as to set about compiling a list of dull books by interesting authors, one could hardly doubt that Ezra Pound's *Pavannes and Divisions* would be his first entry. An incredible performance! Somehow, one has had all these years (for alas, Mr. Pound's indiscretions can no longer be called the indiscretions of youth) the impression that this King-Maker among poets was quite the most mercurial of our performers. One associated with his name the deftest of jugglery, sleights of mind without number, lightning-like tergiversatility, and a genius for finding the latest procession and leading it attired in the most dazzling of colors. Of course, Mr. Pound has himself been at some pains to encourage us in this view. As a publicist he has few equals. But surely it has not been entirely a deception! . . . And nevertheless he comes now upon us with *Pavannes and Divisions*—'a collection,' says Mr. Knopf, 'of the best prose written by Mr. Pound during the last six years'—and therewith threatens, if we are not careful, to destroy our illusions about him forever.

For, regrettable as is the confession, the outstanding feature of this book of prose is its dullness. One reads more and more slowly, encountering always heavier obstacles, and—short of a major effort of the will (and a kind of amazed curiosity)—one finally stops. Intrinsically therefore one may say at once that the book is without value. If one is to examine it carefully, one does so for quite another reason; namely, because Mr. Pound is himself an interesting figure—observe his portrait in this volume, so elaborately and theatrically posed—a curious representative of homo sapiens, and without any doubt a poet who has (sometimes severely) influenced his fellow poets. *Pavannes and Divisions* shall be to us therefore what the soliloquies of the patient are to the psychoanalyst.

If we pass over the unoriginal parts of this book—the clever translation of Laforgue, and the well-selected dialogues of Fontenelle, amusing but nugatory—and if we listen with concentrated attention to the Mr. Pound who chatters to us, alternately, in the lumberingly metrical and crudely satirical doggerel of 'L'Homme Moyen Sensuel,' or the disjointed and aimless prose of the essays and fables, what emerges from this babble? A portrait, sharpfeatured as Mr. Pound's frontispiece, but how infinitely more complex—a portrait which surely not even a Vorticist could compass. One is reminded, indeed, of Mr. Sludge, so inextricably the most sterling platitudes and the most brazen quackeries (no doubt believed in) are here commingled. Add to this that Mr. Pound, like a jack-in-the-box, takes a naive delight in booing at the stately; that he has the acquisitive instincts of the jackdaw (with a passion for bright and shining objects, particularly those spied from a very great distance); that he is unhappy unless he can be rebelling at something or somebody (even at himself of the day before yesterday—and this is healthy); and finally that as a poet he has genius, and has given us more than a handful of beautiful lyrics—and one begins to perceive that Mr. Pound's middle name should have been not Loomis but Proteus. Those to whom Mr. Pound is a thorn in the flesh will say that it is amazing that the poet of *Cathay* should, in *Pavannes and Divisions*, reveal himself so hopelessly as of third-rate mentality: those who are charitable will say that if a poet is to live he must also be a journalist. There is no chance for an argument, since one cannot possibly tell how seriously *Pavannes and Divisions* is intended. But if one cannot read Mr. Pound's intentions, his accomplishment is obvious and disillusioning. If a poet must be a journalist, let him be a good one! And this Mr. Pound is not.

For in point of style, or manner, or whatever, it is difficult to imagine anything much worse than the prose of Mr. Pound. It is ugliness and awkwardness incarnate. Did he always write so badly? One recollects better moments in his history and one even now finds him, as in the first paragraph of his paper on Dolmetsch, making a music of prose. For the secret of this decay one must turn, as in all such cases, to the nature of the man's mind, since style is not a mere application or varnish but the unconscious expression of a nature. And here is encountered one of Mr. Pound's chief characteristics, one that has from the very beginning been steadily growing upon him and—it might be added—steadily strangling his creative instinct. This characteristic is his passion for the *decisive*. His strokes are all of an equal weight and finality. On the sensory plane this first manifested itself, no doubt, as a desire for the single and brilliant image. In logic or dialectics it became a passion for the point, glittering and deadly. In the field of aesthetics it has revealed itself as a need for espousing the out-of-the-way and remote and exceptional, so as to add a sort of impact and emphasis to personality by a solitariness of opinion: it is more striking to play a tune on the Chinese p'i-pa than on the banjo .On these several planes this instinctive appetite has become more and more voracious, more and more exclusive, until finally it has reached a point where it threatens to leave Mr. Pound little else. His poetry has become imageless through excess of image—image too deliberately sought. His prose has become pointless and merely fatiguing because of his effort to point every sentence: it has become a sort of chevaux de frise, impossible to walk through. These are failures which, one would think, the artist in Mr. Pound would have foreseen. In prose it is a failure made all the more complete by the fact that the pointillist style was the last style for which he was intellectually fitted. Without the patience for careful analysis, or the acumen and precision and breadth for scientific investigation, this method makes of him merely a subjectivist pedant, a tinkling sciolist, and—what is more amazing for the man who wrote *Cathay*—an apostle of the jejune and sterile. For so intent has Mr. Pound become on this making of points and cutting of images that he has gradually crystallized from them a cold and hard doctrine, a doctrine of negative virtues, aimed primarily against esthetic excess but in the upshot totally inimical to that spontaneity and opulence without which art is stillborn. In short, Mr. Pound has become, as regards style, a purist of the most deadly sort. So absorbed has he become in the minutiae of esthetics, so fetichistic in his adoration of literary nugae, that he has gradually come to think of style and filigree as if the terms were synonymous. This is the more lamentable because his esthetics, as revealed in his prose, are by no means subtle. One cannot rear a palace of filigree: nor can one compose a Hamlet or a Tyl Eulenspiegel entirely of velleities and evanescent nuances. Young authors, let us grant with Mr. Pound, must learn to be artisans before they can complete themselves as artists. But at the point where purism stifles exuberance and richness (the intense confession of the subconscious) and at the point where, as an esthetic measure, it prefers the neatly-made to the well-felt or the profoundly-thought, it becomes obviously vicious.

It is the critic's license to overrefine his point for the sake of emphasis, and this perhaps, in the present case, we have clearly done. To restore the balance somewhat we should add that, though by no means profound, Mr. Pound is provocative and suggestive in his essays on the troubadours and the Elizabethan translators, and refreshing in his papers on Dolmetsch and Rémy de Gourmont. After all, is he perhaps, in his prose, deliberately a journalist? . . . And we remember with gratitude that he is a poet.

59. Emanuel Carnevali, 'Irritation', *Poetry*

January 1920, xvi, 211–21

Carnevali (b. 1897) was an Italian poet and critic who was briefly on the staff of *Poetry*. He contracted encephalitis and was hospitalized in his native Italy from the twenties until the 1939 war. During this time Pound was in correspondence with him and generously tried to get him financial support (*Letters*, p. 299). Robert McAlmon's Contact Editions published Carnevali's *A Hurried Man* (1925). He has written that 'Carnevali's critical articles . . . in those days were about the best, so far as intellectual content and "sensibility" (however hysterical) were concerned' (*Being Geniuses Together 1920–1930*, revised and with supplementary chapters by Kay Boyle (New York: Doubleday & Co., 1968), p. 151). Kay Boyle has compiled and edited *The Autobiography of Emanuel Carnevali* (New York: Horizon Press, 1967).

There is a word which one associates with Dostoievsky's works—Sorrow; as we think of Walt Whitman the word may be Joy; for Mr. Pound the word is Irritation. Irritation inspires him and he inspires irritation in his readers.

Here are twelve dialogues of Fontenelle, translated. One may say of them that they are just such things as only a man like Mr. Pound could have scooped out of the welter of minor French literature; since if there is a literature in the world to which Mr. Pound is extraneous and foreign, in feelings and ways, it is the French. These dialogues conform surprisingly, and sympathize remarkably, with Mr. Pound—these quarrelsome persons in these dialogues, these not remarkable persons of these not extraordinary dialogues.

Here is a poem called 'L'Homme Moyen Sensuel', parading in a Browning exo-skeleton, with much less than Browning under the skeleton. Here is also a translation from Laforgue by which Mr. Pound has achieved a thing worthy of observation: he has been true to the letter, almost, of the original and at the same time has betrayed and desecrated it. Laforgue's satires are veiled by a delicate and almost haughty modesty, and they have a sorrowfully humble way, which become boisterousness in the translation, reminding one of what Billy Sunday did to Christ.[1]

The book, taken as a whole, is Mr. Pound's profession of faith in art. A faith in art which consists of a few *don'ts* shouted at some imaginary and improbable followers; of repetitions of phrases by old and ancient masters, duly stripped of their original glamour, as all repetitions are. (One finds here a formula almost directly translated from a famous passage of Rimbaud's *Les Illuminations*: 'It is the presentation of such a "complex" instantaneously which gives that sense of sudden liberation'.) A faith in art that becomes militant in a fierce little contempt against America—look! he's throwing pebbles at our skyscrapers, O People!—and a provincial and bourgeois quarrel against the provincial and bourgeois in art. A faith in art that has no love, no ecstasy, not even drunkenness.

It sums itself up mechanically into this: Mr. Pound lets it be known that he is against stupidity, bad art and bad artists. Ask any bad artist: he will tell you that it is *he* who is against bad artists and bad art! Now, the only way to judge whether it is the case of a bad artist disagreeing with himself and objecting to art, or the contrary, is from the style of the objector, from his way of moving about. (As for his tastes in art—in our century one can no longer judge a man from them—faking about them is the most popular of the arts.) What then are the *stride* and the physiognomy of Mr. Pound? Well, he may have written some exceeding good poems, I will not say whether I doubt it or not. But this book is a sequence of false steps made by its author in his effort to gain a recognition that he misses and longs for. And a sulking, aggressive, self-conscious man scowls at you from behind every sentence. Here are some

1 Billy Sunday (1862–1935), fundamentalist American preacher.

of the false steps: He tells us that he takes 'no pleasure in writing this. . . .' He drops, altogether too magnificently, such a portentous formidable new phrase as, 'Art is a science . . . like chemistry,' and as no elucidation or comment follows, but some flat and hollow English instead, one has a feeling of suspicion, as though one had caught a glimpse of a bum with a gold watch-chain strung across his ragged vest. He reiterates that 'obviously this is so, obviously that is so. . . .'; resorts to such stimulants of laughter as three exclamation marks (!!!). Boosting James Joyce, he cannot find a more enthusiastic or enlightening phrase than, 'He gives us Dublin as it *presumably* is'; or, 'He gives the thing as it is.' Giving *the thing* as it is he calls realism, and his criticism proceeds with a quibbling on such words as imagism, impressionism, realism, symbolism; words which, if they ever mean anything, mean one thing only; otherwise, they mean what you understand by them, and if you do not tell us precisely what, they mean nothing.

I might praise the book, and say that there is in it a sort of dignified love for art and art concepts. But how can I?—this love is so cold and so awkward that it inspires no sympathy. It is probably an affair between Mr. Pound and some Grecian wraiths, and we are unable to say just how immoral or lively it is. And is it love? No sincere love-making, no liberating gesture can be awkward; whereas, as Mr. Aiken says, 'awkwardness incarnate' is in this book. Perhaps Mr. Pound's liberation occurred some time ago, in his poems. If it be so, then this is a postmortem restlessness, it is a case of 'pain animating the dust of dead desire.' Yes, that is indeed why we do not stand in awe at the sight of the considerable fight Mr. Pound has put up, that is why we call it a quarrel; a quarrel that is so much and so exclusively nobody's quarrel that there's no chance to sympathize. His problems are unrealities that he has created out of his weariness and spleen, to throw sand in the eyes of the ghost of insignificance and pettiness that haunts him. His anger against the big plagues of the world is so petty, that, I think, he makes petty difficulties out of big ones in order to give himself the sport to fight them. If he saw how enormous the difficulties are that he is making grimaces at, he would become human and there would be a little more sentiment in him—but I suppose he would feel ashamed of it!

It's an ugly love. Rather the crudity and the bombast of an earnest beginner, rather all the pathetic attitudes of self-glorification and self-abnegation with which incomplete artists daily pester the world, than this sophisticated love towards Her; for She is a tough-handed and strong-smelling Woman. Rather the uncouth *gaffes* of an adolescent than this philandering with fawns and nymphs and mouldy reminiscences of Pan—a nasty way of snubbing this great Woman who slings, in passing, streetfuls of dust of today's cities; whose favorite perfume is that of the loam—the loam that soils the hands of dudes and snobs. Rather morbid and talkative love than this ungainly *nouveau-riche* abstinence from raptures for fear of clumsiness; rather coarseness that is tender-hearted, and foolishly weeps and foolishly laughs, than this delicacy and aloofness achieved, or rather striven for, without drama.

Yes, Mr. Pound talks of the experts, of such men as may die of a harsh sound inadvertently caught by their ears. We know them, *ces délicats*. It's Oscar Wilde who wrings new postures and new words out of poor Salome (she was an adolescent and she had a human tendency to be obvious); who writes of men flinging themselves languorously on sofas—and refuses to sit down in Whitman's room for fear of soiling his clothes. It is Rémy de Gourmont, with his perfectly charming receptiveness, who cowers at the sight of such a forsaken, accursed and violent genius as Rimbaud, and gossips about the tragedy of the splendid Youth. It's Gustave Kahn, who quibbles as to whether Laforgue is a symbolist or not, while Laforgue's aloofness and sorrow and death are one of those mistakes or crimes of the world for which the world never gives an account or an apology. It's Ezra Pound who, on the death of Verhaeren, makes haste to tell us that Verhaeren wasn't as good as. . . . I forget the name. What these *délicats* miss, what these choosers, these select selecters and élite-makers and aristocrats miss, is what I call roots. They miss what they intensely long for—a place in the world and the sense of their importance in it. What they hate most is clumsiness, lack of taste, they tell us: to anyone who knows the weight and the majestic stride of this our Earth, to anyone who knows how deep and weirdly gnarled men's roots are, common men's roots, how tormentedly tangled and twisted they are, this lightness and this amenity and this aristocratic giggling are grotesque and funny and sorrowfully clumsy. There was exquisiteness in an Italian mother I saw in Taylor Street biting in a sweet frenzy the mouth of her sloppy child; and she was fat and greasy, too. It is the strong-nosed and big-hearted love which is most delicate. Delicacy is a luxury of the strong-nosed, it is not the privilege of a carefully self-preserving scantiness of heart. *Ces délicats* and 'immaculate perceivers' can never reach that perfect isolation toward which they started when it became impossible for them to be *in* the world; yes, it was their inability to be a struggling part of the world that dropped them out of it. Evidently—the concept of isolation is a theoretical fallacy—isolation that exhibits itself, indifference that meddles with everything and nags and objects!

Ezra Pound's exclusion of his own personal emotion from this book affects to be a feat of dignity, austere lack of sentimentality. It is self-contradictory, and inasmuch as Mr. Pound cannot refrain from shouting and showing signs of emotion, he is most absurdly sentimental. This book is the throttled cry of non-confessed inhibitions. The sentimentality of so many propagandists and radicals who start out, of a day, to settle the troubles of the world—troubles for which they assert they are fundamentally not responsible—this sentimentality is Ezra Pound's. It is the most depraving sort of sentimentality. The idea of self-surpassing, of the Superman, in Nietzsche; and that most frequent and most permanent of colors in art, Sadness—these are furthest from sentimentality, and the best example to set before such noisy self-contradictions as Ezra Pound and the whole bevy of modern purists, professors, learned men and experts!

Mr. Pound is a gentleman who, possessing a good deal of human discrimination, saw what were the things that a great man is concerned about. Thereupon he laboriously set himself to be concerned in such things. Indeed, his art theories have all the requisites: there is the proclamation of art as morals—there is the damning of our present-day ugliness and the longing for the times of Chivalry and the beauty that was Greece; there is an act of faith called *Religio*. It is extraordinary and very deplorable that the same man who speaks of Christ as 'the unpleasing Semite who began to use myths for social propaganda,' who compares disparagingly Blake with Whistler, does not in the least realize that these same men have benignantly given him that which he surreptitiously tried to steal from them, and, without acknowledgment, stalks about calling his own. He does not realize that his art theories are ages old; that the only newness that can be brought into such topics may only be the weight of a personally suffered tragedy, or a golden gift of song, torn out of a man's own heart, his heart of today, of today's sorrow and today's laughter. In other words that only a very *personal emotion* validates and differentiates a man's art theories. Then, when one brings such a gift or casts the shadow of such a tragedy, it matters little that similar things have been said by someone else before; then indeed one may rejoice that they have been said by someone else; then one no longer strives for originality, but for a communion with the great, for the frenzy of the extreme loneliness of being together with the great. And such loneliness is perhaps what is meant by originality. Dignity, aloofness, cool judgment—the dickens! Only eyes of fire may look at the sun. I am thinking that such things as he eventually utters coldly and precisely are the same that were screamed without precision, and with blind illogical heat, by Blake, by Shelley, by Nietzsche, by Rimbaud, and even by the kind and moderate Sir Philip Sidney, who speaks of 'scientists who draw a straight line with a crooked heart.' And I say that it is no longer, in such cases, a matter of words or language, but a flame and an uproar which must unfortunately take the form of questionable and confutable words. Ezra Pound is the soot and the ashes of the fire of what he calls derisively 'the prophetic Blake.'

And as for free verse. Upholding, or apologizing for, free verse is ridiculous and obsolete. There is a song or a scream coming to free verse today, since an image of a *Great Hunt* became song, song of today, song in the ears and song in the throat of a man whom one may see, living and looking sad, if one goes to the office of the Chicago *Daily News* and asks for the 'journalist' Carl Sandburg. The bookish discernment of men who left America 'to seek for intelligent conversation' ought to limit itself to things less alive than free verse is today!

I would praise the book and be pleased at Mr. Pound's sincere love for James Joyce, Hueffer, T. S. Eliot and Laforgue; exult in the fact that he is one of the very few men who spoke at all of Laforgue to the English-speaking-and-not-reading public. But how can I?—I like these men well enough myself; and his enthusiasm is so slack that it disconcerts mine, if anything. And as for Laforgue, I love him so that I am ashamed, for Laforgue, of Pound's indecent flirting. As for the elucidations, which might pass instead of enthusiasm—some of them I have quoted, and here is another: 'If the nineteenth century had built itself *on* Crabbe? Ah, if! But no; they wanted confections.' Naughty child, that little nineteenth century!

This book is the Statute of the American–English élite. The élite is always a self-founded group of self-appointed noblemen. In the fact of this self-appointment there is a bitter realization that no one but the candidates was there to do the appointing. No one ever recognizes the élite; and the élite must therefore come down and make a most undignified show of itself among people whom the élite is supposed to despise and whose opinion it is not to consider. There and therewith the élite commits suicide.

The book has no sadness, no drunkenness, no love, no despair, no whimsicality. No human quality here, nothing but opinions and—an attitude. Attitudes and opinions are such things as may be bought, sold and exchanged, like clothes; they are never contributors to the welfare of the world, since everybody possesses one or more and the world is not helped thereby. Men are forces *within* the world, and when they become conscious one hears an exaltation or a complaint; and these are signs of life. This world is one and ours. These men opinionating assume that they stand out of the world. . . . Well, they do; and each of them ought to look around him and ascertain the space of air he is filling, and make sure what sort of a ghost or reminiscence he is. But, of course, they are not really outside the world—they are an unease of the world, of a kind which is too tenuous to demand a radical cure, and which keeps feeding from itself—its life a vicious circle.

Ezra Pound has estranged himself. It is a task for a broad-shouldered Balzac to state the causes of such a fact; but we who have read his book have suffered from the effects of it, and this is our complaint. And this is our resolution; he cannot talk to us. By us, I mean readers, artists and shoemakers. We—and I stand together with all the fools he so hopelessly curses—acknowledge that there are many things the matter with us; but we realize that he is not really interested and we consider his talk an intrusion: he irritates us.

60. W. G. Hale on Pound's failings as a Latinist

April 1919

W. G. Hale, 'Pegasus Impounded', *Poetry* (April 1919), xiv, 52–5.

In March 1919 'Poems from the Propertius Series' appeared in *Poetry*, printing sections I, II, III, and VI of the 'Homage'. Pound was glad to get the ten guineas which was all Harriet Monroe could pay, but was annoyed that only a 'mutilated piece' (*Letters*, p. 210) of the whole was to be published in America. Hale's attack seemed unfair to him, and he defended the poem in a letter to Orage (*Letters*, pp. 211–13), who was about to publish it in the *New Age*. Pound denied that there had ever been 'any question of translation, let alone literal translation. My job was to bring a dead man to life, to present a living figure.' With the publication of *Quia Pauper Amavi* in October Pound was once again faced with the problem of defending the 'Homage' (Nos 63, 66).

Hale (1848–1928), Professor of Latin at the University of Chicago, was a distinguished scholar, author and editor of many texts, readers and philological and grammatical studies, including *Aims and Methods in Classical Study* (1888).

Dear Madam Editor: A Latinist must naturally be interested when a modern poet translates a Latin poet. Hence my concern in Mr. Pound's experiment with Propertius in *Poetry* for March. I offer certain impressions.

Mr. Pound is often undignified or flippant, which Propertius never is. For example, 'I shall have my dog's day,' 'I shall have, doubtless, a boom after my funeral,' 'There will be a crowd of young women doing homage to my palaver,' 'There is no hurry about it.' Such renderings pervert the flavor of a consciously artistic, almost academic, original. And what, if Mr. Pound is aiming at the colloquial, is the justification of his stilted 'Her hands have no kindness me-ward'?

Mr. Pound often drags, because he pads. Thus the second line is pure addition, and pure delay, in

> Though my house is not propped up by Taenarian columns
> From Laconia (associated with Neptune and Cerberus).

These three Baedekeresque explanations seem to have been gathered, with a modicum of labor, from Harper's *Latin Lexicon*, under the word *Taenarus*.

Mr. Pound is incredibly ignorant of Latin. He has of course a perfect right to be, but not if he translates from it. The result of his ignorance is that much of what he makes his author say is unintelligible. I select a few out of about three-score errors.

In *II* of the translations, Propertius makes Calliope bid him to refrain from writing epic poetry, and to sing only of love. Mr. Pound mistakes the verb *canes*, 'thou shalt sing,' for the noun *canes* (in the nominative plural masculine) and translates by 'dogs'. Looking around then for something to tack this to, he fixes upon *nocturnae* (genitive singular feminine) and gives us 'night dogs'! I allow myself an exclamation point. For sheer magnificence of blundering this is unsurpassable. But other blunders are not without interest.

Where Propertius speaks of the 'purple beaks' (*punica rostra*) of the doves of Venus, Mr. Pound renders by the nonsensical phrase 'their Punic faces'—as if one were to translate 'crockery' by 'China.' He confuses the two Latin words *fugantes* and *fugientes*, and so represents the tutelary gods of Rome as fleeing from Hannibal instead of putting him to flight. Where Propertius says 'I dreamed I lay . . . on Helicon,' he makes him say 'I had been seen . . . recumbent on . . . Helicon.' Where Propertius says, 'The Muses are my companions, and my songs are dear to the reader,' Mr. Pound translates, 'Yet the companions of the Muses will keep their collective nose in my books.' Where Propertius says, 'The trophies of kings, borne in the bark of Aemilius' (the Roman conqueror), Mr. Pound makes him say 'Royal Aemilia, drawn on the memorial raft.' 'Raft' is the school-boy stock-translation of *ratis* (a general word corresponding to our 'craft'). As for 'royal Aemilia,' had there ever been such a lady, Propertius could not have meant her, since the two Latin words are in different cases. These little differences have significance in an inflected language.

Twice Mr. Pound blunders over the word *rigat*, 'moistens' or 'sprinkles', evidently connecting it with English 'rigid,' instead of with English 'irrigation.' Thus where Propertius says, 'Calliope moistened my lips with water from the spirit of Philetas' (a poet who influenced him), Mr. Pound gives us the monstrous rendering, 'Stiffened our face with the backwash of Philetas.' In another passage Propertius says, 'I have no artificial grottoes watered from the Marcian flow' (*Marcius liquor*). The Marcian aqueduct was Rome's best water supply, recently renovated by Agrippa. Mr. Pound seems to have taken *liquor* as spirituous. He must then have thought of age as appropriate, and so have interpreted *Marcius* as referring to the legendary King Ancus Marcius; after which it was easy to add another legendary King, Numa Pompilius. The result is three lines, all wrong, and the last two pure padding:

> Nor are my caverns stuffed stiff with a Marcian vintage
> (my cellar does not date from Numa Pompilius,
> Nor bristle with wine jars).

Of one peculiarly unpleasant passage in Mr. Pound's translation, there is no suggestion in the original. Mr. Pound writes:

> And in the meantime my songs will travel,
> And the devirginated young ladies will enjoy them
> when they have got over the strangeness.

What Propertius says is, 'Meanwhile let me resume the wonted round of my singing; let my lady, touched (by my words), find pleasure in the familiar music.' That is all. (*Gaudeat in solito tacta puella sono*). Just possibly, though not probably, Propertius meant 'young ladies' rather than 'my lady'. But there is no hint of the decadent meaning which Mr. Pound read into the passage by misunderstanding *tacta*, and taking the preposition *in* as if it were a negativing part of an adjective *insolito*. His own context should have shown him the absurdity of his version.

If Mr. Pound were a professor of Latin, there would be nothing left for him but suicide. I do not counsel this. But I beg him to lay aside the mask of erudition. And, if he must deal with Latin, I suggest that he paraphrase some accurate translation, and then employ some respectable student of the language to save him from blunders which might still be possible. If he does not owe this to himself, he owes it to his author, of whose fate otherwise one must think, in Browning's words from *Sordello*, as that of

> Some captured creature in a pound,
> Whose artless wonder quite precludes distress.

QUIA PAUPER AMAVI

London, October 1919

61. A. R. Orage on Pound, Propertius and 'decadence', *Readers and Writers (1917–1921)*

New York, 1922, pp. 33–5

Mr. Ezra Pound's 'Homage to Sextus Propertius' has drawn an American Professor of Latin into the pages of the American magazine *Poetry*. Professor Hale is indignant at the attempt of Mr. Pound to make Propertius intelligible as well as merely accessible to the modern English reader, and in the name of Scholarship, he begs Mr. Pound to 'lay aside the mask of erudition' and to confess himself nothing better than a poet. With some of Professor Hale's literal criticisms it is impossible not to agree. Speaking in the name of the schools, he is frequently correct. But in the name of the humanities, of life, of art, of literature, what in the world does it matter that Mr. Pound has spelled Punic with a capital when he meant a small letter, or that he has forgotten the existence of the Marcian aqueduct? Mr. Pound did not set out with the intention of making a literal translation of Propertius. He set out with the intention of creating in English verse a verse reincarnation, as it were, of Propertius, a 'homage' to Propertius that should take the form of rendering him a contemporary of our own. And, secondly, all criticism based on the text of Propertius is invalid unless it is accompanied by a perception of the psychological quality of Propertius as he lived. But Professor Hale, it is clear, has no sense for this higher kind of criticism, for he complains that there is 'no hint' in Propertius's text of 'certain decadent meanings' which Mr. Pound attributes to him. Is there not, indeed? Accepting decadence in its modern American meaning, Propertius can only be said to be full of it. No literary critic, accustomed to reading through and between an author's lines, whether they be Latin, Greek or English, can doubt the evidence of his trained senses that the mind behind the text of Propertius was a mind which the Latin Professor of the Chicago University would call decadent, if only it expressed itself in English. The facts that Propertius was a poet contemporary with Ovid, that he wrote of the life of the luxurious Roman Empire . . . that he was a child of his age. . . . What, in fact, distinguishes Propertius is his aesthetic reaction against decadence, against the very decadence in which he had been brought up, and with which he had sympathized. But this is not to admit that 'no hint of certain decadent meanings' is to be found in him. . . .

62. Grumbles about the 'Homage', *New Age*

27 November 1919, xxvi, 62

Paul Selver identifies the reviewer as Adrian Collins in *Orage and the 'New Age' Circle* (London: George Allen & Unwin, 1959), p. 40. He describes Collins as 'almost everything that Pound never has been: a scholar (an Oxford double first), a linguist (he translated a volume of Nietzsche . . .) and unpretentious in the extreme. . . . In addition to his other qualities Collins is good-natured and tolerant. So instead of holding Ezra up to ridicule, as I would have been tempted to do, he let him down lightly. He dotted the i's and crossed the t's, but he made this operation painless by the adroit use of gentle persiflage as a local anaesthetic. The result was that Ezra, far from taking offence, invited him to dinner. Collins accepted the invitation and they got on extremely well together.' Pound's reply, in the *New Age* of 4 December 1919, is the following number.

This book consists of paraphrases from the Provençal and from Propertius, together with some original poems. The first, 'Langue d'oc,' are to our old-fashioned taste by far the best, among the most successful being the 'Alba' of Giraut de Borneil and the 'Canzon' of Arnaut, the latter with its seven-fold rhyme-scheme being a real *tour de force*; while in the Borneil Mr. Pound's stanza is even more effective than that of the original. A scattering of words like 'plasmatour' and 'galzeadry' stresses the artificiality of all this poetry, and, if anything, adds to the appreciation of its flavour.

The rest of the book is in Mr. Pound's later manner. 'Three Cantos' are designed to 'go one better' than Browning's 'Sordello', of which they begin with an acute criticism. Mr. Pound then skips through the continents and the centuries, whisking us from Egypt to Provence, and thence to Spain (*via* Japan) in a few pages, coruscating attractively enough as he goes. Yet after these fireworks one may be glad to turn for relief to the simple prattle of 'Sordello.'

There is no 'galzeadry' about the 'Homage to Propertius,' which is very much alive indeed, more modern than the 'Moeurs Contemporaines,' and should be read, by those who have no Latin, with the speed and gusto with which it was evidently written. Mr. Pound has developed the small germ of humour in Propertius—so small that no one else has noticed it—till it overruns his whole work. The new Propertius does not balance his epithets like the old; he has changed his deep organ for the tongs and bones of *vers libre*; he is 'swelled up with inane pleasurabilities, and guzzles with outstretched ears' (is this meant to 'write him down an ass'?), but 'at any rate he will not have his epitaph in a high road'—Mr. Pound has seen to that.

Unexpectedly enough, the method often succeeds. There is a piquancy about the Lygdamus poem that is not in the original ('does he like me to sleep here alone, Lygdamus? Will he say nasty things at my funeral?'), while the effective ending of No. 8 is Mr. Pound's own invention, Propertius saying the exact opposite. Unfortunately, Propertius' dignity and passion have also to be forced into this jaunty mould, with the result that the great lament for 'white Iope, blithe Helen, and the rest,' becomes: 'There are enough women in hell, quite enough beautiful women . . . . death has its tooth in the lot'—and that tooth, we trust, on edge.

It is, however, hardly fair to judge the 'Homage to Propertius' by reference to Propertius. It is obviously not meant as a translation, though it ventures rather too near the original to be taken simply as a free fantasia on Roman themes. Yet the seven major blunders in No. 12 and the five in No. 5 are enough to show that Mr. Pound refuses to make a fetish of pedantic accuracy. The reader is not entitled to expect more than the 'general sense,' even when it is nonsense; as when 'upon the Actian marshes Virgil is Phoebus' chief of police,' or as when Galatea 'almost turns to Polyphemus' dripping horses because of a tune under Aetna.' Even if Polyphemus had had any horses, they probably would not have been able to sing; and, anyhow, why should they drip? Galatea's horses naturally would, as they had just come out of the sea.

Mr. Pound will not finick about tenses, like a mere grammarian, any more than about cases. 'The primitive ages sang Venus, the last sings of a tumult, and I also will sing war when this matter of a girl is exhausted.' But Propertius *has* finished with Cynthia for the time being, and *is* singing of war—in which new amusement Mr. Pound most inconsistently follows him. The palaeontology is, however, Mr. Pound's alone. Again, 'Io mooed the first year with averted head and now drinks Nile water like a god'—which seems a foolish thing for a god to do when he can get nectar; in Propertius, Io merely drank it when she was a cow.

Occasionally a hard word is followed by a comment in the text: as most readers, for example, would naturally like to know where the forests of 'Phaecia' are, these are explained as 'the luxurious and Ionian'; and it is not the fault of Mr. Pound's benevolence that the mythical island of Phaeacia has nothing to do with the Ionian town of Phocaea.

Mr. Pound's world of antiquity is itself as insubstantial as any Phaeacia. While the terrene Marius is conquering the Cimbri, a phantom Marus is drawing spectral dividends from the Welsh mines. The celestial hierarchy, evidently thriving on its Nile water, is increased by 'the Oetian gods,' and a certain Citharaon, who 'shook up the rocks by Thebes'; while Propertius (setting aside Mount Cithaeron) can muster but a single beggarly Oetaean. The small birds of the 'Cytharean' mother have changed their red beaks for 'Punic faces'; there are 'celebrities from the Trans-Caucasus' instead of the simple Romans Propertius knew, and a lady called 'royal Aemilia,' who is drawn on a 'memorial raft'—possibly lent to her by Aemilius, who had used it himself for conveying royal trophies. Xerxes has a 'two-barrelled kingdom' added to his dominions—perhaps the river Ranaus is to be found there, and 'the wood of Aeonium,' which, like Milton, soars above the Aonian mount. There is even a 'trained and performing tortoise' in place of the Propertian lyre, and a 'tune of the Phrygian fathers'—presumably written in collaboration for the tortoise to dance to.

Still, in spite of these delights, it is to be hoped that the shade of Propertius will not stray into Mr. Pound's comic Elysium. That meticulous Alexandrian might not be altogether satisfied with his new liegeman's 'homage.'

63. Pound's defence of the 'Homage'

December 1919

Ezra Pound, ' "Homage to Propertius" ', *New Age*, 4 December 1919, xxvi, pp. 82–3.

While defending the 'Homage' publicly, Pound made many of the same points in a letter to Orage (*Letters*, pp. 211–13).

Sir,—Your reviewer has been so kind to my volume that I am moved to one or two protests. The tacit question of my 'Homage to Propertius' is simply: 'Have I portrayed more emotion than Bohn's literal version or any other extant or possible strict translation of Propertius does or could convey?'

Browning's character Sordello dies a death timely for the great Victorian author, who thereby eliminates the historic Sordello's later life in France. In Browning's preface to that poem he says, if I remember rightly, that all he cares for is the soul, or the portrayal or study of the soul.

Permitted any metaphysics at all, a man's soul is that which he has and which no other man, god, or creature has; the unanalysable quality which makes possible the opinion that 'God has need of every individual soul.' Hence my development of a 'germ' of Propertius, which germ the 'Ride to Lanuvium' and the juxtaposition of the words 'tacta puella sono' and 'Orphea delinisse feras' might have revealed to any sensitive reader. If that last turn is unintentional, then Propertius was the greatest unconscious humorist of the ages. But given the 'Ride to Lanuvium,' even Professor Mackail might have suspected that there was something in Propertius apart from the smaragdites and chrysolites, and that this poet of later Rome was not steeped to the brim in Rossetti, Pater and Co., and that, whatever heavy sentimentality there was in Propertius' juvenalia, it is not *quite* the sentiment of thirteenth-century Florence decanted in the tone of the unadulterated Victorian period.

I don't think I actually turn Polyphemus' horses into vocalists; but, when some horses are able to fly, others might possibly sing, and I think it as likely that Mt. Cithaeron played the flute as that the walls of Thebes rose to magic of Amphion's solo on the barbitos. Also I am tired, very tired, of Amphion and of lyres, whether of tortoise-shell or of some less brittle compost. And there is a perfectly literal and, by the same token, perfectly lying and 'spiritually' mendacious translation of 'Vobiscum est Iope,' etc., in my earlier volume *Canzoni*, for whomsoever wants the humorless vein, which vein, in this particular poem, makes it utterly impossible to translate the 'Votivas noctes et mihi' at its termination.

The quarrel over 'Punic' was started before your reviewer came upon it, and the ancient vestiges of my pedantry beget phantom figures to fill them. Gods deathless and immortal! Is or is not 'Tyrian' used for 'purple' both in Latin and in English? If our forbears took over one such beautiful association of place and colour from the ancients, are we forever forbidden to take over another? Has it not indeed fallen from our own lips into one of the best poems of a friend and contemporary (where I leave your reviewer the pleasure, and no mean pleasure, of finding it)? 'Punic' is not my patent for dark red, and the proof is that I have already lent it, and welcome, to one of the staunchest and oldest of my friends. But I will give your reviewer half of my goods if he can devise me some means of keeping it from the ill-usage of bad poets.

As for Polyphemus' livestock, he had, by tradition, sheep; but as he never existed, and as Propertius certainly had no more belief in the existence of Polyphemus than I have, I cannot be expected to dig up the records of the then controller of agriculture, or mariculture, or arenaeculture for an accurate list of his bloodstock. Did the monocular wooer comb his hair with a hay-rake; did the whale, etc., in Christian mythology . . . did Propertius who brought a new and exquisite tone into Latin care a damn about these things; or did he tremendously care for writing a language that was not the stilted Horatian peg-work or Georgian maunder of Maro?

The philologists have so succeeded in stripping the classics of interest that I have already had more than one reader who has asked me, 'Who was Propertius?' As for my service to classical scholarship, presumably nil, I shall be quite content if I induce a few Latinists really to look at the text of Propertius instead of swallowing an official 'position' and then finding what the text-books tell them to look for.

64. Robert Nichols, 'Poetry and Mr. Pound', *Observer*

11 January 1920, 6

Nichols's review prompted Wyndham Lewis's bitter reply (No. 65), and a further rejoinder by Pound (No. 66).

Nichols (1893–1944) was a minor Georgian poet.

Here is Mr. Pound again proffering a neglectful world a new volume, this time divided into four sections and varying in merit from his best to his abominable worst: all with the Poundian flavour more pronounced than ever. He opens with renderings from the Provençal, in which his impudence, his pedantry, his great redeeming quality of true regard for letters all work in his favour. The following is, I think, Mr. Pound's most successful rendering (from Gilbert Bornello):—

[quotes 'Langue d'Oc', poem I, *CSP*, p. 190.]

I have quoted this in full to show what Mr. Pound can do when he assumes a mask that suits his face. In the second section 'Moeurs Contemporaines,' Mr. Pound comments on life without apparently any mask:—

[quotes 'Moeurs Contemporaines', poem I, *CSP*, p. 196.]

No aesthetic qualities redeem this; for it has none. It is merely poor prose cut into lengths. It is not poetry, though it pretends to be satire. It is merely, in its gross bad taste, a not unfamiliar example of Mr. Pound's pennyweight of pinchbeck impertinence. As for its content, Martial might have extracted one gust of bitter and shrewd laughter from this unhappy theme. But Mr. Pound cannot: he has not the heart, or even the head, for the work. Poor Mr. Pound: he is by no means the finished scourge he would have us think him!

It is with relief that we turn to the 'Three Cantos', where we find the poet, if not at his aesthetic best, perhaps at his most intriguing: that is, at his most intriguing if you are one of those persons who do not like a thing save its taste reminds you of something else. The 'Three Cantos' are an ingenious essay at endeavouring to say a possible something of your own in the words of another. The work is no masterpiece, for masterpieces have a habit of being both readable and understandable. 'The Three Cantos' are barely one and hardly the other. Comprehensibility is a virtue. The greater masters knew this; hence Molière and his valet, Cervantes and his groom. These artists did not necessarily write *down*; they wrote *into* the comprehension of slower mortals. For the master knowing the profound to be expressible makes a certain completeness of clarity his task: his task is to see and record it clearly enough. But our author is inclined to confuse the profound and the obscure. The reader feels he has passed no mild literary examination if he can instantly catch every literary allusion in these 'Three Cantos,' including, as they do, references to or quotations from Joics, the Tolosan, 'The Late Girl's Song,' of Po-Chuin (or was it Li-Po?—I forget), Catullus, Mallarmé, 'The Chronicles of the Cid,' Lopé's 'Inez de Castro,' Doughty's 'Titans,' and Pierre Cardinal. And when all is over, what has been precipitated—of what have we become aware? Story? soul? wit? psychology? No, only of Mr. Pound's potential erudition, of an emotion chopped off short whenever he began, and, alas, ceased so finickly but so pertinently to render choice scraps of other poets. Toward the end, maybe, Mr. Pound himself feels this, for he gives us a lengthy and most admirable fragment from 'One Andreas Divus.' But it is too late: he has smothered the *thing itself* in the tatters of second-hand clothes. Or if the clothes are the *thing*, might we not have them whole? But perhaps Mr. Pound would demonstrate to us that his mind with regard to his theme is merely a ragbag without synthesis.

This synthesis he seems, however, to attempt in the last section of the book 'Homage to Propertius'; homage of a sort that will, I hazard, startle no few professors. For, with regard to Propertius, this is a very odd version of him, the oddness of which is not decreased by Mr. Pound giving us a sense of never being at ease among the acknowledged difficulties of the Latin and by his determination to continue to wear his perverse, ironical, intellectually snobbish panache at all costs.

Let me draw attention to one or two instances which reveal this remarkable opposition of zeal and knowledge. Propertius, in his third elegy in the third book, writes. '*Unde pater sitiens Ennius ante bibit*' ('Whence thirsty father Ennius aforetime drank'). Mr. Pound renders this 'Wherefrom father Ennius, sitting before I came, hath drunk.'

Poor Mr. Pound, if only Propertius had written macaronics he would have had no need of dictionaries, and 'sitiens' might well and truly signify 'sitting'! Unfortunately, Mr. Pound's ineptitudes are not always as amusing as this. How deals Mr. Pound with '*gaudeat insolito tacta puella sono*,' which might be rendered 'Let the girl, much moved, take delight in this music of mine she knows by heart'? Mr. Pound determines to go one better. Here is a chance for his ignorance and bad taste: 'And the devirginated young ladies,' he writes, 'will enjoy them (my songs) when they have got over the strangeness.' Such is the adequacy of equipment in one who seems to think that vulgarity is an aid to incompetence, more especially if used to galvanise a poet of 'melancholy remembrance and vesperal' into a fox-trot briskness. Mr. Pound, indeed, serves his lobster à l'Americaine. In place of the quiet and tender irony we are accustomed to see upon the face of Thomas Campion's favourite Latin poet we behold a mask of mordant gaiety and elegiac irony, sometimes almost saturnine. No matter! though the hand be the hand of Propertius and the voice the voice of Mr. Pound, it is not that of the professional gramophone, being at least a live voice. That is, however, I fear, all that can be said for the version. More and more as we read we become aware of the Poundian personality: that queer compost of harsh levity, spite, cocksureness, innuendo, pedantry, archaism, sensuality, real if sometimes perverse and unfortunate research and honest love of literature. In the end, of course, tedium supervenes, since nothing is more tiring than a tireless *scherzo*. But the work is amusing. Let Mr. Pound stick to the mask. It disguises him just sufficiently and gives to his utterances that slight softness of poetry which in himself he does not possess. For to the man that daily attempts to speak in the tongue of the angels something of the angels' qualities may, temporarily at least, become added. In himself Mr. Pound is not, never has been and almost, I might hazard, never will be, a poet. He is too hard, too clever; he has yet to learn that poetry does not so much glitter as shine.

65. A reply from Wyndham Lewis

January 1920

Wyndham Lewis, 'Mr. Ezra Pound', *Observer* (18 January 1920), p. 5.

Dear Sir—In your last week's issue Mr. Robert Nichols, in reviewing *Quia Pauper Amavi*, referred to Ezra Pound's imprudence in giving an interpretation of Propertius in English: his consequent unfortunate plight ('poor Mr. Pound,' not once, but several times) and to the retribution that it was only to be expected overtook him; for the little word *sitiens* (from a language that 'poor' Pound had, no doubt, supposed to be 'dead') has sprung up, Mr. Nichols alleges, and given him a cuff for his temerity.

Pound's 'true regard for letters,' and his 'honest love of literature,' also enables Mr. Nichols to devote a column and a half to what otherwise would seem to be the work of a very inferior writer indeed. Mr. Pound 'never has been, is not' and, if Mr. Nichols can possibly dissuade him, 'never will be', a poet. Poor Mr. Pound indeed!

One could, of course, point out, commenting on the text of this review, that Mr. Pound, without being a pedant, may conceivably know that Chaucer, Landor, Ben Jonson, and many contemporaries of Rowlandson, found other uses for classic texts than that of making literal English versions of them. Or, again, that the parody of Yeats . . . and the mention of Wordsworth . . . would have indicated to a sensitive or less biassed critic that Mr. Pound in his 'Homage to Sextus Propertius', had some other aim than that of providing a crib for schoolboys or undergraduates.

But a comment on such a review cannot confine itself to indications of that review's technical inconsistency. When Mr. Nichols uses the word 'poetry' (and he refers to the 'softness' that is its inalienable melting attribute) he is using it in an identical fashion to that in which Sir Sidney Colvin uses the word 'beauty' elsewhere, publicly, during the same week. It is part of the same blind conservatism, hatred of a living thing, that men of letters, 'true and honest' ones, painters and musicians, of this community have to bear with when attempting to break through the hybrid social intellectual ring to something that is a matter purely of the imagination or intelligence, and not mixed with officialdom or social attitudes. 'Poor Pound' (more unfortunate in this respect than 'poor Lelian') has had more than his share, I think, of this suffocating and malignant rubbish.—Yours, etc.

Wyndham Lewis

Campden-hill, W.8, January 11

66. Pound defends the 'Homage' again

January 1920

Ezra Pound, 'Propertius and Mr. Pound', *Observer* (25 January 1920), p. 5.

Robert Nichols's reply follows. Nichols defended himself in another letter, printed in the same issue of the *Observer*, against Wyndham Lewis's attack.

Sir,—Leaving aside the personal aspect, the possible merit or demerit of a character sketch which never was, and never was intended to be, an *ad verbum* translation; in which I paid no conscious attention to the grammar of the latin text; and of which all my revisions were made *away* from and not *toward* literal rendering; coming toward the wider issue of academic misinterpretation of the classics:

In the line which your reviewer quotes from Prof. Hale of Chicago

Gaudeat in solito tacta puella sono,

he finds, apparently as Prof. Hale, no trace of anything save Victorian sentimentality. All of which is beautifully academic; the carefully shielded reader, following Professor Mackail's belief that Propertius was a student of Rossetti and Pater, and filled with reminiscences of the Vita Nuova, is asked to read *one* word at a time and one line at a time. Propertius' next statement is:

> Orphea delenisso feras et concita dicunt
> Flumina Threicia sustinuisse lyra.

I can but repeat if this sequence of clauses is wholly accidental, and if the division of *in* and *tacta* is *wholly* accidental, then Propertius was the greatest unconscious ironist of all time. Are we, with all the Greek anthology in background to suppose that irony was invented in 1890 or in the year of grace 1919? Are we, in the face of Propertius' poems on the return of the Praetor and on the Ride to Lanuvium, to suppose that he was always sentimental in the scroll-saw and antimacassar manner so dear to the contemporaries of your reviewer's friend, Mr. Gosse? Are we in the face of Propertius' own lines, Bk. V., poem VIII., 11–15.

> Virginis in palmis ipsa canistra tremunt.
> Si fuerint castae, redeunt in colla parentum,
> Clamant agricolae 'fertillis annus erit.'
> Huc mea detonsis avectast Cynthia mannis.

'Huc mea Cynthia'—my Cynthia, with her *cause célèbre* past, with all that Propertius has matchlessly sung of her and with the remainder of that delectable poem—are we to suppose that he was never ironical, that he was always talking for Tennyson's tea-table, that he attended Dr. Wilson's mid-week prayer meetings, that he was as dull and humorless as the stock contributors to Mr. Marsh's series of anthologies?

Or is the vaunted and recommended 'tenderness' (like the white meat of a young fattened poularde?) supposed to be that quality of feeling which would prevent us from receiving our own Cynthias upon *their* returns from Lanuvium?—Respectfully Yours,

EZRA POUND.

5, Holland-place Chambers, Kensington, W. January 19, 1920.

In reply to the above, Mr. Nichols writes:—

'In reply to Mr. Pound, may I point out that I stated in my review that Mr. Pound, in translating the words 'gaudeat in solito tacta puella sono,' by 'And the devirginated young ladies will enjoy them (my songs) when they have got over the strangeness,' had committed himself to a misinterpretation of the grossest kind. To that statement I adhere. No foolery with 'academic misinterpretations,' with the 'next

statement,' or with lines in a poem two books later, alter the fact that
the above Latin cannot by any possible means whatever bear the com-
plexion Mr. Pound would put upon it. As to the remaining farrago of
Poundian nonsense about 'Victorian sentimentality,' Professor Mackail,
Mr. Gosse, Rossetti, Pater, Dante, Mr. Winston Churchill's private
secretary, and Alfred Tennyson's tea-table, let us be plain; all this has
nothing to do with the subject, which is not Mr. Pound's chronic dis-
gruntlement with all he considers 'beautifully academic,' but the fact
that, as I stated, Mr. Pound has displayed ignorance, incompetence, and
vulgarity in his rendering of the words 'gaudeat in solito tacta puella
sono.'

67. John Gould Fletcher on the decline and fall of an expatriate

May 1920

John Gould Fletcher, from 'Some Contemporary Poets', *Chapbook: A Monthly Miscellany* (May 1920), No. 11, 23-5.

The other poets discussed include Robinson, Frost, Amy Lowell,
Masters, Sandburg, Lindsay, Aiken, Stevens and Kreymborg.

Fletcher (1886-1950), an American poet and writer, was an early
contributor to the *Egoist*. His autobiography, *Life is My Song*
(1937) contains material on Pound's London years. He received a
Pulitzer prize for poetry in 1939. Pound reviewed a volume of
his verse favourably in the *New Freewoman* (15 September 1913).

The first of the exiles in point of time, and perhaps also in eminence, is
Ezra Pound. Pound came to Europe about 1908, and spent a year wandering in Italy, France and Spain before settling in London. There he
published in the following year *Personae*, which was so successful that it
was almost immediately followed by *Exultations* in the same year. After

a return visit to America in 1911, which only served to disgust him completely with his native country (unfortunately for him, this visit antedated the American revival of interest in poetry by two years), he published *Ripostes* in 1912.* In 1913, having been five years in Europe, he collected together most of the pieces later published in *Lustra* (hence the title), and in 1915 he published the results of his work on Fenollosa's manuscript notes (which came into his hands a year before) under the title of *Cathay*. What poetry he has since written will be found in the recent *Quia Pauper Amavi* (1919).

I have made this brief historical note in order to clear away certain misconceptions. In all his work since 1912 (with the sole exception of *Cathay*) Pound has, I think, quite unjustifiably, put greater stress upon his own personal attitude to life, to literature, to members of his own profession, and to society generally, than upon his poetry. He has said in effect that the thing that matters is Ezra Pound and his opinions—not poetry in itself and for its own sake, but poetry for the sake of expressing a man's personal attitude and reaction to what lies about him. This is certainly a mistake on his part. The mere strong expression of one's likes and dislikes does not make any man a poet, and to go about continually thumping the public on its head for its stupidity leads merely to putting oneself on the level of the public, not above it. Nor is Pound in any way well equipped for the job of being a satirist. The earlier volumes show a temperament utterly opposed to the satiric. In these volumes, as in *Cathay*, there is only the restless seeker after beauty—a beauty hard, bright, tangible, vividly American in its abrupt quality of definition, if not in its *mise-en-scène*.

Is it too much to suppose that the search for this beauty, which led Pound back to twelfth-century Provence, to mediaeval Italy, to Greece finally and ancient China, came to him primarily from the keen, vivid atmosphere of America, and from his hatred of the prevailing commercial ugliness, so utterly unsuited to that atmosphere? At all events, in *Personae* Pound had not yet found himself. He was still struggling with vestiges of what he calls the 'crepuscular.' It was in *Exultations* that he became master of his own material, and in this book he produced poetry such as no Englishman could ever write. The nearest things to these poems by an Englishman are some of Richard Aldington's early pre-war poems. Compare these with Pound, and the difference leaps to the

---

* I have omitted *Canzoni*, 1911, and also *Sonnets and Ballate of Guido Cavalcanti*, both of which seem to me slighter work—Pound trying to fit himself into the Victorian order of Rossetti or Yeats.

eye. Aldington is cool, detached, impersonal. Pound, though deriving perhaps nine-tenths of his inspiration from Italian or Provençal literature, lives himself a vivid life in each of these poems:—

> Lo, I have seen thee bound about with dreams.
> Lo, I have known thy heart and its desire;
> Life, all of it, my sea, and all men's streams
> Are fused in it as flames of an altar fire!

This, from the very first poem in *Exultations*, sets the note.

Exultations certainly contains more gold than anything this poet has done. 'Sestina Altaforte', 'Pierre Vidal Old,' 'Ballad of the Goodly Fere,' 'Sestina for Ysolt', 'Portrait,' 'Francesca', 'On His Own Face in a Glass', 'Defiance', 'Nils Lykke', 'Alba Innominata'—it seems strange that the hand which wrote these poems could ever have descended to the trumpery smartness of 'Homage to Propertius' or to the subfusc pedantry of 'Three Cantos'. For these poems have all the vivid energy of a young race. Even at their most bookish, they are bookish in a different sense from European bookishness. The European of the present day when he desires to live in the past surrounds himself with echoes. Pound, you feel sure, might quite easily have lived with Bertran de Born, or even Villon, held rhyming bouts and drinking bouts with them, and broken their pates if necessary.

Strange that the demon of climate, requickening the old shreds of Anglo-Saxon stock, should have produced out of western North America this vivid spirit of flame! Strange, but also tragic. Pound has never been at home in twentieth-century Europe. He can only get life out of books—from the life about him, he can obtain nothing. Something prompts him, therefore, to mock the world he sees, because he hates it; and when he mocks, the vividness utterly abandons him. The smile becomes a leer, the attitude a pose, the dependence on other men's work assumes the dimensions of intolerable pedantry. Technically Pound's later work is even more interesting than his earlier. The *vers libre* experiments of *Ripostes* and *Cathay*, the free, broken blank verse of 'Near Perigord' and 'Three Cantos', are fascinating things to study. But except where he follows faithfully some other work, as in *Cathay*, the poems in these last two volumes are almost valueless. They are 'a broken bundle of mirrors,' the patchwork and debris of a mind which has never quite been able to find the living, vivid beauty it set out to seek. As a pioneer, as a treader in unbroken paths, America can afford to salute the earlier, as it is forced to reject the later Pound; and a whole host of modern American poets could never have done the work they are doing without the inspiration of his influence.

68. Harold Monro, from *Some Contemporary Poets*

London: Leonard Parsons, 1920, 87–93

Monro (1879–1932), English poet and editor, was educated at Cambridge. He founded the *Poetry Review* in 1912, and edited *Poetry and Drama* (1914). He opened the Poetry Bookshop, and was the publisher of the five volumes of *Georgian Poetry*. His *Collected Poems* (1933) contained a biographical sketch by F. S. Flint and a critical note by Eliot. (Pound's review appeared in the *Spectator*, 23 June 1933.) Pound's obituary of Monro appeared in the *Criterion* in July 1932 and in *Polite Essays*.

Ezra Pound, as far as we know, has come under the influence of only two living English poets—Ford Madox Hueffer and W. B. Yeats, neither of whom interfered noticeably with his style, whatever their temperamental effect on his personality.

The sources of his inspiration are bookish, and they are undisguised. Original poems are printed side by side with translations, and some are half original and half translation. After the issue of *Personæ* and *Exultations* in 1909 he wrote *The Spirit of Romance*: 'An attempt to define somewhat the charm of the pre-renaissance literature of Latin Europe.' American, intelligent and arrogant, a most careless scholar but imaginative thinker, he rambles through two hundred and fifty pages of loosely-connected notes on his favourite epoch in European literature. 'I am interested in poetry,' he writes in his *Præfatio ad Lectorem Electum*. 'I have attempted to examine certain forces, elements or qualities which were potent in the mediæval literature of the Latin tongues, and are, as I believe, still potent in our own.'

The intellectual perversity of Ezra Pound has disgusted many of his contemporaries. His influence on the younger poetry of our day is least admitted by many who have been most subject to it. The recognition of his genius will be gradual and tardy, its qualities being, few of them, apparent on the surface, and also because he voluntarily erects a barrier between himself and his readers, and that the standards he has set himself, and the literary obstructions he has himself raised against freedom of the imagination, have so interfered with his production as to reduce him in present appearance to a mere experimenter in unusual rhythms.

He writes (it is as though he were describing himself) of Arnaut Daniel's 'refusal to use the "journalese" of his day,' his 'aversion to the obvious, familiar vocabulary,' of his discontent with 'a conventional phrase, or with a word that does not convey his exact meaning'; that he realised fully 'that the music of rhymes depends upon their arrangement, not on their multiplicity.' In the forms of his *canzoni* he finds an excellence that can satisfy 'not only the modern ear, gluttonous of rhyme, but also the ear trained to Roman and Hellenic music to which rhyme seemed and seems a vulgarity.' But his 'temperamental sympathy' for the pre-renaissance literature of Latin Europe is little shared by his twentieth-century contemporaries. He learnt his art in the school of the Troubadours.

Recently under the title *Umbra*, he has selected all he now wishes to keep in circulation from his earlier books; *Personæ, Exultations, Ripostes*, etc. Glancing down the table of contents we find, among others, the following titles:—

La Fraisne; Cino; Na Audiart; Villonaud for this Yule; Marvoil; Sestina: Altaforte; Aux Belles de Londres; Alba; Planh; N.Y.; Δώρια. Such internationalistic nomenclature will not fail from the outset to irritate the reader, however well-disposed. The beauties of his poetry are disguised among intricacies and wilful complications. Yet, read 'Praise of Ysolt.' Here is the opening:—

[quotes 'Praise of Ysolt', *CSP*, p. 30 'In vain' to ' "Sing a song"'.]

Read 'Δώρια' or 'The Return': both finished specimens of the art of free verse.

[quotes 'The Return', *CSP*, p. 85.]

In other books a strong influence of Chinese poetry takes its place.

Among the Latins Catullus is a predominant source, among the Germans, Heine, and several modern French writers have been carefully studied. Further a 'pact' with Walt Whitman releases his imagination for a number of lively poems in free verse in which he ridicules contemporary habits and persons:—

[quotes 'A Pact', *CSP*, p. 98 'I make a pact' to 'make friends'.]

The series of translations from the Chinese entitled *Cathay* is composed in plain lucid English running in harmonious rhythms, and conveys to the average western mind an extraordinarily clear picture of such a China as travellers and native art have led it to imagine.

Ezra Pound peppers nearly all his writings with archaisms, exoticisms, foreign words ancient and modern, wilful obscurities, and gibes at people less gifted than himself. His very latest poems have the obscurity without the wit or natural intelligence of a Browning.

He seldom misses an opportunity of casting a stone at the 'old bitch gone in the teeth'—this 'botched civilisation' of ours, or, figuratively, of pelting his contemporaries with paper darts, at which, when they do not laugh, but are irritated, he himself becomes the angrier. He seems to have made himself a permanent resident in England, and all his works have been published here, but his intellect has never become acclimatised. Nor, apparently, has he decided whether finally to consider himself a romantic or a realist. Miraut de Garzelas, the 'grave councillor' of his 'La Fraisne' cast aside 'the yoke of the old ways of men,' finding comfort 'by the still pool of Mar-nan-otha.'

> But I have seen the sorrow of men, and am glad,
> For I know that the wailing and bitterness are a folly.
> And I? I have put aside all folly and all grief.

Ezra Pound himself has not learnt the folly of bitterness.

69. May Sinclair, 'The Reputation of Ezra Pound', *North American Review*

May 1920, ccxi, 658–68

Sinclair (1870–1946) was an English novelist and a good friend of Pound's. She is the author of an early, sympathetic note on Imagism in the *Egoist* (1 June 1915) and an article on *Prufrock* in the *Little Review* (December 1917). Walter Allen in *The English Novel* (Penguin ed., 1965, p. 345), attributes the first use of the phrase 'stream of consciousness' to a review by May Sinclair of Dorothy Richardson in 1918.

If the views of some of our more conservative reviewers were immortal Posterity would have an odd idea of Ezra Pound. It would know him, if it were allowed to know him at all, as a literary mountebank; a masquerader looking for something to wear, ransacking the wardrobes of every century but his own; an impudent schoolboy letting off squibs in his back garden.

But what, after all, has Mr. Pound really done? It is true that he has let off squibs, lots of squibs, and some of them have hit one or two respectable persons in the eye. Mr. Pound is not a respecter of respectable persons. He has displayed a certain literary frightfulness in the manner of Laurent Tailhade. He has shown an arrogant indifference to many admired masterpieces of his day. And he has associated himself with unpopular movements. His appearance in *Blast* blasted him in the eyes of respectable persons not hitherto hostile to his manifestations. People become unpopular through association with him. In the interval between the disappearance of *Blast* and the re-emergence of *The Little Review* he published some negligible trifles, which were held up as representative of a trivial talent. Worse still, when various people were forming little groups and creating little organs of their own, Ezra Pound had the temerity to form a group and create an organ more or less his own.

If *The Little Review* had never printed anything but what came to it through its foreign editor it might by this time have ranked as an important international concern; unfortunately it printed many things for which Mr. Pound was not responsible, and when it trespassed, its iniquities were laid on him. Besides he gave opportunities. His critical manner was deceptive. When *The Little Review* announced its Henry James number with an article by Ezra Pound some of us had visions of an irresponsible and agile animal shinning up a monument to hang by his feet from the top. What actually happened?

I do not know any book yet written on Henry James of more solid value than Mr. Pound's 'Brief Note' in *The Little Review*.

[quotes 'Henry James', *LE*, p. 296 'I am tired of hearing' to 'didn't raise this cry'.]

Is not that admirable? Is it not the essential serious truth of his subject? For the sake of it one can forgive Mr. Pound his minor perversities, for example, his dismissal of beautiful *Spoils of Poynton* as 'all that damned fuss about furniture.'

And in relation to his actual *confrères* what has happened? No contemporary critic has done more than Ezra Pound for the work of Gaudier Brzeska, of Mr. James Joyce, of Mr. Wyndham Lewis, of Mr. T. S. Eliot, to admit only four of the names associated with him. For the last seven years he has been more concerned to obtain recognition for other people than to capture any sort of hearing for himself. In this he has shown an absolutely incorruptible devotion to his craft. He may have been guilty of a few blunders, a few indiscretions and impertinences, but he has rendered services to modern international art that in any society less feral than our own would have earned him the gratitude of his contemporaries.

They have not even earned him moderate protection against prejudice.

It has been said of this poet—almost, if not quite the most original, the most individual poet of his century—that he has no originality, no hot, inspired genius, only talent, only an uncanny and prodigious dexterity; that his sources are purely and coldly literary; that he speaks behind a mask and without his mask he is nothing.

Well, Mr. Pound never denied his sources and the author of *Personae* would hardly disclaim his mask. There never was a poet more susceptible to influence, more sensitive to cadences, to the subtle flavors and flying gestures of words; never one who has so absorbed into his system three diverse literatures; of the langue d'Oc, of old China, of Augustan

Rome. With a snatch at the Anglo-Saxon, at Sappho, at the Greek epigrammatists. But there is one literature that he rejects, that by no possibility could he assimilate; the literature of the Edwardian and Georgian eras

As it happened, Mr. Pound's first poems, in *Personae* and *Exultations,* were so amazingly original, so violently individual, that nothing but violent individuality was expected of him. He wrote 'La Fraisne'.

> By the still pool of Mar-nan-otha
> Have I found me a bride
> That was a dog-wood tree some syne,
> She hath called me from mine old ways,
> She hath hushed my rancour of council,
> Bidding-me praise
> Naught but the wind that flutters in the leaves.

He wrote the beautiful 'Praise of Ysolt'.

[quotes 'Praise of Ysolt', *CSP*, p. 30 'Lo, I am worn' to 'seeking a song'.]

He wrote the 'Ballad of the Goodly Fere'. . . . Here was a voice that had not been heard before. Here was a strange, foreign beauty. They made Mr. Pound's reputation.

Then followed the *Canzoni*. In spite of 'The Yearly Slain' and 'The Vision', the *Canzoni* were a set-back to extravagant expectations. The elaborate form, the artificial sweetness, the dextrous technique, the sheer convention of the thing, were felt to be incompatible with unfettered, unpremeditative genius. Instead of warbling native wood-notes wild, Mr. Pound was thinking of his metric. Obviously, Mr. Pound was not a warbler.

There followed the *Sonnets and Ballate of Guido Cavalcanti* to suggest that Mr. Pound was a translator (not too accurate) rather than a poet. And to complete the disillusion people remembered that even in *Exultations* the influence of Mr. W. B. Yeats was discernible in at least four lines:

> But if one should look at me with the old hunger in her eyes
> How will I be answering her eyes?
> . . . .
> And it's a deep hunger I have when I see them a-gliding
> And a-flickering there where the trees stand apart.

There followed *Ripostes* . . . with the grave, uncanny beauty of 'The Tomb at Akr Çaar'; the poignant, almost unbearable passion of 'The Return'; the magic of 'Apparuit':

Green the ways, the breath of the fields is thine there,
Open lies the land, yet the steely going
Darkly hast thou dared and the dreaded aether parted
   before thee
. . . .
Clothed in goldish weft, delicately perfect,
Gone as wind! The cloth of the magical hands!
Thou a slight thing, thou in access of cunning
Daredst to assume this?

Undoubtedly *Ripostes* contains some of his very finest work. It also includes some *opusculi* not so fine which have been remembered against him. Then came his somewhat invidious connection with *Poetry* and his appearance in *Blast*. Mr. Pound there made himself sponsor for Vorticism, and from that day to this alternate fury and indifference have been his portion. Or if any favour comes his way it wears the cold air of controversy and reservation. And, with one exception, every serious and self-respecting magazine is closed to this most serious and self-respecting artist.

He has not been at any pains to open them. It would have been easy enough. He had only to leave Vorticism and every other 'ism' alone. It would have been far the more profitable course. With his uncanny capacity for saturating himself with various styles, his genius for impersonation, he could, if he had chosen, have become one of the most popular poets of his day; he had only to stand on the alert, to snare the familiar sentimental lilt, the familiar charm, the odor and cadence and the sensual thrill; only to follow the strong trail of the bloody realist—you can imagine the exquisite dexterity with which he would have sustained the role—only to write war-songs, to catch the note—he could so easily have caught it—of delicate yearning, or of stark, frightful, abominable truth. Why not? It would have paid him a hundred times over in cash and credit, and he would never have been found out, or not till he was too old and cynical to care.

Instead of which he has adopted the mask of fantastic intellectual Inhumanism. He has written what he has written *Quia Pauper Amavi*. His title is a signboard warning sentimental trespassers that they will not find what they want in his preserves. It points also to his limitations. You cannot conceive him taking a great, passionate human theme and treating it greatly, passionately, tenderly. He would tell you that the great passionate human themes are not to be taken; they no longer stand out nakedly with a simple, immediate appeal. They are caught in a net-work of association. The atmosphere that sustains them has been used up; every breather of the sacred air contributes his share of corruption. This being so, it is obvious that without some reaction art is bound to become an affair of generalized emotions. Imagism, the substitution of the concrete image for the generalized emotion was one reaction, Vorticism, the release of intellectual energy, another.

In associating himself with this movement Mr. Pound increased his natural inaccessibility. All the approaches to this twentieth century poet are difficult. Unless you love sudden, strange, disconcerting beauty and certain qualities that he has brought into literature, of bright hardness, of harshness, of intellectual flame.

In no other volume are these qualities so marked as in his *Lustra* and *Cathay*.

It is, to say the least, surprising that in the years that saw the publication of these poems one should have heard it said that Ezra Pound was 'finished,' so clear it seems that he was only just beginning, only just discovering the medium, plastic, yet capable of the hardness of crystal or of bronze, that was to serve him henceforth. You perceive that between *Lustra* and *Cathay* something has happened to him.

That something was his discovery through Ernest Fenollosa of the old literatures of China and Japan. (Here again, his paraphrases from Fenollosa's translation of the *Noh* plays would have made a noble reputation for any man less dogged by invidious misfortune.)

Of all the influences that he has come under, that of the Chinese poets has been the most beneficent. It has made for clearness, for vividness and precision, for concentration, for the more and more perfect realization of his ideal, the finding of his ultimate self.

> Go, my songs, seek your praise from the young and from the intolerant,
> Move among the lovers of perfection alone,
> Seek ever to stand in the hard Sophoclean light
> And take your wounds from it gladly.

Barring one or two poems in *Ripostes* there is nothing in his earlier work to compare with his translations—or are they paraphrases—of Bunno and Mei-Sheng and Rihaku; of Kakuhaku, Rosoriu and T'ao Yuan Ming.

Take this: Rihaku's 'Lament of the Frontier Guard'.

[quotes 'Lament of the Frontier Guard', *CSP*, p. 143.]

Observe the certainty with which Mr. Pound gets his effect, by the placing of a copula,

And sorrow, sorrow like rain;

by the cadence of his repetitions,

Sorrow to go and sorrow, sorrow returning;

by sheer plain statement,

There is no wall left to this village.

Observe the firm perfection of his own 'Liu Ch'e', written, as if in anticipation, before Fenollosa's work came into his hands.

[quotes 'Liu Ch'e', *CSP*, p. 118.]

After *Cathay, Quia Pauper Amavi* with his 'Three Cantos'.

Hang it all, there can be but the one Sordello,
But say I want to, say I take your whole bag of tricks,
Let in your quirks and tweeks and say the thing's an art form. . . .

Imitating Browning now? Perhaps; but, feature for feature, the new mask fits. Ezra Pound was never more himself than in this 'art-form.' You can see him chuckling as the idea dawned on him. 'At last I can do what I "want to" '! The form gives scope to his worst qualities and his best; his obscurity, his inconsequence, his caprice; his directness, his ease in the attack, his quickness, the shining, darkening turn and return as of a bird in the air or a fish in water; the baffling play of a spirit flying between darkness and light; the resurgence of abrupt, surprising beauty:

here the sunlight
Glints on the shaken waters and the rain
Comes forth with delicate tread, walking from Isola Garda
It is the sun rains, and a spatter of fire
Darts from the 'Lydian' ripples, *lacus undae*
And the place is full of spirits. . . .

Mr. Pound has poured into his Cantos the contents of what he calls his 'phantastikon.' Anything may happen in this art-form. You may come upon anything, from 'Couci's rabbits' to the wars of the Cid. There are as yet but three Cantos published; there may be three hundred before Mr. Pound has done, and no reason beyond the reader's convenience why the endless rhapsody should be divided into Cantos at all. The third proceeds, with no intelligible transition from

John Heyden,
Worker of miracles, dealer in levitation,

to a chunk of the *Odyssey*, translated so incomparably well that one
wishes Mr. Pound would finish what he has begun.

You may pass over the 'Moeurs Contemporaines.' The thing has
been done better by Jules Laforgue and Laurent Tailhade. You might
even pass the 'Langue d'Oc', but that it has something that the earlier
translations lacked: a rough hardness, a twist, a sharp tang overlying the
artificial sweetness. The translator has escaped from the first enchant-
ment of this literature. He is at pains to show up its essential artifice.
By every possible device—the use of strange words like 'gentrice' and
'plasmatour'—he throws it seven centuries back in time. It is to sound
as different from modern speech as he can make it, because it belongs to
a world that by the very nature of its conventions is inconceivably
remote, inconceivably different from our own, a world that we can no
longer reconstruct in its reality.

By this device, this thickening of the veil that hangs between us and
the dead world of the 'Langue d'Oc', Mr. Pound sets in relief the reality,
the modernity of his Propertius. It is as if he said, 'There is the echoed
falsetto of a voice that never rang quite true; here—a thousand years
before it—is the voice of a live man, a man you might meet in Picca-
dilly today.' There is no essential difference between Rome in the
Augustan and London in the Georgian age.

> Annalists will continue to record Roman reputations,
> Celebrities from the Trans-Caucasus will belaud Roman celebrities
> And expound the distensions of Empire,
> But for something to read in normal circumstance?
> For a few pages brought down from the forked hill unsullied?
> I ask a wreath which will not crush my head.
> And there is no hurry about it;
> I shall have, doubtless, a boom after my funeral. . . .

Mr. Pound gives light English for the light Latin. Propertius's
Roman irony rings fresh and English, a modern irony that mocks at
everything, at love and death:

[quotes from 'Homage to Sextus Propertius' III, *CSP*, pp. 229–30
'Midnight and a' to 'in the Via Sciro' and 'What if undertakers' to
'on my pyre'; and 'Homage' VI, *CSP*, pp. 235–6 'When, when, and'
to 'to Persephone'.]

His irony laughs equally at himself and at the conquests of Augustus.

> Oh august Pierides! Now for a large mouthed product.
> Thus:
> 'The Euphrates denies its protection to the Parthian
> And apologies for Crassus,'
> And 'It is, I think, India which now gives necks to your triumph,'
> And so forth, Augustus, 'Virgin Arabia shakes in her inmost dwelling.'
> . . . .
> And I shall follow the camp, I shall be duly celebrated for singing
>   the affairs of your cavalry.

Or take 'A Difference of Opinion with Lygdamus'. Not even the reference to the 'other woman's' incantations disturbs the bright impression of modernity.

Nor should this surprise us. Our imperial politics bring us very near to Augustan Rome. Our intelligentsia, by its psychology, by its ironic detachment, its disenchantments, the melancholy that overlies its increasingly intellectual view of life, is nearer to the intelligentsia of the Augustan era than, say, to that of the Eighteenth Century. And Ezra Pound has never found a mask that fitted him better than his Propertius. In all his adventures he goes out to the encounter with himself; he maintains himself, a salient, abrupt, unmistakable entity, through all his transformations.

On this account his translation is not to be recommended to students cramming Propertius for an exam. He has made blunders here and there that any schoolmaster would have avoided. His 'night-dogs' for *nocturnaeque canes* procured him a rating from at least one professorial chair. There always will be a certain number of inverted minds for which microscopic errors assume supreme importance. Mr. Pound is a poet and he knows that in a foreign poet the essential thing is not always his literal sense, nor yet the structure and agreeable cadence of his verse, but his manner, the way he says things, his gesture, his tone and accent. With rather more brusquerie in this manner, it is this living gesture and tone and accent that Mr. Pound's paraphrasing conveys. You know that it is right because you feel that it is alive; that this *is* an actual Propertius. Mr. Pound should be tried by a jury, not of professors, but of his peers: his defense should be to read aloud Odes VII and IX: and X.

If he had never written anything else: if he had never appeared in *Blast*, never helped to edit *The Little Review*, never expressed his inmost opinion of his contemporaries, but had burst upon the town in innocence with his 'Homage to Sextus Propertius', he would have achieved a reputation, a more solid and enduring reputation than he made by *Personae* and *Exultations*.

To praise Ezra Pound is not to deny that Mr. Drinkwater has charm, that Mr. de la Mare has grace and glamour, Mr. Harold Monro a subtle sense of the ways of trees and animals, that Mr. Siegfried Sassoon is one of the most satisfactory of our war-poets, that there is more passion in four lines of Mr. D. H. Lawrence than in all Elizabeth Barrett Browning, or that Mr. Masefield really can conjure up the smell of a fine hunting morning and the cold, savage magic of the sea. But in this immense and hospitable universe there is room, not only for magic and delight and terror, but for the clear hardness, the civilised polished beauty, the Augustan irony of Ezra Pound.

A poet without passion? There is passion enough in 'The Return'.

[quotes 'The Return', *CSP*, p. 85.]

INSTIGATIONS

New York, 25 April 1920

70. Van Wyck Brooks on Pound as expatriate

June 1920

'Reviewer's Notebook', *Freeman* (16 June 1920), i, 334–5.

Brooks (1886–1963) was an influential American literary critic and historian. This review is collected in *Van Wyck Brooks: The Early Years, A Selection from His Works, 1908–1921*, edited by Claire Sprague (New York: Harper & Row, 1968).

It is quite astonishing still to find young and intelligent persons who can not forgive Ezra Pound for living in England and sticking out his tongue at his native land. It seems to me that if American literature is ever to be really roused it will be largely through the Instigations (to use the apt title of Mr. Pound's new book. . . .) of a band of impenitent gadflies who have nothing to lose and who have got their country into the sort of perspective that comes best from living outside of it. Do you remember in Ibsen's letters how he describes the sensations with which he sailed up the fjord after a ten years' absence from home? 'A feeling of weight settled down on my breast, a feeling of actual physical oppression. And this feeling lasted all the time I was at home; I was not myself under the gaze of all those cold, uncomprehending Norwegian eyes at the windows and in the streets'. That abyss of the exile between Ibsen and his countrymen was indispensable to the growth of a vision that revolutionized in time the whole spiritual life of Norway. I am not suggesting that Ezra Pound is another Ibsen, or that one can not maintain this abyss of exile without crossing the ocean. What I mean is that Ezra Pound has very much at heart the civilization of these United States.

And I am sure he has done more for the new literature in this country than many of those who claim a proprietary right over it.

Horace Brodzky's clever caricature on the paper wrapper of *Instigations* precisely recalls an evening when I dined with Ezra Pound in a little Soho restaurant. I forget whether or not he wore his turquoise ear-rings on that occasion, but the velvet jacket and the protective falsetto voice were enough to impress me. Behind the Struwwelpeter pompadour[1] and the little transparent yellow goat's-beard (in the manner of Watts's Swinburne and the traditional troubadour), one discerned—it was the freckles, perhaps—the Idaho farmer's boy who had cast the skin without losing the spots. Most of Mr. Pound's little expatriate coterie hails from the Valley of Democracy: Mr. John Gould Fletcher is a product of Kansas and Mr. T. S. Eliot of some other quarter in the corn belt. This quite explains their impudence, for there is no sophistication so insolent where it isn't frigid as the sophistication of the exotic Middle Westerner. It was evident that Ezra Pound was on his guard and that his rather insufferable air covered the most familiar of the complexes, but I loved his talk; and while I couldn't at that time make head or tail of his verse, and can't today, I was prepared to believe him a very distinguished man of letters. That was seven or eight years ago. Since then he has emerged from the rather dark and dubious role of the mystagogue, fulfilling the bright and ample promise of his first book, *The Spirit of Romance*.

Mr. Pound is still impudent, he still throws dust in our eyes: in certain characteristics he will probably follow in Whistler's tracks to the end. One has many legitimate causes of complaint against him, not the least of these being that he has all the animus of an outmoded generation in the matter of shocking the grocers. It is really Mr. Pound's loss that he hasn't been able to ally himself with the most vigorous creative forces of our day, on the side, I mean, of the intellectual-proletarian movement. For the first time in generations the aristocrat of the spirit has an opportunity to share, without abating a whit of his artistic conscience, in a great constructive effort of humanity. Because Mr. Pound does not feel this and is consequently obliged to regard humanity as inimical, he expends a good deal of spleen in a manner that strikes us as rather tiresomely out-of-date. He is finical, too, as well as fastidious, as if he wanted to prove his fastidiousness; and he is quite incapable of

---

1 *The English Struwwelpeter: Pretty Stories and Funny Pictures* by Dr Heinrich Hoffmann, an illustrated Victorian book for children, had an illustration of 'Shock-Headed Peter' on the cover, a little boy with an 'afro' hairstyle who 'Never once has comb'd his hair'.

developing an idea. When he downs a victim he stabs him; he can not abolish his prey by a systematic process of reason or ridicule. Nor, on the other hand, can he build up a coherent critique when he most desires the effect of one: witness, in the present volume, the long and brilliant essay on Henry James, a veritable 'chaos of clear ideas.' Finally, he is the most unblushing logroller on record. Ezra's little pound is full of queer stray animals who have become famous because he talks about them so much. He has a way of referring to Eliot and Gaudier-Brzeska as if not to know of them were to inhabit perpetual night.

People used to tell of the extraordinary transformation that took place in Whistler when he set about his work. Off went the tile and the monocle and the swagger stick and the wasp-waisted frock-coat; the paraphernalia of the mountebank vanished; nothing remained but the absorbed gravity of the devoted artist. Ezra Pound's impossibilities are trivial enough beside the conviction that emanates from every one of his pages: of the profound seriousness, I mean, of the business of literature. In this country even the priesthood is a rather pragmatic affair: how can we expect to have the monk of letters? Ezra Pound could hardly have won this conviction even in England where, with few exceptions, the truly devoted writer is devoted because of some extra-artistic element in his work; it is an effect of his association with Paris and the half-legendary example of such men as Mallarmé and Rémy de Gourmont. Grant that his range of sympathies is decidedly narrow, that he makes a perhaps unnecessary parade of his scholarship; you have still to admit that in his atmosphere literature becomes a high, difficult and austere pursuit and that he is within his rights when he speaks to 'the twenty-three students of Provençal and the seven people seriously interested in the technic and æsthetic of verse.' One can not imagine an attitude more vitally important for our literature at the present time than that, not for the generality of writers, but for a few, enough to raise the self-respect of the profession. On one of the obituary notices of Mr. Howells the other day I noticed a quotation from one of his books in which he observed that his early reading gave him, naturally enough, no standing among the other boys. 'I have since found,' Mr. Howells went on, 'that literature gives one no more certain station in the world of men's activities, either idle or useful. We literary folk try to believe that it does, but that is all nonsense. At every period of life among boys or men we are accepted when they are at leisure and want to be amused, and at best we are tolerated rather than accepted.' It was that pusillanimous attitude we found it so hard to forgive in a man of whom we should so gladly have said nothing that is not good, for it vitiated the whole atmosphere of American literature. When I say that Ezra Pound has done us a great service I have in mind the pride with which he upholds the vocation of letters.

Let us also admit that he is an incomparable *causeur*, that he understands the art of literary talk. His criticism is just that. 'Honest criticism, as I conceive it,' he says in the paper on Henry James, 'can not get much further than saying to one's reader exactly what one would say to the friend who approaches one's bookshelf asking: "What the deuce shall I read?" ' Criticism of this kind exacts everything in the way of perception, and Ezra Pound, who is often so extraordinarily clever, is often extraordinarily perceptive too:

If one sought, not perhaps to exonerate, but to explain the Victorian era one might find some contributory cause in Napoleon. That is to say, the Napoleonic wars had made Europe unpleasant, England was sensibly glad to be insular. Emotions to Henry James were more or less things that other people had and that one didn't go into; at any rate not in drawing-rooms.

Most good prose arises, perhaps, from an instinct of negation; is the detailed, convincing analysis of something detestable; of something which one wants to eliminate. Poetry is the assertion of a positive, *i.e.*, of desire, and endures for a longer period. Poetic satire is only an assertion of this positive, inversely, *i.e.*, as of an opposite hatred.

The 'Henry James' exhibits the finest discernment; so does the somewhat arbitrary 'Study of French Poets,' which occupies a hundred pages and offers, with certain rather wayward omissions, a whole anthology of the last forty years; so do the essay on Rémy de Gourmont and some of the reprinted reviews, especially those of James Joyce and Lytton Strachey. There are other pieces in the book that illustrate Ezra Pound's erudition and virtuosity: it is a glittering jumble—'a dance of the intelligence,' to quote a phrase of his own, 'among words and ideas.' A fresh wind of the spirit blows through it from cover to cover, and one has but a single fundamental misgiving. Ezra Pound has inhabited for a long time a universe that consists mainly of Wyndham Lewis, Chinese characters, Provençal prosody, Rémy de Gourmont, *Blast* and the Vortex. These are, quite peculiarly, themes of that limited sort which, if they are pursued too long, turn the best of talkers into a bore. In the name of literature, what can be done to prevent Ezra Pound from becoming a bore?

71. H. L. Mencken, notice, *Smart Set*

August 1920, lxii, 143

Pound's volume is a miscellany of the outlandish—chapters on baroque French poets, very advanced English novelists, and so on. There is even a burlesque on the Book of Genesis. What illuminates the whole is the charm of Pound's unusual personality—his pertinacious bellicosity, his abysmal learning, his delight in the curious. He is perhaps the most extraordinary man that American literature has seen in our time, and, characteristically enough, he keeps as far away from America as possible.

72. 'W. C. Blum' [Dr James Sibley Watson], 'Super Schoolmaster', *Dial*

October 1920, lxix, 422–3

Pound replied to this review: 'Mr. Blum is a wicked man, well disposed toward me, personally, but still wicked. He makes and repeats in slightly altered form, in the *Dial*, the statement that I have pretended that parsing the classics will save American literature, and "make" authors.

' "Parse all the classics, ancient and modern", is the only phrase of his I can verify at the moment. This he calls "Pound's remedy for us", (i.e., American writers).

Mr. Blum is a man of many virtues but that statement is buncumb. The one use of a man's knowing the classics is to prevent him from imitating the false classics.' ('Historical Survey', *Little Review* (Autumn 1921), vii, p. 41.) See also on this the poem 'Cantico del Sole', *CSP*, p. 202.

Dr Watson (b. 1894) was educated at Harvard. He and Scofield Thayer backed the *Dial* during its golden years.

It has been observed that Mr Ezra Pound's critical prose is, as a rule, neither prose nor criticism; and this one is willing to admit, in order to save time and because Mr Pound has admitted it himself with embarrassing frankness. ('This essay on James is a dull grind of an affair, a Baedeker of the continent. . . .') There are still several fixed ideas in *Instigations* and a number of repetitions of cadence that have not been attacked. But a brief and belated review is scarcely the place for this sort of thing, nor for the defence of Mr Pound's method, or lack of it, in judging, which I should some time like to undertake.

An important point, however, about Mr Pound's critical writings, which has been generally neglected, is this: they do satisfy two very conspicuous demands of the American public; the demand for 'constructive criticism,' and the demand for 'first rate school teaching.'

In his essay on James, Mr Pound makes an academic distinction between prose and poetry.

Most good prose arises, perhaps, from an instinct of negation; it is the detailed, convincing analysis of something detestable; of something one wants to eliminate. Poetry is the assertion of a positive, that is, of desire . . .

Well, Mr Pound is a poet. He doesn't write prose; we have admitted that. His destructive remarks are limited to funny oaths and insults; no reasoned attack, no analytic slaughter of the enemy. His time, his energy, he applies to stating, without much fuss, what he finds good, and why.

That people, stupid or not, should demand affirmations and constructive criticism, if only as a novelty, when our young writers are all so busy writing advertisements for a living as to make it impossible for them to praise anything in their off hours, is not surprising. The odd thing is that people should not take pleasure in affirmations when they are handed them. And yet they decidedly do not. We pretend that it is the destructive activities of the Russians of which we disapprove; we were indeed shocked when they murdered the Czar. But we only became really indignant when they began to improvise a government. Thoroughly popular affirmations, one believes, are always either destructive in intent, like patriotism, or insincere, like advertising. Insincerity of tone is the first lesson for the advertiser to learn. Consider the slogans of the day before yesterday: 'All the news that's fit to print,' 'Make the world safe for Democracy.'

All this is intended as an explanation of Mr Pound's failure to impress the multitudes who ask for 'constructive criticism.' If he would wrap up his prejudices in cosmic tendencies and add a little sensational gossip to his technical discussion, he might put over those very unpopular causes, classical learning and modern literature, to a somewhat larger public. But he agrees too well with that public's avowed belief in the necessity for good school-teaching, to do his work in other than schoolmasterly fashion. Apparently he has in mind a special public, a class of students, almost, to whom he is engaged in delivering this correspondence course of lectures. The idea of this class sustains and encourages him. All through *Instigations* we find him admonishing his students: 'Laforgue is an angel with whom our modern poetic Jacob must struggle.' 'If James *had* read his classics. . . .' and so on. He never doubts for a moment that in order to write permanent work, in order to discriminate between permanent and bad work, a man must know the classics from Homer to Gautier. As fast as he can get round to it Mr Pound is filling up the gaps in the curricula of his misguided but indispensable colleagues, the professors; and at the same time he is carrying forward their work from the point where they always leave off and wait for a literary man to clear the way.

Is nobody aware that a contemporary writer is actually giving a course on the Comparative Literature of the Present, that a first rate literary man, a poet, with the rarest gift for translation is bothering to teach school? Poetry lovers may grieve, but Dr Flexner would do well to take notice.

HUGH SELWYN MAUBERLEY

London, June 1920

73. Unsigned review, *The Times Literary Supplement*

1 July 1920, no. 963, 427

The poems of this beautifully printed book have the qualities of structure, rhythm, and sincerity, but they are needlessly obscure. It is an esoteric volume, which evidently has no wish to appeal to more than a small circle of readers, but the author is obsessed by the thought of the greater semi-artistic public; he seems often to be trying to mystify it, and writes always with an eye on it. If he could forget this enmity, his poems would be sweeter and more effective. As they are, they have a mathematical charm.

74. Edwin Muir, review, *New Age*

5 October 1922, xxi, 288

This record of a poet's dealings with his time is full of appropriate acerbity, expressed with an economy which is disdainful. Mr. Pound for some time now has been reduced to throwing his gifts at the heads of his generation; he has made sure beforehand that the bourgeoisie would not applaud, dreading their approbation, justly, more than their resentment. There is no doubt that he is right; it may be, too, that

Philistia is more deeply wounded by something which puzzles it than by something which hits it palpably. One could still wish, however, that the condemnation of our age which is implicitly damning in this book had been explicitly so. The result would have been more illuminating, if not to the Philistines themselves, then to their enemies, who would thus have been strengthened. Mr. Pound's H. S. Mauberley is cryptic, one feels, out of pride, and out of courtesy for the few who will listen to him—a courtesy which takes the form, almost unique in our time, of not assuming that the listener is such a dunce that *everything* needs to be explained to him. It is a kindness which will not be appreciated simply because it will not be seen, for reading has become a special branch of laziness.

Anyone who takes the trouble to peruse this book when he is fully awake will find in it satire without a trace of rhetoric and, in its abnegation of rhetoric, it is more radically moving than it would be with it. Take this bare account entitled 'Ode pour l'Election de son Sépulchre':

[quotes 'E. P. Ode' stanzas 1, 2, 4, 5, *CSP*, p. 205.]

The scorn in these lines is so great that it does not even express itself. And simply because pity is not asked for H. S. Mauberley, our indignation, or, more exactly, our disgust with his time is the greater. There remains that only. The effect of Mr. Pound's lines on the war is the same:

[quotes, with omissions, 'Hugh Selwyn Mauberley' IV, *CSP*, pp. 207–8.]

This indictment, set down with a deliberate contempt for 'literary art,' shows Mr. Pound to be an artist as effective as he was in his early poems. The tragedy is that an artist here tells us that art is no longer possible, and that the only thing we can utter now is our desperation and our contempt.

The tea-rose tea-gown, etc.

says Mr. Pound scornfully.

[quotes 'Hugh Selwyn Mauberley' III stanzas 1–3, *CSP*, p. 206.]

This is not satire, but despair. It is a poet's sin against an age that has sinned grievously against poetry.

UMBRA: THE EARLY POEMS OF EZRA POUND

London, June 1920

75. Edwin Muir, review, *New Age*

22 July 1920, xxvii, 186–7

In this volume Mr. Pound has collected 'all that he now wishes to keep in circulation from *Personæ, Exultations, Ripostes*, etc.' To these he has added a number of translations from Guido Cavalcanti and Arnaut Daniel; and he has appended to the whole the few verses which make up 'the complete poetical works' of the late T. E. Hulme. This collection embodies, we may take it, the author's judgment upon his earlier works, and provides also the material which should enable us to discover what are the qualities which set him apart—so very far apart—from the mass of his contemporary poets.

Mr. Pound's poetry is individual (every critic, of course, says this), and it is imaginative; but it is not in these qualities that it differs so strikingly from contemporary poetry, some of which—a very little, it must be confessed—is also individual and imaginative. The real difference between Mr. Pound and most of the poets of his time is that he is individual and imaginative with distinction. This distinction is never a pose; it is the nuance of the author's individuality which is expressed the more clearly the more sincere is his own expression. It is a sort of fastidious vigour: a subtle form of strength. Mr. Pound's choice of subject-matter and of form, which in many a poet would appear merely precious, appears to be in him perfectly sincere and expressive. He *prefers* the recondite theme and the difficult form, because in dealing with these both his fastidiousness and his vigour find their best opportunity. There is here, once more, no affection, but the desire to find themes and measures which are significant and new, which can be seized imaginatively and made alive.

As an example of the author's combined strength and fastidiousness, perhaps the poem entitled 'A Virginal' could not be bettered.

[quotes 'A Virginal', *CSP*, p. 83.]

How exquisite and how firm that is! The delicacy never becomes mere tenuousness. It is as finished as a sunbeam. Here is another example:—

> subtle as the beauty of the rains
> That hang low in the moonshine and bring
> The May softly among us, and unbind
> The streams and the crimson and white flowers.

The very whispering of Spring showers is in these lines. In another passage in the same poem the author is not so successful:—

> Because of the beautiful white shoulders and the rounded breasts
> I can in no wise forget my beloved of the peach-trees,
> And the little winds that speak when the dawn is unfurled
> And the rose-colour in the grey oak-leaf's fold
>
> When it first comes, and the glamour that rests
> On the little streams in the evening; all of these
> Call me to her, and all the loveliness in the world
> Binds me to my beloved with strong chains of gold.

None of these lines, except the third to the sixth, are distinctively Mr. Pound's. The first two are almost banal, the last two nearer to mere sentimentality than any of the others in the book. The use of the word 'little' twice in four lines is irritating, and in the second instance, at any rate, it does not appear to be relevant. On the next page occur these lovely lines:

> Out of you have I woven a dream
> That shall walk in the lonely vale.

And on the next to that there is this passage:

> The unappeasable loveliness is calling me out of the wind,
> And because your name is written upon the ivory doors,
> The wave in my heart is as a green wave, unconfined,
> Tossing the white foam towards you;
> And the lotus that pours
> Her fragrance into the purple cup,
> Is more to be gained with the foam
> Than are you with these words of mine.

That is fine in its manner, the decorative manner, but, once more, it is not Mr. Pound. Set it against these lines, taken from 'Night Litany':

[quotes 'Night Litany', *CSP*, pp. 40–1 'Yea, the glory' to 'O God of Waters'.]

However artificial the phrasing may *appear*, it will be found that this passage cannot be analysed, nor one jot of its beauty diminished. The purity of the mood, of the words, and of the rhythm is one: the poem is indeed a 'Litany'.

However, the purity—the artistic purity, that is to say—of all the poems in this volume is one of their most striking qualities. Mr. Pound takes art more seriously than it is the custom to take it in this country—or in America; as seriously, in fact, as the French. His artistic severity takes the form of writing upon the theme as the theme dictates. He is sensuous, religious, brutal, romantic, as the subject matter may demand. But, as little as Flaubert's, is his sensuousness or his brutality adventitious. For instance, in the following passage from a rendering of Arnaut Daniel's 'Canzoni' the vigorous curse in the last line is admirable on artistic and not on Masefieldian grounds:

> Disburse
> Can she, and wake
> Such firm delights, that I
> Am hers, froth, lees,
> Bigod! from toe to ear-ring.

Upon Browning, to take another example, he suits the expression to the subject:

[quotes 'Mesmerism', *ALS*, p. 28 'You wheeze' to 'mankin'ards'.]

With this devotion to the theme in its purity, there goes necessarily a total absence of sentimentality. The only two sentimental lines which we have been able to find in the volume we have already quoted. Beside Mr. Pound any poet of to-day will appear sentimental. Occasionally, however, in avoiding the sentimental he falls into the banal. Thus for example in 'Portrait d'une Femme':

> You are a person of some interest, one comes to you
> And takes strange gain away:
> Trophies fished up; some curious suggestion;
> Fact that leads nowhere.

The first line there is written no doubt to get a desired effect. It is written deliberately prosaically, we should say, because Mr. Pound was afraid a more emotional statement would have been sentimental. The result is that it is a banal line, spoiling an otherwise ingenious poem.

It is impossible to do justice to the translations, including the noble 'Seafarer'. They contain, however, not only ingenuity but imagination. They are not renderings, but recreations. The worst poem in the book is the last, 'abbreviated from the conversation of Mr. T. E. H.':

> The Germans have rockets. The English have no rockets.
> Behind the lines, cannon, hidden, lying back miles.
> Before the line, chaos.

Mr. Aldington can do this sort of thing well. But Mr. Pound can write poetry like this:

> Clothed in goldish weft, delicately perfect,
> gone as wind! The cloth of the magical hands!
> Thou a slight thing, thou in access of cunning
> dar'dst to assume this?

76. A. R. Orage on Pound's departure from London

January 1921

'R.H.C.' [A. R. Orage], 'Readers and Writers', New Age (13 January 1921), xxviii, 126–7.

Mr. Ezra Pound has recently gone abroad, perhaps for one year, perhaps for two, perhaps for good. Following the old and, in my opinion, the bad example first set by a man of letters, Landor, Mr. Pound has shaken the dust of London from his feet with not too emphatic a gesture of disgust, but, at least, without gratitude to this country. I can perfectly well understand, even if I find it difficult to approve. Mr.

Pound has been an exhilarating influence for culture in England; he has left his mark upon more than one of the arts, upon literature, music, poetry and sculpture; and quite a number of men and movements owe their initiation to his self-sacrificing stimulus; among them being relatively popular successes as well as failures. With all this, however, Mr. Pound, like so many others who have striven for the advancement of intelligence and culture in England, has made more enemies than friends, and far more powerful enemies than friends. Much of the Press has been deliberately closed by cabal to him; his books have for some time been ignored or written down; and he himself has been compelled to live on much less than would support a navvy. His fate, as I have said, is not unusual: I could parallel it near home and with more than one instance. Taken by and large, England hates men of culture until they are dead. But, all the same, it is here or nowhere that the most advanced trenches of the spirit are to be found; and it is here, I believe, that the enemy will have to be defeated. Mr. Pound has gone, I understand, to France; he is certain sooner or later to find himself in Paris; where the apparent ease of the work of intelligence has flattered many a man of letters that he was contributing to the progress of mankind. A delusion and an illusion! For, in fact, France has long ceased to be in the van of culture and is now, in my judgment, scarcely bringing up the straggling rear. Even with Mr. Pound in it, I expect nothing from Paris for the next quarter of a century. Psychology—I mean psycho-analysis precisely—has not yet learned to speak French, and least of all the French of Paris. And without psychology what is left for Paris but to permute and combine, in ingenious ways but with no essentially fresh results, the pre-war European ideas? Such advance as Europe is capable of making presupposes the taking of a tuck out of the unconscious by a sustained effort of inspiration. The pre-war level or plane of consciousness has been exploited to the last sensation; there is nothing new to be learned on it. The new Europe and the new world depend for their realisation upon the conquest for consciousness of something that has hitherto been unconscious. We look for a dawn that has never dawned before.

Before leaving England, Mr. Pound was generous enough to draw up for publication his intellectual will and testament. On the preceding page is printed, in the form of Axiomata, Mr. Pound's credo, his summary conclusions concerning the nature of the world. I have often expressed the wish that such a statement of philosophy should be made compulsory upon everybody who sets up as critic or creator, as a kind of table of contents or rather potentialities of his mind. Psycho-analysis would know how to make use of such a confession, even if to the general it means little or nothing; for if our dreams are significant for psycho-analysis as indications of our buried thoughts, our thoughts are no less significant as indications of our buried dreams. Creeds, sincerely expressed—and it goes without saying that Mr. Pound's 'Axiomata' are veracious in this sense—define more or less exactly not only the area covered by the mind that formulates them, but, much more importantly, the area of life sought to be included within the mind. They represent more than land under immediate cultivation, they are the stakes that mark out the land which it is hoped one day to bring under cultivation. To put it crudely, the religion, or view of the world, of a race or an individual is nothing more than his or its hopes, ambitions, aspirations, ideals—the kind and extent of which form an index of the amount of vitality of which the race or the individual finds himself or itself in possession. It is from this point of view that it appears to me that a 'Creed' is so desirable in the case of men whose influence, in any event, is likely to be considerable; for we should be able to tell from it, not only what a man is, but what he is on the way to becoming and what, in consequence, he is likely to enable others to become. And since individual self-realisation is the highest purpose of life, it would be no small gain to be able to tell what influences are to be sought and what avoided, whose work is really inspiring and whose deadening, what is 'good' and what is 'bad' in life and, therefore, in art. Literary or artistic criticism, outside a small circle, is altogether too superficial and arbitrary to act as a safe guide. England, for instance, has swallowed rivers of poison in the shape of bad art and literature, much of which has been prescribed as food and tonic by the professional critics. It is possible that the preface of a 'Creed' would save many of these critics their blunders, and put them in the way of realising the character of the spiritual influence under consideration, before they had prescribed it and seen its results in practice.

I shall leave to my readers the pleasant task of interpreting Mr. Pound's 'Axiomata' in terms of life and art, but only after remarking on what appears to me to be the kernel of Mr. Pound's creed—its opening article that 'the intimate essence of the universe is *not* of the same nature as our own consciousness.' Everything else, I think, both in the Creed and in Mr. Pound's work, past, present and future, is implicitly contained in this affirmation, and the more certainly so from the fact that it is at once Mr. Pound's most comprehensive, fundamental and decisive statement. Taking it as the basis of Mr. Pound's Creed, what is to be remarked in it? In the first place, that it is a negative statement, a denial, the reactionary and counter-assertion of a corresponding positive; and, secondly, that the 'consciousness' implied in the phrase 'our own consciousness,' is confined in effect to self-consciousness, waking consciousness, in short, to our normal everyday rational consciousness. But the presence of these elements in the first article of Mr. Pound's Creed is not insignificant; and the evidence is abundant when we transfer our attention from his creed to his work. Writing as a professed literary judge, I should always have said; indeed, I have often said—that the two most serious defects in Mr. Pound's work have been and are his enmity to Religion and his lack of psychological depth. The one has introduced a bizarre atheistic or rationalistic *mannerism* into his style; and the other is responsible for much of his pre-occupation with the *trivialities* of art-forms—studio-talk, as I have called it. The cat is out of the bag for everybody, even without literary judgment, to see for himself now; there it is stalking abroad in the full light of Mr. Pound's explicit article. Mr. Pound's attitude towards Religion (or the world of potentialities—since it is clear that *if* we are not of the same stuff as the 'universe,' the limits of possible knowledge are defined by the actual)—is actively negative, unsympathetic and hostile; and his expectation of 'consciousness' is confined to what may emerge from the self-consciousness alone. Paris, under these circumstances, has nothing to teach and nothing to learn.

POEMS *1918-21*

New York, 8 December 1921

---

77. Maxwell Bodenheim, 'The Isolation of Carved Metal', *Dial*

January 1922, lxxii, 87–91

The massive isolation of Ezra Pound has probably not been surpassed by that of any other poet in any other generation, and seldom equalled. His latest volume gives final emphasis to his position. Coolly immersed in the meanings, deeds, designs, lustres, and peoples of past ages, he regards the present civilization only for moments, and then with a dryly satirical chuckle. His poetry is equally separated from the understanding and appreciation of his generation. The Dadaists dislike his mental coherence, removed from the monotone of careless humour to which they bow, and the conservatives feebly attack him, a little frightened at his erudition and vicious sneer. Between these extremes he must look in vain for greetings. The radicals among young poets and critics, much concerned with the yearnings and turbulence of their day, or with a decorative escape from this turmoil, find him too hard, too dryly aloof. They can take ecstasy from the violently coloured rhetoric of an Amy Lowell—much ado about blues and reds and greens in their relation to overworked emotional significances—or from the chaste miniatures of an H.D., or from the country-lane gossip of a Robert Frost, but Pound, with a cold fire that darts from the intellect, cannot arouse their desire. He insults the surface importance of their own time and their noisily confident relation to this importance; he deals for the most part with past centuries and their contrast with the present one; and his style demands a feverish mental agility on the part of his reader. This combination does not appeal to a young generation that seeks its wisdom from shallower and more brightly tinted substances. His opaque isolation is one of carved metal standing apart from the thin transparencies of a contemporary world, and this position is sternly disclosed in his latest book of verse.

'Homage to Sextus Propertius,' in eleven parts, leads off the volume, but it is the weakest in the collection. Suggested by the Latin of Propertius, this poem has a wearisome length that obeys no visible purpose save to indicate Pound's deliberate fondness for the particular subject-matter at hand—a fondness which in this instance lures him into the polishing of many barren details. Since Pound is noted for the unusual freedom of his translations—a practice that might be profitably adopted by other translators from the Greek and Latin—his poem should be considered as an original creation rising from the hidden foundation of the original work, and indeed, its wording carries the unmistakable stamp of his own style and mental peculiarities. It deals with a Roman's love for a woman, interspersed with passages in which he comments on Roman and Grecian customs, morals, politics, and legends. The result, a mixture of informative volubility and lyrical sensuality, creates a situation in which each element tends to weaken the other, unless one reads the poem twice and effects the separation which has been ignored by the original text. Considering the poem as two poems, the informative one in which the lover remonstrates with his background is coldly verbose, while the more lyrical one is compact, pointed. The latter reveals a sensuality that is self-possessed even in its moments of greatest ardour—a quality also peculiar to Pound's unsuggested work—a sensuality that does not revel with spontaneous blindness, in a manner so dear to the cheated emotions of most critics, but takes the mind into its confidence, desiring a detached and satirical understanding. In its better parts the poem shows an utter absence of rhetoric and a hard, agile style that should not be defended if they have not been detected or appreciated. Criticism should display and embellish without expostulating to those whose ears are bestowed upon other matters, for the latter aim is usually futile and always open to corruption.

Realizing this I shall also avoid an open expostulation with myself in regard to why I do not like 'Langue d'Oc,' the next series of poems in this book. Wittily and candidly, in the enlightened manner of young, modern book-reviewers, I could remonstrate with myself for a time and then return to an adroit reiteration of my original position, but the sport does not move me. Preferring the straight line, I will state that I do not relish folk-songs and ballads, translated or originals, when they are not accompanied by actual music, for their naïve meaning alone on the printed page fails to reward my mind. 'Moeurs Contemporaines' follows the ballads and atones for them with its mild, dry humour, its faintly smiling sophistication. Pound is one of the few men who understand that if you seek to demolish an individual you must do it with an air of abbreviated indifference. The sneer, when extended and detailed, always leaves an impression of frantic animosity that defeats its own purpose. Pound is a master of the indulgent sneer. Lightly, wearily, he points to his subjects; grimaces a moment; and strolls away. The result may be unfair to the person criticized, but it is effective.

The attitude is a natural one to Pound and indicative of his literary isolation from a contemporary world. To him the businessmen, icemen, and housewives, described by American poets and novelists with much detail and emotional gusto, are manikins that barely succeed in becoming amusing at times. This attitude is accentuated and the reason behind it clarified in the next group of poems, 'Hugh Selwyn Mauberley (Life and Contacts)' which is the personal cry of Pound himself. The second part of the opening shows his conception of the background against which his carefully carved isolation stands.

[quotes 'Hugh Selwyn Mauberley' II, *CSP*, p. 206.]

Neatly, gravely, he sums up the defects and limitations of most present-day literature and art, and the broader spirit of the world from which they emerge. In truth, this age 'demands' creations that can be flippant at its own expense without wounding or probing it too deeply, and also asks for a surface realism—'the mould in plaster'—and a feverish succession of gestures that can soothe the prevailing lack of introspective ease. No longer do poets linger over their output. Lady Imagists and novelists, much admired by the younger critics of our day, produce a corpulent volume every year, and often two, seemingly engaged in emulating the men who turn out such an alarming abundance of automobiles and collars in a given period. And this literature, like its more substantial competitors, is apt to be rather monotonous in texture and content. In the course of his summing-up Pound has written the most condensed and deftly sardonic account of the war and its causes that has so far appeared. In thirty-three lines he states the essence of everything that has been written on this subject, compressing the redundant propaganda, realistic horrors, and emotional revolts of all war-poems and novels and stripping them to their effective skeleton. From a variety of emotional motives, most of them surface phantoms, men raced into the strident lies of warfare and then returned to the more passive lies and trickeries of peaceful existence. Their daring, fortitude, and candour exploded with the last roar of the cannons, and those who were still alive returned to the bland subterfuges that had been temporarily abandoned. And the end attained by the dead? Pound answers.

[quotes 'Hugh Selwyn Mauberley' V, *CSP*, p. 208.]

The upheavals and gambles of the present world form a jest to him, and he seeks to escape them by analysing the perfections and ardours of past centuries and by turning his eyes inward upon himself—'the obscure reveries of the inward gaze.' This latter aim is the driving-power of the four Cantos that close his volume. At a first reading, even a careful one, they are apt to appear obscure, and they will be ignored and derided by those who approach poetry for mental and emotional caresses, and quick affirmations of judgement, and not for extremes in mental exercise. Given a mind that is not averse to labouring, provided that a kernel lies beneath the hard shells, you can reach the purpose of these poems. They contain the subconscious matter deposited by years of reading and observation in one man's mind, and in their residence in this sub-conscious state they have blended into the man's mental and emotional prejudices and undergone a metamorphosis, in which they became his visualization and interpretation of past men and events. Legendary heroes, kings, dukes, queens, soldiers, slaves, they live again as this man would have them live, and speak words that are partly his and partly their own, in the manner of übermarionnettes. Their fragmentary and often tangled existence—quick appearances and vanishings—is a distinctive feature of the subconscious state that enclosed them before they were extracted by the poet. The Cantos represent the nervous attempt of a poet to probe and mould the residue left by the books and tales that he has absorbed, and to alter it to an independent creative effect. In places they are far too long, too much a mere catalogue of names and countries, but their purpose is a valid one, and they break into many a passage of hard beauty. They symbolize a quality that rules the work of Ezra Pound—a carved isolation from the men and events immediately surrounding him, and a return to the fundamentals of past creations and ages. He is, indeed, pictured by the last lines of his Seventh Canto:

[quotes *Cantos*, p. 31 'Eternal watches' to 'still features'.]

78. John Peale Bishop, 'The Intelligence of Poets', *Vanity Fair*

January 1922, xvii, 13–14

Eliot's 'La Figlia che Piange' appeared in the Knopf edition of *Poems* (1920).

Bishop (1899–1944) was an American critic, poet and novelist. Edmund Wilson edited his *Collected Essays* in 1948.

Mr. Ezra Pound is not so much a man as a trinity. There is Mr. Pound the poet, Mr. Pound the pedant and Mr. Pound the instigator. The pedant and the author of *Instigations* have frequently of late put the poet out of the house.

I have never doubted that Ezra Pound was a true poet and I do not use the term lightly. 'Blandula, Tenulla, Vagula' from the volume called *Lustra* is pure poetry such as has not often been produced in this country.

[quotes 'Blandula, Tenulla, Vagula', *CSP*, p. 53.]

Mr. Pound knows perhaps better than any living American what poetry should be, and he has been justified in turning to the Troubadours, to the Italian poets of the *dolce stile nuovo*, to Catullus and his contemporaries, as models of that precision which, after the vague rhetoric of the Victorians, it was valuable that poetry should regain. One must, in order not to be a parvenu, find a precedent in the past, or in some literature which has developed upon a different tradition than our own. And once a personal idiom is achieved, no one can gainsay the accomplishment. Masefield found his corrective in Chaucer, and Yeats the model he needed for his plays in the Japanese Noh drama. But Mr. Pound has never stayed long enough in one place to build surely, nor has he been able to secure a permanent color by blending his dyes. It is true that, after all the ransacking has been done in the books read, something still remains which is the essential Pound. And it is this Pound, nervous, harrassed by modernity and yet loving the Attic grace, the Pierian roses, which brings one again and again to whatever he has written.

His failure to realize his high talent, his inability to create a style always at his service, cannot, I think, be wholly charged against him. He is of those poets who must take their images out of old books or legends of the countryside, who cannot deal with life directly but must transmute it into something strange in their own minds. Had he been content to remain in America, and could he have found here some such material as Yeats found waiting to his hand when he returned to Ireland, he might, I think, have been a poet such as is more than any other needed in this country.

'Homage to Sextus Propertius' is a learned account of the love affair whose actual history shines through pages of Roman history, the pilferings from classical literature superfluously pasted across it. Thinking perhaps of the excuse which Propertius made to Maecenas for celebrating his own Cynthia rather than the epic wars of Rome, Mr. Pound offers a precedent for devoting himself to a love poem at a time of such worldly tumult. 'Moeurs Contemporaines' and the carefully distorted self-portraits published under the guise of 'Hugh Selwyn Mauberley' are elliptical, cooly wrought, delicately pointed satires, but there is nothing here so poignant as the poems of T. S. Eliot in a similar genre.

This will perhaps indicate their quality; incidentally it seems a just appraisal on the part of the poet of his own work.

[quotes 'Mauberley 1920' from 'Hugh Selwyn Mauberley', *CSP*, p. 216.]

'Envoi' has a lyricism which Mr. Pound seldom permits himself these days, comparable, perhaps, to 'La Figlia Che Piange' of Eliot. The final appraisal of the book must, however, depend on the six Cantos with which it concludes. I shall have to learn at least three more languages and read seven years before I shall pretend to recognize all the references, but patchwork of erudition, of phrases in five tongues and paraphrased as it is, it still contains much that is pure poetry.

79. Brian Howard on Pound's 'clean, white spirit of disinfection'

March 1922

From 'The New Poetry', *Eton Candle* (March 1922), I, 16–19.

This essay in advocacy of *vers libre* and the 'new poetry' was written when Howard was seventeen and at Eton. Rereading it in 1963, Cyril Connolly, Howard's contemporary at Eton, wrote that 'it might have saved me because it would have brought me Ezra Pound as an influence. Pound's poetry formed a bridge by which one could have crossed over from the classics like Catullus and the early French and Provençal poetry which I loved into the modern idiom instead of remaining bogged down in Flecker and Housman. In 1922 very few senior magazines bothered about Pound and Howard's flair was remarkable' quoted in *Brian Howard: Portrait of a Failure*, edited by Marie-Jacqueline Lancaster (London: Anthony Blond, 1968), p. 56.

Howard (1905–1957) was an English journalist and writer.

Disassociated from any particular movement is Ezra Pound, the greatest living writer of *vers libre*. This genius is deplorably ill read, and having been practically hounded into those refuges of good writers, the American journals, one feels that he has been, in England, very badly treated; not that he cares two hoots—probably. However, I do wish he would write for English papers some of the articles one gathers in those excellent periodicals of New York, the *Little Review* and the *Dial*. But then, of course, he writes *vers libre*. . . .

Ezra Pound has an amazing erudition, an unsurpassable technique, and poetic vision of the first order. Just because he is violently interested in the pre-Renaissance literature of Latin Europe there is no need to murmur things about his being an obscurantist. Nonsense!

It is very upsetting when one realises that here is *another* great writer whose recognition will probably come twenty years late. More

Mammon of Righteousness. . . . It is the same thing, of course, with that most deserving of poets—Ford Madox Hueffer.

Pound is another master of this clean, white spirit of disinfection—this modernist irony. His 'Ancora' is an instance. . . .

> Good God! they say you are *risqué*,
> O canzonetti!
> We who went out into the 4 a.m. of the world
> Composing our albas,
> We who shook off our dew with the rabbits,
> We who have seen Artemis a-binding her sandals,
> Have we ever heard the like?
> O Mountains of Hellas!!

And to 'Formianus' Young Lady Friend' . . . Let us quote some more —'Fish and the Shadow'. . . .

> The salmon-trout drifts in the stream,
> The soul of the salmon-trout floats over the stream
> Like a little wafer of light.
> . . . .
> Light as the shadow of the fish
> That falls through the pale green water.

And that superb piece of *vers libre*, 'The Return'. . . .

> See, they return; ah, see the tentative
> Movements, and the slow feet,
> The trouble in the pace and the uncertain
> Wavering!

I wish there was room to quote the rest.

And now, as an example to the average *London Mercury* poet, with his Varsity *naïveté*, here is a really fresh, charming poem of the ingenuously picturesque type. It is by Pound. 'An Immorality'. . . .

> Sing we for love and idleness,
> Naught else is worth the having.
> Though I have been in many a land,
> There is naught else in living,
> And I would rather have my sweet,
> Though rose leaves die of grieving,
> Than do high deeds in Hungary,
> To pass all men's believing.

Space prohibits me from quoting 'Further Instructions' and 'Deux

Mouvements', but for an end I will rehearse Pound's encouragement to the fighters against Mammons. 'The Rest'. . . .

> O helpless few in my country,
> O remnant enslaved!
> . . . .
> You of the finer sense,
> Broken against false knowledge. . . .
> Hated, shut in, mistrusted.
> Take thought:
> I have weathered the storm,
> I have beaten out my exile.

What enrages me is that he should have been compelled to beat it out. . . .

80. Harriet Monroe, a retrospective view of Pound

May 1925

From 'Ezra Pound', *Poetry* (May 1925), xxvi, 90–7. Two excerpts from the beginning of this article are printed as No. 6.

'Yes, I saw your article', Pound wrote to Harriet Monroe on 30 November 1926, 'if you mean the one that says what a delightful writer I used to be, and what a shame I have probably petered out. Also you blame Wabash for doing in 1907 very much what you did in 1917, n'est-ce pas?' (*Letters*, pp. 278–9).

Re-reading those early poems now, after fifteen years of close attendance upon modern poets, I feel once more that old appeal of strangeness and beauty—'for there is no excellent beauty without strangeness'. Later experimenters have not reiterated Pound's special magic, newer singers have not sung his tune. 'La Fraisne', with its quiet and perfect measures carrying the wistful wisdom of old age; 'Night Litany',

weighted with the wonder of Venice; the slim whiteness of 'N.Y.';
the swift speed of 'The Return'; the splendid wave-pounding of 'The
Seafarer', best translation ever made from Anglo-Saxon; and especially
one of the noblest of all Christ poems, the 'Ballad of the Goodly Fere':
all these keep their power and their surprise for me, as well as the
haunting beauty of their music.

It was somewhat a twelfth-century revival, that music. Ezra Pound's
early poems, after the rich orchestration of centuries of English poetry,
sound to our inner ear like Palestrina after Wagner, Schubert, Beethoven. Their wayward cadences owe something, of course, to the
Provençal poets whom he had so closely studied, something to Villon,
something to Yeats. They recapture primitive simplicities and discard
efficient regularities. They play with rhyme or not, they keep time with
metrics or not, but always they follow their own wilful way and ride
the changing winds of mood as lightly as a swallow.

The same wayward beauty inspires many of the songs in *Lustra*,
published in London in 1916, most of which passed through my hands
to the first printing. The motive here is more audacious, indeed often
satiric; the music more emphatic for either gay or serious emotion,
with less of the Provençal plaintiveness. To the early readers of *Poetry*
these poems seemed to usher in an almost anarchistic revolution in the
art; but today, after a surfeit of free and freer verse, of gymnastic
experiment in poetic motive, rhythm, typography, we read them with
as matter-of-course acceptance of their method as of Shelley's or Swinburne's. And in many of them we feel a surer, though often wilder,
strain of the *Personae* harmonies. Such poems as 'Dance Figure', 'The
Garret', 'The Garden', 'Ortus', 'Preference', 'Fish and the Shadow', the
poignant third part of 'Near Perigord', the high-comedy-perfect 'Villanelle: The Psychological Hour'—these and others are exquisitely
wrought, with added assurance, in a method that rounds out and com-
pletes, sometimes with even keener beauty, the earlier experiments.

Other poems in this book were, of course, a deliberate satiric challenge. It began, for example, with 'Tenzone':

[quotes 'Tenzone', *CSP*, p. 91.]

This challenge the poet repeated, sometimes even more impudently,
in 'Salutation', 'Further Instructions', 'Salvationists', etc.; and with more
confessional feeling in his 'Pact' (with Walt Whitman), and in his
consolatory advice to 'The Rest':

[quotes 'The Rest', *CSP*, pp. 101–2.]

The effect of the challenge, when it was first uttered in *Poetry* in 1913, and re-enforced by other poets of the imagist group, was immediate and dynamic. It was due more to Ezra Pound than to any other person that 'the revolution' or 'the renaissance,' or whatever one chooses to call the freer modern impulse in poetry, was on. Thus, without slurring the quality of his poetry, one may admit that most people who have watched the course of this impulse, think of Ezra Pound first as a force. If, as Carl Sandburg said in a study of his work, 'he has done most of living men to incite new impulses in poetry,' the reason is not only the lithe impassioned *insouciance* of his verse, but still more the ardent professorial rage in him—the love of stirring up and leading forth other minds. There are many so-called educators in our over-instructed world, but few inspired teachers. Ezra Pound is one of the few, and that college in Indiana which once let him go from its faculty must have made the gods weep for its blunder.

Its blunder, but not ours. For the instinct of a great teacher was released from contact with undergraduates and applied to the vivifying of a sleeping art. His method has been fiercely destructive of rooted prejudices, but magically encouraging to every green shoot of new growth. His mind, being imaginatively creative, presented example as well as precept, offered beautiful poems to the world. But not all his work could be printed in books; he must make these books seed the future, he must found a school. So inevitably he gathered a group of poets around him, and reached out through them to ever widening areas of influence; until today there is no one writing the poetry of this age and the next who has not, consciously or not, felt the impact of his mind.

It is this sheer power which made him, to quote Sandburg again, 'the best man writing poetry today'—the best man in the pugilistic sense of utter prowess, in not only writing poetry but making it effective and powerful by ramming it down people's throats. Today 'Salutation,' 'Further Instructions,' etc., having done their work, have lost some of their force; the modern undergraduate, probably, can hardly understand the excitement they aroused—the dust of ages, or at least of decades, which they shook into the startled air. But the modern undergraduate owes to them, for the clearer air he breathes, more than he will ever realize.

Part of Ezra Pound's passion of revolt against Victorian excesses came, as I have hinted, from his study of foreign poetry, especially the light-winged lyrics of mediaeval Provence. Thus translations—from Provençal, early Italian, Latin of the decadence, even Chinese (through

213

Fenollosa et al.)—have gone hand in hand with his own work and have shared its personal and original tang. There be scholars, specialists in these various literatures, who question his competence as a translator; indeed, Professor Hale made out an extremely good case in a certain memorable controversy about the Propertius series. But although Mr. Pound seems proved an inexact Latinist, and for aught I know may be, to a less flagrant degree, inexact in the other languages, he does catch and pass on from those old poets something which usually escapes more careful scholars—he gives us an effluence, an atmosphere, a breath of perfume, more expressive of their feeling and environment than the most literal translation of their precise words. In short, he strives for, and sometimes attains to a rare degree, a poet's imaginative re-creation of another poet's feeling and rhythm; and this is the only kind of translation which can have any value as literature.

But there is danger in this preoccupation with old authors. Of late I have felt that Ezra Pound was sinking too deep in mental easy-chairs of the library, that he was paying the penalty of too much specialization, of isolation with literary groups, apart from the constructive forces which are making the next age. Super-sophistication is more desiccating than ignorance—the artist needs to refresh himself continually at the primal springs of life, by intercourse with simpler people who plant and build and invent, and with powerful people who do these things mightily and direct the energies of the world. Ezra Pound's art of late, instead of broadening out and reaching up, has narrowed down to a merely literary inspiration. It has lost its freshness and become secondary, deriving from books of the past instead of life of the present, and refining often to trivial excess. I cannot follow with sympathy his clever seven Cantos, and in the volume *Poems 1918–21* I find little of that swift keenness of emotional and musical motive which I tried to analyze above. Apparently his inspiration has been intense rather than rich, a youthful fire rather than an enduring light: as with Coleridge, the critical and professorial habit may prove stronger than the poetic mood. And yet—and yet—no prognostication may serve us; at any moment this poet, or indeed any other, may surprise detraction with a masterpiece.

But whether or not he ever offers us more songs, his best work has already the completeness of adequate beauty. As a leader, a revolutionist in the art, he will have a place in literary history; as a poet he will sing into the hearts and minds of all free-singing spirits in the next age—and perhaps in the ages beyond reach of our prophecy.

A DRAFT OF XVI CANTOS

Paris, January 1925

81. Glenway Wescott, review, *Dial*

December 1925, lxxix, 501–3

In a letter to the editor in January 1970 Glenway Wescott recalled that he first read Pound in 1921: 'In the Spring of 1921, Miss Monroe employed me for a while as the magazine's [i.e., *Poetry's*] office boy. All of us at the University [of Chicago], even Yvor Winters, who was my close friend in those years, respected Pound as a poet; [I] yielded enthusiastically to his every critical recommendation; [and] read everything that seemed to him important.' When Wescott met Pound in Paris in 1925, his respect was 'undermined a little by my having realized the bias and limitation of his understanding of French literature'.

Wescott (b. 1901) is an American novelist, author of *The Grandmothers* (1927), *Good-Bye, Wisconsin* (1928); a collection of essays, *Images of Truth*, appeared in 1962.

Not long ago Mr. Pound galloped up and down the frontier of criticism like an early American general, cursing the enemy, firing his recruits, and embarrassing the fearless with decorations of praise. The gallant fighter appears to have withdrawn from the hubbub; precocious children now mature in black ignorance, the makers of plaster casts grow rich, uncursed. He devotes his retirement no less than his notoriety to music and verse; the music is composed in forgotten modes, for the flute, and the poems have all been cantos.

From time to time a canto, like a block of cumbersome, streaked marble, has appeared in one of the few brave magazines, as if on a pedestal of temporary stucco and obscured by scaffolding. Hearsay has numbered them by the hundred; sixteen are here assembled, with pseudo-childish drawings by Mr Henry Strater, in an awkwardly ostentatious volume. Singly, they astounded the reader with tough magnificence; the group is an almost impenetrable mass, for they give each other little aid. The structure of the individual cantos is too subtle to be enjoyed; or perhaps there is no structure, perhaps this is a rag-bag like Sordello. Mr Pound has never been a narrator; as a critic he was rarely able to give an orderly account of an idea; and if they are to multiply until they form an epic, it seems likely to be a labyrinth with a fine, half-materialized ghost for Ariadne.

The epic subject appears to be the birth or births of art; the brevity of perfection; Golden Ages and a present hell. The canto in which Odysseus raises ghosts and that in which the ship's passenger turns into God ('Safe with my lynxes, feeding grapes to my leopards') are very suitably the first; for the whole work's power is that of an hallucination. The civilized Italian brigands quarrel and erect monuments through several cantos: the rudest diction moving in the most royal processions. Kung utters the principles of Mr Pound's passion in a flawless canto:

Without character you will be unable to play on that instrument . . . When the prince has gathered about him all the savants and artists, his riches will be fully employed.

There follows an intimate hell, more horrid than Dante's, and intolerably up to date, full of names from Who's Who spelled with asterisks. It is a bird's-eye view; there is nothing poignant in the spectacle; the mention of death gives refreshment. The horror is redundant, but verbally sonorous.

The common reader is confused by the names of people (Greek, Chinese, Provençal, and fantastic), by the names of places, by a Tower of Babel medley. Row on row of chiselled heads; exploits and emotions of centuries, all having an air of contemporaneity by comparison with which a newspaper is written in a dead language; dates of first editions mingled with dates of suicides from balconies. In between Tuscans and Greeks drift husks of modern men, husks of their voices, and restless Mongolians 'using the long moon for a churn-stick.' Mr Pound's scholarship does not leave one prostrate with faith, but it is unimpeachable. Professors may complain, professors have complained; we still prefer living sculpture to the genuine, dead, stuffed animal. He is not quietly erudite—the pedant approaches knowledge with deference; he is knowledge's lover, speaking of it and to it an intimate idiom which is sometimes gibberish. The slurs and telescopic compressions are like those of one man's memory: reminiscences of a poet who has never died, comparing the courts where civilizations were born as confusedly as a true traveller talks of hotels and views.

Though only a 'draft' of a fragment, the Cantos are one of the most glorious of those long poems in whose construction common sense takes no part, those poems like cities in a vision, swarming and burning and smoky, which are the glory and affliction of this period. The rhythm is breathless and breath-takingly beautiful. Flaubert was not content until he could deliver his paragraphs at the top of his voice; Mr Pound has perfected a cadence which can only be whispered: Southern music reinforced by hard, hyphenated nouns and consonants roughly repeated. A sense of intimate gods:

> Salmon-pink wings of the fish-hawk
> cast grey shadows in the water,
> The tower like a one-eyed great goose
> cranes up out of the olive-grove,
>
> And we have heard the fauns chiding Proteus
> in the smell of hay under the olive-trees,
> And the frogs singing against the fauns
> in the half-light.

An account of evocations which is evocation. A lovely animation among old clothes of 'museum quality':

> With pheasant tails upright on their forelocks,
> The small white horses, the
> Twelve girls riding in order, green satin in pannier'd habits;
> Under the baldachino silver'd with heavy stitches. . . .
> Boats drawn on the sand, red-orange sails in the creek's mouth.

Immortal souls with profiles of well-blown glass:

> Eternal watcher of things,
> Of eyes, of men, of passions.
> Eyes floating in dry, dark air.

An old wisdom in tears. These are his gifts. His early middle-age may be his youth as a poet; and as a civilizer and defender of the arts, he has already a life-time's ardour behind him. 'The blossoms of the apricot blow from the east to the west': he has 'tried to keep them from falling'.

PERSONAE: THE COLLECTED POEMS OF EZRA POUND

New York, 22 December 1926

82. Ford Madox Ford, 'Ezra', *New York Herald Tribune Books*

9 January 1927, sect. vii, 1, 6

Pound referred to this review with pleasure in a letter to his mother on 24 January 1927 (YL, 849).

Ford published it in his *New York Essays* (New York, 1927).

It is now over fifteen years since Miss May Sinclair brought 'Flaming Youth' to the decorative offices of 'The English Review.' 'Flaming Youth' brought with it a poem called 'The Goodly Fere.' . . .

> A master o' men was the Goodly Fere,
>   A mate of the wind and the sea,
> If they think they ha' slain our Goodly Fere
>   They are fools eternally.
>
> I ha' seen him eat o' the honeycomb
>   Sin' they nailed him to the tree.

And the ballad of 'The Goodly Fere' set the Thames on fire.

It set the Thames on fire and then incomprehensible rows began. They were to me incomprehensible and they so remain. 'The Goodly Fere' had not been published a week when the late Edward Thomas, a scrupulous and delicate poet, wrote for me a review of it, in which he declared that it was one of the greatest poems that has ever been written; but the review had hardly got through the press before Thomas wired to me asking me to withdraw the review. Ezra had been treading on his toes. And let that stand for the whole career of Ezra. To-day, once more, 'The Goodly Fere,' with his companions, falls on my no longer editorial desk, and here I am, hoping that it may cause the incineration, if not of the Hudson, at least of the East River. Then Ezra will stamp on my toes good and strong, and so shall history repeat itself.

I have been accustomed to say in my haste that of all the unlicked cubs whose work I have thrust upon a not too willing world, Ezra was the only one who did not subsequently kick me in the face. And so he was a good fellow. I do not mean to say that during sixteen years of close intimacy he has not caused me pain that has amounted to anguish. To begin with, his accent is so appallingly Pennsylvanian—let those who fear expatriates be reassured!—that with all the experience I have had of cis-Atlantic intonation I invariably fail to understand one-half of his talk. He, living in Europe, is so aggressively trans-Atlantic that, mild Briton as I am, I have found him trying at times. In this country I seldom hear America mentioned. But in Paris, God bless you. . . . Once, overwhelmed by, buried under the swarms of Middle Westerners mostly, that there beset the landscape, fill the coffee cup and deafen the ear with endless talk of the wonders that happen where Old Glory flies and of the meagreness characteristic of places where she doesn't—overwhelmed and exhausted I seized a pencil and wrote on the restaurant tablecloth:

> Heaven overarches earth and sea,
> Earth sadness and sea-hurricanes;
> Heaven overarches you and me;
> A little while and we shall be,
> Please God, where there is no more sea
> And no—say—Middle Westerners.

I forget the rhyme. . . . Mr. Ernest Hemingway, I dare say, was holding an immense fist under my nose and assuring me that English is written only to the west of Nebraska, or it may have been Chicago. . . . He was insisting that *we* English change the name of our tongue. . . .

At any rate, the Paris–American, the Rome–American, the London and the Berlin–American could give any fervent home-stayer seven lengths and a beating in the way of patriotism. It must be like that if you think of it. So do not imagine that I am preaching treason to you when I say that you will be something less than a reader of poetry if you do not read the poems of Ezra Pound.

But, indeed, that man has made me suffer. . . . I have had a try a most things, and there was a time when I aspired to be the *arbiter elegantiarum* of the British metropolis. So, of a morning, I would set out on my constitutional, arrayed in the most shining of top hats, the highest of Gladstone collars, the most ample of black-satin ties, the longest tailed of morning coats, the whitest of spats, the most lavender of trousers. Swinging a malacca cane with a gold knob and followed by a gray Great Dane I used to set forth on a May morning to walk in the park among all of rank and all of fashion that London had to show.

Now, to the right of me lived a most beautiful lady. She was so beautiful that Mr. Bernard Shaw broke up the City Socialist Club by drinking champagne out of her shoe. But when she was not wearing sandals on bare feet, draped herself in a tiger's hide and walked bareheaded and slung with amber beads. Of a morning, being a faithful housekeeper, she also carried a string bag, which usually contained red onions, visible through the netting.

Well, almost as soon as I stood on my doorstep Fate would send that Beautiful Lady bearing down on me. At the same moment from the left Ezra would bear down. Ezra had a forked red beard, luxuriant chestnut hair, an aggressive lank figure: one long blue single stone earring dangled on his jawbone. He wore a purple hat, a green shirt, a black velvet coat, vermillion socks, openwork, brilliant tanned sandals . . . and trousers of green billiard cloth, in addition to an immense flowing tie that had been hand-painted by a Japanese Futurist poet.

So, with the Beautiful Lady on my left and Ezra on my right, Ezra scowling at the world and making it fencer's passes with his cane, we would proceed up Holland Park Avenue. The Beautiful Lady in the most sonorous of voices would utter platitudes from Fabian Tracts on my left, Ezra would mutter Vorticist truths half inaudibly in a singularly incomprehensible Philadelphia dialect into my right ear. *And I had to carry the string bag. . . .*

If only he would have consented to carry it, it would have been all right. I have never objected to being seen in the company of great poets and beautiful ladies, however eccentrically dressed. As it was, few of the damned can have suffered more.

I understand that Mr. Pound had to leave London because he sent a challenge—to fight a duel with swords—to Mr. Lascelles Abercrombie, a poet, because Mr. Abercrombie had published in *The Times Literary Supplement* an article in praise of Milton.

In England it is a crime to send challenges to British subjects. I am sure Ezra has committed no other misdemeanor or laches in the course of his career. He is the swashbuckler of the Arts. I rather wish he was not. But most poets take to drink, narcotics, lechery, meanness—to some form of derivative. Ezra takes it out in writing abuse of fools in hideous prose that is seldom quite comprehensible. If there is an abuse to remedy Ezra discharges a broadside of invective in unusual jargon at the head of the oppressor. There is no abuse in the world that he has not sought thus to blot out.

Instead of drugs he stupefies himself with the narcotic of reform. In that he is very American—but what a poet!

For me the most beautiful volume of poems in the world is Ezra's *Cathay*—poems supposedly from the Chinese, but does it matter whether they are from the Chinese any more than it matters whether Fitzgerald's Omar or Baudelaire's Poe are from the East or the West respectively?

[quotes 'The River-Merchant's Wife: A Letter', *CSP*, pp. 140–1; and 'Poem by the Bridge at Ten-Shin', *CSP*, pp. 141–2 'March has come' to 'and girls dancing.']

Now, is not that delicate? Is not that beautiful? Are not the lovely words arranged as only a master of language could arrange them? . . . And if you want the Literature of Escape, to where better could you escape than to Cathay?

The quality of great poetry is that without comment as without effort it presents you with images that stir your emotions; so you are made a better man; you are softened, rendered more supple of mind, more open to the vicissitudes and necessities of your fellow men. When you have read 'The River Merchant's Wife' you are added to. You are a better man or woman than you were before.

My ears are continually deafened by those who object to the work of Mr. Pound—by those who allege that he is erudite! Just heavens! he is no more erudite than any man of considerable knowledge of the world. In literature it is no matter whether your knowledges arises from an intimate knowledge of life in the Bronx or the Tombs in 1926, or from an intimate knowledge of life in China to-day, in France in the fourteenth century, or in Carthage of the time of Hannibal. I have never heard of any one objecting to Miss Mary Johnston because she displayed an erudite knowledge of the seventeenth century, or to myself because I have written novels about the fourteenth, or to Mr. Erskine because he is a classical scholar. It would appear then to be merely captious to object to Mr. Pound placing his poems among the troubadours, the Chinese, or in the days of Sigismundo Malatesta. Time—any given moment of time—goes so swiftly and so irrevocably that there is no day that can proudly claim immortality for itself. The Broadway trolley of to-day is no more permanent a type than was the old horse stage that I can remember running down Fifth Avenue, and the Bowery slang of Stephen Crane is as *fade* as the prose correspondence style of the 1820's. So that it matters very little where or at what date a poet places his poems. What is requisite is that he should be erudite in his knowledge of the human heart.

You *can't* limit literature to New York or even to the Middle West and the year 1927 . . . and young Australian poets in the year 2050 will be complaining of the fatal influence of the poems of Ezra Pound on antipodal verse. But the heart of man will remain eternally the same as, back through endless centuries, it has manifested itself.

I have always myself when writing verse tried to make it like the utterances of an English gentleman of to-day, speaking quietly and intimately into some one's ear. That is my personal ambition, but it has never been my ambition to limit poetry to the utterances of English gentlemen, and I cannot see why the New Yorker or the Middle Westerner should seek to imprison the Muse exclusively in his *parages*.

That is an ambition to me incomprehensible.

And what amazes me in reading right through at a sitting or two the collected poems of Mr. Pound is that more and more he assumes the aspect of a poet who is the historian of the world and who is far more truly the historian of the world than any compiler of any outline of history.[1]

In the Cantos, that intimate work, of which only a portion has been published in the stately and beautiful volume that Mr. William Bird printed in Paris [*A Draft of XVI Cantos*, 1925], Mr. Pound is avowedly writing a history of the Mediterranean basin. The Cantos are not included in the 'Collected Poems' because presumably their series is not completed, but even the 'Collected Poems' cover and illuminate a great space of time and of ground. To read the 'Ballad of the Goodly Fere' is to make the intimate acquaintance of a companion of Our Lord. To read the 'Impressions of Voltaire' is to have a flashlight thrown upon the personality of the author of *Candide*, and to read the 'Alba' that follows is to know a great deal of the frame of mind of the troubadours:

[quotes 'Alba', *CSP*, p. 189.]

As for modernity, from 'Les Millwin' to 'Mr. Nixon', the 'Collected

[1] H. G. Wells's famous *The Outline of History* appeared in 1919-20.

Poems' bristle with it, and what is the 'Homage to [Sextus] Propertius' but a prolonged satire upon our own day, as if Propertius should come to New York or London or any other Anglo-Saxon Capital?

For me, indeed, glancing rapidly through the pages of these 'Collected Poems' is like taking a look through a newspaper. The aggressive titles of the poems give you tidings of wars, atrocities, murders, adulteries—of heaven knows what, taking place heaven knows where. Indeed, should the long-awaited visitor from Mars arrive at last and desire the news for the last two thousand years he could not, if he desired a rapid impression, couched in vivid and often violent phrases, he could not do better than buy and read Mr. Pound's beautiful volume. Let us take 'Mr. Nixon' as a final example of Mr. Pound's satirical methods. It should go home to the hearts of all young poets. Certainly it would go home to mine were I young and a poet.

[quotes 'Mr. Nixon' from 'Hugh Selwyn Mauberley', *CSP*, pp. 211–12.]

So with his collected poems Mr. Pound sets out, another Bertran de Born, splendidly swaggering down the ages. Another Bertran de Born, indeed, poking out his flame-colored forked beard into the faces, menacing with his cane the persons of the Kings of England, of France, of Navarre and of all the big business and of all the meannesses of the universe. They will probably hang him as the Kings of France and Navarre and England so nearly did for Bertran at Alto Forte. But I don't know that one can ask for much better than to have lived a life of sturt and strife and to die by treachery.

One more picture comes back to me, Mr. Pound is an admirable, if eccentric, performer of the game of tennis. To play against him is like playing against an inebriated kangaroo that has been rendered unduly vigorous by injection of some gland or other. Once he won the tennis championship of the south of France, and the world was presented with the spectacle of Mr. Pound in a one-horse cab beside the *Maire* of Perpignan or some such place. An immense silver shield was in front of their knees, the cab was preceded by the braying *fanfare* of the city and followed by defeated tennis players, bullfighters, banners and all the concomitants of triumph in the South. It was when upon the station platform, amid the plaudits of the multitude, the *Maire* many times embraced Mr. Pound that I was avenged, for the string bag and even for the blue earring!

83. William Carlos Williams on Pound's exile

February 1927

From 'Ezra Pound: His Exile As Another Poet Sees It', *New York Evening Post Literary Review* (19 February 1927), vii, 1, 10.

There are men who can tell it by crosses on their hands, who know that all knowledge except a sort is futile. They are not to be discovered under the exigencies of 'the academy': Ezra Pound found it hard going at Penn. He seemed then to be one of the few who have made out what life is about.

Why does one write? One writes and that's the answer. What does one write? That's the sensible question. Pound wrote down fragments for a direction across the dead drift of literature. I mean 'literature' was the chance material which was handy to him as a youngster, and he wasn't going to let them twist it out from between his fingers for any purpose, not even for the sake of 'poetry' or anything else. This, I mean, is what he wrote.

'Literature', 'Science', 'art', 'the museums', 'the universities' are largely conspiracies of dullness against youth and youth is always hard put to escape them—and get informed. Pound was able to do that.

This is about his poetry.

You see people walking the streets in America: they seem all right— fine legs, smart eyes and the rest of it, up and down the scale—so that you really wonder what is the matter with them. But certainly you never think of Poe in connection with them, nor of Walt Whitman, nor even of Emerson, as in Germany you would think of Goethe or some great musician, and in France, seeing them sitting about the cheap cafés or stacking turnips in *Les Halles*, you think, of the Impressionists calling them over on the fingers by name, and so on, to Molière or, it may be, Cocteau. In England it is Shakespeare. In Italy it begins with Dante or Giotto, etc., etc. But here the pageant lacks point. . . .

Quite suddenly you realize that the people have no heads.

This is the effect that produces injuries upon itself like a rooster that bumps the stump of his neck against the block where he was nonplussed: Prohibitions and the especially complicated fire-engine mechanism of the courts made to capture and torment each isolate and individual 'sinner' among us, one by one, enthroning him for a moment, through pressroom madness and efficiency, in the white glare of our adoration before his heart is torn out and the carcass thrown to justice—as we would have liked to have thrown Ezra Pound if we had had the opportunity in the days of his first successes.

The American concept is lacking a head toward life. It is this which Ezra Pound has perceived for nigh onto thirty years in these here parts dod blarst his dirty hide—trying to make us out to be no better than a pack of menials. And so at Penn, while Schelling dogmatically expounded upon the theory of blank verse in the plays of William Shakespeare, Pound would be turning the pages of his own priceless manuscripts or, forbidden that adjustment, he would take out an immense tin watch and wind it with elaborate deliberation. This was Pound at his best in the puppy stage.

Searching for a head to us he finds it logically in the arts and not as Bernard Shaw—who is cracked about one thing, then about another— looking for the same head, might have found it, first in this, then that, then the other. Pound has found the missing head in poetry and, first to last, he has continued the gesture of sticking to that—a fine gesture not entirely accountable to his much-spoken-of inability to write prose.

For purposes of art, naturally, the people of a country do not need to be gifted with heads, but headed or headless, rich or poor, the material becomes plastic in the hands of him who can use it. But if the material is headless, the man who reduces himself to the same condition in order to be 'true' in dealing with it proves himself to be no more than a jackass.

But if a writer, a poet, an artist, exerting his head, intimates that he knows what he is about and why—Pound prefers people with heads. He doesn't find it essential that his material be stupid.

This is subversive reasoning leading top-speed in a republic to bloodshed and revolution. Pound left the university without waiting to complete his thesis for a doctor's degree and in the same year, 1908, I think, settled in London. He had not been exactly driven out of our society, but certainly he was not exactly a voluntary exile either.

So he is spending his life searching in antiquity and elsewhere for proof of his assertions—that the head of America, as in the case of every other country or civilization that ever existed, cannot be elsewhere than in the arts—searching for men who have lived well as proof of the supremacy of a heady life. And that's what his work is, personae: A proof that men still exist as once they existed—blooded through the arts and especially through poetry. This was the firm feeling Pound had always for Browning, whom for many years at this time he deeply admired.

Nothing America could have done to get the intolerable head we so badly needed would have been better than to have enthroned Pound, even for a moment, among us—a thing so hateful to us all that London did it for us, and the Imagist movement was inaugurated (1913)—the most fruitful piece of literary right-handedness the language has witnessed in the present generation.

And so Pound exists where the head is—or where he thinks it is—in London, Paris or Rapallo-near-the-Renaissance, a 'courageous charlatan fooling with the truth' where he thinks the truth is, anywhere but in himself.

And this is the reason Pound is not a modernist—in the best sense—and so has got himself caught in the cross-fire between fools on the one hand and the most capable workers on the other. He is not a modernist, as any one who stays at home must be, in that he does not accept, has not accepted, his local material to make it 'beautiful'. Instead, he fights his material, selects too finely sometimes.

All this is mixed up again with his desire for an intelligent life among intelligent people, a thing not in itself reprehensible, but hard, often, to defend in fact; it requires too much masonry and running for a sensible world. Pound is not interested in a 'perfect' arrangement of stupidities no matter how theoretically satisfying that may be, that is, in the manner of some of the cubist painters of recent remembrance.

Well, the poet is only half the man; never was this truer than in the case of Pound. Pound is full of beauty for people of intelligence—only part of it comes off in verse—sometimes I think not the best part. Pound is inarticulate. It is a new language to him, art. He has difficulty with languages. A good deal of Pound is lost, lost in the come-over from his intelligence into the art. I think much of this could be overcome if the environment were more favourable. Pound might be 'made' by an informed America that knew two or three languages and some of the difficulties of expression.

And the thing is that the place is 'dying' for the lack of what Pound is, and already stinks, the old authentic, fanatical, puritanic stink—

inimical to all life—that will ruin us in the end, spiralling outward until there is nothing left to despoil, and it remains still in the sky, nebulary, a stench still seeking something pure. The pertinence of this being that the fault of the puritan mind, which governs America and has driven Pound out, is the failure of language. Pound has sought to communicate his poetry to us and failed. It is a tragedy, since he is our best poet.

But his work shines most in the reading, not in reading about it.

84. R. P. Blackmur on Pound's 'Variety of Masks'

April 1927

Saturday Review of Literature (30 April 1927), iii, 784.

Blackmur (1904–65), American literary critic, was the author of two other essays on Pound, the most important being 'The Masks of Ezra Pound' in *Hound & Horn* (January–March 1934). See Introduction, pp. 19–20, 22.

These poems are arranged in a rough chronological sequence, and they betray not so much a 'growth' as multiplicity and change. What we have is not the customary single tune played with an increasing intensity and skill, but a measured variety of themes elaborated with an equal skill.

Ezra Pound's poems are not confused in his individual experience; the virtue of his work is not in the expression of his private fervors and dismays. What is personal in his work is the general tone infusing his various styles; and the ultimate value of his poetry should be in the adequacy of his methods and the freshness of his ways of feeling, rather than the novelty or truth of his substance. This sort of statement applies to whole periods of poetry; to the Augustan age in Rome and in

England—to Horace and Propertius, to Dryden and Pope. Thus it is not intended to diminish the poet discussed.

The fact that so great a bulk of Pound's work is translation affects its value very little. Anglo-Saxon, Provençal, Latin, Italian, and Chinese originals wear very new and excellent faces in Pound's English.

Without great original genius, Pound has made more *poetry* than most of his contemporaries; because he has understood better than almost anyone what poetry is not, and because he has perfected an aptitude for the beauty of words and for that beauty in things which is relevant to words and not to paint or carved stone or pianolas. He has kept within his medium, and has thereby achieved a triumph of style varying from a hard radiance to the most limpid image.

'A catalogue, his jewels of conversation;' and there is nothing fraudulent, not a single item pretentious, vain, vapid, or dull in the whole long list here assembled. The temple and the side show are equitably displayed; the glittering, the tenuous, the ironic, the simple breathing of words into being . . . and so on: an index of images and a hierarchy of wit. And all this prompted by an actual poetic talent and not by a wild hankering to shout.

As for innovations, Pound's unfinished Cantos—not printed here—present an anological method of treating widely diverse experience peculiarly appropriate today. And all his work exemplifies a fresh use of language: words used with an amazing aptness and pertinence. The poetry of a thing is its meaning; and while everything else in the world may be suggested, that meaning must be presented *apparently* in terms of the thing itself alone. This Pound has done.

The nub of the matter is in the title. We have several attitudes or moods towards things, and poetry is the mask these moods sometimes wear. *Personae* were the masks of Roman actors. But they were not masks worn to hide character but to show its clearest face. They hid only the irrelevant and unseemly, the unreality of the private individual under the definition and the clarity of a symbol. So Ezra Pound has supplied a variety of masks—some beautiful, some malicious, some ironical—and all better made than any in our generation.

SELECTED POEMS

Edited by T. S. Eliot, November 1928

85. John Gould Fletcher, the neglected assessment

April 1929

Review in the *Criterion* (April 1929), viii, 513–24, of *Selected Poems*, *A Draft of XVI Cantos* and *A Draft of Cantos 17–27*.

On Fletcher see No. 67.

The task of the poet in our day, or in any day, does not differ, except in degree, from the task of the novelist, the biographer, the historian, or anyone else whose life is spent in dealing with words. In any case, the writer makes an attempt to transmit, by means of words, an ordered judgment on the age he lives in, through the medium of his own personality. That is to say, the writer ineluctably expresses himself in relation to his surroundings, even when he is writing about the past. The result is that the completed work, if we take it apart from the accidental circumstances of the author's own life, represents something both greater and lesser than the combination of time, place, and talent that produced the writer in question. It is greater in so far as the writer has succeeded in recreating through the medium of his own experience the experience of others; it is lesser in so far as no writer (not even Shakespeare) has given us the full range of his age. We are therefore, whether we like it or not, obliged to rank authors by means of a very rough-and-ready calculation as to their approximation, or failure to approximate, to what appears to us to have been the central impulse of the particular period they lived in—and this calculation has to be usually performed long after the event. It is for the sake of establishing this approximation—indeed for the sake of establishing reputations that have already clearly established themselves—that histories of literature are written.

The judgment of a contemporary by a contemporary carries very little weight with the literary critic who is attempting to assess dispassionately the value of any particular work or writer. It is a well-known fact that Byron, for instance, preferred Moore, Campbell and Rogers to Wordsworth; that Coleridge acknowledges a debt to the Sonnets of the Reverend Mr. Bowles; that Landor thought Southey important; that Shelley was quite possibly almost as much in debt to Mrs. Radcliffe as to Æschylus; and that Blake enjoyed Ossian as much as the Bible. This list, taken from the writers of a single period, ought to be enough to convince us that every writer has to some extent, his own æsthetic; the question whether that æsthetic remains valuable to a later age depends upon whether the later age can find in it a sympathetic reflection of their own peculiar experience. It is for this reason that literary tradition is, as Rémy de Gourmont has said, 'a choice and not a fact'; tradition as a fact being 'merely a mass of contradictory tendencies'.

One may go even further and say that tradition as a choice is essentially a moral choice; one has instinctively given one's allegiance to this or that side of literary achievement, and one must logically abide the outcome of that choice. And this fact applies not only to great writers, but to minor writers and even bad writers. Perhaps it applies most of all to the minor writers and bad writers. For the great writer gives us the illusion at least of almost complete freedom from traditional bonds. He *is* his tradition at a certain high point in its development; and that being the case, his tradition has had time to assimilate much that was at first foreign to it (as the scholastic tradition of the thirteenth century assimilated Aristotle, or the humanistic tradition of the best writers of the sixteenth century found a place for much popular mediævalism). The question whether such a writer is possible in our age when tradition, as well as much else, seems to have largely broken down, is one that I am not called upon to discuss.

Now no one with an open mind can possibly read Mr. Pound's poetry without realizing that he is above all, a traditionalist. This fact about him has now been discovered by Mr. T. S. Eliot, and has been argued by him in an introduction of great value and interest. It is a paradoxical fact that, to most persons, Mr. Pound's name still represents tendencies covering the entire extreme left wing of literature. How this mistake came about has been largely due to Mr. Pound himself. As Mr.

Eliot very justly observes, 'Poets may be divided into those that develop technique, those who imitate technique, and those who invent technique'. Mr. Pound has always been on the side of those who either develop or invent technique, and has so strenuously opposed those who imitate technique, that he has seen fit to rank himself with the extremists (even the most banally imitative extremists) rather than accept the academically imitative. But in this respect, Mr. Pound has done himself a disservice. It is no part of a poet's business to see that other poets do not imitate; it is only for him to make his own work as good as he can make it.

If we were given the following poem to read, without knowing its author, and were asked to set down the work of the poet whom it most resembled, what would our answer be? Here is the first poem in Mr. Pound's selection:

[quotes 'The Tree', *CSP*, p. 17.]

The answer to that is clearly William Morris. And the careful reader of the poems here culled from Mr. Pound's two first volumes (*Personæ* and *Exultations*) will find many an echo, not alone of Morris but of Rossetti, and of the entire 'æsthetic school' of the close of the nineteenth century. As Mr. Eliot remarks very justly, 'In the background are the nineties in general, and behind the nineties of course, Swinburne and William Morris' . . . 'the shades of Dowson, Lionel Johnson, and Fiona flit about'. The poet, accordingly, that Mr. Pound in this early period resembles most is largely the early Yeats of *The Wind Among the Reeds*; not the later and less easy Yeats of *The Wild Swans at Coole*. But where Yeats was able to refer his alchemical and astrological speculations back to their sources in folk-lore and poetry, Mr. Pound took his materials mostly direct from the books in which he found them.

This however, does not exhaust the tale of early influence upon Mr. Pound. There still remains to be accounted for Robert Browning. Had this influence persisted, I cannot help feeling that Mr. Pound would have been a better poet. For Browning—whatever the young of the present generation may say—was by all odds the most many-sided and intelligent of all the Victorians. Unfortunately, it seems to me that the tale of Browning's influence upon Mr. Pound stopped short at 'Paracelsus' and 'Sordello' and other of Browning's diploma pieces, and did not go on to the mature artistry of the 'Ring and the Book' and 'Parleyings', which raise the ultimate questions of God's justice and man's, and the success of failure. But, in any case, Browning gave Pound the ability to see and depict people like Guido Cavalcanti, Bertram de Born, and Arnaut Daniel as living and breathing—the only unfortunate circumstance being that these were precisely the sort of people with whom Pound was most likely to identify his youthful self.

So far we need not deny Mr. Eliot's contention that 'Pound's originality is genuine in that his versification was a *logical* development of the verse of his English predecessors'. But, it must be added, that those predecessors were, except for Browning, poets of the 'nineties. The result is, that Pound merely further refined upon what had already been refined to the point of becoming tenuous. Moreover, at the time when he started to write, the 'tradition of choice' that the English poets of the day followed, had already altered. A return to the romantic naturalism of Wordsworth, Crabbe, Clare, Cowper and the early Romantics in general was beginning to be felt. This return was due possibly to the influence of Housman and Mr. Thomas Hardy; even more certainly it was due to the general breakdown of the 'art for art's sake' attitude as a way of looking at the world. The new group of poets which it stimulated in England, were determined to cultivate not the 'ivory tower' attitude of Lionel Johnson, but the fresher contact with the local soil which they thought they found in pure lyrists like Herrick. At the same time, the American poets began to cultivate their own local acres, under the influence, now for the first time completely realized, of Browning, Wordsworth, and Whitman.

With neither of these groups did Mr. Pound completely identify himself. Instead of combining more closely with his fellow-Georgians in England in their effort to develop further the tradition of rural naturalism, and instead of uniting with his American fellows in the effort to make poetry about their own local subject-matter, he only burrowed a little more deeply into the past of his Provençal 'personæ'. And in this respect, he was following a side branch, rather than the main stream, of the European tradition. It is all very well to say that Troubadours influenced the early Italian poets before Dante, and that therefore to understand Dante we have to study both the Troubadours and the early Italian poets. The fact remains that Dante acquired nothing from the Troubadours but a technique; into that technique he put a range of experience which had very little to do with the world as the Troubadours saw it. The fact that Dante could not have been the poet he was without that technique, is obvious; but the fact that Dante realized that the technique could be used for means which his predecessors would never have recognized as theirs is equally obvious. By confining his range of experience to what Arnaut Daniel might have felt and thought under the given circumstances, Mr. Pound became what he has remained, even in his latest verses: the most perfect type in our time of a purely 'æsthetic' poet.

II

The attempt to classify writers by means of their conformity to certain clearly defined psychological types, is one that our age has only just begun to make; but some such classification is necessary, in so far as the old distinction between 'classic' and 'romantic' has to a great extent broken down. It is somewhat easier to define poets in this way, than prose-writers; inasmuch as the poets are more directly dependent on the effect of words. And it is through the examination of the vocabulary of writers—as well as their subject-matter—that any fruitful investigations in the direction of the psychology of authorship will be finally made.

In the first forty pages of Mr. Eliot's selection from Mr. Pound's poetry one finds the following verbal forms: *syne, luth, torse, limning, everychone, fleet, foison, lutany, mnemonic, aspen, seneschal, jongleur, emprise, strath, garth, guerdon, terrene, email*, as well as numberless old verb forms such as: *playeth, knoweth, boweth, cometh, holdeth, bestoweth*. There are also compound verbal forms such as *wayfare, swordplay*, and such archaisms as *us-toward* and *we twain*. And the metrical forms are no less complex: canzone, ballade, sestina, alternate through these pages.

The argument that Mr. Eliot brings forward here in Mr. Pound's defence is worth quoting. He says: 'Pound is often most "original" in the right sense when he is most "archæological" in the ordinary sense. It is almost too platitudinous to say that one is not modern by writing about chimney-pots, or archaic by writing about oriflammes. If one can really penetrate the life of another age, one is penetrating one's own.' This statement is quite true, so far as it goes, but we still have to ask ourselves whether Mr. Pound has really penetrated the life of the remote age he has written about, by the means he has chosen, of heaping up archaic diction. We have only to compare Coleridge's vocabulary in 'The Ancient Mariner' and 'Christabel' with the vocabulary of *Personæ*, to find the answer. In these two poems, Coleridge did penetrate the past by means far more sure, economical, and direct. We do not ask whether his diction is precisely that of the old ballads, because we feel all along that Coleridge sees the past that he has chosen to write about and his own life in *relation*; he has a *moral* sense of their points of contact. This moral sense is lacking in Mr. Pound.

Let us turn to the later poems selected from *Ripostes* and *Lustra*. Here we have a considerable clarification of technique, accompanied by a definite loss of power. Some of the poems in *Ripostes* are, nevertheless, perhaps the finest things that Pound has written: 'Portrait d'une Femme', 'Phasellus Ille', 'Apparuit', 'A Virginal', 'The Return'—it is by such things that his reputation as an original poet will finally stand or fall. But over *Ripostes* as a whole, and still more over *Lustra*, there broods the atmosphere of a curious detachment. Pound is growing less interested in Provence, and he has not been able to interest himself profoundly in his own age. This detachment expresses itself throughout the series of short poems which, following Mr. Eliot, I call the Epigrams. Whether these are derived from Martial or Catullus, or simply evolved by Pound himself out of his own inner consciousness, I do not know. But one can say that they have neither the tigerish fury of Catullus nor the wasp-like wit of Martial. They are a detached comment, always from some safe point outside the lives with which they deal, on some of the minor follies of the age. And it is this attitude that gives them their agreeable sparkle, as well as their disagreeable air of pretentious flippancy. One has only to compare them with Blake's private epigrams, or Marston's 'Scourge of Villainy', or the 'Dunciad', to see the difference between this sort of thing and real satire.

So we pass, by way of the brilliant paraphrase of the Anglo-Saxon 'Seafarer', or the even more brilliant paraphrase of *Cathay*, to 'Hugh Selwyn Mauberley' (1920), in which, as Mr. Eliot notes, a fusion between Pound's archæological interests and his more personal feelings finally takes place. And this fusion took place because the war had made the 'ivory tower' attitude finally untenable. 'Mauberley' is—as the Epigrams are not—serious modern work; a document of intense interest for its time.

To say, however, as Mr. Eliot has done, that it is 'a great poem', is a slight—if pardonable—exaggeration. When read as a whole, 'Mauberley' has no cumulative effect. The first five sections of the book, numbered consecutively, are a single poem. Then we drift off at a tangent through a series of contemporary portraits to a discussion of quite a different theme; the relation of the writer to the age he lives in. Here the book halts half-way to interpose an Envoi in an entirely different key and mood from anything preceding. Progress is interrupted, and when we resume again, it is through a sort of coda on personal as opposed to general themes, that we pass to a final 'portrait of a lady' that has very little to do with the mood in which the book started. The experience that began so promisingly has somehow been frittered away.

If we compare this book with 'The Seafarer' or the poems in *Cathay*, we will find, I think, the key to Mr. Pound's failure as a poet. In these translations he not only had material that was congenial to work upon, but a structure already laid down from which his mind could not go astray. With the limits of form already marked off in his mind, he could happily transmute detail into something that was his and yet not entirely his. But when he has been obliged to set up limits for himself, in his own experience, the deficiencies of his purely æsthetic and non-moral sensibility immediately betray themselves. He cannot do so because of

> A consciousness disjunct
> Being but the overblotted
> Series
> Of intermittences.

And further:

> Thus, if her colour
> Came against his gaze,
> Tempered as if
> It were through a perfect glaze,
> He made no immediate application
> Of this to relation of the state
> To the individual, the month was more temperate
> Because this beauty had been.

But surely we have to relate beauty to something, even if it is only to the weather, the food, the traffic, or the day-to-day striving of this disappointing but highly necessary planet?

III

It is only by means of an intensive study of Mr. Pound's 'disjunct consciousness' that we can attain to any understanding and appreciation of his 'Homage to Sextus Propertius' and his Cantos.

These poems are of the utmost importance as critical touchstones for whatever estimate the future will make of Mr. Pound's powers. The

'Propertius' is omitted by Mr. Eliot from his selection, because, as he says, 'if the uninstructed reader is not a classical scholar, he will make nothing of it; if he be a classical scholar, he will wonder why this does not conform to his notions of what translation should be. It is not a translation, it is a paraphrase, or still more truly (for the instructed) a *persona*.'

The reader who has followed my argument about Mr. Pound so far, will here recall that I began by asserting that he was a traditionalist, a statement that I immediately qualified by noting that the tradition he has always followed is a purely æsthetic one, without reference to moral consciousness, leading inevitably to an expressed preference for the side branch, rather than the main stream. This tendency becomes acute in 'Homage to Propertius'. The fact is that to a poet of Mr. Pound's type, the academic classicist is as deeply anathema as the revolutionary innovator. The one takes for granted the substance of the classics, as seen through the perspective of generations of scholars; the other, starting from some illogically personal (hence 'romantic'?) standpoint, gradually approaches the classic author, without ever completely identifying the text of that author with himself. Both are therefore examples of imperfect assimilation. The perfect assimilation, Pound might argue, is to transpose yourself fully into the life and times of the author in question. This attempt, which was begun with the Provençal poets, is carried out fully in the 'Homage to Propertius'.

The difficulty with this poem is that it represents neither Propertius nor Mr. Pound, but only what Mr. Pound might have thought and felt had he *been* Propertius. In the case of the early translations, he had been content to paraphrase the text. But here he assumes that the text already exists in his own mind and the reader's, and that he is free to comment upon it as if he had written it. The result is an extended criticism of Propertius, written by a modern mind temporarily masquerading as Propertius. Technically, the form conveys as accurately as anything in English can, the effect of the elegiac metre:

> Nor at my funeral either will there be any long trail,
> bearing ancestral lares and images;
> No trumpets filled with my emptiness,
> Nor shall it be on an Atalic bed;
> The perfumed cloths shall be absent.
> A small, plebeian procession.
> Enough, enough, and in plenty.
> There will be three books at my obsequies. . . .

The technical quality of these lines must not blind us to the draw-backs of the method of presentation. When anyone writes about a particular epoch of the past, the question always arises whether he has primarily envisaged himself as living that particular life, or has simply let that life be relived as far as possible, without reference to how he might have desired it to be, letting the imagination follow perfectly the accepted details. The latter method is sensational and dramatic; the former intellectualist and static. One finds an example of the intellectu-alist method in Pater's *Marius the Epicurean* [1885]; a perfect analysis of a period seen through Pater's temperament. The sensational method was carried to great heights in Browning.

Now Mr. Pound's 'Propertius' is as purely an intellectualist recon-struction as was *Marius*. The difficulty is that the method is subjective throughout. In other words, it depends entirely upon personal accidents for its successful use. Pater's Romans speak as if they had been to Oxford in the 'nineties; Mr. Pound's Romans speaks as if they had gravitated between modern New York and London. What we get, therefore, in either case is not an example of the poetic imagination at work within a given scheme of historical data, but merely a transposal of certain personal accidents of likeness from one period to another.

But this does not exhaust the dangers of Mr. Pound's method. The mind that tends to transpose itself continually into a series of deliberately chosen pasts, without reference to the needs and exigencies of the pre-sent day, tends to become *temporalized,* and to adopt what Mr. Wynd-ham Lewis calls a 'time-philosophy'.[1] That is to say, juxtaposition in point of times becomes the important element for such a mind, and not association in point of fact. Such a mind rapidly becomes dissociated from everything except time; it lives in a sort of 'continuous present' formed of a number of bygone pasts; and Mr. Pound logically took this step towards the goal he had unconsciously been aiming at from the first, when he began writing his Cantos.

The Cantos as they stand are unquestionably the *selva oscura* of modern poetry. They are an anthology of all the passages in poetry of the past that Mr. Pound has been interested in (I might almost say that they are Mr. Pound's *Golden Treasury*, but decency forbids); they are an extended history of Rimini under the Malatesta dynasty, they are a commentary on Venetian and other history in relation to the artist, they

[1] Lewis's *Time and Western Man* (1927) branded Pound as 'a great *time-trotter*', 'a man in love with the past' and, out-doing himself, described Pound's mind as mixed of equal propor-tions of 'Bergson-Marinetti-Mr. Hueffer . . . -Edward Fitzgerald and Buffalo Bill'.

are a collection of highly recondite and private gibes and japes. But to say that they are a poem in any sense of the word is to say that calisthenics are essentially the same thing as the Russian ballet. There is an element of poetry in them, just as there is an element of the Russian ballet in calisthenics, but the element is not only unsifted out from its less vital context, it does not even affect—in many cases—its context. Let me take two examples. Here is Mr. Pound's portrait of Henry James, in a London club:

[quotes *Cantos*, pp. 28–9 'The old men's voices' to 'as quickly as possible'.]

And so on for several more lines. All that one can say about this is that it is 'merely work chucked away', to quote from Mr. Pound himself, a few lines lower down. Whether it is 'poetical' or not matters little; the fact remains that we have a right to demand something better from a serious poet than the versification of fifteenth-century (or nineteenth-century) business letters.

86. Henry Bamford Parkes on the theories and influence of Pound

December 1932

H. B. Parkes, 'Two Pounds of Poetry', *New English Weekly* (22 December 1932), ii, 227–8. This is a review of *Profile: An Anthology*, edited by Pound, and *An Objectivist's Anthology* edited by Louis Zukofsky. Pound's brief reply, in the issue of 12 January 1933, follows Parkes's essay.

Parkes (b. 1904), English historian, was educated at Queen's College, Oxford. He went to America in 1927 and has been on the history faculty of New York University since 1930. His publications include a history of Mexico (1938), a book on Marxism (1939), and several books about the United States.

These two anthologies provide an opportunity for studying the poetic theories and influence of Ezra Pound. *Profile* contains eighty poems and covers the last quarter of a century. As an anthology, it is not intended to be taken very seriously—Pound professes to have included only those poems which happen to have remained in his memory—and some of the selections are difficult to justify—two pieces of doggerel by Donald Evans, for example. It does, however, illustrate, mostly by rather brief extracts, those writers and tendencies which Pound considers to have been of most importance; and the result is an excellent source-book for the study of the Imagist Movement and of those later poets who were influenced by it. Zukofsky is one of Pound's pupils, and his 'Objectivism' appears to be mainly a restatement, in pretentious and sometimes incomprehensible language, of the aims of the Imagists. His anthology is a collection of those poems, written in the last half dozen years, which are in accordance with the theory of 'Objectivism'. William Carlos Williams occupies twenty-nine pages, and there are pieces by Pound, Eliot and eight others; but more than half of the entire book is occupied by Zukofsky himself and by another young American, Kenneth Rexroth.

Few qualified students of contemporary literature would deny that for the last twenty years Pound has been the most serious and accomplished man of letters in the English-speaking world. The Imagist Movement, of which he was the real leader, may seem, in the light of history, to be comparable in importance to the publication of *Lyrical Ballads*.

On the technique of writing Pound's influence has been wholly beneficial. His early essays, reprinted in *Pavannes and Divisions*, state doctrines which are always true and which are constantly in need of restatement. Poems, he said, should present concrete images, and no word should be used which does not contribute to their presentation. The art of poetry is mainly the art of compressing as much meaning into as few words as possible, and the value of a poem is to be judged by the precision with which the meaning is recorded. Metric does not mean merely conforming to a regular accentual beat; more subtle effects can be obtained by paying greater attention to quantity and pitch, and by writing in the sequence of a musical phrase rather than of a metronome. Pound's own poetry is a successful application of these doctrines. Clichés and rhetorical phrases are altogether avoided. He intensifies and extends the consciousness of his readers by presenting them with objects seen in an unfamiliar light. Instead of drugging them into submission by using an obvious and regular rhythmic system, he keeps them on the alert with the subtlety of his cadences. His versification, based mainly on quantity, is too slow moving for narrative or drama, but as a medium for lyric or elegiac poetry it is unrivalled.

The importance of the Imagist revolution can be seen by comparing almost any good modern poem with the work of the later Romantics or of the Victorians. For a century English poetry had been infested by conventional associations of ideas which were quite as deadening as the poetic diction of the eighteenth century. Certain words and epithets were poetic, and with few exceptions (of whom Browning was perhaps the most notable) poets aimed at producing a vague and sentimental excitement by re-arranging these traditional counters into new patterns. Their descriptions were (by modern standards) intolerably diffuse; and they concealed their failure to convey genuine perceptions and experiences by using accentual rhythms which intoxicated the reader instead of heightening his consciousness. This method could, with such writers as Shelley or Swinburne, secure the acceptance of poetry almost devoid of intellectual content. Poetry of this kind was, at best, an emotional relaxation and not an intellectual discipline.

On the subject matter of poetry, however, Pound's influence has been much less valuable; and the appearance of the *Objectivists Anthology* suggests that a revolt against it is urgently needed. The purpose of an Imagist poem was to distinguish an object or an event from the flux of experience and convey the writer's view of it, and implicitly therefore his emotional reactions towards it, with the utmost possible clarity. The Imagists did, therefore, perform one of the most important functions of poetry; they gave their readers a more vivid awareness of the concrete particulars of which the external world is composed. Good Imagist poems—those of T. E. Hulme, for example—were in their own kind perfect and unsurpassable. And when the Imagist technique was adopted by an American like William Carlos Williams, whose purpose was to break away from inherited and European habits of thought, achieve a closer contact with the objects actually around him, and define the reactions of his sensibility to its unexplored American environment, it was put to a very appropriate and valuable use. Imagism, however, is merely one of the many possible methods of writing poetry, and it cannot, except by a tour de force, produce anything of major significance. The only way to write a long Imagist poem is to describe many objects instead of one, and as long as the poet remains an Imagist, he cannot find among these objects any inherent unity; his poem becomes a kind of catalogue. Pound's Cantos achieve greatness by the excellence of the versification and the skill with which images from different times and places are juxtaposed. But, considered as a whole, the Cantos have no core or central theme, and Pound's statement that the completed work will resemble a Bach fugue does not suggest that the lack will be supplied. The beauty of the Cantos like that of a frieze, is decorative rather than vital. The long poems of Pound's disciples, Zukofsky and Rexroth, are mere catalogues, and the authors do not possess the technical skill with which Pound himself surmounts the difficulties implicit in his method. Zukofsky records a number of personal experiences; his poetry is filled with autobiographical references which the reader cannot be expected to appreciate, and his diction is too undistinguished to counterbalance the lack of any single theme or coherency. Rexroth's diction has a certain splendour, but his poetry is a bare list of objects; most of them he merely names without attempting to describe, and some of them are so abstract and technically mathematical or scientific that any concrete apprehension is impossible. The complete poem is apparently intended to convey some kind of religious intuition, but after reading through thirty-six pages of incoherent imagery, one is left merely bewildered.

The strongest impression which one derives from any long Imagist poem is that its author is not fully alive. One has, of course, other evidence for knowing that Pound himself, as a man, is more alive than most of his contemporaries. But the Imagist method, which is to submit passively to external objects and record the resultant experiences, does not allow whatever vitality the poet may personally possess to be become manifest in his poetry. The same complaint must be made against those writers, who, while adopting Pound's theories and technique, have arranged their observations into a pattern such as a truly Imagist poem never displays. Eliot, for example, has learnt his technique from Pound (although, being also a disciple of the Symbolists, he is more concerned with defining emotions by means of images habitually associated with them than with defining images by means of whatever emotions they may evoke). Eliot's main purpose is to describe, by juxtaposing appropriate images, a state of mind and a state of society. His work, therefore, has coherence. Nevertheless, because Eliot himself does not appear in his poetry as an active personality, because as a poet he is passively receptive to impressions which he merely places side by side instead of organising them into a genuine unity, his work, like that of Pound, seems to lack vitality.

If poets are to surmount this deficiency, they ought probably to forget the doctrine, set forth in Eliot's essay on 'Tradition and the Individual Talent,' that 'the more perfect the artist, the more completely separate in him will be the man who suffers and the mind which creates.' This doctrine leads to the corollary, stated in the same essay, that 'emotions which he has never experienced will serve his turn as well as those familiar to him.' Undoubtedly a great poet is completely self-conscious, but the existence of some kind of separation between his consciousness and his emotions does not mean that he is not interested primarily in himself. The writing of poetry is, in fact, one of the methods by which he discovers what kind of person he is fundamentally, and achieves complete self-consciousness and self-mastery. If a poem has vitality, it is because the author is recording an experience which is, to him as a person, deeply important; and if its imagery has unity, it is because the poem is an expression of a unified experience, attitude, or personality. Any other conception of poetry causes it to degenerate into a mere intellectual amusement, more difficult but scarcely more valuable than designing a tapestry or a vase.

Pound's reply:

Sir,—On the contrary! *Profile* is intended to be taken very seriously, not as a nosegay, but as the definition of a contour.

It contains some of the most condensed criticism I have written. It is possible to criticise by juxtaposition as well as by the braying of an I. A. Richards or the maunderings of a Babbit.

E.P.

87. A supervision with Dr Leavis on 'Mauberley'

1933

Ronald Duncan, from *All Men Are Islands: An Autobiography* (London: Rupert Hart-Davis, 1964), 84–7.

Duncan (b. 1914), English dramatist, was an undergraduate at Downing College from 1933 to 1936. He became acquainted with Pound in Rapallo in the thirties.

At my first supervision, where there were half-a-dozen other under-graduates, he suggested we should read the metaphysical poets—Grier-son's edition—and there was an oblique hint that it would be expedient if we became regular readers of *Scrutiny* and occasionally looked at the *Criterion*. Somebody asked him what lectures we should attend. Leavis studied the questioner with a mixture of tolerance and contempt. 'I suppose you'd better look in on Dr Richards, and I daresay the Bennetts are still murdering Milton, Potts piffling around on Byron, and then there's old Henn getting his lecture-notes muddled with his expletives on the towpath. Basil Willey on the Seventeenth Century isn't bad at all. But avoid Q; he's supposed to lecture on Aristotle's *Poetics* but he never gets nearer than his bottle of Cockburn.'

With this directive I bought a bicycle, told my bedder to get me up early, and by nine was in the lecture-room with a new notebook, looking as keen and naïve as the girls from Girton beside me. I listened to the urbane dilettantism of Dadie Rylands; I observed Richards doing his Dr Caligari act and impressing a row of assiduous nuns. Dr Tillyard was embalming Milton with the same shroud he had used for the last ten years, and was to use for the next twenty. My interest in Milton had been effectively killed at school; it was not profitable to attend the killing of a corpse. Exactly as Leavis had predicted, Sir Arthur Quiller-Couch tottered into the room at Magdalene puffing a cigar and carrying a decanter of port. He reminded me of one of those china pixies with which people spoil herbaceous borders.

But it was the lecturer on English Satire who broke my patience. He gave the usual facetious asides concerning the poets' lives, listed their well known works and never at any point referred to a text or made a direct comment on any lines they had written.

At the end of this performance, which compared poorly with the English master at school, I cycled straight to Chesterton Hall Crescent to see Leavis.

'What's up?' he asked. I had interrupted his luncheon.

'I've called to tell you I'm sending myself down from the university,' I announced.

'What have you been up to—attending lectures?'

I nodded.

'Most of them stick it for a term or two at least,' he said; 'it's only taken you a week to be disgusted. Very promising. What will you do?'

'I'll stay up on one condition,' I offered, 'If you give me two one-hour extra supervisions to myself every week.'

He agreed. He charged me only 7s. 6d. an hour.

My first solitary supervision was held in the orchard. I noticed that the apples still lay where they had fallen. Leavis's manner was as casual as his clothes; only his speech was meticulous and precise. His comments were always direct and unguarded. The very opposite to his writing, where his sentences were as unwieldy as the later Henry James's, without shape, lamed with parentheses. Straight away he gave me the impression that we were not only colleagues but something more—conspirators, whose aim was to blow up the English Faculty.

Leavis had a striking head; it looked as if it contained a brain, and it did. A high forehead, well defined features. His eyes unflinching, something puritanical about the mouth. And though he was almost bald, he had sufficient hair left to wear it long enough to affront the

Fellows. Sideboards added to this Gower Street effect. He never wore a tie even at High Table, and his open-necked collar was, I suspect, maintained by him out of his veneration for D. H. Lawrence.

His first question to me was to the point. Had I read any Pound or Eliot? I had read a little of the latter, nothing of the former. Leavis immediately rectified this by reading 'Hugh Selwyn Mauberley' to me as we sat surrounded by fallen apples. He read poetry more sensitively than anybody: far better than Gielgud or Olivier. He read it better because he never missed an ambiguity, a shade of meaning, and finally because he understood the techniques of poetry, realising that it has little to do with a metre and less to do with scansion.

The superb restraint of 'Mauberley', its urbane flexibility, the way the verse is handled so that the meaning runs against the verse-structure, impressed me deeply. I had never read anything like this before. All the romantic outpourings seemed tame compared to the tough irony of Pound:

> Knowing my coat has never been
> Of precisely the fashion
> To stimulate, in her,
> A durable passion.

Leavis gave 'precisely' and 'durable' just the right emphasis by an imperceptible pause before those two words.

The other verse that impaled me as I heard it was:

> To Fleet St where
> Dr Johnson flourished;
> Beside this thoroughfare
> The sale of half-hose has
> Long since superseded the cultivation
> Of Pierian roses.

The prose, polish and run of the verse with its important pause after 'half-hose has'—and the subtle effect of that half-rhyme—gave poetry a new meaning to me. No longer was it a decoration, it was the window. Leavis told me he thought 'Mauberley' was Pound's masterpiece. 'Unfortunately Pound has never written anything worth reading since.' I wasn't in a position then to question this. I was enormously grateful to Leavis for introducing me to 'Mauberley.'

A DRAFT OF XXX CANTOS

Paris, August 1930
New York, 15 March 1933
London, 15 September 1933

---

88. Dudley Fitts, 'Music Fit for the Odes', *Hound & Horn*

Winter 1931, iv, 278–89

Pound was unofficially connected with *H & H* (see Leonard Greenbaum, *The Hound & Horn: The History of a Literary Quarterly* (The Hague: Mouton, 1966)), but was not pleased with this review: 'Fitts is from my point of view, very nearly hopeless,' he wrote to Lincoln Kirstein, the editor (Greenbaum, p. 118).

Fitts (1903–68) was an American classicist, translator and critic.

A thoughtless reading of the Cantos of Ezra Pound suggests two criticisms, both attractively easy and both superficial. The first of these is that the poem is incomprehensible, a perverse mystification; the second, that it is structurally and melodically amorphous, not a poem but a macaronic chaos. Since my space is limited, I have thought it best to attempt little formal criticism in this review, and to address myself chiefly to a discussion of these two fundamental objections; and since the former is dependent largely upon a misapprehension of Mr Pound's poetical technic, I shall comment first upon the structure, melodic and rhythmic, of the poem.

A key to Mr Pound's method is to be found in his discussion of what he calls 'horizontal music', in his essay on George Antheil*. The valid æsthetic ideal, he observes,

---

* *Antheil and the Treatise on Harmony* (Covici, 1927).

aims at focusing the mind on a given definition of form, or rhythm, so intensely that it becomes not only more aware of that given form, but more sensitive to all other forms, rhythms, defined planes, or masses. It is a scaling of eye-balls, a castigating or purging of aural cortices; a sharpening of verbal apperceptions. . . .*

Music, even as late as Bach, was counterpoint ('horizontal'), rather than harmony ('perpendicular'); that is to say, the emphasis was laid upon the melodic line, upon the simultaneous management of two or more melodic lines, until 'counterpoint' slumped into 'harmony, Lutheran chorales, &c., and progressively into Schönberg, [and] this fundamental drive in music was obscured.'† Melody—whether of music or of verse —is a combination of what Mr Pound calls *raga* (toneless rhythm-arrangement) and *tala* (the sequence of notes at determined pitches). 'Harmony,' the decadent music after Bach, denies *raga* in its preoccupation with *tala*: its tendency is towards a stasis, which rapidly becomes a stagnation. It is no longer active; it is 'atmospheric' (Debussy, Schönberg). The same thing has happened, to even a greater extent, in poetry. The worker in verbal rhythms is denied the possibility of counterpoint (except an artificial counterpoint of echoing and anticipating), and unless he is as careful of the timing as he is of the pitch of his tone-sequences, his verse, like music, will stagnate; lacking motion, it will be inactive, dead.

The motion of Mr Pound's melodic line is the motion of a frieze. He has described it exactly in a passage in the twenty-fifth Canto:

> notes as facets of air,
> and the mind there, before them, moving,
> so that the notes needed not move.

Whether the music passes across the mind, or the mind traverses the music, is immaterial; the important fact is the motion. But the frieze has depth as well as motion. That is to say, there is counterpoint, and there is harmony. What Mr Pound calls 'echo-counterpoint' is managed in various ways; the most obvious device is that of the repetition of pitch and rhythm—'imitation'—and may be observed at its best in such a passage as this, from Canto IV;

[quotes *Cantos*, pp. 17–18 'And by the curved' to ' 'Tis, 'Tis, 'Ytis!'.]

It is hardly necessary to call attention to the echoing of cadences, the recurrent flow of the melody, 'weightless . . . but moving, so that

* *Op. cit.*, p. 44. † *Ibid.*, p. 47.

sound runs upon sound';* what is less obvious, but no less important, is the subtle management of pause (*raga*), the breaking and refashioning of rhythm, indicated with a musician's exactness by the broken lines, the indentations, and the spacing. In spite of its chaotic appearance on the page, the notation is as precise as it can ever be outside of music.†

The contrapuntal effect is complex, but the harmonic is even more intricate. It is a harmony not only of sound, but of image. The former quality is, like the counterpoint, achieved by iteration, by imitation, by a sort of recessive flooding of the phrase with the echoes and associations that have gone before; only, it is denser than the counterpoint, and static: motion is retarded, there is a piling up of resonances, the exact musical analogue is the resolution of cadence into chord:

> (*a*) And all the while, the while, swallows crying
>
> (*b*) Lokka vat youah Trotzsk is done, ειςς
> > > madeh deh zhamefull beace!!
> > 'He iss madeh deh zhamefull beace, iss he?
> > > 'He is madeh de zhamevul beace?'

It is more difficult to define what I have referred to as the 'harmony of the image,' because it is not sonal; it is apprehensible intellectually and emotionally, but it can not be 'heard.' Perhaps I can clarify my meaning by suggesting that the poet uses each image, or each detail of the image, precisely as the musician employs a note, or single pitch. Monolinear verse, then—ψιλὴ μουσικὴ,—would be a single strand of images, or 'scenes,' in juxtaposition; a single melodic line. But if this line is treated, for image, as we have seen that the line may be treated for counterpoint and harmony—that is to say, if the image is broken, echoed back and forth, or adequated substantially or kinetically by another image, the result will be the intellectual equivalent of the metrical and melodic effects I have mentioned.

Manipulation of the Image has this advantage over manipulation of the mélos: it is possible, by a constant fluid intermingling of scenes, ideas, and associations, to make the single strand so flexible, so complex, as to achieve what is to all intents and purposes a true counterpoint, the simultaneous development of two or more lines of image-melody. This

---

* Canto XXVII.

† The nuances of lineation and spacing have never been sufficiently appreciated. How much of the pother attending the criticism of certain of E. E. Cummings' lyrics, for instance, would be avoided if the critics were to consider the poet's apparent eccentricities of typography as attempts at musical notation! So far as I know, only Mr Robert Graves has fully realized this.

particular kind of counterpoint could be illustrated only by long quotation; the curious will find in Canto XXIII, with its parallel treatment of the Homeric and Renascence images, an excellent example. But the harmonization of the image is easier to illustrate. This is from the same Canto:

[quotes *Cantos*, p. 113 'And that was when' to 'mess of that city!']

Here the chord is exceptionally rich. It is a harmonization of several daringly dissident tones: the romantic ballad ('when Troy was down') *plus* the contemporary colloquial ('all right,' 'a bloody mess') *plus* the epic ('superbo Ilion'), and so forth; and of several attitudes, no less antipathetic: the prosaic ('And they were sailing along / Sitting in the stern-sheets'), the 'poetic' ('superbo Ilion . . .'; 'and the wind drifting off from the island'), and the ironic, which approaches burlesque (Anchises' stumbling over '*tetbnéké*'; 'well, they've made a bloody mess of that city'). All of these tones and attitudes entail their own associations, which will be different for each reader. The whole passage is a single image, or, better, an image-chord composed of synthesized details. It is a note in the line of the poem, and at the same time a confluence of various lines of tone and emotion. An example of the inversion of the same device is the finely wrenched dissonance upon which Canto XXIV ends:

> 'Is it likely Divine Apollo
> That I should have stolen your cattle?
> A child of my age, a mere infant,
>   And besides, I have been here all night in my crib.'
> 'Albert made me, Tura painted my wall,
>   And Julia the countess sold to a tannery. . . .'

I have said that the rhythmic balance of individual verses is carefully arranged and accurately noted. This is demonstrable by quotation. What is not demonstrable is the fact that as the individual verse is to the complete cadence, so is the single Canto to the poem as a whole. And as the impasto of detail, or synthesis of contributing images, is to the Image, so is the Image to the Canto, and to the entire scheme. And this raises the question implicit in the first objection. What is the purpose of *XXX Cantos*?

Good poetry, as Mr Pound has pointed out,* is always an assertion. It may be affirmative assertion (assent), or negative assertion (dissent);

* In the essay on Henry James; quoted by Zukofsky: 'Les Cantos d'Ezra Pound,' in *Echanges*, numero 3 (Paris: juin 1930).

but it is always assertion. Negative assertion is invective or satire—both methods are used in the Cantos (see particularly the *Inferno* passages, Cantos XIV and XV),—and it differs from affirmative assertion only in direction. Whether affirmative or negative, the attitude must be positive; that is to say, it must be active. Bad poetry is the poetry of inertia, or of complaint, or of evasion; confronted by the hateful, it denies the existence of the hateful, or it deplores the hateful, or it disregards the hateful and concentrates upon something more agreeable. In any case, it denies reality; it 'does nothing'; whereas good poetry is always the poetry of action.

Taken as a whole, the Cantos illustrate this assertive attitude. The documentation, which at first sight seems so confusing, is simply the affirmation, by means of the recording of facts, of the desirable and undesirable elements of experience. The whole matter is summed up in Canto XIII, the 'image' of Kung and his advisers. Here, Kung is the truly wise man who can approve of each of his counsellors' advice because

> They have all answered correctly,
> That is to say, each in his nature;

'that is to say,' each has affirmed a positive value, though it be no more 'philosophical' than Tseu-lou's

> I would put the defences in order,

or any more 'practical' than the advice of Tian the poet:

> And Tian said, with his hand on the strings of his lute,
> The low sounds continuing
> after his hand left the strings,
> And the sound went up like smoke, under the leaves,
> And he looked after the sound:
> 'The old swimming hole,
> 'And the boys flopping off the planks,
> 'Or sitting in the underbrush playing mandolins.'

But Kung's rebuke falls upon Yuan Jang, his elder,—Yuan Jang being the falsely wise man, the recessive contemplative, the type of intellectual *abisma*, sitting by the roadside 'pretending to be receiving wisdom.' This man answers nothing according to his nature. For action he has substituted the meditation of 'wisdom'; perhaps he has written on the New Humanism,—I don't know; but I am certain that he teaches school, lectures on Beauty and the Eternal Values, and advises his boys to shun the 'sordid things of life.' However that may be, he is bad poetry:

And Kung said
           'You old fool, come out of it,
'Get up and do something useful.'
          And Kung said,
'Respect a child's faculties
'From the moment it inhales the clear air,
'But a man of fifty who knows nothing
              'Is worthy of no respect.'

'Get up and do something useful!' And what is useful? Whatever is 'in your nature': that is to say, whatever is positive. Above all things, it is necessary to be yourself, as the cant phrase has it; and the word to be italicized is 'be.' This is what Kung calls character, or 'order':

    And Kung said, 'Without character you will
        be unable to play on that instrument,
  Or to execute the music fit for the Odes.'

And what is the music fit for the Odes? What is the subject fit for poetry? Again, the assertion of a positive; which, in the Cantos, is the record of the fact, the Image, which is always significant so long as it is true:

    The blossoms of the apricot
        blow from the east to the west,
  And I have tried to keep them from falling.

It seems to me that the two most important elements of Mr Pound's æsthetic are summed up in Kung's observations: his insistence upon *character: order: the assertive attitude;* and his affirmation of the final value of the fact, or Image.

Confronted by this array of scenes and allusions exhumed from dead mythologies and forgotten literatures, of references to experience whose interest is limited to a contemporary few, the thoughtless reader will throw up his hands and exclaim, 'But what is it all *about*? I don't *know* enough to be able to understand this poem. Who is Sigismondo Malatesta? Who is Actaeon? Who is Piere Vidal? But *I* don't know Latin, Greek, Italian, Provençal! Who was Myo Cid, and what has he got to do with Ruth Elder?' But this is the wrong approach, based upon a misconception not only of the nature of the Cantos, but of all pure poetry; and the reader who persists in it may as well take Mr Pound's advice and 'go back and read Tennyson.' In the first place, our baffled friend is misusing the word 'understand.' He is mistakenly assuming that because a tremendous amount of erudition has gone into the making of the poem, the poem must remain an unsoluble puzzle to those who lack an equal amount of erudition with which to unravel the allusions. This, however, is not reading the poem as a poem, but as a sort of historico-archæological cypher. It is as much as to say that no-one can understand Stravinsky's *Sacre*, for instance, who has not (1) a technician's knowledge of musical theory, (2) an anatomist's knowledge of the muscles brought into play during the dance, (3) a painter's knowledge of pigmentation and décor-designing, and (4) an anthropologist's knowledge of ancient Russian folk-rites. 'Les Mariés de la Tour Eiffel,' writes Jean Cocteau,* 'à cause de leur franchise, déçoivent davantage qu'une pièce ésotérique. Le mystère inspire au public une sorte de crainte. Ici je renonce au mystère. J'allume tout, je souligne tout. Vide du dimanche, bétail humain, expressions toutes faites, dissociations d'idées en chair et en os, férocité de l'enfance, poésie et miracle de la vie quotidienne: voilà ma pièce. . . .' 'I have no desire,' Mr Pound observes,† 'either for needless mystery, or for writing equally needless explanations.' (It is to be noted that Mr T. S. Eliot, by appending apparently 'explanatory' notes to the text of 'The Waste Land', obscured what was otherwise perfectly clear because he seemed to suggest that participation in his erudition was essential for the 'understanding' of his poetry.) Obviously, technical information will help in reading the Cantos; it will add a certain richness to the enjoyment, just as information in the fields I have mentioned above will add richness to the enjoyment of the *Sacre*; but no amount of information will bring the reader nearer to the solution of the puzzle. For there is no puzzle.

Mr Pound's documentation is a device, a technic. History and literature are for him a mine of images, and his purpose is to fix certain of these images in a lasting, orderly design, without reference to a philosophy or to any system of teleological principles. Now whether the historical fact, the Image, be the blowing of apricot-blossoms from east to west, or a narcotic charge preferred against Frank Robert Iriquois of Oklahoma City, or the departure of Anchises from Troy, it is a detail of supreme importance to the frieze, a note of supreme importance to the mélos, which is the poem as a whole. The poet, as I have observed, uses images precisely as another poet would use metaphors or, even more simply, chromatic words. These images have no hidden 'meaning.' Malatesta, Frank Robert Iriquois, the apricot-blossoms, are no more 'puzzling' than Shakespeare's 'encarnadine' in the verse about the

* *Les Mariés de la Tour Eiffel: préface de 1922.*
† Note to the Cantos published in the *Hound & Horn*, vol. III, no. 3 [spring, 1930].

multitudinous seas. It is true that if you have enough Latin to be able
to associate 'encarnadine' with 'flesh,' 'carnation,' and the other rich
warm *carn*-words, you will derive more enjoyment from the verse
than will X, who knows only that 'encarnadine' is a euphuism for
'redden'; but you will 'understand' the verse not a whit better than your
less informed friend. Therefore, the criticism that *XXX Cantos* is incomprehensible, is a false criticism; and I have gone into it at some length
simply because it seems to be the objection that is being most strongly
urged against the poem. The Cantos will baffle persons who are willing
to be baffled; but this is so in the case of any considerable poem.

The Cantos may be described as an epic of timelessness. That is to
say, the poem represents Mr Pound's endeavour to manage an arrest of
time. Roughly, the method is that of identification or fusion of image.
And again, I can explain no better than by quoting. Here is a passage
from one of the Malatesta Cantos (XI):

[quotes *Cantos*, pp. 55–6 'Damn pity he' to 'to Enricho de Aquabello'.]

Or this, from Canto XXIII:

[quotes *Cantos*, pp. 111–2 'With the sun' to ' "Yperionides" '.]

In both of these passages, more obviously in the first than the second,
there is a fusion of more than one image-tone (it is a matter of three
vocabularies in the first, of three languages and a couple of jargons in
the second); I might almost say that here is a collision of more than
one plane of writing. What is effected is substantially an identification
of image. The Malatesta episode is taken out of its time-place and located
in our own; and, at the same time, our own time-place is translated to
that of Malatesta. What has really happened, of course, is a destruction
of any time-place whatsoever. It is an arrest of time in a continual
present, a suspension—notes and images

> as facets of air,
> and the mind there, before them, moving,
> so that the notes needed not move.[1]

This is managed here by a fusion of the associations and technics of
tones: the ancient and the contemporary. Sometimes it is effected
simply by transitionless juxtaposition: so, Canto I ends with Odysseus,
and passes with no more than a 'So that': to the *Sordello* of Robert

[1] The text quoted, with errors in the original article, was corrected by Fitts in a letter to
the *Hound & Horn* (spring 1931), iv, 417–18.

Browning; and the Proteus at the end of Canto II is connected by only an 'And . . .' with the modern Venice of Canto III, which immediately, with no transitional phrase at all, takes up the story of Myo Cid before Burgos. At other times it is brought about not by fusion or juxtaposition, but by a complicated interweaving of the strands of fact and association (*cf.* Cantos XIV and XV). Whatever the method, the identification is perfected by Mr Pound's most familiar device: the making himself the agonist of his characters, their mask ('persona'), and, at the same time, the establishment of his characters as *personæ* of himself. He is not only the pilgrim through his cosmos: he is the Virgil pointing out the notable personages to Dante, and, more, he is each one of the notable personages. This, then, is, as I see it, the design and the construction of *XXX Cantos*.

The poem is successful in theory; it is, without any doubt, the most ambitious poetic conception of our day; and it is so nearly successful in execution that fault-finding seems invidious. At the same time, there are unmistakable lapses; and it is curious to observe that these lapses occur inevitably whenever the poet, whether through preoccupation with a detail of fact, or by allowing the intensity of his emotion to degenerate into a personal violence, drops the *persona*, steps away, as it were, from the frieze-stage, and begins to comment upon the actors directly, as Ezra Pound, to the audience. I can account in no other way for the failure of Cantos XIV and XV. These Cantos are the *Inferno* of the poem, and are conceived in the manner of the traditional scatological invective. But for all their vigour (and they are certainly startling!) they carry very little conviction. They do not *assert*: they rant, they snarl. One is always conscious of Mr Pound in these Cantos— of Mr Pound *as* Mr Pound, with scores to pay off, with injuries to redress. The invective is personalized. Worse, the intention to shock and disgust is childishly apparent. Dante, too, could put his enemies in Hell; Dante could shock and disgust; but Dante's method, even when the conception is entirely personal, is always a universalization, unlimited by Dante himself, un-selfconscious.

Preoccupation with a detail for the detail's sake accounts for a more serious, because more fundamental, failure. An example of this tendency may be noticed in the macaronic passage from the beginning of Canto XXIII, which I have quoted. Here Mr Pound is having a perfectly grand time playing with the various meanings of ἅλιος; apparently these maltreated words have overtones of emotional association for him. But he has failed to convey these associations to the reader. For the moment he is indulging pure pedantry—and not very accurate pedantry at that. Again, he has ceased to assert; he has substituted something unconvincingly dead for something convincingly alive. And I would suggest that this tendency is fundamental. Mr Pound's attitude *is* the pedantic, unreal attitude. Throughout the poem he has substituted book-living for actual life. In spite of his realization of what poetry must do—a realization articulate for ever in the beautiful Kung episode—he has failed to make his poetry meet the test of its own formulation: he has failed to assert life because he has chosen only a ghost-life, a life at second hand, to assert.

I have called this poem the greatest *conception* of our day. Aside from what seems to me a fundamental error in attitude, it is a memorable work. Technically it is nearly faultless; as a craftsman Mr Pound is so far in advance of all the rest of us that his book should be universally read, if only as a manual of poetic technic. But it is much more than splendid writing. It is a gallant proud attempt to assert the positive value of experience. It is very nearly the great music, 'fit for the Odes.'

89. Eda Lou Walton on some types of obscurity

April 1933

'Obscurity in Modern Poetry: Ezra Pound's Cantos Provide an example of the Type Which Demands Scholarly Equipment on the Part of the Reader', *New York Times Book Review* (2 April 1933), sect. v, p. 2.

This review indicates Eliot's authority in New York in 1933. He has become (though oversimplified) a weapon to be used against Pound.

Walton (1896–1962), American literary critic and poet, was educated at the University of California, Berkeley. She taught at New York University from 1924 to 1960.

To review these Cantos adequately the reviewer needs a much longer time for study of them than is ordinarily possible. Without this, however, certain points about this volume of Ezra Pound's may be made. The book (there are, we understand, to be 100 Cantos when it is complete) is a kind of odyssey of the literary mind, of that type of mind which has valued reading either above life, or as life itself, and the beauty of language and phrase above everything. Quotations of poetry, allusions to myth, history, famous names, bits of conversation, jokes, spurious documents, are all remembered by the poet and used as reference, but not, we think, in relation to any definite, longer scheme of thought or feeling. The worlds presented are Greek, Roman, Medieval, Italian Renaissance, Provençal, eighteenth century and modern. The nineteenth century, as is true for most modern classical poetry, has been dropped out. The method of the Cantos is in part Joyce's, in part Eliot's. Everything that can be borrowed from other poets, ancient or contemporary, is borrowed and set in Pound's own form, given his own feeling. But it is very difficult, indeed, to determine that Pound has any particular method or any particular philosophical or emotional feeling to express.

A reader of modern poetry may be asked to know several languages, mythologies and histories. He may be expected to remember many names and stories evoked to produce an effect. He may be required to be something of a scholar and something of a collector. But there is no point in his acquiring this training unless through it he is brought to a clear understanding of some new poetic interpretation. Documentation is all right if we know what it documents. But do we—in Pound's case? We know the exact attitude of Eliot as a poet; we understand his artistic position, his feeling, his philosophy of life. It comes through regardless of whether we remember his quotations or have associations with his allusions. The reader, in other words, has no right to object to obscurity in this sense, in poetry, if when that clears there is new light, if the modern poet's addition to what he has quoted, his interpretation of what he repeats, is new and significant. We have come to acknowledge the stream of tradition flowing into modern poetry, but we do expect modern poetry to change and be changed by that stream of tradition. If, however, after going to some trouble to understand the modern poet's literary associations, the reader remains ignorant of the reason for the references used, finds no new light from the particular poet's interpretation of his literary associations, no scheme by which the poet interprets the old and the new, then obscurity becomes obscurity indeed. This particular reader can find (in two or three readings of the 'Cantos') no scheme whereby Pound causes reference to revalue his own ideas or emotions.

It has been said that Pound writes in several planes at once. It has been said that the various ages referred to in the Cantos whirl round like a wheel, whereon Pound, the poet, dashes colors. But why? Joyce uses one plane (the Ulysses story) to tell his modern narrative. Into this plane drop, as if perpendicularly, a number of other planes. But the plane of the narrative movement is always the same and is clear. Eliot has a fixed point of view from which to look on life. We know his scheme of values. Eliot, too, writes on one plane, from one point in time and space. His quotations are used always to confirm his philosophical position in the contemporary world and to clarify his vision concerning modern life.

But what is Pound's philosophy? He has never stated it. What is his prophecy concerning contemporary life? He has never made it. Where does he stand in time or space? If one can judge from his many earlier poems he moves from one place to another very rapidly.

Pound is a superb technician, perhaps the most important modern prosodist. He has contributed much to modern poetry by his many studies in rhythm. He has taught Eliot his technique. He has taught MacLeish a great deal about speech in poetry. He is often a very good lyric poet himself. The best passages in the Cantos are those which attain to sheer lyric loveliness. Pound understands poetry of simple but perfect statement, poetry free of ornateness. But Pound is not a thinker, not a theorist concerning life itself. There are, to be sure, Cantos here to which one can pin a subject: one on Journalists whom Pound hates with a lively hatred, one on usury and the power of money; there are Cantos on Love in its various manifestations, and a Canto defining the Art of Poetry. But all that we can be sure that the thirty Cantos as a whole say is that Pound, himself, can write with extraordinary skill and beauty. Despite frequent references to Dante's scheme, despite references to Ovid, Virgil, Homer, there is no complete scheme of ideas and feelings given to us in the Cantos. Human liberty is stressed, to be sure. Is this the general subject? Is this the general principle of human life set forth?

Pound's meters vary with his subject matter. In the first Cantos he approximates to the classical quantitative meters. Other Cantos take on the meters of various foreign poetry. The language, too, varies from classical serenity of speech to contemporary jargon and slang. This poet's use of meter and language will be studied by many another poet. Perhaps he fills his place as a great experimenter in poetic form.

After all, haven't we gone about as far into obscurity as we dare? Poetry may or may not need to mean anything, but the fact that words have definitions leads one to conclude that words put together have meaning. Anyway, words do produce effects, emotional or intellectual, in the reader. And the modern reader has been asked to follow modern poets down two rather dark alleys. Two types of obscurity prevail. Hart Crane has used that type which results from sinking lower and lower into the subconscious mind. Hart Crane, as a poet, was able to plumb the subconscious depths of associations. His reader can follow him only by repeating the poet's process and institutionally sinking into the uncertain light of subconscious. Therefore, Hart Crane is obscure to the reader who refuses to do this. The reader who is willing may, however, gain considerably in sensitivity to the creative process, and this type of obscurity may be worth while. The second type of obscurity results from a different poetic method. Poets whose minds are a reservoir of bookish memories use and exploit this method. The reader who would pierce this type of obscurity uses not his subconscious mind, but his conscious intellect. He may, thereby, increase his knowledge of poetry in all languages. Does he deepen his own perceptivity? Yes, somewhat. But chiefly, he plays an intellectual game. Having found out and understood every reference, he must come back to the poet speaking. Returning to Eliot, he finds Eliot's own passionate feeling about dearth in life. Returning to Pound, what *does* he find? In the end, it is the modern poet's passionate conviction that *must* count. The modern poet's learning is unimportant save as it enriches his own creative spirit.

90. Geoffrey Grigson, 'The Methodism of Ezra Pound', *New Verse*

October 1933, no. 5, 17–22

Yeats's *A Vision*, quoted by Grigson, appeared in a limited edition in 1927, and was substantially revised and reissued ten years later. The book begins with a few papers titled 'A Packet for Ezra Pound', perhaps meant as a gesture of neighbourliness (they both were living in Rapallo). Yeats here gives Pound's account of the structure of the Cantos before the completion of *A Draft of XXX Cantos*.

'He explains that it will, when the hundredth Canto is finished, display a structure like that of a Bach Fugue. There will be no plot, no chronicle of events, no logic of discourse, but two themes, the descent into Hades from Homer, a metamorphosis from Ovid, and mixed with these mediæval or modern historical characters. He has tried to produce that picture Porteous commended to Nicholas Poussin in *Le Chef d'oeuvre Inconnu*, where everything rounds or thrusts itself without edges, without contours—conventions of the intellect—from a splash of tints and shades, to achieve a work as characteristic of the art of our time as the paintings of Cézanne, avowedly suggested by Porteous, as *Ulysses* and its dream associations of words and images, a poem in which there is nothing that can be taken out and reasoned over, nothing that is not a part of the poem itself. He has scribbled on the back of an envelope certain sets of letters that represent emotions or archetypal events—I cannot find any adequate definition—A B C D and then J K L M, and then each set of letters repeated, and then A B C D inverted and this repeated, and then a new element X Y Z, then certain letters that never recur and then all sorts of combinations of X Y Z and J K L M and A B C D and D C B A and all set whirling together. He has shown me upon a wall a photograph of a Cosimo Tura decoration in three compartments, in the upper the Triumph of Love and the Triumph of Chastity, in the middle the Zodiacal signs, and in the lower certain events in Cosimo Tura's day. The descent and the metamorphosis— A B C D and J K L M—his fixed elements, took the place of the Zodiac, the archetypal persons—X Y Z—that of the Triumphs, and certain modern events—his letters that do not recur—that of those events in Cosimo Tura's day.'

After the esoteric verbiage, the shows of learning, the thick and heavy criticism in which the Cantos have been bedded, it is well to quote this clear exposition of their purpose. The writer is W. B. Yeats, the source his *Packet For Ezra Pound* which is a book strangely unknown to many people.

It may comfort (or irritate) those who are puzzled by Pound to find someone such as Yeats, an 'accepted' (though belittled and misunderstood) poet, considering Pound as an adult, considering him as a poet, and considering his Cantos worth discussion; but an exposition only helps one to read and to criticise the Cantos. It by no means does away with the problems which they provoke or establishes their success.

The two problems are these: how far in its incomplete state is this very long poem justified by its form, and can the material of Mr. Pound's poetry be accepted in the bulk without misgiving? Form in a poem, even a short poem, is the hardest thing to detect and be sure about. On an unfinished poem of the length of the Cantos judgement must be unfinished as well, though as far as it goes the structure should be clear, like the cellular structure of a rounded organism when half dissected. This cellular analogy is important. It would be absurd to condemn the Cantos by deferring to 'conventions of the intellect,' for it is in the nature of contemporary art that it dispenses with the old exaggeration of logic and balance. The Cantos must be as different in structure from *Paradise Lost* as a painting by Braque or a drawing by Henry

Moore differs from a painting or drawing by Poussin. They must be part of an organism, growing from and round certain foci—the archetypal events or fixed elements—but the growth must be firm, the cells full and active.

By this ruler I find the Cantos less satisfactory than they should be. In Cantos I and II the two archetypal events are magnificently stated. Thereafter what appears to me chaotic may, it is true, only appear so because of the extreme intricacy of the irregular but continual intergrowth of fixed elements, archetypal persons, and contemporary events. The difficulty is that the first problem involves the second. The form depends on the substance to a most intimate degree. Where, it might nearly be said, most poets use words, Mr. Pound uses quotations and translations and reminiscence, and single words which are often meant to convey a large burden outside themselves. The method is familiar through 'The Waste Land' (which owes much to Pound), and the total form depends, in more than the immediate sense, in the way in which this peculiar material is put together. As the pieces of material are larger, their link, positive or negative, more obvious, so the pattern in that section of the total form becomes the clearer. Thus in Canto I, given the knowledge of Andreas Divus's translation of Homer in the 1530's, it is clear that Mr. Pound intends one to link classical culture with renaissance and renaissance with mediæval culture. To be sure of his pattern from beginning to end of these *XXX* Cantos, one must be able to catch every thin, delicate shaving of suggestion which Mr. Pound employs. Describing Helen, for example, in Canto II, Mr. Pound says that she

> has the face of a God
> And the voice of Schœney's daughters.

Schœney is Schœnus, father of Atalanta, a fact which five seconds with Lemprière will discover. But why Schœney? The answer is that Golding, in his translation of the 8th book of the Metamorphoses, describes

> Atalant, a goodly Ladie one
> of Schœnyes daughters

and that Mr. Pound intends another cultural link. It is true that he quotes the passage in *Pavannes and Divisions,* but not every reader will have read *Pavannes and Divisions* or Golding's translation, and there is no reason why he should have done. Where, as often, it is possible to discover what Mr. Pound implies by each em, each cell of his material— Provençal, Japanese, Chinese, from Ovid, Homer, Dante, the Poema del Cid, or from contemporary events—it is often possible and essential to admit that he uses it with skill and force.

A lump of dough or a trickle of tar has shape and consistency; and it would be stupid to say that there is not a homogeneity about these thirty Cantos. There is a homogeneity of material, a homogeneity in style or the way in which it is expressed; but remembering again that the thirty Cantos are only a fragment, and affirming that many of the innumerable implications can only be understood after a more thorough study of all Mr. Pound's reading than I have carried out, I doubt still whether the Cantos have, in their splash of tint and shades, the compulsive and pervading discipline, the cellular inevitability that must belong to such a rounded organism. Coleridge's distinction between imagination and fancy detects in many stretches of the Cantos an arbitrary collocation by which they are included in the lesser kind of poetry.

I agree with all who have emphasised it that the writing is often magnificent, but it is best often in the longest passages of unmixed material. It is athletic writing, of a kind which has only been made possible by long severe training and dieting (which is feasting on the right food). Mr. Pound has been finely critical of his own work. A quick way of proving this is to compare the writing in the three Cantos in *Quia Pauper Amavi* with the present strict, abbreviated version. But is it half enough to write well? The Cantos impress me with the fact that Mr. Pound sees rather than thrusts himself deeply into the depth of living and appreciates critically and creatively the implications of human culture as the one safe controller of specific destiny. But I believe that Pound, in his methodist extreme, and Eliot in so far as he has allowed himself to be influenced in this way by Pound, display in their poetry the evils of exaggerated and decadent Humanism. Mr. Eliot (who has used a humanist method for anything but humanist ends) argues the identity of life and literature, that an experience from literature can be as vital as any other. The retort is yes—to the experiencer. Mr. Pound, of course, can see his troubadours as living persons, but a quotation, an allusion, meant to have a big cultural and emotional significance, is not a person, and, more than most symbols or elements in poetry from the simple word to the image, quotations and allusions are inexact instruments. The experience so conveyed is second-hand to the reader, more so than with a carriage of words or of more elaborate personal symbols of a fixed meaning. It is vitiated by a double poetic ambiguity. A satirist could make good points by fancying a poem written in the quotations from a poem written itself in the same quotations from the Cantos which have quoted the quotations from Dante, Ovid and others.

I believe, in brief, that the method of the Cantos and of much of Eliot is a bad one well used. Other poets in the past have used it, but only as an occasional means of imagery. Though capable of great variety, it is a narrow means and one which well accords with inferior perceptive and visual powers, with living in culture rather than creating it.

Both Mr. Eliot and Mr. Pound have talked much about technique. Mr. Eliot has talked of Pound's *Selected Poems* as a text-book of modern versification, of the Cantos as a mine for juvenile poets to quarry; and in Retrospections (*Pavannes and Divisions*) Mr. Pound has talked revealingly of his explorations and experiments, his search for that precision, lacking in Victorian verse, which he finds in the verse of Arnaut Daniel and Cavalcanti. 'If a man's experiments try out one new rime, or dispense conclusively with one iota of currently accepted nonsense, he is merely playing fair with his colleagues when he chalks up his result.' This is true and unfrivolous, but it is going into poetry with too great a consciousness of poetry. Technique is a monstrously hard thing to acquire, but to think too much about it, divorced from its only purpose, is debilitating. Cocteau has said: 'The nightingale sings badly,' but he has also said in large capitals, 'WE SHOULD BE MEN DURING OUR LIFETIME AND ARTISTS FOR POSTERITY.' In no age but our own Humanist fag-end could a poet so much as mention that the writing of his or his friends' poetry can teach other poets.

This is not the proper way of ending an article on the Cantos. They contain, I repeat, much splendid verse, verse stripped of 'rhetorical din and luxurious riot,' verse 'nearer the bone' and as much like granite as it can be, verse of the right kind for a long poem, though verse, I think, too brief, not as it should be through compression, but through deliberate economy. I miss in the Cantos the extreme physical shock which cursory inexpert reading finds at once in an incident or image in Dante, a shock which comes more than once in the work of Mr. Eliot, but there is much in them to admire, much, as Mr. Eliot has injured his case for them by declaring, to profit by. Mr. Eliot and Mr. Pound have restored the understanding of verse and have been good teachers. Yet in as far as they have paradoxically written most original poems which are valuable products of the beginning of a new or at least a transitional art-age somewhat in terms of a dead or dying age, in as far as they adorn art by art and derive art from art, they should by other poets be left alone. This basic idiosyncrasy has damaged what it has made; and Mr. Pound should be allowed to drive his rich, royal coloured coach down his blind boulevard without rearguard or procession. Mr. Ronald Bottrall if he likes can follow on his scooter.

91. D. G. Bridson, review, *New English Weekly*

5 October 1933, iii, 593–5

Pound's testy reply in the issue of 12 October is included at the end of this review.

Bridson (b. 1910) was a radio producer for the BBC. He interviewed Pound for the BBC and the transcript has been published in *New Directions* (1961), no. 17, 159–84.

It is rather late in the day to come forward with the suggestion that present is an integration of past, and that the content or range of present expands in an arithmetical progression. It is also rather late in the day to suggest that awareness of present is tinged and inseparably connected with awareness of at least *some* past. It is a good many years, in fact, since lines were written above Tintern Abbey. All this being so, it is rather difficult to see how one can be fully conscious of present without being equally fully conscious of past. And knowledge of the past being accessible only through the medium of books, paintings, etc., it is difficult to see how one can pretend to know the contemporary world at all surely without being widely read in the literature of the past,— the literature, be it added, of many nations.

All which platitude would not be necessary if Mr. Pound's Cantos had not been decried as—among other things—pedantic. For what is far more difficult to grasp than platitude is downright idiocy,—such as the statement that Mr. Pound—again in his Cantos—had 'substituted book-living for actual living.' In the first place, it is surely significant that the contemporary references of the Cantos are almost invariably first-hand. And just because he has had recourse to others for the actual writing-up of past incident, he can hardly be said to have depended on books, rather than upon life, for his material: even his critics could scarcely supply first-hand reference to Waterloo,—unless, of course, they were actually engaged there. Surely, the very fact that Pound's aim is the establishment of 'an hierarchy of values' stands for something. An hierarchy of values is useful only to those concerned with life, as it could be established—or would be deemed anyway necessary to establish—only by one primarily concerned with the economics of living.

Quite apart from all such considerations, however, it would be difficult indeed to hit on a poem *more* alive than Mr. Pound's 'poem of some length.' Looking back on the Cantos as a whole, one is most of all impressed by their gusto. Their invective (here and there), their idiom, their variety, novelty, oddity, and wild abundance of content, bear witness to a vitality in their author at least unusual. The mere fact of their embracing present *and* past might suggest an overflowing of contemporary consciousness, even if their general tone did not. . . .

For the very obvious fact remains, that however much Mr. Pound may quote or allude, significance is invariably drawn more from the quoter than the quoted. Which is only another way of saying that his knack (among many) is a vitalising of material, contemporary no less than historical. When his material is historical, he vitalises a past not peculiar to himself, but common—did they but realise as much—to all his readers. In fact, the reader of the Cantos (unless he is himself 'literary-minded,' which he generally happens to be) will be conscious far more acutely of the 'personality' of the author than of the 'personalities' which the author absorbs. It is all very well to say that Mr. Pound throws light on the characters he reports: he actually throws far more light on himself. And that he is himself a pedant, only pedants are likely to suggest. Well-read, perhaps,—but that is not *exactly* the same thing. Mr. Pound in his Cantos undoubtedly appears as one of those authors who 'digest a vast mass of subject-matter, apply a number of known modes of expression, and succeed in pervading the whole with some special quality or some special character of their own,'—it being remembered that the 'known mode' of the Cantos was made known by Mr. Pound himself.

Far too much, in fact, has been said about the detachment with which Mr. Pound presents his evidence, and far too little about the quite individual way in which—apart from mental attitude—it is presented. Just because he withholds his comment upon translation or quotation, there is no reason to suppose that a similar effect could be produced by anyone else who happened to translate or quote the same passage with a similar seeming detachment. The manner of presentation, throughout the poem, is Poundian. Nor that in tricks of style only. In this respect, the Cantos make very different reading from 'The Waste Land.' Mr. Pound, it would seem, is not so afraid of his 'personality' as many good folk today. Even if he were, he would be unable to escape from it. It is in his nature to sprawl, and sprawl he does in the 'Cantos' to his heart's content. There are no very memorable lines in them. . . . His effects are effects of whole Cantos rather than of stray lines, his faults those of impatience rather than those of pedantic attention to detail. Whatever the speed of their composition, most of the Cantos convey the impression of having been dashed off in some odd half hour—probably against the clock. It is partly the pace of them, indeed, which leads to their apparent obscurity: the author has no time to explain or qualify, the reader no time to grasp or question. (If Mr. Pound reply, incidentally, that so many lines took him so many days to endite, I shall neither be surprised nor care: he must at least be aware of the effect which his verse produces, consciously or unconsciously.)

What must be at once admitted, of course, is that the Cantos—however easy to read or to appreciate—are difficult to understand fully. From Mr. Eliot we have the following: 'As for the meaning of the Cantos, that never worries me, and I do not believe that I care.' This remark gives rise to the following outburst on the part of Dr. Leavis: 'When Mr. Eliot in "The Waste Land" has recourse to allusion, the intrinsic power of his verse is commonly such as to affect even a reader who does not recognise what is being alluded to. But even when one is fully informed about Mr. Pound's allusions, one's recognition has no significant effect: the value remains private to the author. The methods of association and contrast employed in "The Waste Land" subserve an urgency pressing from below: only an austere and deep seriousness could have controlled them into significance. But the Cantos appear to be little more than a game—a game serious with the seriousness of pedantry. We may recognise what Pound's counters stand for, but they remain counters; and his patterns are not very interesting, even as schematic design, since, in the nature of the game, which hasn't much in the nature of rules . . . they lack definition and salience.'

It is all very convincing to argue like this,—to explain Mr. Eliot's seriousness as 'austere and deep,' and Mr. Pound's 'seriousness' as the 'seriousness of pedantry.' What undoubtedly comes from a reading of 'The Waste Land', side by side with the *XXX Cantos*, is an impression of Mr. Eliot's rather studied and explained effect as opposed to Mr. Pound's rather exuberant carelessness and indifference to understanding or appreciation. The urgency 'presses from below,' far more in the Cantos, I think, than in any poetry which Mr. Eliot has yet set himself to write. As to control and significance,—we can grant Mr. Eliot the former, and wonder how much of 'The Waste Land' Dr. Leavis would have appreciated without the Notes to lay bare the actual plan of the whole. If Mr. Pound would take the trouble to publish an annotated and simplified edition of his Cantos, no doubt their urgency would be more immediately apparent. For myself, I think I can eke out with the edition provided thus far.

What one must wonder, however, is whether the Cantos really achieve what they set out to achieve,—the establishment of 'an hierarchy of values.' An hierarchy is well enough, provided the sheep are actually sorted from the goats. If, on the other hand, the eyesight of the judge is none too sure, unless the sheep and the goats are actually separated for him, he is apt to confuse them for himself. In other words, even if the Cantos assemble the values, the latter must be sorted out clearly before they can truly be said to have been ranked at all. And here, I fancy, Mr. Pound has expected rather too much of his readers. To quote Mr. Eliot once more: 'I know that Pound has a scheme and a kind of philosophy behind it; it is quite enough for me that he thinks he knows what he is doing; I am glad that the philosophy is there, but I am not interested in it.' But that, unfortunately, won't do! If the Cantos are so written that they are more interesting as pure poetry than as significance, then they are not fulfilling their purpose. The audience addressed in 'The Waste Land,' was far smaller than the audience we may assume to be addressed in the Cantos. 'The Waste Land,' like Gower's 'Vox Clamantis,' is a warning addressed to the selected few in what is to all intents and purposes a private code. The Cantos, on the other hand, aim at something far more ambitious. Their appreciation should, accordingly, be far more general. The control and atmosphere of restraint discernible in Mr. Eliot's poetry, are perfectly suited to his poetry. The hit or miss method of the Cantos is not so perfectly suited to Mr. Pound's. If we can appreciate the Cantos for their surface value, that is more than their critics would have us suppose. If we cannot appreciate them for all that they contain for their author, the fault is perhaps ours. But if Mr. Pound's intention is that the content assume sociological significance, then he is to be blamed for using a method which—however well handled—is unsuited to his intention. He has far too much of importance to say for him to rest content in the appreciation of a few. Human nature and intelligence being what it is, he would have been well advised to compromise by meeting his audience half way.

Pound's reply:

Sir,—Perhaps Mr. Bridson would be generous enough to explain WHAT audience I ought to 'meet halfway.'

London, is, as you know, full of pimps who do not want to look either facts or ideas in the face. Back from 1908 they smothered discussion of KNOWN FACTS about literature; stifled comparison of British metric slop and bombast with good writing in other languages; from 1918 onwards they did their filthiest to prevent the distribution of C. H. Douglas' ideas.

Are these the vermin for whom one should write footnotes?

On these spirochetes rests the blame for ten years' utterly needless prolongation of poverty, for 15 years of competitive armament and treason. I don't mean merely the gun-touts, but the journalists engaged in suppressing news and in keeping language so indistinct that it cannot serve as efficient medium of communication.

92. Marianne Moore, review, *Criterion*

April 1934, xiii, 482–5

Marianne Moore reviewed *A Draft of XXX Cantos* in *Poetry* (October 1931) (see Bibliography), and recast the review for the *Criterion*.

Miss Moore (1887–1972) graduated from Bryn Mawr College in 1909. She was editor of the *Dial* (1925–9) and is the author of several collections of poetry. She and Pound first met in New York in May 1939, though they had been in correspondence for twenty years.

'It is a disgraceful thing', Ezra Pound says, 'for a man's work not to show steady growth and increasing fineness from first to last,' and anyone alert to the creative struggle will recognize in the Cantos under later treatment as compared with earlier drafts, the rise of the stormwave of literary security and the tautness obtained by conscious renunciation.

We have in them 'the usual subjects of conversation between intelligent men'—'books, arms . . . men of unusual genius, both of ancient times and our own'—arranged in the style of the grasshopper-wing for contrast, half the fold against the other half, the rarefied effect against a greyer one. Mr. Pound admits that he can see, as Aristotle did, a connection sometimes where others do not: between books and war, for instance. It is implied that if we were literally in communication, at home and internationally, we should be armed against 'new shambles'; against 'one war after another', started by men 'who couldn't put up a good hen-roost'. And, obversely, 'if Armageddon has taught us anything it should have taught us to abominate the half-truth, and the tellers of the half-truth in literature'. The Cantos are both a poring upon excellence and a protest against 'the tyranny of the unimaginative'. They are against 'the vermin who quote accepted opinion', against historians who ought to have 'left blanks in their writings for what they didn't know'; and are for work charged with realness—for a 'verity of feeling' that releases us from 'the bonds of blatant actuality'.

'The heart is the form,' as is said in the East—in this case the rhythm which is a firm piloting of rebellious fluency; the quality of sustained emphasis, as of a cargo being shrewdly steered to the edge of the quai:

> Under the plumes, with the flakes and small wads of colour
> Showering from the balconies
> With the sheets spread from windows,
>   with leaves and small branches pinned on them,
> Arras hung from the railings; out of the dust,
> With pheasant tails upright on their forelocks,
>   The small white horses, the
> Twelve girls riding in order, green satin in pannier'd habits. . . .

'Every age yields its crop of pleasant singers', Mr. Pound says, 'who write poetry free from the cruder faults', and in the Cantos the quiver of feeling is not conveyed by 'rhyming mountain with fountain and beauty with duty', though in the present evolved method the skill of the more apparent method remains. The edges of the rhetoric and of sound are well 'luted', as in good lacquer-work, and the body throughout is ennobled by insinuated rhyme effects and a craftily regulated tempo:

> *Di cui* in the which he, Francesco. . . .

One notices the accelerated light final rhyme (lie), the delayed long syllable (grass),

> The filagree hiding the gothic,
>   with a touch of rhetoric in the whole
> And the old sarcophagi,
>   such as lie, smothered in grass, by San Vitale;

the undozing ease of

> And hither came Selvo, doge
>   that first mosaic'd San Marco,
> And his wife that would touch food but with forks,
> Sed aureis furculis, that is
>   with small golden prongs
> Bringing in, thus, the vice of luxuria.

There is many a spectacular concealment, or musical ruse should one say, in the patterns presented of slang, foreign speech, and numerals—an ability borrowed as it were from 'the churn, the loom, the spinning-wheel, the oars'; 'Malatesta de Malatestis ad Magnificum Dominum Patremque suum, etc.' about the gift of the bay pony. We have in some of these metrical effects a wisdom as remarkable as anything since Bach.

To the motion of the verse is added descriptive exactness which is, like the good ear, another indication of 'maximum efficiency':

> The gulls broad out their wings,
>   nipping between the splay feathers;
> Gold, gold, a sheaf of hair,
>   thick like wheat swath;

and 'the old woman from Kansas . . . stiff as a cigar-store Indian from the Bowery . . . this ligneous solidity . . . that indestructible female . . .'

Mr. Pound has spent his life putting effort and impudence into what people refuse to take time to enjoy or evaluate: in demonstrating 'the *virtu* of books worth reading'; in saying by example, that 'the thing that matters in art is a sort of energy'; that 'an intensity amounting to genius' enters into the practice of one's art, and that great art is able to overcome 'the fret of contemporaneousness'. Horror of primness is not a crime, 'unvarnished natural speech' is a medicine, and it is probably true that 'no method is justified until it has been carried too far'. But when an author says read what you enjoy and enjoy what you read, one asks in turn, can a man expect to be regarded as a thing of superlatives and absolutes when he dwells on worthlessness as in the imprecatory cantos, forsaking his own counsel which is good! One may vanquish a detractor by ignoring him ('he could have found the correction where he assumed the fault'); or may 'turn to and build'. And one may embarrass with humour, which is in the Cantos a not uningenious phase of dogma. At least we infer that an allusion to easy science, namely easy art, which 'elected a Monsieur Brisset who held that man is descended from frogs', is not a compliment; and that the lines about 'sucking pigs, pigs, pigs, small pigs, porkers throughout all Portugal' is more than mere decoration. But rather than blunt the point of his wedge, a writer is sometimes willing to seem various things that he is not; and Mr. Pound is 'vitally interesting'. His feeling for verse above prose—that for prose 'a much greater amount of language is needed than for poetry'—is like Schönberg's statement: 'My greatest desire is to compress the most substance into the least possible space', and Stravinsky's trick of ending a composition with the recoil of a good ski-jumper accepting a spill. Furthermore, as art grows it deviates. 'I know of no case when an author has developed at all without at least temporarily sacrificing one or several of his initial merits,' Mr. Pound says. In the Cantos the 'singing quality' has somewhat been sacrificed to 'weight'—to 'organ base'. The automatic looser statement of primary impulse penetrates better usually than the perfected one of conscious improvement and the undevout reader might perhaps see the water better in the following lines of prose criticism: 'the cross run of the beat and the word, as of a stiff wind cutting the ripple-tops of bright water' than in: 'the blue-grey glass of the wave tents them' and 'a tin flash in the sun-dazzle'. But the day is coming when spareness will seem natural.

The test for the Cantos is not obstinate continuous probing but a re-reading after the interval of a year or years; 'rhythmic vitality' needs no advocate but time. 'The great book and the firm book' can persuade resisters that 'good art never bores one', that art is a joyous thing.

GUIDO CAVALCANTI RIME

Genoa, January 1932

93. Etienne Gilson, review, *Criterion*

October 1932, xii, 106–12

Pound mentioned having briefly been in contact with Gilson in
Kulchur (1938), 54–5: 'Even in my own case I have struggled in
vain for corrections, I have howled in vain for odd bits of supplementary knowledge. The eminent professor and historian
G. promised me light on Mediaeval philosophy. I sent him
vainly my best set of photographs of del Garbo's commentary
on Guido. And there have ensued years of silence'.

Gilson (b. 1884) is a distinguished French scholar of mediaeval
philosophy. Pound's editorship of *Guido Cavalcanti Rime* is indicated only by the initials 'E.P.', and Gilson did not, apparently,
realize who this was.

This maganificent edition of *Guido Cavalcanti* will certainly be wel-
comed by all students of Italian literature. It seems to be his author's
desire to remain anonymous; whoever he may be, I want to assure
him that I fully realize what a claim he has on the gratitude of his
readers, even where they feel inclined to disagree with some of his
interpretations. The text of the *Rime* in a critical edition, photostatic
reproductions of the most important manuscripts, English translations
of several poems, learned commentaries on their meaning, the whole
enterprise carried on with a care and accuracy deeply rooted in the
passionate love of the editor for his poet, all this is enough to put the
book on a higher level than the ordinary reprint of an old text. I am
not quite sure that *Guido Cavalcanti* 'is not inferior to Dante in quality'
(p. 9), but I am glad his editor and translator felt that way. Believing in
his subject, he certainly has done his utmost to impart to others his own
conviction.

273

Of the text itself, I have very little to say. Descartes once observed that a fool can raise more questions in an hour than a wise man can answer in a life. The text of *Cavalcanti* was already practically established, there always will be divergences in the selection of some readings and as we have been provided by the new editor with a very good choice of variants, it is up to us to pick up the best among them, when we do not agree with his own decision. I wish rather to consider the general interpretation of *Cavalcanti* which is everywhere implied in this new edition and to submit a few remarks concerning what might possibly be a safer approach to such a subject.

In doing so, I am simply yielding to the suggestions of the editor. Having attempted a translation of the famous Canzone, *Donna mi prega*, he knows better than anybody else that: *the poem is very obscure* (Partial explanation, p. 12). More than that, he knows very well one of the chief reasons why it is obscure. Guido is not a philosopher, but there is philosophy in his poem, and 'as the philosophy of the time has been completely scrapped, there are very few specialists who can help us. I should be glad to hear from anyone who has more definite knowledge. Up to the present time I have found out by concentration on the text, and not by reading commentators, and I strongly suspect that is the road that the next man will have to follow'. This is perfectly true. The only trouble is that even those who are acquainted with mediæval philosophy feel helpless before such a text, and will continue feeling thus, so long as they are not provided with the text of the commentators. I dare say that, if we had it, we could get rid in a very short time of the worst obscurities involved in the text. So long, on the contrary, as we do not find it at our disposal, the only method left open will be 'concentration on the text'; that is to say, concentration on poems written in a language whose words have for us no meaning. It would be much better, indeed, if they had none; we are not tempted to 'concentrate' on Japanese texts, because we do not know Japanese; we know, on the contrary, a little of the language in which Cavalcanti's poems are written, and this is what makes concentrating on his text to be so dangerous.

What the religious opinions and philosophical convictions of Cavalcanti can possibly have been, I don't know. I knew, at least, my own ignorance before reading this new edition, and I am still more conscious of it after re-reading the text, its translation and its explanations. The Canzone *Donna mi prega* was known, so we are told, as the 'philosophic canzone'. When it appeared, Guido was called a *natural philosopher*, which seems to be practically identical, in the mind of his contemporaries, with 'atheist' and 'Epicurean'. Not that anyone had then any clear idea or has now any very definite notion of what Epicurus taught. But a natural philosopher was a much less safe person than a moral philosopher. Why this should be said of the state of public opinion in and about 1290, I am unable to guess. Albertus Magnus and Thomas Aquinas, with many others, had written treatises in physics and natural philosophy without having to face the slightest opposition. But this is not even the question; I rather wonder if we have any good reasons to call Cavalcanti a 'natural philosopher'? If he was, which can perhaps be proved on other grounds, we do not find much of it in his famous canzone, no more, indeed, than was commonly known and accepted by any man who had attended schools in his time. Let us consider some of the controverted statements and see what they mean.

The editor himself acknowledges that it is difficult to find real boldness of thought in the doctrine of Cavalcanti; but beside the doctrine, there is the spirit: 'It is not so much what Guido says in the poem, as the familiarity that he shows with dangerous thinking: *natural demonstration* and the proof by experience or (?) experiment'. All this because, according to Cavalcanti, love is known 'not by the reason, but 'tis felt, I say'. Hence the commentary: 'The *non razionale ma che si sente* is for experiment, it is against the tyranny of the syllogism, blinding and obscurantist'.

So many things in so few words! As we shall see later, the text does not mean anything of that kind, it has no relation whatsoever to the opposition between experience and reasoning, but even supposing it has, and means what we are told, was it necessary in 1290, to be up against syllogisms, to realize that love is not known by arguing, and that unless a man has felt it, no abstract description will ever teach him what it is? What is real 'obscurantism', is believing that men have ever been so stupid as not to be aware of such an elementary truth. Besides if there were any naturalism in this statement of Guido, we could find much more naturalism in the conception of mystical love developed in the twelfth century by St. Bernard. It is entirely based on personal experience or (?) experiment: 'Hodie legimus in libro experientiæ' (*In Cant., Cant.,* iii, 1). 'Pozzo in hujusmodi non capit intelligentia nisi quantum experientia attingit' (*op. cit.,* xxii, 2). And who is the real master of love in the Divine Comedy, if not St. Bernard? To think that because Guido applies it to human love, he is fighting against a classical tradition, amounts to building a general interpretation of the man's character on our complete disrespect for some fundamental facts.

Another critical passage bears on the origin of love:

> Vien da veduta forma ches s'intende
> Che'l prende
> nel possibile intelletto
> Chome in subgetto
> locho e dimoranza
> E in quella parte mai non a possanza

Which the English translation renders thus:

> From form seen doth he start, that, understood,
> Taketh in latent intellect—
> As in subject ready—
> place and abode,
> Yet in that place it never is unstill.

With all due apologies for my boldness, I must confess that I can not reconcile the translation with the text. In the first place, it seems obvious that 'possibile intelletto' cannot be rendered by 'latent intellect'. This part of the text is not really obscure, for it is a commonplace application of a conception of human knowledge almost universally admitted in the thirteenth century. The origin of our concepts is a form perceived by our senses (veduta forma), abstracted from the sensible image by an act of understanding (ches s'intende), and impressed by the active intellect in the possible intellect (nel possibile intelletto), where it stays as in its receiving and conserving subject (chome in subgetto locho e dimoranza). Considered as a form that is simply understood in the intellect, love has no real power (e in quella parte mai non a possanza); in other words, being then a purely rational quality, it does not generate delight, but knowledge (non a diletto ma consideranza); quite different is the sensible emotion generated by the contemplation of a beautiful form, it delights and, sometimes, it kills.

The translator of Guido was on the right track when he quoted Avicenna in his commentary on the vocabulary of the poem (p. 28). He was still nearer the truth when he wrote that the terms '*intellectus possibilis*, POSSIBLE, and the *Passive* intellect belong to two different schools'. Why not, then, stick to the technical term in the translation? The *passive* intellect belongs to Aristotle and Alexander, the *possible* intellect to Albertus Magnus and Thomas Aquinas, *passive* implying the materiality, possible, on the contrary, the immateriality of the intellect: 'Intellectus noster possibilis est in potentia tantum in ordine intelligibilium: fit antem actu per formam a phantasmatibus abstrac-

tam' (ST. THOMAS, *In Arist lib. de anima,* II, lect, vi., ed. Pirotta, n. 303).
I do not say that Guido was a Thomist, but there is not the slightest
evidence that he was an Averroist, still less an Epicurean. I feel very
strongly inclined to think that he was a poet, using a commonly received terminology and trying to turn it into beautiful verses.

The same remark would apply to the difficult expression:

> Perche non pote laire simiglglianza (p. 17)

The variant reads:

> Si, ch'ei non uot largir simiglianza.

I would not commit myself beyond what I know. If the printed
verse is the right reading, we must keep it, with the hope that its
meaning will be discovered by a better man; but the variant seems to
be at least intelligible. It alludes to the mediæval notion of *similihido.*
Every form generates its own likeness, by a process more or less ana-
logous to what we call-today irradiation. So far as I can grasp its meaning, the stanza expresses the idea that a purely abstract form, as it is
conceived by reason, does not produce a sensible likeness of itself, so
that it is not a cause of pleasure, but an object of contemplation (non
a diletto ma consideranza, Perche non pote largir simiglglianza).
Whether it means exactly this, or something of that kind, could probably be ascertained by the publication of old commentaries on Guido's
text.

Another translation that seems to me dubious is that of the two
frightfully obscure verses:

> Elgli é creato
> > e a sensato
> > > nome
> D'alma chostume
> > di chor voluntade.

The translator (and here my whole sympathy is with him) renders
the text in the following way:

> Love is created, hath a sensate name,
> His modus takes from the soul, from heart his will.

I am just wondering if we have not here a case of mediæval ety-
mology, very cheap indeed, but in no way cheaper than: *mulier—
mollis aer,* or *molliens herum,* etc. Guido means, perhaps, nothing deeper
than this: 'Love is created, it has taken its name, *amor,* from *anima* (for

it has its seat in the soul) and *cor* (for it derives its will from heart).'
Deriving *amore* from *alma* and *chor* is by no means absurd in the thirteenth century; I would not affirm that this is the real meaning of the
verses, it is at least very likely that Guido had something of that kind in
mind when he wrote them.

What is, finally, the outcome of the discussion? That the first thing
for us to do is turning back to Garbo's Latin commentary. We must not
believe that everything we will find there is necessarily true, but it
should undoubtedly help us a good deal in discovering the truth about
Guido's meaning. One of the best things the new editor has done, in
this respect, has been to reproduce three folios of Garbo's commentary
(plates, 2, 3 and 5). Unfortunately, the second strophe, on which I
tried to 'concentrate' is not to be found there, so that I am not in a
position to check up my own mistakes, but we have a long stretch of the
commentary on the third strophe (plate 3). And I must say that I
found it, in its scholastic honesty, quite illuminating. A few extracts
will show what I mean:

*Nou e virtute, mà da questa vene Perfezione ches si pone tale Non razionale ma che si
sente dico.*—In the first part Guido means that love is not a virtue, but proceeds
from the operation of some virtue. . . . For love is not one of those virtues
that belong to the natural faculties of the soul, nor is it one of those virtues that
are intellectual or moral habits; but love is the passion of a certain habit, exactly
as anger (*ira*) or sadness (*tristitia*) are not virtues, but passions of the appetite.
Though, nevertheless, love be not a virtue, it proceeds from a virtue, for which
reason Guido adds: *ma da quella viene.* Now, by saying that love proceeds from
a virtue, he does not mean a virtue that is an intellectual habit, since it has been
said earlier that love abides in the possible intellect; it does not either proceed
from that kind of virtues we call moral habits, since those are to be found in the
appetite as regulated by reason, and Guido himself will presently say that an
appetite where there is love is *not* regulated by reason. When Guido says that
love proceeds from virtue, he means, therefore, big 'virtue', a power (or faculty)
of the soul, for indeed it proceeds from the operation of the sensitive faculty
which is in us. In other words, love is a certain passion of the appetite, which
appetite (or desire) follows the apprehension of the form of a thing, firstly by
external sense, next by our internal faculties of perception. . . .

Let us now come back to the English translation:

> It is not virtu, but perfection's source
> Lying within perfection postulate
> Not by the reason, but 'tis felt, I say.

It seems too clear that it bears no relation whatever to the text, which simply means:

> It is not a virtue, but it comes from that
> Perfection which is posited as such (i.e. as a virtue),
> Not from the rational virtue, but from sensibility.

This interpretation is confirmed by Garbo's conclusion in his commentary: since love is a passion, it cannot abide in reason, nor even in sensations considered as pure knowledges, but in the sensible appetite (or *desire*) only. This is why love is *fuor disalute*. A blind desire, not regulated by reason, as Garbo says a little farther, is a passion that puts man's judgment 'extra salutem', for 'in love, judgment is not sound but is on the contrary corrupt'. Hence the famous statement about 'intenzione' which has so much puzzled the translator:

> E l antenzione
> > per ragione
> > > vale
> Discerne male
> > in chui é vizio amico.

It does not mean:

> Maintains intention reason's peer and mate;
> Poor in discernment, being thus weakness' friend.

Unless I do not understand either Italian or English (and I am quite willing to admit of it in this case), I would simply translate, with old Garbo's help:

> For intention's value rests on reason
> And it sees but little in whom has vice for friend.

I quite realize the absurdity there is, for a Frenchman, to attempt an English translation of Italian verses, interpreted through the photostatic reproduction of a mediæval latin commentary. To make up for such bad manners I shall conclude these remarks by offering to the new editor of *Cavalcanti*, if he helps me in securing a complete set of photographs of Garbo's commentary, to provide him with a transcription of the latin text. It will be very easy, then, to compare it with Guido's poem and I quite agree with him that concentration would be much more fruitful if it were preceded by erudition.

94. John Sparrow, doubts about Pound and 'Mauberley'

1934

From *Sense and Poetry: Essays on the Place of Meaning in Contemporary Poetry* (London: Constable, 1934), 122–32.
'Phallus in Wonderland', a dialogue in verse by Gavin Ewart, appeared in *New Verse* (May 1933), no. 3, 4–11.

Sparrow (b. 1906), Warden of All Souls, Oxford, is the author of several collections of essays and other scholarly work.

An excellent example [of those writers whose 'novelty of method' is explained by their desire to avoid, not to improve upon, 'an orthodox method'] is the work of Mr. Ezra Pound, who by a somewhat ironic fate has gained his great reputation chiefly by his innovations, though it is where his work is least novel that it is most successful. His translations from the Chinese are simple and elegant, but it seems that the fear that this should be the only distinction of his writing has led him to adopt in his original poems a more personal style. This style has won him high praise in high quarters: 'No one living has practised the art of verse with such austerity and devotion, and no one living has practised it with more success'—is the verdict of Mr. T. S. Eliot himself, who has done Mr. Pound the signal honour of dedicating to him 'The Waste Land' and acclaiming him in the dedication with the title *il miglior fabbro*.

It is not therefore an injustice to take as an example of Mr. Pound's work his 'Hugh Selwyn Mauberley,' which, though it is not itself an unintelligible, though it is often an obscure, poem, has undoubtedly exercised a deep influence on writers who seek to exploit idiosyncrasies of feeling at the expense of intelligible content.* 'This seems to me,' says Mr. Eliot, 'a great poem . . . It is compact of the experience of a

---

* The more suggestive manner of 'The Waste Land' is used by Pound in his long unfinished *chef d'oeuvre*, the *Cantos*.

certain man in a certain place at a certain time, and it is also a document of an epoch; it is genuine tragedy and comedy; and it is, in the best sense of Arnold's worn phrase, a "criticism of life." '* A more recent admirer† writes, ' "Hugh Selwyn Mauberley", it must be repeated, is a whole. The whole is great poetry at once traditional and original. Mr. Pound's standing as a poet rests upon it, and rests securely.'

Whole though it be, the short pieces of which 'Mauberley' consists treat for the most part of separate subjects and are easily detachable. If the following poem, the third of the series, loses anything through being taken separately, sympathetic imagination will readily supply the loss:

[quotes 'Hugh Selwyn Mauberley' III, *CSP*, pp. 206–7.]

The treatment of the theme in this poem is a little strange, but in the theme itself there seems to be nothing extraordinary: Mr. Pound is dealing, as many of his contemporaries and even his predecessors have dealt, with the 'modern world of mass-production and levelling-down, a world that has destroyed the traditions and is hostile, not only to the artist, but to all distinction of spirit.'‡ This poem clearly belongs to the second of the two classes indicated by Mr. Eliot when he says that in some of Mr. Pound's verse 'the content is more important than the means of expression, in the others the means of expression is the important thing.' Here it must be the treatment and not the content that claims our attention. We know well that the pianola with all it stands for has replaced the lyre: we are interested to see what is the peculiar magic by means of which Mr. Pound has invested this theme with poetry. Let us see how the same theme has fared in other hands: when Mr. Pound says that 'We see τὸ καλὸν decreed in the market-place' another said before him, expressing not, it is true, the identical contrast between a pure and a commercialized standard of beauty, but, in a very similar spirit, the opposition between a world dominated by the Stock Exchange and the beauties of a pagan and Hellenic world:

> The world is too much with us; late and soon,
> Getting and spending, we lay waste our powers.

And Mr. Pound's invocation of Apollo, his hankering after the 'mousseline of Cos'—are akin to the impulse which was expressed in the words:

---

* Ezra Pound, *Selected Poems* with an introduction by T. S. Eliot, 1928, pp. xxiii–xxiv.
† Mr. F. R. Leavis, in *New Bearings in English Poetry*, 1932, p. 150.
‡ *New Bearings*, p. 145.

Great God! I'd rather be
A Pagan suckled in a creed outworn;
So might I, standing on this pleasant lea,
Have glimpses that would make me less forlorn;
Have sight of Proteus rising from the sea;
Or hear old Triton blow his wreathed horn.

The thought expressed in Mr. Pound's poem is a little more complex, a shade more interesting than that; and in his poem he has avoided using such words as 'pleasant lea', which he would no doubt regard as a worn-out *cliché* (though when his poems are as old as Wordsworth's, his own 'Phallic and ambrosial' may itself have come to sound a little worn); but is he, on the whole, a gainer? No one will suggest that because his mood was in some respects identical with Wordsworth's, he should himself have written Wordsworth's poem or something like it. But it may well be asked whether it is possible to detect in the studied idiosyncrasies of his manner that advance upon the orthodox, that fruitful poetic exploration, which commands the homage of his admirers. Can we recognize in the 'means of expression' that 'importance' which Mr. Eliot would have us see there; or must the performance be adjudged at best a failure, at worst a sham? The uninstructed reader might be tempted to say that the expression of this commonplace thought is itself redeemed from the commonplace only by two peculiarities: it is peculiarly pretentious and it is peculiarly cheap.

Mr. Leavis, however, knows better. In 'Mauberley', he says, 'The rhythms, in their apparent looseness and carelessness, are marvels of subtlety . . . and the verse has extraordinary variety. The subtlety of movement is associated with subtlety of mood and attitude. "Wit" is present. Critical activity accompanies feeling and remembering.'* Where wit is present and critical activity accompanies feeling and remembering, there are certainly the makings of a delightful poetic gathering, and this poem is singled out by Mr. Leavis for especial admiration, in order to show that Mr. Pound's 'poise, though so varied, and for all his audacities, is sure; how sure, nothing can show better than the last stanza of the third poem:

> O, bright Apollo,
> τίν' ἄνδρα, τίν' ἥρωα, τίνα θεὸν
> What god, man, or hero
> Shall I place a tin wreath upon!

* *New Bearings*, p. 143.

In what poet, after the seventeenth century, can we find anything like this contributing to a completely serious effect (the poem is not only tragically serious but solemn).'*

The influence of Mauberley can be gauged from the following typical stanza, taken from a 200-line poem, entitled (I suppose wittily) 'Phallus in Wonderland' and printed in *New Verse*, a periodical printed in Cambridge which claims to represent all the valuable elements in contemporary poetry:

> 'Prima coitio est acerrima' (Terence);
> In 1889 I first encountered woman
> And copulated unsatisfactorily
> Owing to ignorance.

It would be unfair to judge 'Mauberley' by a section which is admittedly not the finest of the series. That praise is reserved for a piece in the second division of the poem, 'Mauberley' II. To do justice to this poem it must be quoted in full:

[quotes 'Hugh Selwyn Mauberley' (Mauberley 1920) II, *CSP*, pp. 217–18.]

The detached critic, ready always to find merit in new fields, may pause for a moment before this performance, asking what in it he is to admire. Is it beauty of sound? hardly, where every line is harsh and grating. Is it a sequence of lovely images? That will be sought equally in vain. Nor can the piece lay claim to intellectual interest: the thought that appears to inform it is singularly commonplace. Mr. Leavis, however, can tell us why Mr. Eliot thinks this 'great' and the ordinary reader may welcome his explanation (though according to Mr. Leavis 'it seems impertinent to explain what so incomparably explains itself, and all elucidation looks crude').† 'The poem is poignantly personal, and yet, in

---

* *New Bearings*, p. 144. It is a pity that Mr. Leavis has not explained the effect aimed at by Mr. Pound in his mis-accentuations (carefully preserved by himself when he quotes and Mr. Eliot when he edits the poem) in the second line. Of four different words, three are wrongly accented. Mr. Pound's Latin is also sometimes strange: cf. *Selected Poems*, pp. 81 (Gaudero); 134 (vir quidem); 180 (Secut). The way in which Mr. Pound attempts to quote Catullus on p. 83 suggests that his knowledge of the language is elementary. It would be captious to call attention to such points as these, if it were not that much of the respect accorded to Mr. Pound is apparently due to his reputation for scholarship in Latin, Greek, Provençal, and Chinese. His learning in the latter pair of languages I take on trust; it is difficult to believe that the mistakes which occur almost as often as he ventures into the former pair are due invariably to the printer.

† *New Bearings*, p. 139.

its technical perfection, its ironical economy, impersonal and detached. Consider, for instance, the consummate reserve of this:

> Unable in the supervening blankness
> To sift TO AGATHON from the chaff
> Until he found his sieve . . . .
> Ultimately, his seismograph:

—With what subtle force the shift of image in the last line registers the realization that the "orchid" was something more, the impact more than æsthetic! And with what inevitability the "seismograph" and the scientific terminology and manner of what follows convey the bitter irony of realization in retrospect!'*

One of the most admired of modern critics is here appraising the *chef d'œuvre* of one of the most successful of modern poets; and yet it sounds much as if an impostor had duped a clever fool into writing high-sounding nonsense. 'And this'—we are tempted when we see such work thus praised, to repeat the words of an earlier critic—'is fine poetry!† This is what ranks its writer with the master-spirits of the age!‡ This is what has been described, over and over again, in terms which would require some qualification if used respecting *Paradise Lost.*§ [This is] to be held to admiration as an inestimable specimen of art.‖ And what must we think of a system by means of which verses like those which we have quoted, verses fit only for the poets' corner of the *Morning Post*, can produce emolument and fame?' What word of this, except perhaps the reference to the *Morning Post*, is not applicable to the passages that have been quoted from the works of Mr. Pound and of Mr. Pound's admirers?

* *Ibid.*, p. 148.
† 'a great poem,' Mr. Eliot; 'great poetry,' Mr. Leavis.
‡ 'a document of an epoch,' Mr. Eliot.
§ 'genuine tragedy . . . a criticism of life,' Mr. Eliot.
‖ 'marvels of subtlety . . . technical perfections,' Mr. Leavis.

MAKE IT NEW

London, 27 September 1934
New Haven, 12 March 1935

95. G. M. Young, review, *Observer*

7 October 1934, 7

Young (1882–1959) was an English historian and essayist, best known for his *Victorian England* (1936).

Oft had I heard of Ezra Pound, and when he came my way I opened the book with something like excitement. From allusions to his other works in the writings of our living critics I knew, or perhaps I should say I had 'a growing awareness,' that Mr. Pound was a figure and an influence of considerable importance; but whether he owed his eminence to his poetry, his prose, or his knowledge, much insisted on, of the Provençal tongue, I could not exactly make out. Nor does the book itself make it easy to come to a decision. It contains, after the introduction a very slight essay on the Troubadours, a remarkably ingenious translation of Arnaut Daniel, some scrappy remarks on Elizabethan and other translators, originally printed in the *Egoist*, ce qui ne surprendra personne, an anthology of Modern French verse with critical observations, two fulldress, but only partly composed reviews of Henry James and Rémy de Gourmont, and an erudite analysis of Guido Cavalcanti. Of this last, let those judge who are able. An addiction to minor poets of such intense obscurity as Arnaut and Guido is characteristic of Mr. Pound's independence, and has, I think, not been without influence on his own manner, and the manner of those who follow him.

> At midnight mirk
> In secrecies
> I nurse
> My served make

285

In heart; nor try
My melodies
At other's door nor mearing.

does not seem to me to be very good poetry, but I have seen a great deal like it in these last few years.

A style so personal, wielded with such confidence and backed by such wide erudition, was destined to exercise a large influence on the immature. In prose, Mr. Pound seems less at home. In fact, an observation on one of Henry James' books that 'it is damn badly written: atrocious vocabulary' surprised me a little, because up to that point it had not occurred to me that Mr. Pound recognised any difference between good writing and bad, or acknowledged any obligation to the canons, practices and decencies of English prose. I am not referring to the callow exhibitionism of his diction, or 'the katachrestical vigours' of his syntax. Let every man write his own style. But a sentence framed in this manner:—

> Greece and Alexandria may have been embedded knee-deep in Sapphics.

is peculiarly disconcerting because it suggests that the writer has never seen a bed and does not know where the knees come. And with such 'verbal manifestation,' Mr. Pound's pages teem. If the prose of James is damnable, blasphemy herself might fail to characterise some of the personal contortions to which Mr. Pound's Muse is reduced, while Mr. Pound, like Mrs. Micawber, 'abets her unnatural feats by playing the barrel organ.'

Of Mr. Pound's learning only his equals will speak with confidence. I do not myself think that tribus cimicium is a good genitive or tribus Britannicus a good concord. But as Mr. Pound claims to have been well taught in Latin, very likely he is right and the Latin grammar wrong. I had never noticed the 'Syrian syncopation' in Bion's Adonis, and when Mr. Pound remarks on the heavy accentuation of some of Valla's hexameters, I wondered whether perhaps they were not groaning under the false quantities they had been made to carry. Nor do I see how Raphael and Ideal can, even unintentionally, rhyme, unless in Mr. Pound's lingua materna, they both rhyme with squeal. But these trifles are not germane, I know, to Mr. Pound's 'coherent defence of essential literary values.' They are part of the game of putting it across the Gobemouches [simpletons], a game which, to my great disappointment, Mr. Pound does not play well enough to make the performance amusing to the onlooker.

96. G. K. Chesterton, review, *Listener*

28 November 1934, xii, 921

This review encouraged a rapprochement between Pound and Chesterton. Pound had described him as one who 'creates a milieu in which art is impossible' (*Letters*, p. 171). In 1935 he was writing to Chesterton that 'I take it that we are all three [Pound, Chesterton and Hilaire Belloc] definitely against Shaw, Wells etc., paucity of perception' (letter of 17 December 1935, quoted in 'Verse is a Sword: Unpublished Letters of Ezra Pound', edited by Noel Stock, *X: A Quarterly* (October 1960), i, 263).

Chesterton (1874–1936) was an English essayist, poet and controversialist.

The book I like best is Mr. Ezra Pound's essays . . . There are two things about Mr. Pound that I like: he is very learned, which I am not; and he has furious likes and dislikes, which I have but should hesitate to state so furiously He is so much at home in antiquity that he can say he likes Æschylus and dislikes Virgil, as you and I might say we like Michael Arlen's stories but not Noel Coward's plays—or *vice versa*. But I put his book first, not only because it is best, but because it gives me a sort of text. The *Agamemnon* of Aeschylus leads him to exclaim suddenly, 'Damn ideas!' and 'An idea is only an imperfect induction from fact'. Well, that is an idea; and certainly a very imperfect induction. But ideas are not too common. Anyhow his point is that there is something more alive than abstractions: and he finds it in 'The whole wildness of Kassandra's continual shrieking "τροίαν 'Αχαιῶν οδσαυ Troy is the Greeks". Even Rossetti has it better than Browning: "Troy's down, tall Troy's on fire", anything, literally anything that can be shouted . . . anything but a stilted unsayable jargon . . . "Troia the Achaioi hold".' That is very good; and that is the question I want to ask about these twentieth-century summaries: Have they anything short enough to be shouted? Have they anything anything to shout about?

It would be very absurd to call Mr. Pound futile; on some points of economics especially he is really constructive; but even he has just a touch of the sort of thing I want to describe. Thus he affirms admirably, 'Most good poetry asserts something to be worth while, or damns a contrary', but adds that it becomes objectionable when somebody 'suggests some quack remedy (Prohibition, Christianity . . .), the only cure being that humanity should display more intelligence and goodwill than humanity is capable of displaying'. Being an American, he probably means by Christianity the Puritanism of Tennessee; but when the most brilliant thinker says our only cure is to be what we cannot be, even a Puritan should hardly be called a quack for suggesting something that we can be.

97. Bonamy Dobrée, review, *Criterion*

April 1935, xiv, 523–6

Dobrée (b. 1891) was Professor of English Literature at Leeds from 1936 to 1951. He was educated at Haileybury and Cambridge, and is the author of *The Lamp and the Lute* (1929), *Modern Prose Style* (1934) and *The Early Eighteenth Century* (1959).

Criticism is not a circumscription or a set of prohibitions. It offers fixed points of departure. It may startle a dull reader into alertness. That little of it which is good is to be found mostly in stray phrases; an older artist helping a younger in great measure by rules of thumb or cautions gained by experience.

It is a comment on Mr. Pound's own alertness that he does not hesitate immediately after these remarks to print five pages headed 'A Few Don'ts'. It would seem that the cautions gained by experience resolve themselves into a set of prohibitions. This may seem a confusion, but the fact of the matter is that there are two kinds of criticism, that meant for the reading man, and that for the writing one. There is, however, one thing which Mr. Pound overlooks, and that is that the stray phrases which seem so good have to be led up to, just as do the sentences of staggering simplicity which mark the culminating point of a drama or poem, such as 'He has no children', or 'Ils s'aimeront toujours', or 'e mangia e bee e dorme e veste panni'. Mr Pound himself gives us several examples, but they lose half their force taken out of their setting: for instance—

Ovid indubitably added and invented much that is not in Greek and the Greeks might be hard put to it to find a better poet among themselves than is their disciple Catullus. Is not Sappho, in comparison, a little, just a little Swinburnian?

These quotations are taken from the body of the book, but it is in his preface, his 'Date Line' that Mr. Pound lays down what he considers the function of criticism to be, and makes it clear that the sort of criticism he writes is only for such as are keenly interested in method and who love literature to the extent of wanting to know the how of it, not the motive nor the end. His criticism, in fact, is that rare and delightful thing pure literary criticism, and neither psychological, as the seeker for motive would make it, nor philosophical as the pursuer of ends, the moralist, would like it to be. For him there are five methods of criticism: (1) by discussion 'extending from mere yatter up to . . . the clearly defined record of procedures and an attempt to formulate more or less general principles': (2) criticism by translation: (3) by exercise in the style of a given period: (4) by the setting of a poet's words to music: (5) criticism in new composition. Mr. Pound, as we know, has practised all five, but in this book he confines himself to two, criticism by discussion and by translation. He imposes a further limitation upon himself. Acting on the principle that the critic, like the biologist, at best expects to explore a limited field—'No biologist expects to formulate a WHOLE NEW biology'—he has confined himself to a close study of certain writers, and he states that 'the present volume is a collection of reports (in the biologist's sense) in specific bodies of writing'. He discusses the Troubadours, Arnaut Daniel, Elizabethan Classicists, Translators of Greek, French Poets (recent), Henry James, Rémy de Gourmont, and finally Cavalcanti.

The first on 'the Troubadours: their sorts and conditions', is short and descriptive, and very informative. The best 'by the way' there is the remark that:

thoughtful men have in every age found almost the same set of things or at least the same sort of things to protest against; if it be not a corrupt press or some monopoly, it is always some sort of equivalent, some conspiracy of ignorance or interest.

This essay is not characteristically Mr. Pound's: it might, as far as matter goes, have been written by any critic of the Gosse variety, or even by a University professor. But in the one on Arnaut he gets closer to his subject: he approaches the realm of technical criticism, and gives some admirable examples of criticism by translation. The next two on Elizabethan Classicists and Translators of Greek (Poetry should be added) are interesting and suggestive, but rather slight: this is not to say that acute *obiter dicta* are absent, but that the ground has been only patchily covered. There follow the appreciative little essays on a number of French poets, descriptive rather than analytic, excellent introductions but no more: they may, however, serve to clear the ground of a lot of nonsense. In dealing with Henry James, Mr. Pound first makes some very sensible general observations on James, pointing out certain aspects that are usually forgotten when discussing him, and then proceeds to perform another function of criticism, that of weeding out the good from the bad, so that one need not trouble about the latter—provided, of course, that Mr. Pound has won our confidence. Rémy de Gourmont, chosen because he was so opposite to James, is made the occasion of an appreciation, backed by a number of quotations. 'A Stray Document' consists almost entirely of the useful prohibitions, and is still fresh. The book concludes with the essay on Cavalcanti.

This last is a first-rate piece of critical work. It begins with a short introduction on mediævalism, and a longer excursus on the mediæval Italian poets. This is followed by a translation of 'Donna mi Prega', offered not as an equivalent, but as an instrument that may assist the reader unfamiliar with old Italian in gauging *some* of the qualities of the original. So Mr. Pound admits, wisely, for to translate the melliflous music is impossible, though we might think that

> In quella parte dove sta memoria
> Prendo suo stato

and

> D'alma chostume [e?] di chor volontade

might be more happily rendered than by:

> In memory's locus taketh he his state

and

> His modus takes from soul, from heart his will.

The 'partial explanation' which comes next is illuminating in its delving both into mediæval thought and Cavalcanti's poetic qualities. Most valuable also is the scholarly text of the famous *canzone*, with variants in the margin, which Mr. Pound prints in such a form as to reveal much of the internal structure of the poem, thus:

> Donna mi priegha
> > perch' i volglio dire
> D'un accidente
> > che sovente
> > > é fero
> Ed é sí altero
> > ch'e chiamato amore . . . etc:

This leads him on to the form, especially in connection with music, a consideration of the vocabulary, and a large and important sheaf of valuable notes.

Whatever one may think of some of Mr. Pound's conclusions, and criticism of criticism becomes wearisome, these collected essays are for the reader a valuable exercise in intelligent criticism, useful to the poet, but probably more useful still to the reader of poetry: they provide intellectual pleasure. Besides this, of course, they allow Mr. Pound himself to come through, and show him to be, what few of any generation are, really devoted to poetry, eagerly seeking it in every phase, lovingly searching out every corner of its anatomy. Nor is he able to keep his prejudices out, particularly those against Christianity, the academic teaching of literature, and Milton. I might, perhaps, put in a plea for some professors of literature, but the only serious quarrel I have with him is on the score of Milton. Admitted that much of what he did was horrid, much also is of the best: he was not always contorted into repellent latinisms. To argue the case would take more room than is here possible to grant me, but I would take the liberty of asking him to do something, and as he on more than one occasion remarks that we should all be the better for doing it, I have no hesitation in turning the injunction back upon him: and that is, to read Landor. Landor was an admirer of Milton, but no infatuate; and I would like to think that if Mr. Pound were again to read the two conversations between Landor and Southey dealing with Milton, he might a little, just a little, revise his opinion. Perhaps by so doing he might forfeit something in the esteem of Dr. Leavis, but that is a risk he may be prepared to take.

ELEVEN NEW CANTOS XXXI-XLI

New York, 8 October 1934
London, 14 March 1935

---

98. Philip Blair Rice, 'The Education of Ezra Pound', *Nation* (New York)

21 November 1934, cxxxix, 599–600

Rice (1904–1956), American philosopher and critic, was educated at the University of Illinois and Balliol College, Oxford. He taught at Kenyon College and was on the staff of the *Kenyon Review*.

About the time the first thirty Cantos were published, Mr. Pound was reported to have declared that he was giving up poetry for political economy. It is gratifying to find that this report was slightly exaggerated. Even if the term is used with the utmost latitude, only a small portion of the new Cantos can be called poetry, but one is thankful for such small favors as are forthcoming.

Of the eleven new sections of Mr. Pound's amazing scrap-book, seven almost in entirety and two more in large part consist of snippings he has made in pursuance of his present interests. At first reading, it might appear that he has been taking correspondence courses in such subjects as the History of the United States Treasury from the Revolution to the Civil War (from the Original Documents), Banking and Public Finance in Fifteenth Century Italy, Psychopathology of the Crowned Heads during the Napoleonic Era, and Sales Methods in the Munitions Industry; that he has come across a number of sometimes very dull and sometimes very interesting facts, which he has not yet digested; that he has made notes diligently on small pieces of paper; and finally that, an Apennine gust having scattered these papers over the hills about Rapallo, Mr. Pound has picked them up and sent them to the printer as he found them. On maturer consideration, traces of connection between the fragments can be discovered here and there, along with an illuminating comment, but in general the significance does not emerge. Major Douglas of Social Credit, Mr. Pound's present mentor, is sensed dimly in the background, although he is cited by name only once. Even a good thumping apotheosis would be a relief. But one awaits in vain an apocalyptic vision of the transfigured major waving his national-dividend slips, attended by Mr. Munson and Mr. Orage *en séraphin*, with Mr. Pound himself, perhaps, leering from a corner of the picture in the guise of a gargoyle.

Of the remaining Cantos, XXXVI appears to be a translation of a medieval treatise on love in the neo-Platonic manner, XXXIX is another variation on the Circe passages of the Odyssey, about half of XXXV consists of gossip overheard in Central Europe, and part of XL is a reworking of an ancient account of the founding of Phoenician colonies, the point of which seems to be a comparison of ancient and modern imperialism. Mr. Pound's personal contributions here are greater, and they prove that he can write in his old manner when he wishes.

For the sake of these passages, at least, those who found in the previous Cantos one of the richest poetic stores of our time will want the present volume too. As to the rest, it is always wise to listen when Mr. Pound, in his role of 'instigator', tries to call something to our attention. It remains a matter for regret, however, that he seems to have been stumped by the problem of combining poetry and economics, when younger poets, most of them his own disciples, are already proving themselves equal to the task. Is the reason this, that it takes a great philosophy to produce a great vision, and Mr. Pound's social tenets do not go deeply enough into the needs of our time to supply adequate stimulus to the imagination?

99. John Crowe Ransom, 'Pound and the Broken Tradition', *Saturday Review of Literature*

19 January 1935, xi, 434

Ransom (b. 1888) is a distinguished American poet and critic, author of *The World's Body* (1938) and *Selected Poems* (1945). He was an influential editor of the *Kenyon Review*.

The new Cantos of Mr. Pound's, XXXI to XLI, are very much like the others. If there is a difference it is that the new ones have gone a little further still from any accepted tradition of what poetry is; direr, as if a little wearier, yet more resolute than the old ones. Evidently it is hard to sustain the role of poet nowadays, even of modernist poet. But the father of modernism is still substantially himself. Perhaps it should be added quickly, for the benefit of unbelievers, that he is not exactly a mountebank.

As for the tradition, it may look as if modernist poets cared nothing about that, but so far as Mr. Pound is concerned this is not so; and to prove it here is his *ABC of Reading*. Few scholars know so well the many collateral forms of European poetry, and the parent tree from which they have stemmed. For what purpose then does he exhibit this literature to possible readers? Not for mockery. His writing about poetry is smart and journalistic, rather in the manner of an Elbert Hubbard,[1] but his readers should guard against error by repeating to themselves: His receptivity is acute, and his attitude toward the tradition is piety.

As a reader, orthodox; as a poet, revolutionary. It is a great paradox. Why should Mr. Pound divide himself like this? Is it not painful? I should think it is painful, but I should think also that it is not peculiar to Mr. Pound but is, after Mr. Pound, characteristic of our generation. I have in mind the same sort of ambivalence in certain other living

[1] Hubbard (1856–1915) was an American journalist and editor of the *Philistine*, a popular pseudo-arty magazine.

poet-critics, such as Mr. T. S. Eliot and Mr. Allen Tate. Few poets define their critical position so accurately as these, and fewer novelists; but I imagine it is a common thing in our time for the creative artist, steeped in the past, to feel wretchedly obliged to turn his back upon it; and I judge that this occurs as a general phenomenon for the first time in history. The explanation would be difficult and long, and it would not make a pretty story, for it would show the Eumenides visiting our generation with a new sort of vengeance. The generation does not quite understand it, just as it only half realizes the obscure crime it has committed; but at any rate it begins now to observe with alarming repetition that its most sensitive spirits seem doomed to love one thing and perform another.

Mr. Pound may attempt, though I think unsuccessfully, to derive his modernism from the tradition. His list of recommended readings from English poets is supposed to present a continuous history, and it is very interesting. Here are the chief items: Chaucer; Gavin Douglas's translation of Virgil and Arthur Golding's translation of Ovid, the latter twice described as the most beautiful book in English; a little of Marlowe; Shakespeare's Histories and songs; a little of Donne; the Stuart song writers; Butler, Pope and Crabbe as author of the satiric couplet, Landor, Browning's 'Sordello'; and finally, as if borrowing from another literature where the English is lacking, in order to bring the history down to date, four French Symbolist poets. Now the really suspicious feature of the list is the inclusion of the Symbolist poets. Traditionalists would be inclined to reject them from the company, just as unquestionably they would reject Mr. Pound, their English successor, whose practice is anti-traditional in a much more precise and demonstrable manner. With the advent of the Symbolist poets during the last century there is a break and the history of poetry becomes discontinuous; poetry, in the inherited sense, is about to disappear. With Mr. Pound's late Cantos it has disappeared.

As if not quite prepared to admit that the break has occurred, still trying to relate the new to the old, Mr. Pound is at pains to show how fastidiously, how exclusively, he takes his sustenance from the banquet of tradition. He appears to think that the ruling quality which makes any poetry poetic is its condensation. The poets he admires speak straight to the point, without padding and ornaments. Such a poet as Shakespeare is often at fault here, and Mr. Pound is right in saying so. But density is not the single cause of poetry. All is not poetry that is dense; this is proved in most of Mr. Pound's new Cantos, which are condensed to the point where the explicit relations and the musical phrases are squeezed out, and the solid material ingredients remaining involve the reader in a gigantic feat, not only of explication, but even of projecting out of his own mind the necessary solvent of tone, of psychic harmony.

What has really disappeared in the condensed poetry of Mr. Pound, of course, is both a certain spirit and a certain music, until the old product and the new differ not quantitatively but qualitatively. I cannot define on short notice the spirit; but as to the music, Mr. Pound, in his capacity of guide to literature, never wearies of telling us about the troubadour songs of Provence, which he reveres. He lays down the law that, the further the poem goes from its original character of song, the more dubious its estate. But what if we apply that canon to the Cantos? More or less consciously, we do apply it all the time. The result is that we find ourselves sometimes admiring in Mr. Pound's poetry an effect of brilliance, and nearly always missing the effect of poetry; that is, the effect we have loved as poetry, and the one, in fact, to which Mr. Pound the teacher of poetry has referred us.

So far as English poetry is concerned, it may come to be the common opinion, after we are gone, that Mr. Pound was the very man in whose hands the tradition broke. But perhaps it will not be argued that it broke because his loyalty to it was too weak; for his loyalty is intense. It broke because of another competing loyalty: he was responsive to the spirit of his own generation, to the spirit, perhaps we should say, of his lost generation. A new age, harder than previous ages, either above them or below them in its power of sustained inhumanity, required another poetry, and the old poetry could not be saved. That is the thesis which his honorable if bewildered career suggests.

100. George Barker, review, *Criterion*

July 1935, xiv, 649–51

Barker (b. 1913), English poet, is the author of *Poems* (1935),
Calamiterror (1936) and *Collected Poems* (1957).

The creation of a personal cosmology cannot legitimately be said to
distinguish the poet or artist in general from other kinds of people:
rather it appears to distinguish a type of mind which although not
invariably commonplace is not necessarily conspicuous for its creative
fecundity. Thus those who live, more or less literally, in worlds of their
own, prove, more often than not, to be, for example, frustrated spin-
sters, lunatics, children, paralytics, etc. But the rendering of portions of
unreal worlds—worlds caricaturing or representing by symbol that
which the agent takes to be the factual world—provides the more
interesting type of artist with abundance of subject. Such an artist is,
indeed, as much of the purely objective artist as it is possible for him to
be; for it is not possible for the poet, for instance, to portray in words the
world upon which he knows he walks and in which he feels he functions;
for this world cannot be transferred into words without having passed,
like a conjurer's swallowed ball, through his head; and, like the conjurer's ball, it appears it cannot pass through his head without suffering
or attaining to some degree of change, emerging either roseate from
red, obloid from round, or noticeably diminished in size. It is usual, I
think, for the latter transmogrification to overcome reality as digested
by the majority of poets: as instance, allowing that one might liken the
poetical work of, let us say, Hopkins, to an incomplete circle (incomplete
insofar as his work as a poet was externally restricted), one observes that
the periphery of his possible circle cannot and could not equal in scope
that, for instance, of Mr. Ezra Pound (whose work as a poet appears to
have been quite prolifically encouraged). Not, it follows, that any
intrinsic superiority over Hopkins therefore lies in Mr. Pound's work—
but there does lie, I feel, a superiority in the poet who can deal with a
larger repertoire of experience as adequately as the poet who can no
more adequately deal with a lesser repertoire. Whether Mr. Pound deals

as adequately with his material as Hopkins dealt with his, is not, at the moment, acutely relevant. It may be simply that Mr. Pound has advanced the boundaries of subject in poetry. There is, I suspect, an indisputable startling investigation of provinces hitherto untouched in poetic experiment obvious in the Cantos. Certainly this was, to a minor degree, bound to occur in a work of such dimensional magnitude; but in fact the scope exceeds the accidental; states in characteristic language that the poet pertains to that superb species the explorers such as Marco Polo, Cézanne, Walt Disney, etc. It is illuminating to introduce here a sentence from Mr. Louis Zukofsky's essay on Mr. Pound's Cantos (*Criterion*, April 1931), in which he remarks: 'In short, Pound has . . . made the subject matter his style': for in no other contemporary writer (with the accepted exception of James Joyce) does one find those brilliant and unprecedented runs of words which render verbal aspects of a world as brilliant and as unprecedented—from his private regions of poetic material he obtains stuff indigenously extraordinarily by which, quite naturally, one is fascinated, if not invariably charmed. And this in itself corroborates the newness. It is because Mr. Pound has actually accomplished a discovery of new subject matter (and has not, like so many innovators, merely purloined it) that his poetry excites and presages.

The impression of richness which is imparted by these particular Cantos is due to their indefatigable dealing with proper things such as Napoleon, money, Mr. J. Q. Adams, etc. Whereas much contemporary poetry explores or seeks to explore quandaries in the main abstract, the poetry of Mr. Pound, and these eleven Cantos in particular, encrusted as it were with facts, establishes a kind of actuality which it is not difficult to admire (if one likes facts) or deride romantically (if one does not). Mr. Pound's apparently inexhaustible ritual of facts signifies, I have no doubt, limitation in a sense—but it is, certainly, limitation of a sort from which most poets could suffer only with ultimate benefit. The critic who observed that what art needed was a revolution in subject matter had his eye on painting and not on poetry. For Mr. Pound, in his finding of new poetic matter, has vindicated the act by using a tone of poetry and a gait of rhythm adjusted with exactitude and sincerity to the nature of the find. In Cantos XXXI–XLI the subject, which is mainly that of economics, has obviously presented him with difficulties less tractable then heretofore:—but all's grist—coming out on the page with a fluency that is momentarily alarming: until one remembers that this is narrative verse. What ought that to do but flow? Well, it ought to narrate:

Men of Lixtae came with us to interpret
for 12 days sailing southward, southward by desert
one day sailed against sun, there is an harbour
with an island 15 miles in circumference,
We built there, calling it Cyrne
believing it opposite Carthage as our sailing time
was the same as from Carthage to the Pillars.

The reader who finds either these lines unsatisfactory narrative verse or the Canto in which they occur poetically empty should adjust his standards to accommodate them: the chances are that in the long run he will not choose to revoke his advance.

101. Stephen Spender, review, *Spectator*

14 December 1934, cliii, 938

Spender (b. 1909) is an English poet and critic. His *Poems* appeared in 1933, and an autobiography, *World Within War*, in 1951. He was co-editor of *Encounter* from 1953 to 1965.

This poem stands between 'Mauberley' and the *XXX Cantos* of Mr. Ezra Pound. It is the most interesting and the most sustained of his translations, and in the technique and beautiful surface it is the finest development of his early work. For Mr. Pound's writing is essentially surface writing: it contains no profundity of thought, and little obscurity of meaning. The only difficulty which it presents to the 'common reader' is one of reference, since it refers frequently to a background of history and art which is unequally known to him. It is a mistake though to suppose that this knowledge is essential to an appreciation even of the Cantos. For such poetry has an existence of its own which is independent of the writer's sources, however important they are. It creates its own conditions, even while it is referring to another environment.

Nevertheless, for the purposes of this review, light may be thrown on the 'Homage to Sextus Propertius', if one troubles to look up Books II and III of the Elegies of Propertius. One sees the force of Mr. Pound's method if one compares the prose version by H. E. Butler in the Loeb Library with his free rendering:

> Callimachi Manes et Coi sacra Philetae,
> in vestrum, quaeso, me sinite ire nemus.
> Primus ego ingredior puro de fonte sacerdos
> Itala per Graios orgia ferre choros.

Here is the prose:

Shade of Callimachus and sacred rites of Philetas, suffer me, I pray, to enter your grove. I am the first with priestly service from an unsullied spring to carry the Italian mysteries among the dances of Greece.

Here is Mr. Pound:

> Shades of Callimachus, Coan ghosts of Philetas
> It is in your grove I would walk,
> I who come first from the clear font
> Bringing the Grecian orgies into Italy,
> > and the dance into Italy.

He has not made a literal translation, but he has created, in his own version, what he finds to be the *quality* of Propertius. His function then is not merely that of a translator, but, in the most literal sense, that of a creative critic. He has not copied meaning any more than he has copied metre. He has invented a Propertius of his own with an English metre and an English diction: this is the highest and most daring function of a translator.

Readers who are not interested in the problem of translation will still find much to enjoy in the poetry, as English poetry .The poem is full of extremely beautiful passages, such as the end of the first section:

[quotes 'Homage to Sextus Propertius' I, *CSP*, p. 227 'Happy who are mentioned' to 'out with the years'.]

102. John Speirs, 'Mr. Pound's Propertius', *Scrutiny*

March 1935, iii, 409–18

Speirs (b. 1906), Scottish literary critic, was educated at the University of Aberdeen and Emmanuel College, Cambridge. He is Reader in English Literature at the University of Exeter, and is the author of *The Scots Literary Tradition* (1940) and other books of criticism.

It is tempting, and also instructive, to compare Mr. Pound's 'Propertius' with the original Propertius, but it must be emphasized that it is to 'Mauberley' rather than to the Latin verse of Propertius that Mr. Pound's 'Propertius' is related. Interesting affinities may, perhaps, be detected between the Latin poet and the English poet. A good deal of Propertius (there seems reason to believe) was as much 'translation' from the Greek of Callimachus as Mr. Pound's 'Propertius' is from Propertius. Only a small proportion of Callimachus has been preserved; but the three poets appear to have this quality at least in common that they are, in a sense I shall return to, 'late'—the Latin poet 'late' in his civilization, our contemporary in his. Nevertheless it remains the case that the reader who seems to 'appreciate' the Latin will not necessarily appreciate Mr. Pound; whereas the reader who already appreciates 'Mauberley' will at once appreciate also the 'Propertius'. The latter reader is, probably, the 'instructed' reader whom Mr. Eliot implies in his Introduction to his selection from which he omits the 'Propertius'—

If the uninstructed reader is not a classical scholar, he will make nothing of it; if he be a classical scholar, he will wonder why this does not conform to his notions of what translation should be.

It should be added that nothing in this Introduction sheds so much light on the 'Propertius' as certain things in the three essays which appeared as the pamphlet *Homage to John Dryden*. The 'Propertius' (though it will only now become generally accessible) first appeared as early as 1918.

The three essays belong to 1921 and 1922, so that it is reasonable to assume that Mr. Eliot was familiar with the 'Propertius' when he wrote them. More significant is the fact that 'Mauberley' first appeared in 1920, two years after the 'Propertius'.

There is, in addition, the earlier verse and there are, since the 'Propertius' and 'Mauberley', the Cantos. This is not the place for a detailed consideration of the relative merits of these. I can only testify, here, that the earlier verse and, in spite of Mr. Eliot's enthusiasm for them, the greater part of the Cantos seem to me very inferior verse in comparison with the 'Propertius' and 'Mauberley'; and in this I find myself still in agreement with Mr. Leavis's judgment in *New Bearings* and also, to this extent, with Mr. Blackmur's in the *Hound & Horn* (Jan.–March, 1934). The idea has, however, got about (I think Mr. Eliot's Introduction is partly responsible for it) that even if the Cantos are in certain respects deficient the younger men may learn an enormous amount from a close study of the versification. But it is precisely because I seldom find in the Cantos (in spite of the labour which has obviously been expended on the versification) anything like the varied metrical subtlety I find in the 'Propertius' and, especially, 'Mauberley' that I find the Cantos deficient by comparison. It seems to me, therefore, that it is from the 'Propertius' and 'Mauberley' rather than from the Cantos that whatever of the value may be learned from Mr. Pound will be learned, and that this is as much as to say that they are the better poems.

It is at this point that I am forced to record a disagreement with Mr. Blackmur, the more reluctantly as he was one of the first in America to recognize Mr. Eliot and to give good reasons for that recognition. He says (in the article to which I have referred):

For Mr. Pound is at his best a maker of great verse rather than a great poet. When you look into him, deeply as you can, you will not find any extraordinary revelation of life, nor any bottomless fund of feeling; nor will you find any mode of life formulated, any collection of established feelings, composed or mastered in new form.

Mr. Blackmur agrees that Mr. Pound is 'at his best' in the 'Propertius' and in 'Mauberley.' He agrees also that they are 'great verse.' That 'great verse' seems to me itself the most reliable evidence there can be of the presence of those things which Mr. Blackmur, in the passage quoted, says are absent. The 'verse' seems to me 'great' as the result of a pressure of experience against it which it composes and the 'Propertius' and 'Mauberley' therefore 'great poetry' because 'great verse.'

I cannot, either, accept Mr. Blackmur's preference of the 'Propertius' to 'Mauberley'—

The first ['Mauberley'] is Mr. Pound's most nearly, in the ordinary sense, 'original' work, and the second [the 'Propertius'] as a translation, the least. The reverse ascriptions are in fact more accurate; and the paradox is verbal not substantial. The substance of 'Mauberley', what it is about, is commonplace, but what the translator has contributed to 'Propertius' is his finest personal work.

The 'Propertius' and 'Mauberley' seem to me to be great in the same kind of way. But because 'Mauberley' seems to me to possess in greater degree what the 'Propertius' also possesses I consider it the greater poem. When Mr. Eliot said of 'Mauberley', 'It is compact of the experience of a certain man in a certain place at a certain time; and it is also a document of an epoch; it is genuine tragedy and comedy; and it is, in the best sense of Arnold's phrase, a "criticism of life," ' he said something which could be said to a lesser extent also of the 'Propertius' but which, as Mr. Leavis pointed out, could scarcely be said of the earlier verse or of the Cantos.

There remains to reinforce these opinions by some more particular consideration of the 'Propertius' itself. The sophistication of the verse here is no surface thing. It indicates the deeper sophistication of one who is 'expert from experience'—centuries of experience. A critical self-knowledge is his reward:

> For I am swelled up with inane pleasurabilities
> > and deceived by your reference
> To things which you think I would like to believe

is, of course, said ironically. The constant 'inspection' of his experience is indicated, also, by the frequent employment of non-emotive words.

This is what I meant when I called Mr. Pound 'late'. The urbanity of tone belongs to one who is exceedingly (I would not say excessively) civilized. A sense that the experience he is temporarily concerned with is relative to the sum of experience and is not absolute, a sense of proportion, a poise, proceeds from this 'lateness,' this sense of centuries of experience. In No. VII, for example, where there is a tendency to passionate excess, the balance is redressed first by the suggestion of satiety, then more particularly by the phrase

> such at least is the story.

There follow magnificent lines, the theme completely traditional, Epicurean, and the poem ends—

God am I, for the time

—the final emphasis on 'for the time.' No. IX is again completely traditional in theme, and ought on that account to be readily appreciated: also it opens with canorous splendour:* it continues—

I shall live, if she continue in life.
   If she dies, I shall go with her.
Great Zeus, save the woman,
   Or she will sit before your feet in a veil, and tell out the long list of her troubles.

The intensity of concern in these lines is not mitigated because controlled by the apparent levity of the last two. The poem continues—

> Persephone and Dis, Dis, have mercy upon her,
> There are enough women in hell, quite enough beautiful women
> Iope, and Tyro, and Pasiphae, and the formal girls of Achaia,
> And out of Troad, and from the Campania,
> Death has its tooth in the lot.

These lines have behind them not only Latin poetry (and Greek) but also Provençal poetry and Villon. What transforms the traditional theme, gives it a new body of strength, is that 'hell' and, more especially, the colloquialism at the end.

But this balance between the formal and the informal, between conventional elegance and conversational ease, is not merely a matter of the insertion of contemporary colloquialisms. The diction includes, for example, the 'scientific' Latinisms 'torridity' and 'canicular' (No. VIII).

> The time is come, the air heaves in torridity,
> The dry earth pants against the canicular heat.

It is, rather, a freedom from Poetic Diction which allows of this wide range of selection. The result is that a total variety (and also a complexity) of mood finds its expression, and this is what is pointed to not only by the variety of the diction but by the variety also of the versification (contrast the comparatively monotonous versification of the Cantos). The mood modulates between the tragic and the comic. There is broad comedy, broadening in places to farce, in No. IV:

> Damp woolly handkerchiefs were stuffed into her undryable eyes,
> And a querulous noise responded to our solicitous reprobations.

Cynthia's supposed abuse of her rival follows:

* For the nobleness of the populace brooks nothing below its own altitude.
  One must have resonance, resonance and sonority . . . like a goose. (No. XII).

> she twiddles the spiked wheel of a rhombus,
> She stews puffed frogs, snake's bones, the moulted feathers of screech owls,
> She binds me with ravvles of shrouds.
> > Black spiders spin in her bed!
> Let her lovers snore at her in the morning!
> > May the gout cramp up her feet!
> > Does he like me to sleep here alone, Lygdamus?
> > Will he say nasty things at my funeral?

The poem ends with an ironical comment. In No. X there is again broad comedy. The poet is drunk and loses his way.

> And she has been waiting for the scoundrel, and in a new Sidonian night cap,
> And with more than Arabian odours, god knows where he has been.

He arrives in the early morning instead, curious to know if Cynthia has been faithful or not—'And Cynthia was alone in her bed'—

> > You are a very early inspector of mistresses.
> > Do you think I have adopted your habits?

I need not labour the contrast between these and any earlier quotations.

Before passing finally to indicate what seem to me the more significant Numbers I ought to stress the element of 'mockery' in Mr. Pound's 'Propertius' (whether or not, as Mr. Eliot thinks, it is present also in the Latin Propertius) for it, perhaps, has its significance in relation to them. It is markedly present in the earlier part of No. XII.

> > Who, who will be the next man to entrust his girl to a friend?
> > > Love interferes with fidelities;
> > The gods have brought shame on their relatives;
> > > Each man wants the pomegranate for himself.

It comes (it will be noted) from a knowledge of human—and Divine— weakness. The Olympians are not exempt (No. VIII)

> > Was Venus exacerbated by the existence of a comparable equal?
> > > Is the ornamental goddess full of envy?
> > Have you contempted Juno's Pelasgian temples,
> > > Have you denied Pallas good eyes?

nor the heroes from disrespect (No. XII):

> and there was a case in Colchis, Jason and that woman in Colchis.

But because no one is without weakness there is a certain tolerance. The poet is disillusioned enough to expect the worst, even of his friend

Lynceus, and is therefore not annoyed, or ever surprised, when he finds it. The mockery of Lynceus (No. XII) is playful rather than serious; there is at any rate no question of the termination of the friendship as the result of what has happened. The poet can say also of his mistress (No. XI):

> All things are forgiven for one night of your games . . .
> Though you walk in the Via Sacra, with a peacock's tail for a fan.

Numbers I, II, V, VI, XII, seem to me the more personal Numbers, in the sense not that they are the less, but the more, significant Numbers. In these the interests are recognizable, beneath the disguises, as substantially those of 'Mauberley.' The poetry seems to derive (as Mr. Leavis remarks of 'Mauberley') from a 'recognition of bankruptcy, of a devoted life summed up in futility.' The poet cannot believe in the 'importance' of 'Cæsar's affairs,' War (the poem was written during the War) and Empire, the things which seem most 'important' and are, of course, not.

(No. I)   Annalists will continue to record Roman reputations,
        Celebrities from the Trans-Caucasus will belaud Roman celebrities
        And expound the distentions of Empire,
        But for something to read in normal circumstances?
        For a few pages brought down from the forked hill unsullied?
          I ask a wreath which will not crush my head.

(No. II)   Alba, your kings, and the realm your folk have constructed with such
          industry
        Shall be yawned out on my lyre—with such industry.

(No. V)   And I shall follow the camp, I shall be duly celebrated for singing the
        affairs of your cavalry.

But in spite of the best of intentions, he is in fact not equal, he says, to the 'heroic' (No. II)

> And Phoebus looking upon me from the Castalian tree,
> Said then 'You idiot! What are you doing with that water;
> Who has ordered a book about heroes?
>   You need, Propertius, not think
> About acquiring that sort of a reputation.'

'Cæsar's affairs' and 'everything else of importance' are weighed down in the balance by 'a girl'—'I also shall sing war when this matter of a girl is exhausted.'

[quotes 'Homage to Sextus Propertius' V, *CSP*, p. 234 'Neither Calliope' to 'out of nothing'.]

He continues, later in the same Number;

> I should remember Caesar's affairs . . . for a background,
> Although Callimachus did without them, and without Theseus,
> Without an inferno.

It amuses him (No. XII)

> Of all these young women
>   not one has enquired the cause of the world,
> Nor the modus of lunar eclipses
>   Nor whether there be any patch left of us
> After we cross the infernal ripples,
>   nor if the thunder fall from predestination;
> Nor anything else of importance.

The deepest thing in the 'Propertius' is this sense of emptiness, of there being nothing whatever left after one has 'looked into the matter.' It is related to the poet's sense of personal failure

> (No. VI)   Nor at my funeral either will there be any long trail, bearing ancestral
>   lares and images;
>   No trumpets filled with my emptiness,
>   Nor shall it be on an Atalic bed;
>   The perfumed cloths shall be absent.
>   A small plebian procession.

> (No. XII)   And behold me, small fortune left in my house.
>   Me, who had no general for a grandfather!
>   I shall triumph among young ladies of indeterminate character,
>   My talent acclaimed in their banquets,
>   I shall be honoured with yesterday's wreathes.

Beneath the surface trifling and frivolity of the poem there is an agonized sense of tragic waste.

It remains only to say that, in my judgment, the 'Propertius' will hereafter be recognized along with 'Mauberley' and, therefore, along also with the poetry of Mr. Eliot and the later poetry of Mr. Yeats as one of the few remarkable poetic achievements of the time.

THE FIFTH DECAD OF CANTOS

London, 3 June 1937
New York, 29 November 1937

---

103. Stephen Spender, notice, *Left Review*

July 1937, iii, 361

Ezra Pound goes on and on with his Cantos. If one imagined a person called Rabbi Ben Ezra Pound writing an immense poem suggested by the antique flavour of his first name plus the sense of money civilisation suggested by the second—well, that poem might be very like the Cantos. In these Cantos, as in the early ones, there are passages of classical beauty inserted amongst great tracts of the Social Creditor looking at history and life. A certain dullness weaves together these divergent interests and ages into a sort of whole.

104. Edwin Muir, review, *Criterion*

October 1937, xvii, 148–9

The third instalment of Cantos takes Mr. Pound just across the middle line of his poem, and also (if I have read him rightly) concludes its first phase, the phase dealing with usury, banks scarcity, and their consequences. The first three Cantos consist mainly of rough notes and excerpts dealing with financial ordinances in certain Italian cities in the seventeenth and eighteenth centuries. Then comes a fine canticle on usury:

[quotes *Cantos*, pp. 239–40 'With usura' to 'her bridegroom CONTRA NATURA'.]

There follows another mixed financial Canto, one of the best in the present volume, which is given a fine accumulative effect by what precedes it, the difficult and crabbed jottings from the seventeenth and eighteenth centuries, and by the refrain:

17 years on this case, and we are not the first lot!

Mr. Pound continues:

[quotes *Cantos*, p. 243 ' "Can we take" ' to ' "Jury convict 'um" '.]

Then comes a variation on the theme of Ulysses' descent into Hell, then another monetary Canto, then a transcription from or improvization on the Chinese, then yet another monetary Canto; and last of all the canticle on usury is repeated with variations and additions.

Taken by itself this volume certainly presents a pattern; whether excessively encumbered with detail is difficult to judge. The first two Cantos are hard to follow because the mass of detail is presented without order, or in an order which is strange to the reader; yet they have a powerful delayed effect when we come to the fifth Canto with its question:

Will any jury convict on this evidence?

They definitely affect also our reading of the intermediate cantos, particularly the Chinese one; for we feel that all the events in the poem are contemporaneous; that they are all together in one place. In his account of the symbolism of the poem Mr. Yeats mentions the fixed elements, the archetypal persons, and contemporary happenings as its three main constituents. Actually everything in the poem tends to be archetypal and fixed; everything is on the same plane and in the same time, a prolonged present. If this is true, a short notice is not the place to follow out its consequences. A prolonged day has something of the effect of a day of judgment, for it effaces temporal differences and with these what Nietzsche calls the pathos of distance. One may admit the day, while remaining doubtful of the judgment. Everything is brought immediately before us; the seventeenth century is just as close as the present, and China as near as London; the resulting world is the world of this poem. To judge it as a work of imagination one would have to follow out the implications of a prolonged present. There is little doubt that it is one of the most remarkable poems of our time.

105. Delmore Schwartz, 'Ezra Pound's Very Useful Labors', *Poetry*

March 1938, li, 324–39

Schwartz (1914–66), American poet and critic, was educated at New York University. See Introduction, pp. 22–4. This review is included in *Selected Essays of Delmore Schwartz*, ed. Donald A. Dike and David H. Zucker (Chicago, 1970).

This is the thirtieth year since the publication of Ezra Pound's first book of poems. The occasion, for it is an occasion, is marked, as it should be for so faithful a poet, by the publication of ten new Cantos of his long poem, and it is obvious that a response of congratulation and gratitude is precisely what he deserves. The fact that Pound himself has from time to time fired twenty-one gun salutes to his own efforts ought not to deter us. An enormous transformation of sensibility has occurred since the printing of the first volume of *Personae*, and no man can have had more to do with this transformation than Ezra Pound. The contrasting states of culture in 1908 and 1938 are subjects for the literary historian, but what has happened can be suggested briefly and by a mere array of names. No complacency, no great satisfaction with 1938 need be assumed. Some of the names for 1908 are Hamilton Wright Mabie, William Dean Howells, Richard Harding Davis, and George Woodberry. American culture was an insupportable desert from which Pound, and before him, Henry James, and but a few years later, George Santayana and T. S. Eliot found it necessary to depart. They left for various reasons—both Eliot and Pound seem to have gone merely for a year of study—but the significant fact is that they did not return. What has happened in the interim cannot, it is clear, be attributed to the operation of any individual mind; the World War, to take the big example, broke down a great deal in the region of attitudes and feelings which Pound, though he had shouted one hundred times more loudly than his usual wont, could never have moved. But here is another array of names: James Joyce, William Butler Yeats, Robert Frost, Wyndham Lewis, William Carlos Williams, Marianne Moore, and many more

311

could be added. They have at least this fact in common, that at one time or another, one way or another, Pound helped them very much, often howling their merits in the ineffable jargon of his public epistles. Joyce has said publicly that it was Pound who secured a publisher for *Ulysses*, and there was, before this, all that Pound said and wrote about Joyce's first two books. There is also the famous story of how, after years of the hardship of loneliness, Robert Frost went to England and was discovered by Pound immediately upon the reading of his poetry. Besides these quasi-editorial activities, there is the profound effect which Pound's verse has had upon the writing of T. S. Eliot: not only obviously in poems like 'The Journey of the Magi', and 'The Waste Land', but in the most minute details: the first line of 'Ash Wednesday', 'Because I do not hope to turn again', is a translation of Cavalcanti's *Perch'io non spero tornar già mai*, and thus probably derives from Pound's early translation of Cavalcanti. The very variety of Pound's services is impressive and one cannot but be amazed at the examples of generous attention on Pound's part which crop up from time to time. To take an instance which is not well known, John Peale Bishop writes in his essay on Hemingway[1] that 'in Paris Hemingway submitted much of his apprentice work in fiction to Pound. It came back to him blue-penciled, most of the adjectives gone'. And then there is all that Pound has done in Chinese poetry, in Provençal poetry, in Latin poetry, and from the very beginning in 1912, in *Poetry: A Magazine of Verse*. So many more fruitful activities of this nature could be rehearsed that it is necessary to stop here in order to avoid a mere list.

The Cantos ought to be regarded as arising from this whole complex of interests. They are the production of one who has devoted himself almost wholly to literature, setting up literature, whether knowingly or not, as his ruling value. When in 1934 Pound declared that he was giving up literature for economics, no one really interested in the matter was disturbed, and there was no reason to be, for ten new Cantos appeared a short while after. When we consider this devotion to literature, we come upon the essential characteristic of the Cantos; their philological discussions, their translations, their textual references, their peculiar and increasing interest in how things are said, not to speak of the various dialects and slangs which are introduced, and the habitual quotation, of letters, codices, and other documents.

[1] Bishop's 'Homage to Hemingway' appeared in the *New Republic* (11 November 1936); it has been reprinted in Malcolm Cowley's *After the Genteel Tradition* (1936) and Bishop's *Collected Essays* (1948).

The standpoint from which the various heroes of the Cantos are represented is also a good indication of this point. Mozart is celebrated in Canto XXVI not as the great musician, but because of an insulting letter to the Archbishop of Salzburg, Mozart's epistolary style of invective being so interesting that it must be quoted. T. E. Hulme, whose thought affected so many of Pound's generation so much, is mentioned not as a philosopher of great promise, but as the soldier who went to the trenches with books from the London Library, and when the books were lost in a trench explosion, the London Library became very annoyed, and when Hulme was wounded and in the hospital, he read Kant 'and the hospital staff didn't like it.' Andreas Divus is mentioned because he was a good translator of Homer, and Helen of Troy is introduced briefly by means of several puns in Greek and a quotation, finely translated, from *The Iliad*. Another figure held up for admiration is old Levy, a German scholar of Provençal whom Pound visited in order to find out the meaning of the word 'noigandres': Levy's dialect is reproduced and the sensuous character of the place where the interview occurred, Freiburg, is described, the philological interest apparently giving rise to the whole passage, which is one of the most beautiful in the Cantos. The Italian villains of the Renaissance and Thomas Jefferson are both sung by the poet partly because they were patrons of the arts, partly because they wrote interesting letters. And as for the villains, the same attitude determines their choice, and we get as an example of complete stupidity such an anecdote as this one from Canto XXVIII:

> 'Buk!' said the Second Baronet 'eh. . . .
> 'Thass a funny lookin' buk' said the Baronet
> Looking at Bayle, folio 4 vols.,, in gilt leather,' Ah. . . .
> 'Wu . . . Wu . . . wot you goin' eh to do with ah . . .
> '. . . ah read-it?'

The generalization which flows from these instances is almost too obvious to be mentioned: Pound has been the pure literary man, the complete man of letters; the concern with literary things, with the very look of print upon the page, is at the center, the source, of his writing. It would be possible, but difficult, to exaggerate this attachment, for it infects the Cantos at every point, and even in this latest volume under review, which is devoted to a long history of the origins of usury proceeding through many cantos (with typical interruptions), the presentation of the facts is made in terms of textual references, signatures upon documents, their dates, and the idiom in which the documents were written. From this standpoint the Cantos are the long poem of a wandering scholar without chair, without portfolio. And it is tempting, but not sufficiently tempting, to attribute this kind of prepossession to the fact that when Pound went to Europe to study texts for a thesis on Lope de Vega, he left a country where a thoroughgoing devotion to literature as an important element in the life of an educated man had for a long time been a rare or academic or sterile thing.

Much is to be gained by keeping this in mind when we read the Cantos. We understand why a poet with such interests resorts so often to allusion, and we see that if we want to know what the poem is about, we had better read it as it was written, in the shadow of many books. But more than that, the values by which men and things are judged seem actually to be determined by a belief, or rather feeling that literature is the greatest good in the life of mankind. In the Kung Canto, where the dominant values of the poem are explicitly declared, we have, to begin with, a quotation from the books of Confucius. And among the emphases, order, fit ritual, a temple, mandolins, and other things related to art, we are given the key statement about government:

> And 'When the prince has gathered about him
> 'All the savants and artists, his riches will be fully employed'

and this is one of the central motives behind the later concern with usury and economics, the fact that good writers are not adequately supported and published, as Pound has explained in his prose. Or again, as Kung says in conclusion:

> Without character you will
> be unable to play on that instrument
> Or to execute the music fit for the Odes.

The implication is that we ought to have character merely for the sake of being good poets. The opposite extreme, as of I. A. Richards, is to suppose that the Odes exist in order to make character possible.

The facile thing would be to say that Pound's vision was 'one-sided,' or a version of the ivory tower and sheer aestheticism, or a picture of the nature of things through the medium of books. The truth, however, is that Pound has been standing still on this basis, occupying this particular balcony, but has turned his gaze in a great many directions, so that the Cantos represent and contain a good deal more than the perspective from which they were written, although so much of what they contain is naturally in terms of that perspective. If, then, before going on to consider the Cantos in themselves, we examine them as a source of literary influence and a profound modification of poetic practice, we find immense profits. The most important and impressive fact about what Pound has done to extend the medium of poetry is clearly the versification. It is not only that some great modes of poetry—direct statement, description, speech, and the movement of the poem itself— have been given fresh kinds of rhythm, but that, above all and extreme as the claim may seem, our capacity to *hear* words, lines, and phrases has been increased by the Cantos. In this new volume, for example, in Canto XLV and again in Canto XLI, there is this chant:

[quotes *Cantos*, p. 239 'With *Usura*' to 'from incision'.]

and so, through many repetitions and specifications which heighten the song, concluding with

[quotes *Cantos*, p. 240 'Azure hath' to 'CONTRA NATURA'.]

> They have brought whores to Eleusis
> Corpses are set to banquet
> at behest of usura.★

To observe the way in which the emphasis is variously shifted and the key word brought in differently and monotony avoided, it would be necessary to quote the whole Canto. There is nothing like it in English, except perhaps for a like chant against pity in Canto XXX. And in order to show adequately how many times and with what variety the Cantos display a progress, actually, in hearing, it would be necessary to quote at great length. No one seriously interested in writing ambitious poetry during the next hundred years will fail to be affected by these aural developments; if not directly, then through some poet who has himself digested Pound. T. S. Eliot is in part an example of such a poet, and it is Eliot who has pointed out that the Cantos 'are a mine for juvenile poets to quarry.' Related to this aspect of Pound's writing, and perhaps merely the same thing at another point is the effort throughout the Cantos to incorporate speech, to make verse out of speech, and if in this the poem is often distorted by Pound's love of the weirdest slangs

★ It is interesting to observe in passing that in this particular Canto the attack on usury as a poetic statement can be separated from its connection with a particular economic theory by the mere device of substituting another three-syllable word with the same accents, for example, 'capital.' The point cannot be pressed very far, since the Canto in question ties up with other discussions of economic theory throughout the poem, discussions which would prevent such a substitution. Nevertheless the possibility of substitution may exist wherever we are confronted with a good poem whose beliefs we do not accept.

and dialects, represented in his own kind of phonetics, the experiment is valuable even in its failure, and provides the basis for a dramatic verse which would attempt to display contemporary speech. And there is, in addition, what has been noted often before, the demonstration of style which is clean-cut, hard, sharp, and visual, the utter rejection of certain types of rhetoric, and the use of subject-matters which have not previously or recently been considered 'poetic'.

But most of all, literary practice benefits by the effort of the Cantos to digest a great many diverse elements, and to speak, in one poem, of many different *kinds* of things. This is a matter important enough to deserve a digression. It is clear that at the present time, the poet is confronted by an environment which, on the level of perception at least, is extremely disordered; perhaps one should say: un-ordered. One who rides in a subway train knows very well how advertisements, lights, stations, the faces in another passing train, are all shuffled together. Or when one walks in crowds one is amid thousands unknown to each other. Or in reading the daily newspaper, one is faced with a fund of events which are together mainly because they occurred upon the same date. The subway, the crowds, and the newspaper are merely easy examples. The point is that the writer who has a sense of his own time and a sense of intellectual responsibility toward his own experience must of necessity attempt to digest into his poetry these types of disorder. It is not a question of yielding to modern experience and merely reflecting it in one's writing by an equivalent disorder upon the verbal level; nor, except for certain kinds of lyric writing, is it possible merely to disregard the kind of experience which has become a part, to put it bluntly, of the nervous system. The difficult and ineluctable task is to say something intelligent and just about modern experience, and to be sure that modern experience is actually contained in the poem and the intelligence and the justice made relevant to it; not, on the contrary, to permit the poem to be absorbed wholly in edifying sentiments.

When, then, the *unrelatedness*, on all sides, of modern experience is recognized, it becomes simple to understand the way in which the Cantos are put together, and we can see what a lesson they afford for further acts of ordering. 'The Waste Land', 'The Orators', of Auden, and 'The Bridge', of Hart Crane, are further examples of the actuality of the problem, and if it is only in the instance of the first poem that anything has been gained from Pound, all these poems reinforce our understanding of what confronts the modern poet and of how the Cantos have to do with it. Thus in this new volume which brings us to

Canto LI, we find Pound attempting to get no less than the subject-matter of economics into his poem.

Once, however, that we narrow our attention to the Cantos in themselves, forgetting their usefulness as a basis for future poetry, a somewhat different story seems to present itself, at least to one reader. Taking this long poem in itself, we must of necessity see it not as an integral part of a literary period, but in the company of other long poems of like ambition. The first lack to be noted from this standpoint is the absence of a narrative framework such as sustains every long poem which has become a portion of the whole corpus of poetry. Pound himself has declared that it is above all by its story that a literary work gains its lasting interest,[*] and it is difficult to see what basis for unity in an extended poem would be superior to that of plot. Pound's own words, in a letter to *Poetry* for August 1936, can be used against him:

Whether the present generation of local talents think they are being superior in eschewing topics which interested Dante, Shakespeare, and Ovid, must be left to the local book trade to determine. . . . Whether anyone will rise to VITAL ethics remains to be seen. Whether poetry can get on without taking count of those motivations without consideration of which no novel can rise to being *histoire morale contemporaine* I very considerably doubt.

Pound's object in this letter is merely to state that he thinks other poets ought to write about economics, and in passing it ought to be noted that the purposes of the Cantos is stated in two succinct phrases, 'VITAL ethics' and *histoire morale contemporaine*, but the citation of authorities, Dante, Shakespeare, Ovid, is very interesting since all of these poets depended upon plot in one fashion or another. The Cantos have no plot, although as the poem continues, the repetition of key phrases, characters and situations, makes more and more clear the kind of unity which the Cantos do have, a wholeness based upon certain obsessions or preoccupations, deriving itself from the character of Pound's mind, and displaying itself not in conjunction with the numerical order of the Cantos, but, so to speak, against the grain of continuity, which itself seems to be determined by the requirements of musical order, *melopoeia*, as Pound calls it. Or to put the whole issue differently, here we have a long poem without a hero, such as Achilles or Odysseus or *Virgilio mio*, or Agamemnon or Hamlet. Or if there is a hero, it is not Thomas Jefferson, Sigismundo Malatesta, and the other letter writers, but it is, in

[*] 'Narrative sense, narrative power can survive ANY truncation. If a man have the tale to tell and can keep his mind on that and refuses to worry about his own limitations, the reader in the long or short run, will find him.'

fact, Pound himself, the taste of Pound, above all his literary taste, that is to say, his likes and dislikes among books and the men who in some way have had to do with books or documents of some kind.

And when we examine the texture of the verse, we find lacking, amid much beauty of language and observation, other elements which have been characteristic of great poetry. The Cantos, as others have noted, consist of many surfaces, presented with great exactitude, but with nothing behind them. We get what is upon the surface, whether the idiom of a text which Pound is translating or the particular quality of the sunlight upon the water which Pound is describing; but we do not get anything more than this. Many touchstones from very different poets could be cited for comparison, but one example, the following line from Yeats, may suffice because the meaning itself states what is wholly absent from the Cantos:

The uncontrollable mystery on the bestial floor[1]

and as against this, as an example of the moments when the Cantos are seeking sublimity, the following passage may be taken as characteristic:

[quotes *Cantos*, p. 246 'The small lamps' to 'float seaward'.]

Beautiful as is this writing, the difference must be apparent. It is not the absence of a particular belief in any 'uncontrollable mystery'—Yeats is no more a Christian than Pound—but the lack of interest in some of the most significant attitudes of the human spirit, which displays itself at times in the absence of seriousness as a *literary* quality. What is held up for our gaze most often in the Cantos is one man's brutal forthrightness, another's explosive speech, 'verbal manifestations' of all sorts, and the quality of Mediterranean seascapes. We get as an interesting personality:

(Az ole man Comley wd. say Boys! . . .
Never cherr terbakker! Hrwwkke tth!
Never cherr terbakker!)

It is the entrance of the cuspidor into the medium of epic poetry, and it is a very interesting entrance, witnessing Pound's wide sense of fact, but if *The Iliad, The Divine Comedy*, and the plays of Shakespeare are our actual criterion of good, better, best in literature, then we must say that such presentations (and the Cantos abound in them) are sometimes good, but never best. And sometimes they show a triviality of interest, and they show how oppressive 'personality' often must be.

[1] The final line of Yeats's 'The Magi'.

The obscurity of the Cantos, their dependence upon quantities of information which are not readily available is at once another definition of the poem, and yet not at all as important a handicap and burden as some suppose. The amount of learning necessary in order to understand the manifold allusions of the Cantos can easily be exaggerated, and could quite simply be put together in one supplementary volume such as has already been provided for Joyce's *Ulysses*. Pound is not as learned as he seems to be—the scattered character of his learning leads to the mistaken impression—and at any rate the amount of information which must be acquired is nothing compared to what must be done in order to read *The Divine Comedy*, or the effort we make when we learn a foreign language. It is curious, of course, that a writer of our own time and language should require so much external help, but the only question is: is the poem good enough? It is.

Another fact to be remembered is that if we take Pound's writing as a unity and read his criticism as well as the Cantos, we have another good light in which to read the poem. Piere Vidal, Actaeon, Andreas Divus, Henry James, Sordello, the Homeric Hymns have all been mentioned explicitly in the criticism before the poem had been written, a point significant with regard to the whole pattern. And most of the relevant essays are to be found gathered together again in the book called *Make It New*, which selects from the previous books of criticism. Here, for example, there is a statement which illuminates the whole intention of the poem: 'Most good poetry asserts something to be worthwhile, or damns a contrary; at any rate asserts emotional values.' And here as one more example we find the very beginning of passages in the Cantos, such a passage as

[quotes *Cantos*, p. 28 'And the great' to 'an endless sentence'.]

It is Henry James, a patron saint of all literary craftsmen, as we are told in the prose:

The massive head, the slow uplift of the hand, *gli occhi onesti e tardi*, the long sentences piling themselves in elaborate phrase after phrase, the lightning incision, the pauses, the slightly shaking admonitory gesture. . . . I had heard it but seldom but it is all unforgettable.

Thus the poem rests upon the various stilts of Pound's criticism and other sources of information. But very few things are not so crippled in one way or another.

The justification of the whole is thus not the poem taken in itself, not yet, at any rate, before the poem is completed. The virtue which we can be certain of at present is, to sum up and repeat, the immense usefulness for future writing. Pound fits one of his own categories: he has been a great *inventor* in verse, and we know how few can be supposed to know the satisfaction of fulfilling their own canons of excellence.

106. James Laughlin IV, 'Ezra Pound's Propertius', *Sewanee Review*

October–December 1938, xlvi, 480–91

Laughlin (b. 1914), American publisher, was educated at Harvard. He founded New Directions in 1936, and became the leading American *avant-garde* publisher. He has played a crucial role in establishing Pound's reputation in America.

Ezra Pound completed his transcriptions from Propertius in 1917. At the time he was living in London with his wife, and he was very poor. His books of verse had stirred up critical controversy, but there was no money in them. He made a few pounds a month doing reviews for respectable journals and spent much time in the reading room of the British Museum—which is free. 'Quia Pauper Amavi' was his first title for his 'Propertius'; 'Love on the dole', we say nowadays. 'Sollicitate tu causa pecunia vitae' wrote Propertius, but it doesn't appear that he starved in an attic: it is known that he was a knight, Maecenas was his friend, and he seems to have had enough money now and then to entertain the 'mixtas puellas' who so delighted him. Nevertheless, Pound in part identified himself with Propertius in these terms. It was not till some years later, when Pound had crossed to the continent and things were better for him (there were American editions then and his own Maecenas in the person of John Quinn, the bachelor corporation lawyer who backed *The Little Review* and built a collection of modern French painting worth two millions), that the title was changed to 'Homage to Sextus Propertius'. I should say that the further basis for his self-identification with Propertius lies close to such typical Propertian lines as:

> me iuvet in gremio doctae legisse puellae
> auribus et puris scripta probasse mea

The inspiration for Pound's early lyrics was Venetian and Provençal; before the Cantos cast their epic spell upon him he must have thought of himself as a love poet. There are many grounds for comparison between Propertius and Villon, of whose 'Grant Testament' Pound has made a short opera, composing the music himself, fitting the music to the sound-values of the words.

I have used the word 'transcription'; Pound's 'Propertius', though it follows the original text, cannot be called a translation. He would not call it that himself. Of some ninety-two elegies he has used only fourteen. There are frequent transpositions of lines, not only within a poem, but from one poem to another. There are constant omissions of uninteresting sections. There are Poundian interpolations, entirely extraneous, on every page. And there is no attention whatever to accuracy of detail. Also the boners, real schoolboy boners, half a dozen of them: 'sitiens' (thirsty)—'sitting'; 'vota' (vows)—'vote'; 'fugantes' (putting to flight)—'fleeing'; 'vela' (sails)—'veil'; and the PRIZE, the *grand* prize!

> Cimbrorumque minas et benefacta Mari

(roughly: 'the threat of Cimbrian invasion and Marius' public service and the profit in defeating them')

> Welsh mines and the profit Marus had out of them

Believe it or not!

A mess, you say? A hash? Yes, definitely a hash, but, strangely enough, a very tasty one, an excellent Sunday supper. Academics will certainly sneeze and snort over Pound's distortions, but if they have trained ears his verbal music will move them. Flashes of superb diction intercede for him. Several responsible critics (R. P. Blackmur is the latest) consider that Pound is at his best in the 'Propertius', and T. S. Eliot did not hesitate to have his firm (Faber & Faber) put out last year a new edition of the book uncorrected. Propertius might never recognize himself in this new overcoat but he couldn't complain of the quality of the goods. As a sample of this cloth look at Pound's construction from Propertius' wonderful 'O nox mihi candida', a poem which I value just twice as much as Catullus' better known 'mille basia'. Here it is entire:

[quotes 'Homage to Sextus Propertius' VII, *CSP*, pp. 237-8.]

Studying that third stanza I feel that it alone justifies all the crimes that free verse, of which Pound is a major uncle, has committed. Pound's faultless cadences have no resemblance metrically to Propertius' alternating hexameters and pentameters, but they manage to transmit, to the limit of possibility, the noble beauty of the Latin lines. The voices speak in different tongues, but the speakers' expressions are identical. On the whole, Pound is not half the poet that Propertius was—he has a similar sort of sensitivity (a trifle precious?) but never so deep or so flexible— but I think his

> Today we take the great breath of lovers,
>   tomorrow fate shuts us in,

rises to equal Propertius'

> sic nobis qui nunc magnum speramus amantes
>   forsitan includet crastina fata dies.

perhaps even the verbal valence of the English is a grain higher than the Latin. There is real magic in those two lines of Pound's; that is poetry and even the fact that its best image was spawned from a textual corruption (evidently Pound read 'spiramus' for 'speramus') cannot taint it. Those lines would make Propertius' spine tingle just as much as his own do Pound's.

The basis of good hash is good meat. Pound, by luck or intention, has tampered least where Propertius was best. But tamper he does, freely, both with words and with ideas. There is not a single elegy where the general sense has not been slightly or severely wrenched. Pound uses Propertius' ideas as a springboard for his own. He uses the Latin imagery as a catalyst for his own. There are spots where he seems only to have glanced at the texture of a word, ignoring its dictionary meaning, to form his version. It has occurred to me that 'Variations on themes of Propertius' would be a more accurate title than 'Homage to Propertius'. It is sometimes just as hard to locate Propertius' figure in Pound's recreation of it as it is to detect Handel's theme in Brahms' variations on it. There is a good example in Pound's second book. Here

Pound has inverted the theme as well as varied it. Where the original reads

> cur tua praescripto sevecta est pagina gyro?
>   non est ingenii cumba gravanda tui.
> alter remus aquas alter tibi radat harenas,
>   tutus eris: medio maxima turba mari est.

Pound has written

> Why wrench your page out of its course?
> 'No keel will sink with your genius
>   'Let another oar churn the water,
> 'Another wheel the arena; mid-crowd is as bad as mid-sea.

Do you see what has happened? I think it is worth-while to put this specimen under the microscope because it affords such a perfect opportunity to see just how Pound's mind operates in the process of composition. Here you can watch the metamorphosis of observation into imagination in close-up; literature, as Eliot has pointed out, is as much a product of other literature as of life.

It must be said first of all that Pound's mind is unbelievably quick. It is of the comprehensive, as opposed to the logical, type, and it works like lightning, often carelessly. Here he has read the first two lines accurately, but in the third he has gotten ahead of himself, his imagination has already run away with him. He has caught sight of half the line and formed his image without reading the rest. Propertius' image is that of an oarsman playing safe with a rough sea by keeping always close enough to shore so that the landward oar scrapes sand. It is a good image; you've done that yourself. It means that Propertius should stick to safe lyrics and not try turbulent epics. But Pound's Pegasus, in its haste to be off, misses the point entirely. He tells Propertius to sit on the beach and let somebody else go rowing. Then in the next line he puts in something that isn't in the Latin at all. The word 'gyro'—'course'—has suggested a parallel image: a dangerous chariot race in the arena. In it goes in place of the dull 'you will be safe'. Then with a fine disregard for syntax he deftly, very deftly, misturns the sententia.

And so it goes. Hugh Porteous, the English Sinologue, has discovered that Pound is equally cavalier in his translation of the Ta Hio. His Cavalcanti, on the other hand, is more careful, possibly because he did detailed comparison of the existing manuscripts. Pound's edition of Cavalcanti is a sort of rebuttal to the many critics of his careless scholarship.

It contains a very sensible and serviceable chart of variant readings. much more practical than the footnote method, en-face translations, and large, clear photographs of the disputed manuscript pages. Its weakness is typical: a preface on the essence of medievalism which is Poundianly an-historical. Pound paid for the book's production himself and doled it out to scholarly reviewers; he wanted to be sure that his reputation included scholarship. This admiration for versatility (he has *not* written on Da Vinci) has carried him into music (a book on harmony and two operas), into economics (he lectured on money at the University of Bologna and is a mainstay of the Social Credit movement), into politics (his newest book is subtitled *L'Idea Statale*), into art (his book on Gaudier-Brzeska), into philosophy (the *Ta Hio*), into literary criticism (three books), into sexology (he translated de Gourmont's *Physique de l'Amour*), into education (*The A B C of Reading*), into architecture (he outlined a model city in one number of *Exile*), and into history (the Cantos). Perhaps there are a few more; mathematics too, I think.

That is a long way from Propertius but perspective requires background. Now to go back through the telescope, notice how Pound's skill with verbal sound-effects has conditioned the second line of the last citation. The word 'keel' suggests a large vessel, while 'cumba' means a small one, a rowboat; however, 'keel' was musically necessary to fit in with 'sink'. This terminal syzygy is a favorite Pound device, here heightened by the repetition of consonants, and the assonance of the three thin vowel-sounds, which themselves suggest the lightness of Propertius' poetic skiff, in contrast with the heavier vowels—'oth', 'oa', 'ur', and 'a'—of the epicist in rough water. It is wrong to suppose that minute devices such as these are accidental. In Pound's case they are part of the conscious, laboriously developed, technique. He has not reached his pre-eminence as a verbal musician without effort; for years he practised writing verse with an accelerated metronome in order to memorize the exact length and weight of the basic sounds of language. Pound builds his lines like a mason laying bricks. The artistry is there if you look for it; Edith Sitwell has done an extended study of the detailed sound-effects in one of the Cantos.[1] There are other examples of sound slighting sense in the 'Propertius'. In the panegyric to Virgil at the end of the second book (part of which, by the way, Pound mistransfers to Lynceus) the walls ('moenia') on the Lavinian shore become 'stores' to go with 'casts' ('iacta') for another syzygy. There are a few other such

[1] In her *Aspects of Modern Poetry* (1934).

wrenchings, but for the most part the mating of sound and sense is happier.

It is in the larger matter of ideas that the principal distortions occur. Pound has not given an interpretation of Propertius' *weltanschauung* so much as he has projected the Roman's life into his own. He has not put Propertius into modern dress (except for a few colloquial expressions here and there) but he has applied the classic properties to his own personal plot. Pound entitled one of his books *Personae*, and it is frequently said that his muse speaks through the stage-masks of others. This is true in the case of his Chinese poems where there is no apparent self-interpolation, and largely true of the Troubadour poems, but with the 'Propertius' the case is exactly the reverse. It is Propertius who is made to speak through the mask of Pound. A few instances will illustrate.

Propertius was undoubtedly cynical at times. He seems to have been an ill-disciplined person subject to rapid and violent changes of mood. He was the Dionysiac type like D. H. Lawrence, the emotionally-minded writer, as opposed to the Apollonian type, the rationally-minded writer, like James Joyce. As a result we find his poems alternating (often within a single elegy) between the cynical and the ideal (a terrestrial idealism, of course). Pound catches this alternation but he greatly extends the cynical phase of it, reading it into lines where it is not conceivably inherent. It is true that Pound has chosen his selections from the part of the work which describes the stormiest, most bitter-sweet, phases of Propertius' relationship with Cynthia, but even this does not validate the extreme acidity which he imposes on his hero. Pound does not stretch Propertius' suspicions about the courtesan Cynthia; he deals sympathetically with her. But he does make Propertius much more of a socially-minded poet than he probably was. He twists the lines till they bear on social injustices or hypocrisies with which Propertius was certainly not concerned, supposing he was even aware of them. On analysis these faults of society prove to be precisely the ones which have weighed most heavily on Pound throughout his life. Probably by this time Pound knows that his translation of 'Cimbrorum minas' as 'Welsh mines' is incorrect. But I think it doubtful if he would change it now. Pound is aware of and despises the pilferage of public wealth by private persons and he intends that Propertius, with whom he has allied himself (there is no stigma of metempsychosis) shall do the same. If he didn't then he does now!

That is an extreme case but it is typical. A more extended one revolves on Propertius' feeling about epic poetry. In a very fine passage in

Book Three the poet converses with Phoebus and is advised to confine himself to lyric poetry, his talent being unsuited for the panoramic
canvas

quis te
carminis heroi tangere iussit opus?
non hinc ulla tibi speranda est fama, Properti:
mollia sint parvis prata terenda rotis;
ut tuus in scamno iactetur seape libellus,
quam legat expectans sola puella virum.

This point of view is frequently repeated briefly in other elegies.
The attitude is temperate: Propertius respects the epic poets, especially
Virgil and Father Ennius, but realizes he cannot rival them; he consoles
himself with the knowledge that poets like Varro, Calvus, Gallus, and
Catullus have become famous on love poems alone. But Pound trans-
mutes this attitude into one of extreme scorn and hatred. Writers of
epics are made to appear as Chamber of Commerce poets, bangers and
clangers on the big Roman cymbals, hangers on the martial bandwagon,
intellectual profiteers like Paul Engle. 'Outweariers of Apollo will, as
we know, continue their Martian generalities.' is a sample. In the second
poem a reference to the three Horatii is very artfully twisted to provide
a jibe at Horace for supposed militarism (Pound dislikes Horace almost
as much as he dislikes Milton). But the perversion reaches its climax in
the way Pound handles Propertius' feeling for Caesar. Propertius was
not a militarist. In one poem he pities the soldier's hard life, and in
another he writes, 'All the hard fighting I want is the battles with my
mistress', but there is evidence that he had a real admiration for Caesar
as a man of action, praising him above Maecenas. Yet this Pound rejects,
as he wishes Caesar to play the part of his arch-enemy Sir Basil Zaharoff.
Thus we have Propertius ridiculing Caesar's (political?) Trojan lineage,
and saying that his 'ventricles do not palpitate to Caesarial *ore rotundos*',
whereas Propertius actually said that he would try to describe Caesar's
accomplishments if he thought he could do them justice.

It is interesting to compare in this respect the Pound of the 'Propertius' and the Pound of the Cantos period. The idea of a Caesar has
changed color, for Pound is a profound admirer of Mussolini and a
strong supporter of Italian fascism. His scatalogical attacks on ineffectual pacifists and munitions kings still continue, but apparently there
are now wars and wars. A war in Africa, for example, is not a crime
against civilization but a civilizing mission. Italy must do her duty and
save the blacks before they all castrate themselves. The Cantos began on

a lyric note, but as they progress arms play as great a part as men and books. They carry no burden of nationalism, it is true, but the last dozen have been little more than propaganda for a specific economic system. Propertius, when his love for Cynthia had waned, turned in his last elegies to matters public and archaeological; there are long passages of early Roman history in chauvinistic vein. 'I also will sing war when this matter of a girl is exhausted', he had said back in Book Two. But if he thought his talents had increased, that it was now safe to paint with the big brush, he was mistaken. 'Ingenium nobis ipsa puella facit', he wrote when he was in love with Cynthia. The conceit was deeper than he imagined. His last book is heavy as a damp feather bed. Cynthia *was* his genius. Without her it went thin.

Cynicism permeates Pound's 'Propertius', but it takes its most curious form in the treatment of deities and mythological personages. Pound, who is a professed Confucian, wastes no reverence on Christian theolatry, and accordingly Propertius is made to treat Roman divinities rather as though they were stock characters in the Sunday comic section. Cynthia is ill: 'Old lecher', says Ezra Propertius to Jove, 'let not Juno get wind of the matter!' But this is an exaggeration, I admit; on the next page Pound finds the ton juste for

> There are enough women in hell,
> quite enough beautiful women.

In any case Pound puts Propertius' proper names to another use than that for which they were intended. He uses them largely for their surfaces, which provide color, sonority, and richness to his diction; and many of them as the original supplies he often tacks on a few extra ones of his own. But Propertius used them chiefly for their meanings. Roman literature had a tradition of mythological allusion quite as pernicious as that which has afflicted some periods of English literature. Mythology is proper matière for poetry when it can take the form of Catullus' 'Attis', but not when it is used for stuffing, to parade erudition. Propertius, to his discredit, often used it in this way. From frequent references to Callimachus and Philetas we know that he admired the Alexandrinian tradition, which (Callimachus, as head librarian at Alexandria, naturally fell into erudition) included recondite allusion as a method for poetry. Propertius was also given to obscure puns depending from other poets' work, particularly from Virgil. Pound lets these lie, happily.

Only Yeats and Eliot can compare with Pound among living poets for richness of diction. And his diction is at its richest in the 'Propertius'.

It must be seen to be understood, but certain technical formulae can be deduced. I should say that the basic difference between the verbal aspects of English and Latin poetry was the variance in compression. In a highly inflected language like Latin almost all the words are live words, carrying meanings. In a positional language like English at least half the words are merely nuts and bolts joining the live words together. Hence Latin's verbal interactivity is twice that of English and the poet's burden is doubled. It is interesting to see how often Propertius attempts to lighten his load by separating the parts of adjectival phrases at different ends of a line, that is, beyond the exigencies of his metric. There is almost a regular pattern; it is the most marked characteristic of his style. In English the verbal pressure is far below; in Pound's verse there are usually only two high pressure points per average line. An examination of these pressure points shows at least four distinguishable procedures which combine with many others less distinct to form Pound's stylized diction, his poetic language. Of particular interest here are two formulae employing Latin roots. One is the use of the English cognate of a Latin word without regard to its current usage. This Pound does repeatedly, as 'Have you *contempted* Juno's Pelasgian temples?' and '*combusted* Semeles'. This device may be awkward but it generates a high charge of meaning; in its weaker forms it serves well as a roughener breaking up monolingual smugness. Another formula is the use of rather pretentious Latin-root words for pure decoration, as: '*devirginated* young ladies'; and '*canicular* heat'.

Another frequent device I have labelled for want of a better name a 'colloquial force-image', of which fair examples are 'neither would I *warble* of Titans' ('canerem') and 'if she goes in a *gleam* of Cos, in a *slither* of dyed stuff' ('fulgentem incedere'). And the fourth device is simply the expression of Pound's peculiar wit. To him, and him only, could have occurred such figures as: ' "You are a very early inspector of mistresses".'; 'Zeus' clever rapes, in the old days,'; 'Upon the Actian marshes Virgil is Phoebus' chief of police'; and 'We have kept our erasers in order' ('exactus tenui pumice versus eat'). The general tone and the pitch of Pound's poetic diction are best suggested by a quotation from his late friend A R Orage: ' . . . the conscious aim of the greatest writers of English was to make their written word correspond more and more precisely, not of course to the casually spoken word, but to the art-carefully chosen spoken word.' As an example of Pound's 'art-carefully' fashioned diction which can naturally be 'spoken', take this stanza from the twelfth poem:

[quotes 'Homage to Sextus Propertius' XII, 11.1–13, *CSP*, p. 245.]

It is hard to come to a decision on the final value of Pound's 'Propertius' because it includes such extremes. It is rather like the case of the little girl in the nursery rhyme who when she was good was very good and when she was bad was just HORRID. At times there is something definitely horrid about Pound's mis-treatment of Propertius: he has taken away the 'mollis liber' and replaced it with a case history by Dr. Freud. Yet, on the other hand, some of his cadences are perhaps the finest yet done in this century. It is a hard choice, a hard one. Perhaps it is best to leave the last word to Ezra Propertius himself:

> I ask a wreath that will not crush my head.
> And there is no hurry about it;
> I shall have, doubtless, a boom after my funeral,
> Seeing that long standing increases all things
> regardless of quality.

(Nota bene that that last line, that one on the right there, is *not* found in Propertius.)

107. Archibald MacLeish on Pound's revolutionary modernism

June 1939

From 'Poetry and the Modern World', *Atlantic Monthly*, clxiii, p. 829.

MacLeish (b. 1892), American poet and dramatist, has written a dialogue on the Bollingen controversy, *Poetry and Opinion* (1950), as well as discussing Pound in *Poetry and Experience* (1960). During the war MacLeish was Librarian of Congress and was closely associated, in Pound's mind, with F. D. Roosevelt. Pound attacked him in a broadcast over Rome Radio on 23 April 1942 (printed in C. Norman, *Ezra Pound*, pp. 391–3). MacLeish was able to play a modest role in securing Pound's release from St Elizabeth's in 1958.

The French poets called *Symbolistes* had one thing in common and only one—a common hatred of the formal and rhetorical poetry of Parnasse '*avec sa perfection technique, ses vers sculpturaux, ses rimes opulentes, son archéologie hellénique, romaine et hindou.*' Their common purpose was, as Verlaine put it, to '*tordre le cou a l'Eloquence.*'

Pound, the first of the American poets justly called 'modern', was also a hater of rhetoric and a twister of tails. Pound was the great dismantler, the great wrecker of brownstone fronts, the great tearer down of imitation French châteaux and imitation Gothic railroad stations. He was a wrecker to whom not merely the politely dead poetry of the generation immediately prior to his own, but the whole world which accepted that poetry, was an obsolescence, a solecism calling for the crowbar and the sledge. He was a dynamiter who hated not only the Georgian Anthology and the overstuffed verse of the years before the war, but the whole Edwardian organization of experience out of which all the experience and most of the poetry had long since leaked like the horsehair out of an old family sofa, leaving nothing but a stiff brittle shape which dogs avoided and even lovers would not use. He was, as he himself said of Laforgue, an exquisite poet, a deliverer of the nations, a Numa Pompilius, a father of light. His dreams at night were of words chipped clean of the rhetoric which staled them, words planed clean of the literary varnish which had tinted them to golden oak, words scraped back to the white pine with the white pine odor. He was, and he still is, one of the great clearers and cleansers of cluttered earth. If a new generation does not see him in these terms it is because a new generation does not know the architecture he has overthrown. These poems which are wall ornaments now that the old buildings have gone down were tools once—hooked iron crowbars and mallet-headed sledges and cold steel chisels of destruction.

GUIDE TO KULCHUR

London, 21 July 1938
Norfolk, Conn., 11 November 1938

108. Philip Mairet, review, *Criterion*

January 1939, xviii, 326–9

Mairet (b. 1886) was educated at the Hornsey School of Art and worked as a draughtsman and designer of stained and painted church windows. He became the literary editor of the *New English Weekly* when it was founded in 1932, and succeeded A. R. Orage as editor in 1934. Mairet is the author of *A. R. Orage: A Memoir* (1936) and translator of various works from the French. He reviewed Pound's *ABC of Reading* in *New English Weekly* (14 June 1934).

His *ABC of Reading* was a specialized matter. It exhibits fully the sensibility, and the independence, of a mind which, applied to the history of letters, reflects another set of qualities, different from those usually recognized: suggests the possibility of new anthologies, is itself a brilliant new anthology. Such a mind can be genuinely re-formative: its re-valuations may enable portions of the past, inoperative in the present, to swing into action; and nothing is more healthily revolutionary. The present book attempts to extend this kind of operation to the entire tradition of human learning, however cursorily. But it would be a blazing divine dragon of wisdom indeed, who in such an effort could demonstrate anything half so clearly as his own limitations.

Mr. Pound tries to disarm us by a kind of modesty: the book is frankly table-talk, the spelling of the title facetious, he talks mostly from memory, seldom even troubling to get up and go to the bookshelf. Our guide's brain sparkles and crackles away at its usual high cerebral voltage, and yields the usual lack of steady illumination, despite such flashes as:

When the usurer climbs into the saddle you have attention absorbed by detail, colour, lighting etc. to DETRIMENT of the total reason for the work's coming to be [p. 90].

which piece of perspicuity is culled at random, the book holding perhaps a hundred as good and better. It is the wisdom of sensibility with a certain (or uncertain) generalizing power. Real sensibility is rare: only artists and a few others have it, and it may co-exist with the intellectual equipment of a thorough eccentric—a crank. It is perhaps unlikely that even the youngest pupil will take Mr. Pound's book for a serious anatomy of culture: the title alone is warning. Nevertheless, it is perforce a wider critical conspectus than he has before attempted, and hence reveals his mind more fully. We get near the very springs of his motivation as a cultural revolutionary, for example, as we watch him instilling distrust for the Hellenic and Judaic—but oddly, not the Roman—bases of European learning. His instrument for doing this is Confucius.

The present reviewer, whose enthusiasm for Chinese writers did not carry him beyond the oft-abused but excellent translations in English and French, is suitably abashed before one who sprinkles his text with Chinese in the original. He is perplexed, however, at no mention of Lao-tze, without whom Kung-fu-tze is as inconceivable as Aristotle without Plato. But this throws light upon Mr. Pound's treatment of those twin luminaries of Greek learning, with whom of course, his subject compels him to reckon.

To begin by reference to 'Platonic inebriety' and to class Plato with Balzac as 'probably an adolescent enthusiasm' indicates an attitude, a *parti pris*, and not quite a critical one. But as we read on, we find it is not Plato but Aristotle whom Mr. Pound indicts as the misleader of youth. Plato gets at first grudgingly and at last rather handsomely reinstated, for having proved able, Mr. Pound admits, to generate states of enthusiasm in many minds in various periods, states conducive to socially meritorious action. Why, Mr. Pound knows not, perhaps it is a human weakness, but so it is. But whilst he thus softens a little towards Plato, and allows to Platonists, gnostics and metaphysical minds generally, a possible cultural value, he transfers his severity to Aristotle—and for the first time works with both elbows and a book on the table.

Whatever a Greek scholar of competence might make of the textual criticism that ensues, to the general reader it is almost unreadable without the original of the Nichomachean Ethics at hand, would be difficult with it, and is, I dare swear, a pretty slipshod performance anyhow. What it does reveal though, is that the element in Aristotle that Mr.

Pound can not abide is that root of gnostic traditions which Plato and the Stagirite shared. 'Arry' is *not*, after all, wholly and solely an inductive objectivist. Mr. Pound's horror, quâ philosopher, at anyone who thinks meanings may be as important as facts is such that we begin to see that his motive is really more of a desire to get away from something than to arrive anywhere.

Hence such absurdities as—'the truth of a given idea is measured by the degree and celerity with which it goes into action', and, on the very next page, '19th century mostly MESS'. Can Mr. Pound tell us of an epoch whose main ideas—in this case, humanitarianism, utilitarianism, parliamentarism, financialism—had a realization more sudden and extensive? And were they therefore true?

'After Leibnitz' time the professional philosopher was just a bloke who was too dam lazy to work in a laboratory' shows this mind in typical flight from a certain order of reality, especially after approving use of Schopenhauer. Only his Confucian leaning protects Mr. Pound from the suspicion of a post-war-baby desire for up-to-dateness. 'Nothing could be more hostile to any degree of polite civilization than the tribal records of the hebrews. There is not a trace of civilization from the first lies of Genesis up to the excised account of Holophernes.' I fear that in a guide to culture, this is just pure bosh in an excited tone of voice.

What is he running away from? Doubtless the realization of mortality, the eternal questioning, the everlastingly provisional nature of human things. But an attitude to these infinites is important, you cannot afford simply to be without one. Fully half of all and every human culture depends upon it. The cult of an attitude to the dark half of things is just as vital as the finding of your place in the light half. You may make a 'Kulchur' of facts, reasons and personally conceived good taste. But culture implies cults, and recognition of the weaker side of life.

What has such a writer to do with China, where yinn and yang are equal and opposite? Was the master Kung no more than a totalitarian intellectual? He was not; but anyhow Kung is not the whole story. When Mussolini said to Ezra Pound '*Why* do you want to put your ideas in order?' I could not help thinking of the Taoist tale, of Kung's total discomfiture when he went to convert the robber Chee.

109. Dudley Fitts on a bad boy strutting and shocking

May 1939

'Right Thinking', *Saturday Review* (13 May 1939), xx, 16–7

This review shows Fitts in the process of making a substantial second judgment about Pound (see No. 88).

This is a book to which one can say neither yes nor no. It is a compound of profundities and balderdash, pretty evenly balanced. It is a guide to right thinking, right behavior moral and political, right reading. The ground covered is enormous; the method is aphorismic. Mr. Pound begins by saying that he is 'not trying to condense the encyclopedia into 200 pages'; but there is so much leaping about from topic to topic, and so much eccentric digression within individual topics, that the total effect is that of condensation, and rather improvisatory condensation into the bargain.

No one who cares anything about poetry, ancient or modern, can afford to disregard Mr. Pound's contribution to it both as poet and as critic. I suppose he has a better ear, a subtler, more assured feeling for language, than anyone writing today. Of his scholarship, on the other hand, one can be less sure. The evidences are all too fragmentary: a playing about with Greek phrases in combination with Chinese ideographs; the *ipse-dixit* pronouncements on Greek tragedy in translation (especially the *Agamemnon*; but he might take a look at Louis MacNeice's recent version); above all the familiar use of tags which (as in the case of 'Homage to Sextus Propertius' and certain of the Cantos) suggests the familiarity of uneasiness. And his criticism of painting and music, especially of music, is neither more nor less than clever.

And these add up to a breathless and stimulating book. But it isn't the book that we have been waiting so long for. If only Mr. Pound could forget that it is not necessary to sustain the proud scolding pitch for ever! If he would only forget—for more than ten pages or so—his beloved role of yokel-scarer in the name of Douglas and the Fascist

State! Does he want an audience? I should think he would. And no one has more to give an audience. But timidity, or self-consciousness, or something, gets in his way. Then we have the sneers about the profs, the linguistic rough stuff, the bad boy strutting and shocking; and we remember the Duke of Cornwall's remarks on the brusque Kent:

> This is some fellow,
> Who, having been prais'd for bluntness, doth affect
> A saucy roughness, and constrains the garb
> Quite from his nature: he can not flatter, he,
> An honest mind and plain, he must speak truth:
> An they will take it, so: if not, he's plain.

Well, the only kind of person that Mr. Pound cares about—that is worth caring about—will take it, so. It's a pity, though, that his plainness shuts him off from so many others who might be helped.

110. William Carlos Williams on Pound's great risk

June 1939

'Penny Wise, Pound Foolish', *New Republic* (28 June 1939), xcix, 229–30.

A man does not have to agree with Pound to acknowledge the excellence of what he has written. For myself I disagree with him fundamentally and finally in what I believe he, as a man of responsibility, represents. But I cannot disagree with him when he says such things as 'The magic of music is in its effect on volition. A sudden clearing of the mind of rubbish and the reëstablishment of the sense of proportion.' That's what can be got from this book.

I believe it to be one of those essential books. Though in itself it may seem to carry little weight, yet, so long as it is there and *heeded*, a writer will be bound to go right in his writing. There's more good sense for him packed here than you will find in all the colleges of Christendom put end to end until they reach completely around the alphabet.

Pound begins with Confucius and the complete corrective to false knowledge inherent in the Chinese ideogram. Thence he sweeps zig-zag through the entire field of culture . . . as only Pound would dare to do and get away with it. Aristotle comes next to Confucius, so far as I can see, though with all manner of texts and personalities between them. And the man continues—with enough damn silliness to purge a constipated mule by way of laughter. He flops about from lap to lap of some of the shoddiest fakirs of our time, frantically seeking to *discover*. He raves about his perverse preferences as though he were a pale schoolgirl with her first male teacher and then . . . brings himself back to seriousness by sheer muscle power of the understanding, raising his chin once again above the bar, for the hundredth time. It's heartbreaking to watch him and a relief when he comes, as he always seems to, once more through.

What Pound is attempting brilliantly in his book, for all its follies, is to cut short the awful waste of life we suffer to gain knowledge. He is attempting to make it good form to find a way to the gist of learning before we are crippled by age and cannot make use of it. The swiftness with which we get knowledge should be one of its major virtues.

†The monumental futility of our schools, holding a man back when, in the name of learning, he ought to be going forward as swiftly as he can in his short life, to knowledge, makes Pound mad. Delay, delay—until it is too late to do anything about it. He thinks that the reason for this delay lies in the economic impasse that usury has forced upon us. The reigning powers of what Pound calls 'the bank and gun business' are afraid that people will see through them. They say to themselves, 'Don't let knowledge increase too fast; don't let them find out while they may still be of a mind for action.' *Usura* is the devil of Pound's story, the mark of the destroyer in our age. The schools hold that knowledge and action are of different natures. Pound shows them united into one.

And his conclusion from all this is totalitarianism! The failure of the book is that by its tests Mussolini is a great man; and the failure of Pound, that he thinks him so. The book should be read for its style, its wide view of learning, its enlightenment as to the causes of many of our present ills. The rest can be forgiven as the misfortune of a brave man who took the risk of making a bloody fool of himself and—lost.

CANTOS LII-LXXI

London, 25 January 1940
Norfolk, Conn., 17 September 1940

---

111. 'H. H.' [James Laughlin IV] and 'S. D.' [Delmore Schwartz], Notes on Ezra Pound's Cantos: Structure and Metric

1940

This pamphlet, published by New Directions, was prepared as a promotional aid for the New Directions edition of *Cantos LII–LXXI*, and was included in review copies. Laughlin had asked Pound to consider a preface for the new Cantos. Pound refused, writing in February 1940: 'Dear Jas: Cantos 52-71 can NOT have a preface in the book. Cover gives ample space for blurb. The new set is not incomprehensible. Nobody can summarize what is already condensed to the absolute limit. The point is that with Cantos 52-71 a NEW thing is. Plain narrative with chronological sequence. Read 'em before you go off half-cocked' (Stock, *Life*, pp. 375-6). Laughlin was the author of an essay on the 'Homage' (No. 106), and Schwartz had reviewed the *Fifth Decad* (No. 105).

NOTES ON THE CANTOS

What follows should not be taken as an official statement. Mr. Pound consented to these notes but did not provide data for them and has not passed on them. He takes the attitude, naturally enough, that the Cantos are self-explanatory. In a sense, this is, of course, true; to paraphrase Mr. MacLeish, a poem does not mean, it *is*.* On the other hand, if the

* MacLeish's 'Ars Poetica' ('A poem should not mean/But be') was published in his *Streets in the Moon* (1926).

reader's enjoyment can be increased by a few hints and suggestions, why not provide them? But these are suggestions, and nothing more. The Cantos are still in mid-course; it would be foolish to attempt any complete study until the whole structure of the poem is visible.

What are the principal difficulties for the reader of the Cantos? But first, let us take up a position on the subject of difficulty itself. People say, 'The greatest writing is always the simplest.' That simply isn't so. Look at Dante, or Donne, or any one of a dozen others who have stood the test of time. Isn't the right answer this—that they are both simple and difficult? that there is more than one level of meaning? that simple things are said with simplicity and more complicated things are said with the precision which their complexity dictates? Why not take this position—that difficulty in a poem is justified when it enriches and does not obscure the meanings involved?

The first difficulty which strikes the reader of the Cantos is the frequent use of quotations from ancient or foreign languages. Pound is at home in many languages and he does not hesitate to use them. The reader who doesn't know the language thinks he is missing something . . . . he feels he is being 'snooted' . . . but, for the most part, he isn't, because Pound is almost always using the alien phrase as an echo: he expresses the particular theme in English and then brings in the source phrase as an echo, for color or music or to make an 'intellectual chord.'

That term 'intellectual chord' is undoubtedly offensive to the purist, but it is useful for describing one of the principal characteristics of the Cantos—the juxtaposition of superficially unrelated material. As we read along in, say, the *Odyssey* we are carried from point to point by a narrative sequence. In a poem like the *De Rerum Natura* the sequence is logical. In the *Commedia* the sequence is organized from a plainly recognizable hierarchy of moral values. But as we read along in the Cantos we cannot at first discover any system in the arrangement of episodes; in a single page we may find themes from colonial American history, modern London and the Italian Renaissance all fused together. The youngest generation of readers may not be so startled by this situation because they have grown up in a cultural milieu in which the importance of free association has been demonstrated by Freud, and in literature by Joyce, and in art by the Surrealists. Further, they may have noted the germs of this type of construction in writers like Rimbaud, who attacked not only the conventional patterns of language and verse form but also those of bourgeois thought. But to older readers Pound's construction must seem a hopeless riddle. So, for them, let us develop the musical analogy. A sequence of notes, a melody, gives pleasure. But two or more notes struck together, when they are harmonically related, give more pleasure. They elicit from the hearer a kind of tonic judgment, a recognition of the fitness of their relation, which, in itself, gives pleasure. Similarly, as modern composers are proving, there are dissonant relationships which also induce a kind of pleasure. In music these judgments are so rapid that they are not consciously noted. But when, in the poetical music of ideas, the same principle is carried over into language in timing is enormously slowed down—the 'notes' hang in the air and can be thoroughly compared and savoured. And thanks to this lengthening of the period of apperception their relationships can be tested on a number of different levels. Take a typical Pound chord— the juxtaposition of a political idea of John Quincy Adams' with one of an ancient Chinese emperor. Each idea is a note. Considered separately they are interesting in themselves, but, taken together, they open up fascinating avenues of comparison and contrast—historically, philo-sophically, humanly.

That is what is meant by an 'intellectual chord' and, while it is not Pound's term and he may resent such a simplification, it does illuminate the constant mixing of material in the Cantos. The reader might ask, 'What is accomplished by such a chord?' and 'Is that poetry?' Those are fair questions. Perhaps we can best discuss them by asking ourselves a third question: 'What is an epic poem anyway?'

Pound likes to say that an epic 'is a poem containing history'; but that seems only a partial definition. Would it not be better, with the great classic epics in mind, to say that an epic is a poem which attempts a fairly complete presentation of the state of mind, the *weltanschauung*, of a culture? When we have finished the *Commedia* we know, about as well as we can, what it must have been like to be living in the Middle Ages—beliefs, hopes, fears, interests, problems, pleasures . . . The *Iliad*, The *Aeneid*, even *Paradise Lost* achieve, in their different ways, the same result. And Pound is attempting the same huge aim in the Cantos; he is painting, in vast detail, the mind-body-soul of Twentieth Century man. But, you protest, how can that be when two thirds of the poem deal with remote periods of history? The answer to that paradox lies in the very nature of history itself . . . a force which has a kind of continuous life. A novelist, building the character of a man, is likely to deal heavily with his childhood, to show the roots and hidden causes of his actions. Pound, focussing on modern man, turns the spotlight on the phases of history that have conditioned the nature of his being. Hence the long passages on Fourteenth and Fifteenth Century Italy, the crucial period in history when the Medieval conception of man as directed toward the after-life was supplanted by the individualism and this-worldliness of the Renaissance. Hence too, the emphasis on the American founding fathers like Jefferson and Adams, the men who set the stage for democracy. And hence the concentration on the history of money and banking, since, as we shall see, Pound considers money, or the misuse of money, as the main determinant of our social maladjustments.

We have then in the Cantos an attempt to x-ray the modern mind, to go deep into it by an examination of the roots in history of its patterns of action. And the technique of this examination is a continual cross-reference, a sort of evaluation by comparison. But when we speak of evaluation we infer a standard of values. What is the moral structure of the Cantos? The Hell cantos—14–16—give a ready clue; the people most thoroughly damned are the modern usurers, the bankers and financiers who have perverted public credit to private ends. Theirs is the diabolical principle. Pound early rejected Marxism because he believed that Marx never really understood the nature of money. Coming under the influence of Guild Socialism and later of A. R. Orage, Pound became interested in the Social Credit economics of C. H. Douglas. But he did not limit himself to Douglas. Becoming more and more deeply involved in economic speculation he evolved a system compounded from four main sources: Douglas Social Credit; Silvio Gesell, the South African who developed the theory of velocity by stamp scrip; certain of the Canonist writers on economics; and certain of the economic theories of the Corporate State. There is not space here for a full discussion of Pound's economic ideas; they can be found in his books *A B C of Economics* and *Social Credit, An Impact*. What we need to know are his bases for moral judgment in the Cantos very briefly, they are these: credit and money, of which gold is only a yardstick, are public—social—commodities, and their value and volume should be controlled by the state as trustee for the people. Instead, thanks to the way the modern banking system has developed, credit and money are controlled and misused by private forces; whence, depressions (resulting from an uneven flow of new money) and wars (resulting from the struggle for markets). Evil, then, is the force which promotes or condones the anti-social use of money; good, that which opposes it. When we understand this, the recurrent passages in the Cantos on the history of money and banking—traced from the origins of banking in Siena, through the perversions of finance back of the Napoleonic Wars (the period in which private bankers set the precedent for their credit franchise), through Jefferson's fruitless struggles to provide a clean money system for the United States, through the 'merchants of death' of the World War, and finally, the monetary reform movements of the past few decades—become clear and their purpose obvious.

In the past decade—the heyday of Marxism—it has been customary for liberal critics to sneer at Pound's economic ideas. Current events, with a sinister irony, give them the lie—the success of Hitler's national inflation has proved that the idea of a socialized credit system is not ridiculous. Perceptive observers have pointed out the salient aspect of the present war: it is a struggle between two concepts of money, privately controlled money and state controlled money. While fundamentalist economists declared from month to month that Germany was bankrupt Hitler systematically cleaned out private banking (he calls it *leikapitel* in *Mein Kampf*) and built his war machine, proving what Pound has been saying for years—that a statal money system would work. Naturally, Pound never hoped to see the theories he advocated put to such horrible uses—he has always been against war—but the cold facts give the Cantos an unintended but undeniable new interest. If the democracies are not totally stupid, think Pound, they will fight fire with fire—they will learn from Hitler's experiment and finance their war and defence with a statal economy; they will suppress the private banker in his role as war profiteer. And if they have real vision, when this war is over the democracies will never return to their old follies—they will use the technique of a social credit system for humanitarian ends. Consider what Germany might be today if her inflation had been devoted to social reconstruction rather than a military machine! That, of course, is Pound's dream—that the democracies, and particularly America, should lead the way into an age of plenty through the development of a decent money system. Often Pound is branded a fascist because he likes to live in Italy and has not hesitated to commend the good points that do exist, among the bad, in the fascist program. But he is no fascist at heart— let the cantos on John Quincy Adams bear witness to that. Pound's dream for America is of a country in which democracy will really be made operative by a democratic money system, a system which does not vest the power to create and rent money in a limited group but in the responsible representatives of the whole people. That is the 'material morality' behind the Cantos.

There is also a morality for the individual, based on the teachings of Confucius. Pound became engrossed in Oriental literature through the influence of Ernest Fenollosa, who, on his death, left Pound his notebooks. Pound's first 'translations' were really adaptations of Fenollosa's, but in subsequent years he became a serious student of Chinese language and thought. The Confucian 'order' is a hierarchy of disciplines beginning in the individual and extending through his various faculties to the social organism. The Confucian principle interlocks with Pound's morality of money to inform the moral values of the poem.

The influence of Chinese thinking is extensive in Pound and has much to do with both his poetic and later prose styles. The reader of the Cantos will be continually struck by the constant use of extreme ellipsis. Pound has whittled away all but the skeletal essentials of what he wants to say. Sentences do not end. Phrases are left hanging. References are not fully developed. It is almost a shorthand—but a very beautiful one, for Pound's metrical powers are superb. This elliptical style, which has its counterpart in the short, stabbing, graphic 'word-punches' of his critical prose, Pound refers to as his 'ideogrammic method' and it stems from his interpretation of the fundamental nature of Chinese picture-language. Pound was greatly influenced by Fenollosa's remarkable book *The Chinese Written Character*, which traces the growth of Chinese ideograms from simple descriptive pictures to complicated mixtures of phonetic and graphic roots. Later Pound discovered a high poetic tension in Chinese poetry where the juxtaposition of visual meaning-charged words with little interference from purely syntactical connectives produced great compression of imagery. He then set out to do with English as much as he could in the same direction—making each syntactical unit as much of a picture as possible and eliminating as much of the conventional linguistic framework as he could. This streamlining is at first very confusing, but when the reader becomes accustomed to it he is apt to like it. The amount of matter which the mind must absorb is reduced to a minimum and does away with much that is non-poetic in a long poem.

In his little essay *A Packet For Ezra Pound* W. B. Yeats spoke of the architecture of the Cantos as a fugue, with a series of recurring themes which are variously rephrased. Pound is quoted as dissenting from his great friend's analysis and wishing it were not on record. While the recurrent themes are obviously an important factor in the plan, musical structure is probably not the final key. Certain of Pound's revelations to his publisher about the work in progress seem to indicate a more than casual influence of the structure of the *Commedia*. A recent letter stated that two thirds of the poem were completed and that he (Pound) was ready to plunge into the Empyrean. The reference to the *Paradiso* is fairly plain and prompts such a possible comparison as the following:

I	*Inferno*	The Greek, Italian, Renaissance, European, and World-War-Hell cantos.	Physical and psychological factors conditioning the modern mind.
II	*Purgatorio*	History of money and banking, American Colonial, and Chinese cantos.	Material factors.
III	*Paradiso*	The Cantos to come.	Philosophical and spiritual factors and effects.

Such a scheme is of course merely tentative, and may be completely mistaken; nevertheless it presents interesting lines of speculation.

The final difficulty which troubles the reader of the Cantos is Pound's extensive 'mythology'—his continual citation of historical and imaginary figures, few of whom are familiar to most people. Complaints are heard that an encyclopedia is needed to read the Cantos. There is no question that an encyclopedia does help, but is it really necessary? It is not, if the reader can exercise, for the first reading, a certain limitation of curiosity. It isn't necessary to hear the line of every instrument to enjoy a symphony. For the most part, when he uses an historical character—say Sigismundo Malatesta—Pound fills in enough background and coloring to make him a convincing figure and his story revealing of the idea Pound wishes to get across. Similarly, with the imaginary figures Pound has invented as vehicles for his episodes of modern history— where his dramatic sense, his selectivity, is at its best, it is hardly necessay to identify the characters. Take the passage on Corles, the Austrian artillerist who refuses to fire on the enemy and is 'put away' in an asylum for the duration. The reader does not need to know that Corles is Alfred Perles, Parisian exile and author of *Sentiments Limitrophes*, to appreciate the point of the episode. Unquestionably, a guide to the Cantos will at some time be compiled, and will add to the pleasure of reading them, but in the meanwhile, and for the casual reader, the poem does stand on its own feet as intellectual entertainment, providing that the reader does not insist on trying to recognize instantly every detail and relationship .

For detailed analysis of the Cantos, the interested reader is referred to R. P. Blackmur's essay on Pound in *The Double Agent*, Allen Tate's essay in *Reactionary Essays On Poetry And Ideas*, and the chapter on Pound in Delmore Schwartz' forthcoming book of criticism, *The Imitation Of Life*.

H. H.

NOTES ON THE VERSIFICATION
OF THE CANTOS

Perhaps the most interesting thing about the Cantos from the very start has been the meter. Not only is there like it in English, no poem which seems to resemble it, even at a distance; but one can say that no other poem in English attempts to take hold of so great a variety of subjects. Whether or not the poet's insight is equal to his scope is a different and difficult question. Whether it is or not, the scope is a fact and a very important one in the history and the future of English and American poetry.

Most types of versification have tended to draw a circle about a definite region of human experience, which then becomes, for the time being, 'the poetic' realm. The rest of experience is excluded as not suitable, appropriate, or elevated enough for the poet. No doubt, this kind of limitation is often the source of great strength. But times change; the world moves on; and the poetic idiom which was an adequate instrument for one age becomes a dead weight for the new age. This need not be so, if the mode of versification is developed freshly by the new generation; but most of the time it is not, and it merely serves to prolong habits of thought and perception and feeling which belong not to the life of the present, but only to its literary past. This is what happened in the Eighteenth Century before the debut of Wordsworth and Coleridge, and it happened again during the first decade of the Twentieth Century, before the beginning of the Imagist movement.

It is Pound, however, who has given the completest demonstration of how the Victorian modes of versification, the Victorian poetic realms, can be broken down, and his instrument, which seems to have developed over a period of ten years, has been metrical. Whether it is the letters of Jefferson, or a translation of Cavalcanti, or a history of usury in Renaissance Italy, or conversation heard in a London street in 1916, what the Cantos show us is how extensive is the field which can be poetic. No matter what Pound writes about in the Cantos, and he writes about almost everything, it always sounds like verse. *Sounds like verse* is the kind of statement which often expresses a lack of discrimination and

345

taste; in fact, it is sometimes precisely the expression of a feeling that the poetic is limited to certain areas of human experience. In the case of the Cantos, it witnesses the endless extent of the poetic. The Cantos destroy, by means of their versification, the division between the poetic and the unpoetic.

When we stop, after the third or fourth reading of the Cantos, and ask what meter or meters Pound is using, we are likely to be perplexed. It makes little difference if Pound consciously adhered to metrical forms or if he depended for the most part upon his ear, his aural imagination, as T. S. Eliot would say. We get the incontrovertible impression of a consistent rhythm in the way that the words in the line and the lines in the verse-paragraph are organized. It might be added that it is difficult, at least for the present writer, to feel any such consistency, in the way that the poet passes from subject to subject and from canto to canto; some controlled form of free association is evidently at work, and perhaps also certain analogies with musical form.

An analysis of various cantos in terms of traditional metrics, that is, in terms of accented and unaccented syllables, offers some light. We notice, to begin with, that unlike most poetry in English, the Cantos have an extraordinary number of feet which are trochaic, dactylic, anapestic, and spondaic. Now we know that the dominant meter in English is iambic; that the unaccented syllable, first, and the accented syllable, second, is the typical foot in English to such an extent that all other kinds of feet can only be regarded as variations upon the norm. It is true that late Elizabethan blank verse tended to eliminate the unaccented syllable; Milton developed a consistent trochaic variation; Coleridge, in writing 'Christabel', counted *only* the accented syllables; Hopkins, in working out 'sprung rhythm', decided that a foot might have any number of unaccented syllables, not merely one or two; and other poets, such as Bridges, Swinburne, the appalling Longfellow and the authors of free verse, have tried to get away from the iambic base of English poetry.

No one, however, has gone so far or been so successful as Pound in the Cantos. A good deal more analysis will be necessary before one can be prepared to advance more than a hypothesis as to the metrical system of the Cantos, but tentatively and as an initial hypothesis, one can say that they show at great length a dominant rhythm which has its roots in a trochaic base. When we remember that most English poetry has an iambic base, the radical nature of the change becomes obvious. In the Cantos, the dominant foot is trochaic and the chief variations become

346

anapestic and spondaic; while in most English verse the chief variation is the trochee. A number of observations tend to confirm this view of the Cantos' meter. For example, when line-endings are continually trochaic, the verse becomes an intolerable jingle, and this is avoided beautifully in the Cantos by line-endings which are never consecutively trochaic for more than two or three lines at a time; but after two or three lines which end in trochees, the dominant movement of the verse is strengthened and corrected by an iamb or a spondee. This too explains some of Pound's syntactical habits; the omission of 'the's and 'and's is a device which helps to eliminate the natural tendency of the language to fall into iambic feet.

There is much more to be said and much more study is necessary. But it should be clear that what we have in the Cantos is nothing less than a revolution in English versification, a new basis for the writing of poetry, which, when it has been dissociated from Pound's particular vision, should have an immense influence on the poetry of the next hundred years.

S. D.

112. Edwin Muir on the Cantos as a political poem

1940

From 'Recent Poetry', *Purpose* (July–December 1940), xii 149–50.

Mr. Pound continues to build up the most miscellaneous and conglomerate poetic structure of our time. The material in these latest cantos is drawn mainly from ancient China and eighteenth-century America. It is political, and is embodied in an elliptical statement of the ways in which societies are ruled, well and badly. Mr. Pound has a clear idea of good rulership and bad; the first thing being to him in accordance with

Nature, and the second against it. The Chinese Cantos are vivid and condensed, and present history in a series of concrete images, the choice of detail showing marvellous skill. The American section reads like a prolonged footnote to a detailed history, and demands a specialised knowledge from the reader which he is unlikely to possess. This volume, like its predecessors, shows that Mr. Pound is capable of imposing style on the most heterogeneous material. As a technician there is no one to touch him. The full shape of the poem is still scarcely to be guessed at, but it is clear that this is the main political poem of our time, and political in the sense that it is concerned with the nature and the end of politics, not with specifics or ideals. Why Mr. Pound's criticism of human society required the inclusion of such a mass of detailed matter may become clear when the poem is finished.

113. Randall Jarrell on the deterioration of Pound

December 1940

From 'Poets: Old, New and Aging', *New Republic* (9 December 1940), ciii, 798–9.

Jarrell (1914–65) was an American poet, critic and novelist.

I had thought of Ezra Pound as the one thing constant in this fleeting world. Continents sank under the sea, empires fell: Vienna fell, Canton fell, Warsaw fell: the unmoved sage sat on at Rapallo, like Idiosyncrasy on a monument—the warm Italian breeze bore out over a universe of cretins his condemnations and invective, his economic panaceas, his *wd's* and *cd's* and *shd's*, his American slang unparalleled outside the pages of an English novel. But as Hitler says, *there are no more islands*: Mr. Pound has deteriorated with the world. *Cantos LII–LXXI* contains the dullest and prosiest poetry that he has ever written. These Cantos are so bad that they would not seem his at all, if they were not so exactly like the very worst portions of the old ones. Mr. Pound has become himself to the ∞th degree, his day-dream is at last absolute. One sees implicit in every page: 'Le droit, c'est moi'. Prejudice, whim, idiosyncrasy, have been hypostatized into a universal imperative. Mr. Pound is obviously one of the most talented poets of our time; yet these Cantos are almost unreadable. What has happened?

That would take a book to tell. Mr. Pound has always had likings or prejudices rather than standards—his strength has lain mainly in disconnected insights. Organization and logic have been his weak point; the Browning monologue (which was designed to be effectively dramatic precisely because of its formlessness) has been his favorite form almost from the beginning, and his and Eliot's use of it has made it and its variants standard for the age. His talents are primarily lyric—not narrative, certainly not expository or didactic. He is not really a 'thinker' at all: any sort of thinking, outside of the German system-making Heine makes fun of, requires a certain submissiveness to facts, and Mr. Pound has never submitted to a fact (or anything else, for that matter) in his life. He has taken all culture for his province, and is naturally a little provincial about it: one of the touching things about him is his entire Americanism, an Americanism that could survive unimpaired fifty years in a lunar crater. He has an enormous amount of talent, wit and courage, but he has the literary man's characteristic vanity and omniscience, a magpie's eclecticism, a mania for absolutes and a conviction that they are accessible: to him everything is fairly simple Black or White. He repeats, *Hold to the middle*—meanwhile the middle hardly exists for him; his feeling for Confucius is less appreciation than identification. He is not the Fool-Killer—life is a short blanket—but the Fool-Damner; he has shouted so long into the intense inane that his yells, by a natural protective metamorphosis, have taken on something of the character of their surroundings.

Early in his life Mr. Pound met with strong, continued and unintelligent opposition. If people keep opposing you when you are right, you think them fools; and after a time, right or wrong, you think them fools simply because they oppose you. Similarly, you write true things or good things, and end by thinking things true or good simply because you write them. For Mr. Pound, both circumstance and predisposition made the process inescapable. His friends and disciples were eager to encourage him in his worst excesses; and modernist poets or critics hated, by caviling at the work of their talented fellow, to expose him to the jeers of the academic masses, who already condemned indiscriminately all that he had done. (Eliot for, instance, has written appreciations, not criticisms, of Pound.) Mr. Pound's universe became more and more a solipsistic one; the form, logic and amenities of his criticism some time ago assumed the proportions of a public calamity. And his special poetic gifts—and performance—succumbed in their turn. Writing good poetry is only occasionally difficult: usually it is impossible. But writing what seems to you good poetry is always easy, if only, somehow, your standards of what constitutes a good poem can be lowered (and specialized) to what you write; this unconscious and progressive lowering of taste, a sort of fatty degeneration of the critical faculties, is the most common of ends. Mr. Pound seems no longer able to discriminate between good and bad in his poetry: to him it is all good because it is all his.

Half of *Cantos LII–LXXI* is a personal, allusive and wildly eccentric retelling of Chinese history, full of names, dates, quotations, ideograms, abbreviations, underlinings and slang. Everything is seen as through a glass darkly, the glass being Mr. Pound: 1766 B.C. talks exactly like 1735 A.D., and both exactly like Ezra Pound. To the old complaint, 'All Chinamen look alike,' Mr. Pound makes one add, 'And talk alike, and act alike—and always did.' Little of the intrinsic interest of the events manages to survive the monotonous didacticism of the account. The rest of the book is more interesting, since it consists mostly of quotations—intelligent, informative or just odd—from John Adams, its subject. (On the dust-jacket New Directions twice insists that Pound's subject is John Quincy Adams—a queer mistake to make; whoever made it must have found Pound's style too entrancing ever to determine what he was writing about.) Mr. Pound has a fine feel for anecdotes that carry the quality of a person or an age; but I should prefer to see a collection of his favorites in some more appropriate form.

The versification of these cantos is interesting: there is none. The prose is an extremely eccentric, slangy, illogical, sentence-fragment, note-taking sort of prose—but prose; the constant quotations from letters or documents or diaries are no different from the verse that frames them. The technical skill that went into some of the earlier Cantos has almost disappeared.

114. Robert Fitzgerald, 'Mr. Pound's Good Governors', *Accent*

Winter 1941, i, 121–2

Fitzgerald (b. 1910) is an American poet and translator. He reviewed *The Pisan Cantos* in the *New Republic* (No. 116), and is the author of 'Gold and Gloom in Ezra Pound', *Encounter* (July 1956).

Merely try to imagine Mr. Pound's *Cathay* being published in 1940 instead of in 1915, and you are well prepared for the study of these Cantos. *Cathay* is a fine work of art, matchless of its kind, modest in its scope but probably definitive. Owning it, you need own no porcelains. Very good. The poet meanwhile has lived a quarter century; no one who has survived the same period can sensibly reprove the direction his interests have taken. In the first ten and I believe the best of these Cantos, LII to LXI inclusive, he has attempted a rendering, not of certain poems of Rihaku or notes of Fenollosa, but of China's entire dynastic history from the third millennium before Christ to the eighteenth century A.D. A rendering: i.e., a poem making palpable the essentials of the subjects. The essentials: whatever in men, deeds, and policies casts light on the practice of wise government.

Anyone unfamiliar with the preceding Cantos may get his footing fairly easily in Canto LII, which opens with a summary of the plight of Europe according to Pound. It is 'sin drawing vengeance,' and the sin is *neschek*, a word that the active reader may be tempted to interpret (and half rightly) through the Latin *nescio* (i.e., as 'ignorance') until the meaning becomes plainer in 'poor yitts paying for / . . . a few big jews' vendetta on goyim' and is finally made explicit: 'of the two usuries, the lesser is now put down' (i.e., in Germany and Italy, which have deprived private bankers of credit-control but not yet put down 'super-*neschek* of the international racket'). Furthermore, 'the groggy church is gone toothless / no longer holds against *neschek*,'—i.e., does not, as in the Middle Ages, condemn the taking of interest as a sin. After this little exercise in contemporary analysis and in Pound's methods of exposition, the reader is abruptly introduced to the poet's true values through a long and beautiful poem that is a sort of Chinese *Works and Days*, representing the hallowed observances of the seasons among an uncorrupted people. If Pound's ascription of our political ills to money-lending has seemed preposterous to the liberal reader, this passage should at least make him think again as to the poet's standards. Pound closes the Canto with an adjuration: 'Begin where you are said Lord Palmerston / began draining swamps in Sligo / Fought smoke nuisance in London. . . .'

All right. The good governors are those who begin where they are, who act usefully for the well-being of the people. The next nine Cantos, in which the good governors of China are plucked from the past and celebrated in their setting, constitute one of Pound's most sustained and fascinating stretches. For the reader who will keep his mind on the poem and perform his own cross indexing as he goes along, not much of it will remain finally obscure, nor will the asides and outriders of freely associated material distract him from the main drive. I imagine that there are two principal reasons for this coherence: the Cantos pursue a chronological structure, and afterthoughts as to the English reader's need for enlightenment seem to have dictated many verses. Metrically the Cantos are not only elaborate but rich in the saving imagery that Pound in other cantos has deleted or omitted with unfortunate results.

I am afraid that half at least of the second decade of Cantos here published, LXII to LXXI, fall into that category. It is clear, orderly, appropriate, and interesting that these Cantos should without prelude launch into the career of John Adams, which began mid-eighteenth century at precisely the period when Pound drops his Chinese, and that the space given to Adams should precisely equal that given to four millenniums of Chinese history. It is perhaps just that American readers should be presumed to know a great deal more about Adams and his contemporaries than about Kung-fu-tsu (Confucius). Certainly, 'without knowing their actions / you know not what made us our revolution / *magis decora poeticis fabulis*. . . .' Nevertheless, there are here long passages shuffled in chronology, composed wholly of snipped lines from Adams' letters, isolated curiosities of detail cryptic, contemporary references and a liberal use or implication of *et cetera*. These passages seem to me not merely arid but, in effect, perfunctory and thoroughly dull. More's the pity, because elsewhere the man and his time come through inimitably, supporting through the mouth of the Founder Pound's great hymn of hate: 'I abhorred over our whole banking system / Every bank of discount is downright corruption / taxing the public for private individuals' gain - and if I say this in my will / The American people wd / pronounce I died crazy.'

115. Paul Rosenfeld: 'The Case of Ezra Pound', *American Mercury*

January 1944, lviii, 98–102

Rosenfeld (1890–1946) was an American critic of music and letters whose most influential years were in the twenties, when he was a regular contributor to the *Dial*. Pound apparently disliked Rosenfeld, referring to him as 'Mr. Rosie Field' in a letter to Lincoln Kirstein of 26 October 1930 (quoted by G. A. M. Janssens, *The American Literary Review: A Critical History 1920–1950* (1968), p. 48).

I

A poet, but long desirous of leading poets and dictating to men; a propagandist for poetry and later for the Social Credit System, Ezra Pound finally has been indicted for treason to the United States. For twenty years a resident of Italy, he has openly been a convert to Fascism since 1936, when, in his booklet *Jefferson and/or Mussolini*, he proclaimed Mussolini the embodiment of Jefferson's political ideals. Before Pearl Harbor he began speaking over the radio in a spirit unfriendly to us. Since that date—until Mussolini's fall—he has continued voicing his sentiments over the air. Listeners-in on the Rome radio got the impression that he was speaking in a cryptic language reminiscent of that of

James Joyce in *Finnegans Wake*. But among his constant audience has been the F.B.I. and, it appears the office has succeeded in interpreting this mysterious, private language of his and made a sense of it not altogether healthy for Ezra.

He is clearly Fascism's great prize among the American intellectuals. And many persons have been asking, and many more are certain to ask. What kind of a first-rate intellectual is this American, to whom the fantastic business of adherence to that assassin of human liberty, Il Fascismo, did not seem monstrous and impossible? What manner of man, indeed, is the fine poet, Ezra Pound?

By way of an answer to this question, the present writer begs leave to introduce a personal impression of the poet. It dates from the Anglo-American Paris of the early 1920's. On the evening of my arrival in that city, sitting behind the privet-hedge of a small restaurant in the Latin Quarter, I became aware of something slightly disturbing on the side-walk. This was a tall individual in the later thirties who, while obviously an Englishman or an American, appeared to have stepped straight out of the opera *La Bohème*. A swarthy sombrero covered his head. The collar of his Wotan-blue shirt lay widely open on the lapels of his coat, which had a good English cut, setting off a ruddy, well-trimmed beard. He sported a cane. Resembling the 1830 artists in Puccini's opera, he also resembled a Norse pirate, but an ornamental Norseman, who infrequently had been to sea. His glance, as momentarily he lingered, took in the diners: not, however, it seemed to me, so much in order to gather their identities as to gather the impression he was making.

Two days after there was a knock on the door of my hotel room. In the corridor stood my old friend Sherwood Anderson, who with his wife was occupying a room on a lower floor, and incidentally seeing something of the English and American men-of-letters in Paris. 'Come on down', said he. 'Ezra Pound is here'. Willingly I accepted. Some years previously there had come into my hands a much-remarked book of original verse, called *Provença*, the work of a student of romance philology from Idaho, Ezra Loomis Pound, who had gone abroad in 1908 and remained in Venice, Paris and London. The contents of the volume largely were dramatic monologues descended from Browning's famous ones. But the personages addressing the reader were trouba-dours of the period when the love of beauty awoke in the South of France from its deep sleep during the dark ages. The diction was re-cherchée, emphatically archaic and Anglo-French. Some poems even were couched in poetic forms employed by the Provençal minstrels but never hitherto used in English. Among these were the aubade and the canzone. A flowering period sunken these last six hundred years breathed again through the performance.

II

Since then, Pound has become a champion of modern art. In London, onwards from 1912 he had assumed the leadership of Imagism, the first artistic movement in England to succeed that of the nineties and *The Yellow Book*. Characterized by its search for words and expressions which create images, the movement was an off-shoot of French Symbolism; yet it made English poetry fine art once more. It liberated prosody; expelled commonplaces and grandiloquence from phraseology; brought back precision of language, concreteness of vision, concreteness of thought.

But down on the second floor of the small Parisian hotel, Sherwood Anderson opened the door to his room. There by the table sat my Rudolpho of the Boulevard St. Germain. It had been Ezra Pound. The man, as we talked with him, proved attractive enough. He had dash and experience. His synthetic vocabulary; his phraseology's fulness of literary color: his elocutionary manner—that of an improved Shakespearean barnstormer—were almost wonderful. He seemed pleased with existence, affable, clever, communicative—quite the opposite of poor James Joyce, who had been polite, dismal, austere and remote. But a literary dandyism grew plain.

The social dandy is of course a graceful, charming individual whose grace and charm draw attention to themselves and betray the satisfaction of a vanity. The literary dandy is his counterpart on the intellectual plane. Thus, Pound gave evidence of a desire to please and simultaneously to dazzle. Detecting my interest in music, he volunteered a little talk on the way in which the troubadours notated the melodies to which they intoned their verses. Growing egotistic, again and again his conversation displayed his self-satisfaction. 'What are you working on now, Mr. Pound?' inquired Tennessee Anderson. 'Dante composed the Poem of Faith. I am writing the Poem of Doubt', said he. The poem he thus modestly compared to the *Divine Comedy* was his amorphous Cantos. Pleasantly he added, 'I'm also composing an opera. That is, I have an idea for the melodic line, and I am thinking of going out to see a friend, to ask whether he can fill it in for me'.

It was sheer folly. In good music, melody, rhythm and harmony are inseparable; either born together or not at all. But Pound was serious.

I liked him better on a later occasion, in the little restaurant on the Boulevard. His English wife was with him, and his sprightly little mother-in-law, a Mrs. Shakespeare. Jovially he turned himself into a handbook for the American traveller. He waxed amusingly satiric over literary London. But his arrogance grew plain again. To Paris recently there had come a young English author, begloomed by a domestic catastrophe. And Pound felt called upon to boast 'R—— has come over to Paris just to sit at *my* feet'. The last view I had of him was in the Champs Elysées. In a *fiacre* trotting up the stately avenue reclined a lanky figure suggestive of an Egyptian pharoah taking the air. Outspread, the man's arms rigidly rested on the wagon's lowered hood. His bearded head lay back, facing the clouds. Of course it was Pound.

III

And my reason for trotting out these somewhat melodramatic pictures? It is the fact that they succinctly give the answer to our problem: what manner of intellectual, what manner of man is Ezra Pound? The answer is a bit of a literary actor and peacock. The histrionic and dandified traits imprinted on these memories indeed are of the essence of the man and characteristic of his work. Certainly he is highly talented. He has a mind; the ability to act and execute.

He is a master of verbal and metrical expression. His visual and acoustic sensitivity is exquisite. His verse is wonderfully lean, clean-cut, packed, intense: supple in rhythm and style; sometimes fiercely, but always clearly expressive of agreeable or disagreeable sensations through sharp vivid images. For all its shapeliness, it nonetheless achieves deep meaning and moves the reader mainly in instances where Pound has merged his personality in that of former poets and adopted their language and thought—as in *Provença*, or in his paraphrases of the Anglo-Saxon 'Seafarer', the elegies of Propertius, the water-color-like poems of the old Chinese. Certainly the significations of his directly lyrical poems of the London period, say the gay, satiric epigrams, are fairly trivial. To achieve self-expression, we mean, Pound has always had to wear a costume, to enact some rôle proposed to him by other minds.

And all his work has called attention to himself. Naturally, every lyric poet conveys his own emotions; and the work of many a great writer has been an almost unbroken autobiography. But this lyricism is not the subject of our reference. Rather it is the fact that, ever a bit of a smart-aleck, Pound has preened and swaggered in his poetry. To Ford Madox Ford he once remarked, 'What the public wants is Me, because I am not an imbecile like the component members of the public', and he has conformed to this idea with exceeding narrowness. His poetry and prose are frequently humorous; but they are mannered, never conceal art, and persistently and complacently have brought us face to face with the personality of Ezra Pound frequently represented as that of a selfless champion and martyr of pure art and a sage of social economy in the footsteps of Major Douglas. No object sufficiently has awakened humility in him, not even the literature he has loved.

Not that this dandyism sets him in a necessarily frivolous class of artists. Byron, too, was a self-worshipper. So also was Whistler, and Oscar Wilde.

But, it may be asked: granting the histrionic character and self-complacency of Fascism's outstanding recruit, can any connection be thought to exist between them and his Fascism? Can either the actor's psychology, or elated vanity, be considered the cause of his adherence to that sorry system? Now, the source of Pound's fantastic, horrid act indubitably is a complex one; he pretends it was entirely disinterestedness and social-economic philosophy. Conceivably, a contempt for the facile, opportunistic Marxism of so many English and American writers may have been a part of it. To ourselves, nonetheless, the man's histrionic temperament and foolish vanity, do seem possible, unconscious motives. Fascism, like the Social Credit movement before, may well have interested him as another of the external ideas able, as it were, to provide him with an intellectual costume and a rôle to play. Simultaneously it may have proffered itself to him as a means of displaying his self-esteeem. All dandies feel themselves superior to humanity; and the special reverence which Pound all along has been demanding of his compatriots had materialized to but a small degree. And Fascism opposed the democratic sentiment that all men should be free; fundamentally are equal; that humanity is a whole formed in the Creator's likeness. It claimed to be a government of the élite, the socially and intellectually superior.

Publicly to espouse Fascism thus was simultaneously to acquire a new rôle permissive of expression, and to associate oneself conspicuously with 'the few', to attest belief in the hypothesis of 'the superior man', to defy and humiliate the recalcitrant democratic public.

For these reasons, we think, Pound took the jump: in any case, for the present it does seem the part of charity to assume these were his motives, and no others.

THE PISAN CANTOS

New York, 30 July 1948
London, 22 July 1949

116. Robert Fitzgerald: ' "What thou Lovest Well Remains"', *New Republic*

16 August 1948, cxix, 21–3

We find ourselves, again, in debt to New Directions, now that the latest cantos of Ezra Pound are available in a volume to themselves, printed from the same fonts as the preceding Cantos, and also in a collected edition. This publication is admirable—and far from being simply an admirable act of piety. The poet remains in St. Elizabeth's Hospital, Washington, adjudged too ill in mind to stand trial for treason; and it is easy to look for and discover in the poetry evidence of his illness. That evidence is almost certainly there in quantities strongly confirmatory for the diagnostician. As for the average, untuned reader, long since put off by Pound's polylingual reveries and idiosyncratic structure, he may not see any greater reward for patience in the new Cantos than in the old. But this is not inevitable nor desirable.

Critics, and most creators when acting as critics, tend to overestimate the role of schematization and design in the production of works of art. All artists recognize, I think, that much is always given, or formed out of thin air as if by some independent demon, while the materials are being worked or played with, and that no matter with what clarity the form is seen beforehand, the object as it finally issues represents the lucky catch as much as it represents the intention. Pound's Cantos are the work of a man for whom the thing given has, in general, had the upper hand over deliberation, a man whose long isolation in Rapallo and unfretful assurance as to his own technical power have allowed unusual freedom in moving here or there, up or down, forward or backward (like a swimmer in clear water) among verbal or substantial intimations and *seizing* them, putting them down, when a more hesitant—or sluggish—artist would have left them in the air.

Pound was born to be a workman in verse, and, if it is manipulation you ask, there is proof of many years' tinkering in his successive recastings of the great Cavalcanti canzon, *Donna mi prega*, into English, of which the last version now stands as Canto XXXVI. The detail is often worked, and worked very hard in some instances. But in compositional art, in the whole affair of placing, accenting, subordinating and linking details, there has apparently been operating something that could be called 'the principle of the plenum': all the intimations have had to be got in. Aware of his detractors, he once wrote of his prose structure, 'I am not proceeding according to Aristotelian logic but according to the ideogrammic method of first heaping together the necessary components of thought. None of these "incoherent" or contradictory facts can be omitted.' This applies perfectly to the Cantos.

Once you start thinking, however, you are irrevocably committed to logic; you think well or ill according as you think coherently or not; and so one notices in this statement Pound's perhaps involuntary use of the word 'first.' He is saying, in effect, that he has undertaken a labor that other men would regard as purely preliminary; for him it has been an end in itself. And why should it not be an end in itself? The ability to think consecutively, to dispose ideas in a really progressive order, is more uncommon than most people suppose; the appearance of doing so can be faked, and constantly is, with the aid of a little rhetoric. Pound was being comparatively honest; he merely dignified his own limitation of ability or interest as 'ideogrammic method'; and it is proper, after all, for a man to insist on the dignity of what he does. Moreover, nobody questions that in his notes Pound *did* hit on a good many 'necessary components of thought.'

All that must be said is that he rarely went on to think very well about them, and that this is a great defect in critical or argumentative prose. It is not merely that he thought badly enough to behave fantastically. We have lived in a time when no subject was thoroughly learned, no argument pursued until it was settled; and Pound abetted this tendency. But is the defect of the prose likewise a great defect in the Cantos? The answer is Yes, if that is what you demand; but it is not a wise demand to make.

The fine artist is drawn to the impossible as the mystic is drawn to the inconceivable. It has been said that it is impossible to use a logical language, like English, as if it were a picture language, like Chinese, or as if it were an abstract musical medium. It has also been said that it is impossible to write, in English, Homeric hexameters. Perhaps Pound's disregard of the first kind of impossibility may be illuminated by his triumph over the second.

'I have never read half a page of Homer,' he has declared, 'without finding melodic invention. . . . There are, mathematically, 64 basic general forms [of the so-called dactyllic hexameter] . . . a variety which will naturally accommodate a vastly greater amount of real speech than . . . ti tum ti tum ti tum ti tum. . . . The legal number of syllables in a classic hexameter varied from 12 to 18.' Here, on a silver platter, is a key to much of the verse in the Cantos, and especially to the Pisan Cantos, in which the hexameter is practically a norm—established, I will go so far as to say, in the first line: 'The enormous tragedy of the dréam in the peásant's bént shoúlders.' Taking this basic six-beat pattern, actually three and three, Pound has modulated it *ad infinitum,* dropping the second half line, echoing it, slowing, speeding or exploding the component feet, suspending and delaying the completion of the measure by parenthetical inserts, relieving it with the familiar English pentameter (blank verse) line, but returning often enough to the long line to keep it alive in the reader's ear:

> And when the morning sun lit up the shelves and battalions
> of the West, cloud over cloud
> Old Ez folded his blankets.
> Neither Eos nor Hesperus has suffered wrong at my hands.

Everything here is typical: the evocation of brightness, the sun in the air; the suggestion in 'cloud over cloud' of nature's own plenum or plenitude; the swift astringency of sense and hidden pleasure in the 'Old Ez' hemistich ('folded his' echoes 'Old Ez'); the Greek names for dawn light and evening star and the artist's pride stated at the end. Of such details, minutely melodic, is the long web woven.

But few of the details are as simple in their allusiveness as this one. Not only in melody, in shifts of key, but in shifts of reference also, they require at almost every point an agility in the reader's mind like the agility of a performer reading a difficult score. And this is, indeed, the nature of difficulty in the Cantos. To read at sight a sonata of Mozart's, a pianist must have trained his eyes and mind and fingers; he must be equipped for the exertion. Both the system of notation and the instrument are standard, and the equipment can be acquired by hard work in a conservatory. But the equipment needed for a perfect reading of Pound's Cantos is, to say the least, much less accessible.

Latin, Greek, Italian, French and Chinese are requisites if the cantos are even to be read aloud correctly, and few of us live with all these languages. This, however, is not the poet's fault. In an earlier Canto he represented John Adams as saying, circa 1820:

> I begged Otis to print it (the Greek prosody)
> He said there were no Greek types in America,
> and if there were, were no typesetters cd/ use 'em.

To judge by the errors in the Greek passages of the Cantos as printed, Otis could say the same today; and it seems less excusable that in the first few pages of the Pisan Cantos the Latin *veneno* is printed *veleno*, *nox animae* is printed *nux animae*, and 'Thames bank' becomes 'Thomas bank.' Aside from the language difficulties, in Pound's *plenum* there are so many data of an elliptical and evanescent kind that it seems impossible in some cases to discover just what the 'necessary components' are. In other cases it is hard to see what interest or value they may have apart from the sheer fact of their presence in the poet's mind or on the page.

But, even as I complain, I insist that we ought to be grateful for what we have, mindful that if it were otherwise we wouldn't have it. A very imperfect reading can nevertheless be rewarding. On the whole, too, the latest Cantos are plainer sailing than many of their predecessors. A 'sailing around' or 'periplum' is one of the descriptions the writer offers for his work. In all eleven of the Pisan Cantos the writer speaks from an Allied detention camp in Italy in 1945, within sight of the tower of Pisa. It is late summer going into early autumn; he is quartered in a tent, and a colored American soldier has made him a table to write on. The form of his writing is fluid notation and revery. There are many themes and motifs and echoes, some of them only recognizable if you are familiar with preceding Cantos.

The poet identifies himself with Odysseus, as he has before, but this time it is in his role as 'Ou Tis' (Greek for No Man), and he speaks of himself as 'a man on whom the sun has gone down.' He is, again, Odysseus among the shades of the heroes; 'Lordly men are to earth o'ergiven'; he summons to mind Ford, Yeats, Joyce and other 'men of unusual genius' whom he has known. Like a grasshopper (another early image for himself) he flies back and forth in time (for 'Time is not, time is the evil, beloved') amid scenes and ideas from the past.

Against 'capitalism' he repeats the quotation from John Adams that pleased him two decades (of Cantos) ago: 'Every bank of discount is downright corruption'; and he has words also for the corruption of fascism: 'jactancy, vanity, peculation to the ruin of 20 years' labor.'

He addresses a spider, a cat and a butterfly, his companions in captivity; he touches lightly on his age and fatigue, expatriate for so many years in a country he has loved and seen defeated, with 'stone after stone of beauty cast down.' Like Odysseus, he tells of his wanderings, but obliquely, in another strand of discourse, taken up, dropped, and taken up again: New York of 40 years ago, Spain, Provence, Paris and London: beautiful place names, odd images, fragments of anecdote, and endearing personal memories:

> So that leaving America I brought with me $80
> and England a letter of Thomas Hardy's
> and Italy one eucalyptus pip. . . .

for he is leaving Italy, and knows it:

> As a lone ant from a broken ant hill
> from the wreckage of Europe, ego scriptor. . . .

So impersonal is this polylingual surface, and so brisk the poet's taste, that the reader does not at once realize that in certain passages Pound is for the first time expressing a personal desolation and a kind of repentance, that is enormously moving:

> Tard, tres tard, je t'ai connue la Tristesse
> I had been hard as youth sixty years. . . .

and lines of this stamp, recurring, come to a culmination in a long passage, at the end of Canto LXXXI, which will stand as one of the peaks of all Pound's writing, and of which I quote only the noble beginning:

[quotes *Cantos*, pp. 556–7 'What thou lovest' to 'I say pull down'.]

'It is not man made courage or made order or made grace.' If I read these lines aright in their whole context, the reason Pound began calling his poetry 'Cantos' 20 years ago becomes clearer. In perception or vision he would mount to a *paradiso* as his master, Dante, did; and he observes that 'le paradis n'est pas artificiel': it exists. Well, the moral universe of the *Divine Comedy* was orthodox, graded, and public, firmly conceived to its uttermost corner; and this of Pound's is quite a different thing. But at their least valuation I submit that these Cantos in which light and air —and song—move so freely are more exhilarating poetic sketch books, 'Notes from the Upper Air,' than can be found elsewhere in our literature.

117. Louis L. Martz, review, *Yale Review*

Autumn 1948, n.s. xxxviii, 144–8

From 'Recent Poetry', a review of the New Directions edition of the *Cantos* and the *Pisan Cantos*.

Though continuing the concern with the unity of the Cantos, Martz here applies for the first time a chronological analysis of theme and organization, in the hope of answering the larger question of form. He is the first critic to glimpse the idea that the later Cantos could not, in some senses, have been predicted by the earlier, and that they modify our sense of the organization of the whole.

Martz (b. 1913), American literary critic, teaches at Yale University and is the author of various studies of seventeenth century and modern poetry.

Here in one volume are eighty-two of the projected hundred cantos in Ezra Pound's human *Commedia*, including the new *Pisan Cantos* (also published separately) written during Pound's confinement in the prison camp near Pisa. Viewing the more than five hundred pages in this volume, we may well feel that there is no longer any need to suspend appraisal of Pound's achievement 'until the "Cantos" are completed'; here is enough, and to spare. Is Pound succeeding in his aim of giving to the world an epic poem in an art form new to the English language? Or is he simply giving us a huge anthology, a load of junk and jewels, from which every reader may take his choice? Some of the variant 'keys to the whole design' that have been suggested may help in deciding whether the new Cantos serve to develop a poetical unity, or merely offer another instalment of chaos.

In 1928 Yeats recorded the famous impressions of the Cantos (later prefixed to his *Vision*) which he had drawn from conversations with Pound at Rapallo: here, when completed, would be a poem without plot, chronicle, or 'logic of discourse,' but a poem that would 'display a structure like that of a Bach Fugue'; a poem that would resemble an Impressionist painting, 'where everything rounds or thrusts itself without edges, without contours'; or, a poem that would resemble a 'Cosimo Tura decoration' in compartments. Pound himself, however, has insisted that the poem proceeds by the 'ideogrammic method' of Chinese poetry, and has referred us to the remarkable essay by Ernest Fenollosa on 'The Chinese Written Character,' an essay that Pound edited. Fenollosa's essay is certainly Pound's Art of Poetry: it contains indispensable clues to Pound's poetic method in the Cantos and shows the meaning of the analogies suggested by (or to) Yeats. Parts of the essay, for example, read like a description of Impressionist painting: 'Sentences must be like the mingling of the fringes of feathered banners, or as the colors of many flowers blended into the single sheen of a meadow.' These analogies, then, all point to one end: a poem that, by fluent association of disparate elements, creates a grand unity of the whole. That whole will contain, Pound has said, 'the tale of the tribe,' the human race. But more recently (1940) Pound's publisher has reported that the poet now dissents from Yeats's account of the poem, and instead hints at a threefold structure of 'Inferno,' 'Purgatorio,' and 'Paradiso.' Can this view of the structure be reconciled with that suggested by Yeats?

Reading through the Cantos, a few every evening for several weeks, one can begin to reach conclusions. One can feel that the work has in places a unity that binds many Cantos together, and that it has everywhere some kind of coherence, though not everywhere the same kind: during the twenty years of the work's gestation Pound has clearly modified his methods and aims. The threefold division of the *Divine Comedy* does not appear; yet the analogy is valid, for Hell, Purgatory, and Heaven are there, laminated, interlarded with each other. Canto I presents the descent of Ulysses into Hell, with this glimpse of Elpenor saying,

> I fell against the buttress,
> Shattered the nape-nerve, the soul sought Avernus.
> But thou, O King, I bid remember me, unwept, unburied,
> Heap up mine arms, be tomb by sea-bird, and inscribed:
> *A man of no fortune, and with a name to come.*

It seems a bitter prophecy, for now, in the *Pisan Cantos*, Pound sees himself among those 'who have passed over Lethe,' and refers to himself and his companions in the camp, repeatedly, as 'men of no fortune and with a name to come.' Hell is the substratum, the groundtone, upon which one sees the visions of Purgatory and Paradise. Thus the Confucian Canto (XIII), in itself a fine example of unity formed out of fragments, presents the Heaven of moral wisdom; it is set off on either side with scenes of commercial ugliness (XII) and with the scabrous Hell of the usurers (XIV and XV, with echoes of Dante). Usury, of course, is Pound's version of the Devil at work in the modern world. Canto XVI, then, presents a kind of Purgatory, where 'I bathed myself with the acid to free myself of the hell ticks'; XVII gives a different view of Paradise through the medium of cool, classical imagery; and XVIII returns to the commercial Hell of the modern world. These are merely instances, but they may suggest why this reader feels that the first thirty Cantos (published together in 1933) form an impressive unity of association, despite some passages that one regrets.

In the *Eleven New Cantos* (1934) it appears that a modulation is being introduced. These fragments from American and modern European history, excerpts from letters, glimpses of raw life, seem to form an extended sermon on the evils of usury, a bad banking system; they present a world that is 'irritable and unstable.' But the sermon goes on too long: it is too consistently prosy, flickering, and ragged. This erring from poetry results from a basic flaw that Pound clearly saw in himself, when, in his essay on William Carlos Williams, he contrasted their two temperaments: 'If he wants to "do" anything about what he sees, this desire for action does not rise until he has meditated in full and at leisure. Where I see scoundrels and vandals, he sees a spectacle or an ineluctable process of nature. Where I want to kill at once, he ruminates.' This impatient desire for direct action does heavy damage to the Cantos from XXXI to LXXI: the continuity here is too often merely one of abstract theme—the very error that Fenollosa warned against. The long history of China (LII–LXI) is an extended illustration of how a high culture can be maintained century upon century, against the heaviest odds; in contrast, the following section, entitled 'John Adams', (LXII–LXXI) attempts to show a balanced, 'Confucian' mind analyzing the mistakes that threaten (Pound would say) to bring American democracy to a quick end. But the low pulse of the writing in the Chinese sequence will not sustain a section of this length; and the Adams sequence is the one section of the Cantos that may fairly be called unreadable. In these middle Cantos one is forced to anthologize, choosing, for instance, the ode on the definition of love from Canto XXXVI; Canto XLV, the ode against usury; XLVII, a sustained elegy on man's fate, and one of Pound's finest poems; XLIX, a 'Chinese poem,' and a fine example of the ideogrammic method.

After the growing tedium of Cantos LIII–LXXI, one comes with pleased surprise to the new *Pisan Cantos* (wondering why Cantos LXXII and LXXIII do not appear). For at Canto LXXIV Pound returns to the fluent association of diversities that produced the greatest poetry of the earlier Cantos. In the first three or four of the new Cantos one may be bothered by incoherence, though startled and moved by some of the finest passages in recent poetry. But if we read on, the details begin to flow together until in Cantos LXXIX, LXXX, and LXXXI we come to the best of all the new Cantos; and a total impression emerges as if we had moved away from too close a view of a Pissarro landscape. We see, vividly, the aging prisoner amid the ugliness of the camp ('so lay men in Circe's swine-sty'); it is Hell; and yet it is full of charity, both in the poet and in his fellows. We are impressed by the essential humility of the poet's attitude, by his flashes of wry humor, and above all, by his belief in the power of artistic achievements to live 'in the stillness outlasting all wars.' 'Gaudier's word not blacked out/ nor old Hulme's, nor Wyndham's.' Here, I think, is the essential Pound. He has always been, as Eliot has recently said, quite unassuming about his own poetry; his arrogance has sprung mainly from his zeal for artistic creation, wherever it is found. That almost impersonal zeal has carried him through his appalling crisis to a calm in which he appears 'As a lone ant from a broken ant-hill,' recalling the culture of the period 'before the world was given over to wars,' the period when he was a driving muscle in a literary revolution. Famous figures stream before us in ideogrammic scenes: writers, painters, musicians, philosophers, who were makers of an era, with others now nearly forgotten, all drawn together by the elegiac mood. And amid these actors there are places, views that recall the era gone:

> and at Ventadour and at Aubeterre
> or where they set tables down by small rivers,
> and the stream's edge is lost in grass.

It is perhaps true that our interest in a great part of the new Cantos lies at the edge of the poetical; we feel the interest aroused by the journal or the letters of an important writer who has intimately known the greatest artists of his time. It is perhaps true that the *Pisan Cantos* are really a brilliant note-book held together by the author's personality, with poems scattered throughout:

> and there was a smell of mint under the tent flaps
> especially after the rain

> and a white ox on the road toward Pisa
>   as if facing the tower,
> dark sheep in the drill field and on wet days were clouds
> in the mountain as if under the guard roosts

But the poetry can also be sustained for many lines, as in the great lynx hymn that concludes Canto LXXXIX, or the ode on vanity that concludes Canto LXXXI with these significant lines:

> To have gathered from the air a live tradition
> or from a fine old eye the unconquered flame
> This is not vanity.
>   Here error is all in the not done,
> all in the diffidence that faltered . . .

This and a notable sentence from Pound's essay on Williams seem to summarize all that need be said of Pound's failures and achievements: 'Art very possibly *ought* to be the supreme achievement, the "accomplished", but there is the other satisfactory effect, that of a man hurling himself at an indomitable chaos, and yanking and hauling as much of it as possible into some sort of order (or beauty), aware of it both as chaos and as potential.'

118. Reed Whittemore, review, *Poetry*

November 1948, lxxxiii, 108–10

Whittemore (b. 1919), American poet and critic, was educated at Yale University. He edited *Furioso* from 1939 to 1953, taught at Carleton College, and is literary editor of the *New Republic*.

Pound has always placed great emphasis upon *integrity*. His own has now carried him to Washington under conditions which will presumably be the subject of his next sixteen cantos if he writes them, and which may very well be the most appropriate conditions for a last statement about the results of integrity in this world. But the question, 'what is integrity?' or 'how does one get that way?' has been answered differently by Pound in various sections of the Cantos, so differently that it is possible, I think to find in the Cantos several Pounds, all men of integrity but not all, for my money, equally convincing. At the risk of appearing glib and pretentiously expert about a poem I cannot profess to understand, I shall therefore casually divide the Cantos into three parts.

The first thirty are the finest of what I will call, after Matthew Arnold, the Hellenistic Pound. Here he received and transformed into his own idiom The World. No solutions were offered, no programs defended. If there was an assertion of any kind it was Kung's in Canto 13: 'If a man have not order within him / He cannot spread order about him.' It was Kung's assertion, however, not Pound's, since Pound's ostensible role in the early Cantos was that of observer, recorder, he who sees 'things as they are' and is moral (a man of integrity) in so doing.

But then his role changed. In the middle Cantos it was clearly no longer moral for him to be merely the moral poet. Hebraic compulsions assailed him. It became necessary for him to 'spread order about him.' Following Kung's advice in a way Kung may not have anticipated, he must have said to himself, 'You old fool, come out of it, / Get up and do something *useful*.' Thus he committed himself to a program which came to occupy his time and talents increasingly until, in Canto 71, he suggested that he might go so far as to include the central plank of that program in his will. It was a position which he, a man of integrity, was prepared to proclaim and defend to the death—but it was also a contradiction of his previous position.

The Pisan Cantos clearly constitute a third phase, though the neat label for it escapes me. To the integrity of the artist and the integrity of the reformer (or from these two) has been added (or subtracted) all the problems which attend the integrity of the man. Nothing could be more natural. Pound has never been so much Hellenist or Hebraist, Imagist or Economist as he has been Pound; the world has been disposed to think of him so; Pound has been disposed to have it think of him so. And the events of the past few years have only served to magnify both for Pound and for his public his person rather than his positions. What is most strange about *The Pisan Cantos* is not that they are a 'revelation of the poet's personal tragedy' (dust jacket) but that they are not more personal than they are. Hellenism and Hebraism are still with us; usury is still downright corruption; Swinburne is still a villain; and our higher institutions of learning are still 'kawledges' where 's.o.b.'s' discuss 'moddddun opohetree.' All his concerns of the past thread through the new Cantos as if they were as current, as vital, as when he first wrote of them. Nothing has changed except (the all-important exception) Pound's attitude toward them. They are no longer central. They are the inert ingredients of his own past.

As a result of this shift in emphasis the new Cantos are perhaps more like the old than the middle Cantos. Having in effect despaired of his Program (without rejecting it for a minute), he regards it occasionally with the kind of detachment so effective in his earlier treatment of reformers—of the people who 'went to it,' for example, in Canto 16, or of the various enterprising gentlemen who failed to save England or Russia or any place in Canto 27. Since his Program is no longer primary he is at liberty to look upon it, if not dispassionately, at least with such objectivity as one may bring to bear upon matters which have become old hat.

Unfortunately the Hellenistic morality of phase one is also old hat. So little is Pound any longer engaged by the 'details' of expression—the craftsmanship involved in describing 'things as they are'—that much of the late work has the finish and texture of a diary. Not the poem but the poet is now primary; not 'moddddun opohetree' but the memories of former engagements in that industry are his real concern. As he says himself, 'the drama is wholly subjective'. Being subjective it is a drama which only an intimate knowledge of Pound's own life can satisfactorily explain. And more important, it is a drama containing excessively private interpretations of 'things as they are,' so private that the 'things' only get on paper in fragmentary form. There are notable exceptions. There are fine passages. But the whole seems to me to be much too disorderly, incomplete, unfinished to be more than a useful text for a biographer.

119. William Carlos Williams, from a review, *Imagi* (Allentown, Pa.)

Spring 1949, iv, 10–11

I have not (even yet) read every word of the *Pisan Cantos*, nor deciphered half those I have read.

But I have seen enough to be indifferent to many of them and to find myself wonderfully enlightened by the art of the others.

Beauty may be difficult—as Ezra insists, but a sense of reality in the words is even more difficult. A sense that *connects* the past with the present so that the deepest past starts to life is (to say the least) astonishing.

Pound's words are his currency. He hates everything that is less than living (totally living), living back into the remoteness of all the past. . . .

My brief criticism of these Cantos remains the words of it. No one in our day has so used the words: they get a new light over them, a new application to the objects, a new *lack* of the stereotyped official use of poetic reference.

A new hygiene of the words, cleanliness.

In short, they live, the sentence lives, the movement lives, the object flares up (out of the dark). That is what I mean by reality, it lives again (as always) in our day.

The words get a freshness over them that I find in no other lines written in our day. But I will not deny, there's as much trash as excellence. But why stress, as they do in 'Books', the trash merely to reveal the ready audience for trash?

The OTHER is that which needs to be seen. . . .

Trash: incommunicable personal recollections—names, words without color. Tho' I have met one Canadian of good ear who reads *all*, right on through for the pleasure of the *sound*.

(But you can't *sound* the Chinese ideographs: Pound sez we're lucky to get as much of that as we have got and that the sounds will be given later.)

—and it is the most authentically sounding language (reality again) of our present day speech: far more likely than the stupidity of journalese—with which he is attacked.

Give him the prize and hang him if you like, but give him the prize.

That's the way it should be read, 'right on through' for the delight of the sound. More than 'delight', the illumination brought on by the reality of the sound, the well based quality of the language itself—even, yes, apart from the 'meaning'—and this *alone*. It is unbelievably good.

—with the eye (that is, the mind) directed flexibly *inward*. Look *into* the poem (as poems that deserve to be read should be read) and you will *see* the sun rise and hear the winds blow, smell the air, the pure air that is beyond the air—and know the men who are talking.

Finally there is the curious fact that much that is said of usury (Pound's special bug) is so flamingly true that the perceptions of the poem form an actual, practicable modus operandi, a sound and workable mode of procedure which would—save the world for us (if followed) and so as he believes, the country. Money as we use it (usury) is our hell.

They might (Pound's fiduciary conceptions) if correctly paid attention to even save us from Russia! Those bears!

The poem (the Cantos) accidentally, thus, happens to be true, true to the facts which, being overridden in the past have continued to destroy us through the ages—bringing on wars.

Heeded, Pound's loyalty, humanity (conspicuously revealed by the devotion he inspires in other men who devote themselves to him), kindness and good sense, would strike like lightning into us.

So we procede to legally slaughter him (in the face of the lice and swine we let live) that we may escape the implications of his genius. We might better acquire stronger stomachs against his peccadillos.

120. C. M. Bowra, 'More Cantos from Ezra Pound', *New Statesman and Nation*

3 September 1949, n.s., xxxvii, 250

This is a review of *The Pisan Cantos* and a reissue of the *Selected Poems*.

Bowra (1898–1971), English critic and scholar, was Warden of Wadham College, Oxford, from 1938 to 1970.

It is almost impossible to be impartial about Ezra Pound. For a small, very select circle, which includes the greatest poets of our time, such as W. B Yeats, T. S. Eliot, and Edith Sitwell, he has been not only an inspiring critic but no mean practitioner of poetry. To most other poets and lovers of poetry he is, if not something much worse, at least a mountebank and a buffoon. The appearance of *The Pisan Cantos* and the reprint of *Selected Poems* is a challenge to look at him again and try to decide what he is worth. This is not easy. Many powerful, if irrelevant, considerations push themselves forward and obscure the vision. We must forget Pound's politics and his war-record; we must also forget his disagreeable personality on paper, his cockiness and offensiveness, his pretences to a scholarship of which he is almost totally deficient (even in *Pisan Cantos* most of the Greek quotations are ungrammatical), his contempt for anything that might be thought pretty or warm-hearted or ordinarily human. If we can make this effort, we may then turn to *Pisan Cantos*.

From the start we are struck, almost overwhelmed, by two contradictory impressions. The first impression is that, despite everything, Pound has an ear for rhythm and an eye for words which assert themselves in every poem. His hatred of an out-moded, literary speech is justified by his own efforts to make words clear and clean and direct. More than this, he makes them move to his own music. The first line of the book shows of what he is capable:

The enormous tragedy of the dream in the peasant's bent shoulders.

373

There are many such lines, and there are even passages of this quality. As we read the Cantos, we see why Mr. Eliot saw so much in Pound; for their voices are very similar. Pound can write the slow, melancholy line like

> As a lone ant from a broken ant-hill
> from the wreckage of Europe, ego scriptor,

or lines lighter and gayer like

> O lynx, guard my vineyard
> As the grape swells under vine leaf
> This Goddess was born of sea-foam
> She is lighter than air under Hesperus.

At intervals we find many such excellent lines, and we can see why Pound has had so great an influence in our time. When one of the chief problems of poetry has been to find a vocabulary which shall be fresh and precise and pointed, Pound has done much to show how it can be done.

This impression of excellent craftsmanship is countered and for the present reviewer ruined by the content of the poems. This excellent gift for words is applied on the whole to experiences which are dull or distasteful, usually dull. Pound rambles on, without plan or design, about a series of dreary subjects—the bad influence of bankers, gossip, seldom interesting, about men of letters and artists, stray bits of reading, conversations in American all too like actual conversations with Americans, semi-symbolical figures of hostesses and tourists and rich men, who are interesting neither as human beings nor as symbols, and of course political comments of a 'blimpish' kind with a smack of Wall Street. Pound has a great deal to say, but he arranges it into no pattern, assuming perhaps that the stream of his consciousness is some golden stream. Alas, it is nothing of the kind. Pound's comments on life are peculiarly tedious, and, when they are spread over a whole book, they are deadly. Pound, after all the fuss and trouble, is nothing but a bore and an American bore. Read his poems in his own language and the voice is all too familiar. The unceasing rattle, the chaotic flow, the pointless gossip, the feeble generalisations, the 'knowing' air, the inside information, the culture—these things are known to us and give no pleasure. The disaster of Pound is that he, to whom the gods gave a remarkable gift of words, has been denied the experience worthy of them. In the end he has very little to say that is worth saying.

121. Richard Eberhart on the character of Pound's work

1949

'Pound's New Cantos', *Quarterly Review of Literature* (1949), v, 174–91.

The initial publication of this essay was accompanied by a note: 'In the Fall of 1946 J. Laughlin sent me the manuscript of Pound's *The Pisan Cantos* asking if I would like to write something about them. In the light of subsequent controversy it should be stated that [this] article appears as it was then written.'

Eberhart (b. 1904) is an American poet and playwright. His *Collected Poems 1930–1960* appeared in 1960, and *Collected Verse Plays* in 1962.

I am not interested in what was reported to be another incident in the life of Ezra Pound. I am interested in the Cantos as poetry. I am not concerned with Pound's political beliefs, nor with his social pronouncements, which have not seemed logically to cohere. To what extent one can abstract these from the total impact of his late Cantos, I am not certain. An approach to the work as poetry is necessary and more rewarding, at least to me, than reading the Cantos as political, economic, or sociological manifestoes. Fifty years will remove the politics and leave the poetry. The Cantos can be read disinterestedly, which is only to pay them their due as art, and indeed in these new Cantos one would assume a task of special pleading to overestimate the political or sociological as predominantly significant.

The eleven new Cantos (74–84) carry on much in the manner as they do in the type of matter of the former Cantos. If anything, they are more lively and more lyrical than their predecessors; some might assess them as more violent in places, more nervously jumping from point to point in a kind of insistent distraction, with less cohesive order, throwing off shoots and flares of lyric. The dates come up into the last few years, imparting an interest of the immediate to the work. One wonders when the century will be reached and what will then be able to be made of the whole work.

We are invited to compare the later work of Pound with that of Eliot. These works represent two major approaches to life, the religious and the secular; contemplation versus action; the feminine set against the masculine; the inner against the outer world; the world of spiritual timelessness against an artistic reconstruction of history.

The last quartets of Beethoven have been witnessed in regard to Eliot's. Beethoven's last quartets have the power to excruciate. They are excruciating. The word could not be applied to Eliot's later work. His trilling wire in the blood is a small wire, with not maddening vibration. Beethoven was straining at the bounds of sensibility. Eliot does not strain, even at the bounds of grammar; the form is placid, controlled, studied, considered, in keeping with the gentle, deep aspiration of his spiritual wish. He is not angry. He has denied such things, and that is his criticism.

It is more difficult to write good poetry of acceptance than it is to write good poetry of revolt. The 'Four Quartets' do not shock us. They are to speak beyond such things. The allusions are provocative, as before. I will not point out the selection of 'Erhebung', the careful admission of 'smokefall', the masterful perception of the word 'twittering.' Nor exclaim the niceness of 'where the field-mouse trots'; the newness of 'haruspicate and scry'; the syllabic delicacy and nuance of 'sortilege, or tea leaves'; nor the resurrection of 'Behovely' ('Sin is Behovely').

I would point up some solemn comments: 'human nature / Cannot bear very much reality.' We are so much of our age, and Eliot has expressed it so dominantly, that I have heard no one object to this statement. It is taken as a matter of fact, as basically acceptable or accepted truth, the truth about human kind. Yet if we look with detachment at this statement, we do not necessarily believe it. It becomes a pseudo-statement, the best poetry can do, unscientific. Actually we do not know what 'reality' means, and we have no measuring rod for 'very much.' But, even if we could be satisfied on these points, the possibility arises of transcending our times, which could mean transcending Eliot's statement, with attendant removal from the subtle intoxication of its persuasion, from the very tone, from the very texture. It would then be possible to see this statement, from some future point of view, as period writing. It would be possible to refuse it total assent as feminine, soft, weak. It would be possible to consider certain past, heroic times as perhaps having equal value, differently emphasized. Some Greek, some Elizabethan, or our present Pound could announce the opposite with telling effect. For human kind can, and has, borne, and will bear, very much reality, by whatever semantic gist. There is a core of man's humanity which Eliot's statement does not reach. Blackmur (*Sewanee Review*, Autumn 1946) would have the statement modified by addition of 'that human kind cannot *know* very much reality' and that in his inability he rushes 'heartlong into the arm of authority, if not the authority of some past revelation then the nearest spatch-cock authority to hand, when it is asserted as genuine and its own. Authority is ostrich.' The switch to cognition is plausible, but takes away from the feeling of having to bear what he knows, and it would not seem that man's inability to know very much reality is cause which results in his rush to authority. Eliot's emphasis on the feeling in 'bear' would seem the more profound, whether or not we are concerned with the authority. But my point is that Eliot's statement remains aloof from the deepest human suffering, affronting our profound recognition of this, and does not belong with the endlessness of humility.

The positive, the masculine, and the heroic (or its inversion in satire) are in the realm of Pound. The end of Eliot's vision in the Quartets is a state of grace shining from a line Tennyson could have written: 'And all shall be well and / All manner of thing shall be well.'

As yet we have no feeling that this state is available to Pound; nor that he would welcome it; nor that he could make poetry of it. He is the militant mind still protesting, still aggressive, dominating his forms, making an objective picture of the world out of intellect and feeling, in which there is great spirit, but in an entirely different sense from the technically religious spirit. There is a sense that man has borne very much suffering, and can bear it, but as against Eliot's statement we have the typically Poundian, individualistic, intellectual, aggressive comment:

> I don't know how humanity stands it
> with a painted paradise at the end of it
> without a painted paradise at the end of it.
> the dwarf morning-glory twines round the grass blade

The poetry of Eliot's statement depends from the whole structure of Christian doctrine, less a made thing than Pound's. Here the ideas stand up in their own right. The method of the make is evident. The trouble is that it is a squib. To what extent is it deeply felt in Pound's philosophy?

These are four lines in a welter of lines quickly running through all sorts of ideas and sensations. Either Pound has so much to say that he hurtles us along in his hectic, headlong pursuit of his exuberant, prolific world, as if his magic would break should we stop for months to consider, say, these four lines. Or, Pound is not interested in penetrating, or cannot penetrate, the depths of life and will cast out these laconic lines, for instance, for the sake of laconism. Either–Or. The fallacy of either–or is also evident, and not final.

One is harassed by the squib-writing and can scarcely find three pages of unbroken coherence. This is probably to misunderstand, out of imperfection, the niceness of musical structure, the necessity of every line and phrase being precisely where and as it is.

To return to an Eliot-Pound contrast, it could be substantiated that in his poetry Eliot has little love of individuals. The compassion, and the passion, Hopkins had for specific human beings in his poems, the deep realizations he erected of their essential humanity, as, to name one instance, Felix Randall, marks him. Where Eliot is deficient in this respect, where Hopkins applied to individuals deep love, Pound is objectively interested in all kinds and conditions of men, historical and contemporary, those in old legends, old courts, or modern states and senates, and lays about him with hatred as well as with sometime affection. This is to be expected, granting the objective, secular, history-redacting nature of the work. It also marks the poet interested in this world, the world, rather than in the soul, the after-world.

As for the polylinguality of Pound, one becomes used to it. The constant repetitions, cries, tags, pointers mingle in with the plain (or rather Poundian) English of the text. One finds accountably that Pound relies more heavily in places on Italian than on other Romance languages; that his Spanish is sparse; that his German is as it were unfriendly. The Greek is always slightly, if not as I am told always accurate. He has a real love for old French, early English. I am not prepared to comment on the Chinese.

Instead of the English being cluttered up with foreign tongues, one would like there to be more of them, in denser proportions, which is to ask for a radical attempt to write in half a dozen languages. Joyce more nearly did this than Pound does, with radical aim of a new synthetic language. In Pound the importations, poetically, are embellishment and ornamentation, and are not organic in effect. The meaning is organic with the whole, yet the effect is often of the cymbaler, of glissando. The intellectual lie is given to the method in Pound's resistance to any method more formidable. He uses only a few languages, and these up to a certain point. He eschews Siamese, Swahili, Russian. The ordinary informed Westerner would be baffled by a more formidable system, who is intrigued with Greek, Latin, or old French tags. No new language has been created, as in Joyce, but conventional languages imported into English. The effect is stimulating and pleasing, the method highly developed as Pound's own, and perhaps a more radical departure should not be desired. Polylinguality is relative, absolute polylinguality futile, partial polylinguality pleasing. It is to be noted that the heavy bulk of the work is to be understood in plain English.

Plain English in Pound is not plain English elsewhere. As we know, it is inspissated, whirled around with abbreviations, slants, grammatical oddities, capacious quirks and tricks of spacing, indentation and repetition; time is scrambled and comes out like meaning, like history, sometimes translucent, sometimes cryptic. Pound has hem-stitched a new style, quite his own, which nobody would want to copy and would do so disastrously. It does not seem a great new direction in English verse, but a mind-like vehicle and necessity of the author. One would like to hear the Cantos declaimed by loudspeaker from the Greek theater at Taormina, or at Berkeley, preferably by Pound himself. His reading of 'The Seafarer' was powerful, strident, exhilarating; the Cantos would lean to the dramatic so declaimed. But they are best enjoyed in the solitude of the study in a collation of discriminations over a long period of time.

The problem of Pound's redaction of history should be attempted. Is Pound's history true? This poses the problem of the relation of art to life. History is always changing. The imposition of his art changes the way of looking at it, not only within the framework of the Cantos, but outside that framework as well. Yet the question is not fundamentally of the validity of the method, but of the value of the work as art, as poetry.

Aristotle says,

It is not the function of the poet to relate what has happened, but what may happen,—what is possible according to the law of probability or necessity. The poet and the historian differ not by writing in verse or in prose. The work of Herodotus might be put into verse, and it would still be a species of history, with metre no less than without it. The true difference is that one relates what has happened, the other what may happen. Poetry, therefore, is a more philosophical and a higher thing than history: for poetry tends to express the universal, history the particular.

Pound creates a species of history in verse. The history is not the first consideration, but the poetry. We are challenged by him as to the universality of the poetry.

The secular nature of Pound's work and the time in which he is constrained to live work against the unification of ideology and poetic means known to Dante. It is not for nothing that we often cannot see the wood for the trees, the master plan in a Canto or number of Cantos, the totality of design in episodic content.

Universality in secular work I should judge to be more difficult of attainment than universality in a Dantesque sense, where what is given, the Church, is the very altar of absolute meaning. Pound thus, in a sense, has chosen a more difficult task for our times than Eliot; perhaps choice is the wrong term, since each is compelled by the necessities of his own nature: choice is not pure. But Eliot, in assuming the Church (whether of England or Rome would not be radical here), has not only the likelihood of a greater unity in his performance, but of a greater potentiality of credibility in that he has penetrated to, or attempted to penetrate to the heart of Christian feelings in a Western world largely Christian.

Pound is the masculine, aggressive writer, attempting to dominate an immense secular scene and field, to wrest from many centuries, several languages, and multifarious events a pattern of significance, his own, but related to these, whereas Eliot is the feminine passive writer (in his later period) who accepts the strictures of a predetermined way of life, in which there is paradoxically the greatest and the richest freedom, within the confines of which he is able to submit his art to values which he cannot, nor would wish to supersede. Eliot can arrive at a statement of the deepest poetry in 'Humility is endless.' The truth of this statement is incontrovertible, granted, of course, a Christian premise. It comports with the highest type of action in a Christian society. It is a wisdom at the base of passion and thought. Eliot's given type of being and character has allowed him to arrive at this, as one conclusion, in which many can share, and have done for centuries. A pagan, however, or a Communist, or any enemy of Christianity, anyone who conceives of life without the necessity for Christianity, would not grant the premise, and to him Eliot's statement, although it still might be valid poetically, could be without deep significance. It is gratuitous to attempt to judge what would be Pound's allowance of significance to this phrase, but there is the point that in secular life, in the use of facets of history explicitly, it would be difficult to find a trope as profound as this, as indeed one is haunted all through the Cantos with the question of Pound's profundity.

How profound is Pound? Reading the Cantos hour after hour crosses the mind with the notion that they are not profound, if the bias can be permitted that secular work of this kind, being pagan, is of less value than work of the deepest Christian meaning. Reading the Cantos is like walking through a jungle in Yucatan. Not profundity, but an efflorescent spectacle. As if we in some Rousseau-super world were to view historical tags, Chinese mementoes, personal histories hung on febrile trees, lambent Soutine beasts beside, with an orator flinging imprecations, proffering hortatory truths through a screen and forest of live oaks hung with Spanish moss.

To return to Aristotle.

By the universal I mean how a person of a certain type will on occasion speak or act, according to the law of probability or necessity, and it is this universality at which poetry aims in the names she attaches to personages. The particular is—for example—what Alcibiades did or suffered.

In the Cantos we hear many personages speak through Pound: the question is how fully we assent to the validity of his shiftings of emphasis and meaning, revising what seemed to be historic truth to make his own artistic truth; how credible the made artistic truth is; whether it is universal in the Aristotelean sense.

There can be no doubt about the validity of Pound's method. A poet can do anything that he can do. The assessment of values comes later. You cannot expect Beddoes to be Hardy, Webster to be Shakespeare, or Pound to be Eliot. Aristotle again,

It clearly follows that the poet or 'maker' should be the maker of plots rather than of verse; since he is a poet because he imitates, and what he imitates are actions. And even if he chances to take an historical subject [note the suspicion of unlikelihood] he is none the less a poet; for there is no reason why some events that have actually happened should not conform to the law of the probable and possible, and in virtue of that quality in them he is their poet or maker.

That Pound is a maker of plots in a sense, on a vast scale and forcibly conceived, though not of course tragic-dramatic ones, is evident. Blackmur in 'Masks of Ezra Pound' has given us 'an exhibition of the principal subject-matters in summary form' (1934), dealing primarily with the then thirty Cantos, to a lesser extent with the following eleven. And codes for ensuing Cantos in the form of concurrent criticisms are available.

Aristotle continues,

Of all plots and actions the episodic are the worst. I call a plot 'episodic' in which the episodes or acts succeed one another without probable or necessary sequence [cf. *Anthony and Cleopatra*]. Bad poets compose such pieces by their own fault, good poets, to please the players; for, as they write show pieces for competition, they stretch the plot beyond its capacity, and are often forced to break the natural continuity.

These remarks are not directly relevant to an epic poem, but carrying over from a play to a long poem they allow us the authority of Aristotle (we do not have to accept it) upon which to hang or fit the continuous but sometimes poorly hanging and incompletely fitting episodes of the Cantos.

While Aristotle ends by holding that Tragedy is a higher mode of imitation than Epic, he has cogent things to say of Epic before he reaches that conclusion. As regards length of scale,

The beginning and the end must be capable of being brought within a single view. This condition will be satisfied by poems on a smaller scale than the old epics, and answering in length to the group of tragedies presented at a single setting.

It would seem that the Cantos are epical in dimension, but the condition will not be satisfied. This, however, for the avid will be a favor to the Cantos, rather than the reverse. He says, however, that Epic poetry has a special capacity for enlarging its dimensions, for

In Tragedy we cannot imitate several lines of action carried on at one and the same time; we must confine ourselves to the action on the stage and the part taken by the players. But in Epic poetry, owing to the narrative form, many events simultaneously transacted can be presented; and these, if relevant to the subject, add mass and dignity to the poem.

In a sense, the many events of all the Cantos are simultaneously trans-acted and can be simultaneously held in the mind by the skilled reader, since it is part of the musical structure to move forward and backward through history. They can be held thus, not in particularity, but in their type of tactile scope, their peculiarity, giving us the weight of their mass and dignity.

Aristotle says Homer is the only poet who rightly appreciates the part he should take himself. 'The poet should speak as little as possible in his own person, for it is not this that makes him an imitator.' He would give Pound bad marks for the interwoven anecdotal intrusions of what 'Bill Yeats' said, or 'J. B.', his conversations with 'Fordie', what he thought of a dinner at Hewlett's, an endless series. Yet these pertain to Pound's love, aforementioned, and endear the objects of his affections to the mind.

Things as they were or are. Things as they are said or thought to be. Things as they ought to be. Aristotle, lastly here, says a poet must of necessity imitate one of these three objects. Pound's history eschews the first. He cannot encompass the third, due perhaps to the secular nature of the intentions of the work. His tirades against banks, money, political machinators, would come under this category, but announce artistic limitations. There is no entire moral or ethical view of man in the sense that Pound is presenting the world as it ought to be. He harangues against usury, but offers no complete economic platform, only negative criticism. There is no espousal of a Gandhian agrarianism, or of a world state, or any solution theoretically posed. Indeed, it seems a rebuke and limitation that Pound, so roundly smashing idols as he thinks with negative criticism, has not been inventive enough to propose an imaginative solution to the dilemma of man. But where is there one, from a secular departure? He is much too intelligent to think that there is any. But he is not as wise as the makers of scripture. And the Cantos can be richly enjoyed as poetry.

Things as they are thought to be. Pound is the maker of his own conception of events as he thinks them to be. His conception embraces entire histories East and West, the rise and fall of civilizations, the re-appearance in one country of political intrigues, known in another in a different century, the evil in man cropping up everywhere, the aristocracy of art also recurrent ('to sort out the animals'), Chocorua equated with Taishan, 'The enormous tragedy of the dream in the peasant's bent shoulders', but 'Fear god and the stupidity of the populace'; 'Entered the Bros Watson's store in Clinton, N.Y.' related to 'The cakeshops of the Nevsky', et sic de similibus.

Pound has a handle on the truth and carries history along with him in his case, wearing a gaudy suit of motley. As history, the Cantos are not impressive; as reconstructed history they are a vessel of wonder; as poetry, they are in their element. History, linguistics, economics, sociology, myth are all brought together documentarily, in the weaving of a rich tapestry. I think of the Cantos as a mosaic, or a tapestry, as of an intricate ancient work put together with incredible skill and patience over a long period of time, a Uccello in colored silks.

The new Cantos (74–84) are in some ways more nervous, elliptical, incoherent, lyrical than their predecessors. The lyrical quality is a boon, and the wiry liveliness is highly stimulating. One might make out a point that his later work in some way approaches surrealism, although it does not arrive there. This is odd in view of the hard, prosaic actuality of much of the past writing. Someone might study the more effusive, lyrical quality discoverable in the present Cantos in comparison with the more nearly incipient lyricism in the earlier. Also cogent would be a study of the Cantos in relation to musical structure; the present Cantos abound in melody, in melodic refrain. The subtlety of the spacing of the repetitions of phrase, and their metamorphoses, are cunningly contrived in an orchestration of sound and sense.

The art of teaching is to suggest. Pound is in one facet the frustrated teacher neurotically forced because his pupils do not know about, or enough about, or qualitatively enough about Padré José Elizonida, Kung, taou, Chung, Kung futsen, Tangwan Kung, or Tsze Sze's third thesis. He wants them to know about these. He lays them out to view in a long fury of explication. He ends by stuffing them down the throats of his readers. After the *nth* reference to *x*, how many of his readers will be provoked to refer to, study, and inwardly digest that individual or datum? The error is that of explication, and of explication, of incomplete explication. And of explication, perversely that it is not evocation. Pound is all on the outside of the mind. The work is all brains, no soul. Or better, not sufficiently humane in brain, not deep enough in soul. We do not go to the Cantos for knowledge. We go to them with our own knowledge for revisions of feeling, for accretions of new feelings.

Hopkins wrote of Duns Scotus's Oxford. The implication was so profound as to move a generation of young poets. Duns Scotus became a point of entrance and departure in reference to the totality of Hopkins's mental life. There is more weight in Rilke's reference to Gaspara Stampa than in two dozen assorted references in Pound. The Cantos are a depot of references. A key is in the unselectivity, the sporadic, chaotic growths; in the fact that scarcely one of them seems to have as significant an equation with deep influence on Pound's mind as have those of Hopkins or Rilke on theirs, and where they are significant, they seem objective, exterior, secular, rather than profoundly inner, as in the others.

Eliot provoked a generation to new consideration of Webster, Dante, Dryden, Donne, Marvell, and others; he changed the times in his own fashion. It was performance, in some manner unknown to Pound, by implication, by suggestion, by evocation. How many actually go to Fenollosa because of Pound's use of him? Pound piques the scholar, but there has been no concerted movement of the contemporary mind to make his personages a part of its innermost life; they have become a part of its life, but not of its inner life. A concerted movement may or may not be of qualitative value, but in any event the value of Pound's personages and references to historical events is a poetic value.

To turn to a minor point, the four-letter language of D. H. Lawrence was used with a spiritual aspiration to cleanse the mind. His was a cathartic and a revolutionary principle. We have seen that he did not revolutionize prejudices too deeply ingrained to accept his proposed usages. Pound scatters about him four-letter words and abbreviations without a cathartic or revolutionary principle. They estimate themselves as pinpricks.

The Cantos cannot warm as Eliot's later work fully warms. One gives the Cantos respectful, purely intellectual admiration. They are unique in modern literature. One has admiration for the daring of such scope, for the amassing and reforming of such an interesting totality of matter, for the full-bodied feel of dense work in a time of partial insights. 'Here error is all in the not done' cannot name a perfection of all the Cantos, but 'To have gathered from the air a live tradition' is massive gain to modern letters. The Cantos are a market place. They are not a cathedral.

Let us choose now, at random, arbitrarily, from the plethoric images one set of ideas for partial explication of Pound's method and use of counterpoint. The Cantos are a music of ideas ('Some minds take pleasure in counterpoint'). The interweaving of melodic ideas, of rhythmic ideas, could be shown in any number or combination of tropes, the peculiarity of the linguistics residing in the evocative power of phrases in spite of their frequently explicit, objective nature, and some lines quoted hereunder will be found to have a sensuous, lyric yield as of Pound's early period.

Let us point out and up his play on Mt. Taishan, the interweaving ideas of periplum, light, clouds, wind, rain, mist, classic images, the sun, the moon. Note, in the present Cantos, how these are heavy in Canto 74, are light in 76, increase in 77, lighten again in 78, are absent in 79, echoed in 80 in a new way, begin Canto 81 but stop abruptly, die out but for one word in 82, return sonorously and fully in 83 and then die down in 84. Thus this particular set of ideas is worked in each Canto. . . .

Pleasure in reading these latest of Pound's Cantos can be extreme. The student is recommended to read them about six times before their flavor can diffuse through the blood: after that their structures may inhere to the delight of the mind. The readings have invited resubmission to the entire body of the work, as indeed to all Pound's poetry. It should be said that certain prejudices have been mitigated in the process, since for twenty years I have not been deeply moved by Pound—as I have been deeply moved by the spiritual depth of Eliot. I never enjoyed temperamental affinity with Pound's work, excepting certain examples of the early lyrical strain, although his excellence and value were not questioned. There is a freshness, an easy flow, a splendid orchestration in these new Cantos, flashes of lyrical intuition and powerful chance statements about life and people, which rebuke my former obtuseness; in reading the earlier Cantos by book-lengths it seems that their variability is not extreme, yet I prefer the sometime abandonment in these new Cantos. I have tried to indicate this feeling only by quotation from the Taishan motif, but assure the reader of literally scores of similar sets of notions as brilliantly woven, unwoven, rethreaded, arranged, shifted, played upon, in a most lively intellectual grasp of Pound's chosen cyclorama.

Not to be resisted, lastly, is an attempt to point out some of the rich examples of Pound's philosophy, wisdom, and wit. Note the comment on Possum-hang-whimper. 'And with one day's reading a man may have the key in his hands.' 'and in this war were Joe Gould, Bunting and Cummings as against thickness and fatness.' This is the 'as if' method with a vengeance; the selectivity of art here inhumanly striking the nameless dead. 'Lordly men are to earth o'ergiven.' There is the anecdotal tag, Mr. Adams on teaching at Harvard. 'filial, fraternal affection is the root of humaneness / the root of the process.'

I refrain from quoting the Yidd-Goyim passage, hateful deposition. One despises that attitude, but there are only a few lines of it: 'every man to his own junk-shop' Flash-backs like 'Until I end my song', 'We who have passed over Lethe.'

'no unrighteousness in meteyard or in measure (of prices)' Cf. Leviticus, 19, 'ye shall do no unrighteousness in judgment, in meteyard, in weight, or in measure.' Then 'and there is no need for the Xtns to pretend that / they wrote Leviticus / chapter XIX in particular.' 'just getting stupider as they get older'.

For long keeping: 'nothing matters but the quality of the affection / in the end—that has carved the trace in the mind / dove sta memoria'

> 'and Gaudier's eye on the telluric mass of Miss Lowell'
> 'the wind mad as Cassandra / who was as sane as the lot of 'em'
> 'theatre of war' . . . / 'theatre' is good. There are those who did

not want / it to come to an end.' 'There / are / no / righteous
'wars' 'can that be the papel major sweaten' it out to the bumm
drum?' 'Athene cd / have done with more sex appeal'

The comments on Hovey, Stickney, Loring, Mr. Beddoes in re Mr.
Eliot. 'Tune: kitten on the keys / radio steam calliope / following the
battle hymn of the republic', 'Les moeurs passent et la douleur reste',
'Orage, Fordie, Crevel too quickly taken', 'I have been hard as youth
sixty years', 'what thou lovest well remains, the rest is dross', 'the
loneliness of death came over me / (at 3 P.M., for an instant)', 'the humane
man has amity with the hills'.

And two superb lyrics:

> A lynx, my love, my lovely lynx,
> Keep watch over my wine pot,
> Guard close my mountain still
> Till the god come into this whiskey.
> Manitou, god of the lynxes, remember our corn.

> Ere the season die a-cold
> Borne upon a zephyr's shoulder
> I rose through the aureate sky
>
> Lawes and Jenkyns guard thy rest
> Dolmetsch ever be thy guest,
>
> There I heard such minstrelsy
> As mocketh man's mortality
>
> Lawes and Jenkyns guard thy rest
> Dolmetsch ever be thy guest

Note too the quatrain on who has passed a month in the death cells;
the statement again that the Brothers Adam are our norm of spirit; what
'Stef (Lincoln Steffens)' said you can (cannot) do with revolutionaries;
and the last lines

> If the hoar frost grip thy tent
> Thou wilt give thanks when night is spent.

122. John Berryman, 'The Poetry of Ezra Pound', *Partisan Review*

April 1949, xvi, 377–94

Berryman (1914–72), American poet, contributed 'A Tribute' on Pound to *Agenda* (October–November 1965).

Since Pound has been for several generations now one of the most famous of living poets, it may occasion surprise that an *introduction* to his poetry, such as I was lately invited to make for New Directions, should be thought necessary at all. It may, but I doubt that it will. Not much candor is wanted for the observation that though he is famous and his poetry is famous his poetry is not familiar, that serious readers as a class have relinquished even the imperfect hold they had upon it fifteen years ago, and regard it at present either with hostility or with indifference. The situation is awkward for the critic. Commonly, when the object of criticism is at once celebrated, unfamiliar, and odious, it is also remote in time; the enquiry touches no current or recent passion. Our case is as different as possible from this enviable condition.

> In a few years no one will remember the *buffo*,
> No one will remember the trivial parts of me,
> The comic detail will be absent.

After thirty-five years neither comic nor tragic detail is absent. Whatever the critic may wish to say of the poetry runs the risk of being misunderstood as of the poet; one encounters *eager* preconceptions; and no disclaimer is likely to have effect. I make, however, no disclaimer just yet. Let us only proceed slowly—remembering that it is the business of criticism to offer explanations—towards the matter of hostility, beginning with the matter of indifference.

It *is* very surprising, perhaps, that readers of poetry should remain indifferent to the verse of a poet so influential as Pound has been. As one of the dominant, seminal poetries of the age, one would expect readers to want to become acquainted with it as a matter of course. That many

388

do not want to, suggests that they do not in fact so regard it, or regard it as only in some special sense an influence; and I think this is the case. They regard *Pound* as a dominant influence. They are quite right, of course. But even this is often disputed or ignored, so we cannot avoid some discussion. It is necessary to see Pound under two aspects: as he worked upon poetry and as he worked upon the public. The notion of him as publicist for Joyce, Eliot, Frost, a hundred others, being still current, I feel free to select instances displaying rather the first aspect, and take his relations with W. B. Yeats, with Imagism, and with 'The Waste Land'—with the major poet, that is, the major movement, and the major poem, of the century so far.

Pound went to London in 1908, at twenty-three, to learn from Yeats how to write poetry, in the belief that no one then living knew more about it. Swinburne was just alive (when he died the following April, 'I am the King of the Cats,' said Yeats to one of his sisters meeting her in the street), inaccessible behind Watts-Dunton.

> Swinburne my only miss
> and I didn't know he'd been to see Landor
>   *and* they told me this that an' tother
> and when old Mathews went he saw the three teacups
>   two for Watts Dunton who liked to let his tea cool
> So old Elkin had only one glory
>   He did carry Algernon's suit *once*
> when he, Elkin, first came to London. . . .

Pound was a most odd disciple; he regarded himself as the heir of Browning, he was stirring free of Fitzgerald and the Nineties, he had already begun the war on the iamb and the English heroic line that would never end (consider the two opening dactyls here and then the spondee-two-dactyls-and-trochee of the beautiful sixth line), he was full of the Troubadours, and he was becoming obsessed with the concept of verse-as-*speech*. He had as much energy as Yeats. The older poet has recorded his debt to the younger for advice against abstractions, underlinings of them, help in revision, and so on. But the change that began to move in Yeats' verse about this time was towards speech, the beginning of his famous development, and like one or two others I have always supposed Pound the motor. What seems to have happened was this. Pound was going in the afternoons to see Ford Madox Hueffer (Ford), and in the evenings to see Yeats; the older men did not get on. Of four 'honourable debts' he acknowledged later, the chief was Hueffer, who 'believes one should write in a contemporary spoken or at least speakable language'—not the same thing, it will be observed, as Pound's famous earlier formulation of 'Mr. Hueffer's realization that poetry should be written at least as well as prose.'

So old Ezra had only one glory

here, that he passed on without source in the evening what he had heard in the afternoon.

Then Imagism. There were two 'Imagist' movements (besides a dilution of the second, conducted by Amy Lowell, which reached the public), both in London. The first was started in March 1909 by T. E. Hulme who was insisting on 'absolutely accurate presentation and no verbiage', F. S. Flint who had been advocating 'vers libre,' Edward Storer who was interested in 'the Image,' and others, all strongly under the influence of French Symbolist poetry. Pound joined the group on April 22nd—Elkin Mathews had published the week before a third collection of poems, *Personae*, his first book proper, which would establish him. Pound read out to the startled Soho cafe a new poem 'Sestina: Altaforte.' *Exultations*, issued later that year and *Canzoni* (1911), continuing his Provençal investigations, display no Imagist affiliation; *Ripostes* (1912) does, and at the end of it he printed Hulme's five poems and named the movement, which had passed away meanwhile, perhaps because none of its other members could write poetry. Through Pound personally the first movement reached the second. The second consisted of H. D. and Richard Aldington, who were inspired not by French but by Greek verse, in 1912; Pound got their work printed, wrote the movement's essential documents (in *Poetry* for March 1913, 'A Few Don'ts' and an interview with him signed by Flint), and edited *Des Imagistes* which appeared in March of 1914. By the time Miss Lowell arrived with her retinue that summer, Pound, joined now with Wyndham Lewis and the sculptor Gaudier-Brzeska, had launched Vorticism, in the opening *Blast*. The importance of literary movements is readily exaggerated; conceivably in the end Imagism will seem valuable above all as it affected Pound's verse. Still, with a doubtful exception for the unnamed movement of the Auden group about 1930, it is the migration to a new position, for our time, that retains most interest, and is a fair sample of Pound's activity.

His now celebrated operation some years later upon 'The Waste Land', disengaging that work as we know it from what its author describes as a sprawling, chaotic poem twice as long, is another. Keeping our wits and facts in order, we need not follow a critic sometimes so penetrating as Yvor Winters in seeing Pound as the 'primal spirit' behind every gesture, every deplorable gesture, of the deplorable Mr. Eliot. 'The principal influence' upon Eliot's verse, Mr. Winters writes, 'is probably that of Laforgue, whose poetry Pound had begun to champion at least as early as 1917.' This is very early indeed, only seven years after Eliot's 'Humouresque, After J. Laforgue' in the *Harvard Advocate*. No, Eliot started alone. The two poets met first, and Pound persuaded *Poetry* to print 'The Love Song of J. Alfred Prufrock,' in 1915, by which date Eliot was nearly through with Laforgue. Mr. Winters' remark neglects also the serial character of the influences on Eliot's poetry, which include Laforgue, Webster, James, Baudelaire, Pound, Gautier, Joyce, Apollinaire, Dante. It is emphatically not a mistake, however, to regard Pound's personal influence as great from 1915 on; and great on the period as a whole.

The reader who is not a student of poetry has another ground for indifference. Pound, he has always heard, has no '*matter*.' Granting the 'importance' of his verse, granting the possibility that having been for poets fertile it might prove on acquaintance agreeable or beautiful, what has he to do with this sport, a matterless poetry? This is a much more sophisticated dissatisfaction, and can claim the highest critical support. 'I confess,' Mr. Eliot once wrote, 'that I am seldom interested in what he is saying, but only in the way he says it'; and R. P. Blackmur, 'he is all surface and articulation.' We notice Mr. Eliot's qualification ('seldom') and we are puzzled by an ambiguity in Mr. Blackmur's 'articulation' (is this jointing or merely uttering?); but on the whole they put authoritatively the established view. Now there can be no question of traversing such authorities directly. But it is a violent and remarkable charge; I think we are bound to look into it a little.

If his critics are right, Pound himself misconceived his work from the beginning and has continued to do so. This is of course not impossible; in fact I shall be arguing presently, in another sense, that it is just what he has done. But let us hear what he has said. In a very early poem, 'Revolt Against the Crepuscular Spirit in Modern Poetry,' he says:

> I would shake off the lethargy of this our time, and give
> For shadows—shapes of power
> For dreams—men.

If the poem is bad, the programme is distinct. Then one of his debts, he records later, 'may be considered as the example of or hint from Thomas

Hardy, who, despite the aesthetic era, has remained interested in his subject, i.e. in distinction to being interested in "treatment." ' Among other passages to the same effect, I give one more, later still, which readers must have come on with surprise. Speaking of Mr. Eliot and Miss Moore, Pound remarks, 'Neither they nor anyone else is likely to claim that they have as much interest in life as I have, or that I have their patience in reading.'

The 'literary' or 'aesthetic' view taken of Pound now for many years will not be much disturbed by such assertions, until we observe how oddly they are confirmed by the opinions expressed in 1909 about *Personae*. These opinions are worth attention, because Pound's literary personality became known as a leader's thereafter, and most reviews his books have received, since, show the impress of this knowledge; they are impure. It is hardly too much to say that the first *Personae* was the last volume of Pound's that was widely judged on its merits. What did the old reviewers say? 'He writes out of an exuberance of incontinently struggling ideas and passionate convictions. . . . He plunges straight into the heart of his theme, and suggests virility in action combined with fierceness, eagerness, and tenderness'—so R. A. Scott-James whose excitement, by the way, about 'the brute force of Mr. Pound's imagination' did not prevent his noticing the unusual spondee–dactyl use which he exemplified with a lovely line from 'Cino':

Eyes, dréams, / líps, and the / níght góes.

It is absolutely unnecessary, and appears to a scholar probably very ridiculous, to patronize the reviewers of an earlier age. The 'beauty of ("In Praise of Ysolt") is the beauty of passion, sincerity and intensity,' wrote Edward Thomas, 'not of beautiful words and images and suggestions. . . . the thought dominates the words and is greater than they are.' One hardly recognizes here the 'superficial' or 'mindless' Pound whom critics have held up to us since. Faced with a welter of Provençal and Browning and early Yeats, not to mention Villon, the reviewers nevertheless insisted upon the poet's strong individuality: 'All his poems are like this, from beginning to end, and in every way, his own, and in a world of his own.' Faced with this learning (the notes quote Richard of St. Victor, etc.), they admired 'his fearlessness and lack of selfconsciousness,' 'the breath of the open air.' 'He cannot be usefully compared,' Thomas went on, 'with any living writers . . . full of personality and with such power to express it, that' and so on. The Oxford *Isis* agreed that 'physically and intellectually the verse seems to reproduce

the personality with a brief fullness and adequacy.' Instead of pursuing
the engaging themes thrown up by this medley of exaggeration and
justice, culled mostly from the back leaves of *Exultations*, let me pass to a
third, more serious difficulty with the view that Pound has no 'matter'.

Pound's poetry treats of Provence, China, Rome, London, medieval
living, modern living, human relationships, authors, young women,
animals, money, games, government, war, poetry, love, and other
things. This can be verified. What the critics must mean, then, is that
they are aware of a *defect*, or defects, in the substance of the poetry.
About one defect they have been explicit: the want of originality of
substance. Pound has no matter *of his own*. Pound—who is even in the
most surprising quarters conceded to be a 'great' translator—is best as a
translator. 'The "Propertius" is a sturdier, more sustained, and more
independent poem than "Mauberley," ' writes Mr. Blackmur. 'Craftsmanship may be equally found in both poems; but Mr. Pound has
contributed more of his own individual sensibility, more genuine personal voice, in the "Propertius" where he had something to proceed
from, than in "Mauberley" where he was on his own. . . . This fact,
which perhaps cannot be demonstrated but which can be felt when the
reader is familiar enough with the poems, is the key-fact of serious judgment upon Mr. Pound.' I do not feel sure that time is bearing out the
first part of this careful judgment; the finest sections of Pound's post-
war farewell to London, where the grotesquerie of Tristan Corbière is
a new element in the complex style, naive and wily, in which he
celebrates the modern poet's difficulties and nostalgia, seem to me somewhat more brilliant, solid, and independent, than the finest sections of
the Roman poem. But my objections to the point of view begin well
behind any value-judgment. *All* the ambitious poetry of the last six
hundred years is much less 'original' than any but a few of its readers
ever realize. A staggering quantity of it has direct sources, even verbal
sources, in other poetry, history, philosophy, theology, prose of all
kinds. Even the word 'original' in this sense we find first in Dryden, and
the sense was not normalized till the mid-century following. A few
hours, or days, with several annotated editions of *Lycidas* will transform
the reader's view of this matter, especially if he will bear in mind the
likelihood that the serious modern poet's strategy resembles Milton's—
exceptional as Milton was—far more closely than his (the reader's)
attitude and knowledge resemble Milton's contemporary reader's attitude and knowledge. Poetry is a palimpsest. 'The old playwrights took
old subjects,' remarks a poet who has not been accused of want of

originality, 'did not even arrange the subject in a new way. They were absorbed in expression, that is to say in what is most near and delicate.' So Yeats; but our literary criticism, if at its best it knows all this well enough, even at its best is inclined to forget it and to act as if originality were not regularly a matter of *degree* in works where it is worth assessing at all. A difficulty is that modern critics spend much of their time in the perusal of writing that really is more or less original, and negligible. This African originality is very confusing. One of the writer's favourite poems is perfect Thomson in manner as well as perfect Wordsworth, the substance is all but purely Wordsworth's, and how are we accustomed to deal with this? The answer is that we are not. It clearly troubles Mr. Eliot that the two first sections of 'Near Perigord' resemble Browning, Pound's master, though the poem seems to him (as to me) beautiful and profound; this poem is extremely original in substantial development. Now though Mr. Blackmur is preferring derivation and Mr. Eliot is deprecating it, they appear to illustrate an identical disorder of procedure, that of a criticism which is content to consider in isolation originality of either matter *or* manner, without regard to the other, and with small regard to degree. I term this a disorder rather than a defect because with regard to a poetry as singular as Pound's, and with such diverse claims upon our attention, it is all but fatal to criticism. The critics were writing, one fifteen years ago, the other twenty, but I do not know that our situation has much improved, and it goes without saying that the best criticism of the period has addressed itself almost exclusively to manner, except for the proliferation in the last decade of an exegetical criticism similarly limited and comparatively abject. Until we get a criticism able to consider both originalities, in degree, Pound's achievement as a poet cannot be finally extricated from the body of his verse; and prepossessions should be avoided. That he has translated so much has no doubt cost him many readers, who (despite Dryden and Pope) cannot imagine that a 'real poet' would be content to translate so much; but criticism should be wiser.

Why *has* Pound translated so much? The question is an important one, and the answers usually given ignore the abyss of difference between his just-translations, like the Cavalcanti (the Canzone aside, of which his final version opens Canto XXXVI), such as might have been made by another poet of superlative skill, and renderings like those in *Cathay* and 'Propertius', which are part of Pound's own life-poetry. The first class may be considered as exercise, propaganda, critical activity, taken in conjunction with his incoherent and powerful literary criticism. The second class requires a word about Pound's notion of *personae* or masks, which issued successively in the masks of Cino, Bertran de Born, various Chinese poets, Propertius, Mauberley, fifty others. They differ both from Yeats's masks and from the dramatizations, such as Prufrock and Auden's 'airman,' that other poets find necessary in a period inimical to poetry, gregarious, and impatient of dignity.

We hear of the notion in two of his earliest poems, a sonnet 'Masks' about

> souls that found themselves among
> Unwonted folk that spake a hostile tongue,
> Some souls from all the rest who'd not forgot
> The star-span acres of a former lot
> Where boundless mid the clouds his course he swung,
> Or carnate with his elder brothers sung
> E'er ballad makers lisped of Camelot . . . .

and 'In Durance':

> But for all that, I am homesick after mine own kind
> And would meet kindred even as I am,
> Flesh-shrouded bearing the secret.

The question is, what the masks are *for*.

Does any reader who is familiar with Pound's poetry really not see that its subject is life of the modern poet?

It is in 'Faman Librosque Cano' and 'Scriptor Ignotus' of *Personae*—

> And I see my greater soul-self bending
> Sibylwise with that great forty-year epic
> That you know of, yet unwrit
> But as some child's toy 'tween my fingers.
>
> If my power be lesser
> Shall my striving be less keen? . . . .

It is in 'Histrion' of *Exultations*—

> 'Tis as in midmost us there glows a sphere
> Translucent, molten gold, that is the 'I'
> And into this some form projects itself
>
> And these, the Masters of the Soul, live on.

It is in one of the few good lines of *Canzoni*—

> Who calls me idle? I have thought of her.

395

It is in 'N.Y.' of *Ripostes* (1912), the volume in which Pound established his manner and the volume with which modern poetry in English may be felt to have begun—

> My City, my beloved, my white! Ah, slender . . .
> Delicately upon the reed, attend me!
>
> *Now do I know that I am mad,*
> *For here are a million people surly with traffic:*
> *This is no maid.*
> *Neither could I play upon any reed if I had one.*

It is everywhere (as well as in the Chinese work) in the more 'original' poems and epigrams of *Lustra*, written 1913–1916. (A lustrum is 'an offering for the sins of the whole people, made by the censors at the expiration of their five years of office.' It has not perhaps been sufficiently observed that Pound is one of the wittiest poets who ever wrote. Yet he is serious enough in this title. In certain attitudes—his medieval nostalgia, literary anti-semitism, others—he a good deal resembles Henry Adams; each spent his life, as it were, seeking an official post where he could be used, and their failure to find one produced both the freedom and the inconsequence that charm and annoy us in these authors.) It is in the elaborate foreign personae that followed, *Cathay* (1915)—

> And I have moped in the Emperor's garden, awaiting
> an order-to-write!

and 'Propertius' (1917)—

> I who come first from the clear font
> Bringing the Grecian orgies into Italy
>   and the dance into Italy.

It is in 'Mauberley', of course—

> Dowson found harlots cheaper than hotels;
> So spoke the author of 'The Dorian Mood,'
>
> M. Verog, out of step with the decade,
> Detached from his contemporaries,
> Neglected by the young,
> Because of these reveries.

Meanwhile Pound's concept of method had been strongly affected by Ernest Fenollosa's essay on *The Chinese Written Character as a Medium for Poetry* ('Metaphor, the revealer of nature, is the very substance of poetry. . . . Chinese poetry gets back near to the process of nature by means of its vivid figure. . . . If we attempt to follow it in English we must use words highly charged, words whose vital suggestion shall interplay as nature interplays. Sentences must be like the mingling of the fringes of feathered banners, or as the colors of many flowers blended into the single sheen of a meadow. . . . a thousand tints of verb') and for years he had been trying to work out a form whereby he could get his subject all together; by the time of 'Mauberley' he had succeeded, in the final version of the opening Cantos. And it is, as we shall see, in the Cantos also.

Above all, certain themes in the life of the modern poet: indecision-decision and infidelity-fidelity. Pound has written much more love-poetry than is generally realized, and when fidelity and decision lock in his imagination we hear extraordinary effects, passionate, solemn. A lady is served her singer-lover's heart, eats, and her husband tells her whose:

> 'It is Cabestan's heart in the dish.'
> 'It is Cabestan's heart in the dish?
> No other taste shall change this.'   (Canto IV)

She hurtles from the window.

> And in south province Tchin Tiaouen had risen
> and took the city of Tchang tcheou
> offered marriage to Ouang Chi,
> who said: It is an honour.
> I must first bury Kanouen. His body is heavy.
> His ashes were light to carry
> Bright was the flame for Kanouen
>   Ouang Chi cast herself into it, Faithful forever
>   High the hall TIMOUR made her.   (Canto LVI)

'His body is heavy.' The theme produces also the dazzle and terror of the end of 'Near Perigord,' where we finally reach Bertran *through Maent*, whom we'd despaired of. If there are a passion and solemnity beyond this in poetry—

> Soul awful! if the earth has ever lodg'd
> An awful soul—

we have to go far to find them. If Pound is neither the poet apostrophized here nor the poet apostrophizing, not Milton or Wordsworth, his place will be high enough. These themes of decision and fidelity bear on much besides love in his poetry, and even—as one would expect with a subject of the poet-in-exile (Ovid, Dante, Villon, Browning, Henry James, Joyce, Pound, Eliot, as Mann, Brecht, Auden) whose allegiance is to an ideal state—upon politics:

> homage, fealty are to the person
> can not be to body politic . . . .   (Canto LXVII)*

Of course there are other themes, strong and weak, and a multiplicity of topics, analogies to the life of the modern poet, with or without metaphor the *interests* of the poet. But this would appear to characterize any poet's work. I mean more definitely 'Life and Contacts,' as the sub-title of 'Hugh Selwyn Mauberley' has it.

It is not quite Ezra Pound himself. Yeats, another Romantic, was also the subject of his own poetry, himself-as-himself. Pound is his own subject *qua* modern poet; it is the experience and fate of this writer 'born / In a half savage country, out of date,' a voluntary exile for over thirty years, that concern him. Another distinction is necessary. Wallace Stevens has presented us in recent years with a series of strange prose documents about 'imagination' and 'reality.' If Mr. Stevens' poetry has for substance imagination, in this dichotomy Pound's has for substance reality. A poem like 'Villanelle: the Psychological Hour' or the passage I have quoted about Swinburne could have been made only by Pound, and the habit of mind involved has given us much truth that we could not otherwise have had. Two young friends did not come to see the poet! The poet missed a master! This is really in part what life consists of, though reading most poetry one would never guess it.

> And we say good-bye to you also,
> For you seem never to have discovered
> That your relationship is wholly parasitic;
> Yet to our feasts you bring neither
> Wit, nor good spirits, nor the pleasing attitudes
> Of discipleship.

It is personal, but it is not very personal. The 'distance' everywhere felt in the finest verse that treats his subject directly has I think two powerful sources, apart from the usual ones (versification and so on). First,

* Without allusion to the poet's personal situation, which is rather a matter for courts, which have reached no verdict, and psychiatrists, who have declared the poet insane, than for literary criticism, it will be recalled as a gloss for these lines that when the Irish patriot Sir Roger Casement was tried for treason a war ago he had to be tried under a statute centuries old, the charge being based upon a conventional oath of *personal* loyalty to the King made when Casement was knighted for services 'to the Crown' as a civil servant investigating atrocities in the Putomayo.

there is the peculiar detachment of interest with which Pound seems to regard himself; no writer could be less revelatory of his passional life, and his friends have recorded—Dr. Williams with annoyance—the same life-long reticence in private. Second, his unfaltering, encyclopedic mastery of tone—a mastery that compensates for a comparative weakness of syntax. (By instinct, I parenthesize, Pound has always minimized the importance of syntax, and this instinct perhaps accounts for his inveterate dislike for Milton, a dislike that has had broad consequences for three decades of the twentieth century; not only did Milton seem to him, perhaps, anti-romantic *and* anti-realistic, undetailed, and anti-conversational, but Milton is the supreme English master of syntax). Behind this mastery lies his ear. I scarcely know what to say of Pound's ear. Fifteen years of listening have not taught me that it is inferior to the ear of the author of *Twelfth Night*. The reader who heard the damage done, in my variation, to Pound's line—*So old Elkin had only one glory*—will be able to form his own opinion.

We write verse—was it Renoir, 'I paint with my penis'—we write verse with our ears; so this is important. Forming, animating, quelling his material, that ear is one of the main, weird facts of modern verse. It imposes upon the piteous stuff of the *Pisan Cantos* a 'distance' as absolute as upon the dismissal of the epigram just cited. The poet has listened to his life, so to speak, and he tells us that which he hears.

Both the personality-as-subject and the expressive personality are nearly uniform, I think, once they developed. In Yeats, in Eliot, we attend to re-formations of personality. Not really in Pound; he is unregenerate. '*Toutes mes pièces datent de quinze ans*,' he quoted once with approval from a friend, and the contrast he draws between the life of the poet as it ought to be (or has been) and as it is, this contrast is perennial. But if this account of the poet's subject is correct, what can have concealed it from most even sympathetic and perceptive critics and readers? With regard to critics, two things, I believe. All the best critics of Pound's work themselves write verse, most of them verse indebted to Pound's, much of it heavily; they have been interested in craft, not personality and subject. Also they have been blinded, perhaps, by the notion of the 'impersonality' of the poet. This perverse and valuable doctrine, associated in our time with Mr. Eliot's name, was toyed with by Goethe and gets expression in Keats's insistence that the poet 'has no identity—he is continually in, for, and filling some other body.' For poetry of a certain mode (the dramatic) this is a piercing notion; for most other poetry, including Pound's, it is somewhat paradoxical, and may disfigure more than it enlightens. It hides motive, which persists. It fails to enable us to see, for instance, that the dominant source of inspiration in Keats's sonnet on Chapman's Homer is *antagonism*, his contempt for Pope and Pope's Homer. (This view, which I offer with due hesitation, is a development from an industrious and thoughtful biography of the sonnet by a British scholar in *Essays and Studies* for 1930.[1])

The reader is in one way more nearly right than the majority of critics. He is baffled by a heterogeneity of matter, as to which I shall have more to say in a moment, but he hears a personality in Pound's poetry. In fact, his hostility—we reach it at last—is based upon this. The trouble is that he hears the personality he expected to hear, rather than the one that is essentially there. He hears Pound's well-known prose personality, bellicose, programmatic, positive, and he resents it. Mr. Pound is partly responsible. This personality does exist in him, it is what he has lived with, and he can even write poetry with it, as we see in 'Sestina: Altaforte' and elsewhere early and late. A follower of Browning, he takes a keenly *active* view of poetry, and has, conceivably, a most imperfect idea both of just what his subject is and of what his expressive personality is like.

This personality is feline, supra-delicate, absorbed. If Browning made the fastest verse in English, Pound makes the slowest, the most discrete and suave. He once said of a story in *Dubliners* that it was something better than a story, it was 'a vivid waiting,' and the phrase yields much of his own quality. There is restlessness; but the art of the poet places itself, above all, immediately and mysteriously at the service of the passive and elegiac, the nostalgic. The true ascendancy of this personality over the other is suggested by a singular fact: the degree in which the mantic character is absent from his poetry. He looks ahead indeed, looks ahead eagerly, but he does not *feel* ahead; he feels back. (Since writing the sentence, I come on the phrase in Fenollosa, an impressive remark, 'The chief work of literary men in dealing with language, and of poets especially, lies in feeling back along the ancient lines of advance.') It is the poetry of a late craftsman; of an expatriate—

> Moaneth alway my mind's lust
> That I fare forth, that I afar hence
> Seek out a foreign fastness.   ('The Seafarer')

[1] B. Ifor Evans, 'Keats's Approach to the Chapman Sonnet', *Essays and Studies* (1930), xvi, 26–52.

> Here we are, picking the first fern-shoots
> And saying: When shall we get back to our country?
>
> Our sorrow is bitter, but we would not return to our
> country.   (Cathay's first lines)

—of a failing culture. The personality is full already in 'The Return'
from *Ripostes*,—return of the hunters, or literary men, for like others of
Pound's poems this is a metaphor: those who in an earlier poem had
cried

> 'Tis the white stag, Fame, we're ahunting,'

now come back illusionless.

The Cantos seem to be a metaphor also. This immense poem, as yet
untitled and unfinished, is seriously unfinished: two cantos are missing,
and sixteen are to come, if the poet recovers sufficiently to be able to
write verse again. Since Canto LXXIV alone is twenty-five pages long,
it is clear that the last sixteen of the hundred may alter radically views
we have formed of the work as a whole from the part we know; and we
want to avoid the error (if it was one) of Mr. Pound when he hazarded
in 1933, of the still untitled and unfinished *Finnegans Wake*, 'It can
hardly be claimed . . . . that the main design emerges above the
detail.' Nevertheless I must say something of the subject and form of this
epic. I believe the critical view is that it is a 'rag-bag' of the poet's interests, 'A catalogue, his jewels of conversation.' It can be read with delight
and endless profit thus, if at any rate one understands that it is a work of
versification, that is, a poem. The basal rhythm I hear is dactylic, as in
the Swinburne and Ouang Chi passages and in the opening line 'And
then went dówn to the ship,'—in this line we see the familiar tendency
of English dactyls to resolve themselves into anapests with anacrusis, but
the ambiguity seems to me to be progressively avoided as the poem ad-
vances. But the rag-bag view depends for support upon lines that Pound
cut out of the primitive printed versions of the earliest Cantos; the form
greatly developed, the form *for the subject*. For a rag-bag the poem sets
out very oddly. I will describe the first three Cantos.

I. The Poet's, the Hero's, physical and mental travel: what can 'I'
expect? Persona, Odysseus-in-exile; antagonist, Poseidon (the 'godly
sea'—an ironic pun). Material: escape-from-transformation, sacrifice,
descent to Hell, recognition of an obligation to the Dead (parents,
masters), prediction of return *alone* over the seas, 'Lose all companions.'
(This is exactly, thirty years later, what happened to the poet.) Form:
a depth-introduction, heroic Greek (*Odyssey* xi) through Renaissance

Latin (Divus) in old-heroic-English-style as modified by modern style. So the first Canto, about sacrifice to the enemy, acknowledgment of indebtedness, and outset.

II. The orchestra begins, the poet's nineteenth-century English master to Provençal to Chinese to ancient British to modern Spanish (another exile) to ancient Greek, very rapidly; then the Poet's theme and temptation, Beauty, a faithless woman (Helen); then an exquisite, involved color- and sense-lyric (the first of dozens) in honor of Poseidon's beloved; then the Canto proper, about *betrayal,* the metamorphoses into 'Sniff and pad-foot of beasts' of all those who do not recognize and wish to *sell* (sell out) the God—Dionysus and Poseidon are linked as having power each over the sea, and those false to them are the 'betrayers of language' of Canto XIV, Mr. Nixon of 'Mauberley'—'I' (Acoethes, the persona) alone have not. Exilic Ovid is the fable's source.

III. Three themes: (1) A stronger sea-ceremony than sacrifice, *embracing* of difficulties, the Venetian *'sponzalizio de mar'* ('to wed the sea as a wife,' Canto XXVI), *'voce tinnula'* below being Catullus' 'with ringing voice' for nuptial songs; (2) enmities and poverty that beset the Poet or Hero (persona, the Cid), *proscription*; (3) artistic mortality, a Mantegna fresco flaking, and just before, an opposite example, Ignez da Castro stabbed by her lover's order (Pedro I of Portugal) in 1355, then avenged by her son, exhumed and *crowned* ('here made to stand')—

> Time is the evil. Evil.
> A day, and a day
> Walked the young Pedro baffled,
> a day, and a day
> After Ignez was murdered.
> Came the Lords in Lisboa
> a day, and a day
> In homage. . . .
>
> (Canto XXX)

This kind of interpenetration of life and art, in metaphor, is one of the poem's triumphs, a Coleridgean 'fusing.'

Such, according to the notes I once made in my margin, is the beginning of this famous 'formless' work which is, according to one critic of distinction, 'not about anything.' Reviewers of The Pisan Cantos have showed surprise that they were so 'personal,' and yet very fine,—fine,—it is the most brilliant sequence indeed since the original thirty. The Cantos have always been personal; only the persona increasingly adopted, as the Poet's fate clarifies, is Pound himself. The heterogeneity of material every reader remarks seems to have three causes. The illusion of Pound's romanticism ('—if romanticism indeed be an illusion!' he exclaims in *Indiscretions*) has given him an inordinate passion for ages and places where the Poet's situation appears attractive, as in the Malatesta cantos, where Sigismondo is patron as much as ruler and lover (VIII–XI), and the Chinese cantos (XIII, XLIX, LII–LXI); here he is sometimes wonderful but sometimes ungovernable. Then he is anxious to find out *what has gone wrong*, with money and government, that has produced our situation for the Poet; several of the money-cantos, XLV and LI, are brilliant, but most of the American historical cantos (XXXI–IV, XXXVII–VIII, LXII–LXXI) are willed, numb, angry—the personae Jefferson and John Adams are not felt and so the material is uncontrolled. The rest of his heterogeneity is due to an immoderate desire, strong in some other modern artists also, for mere conservation—

> And lest it pass with the day's news
> Thrown out with the daily paper.   (Canto XXVIII)

Once the form, and these qualifications, are understood, Pound's work presents less difficulty than we are used to in ambitious modern poetry. Pieces like 'A Song of the Degrees' (an anti-Psalm) and 'Papyrus' (a joke, for that matter a clear and good one) are rare. Occasionally you have to look things up if you don't wish to be puzzled; and it does no harm to use the index volume of Britannica Eleventh, and various dictionaries, and to be familiar with Pound's prose, when you read the Cantos; the labor is similar to that necessary for a serious understanding of *Ulysses*, and meditation is the core of it. To find out what a modern poet has done we have often to ask *why* he did it.

The poet's own statements must be accepted with a certain reserve, which neither his admirers nor his detractors have always exercised. Thus the Cantos are said to be written in an equivalent for ideogram. We have recognized their relation to parts of Fenollosa. But Fenollosa's technical center is an attack on the copula; I observe that four of the lines about Ouang Chi successively employ the copula without loss to characteristic beauty, and I reason that we must inquire into these things for ourselves. More interesting, far, are the equivalents for musical form, and the versification. So with Pound's remark that the Cantos are 'the tale of the tribe'; they seem to be only apparently an historical or philosophical epic, actually a personal epic—as he seems to understand himself elsewhere in *Culture*[1] when he suggests that the work may

[1] The genteel title of the New York edition of *Guide to Kulchur*.

show, like Beethoven's music, the 'defects inherent in a record of struggle.' Mr. Pound too may really, like his critics, regard the work as nearly plotless and heroless. Writing of Dr. Williams he says, 'I would almost move . . . . to the generalization that plot, major form, or outline should be left to authors who feel some inner need for the same; even let us say a very strong, unusual, unescapable need for these things; and to books where the said form, plot, etc., springs naturally from the matter treated.' 'Almost,' and he is not speaking of the Cantos directly, but the passage is a very striking and heretical one. I put in evidence against it his long labors on the opening Cantos, and the Cantos themselves in my simple analysis, where the arraying of themes is quite different from casuality. The Hell-allusions in the first half of the work, with the allusions to Heaven in recent Cantos, also strongly imply a major form. But all present discussion must be tentative. I have the impression that Pound allowed, in whatever his plan exactly was (if it exactly was, and if it was one plan), for the drift-on-life, the interference of fate, inevitable in a period of violent change; that this may give us something wholly unpredictable in the Cantos to come, as it has given us already the marvellous pages of *The Pisan Cantos*. Here we feel the poet as he felt D'Annunzio in 1922: D'Annunzio, he wrote from Paris to the *Dial*, 'lies with a bandaged eye in a bombarded Venice, foaming with his own sensations, memories, speculations as to what Dante might or might not have done had he been acquainted with Aeschylus.' Foaming, yet always with the limpidity, *clarté*, the love against rhetoric, for which his poetry is our model in this century. It would be interesting, if the Cantos were complete, to compare the work with another poem, not more original in conception, exhibiting, if a smaller range of material and technical variety, greater steadiness, a similar substance and a similar comprehensive mastery of expression, 'The Prelude'; but the argument of my very limited essay is ended. Let us listen to this music.

123. Malcolm Cowley, 'The Battle Over Ezra Pound', *New Republic*

3 October 1949, cxxi, 17–20

The award of the Bollingen Prize to Pound in 1949 brought forth, as Cowley indicates, an outpouring of argument (see Introduction, pp. 25–7). This article is a judicious account of the controversy and of the issues it raised.

Cowley (b. 1898), American critic and poet, graduated from Harvard after serving in the First World War. He was an influential staff member of the *New Republic* from 1929 to 1944. Cowley has written about meeting Pound in Paris in the early twenties in *Exile's Return* (1934).

The literary battle of the year is being fought over Ezra Pound and the Bollingen Award. Since the end of the Federal Arts Projects it is the only battle among and against the bookmen that has reached the floor of Congress or, as the cannon thundered, has forced an agency of the United States Government to sue for peace.

Hostilities started late last winter with a statement by the Fellows of the Library of Congress. Under a grant from the Bollingen Foundation they were offering a $1,000 prize, which was to be awarded annually to the best new book of poems by an American citizen. They announced on February 23 that the first year's prize had gone to *The Pisan Cantos*, by Ezra Pound, who is a citizen under indictment for treason. Judged to be insane by a medical board, he has been confined in St. Elizabeth's Hospital in Washington.

At first there were only mild skirmishes over the award. A few newspapers printed favorable editorials, while others were puzzled rather than angry; they wondered who were the Fellows of the Library of Congress and why they had chosen a book by a guaranteed-to-be-crazy poet who had given radio broadcasts for the enemy, like Axis Sally and Tokyo Rose. It was learned that the Fellows were an unpaid advisory group of poets and critics appointed by the Librarian of Congress; at present the group has fourteen members. Two of them, Karl Shapiro and Paul Green, announced that they hadn't voted for Pound's book and apparently there was one other vote against it, leaving it as the first choice of eleven Fellows. Dwight Macdonald, the editor of *Politics*, praised their decision for its freedom from prejudice; he called it 'the brightest political act in a dark period.' William Barrett dissented in *Partisan Review*, on the ground that the form of a poem cannot be judged apart from its content. He quoted passages to show that the content of *The Pisan Cantos* was fascist and anti-Semitic.

Three of the Fellows stated their various positions in the correspondence columns of the same magazine. The battle was dying away in scattered shots and letters to the editor when suddenly the *Saturday Review of Literature* marched in with fresh battalions, like Blücher at Waterloo.

In two long articles (the *SRL*, June 11 and 18) Robert Hillyer charged that the award to Pound was an insult 'to our Christian war dead'—that was one of his phrases—besides being part of a far-flung conspiracy against American ways of life and literature. He did not state, but he took time and space to imply, that the conspirators included Paul Mellon the financier, T. S. Eliot the Nobel prize-man and Dr. Carl G. Jung the psychoanalyst, besides the Bollingen Foundation, the Pantheon Press, at least half the Fellows of the Library of Congress, all the poets who admire Pound or Eliot, all the 'new critics,' most of the literary quarterlies and I don't know how many other persons and institutions. Their common aim, he said, was the seizure of power in the literary world, and beyond that 'the mystical and cultural preparation for a new authoritarianism.'

Those are big words and the editors of the *Saturday Review* supported them. In the same issue as the first of Hillyer's articles they printed a statement which, defying lightning and suits for libel, was doubly signed for the editorial board by Norman Cousins, Editor, and Harrison Smith, President. 'The Bollingen Prize given to Ezra Pound will eventually set off a revolution of no mean dimensions,' they prophesied. It has indeed set off a revolution in their correspondence columns, where hundreds of readers have leaped into print and combat.

This revolution by letters to the editor has been rich in patriotic slogans: 'Up with the English classics!'—'Down with the cult of unintelligibility!'—'Down with the new criticism!'—'Down, down with expatriates!'—'Save our college girls from reading T. S. Eliot!' Even

here in the Connecticut hills one hears the drums of conflict inter-
rupting the Yankee twang of the mowing machine; and it is hard for
us not to join the cultured mob that is apparently getting ready to storm
the Library of Congress, drive out the new authoritarians and hang
Eliot to the nearest, if any, lamp post. But another voice, perhaps that
of the mowing machine, warns us to stop and see what the issues are
before we begin to fight.

Is there any real conspiracy in the literary world to promote what
Hillyer calls 'a new authoritarianism'? Look as hard as I could, I found no
signs of it; nor could I find many connections among the persons and
institutions listed in Hillyer's two articles. Besides Ezra Pound there is
one man on the list, one only, who may have been a fascist sympathizer
at one time. It seems that Dr. Jung spoke well of Hitler before 1938, but
his American disciples insist that he afterwards changed his mind.
Incidentally there are very few of these disciples and none of them is a
'new critic' or a Fellow of the Library of Congress.

Let us consider some of the others indicted by Hillyer as members of
a conspiracy against the American way of life. Paul Mellon, the son of
Andrew Mellon, is a public-spirited man who has done a great deal for
American literature, chiefly through the Bollingen Foundation. I know
several writers who have received grants from the Foundation and not
one of them shows a trace of fascist thinking; they include the usual
mixture of liberals, conservatives and political bystanders. Although the
Foundation gave money to the Library of Congress with which to
make a poetry award, it did not know—nor did Paul Mellon know—
that Pound was being considered for the first year's prize.

And the Pantheon Press: what malice or misinformation prompted
Hillyer to drag it into his articles as if into the prisoner's dock? It is a
small publishing house founded by two refugees from Hitler and very
favorably known for its editions of the European classics. By now it has
received the apologies of the *Saturday Review*. The editors should also
offer their apologies to T. S. Eliot. Hillyer implied that he exercised a
malign influence over the other Fellows and persuaded them to give
the award to Pound; whereas it is a matter of record that he neither
nominated *The Pisan Cantos* for the prize nor argued that it was the best
book to choose; he merely cast one vote for it among eleven. Hillyer
also called him 'a disciple of Dr. Jung,' an author whom Eliot has not
read. His own political convictions are traditional, conservative and not
in the least totalitarian. Eliot is a pluralist who believes that we owe
our loyalties, not to the state alone, but also to church, class, family,

region and profession. He thinks it is a symptom of decay and a catastrophe in itself for the state to become all-powerful.

And what about the other Fellows of the Library? I have known most of them for years and respect them all as men and writers. It is ridiculous to charge them with anti-Semitism or with having fascist sympathies. Since the award was made I have talked with some of them; they said that Pound's politics was crazy and contemptible. One Fellow had read the text of Pound's broadcasts for the Italian government and thought that the poet, if he recovered his sanity, should be tried for treason. 'But that is a matter for the courts to decide,' he said. 'Our job wasn't to pass on the question of Pound's loyalty; we were giving a prize for a book of poems.'

On account of statements like this the Fellows have been accused of advancing the false principle that art is entirely separate from life. Those with whom I talked insisted that they had no such intention. To paraphrase what some of them said—for I cannot remember the exact words—they felt that too many second-rate authors had been given prizes for expressing the right opinions. We criticize the Russians—and rightly, they added—for making poets follow a party line; yet recently some American critics have been treating our own poets in the same fashion, demanding that they be wholesome, popular and patriotic. The Fellows insisted that there are other virtues in literary works than those of the good citizen or the government official. Originality, learning, sharpness of image, purity of phrase and a strict literary conscience: these are virtues, too, and they are present in Pound's work along with his contemptible politics. By giving him the prize, the Fellows said, they were defending 'that objective perception of value on which any civilized society must rest.'

After listening to their arguments I am certain that the Fellows were trying hard to perform their double duty as citizens and men of letters. It is silly to accuse them of weaving plots and harboring dire motives. The real questions about their choice are literary rather than political; or rather the literary and the political questions are so intermingled that by answering the first we also answer the second. What we should ask is whether, in giving their prize to *The Pisan Cantos*, the Fellows were choosing the right ground on which to defend the objective perception of value. Under the stated terms of the award, do Pound's last Cantos represent 'the highest achievement of American poetry' during the year 1948? If they fail to represent that achievement, then the Fellows were wrong by their own standards and the great arguments about poetry and treason, form and content, the new poets and the new criticism can all be deferred to a better occasion.

So let us consider the book, the author and the curious position he occupies in the history of art in our time. For some thirty years after 1907 Pound was an explorer, a precursor, a discoverer of new moods and manners and critical standards. He exerted a decisive influence on the work of several authors greater than himself, including Yeats, Eliot and Hemingway. And he continued to write, write in various fashions, classical, medieval, Japanese and Mandarin, until he finally patched together a multilingual style of his own and accumulated an imposing body of work—imposing in its bulk and in the brilliant phrases scattered through it like sunbeams in a fog; and yet how much of it will survive?

My friends keep praising his 'Mauberley' poems, first published in 1920; and I read them again last week with a good deal of admiration, it is true, but also with the feeling that they had inspired better poems by Eliot and E. E. Cummings. There are fine lyrics scattered through the rest of his work from beginning to end, with three of them even in the bumbling *Pisan Cantos*; but he usually spoils the lyrics by some in-trusive gesture of pedantry or self-assertion, like an actor who insists on taking his bows before the play has ended. Spoiled work: that is the phrase for most of Pound's poems and I think for all the Cantos; they are never cheap or easy, never lacking in new phrases, but they are spoiled—and spoiled by vices that are inseparable from the virtues of his poetry; spoiled like the man himself by arrogance, crotchets, self-indulgence, obsessive hatreds, contempt for ordinary persons, the in-ability to see the world in motion (everything in Pound's poems is frozen as in a gallery of broken plaster casts) and finally by a lack of constructive power that keep him from building his separate perceptions into uni-fied works of art.

Arrogance, crotchets and self-indulgence are also the faults that mark his brief political career. Since his personality is the same in all fields, it is hard to draw a distinction between his art and his life, between the form and the content of his work or between his poetry and his politics. I confess to being less excited than others by the public implications of his disloyalty. The London *Times Literary Supplement* wasn't altogether frivolous when it said that his worst crime wasn't his broadcasts for Mussolini but his translations from Propertius. The broadcasts were silly and ineffective. They did not succeed in persuading American soldiers to desert or malinger—the GI's weren't even amused by his thirty-year-old American slang—nor can I believe that his anti-Semitic outbursts caused the death of a single Jew among the millions who perished. This brilliantly gifted man who had failed to become another Propertius or Ovid failed again in the role of Coriolanus; the spoiled great poet was also a spoiled traitor, despised and laughed at by his foreign masters. After being arrested by his own countrymen he was sent to a mental hospital without being granted the dignity of a public trial. It was the perfect retribution, a spoiled punishment for a spoiled crime.

The Pisan Cantos is the weakest of his books, the most crotchety and maundering. It contains two almost-fine lyrics, both spoiled by pedantry, and a third lyric of twenty lines that belongs with the best verse of our time:

> The ant's a centaur in his dragon world.
> Pull down the vanity, it is not man
> Made courage, or made order, or made grace,
>   Pull down thy vanity, I say pull down.
> Learn of the green world what can be thy place. . . .

That is superb, but there is not enough of it to redeem a disordered book of disordered observations, an old man's mutterings. In American poetry 1948 was not distinguished, but still it was the year when William Carlos William published the second long volume of his *Paterson*. Archibald MacLeish had a new book of poems, *Actfive*, and Peter Viereck a very lively first book. It seems to me that *The Pisan Cantos* was the worst of several possible choices; but my chief grievance against the Fellows is that by giving a prize to Pound they forced him back into the limelight, thus destroying the symmetry and perfect justice of his fate.

Against Hillyer one is justified in having other and more serious grievances. For thirty years he has been a poet and professor involved in many of the literary and academic struggles of his time. He regards Eliot and W. H. Auden as his poetic rivals and he has attacked them often, in articles that revealed an obsessed rage. Some of the 'new critics' have been his academic rivals, at Harvard and now at Kenyon College, and he has battled with them, too. It would seem that his two articles in the *Saturday Review* are an attempt to carry this private warfare into a national or international field where all the issues become inflated and falsified.

Let us put the articles to the semantic test of seeing what courses of action he was advising, and to whom.

To Congress he was saying quite plainly, 'Investigate the Bollingen Award and force T. S. Eliot to resign as a Fellow of the Library.' Representative Jacob K. Javits (R, N. Y.) had no sooner read the articles than he demanded such an investigation. Eliot hasn't been asked to resign, a demand which would be a grave discourtesy, and the investigation seems to have been cancelled; but the mere threat of it has forced the Library of Congress to withdraw the Bollingen Award, as well as two other annual prizes it had offered, for prints and chamber music. Historically this withdrawal is almost the end of the effort, started when Archibald MacLeish was Librarian, to create a living relationship between the Library and the artists and writers of our time. So far as Hillyer is responsible for the retreat, I do not think that he should be proud.

But he had messages for others besides congressmen and government officials. Thus, he was saying to Paul Mellon and other wealthy men who had made or thought of making grants to encourage American writing, 'Be careful, save your money, the *Saturday Review* is watching you.' The Rockefeller Foundation has helped two of the literary quarterlies to pay fair rates to their contributors. Hillyer was telling the Foundation, in effect, 'These quarterlies print the "new critics," who don't like my work and I'm sure are tainted with fascism. Don't renew their grants when they expire.' Many of the universities have been adding poets and critics to their faculties. Hillyer seemed to be warning their boards of trustees, 'Make sure that the poets and critics don't admire Eliot or I guarantee that you'll get into trouble.'

Writers are like doctors and priests and judges in that they have a double duty, to the public and to the values of their own profession. With his muttered threats and his charges of a vast conspiracy, Hillyer has been false to both obligations. He has misled the public about the nature of an argument among poets and critics, while he has harmed all writers in his attempt to punish a few. Today there is a war in which the battle over Ezra Pound is merely an episode. The little American republic of letters is under attack by pretty much the same forces as those to which the Russian writers have already yielded: that is, by the people who prefer slogans to poetry and national self-flattery to honest writing. Hillyer has gone over to the enemy, like Pound in another war. Worsted in a struggle among his colleagues and compatriots, he has appealed over their heads and under false colors to the great hostile empire of the Philistines.

124. Kathleen Raine on Pound's Confucius and modern poetry

March 1952

'There is No Trifling', *New Republic* (24 March 1952), cxxvi, 17, 22. This is a review of *The Confucian Analects* (1951).

Miss Raine (b. 1908), English poet and critic, was educated at Girton College, Cambridge. Her *Collected Poems* appeared in 1956.

To Chinese scholars the accuracy of Pound's translation will be of first importance, and about this I am not qualified to hold any opinion, for to me the Chinese text interleaved with the English has only the potency of the unknown. For such as myself (typical, unfortunately, of my generation) these beautiful ideograms, reproduced from the stone tablets formerly set up by the great Emperors and renewed from time to time over a period of nearly two thousand years, merely indicate a relatively unexplored field of human thought. Ezra Pound sees no reason why the study of philosophy in our universities should be confined to the Greeks and their European successors; and when a poet of major status thus points the way to a body of philosophy or poetry that be believes to have relevance to his own period—as did the Elizabethan translators of the Classics, or Yeats with the Upanishads—the issue is of more than academic interest. Mr. Pound's work on Confucius (along with Arthur Waley's great contribution to Chinese studies) has introduced a new element into the literary context of our time. As with Chapman's Homer or Dryden's Virgil, Pound's Confucius is to be read as much in relation to its translator as to its original author: it is a twentieth-century reading of Confucius—a contemporary work to be considered not in the context of ancient China but along with Pound's Cantos, the writings of Eliot and Yeats, and in the light of current social theories.

History, as Pound sees it, is a natural and not a supernatural phenomenon. This historical sense of Pound's may not have revealed to him an eternal truth. But the question is not whether or not Confucianism contains the whole of truth for all time, but its particular relevance in our particular society. It seems to me that in this respect Pound has put his finger on the vital spot.

Not that Confucianism in any way resembles the ideologies current in either the American or the Russian halves of the modern world. Perhaps societies have always been more remarkable by reason of the anti-bodies that they produce, in resistance to or revolt against current modes of thought, than in their majority cultures. Majorities most always consist of the most unreflecting, and are likely to be wrong; whereas the diagnosis of an intelligent critic is seldom wholly wrong. So with Pound—the relevance of Confucius to contemporary democracy is not one of affinity, but rather, perhaps, one of need. 'Government is rooted in man, it is based on man, and one reaches man through oneself. . . .' This social philosophy, based like contemporary science on the natural, is the diametrical opposite both of doctrinaire Marxism and empirical behaviorism. It embodies an organic, not a mechanistic view of nature.

Society, according to Confucius, grows from within outwards; while (explicitly in Marxist theory, and implicitly in a society whose instruments are the advertisement, the radio and the television-set) the modern world aims at conditioning human behaviour from without inwards. No one (unless the psycho-therapists who have to deal with the casualties) seems seriously to have considered the dangers of this wholesale conditioning of human mental reflexes. Confucius, on the contrary, begins with a long look at what man is: the virtuous man 'looks straight into his own heart at the things wherewith there is no trifling.' This truth of the deepest nature of man is the 'unwobbling pivot' upon which the affairs of families, societies, and states ultimately depend. A virtuous man will have right family relationships; and 'one human family can humanize a whole state; one courteous family can light a whole state into courtesy.' It is a form of humanism, at the same time, with strong affinities to certain kinds of European and American humanism. Such a society is stable because it rests upon the real nature of man.

The secular behaviorism upon which our own society is (implicitly) more and more based is itself the successor and counterpart of the hieratic forms of Christianity for which, also, authority is external to man. There has always been a minority who appealed to the Gospels, which are in this respect Confucian rather than Roman, deriving order from within. On this truth, great philosophies would seem to be agreed, while lovers of power have at all times dissented. Coleridge's theory of the imagination, for example, envisages an inborn nature such as Confucius saw it. This inborn nature is a mystery; it may be a divine mystery, the God within as Blake and Coleridge both affirmed; but the Confucian social ethics deliberately confines itself to the human, drives no wedge between the spiritual and the material, since both are in man.

Since those things 'with which there is no trifling' are innate, true education can never be a process of indoctrination; it can only be a bringing to light of what is already implanted in man.

What heaven has disposed and sealed is called the inborn nature. The realisation of this nature is called the process. The clarification of this process (the understanding or making intelligible of this process) is called education.

In comparing the opposed views, of forms of thought and behavior imposed from without inwards, or unfolded from within outwards, we must not be misled by the excellence or otherwise of the ethics or doctrines inculcated. What is important is a habit of mind, an orientation towards the real.

The great learning takes root in clarifying the way wherein the intelligence increases through the process of looking straight into one's own heart and acting on the results; it is rooted in watching with affection the way people grow.

You cannot, in fact, teach people what they do not already know—you can only help them to know that they know it.

However wrong-headedly and illogically Pound may have sought to identify this organic philosophy of social order with Mussolini's regime, we should not therefore overlook the fact that the main elements of that philosophy are a penetrating and accurate criticism of the worst heresies of our own society. Pound by his translations and critical prefaces has done more perhaps than any living man of letters to create a context of ideas in which poets have been working for some thirty years. Because of Pound that context of contemporary poetry is now world-wide in a sense that it has never been hitherto. It is in relation to this creation of an intellectual framework for our time that his *Confucius* should be considered, and is likely to be remembered.

125. Ronald Bottrall, 'The Achievement of Ezra Pound', *Adelphi*

May 1952, n.s. xxviii, 618–23

Bottrall (b. 1906), an English poet, has for some time been an executive of the British Council. His *Collected Poems* appeared in 1961. Bottrall is the author of an earlier essay on Pound (*Scrutiny*, September 1933).

During the last twelve months or so in addition to a collection of essays on Ezra Pound, there have appeared the collected edition of the first 70 Cantos; a volume of Pound's letters, edited by D. D. Paige; and a full-length study of Pound's poetry by Hugh Kenner. All this does honour to a neglected writer and is an encouraging riposte to the attacks made by large sections of the American press on Pound and the judges who awarded him the Bollingen Prize. But I sense in a good deal of the criticism the hushed atmosphere of the cult, and this I cannot believe that Pound himself would welcome. He has always been a plain speaker and a hard hitter.

In an essay that appeared in the *Dial* in January 1928, T. S. Eliot wrote: 'I cannot think of anyone writing verse, of our generation and the next, whose verse (if any good) has not been improved by the study of Pound's.' This has always puzzled me. A generation is usually taken to be about thirty-five years. Let us assume that a literary generation is fifteen years; even then I can think of hardly anyone born about 1900 who was in 1927 exemplifying the influence of Pound; Allen Tate's is, indeed, the only name that comes into my mind. If Eliot was speaking prophetically, he was still off the track. The new generation which began to write in England in 1928–29—Auden, Spender, Day Lewis and Empson—were fertilized by Donne, Hopkins, Hardy, Wilfred Owen, Laura Riding and Eliot himself, not Pound.

In 1929, however, when I was teaching in Finland and trying to learn to write verse, F. R. Leavis recommended me to read Eliot's selection of Pound's poems and to give special attention to 'Hugh Selwyn Mauberley'. I can never be sufficiently grateful for this advice. As I read 'Mauberley' and I saw, or thought I saw, how contemporary verse should be written, I worked through Pound's poetry and I tried to discover how he had arrived at the perfection of 'Mauberley'. His poetic progress seemed to me to be a movement from unnecessarily simplified imagist statement to unnecessarily complicated ellipsis. 'Mauberley', 'Homage to Sextus Propertius', and the early Cantos come at a point of equilibrium in this progress. About 'Mauberley' Leavis and Hugh Kenner have written admirably. It will be sufficient here if I draw attention to the superlatively controlled rhythms, the delicate irony and the exquisite modulations of tone in this great poem. Kenner has rightly pointed out that Mauberley is not a self-portrait, but a *persona* with whom Pound would wish not to be confounded. This reading strengthens the ironies of the poem and re-emphasises its suppleness and subtlety.

The early poems lead up to 'Propertius' and 'Mauberley'. The methods of these two poems, superimposed, lead to the Cantos. The principal difficulties confronting any reader of the Cantos are to make out the pattern of the poem and to keep in mind the appearances and re-appearances of certain basic characters, incidents, attitudes and phrases. Pound's later writing is remarkable for his use of ellipse in syntax and image and for the bareness of his phrasing. The surface simplicity of the Cantos is full of pitfalls, and the connection between an incident and an image, presumably evident to Pound himself, too often fails to penetrate to the reader. Events and persons of trivial or ephemeral importance are introduced at random in language charged with very little poetic pressure; such references can only be justified if they are supported by adequate tension in the verse or by being clearly placed in the thematic pattern of the poem. Pound's frequent failure (or refusal) to provide the tension or the referential nexus cannot fail to be a source of irritation to many readers.

Although Pound has modestly called them 'a poem of some length,' the Cantos are persistently referred to by his idolaters as an epic poem. What is an epic? A conventional definition would be, 'a poem celebrating, in the form of a continuous narrative, the achievements of one or more heroic personages of history or tradition.' In short, the Heroic Poem, of which Dryden in his *Dedication to the Aeneid* says, 'The design of it is to form the mind to heroic virtue by example. . . . the action of it is always one, entire and great.' Whatever Pound's intentions are, this is far removed from the actual achievement of the Cantos, of which the fine Greek poet George Seferis has said that 'never perhaps has poetic material been collected so indiscriminately.' The Cantos, in fact, may more usefully be likened to a series of confessions, either *in propria persona* or through the *persona*, or mask, of characters, fictitious, living or dead. Like most confessions, they are involved, anecdotal, misleading and repetitive.

Eliot has not helped matters by contending that as we go on reading the Cantos we become habituated to Pound's methods as we have become habituated to Joyce's by re-reading of *Ulysses*. Joyce has written something far nearer an epic than Pound. Difficult as *Ulysses* was at a first reading, the figure of Ulysses-Bloom stood out clearly and we could work out an exegesis from this starting point. No exegesis that I have read can persuade me that because Pound starts off by translating sixty lines of a Latin version of the *Odyssey*, and refers to Odysseus from time to time throughout the Cantos, he has achieved an epic and an ordered work of art. We soon leave the sea and become bogged down, not so much by allusions as by the ellipses, the interruptions, the failure to knit together the basic themes, as Joyce so triumphantly knitted his. Every detail in his *Ulysses* is relevant to the main themes; for Pound, the digression, the anecdote (preferably glossed in a foreign language) is the fatal Cleopatra for which he will gladly sacrifice an epic. In Canto XIII Kung (Confucius) says:

> Anyone can run to excesses
> It is easy to shoot past the mark,
> It is hard to stand in the middle.

It is hard and it is just what Pound cannot do.

Pound is still the old-style optimist, the believer in the good society, which is just around the corner, ready to hand if we only get rid of the financiers and the armament manufacturers and restore order. His own personal tragedy, even, has not brought home to him that he has only scratched the surface of evil, never looked into its depths. He has a bewildered sense of human waste and corruption, but no tragic sense of the human predicament. Pound is very ready to consign people he does not like to their appropriate place in his private inferno. But he himself (apart from some strangely humble passages in *The Pisan Cantos*) is buoyantly and confidently free from self-criticism. It is, surely, a very unreal hell that only houses the 'others;' the only hell that matters in art or religion is the one where one is and where, but for the grace of

417

God, one will remain. If Pound reaches Paradise in the Cantos it will be an earthly paradise.

In his later poetry and in all his criticism Pound (like Browning, from whom he learnt a good deal) sets out to convince. In the Cantos he too often presents particular instances of 'ideas in action,' conduct, taste, or artistic creation, to exemplify those general laws which he himself has postulated *a priori*. Only rarely does he allow his instances to develop organically and enrich his poetic pattern; he prefers to set them down baldly as a re-inforcement of his dogmatic assumptions. He is primarily concerned with opinions and events, not human relationships, and this devitalises his later work. The strange argument put forward by Eliot to excuse Pound's reiteration of his *idées fixes* is that he writes so well: 'No-one living . . . . can write like this: how many can be named, who can write half as well.' In fact, his rôles of impresario and teacher all too often bedevil the poetry. Pound has from the beginning impressed on his disciples that poetry should be as well written as prose. After a recent re-reading of 82 Cantos I can but wish that the opaque mass of much of the American history and the economics had been even half as well written as the prose of Swift.

This is not to say that we are not all in the debt of this great practitioner of verse, or that I do not admire the finest passages of the Cantos. What I am trying to re-affirm is what I said in an essay written early in 1933, one of the first lengthy appraisals of *A Draft of XXX Cantos*, that Pound has suffered more from his admirers than his detractors. Pound's healthy and exuberant love of the arts, his just contempt for academic reputations, his fine sensibility, his acute nose for worthwhile things lost in the byways of literature, his untiring search after the best modes of expression—these have fired his advocates to declare that he has a better understanding of Chinese poetry than Arthur Waley and a more profound insight into the writings of Cavalcanti than the greatest living Italian poet, Eugenio Montale. We may not have long to wait before some neophyte unearths, with a murmur of approval, Ernest Hemingway's judgment of 1925 that Pound is the major poet and Eliot the minor one. Pound, probably rightly, is credited with having been the principal influence in causing Yeats to change his poetic style. This affords a useful ground for comparison. After 'Mauberley', Pound might have gone on writing as finely as in this poem, where he matches, even surpasses, the later Yeats; but he did not, and in my opinion 'Among School Children' and the two 'Byzantium' poems are greater than any Canto or any part of any Canto. However much they may have owed to Pound, it is Yeats and Eliot who write the exquisitely-organised, the greatest poetry after 1920, and not Pound himself.

This fact has been obscured by the authority of Eliot who has dubbed Pound 'il miglior fabbro.' Eliot rightly insists that it is on his total work for literature that Pound must be judged: 'on his poetry, *and* his criticism, *and* his influence on men and on events at a turning point in literature.' Judged by these criteria, Pound is a major figure. It has been to me an exhilarating experience to read the new collection of his letters and to re-read his criticism. Both are so salty and full of bite. Pound's incursions into European art, literature and music have a vigorous, buccaneering quality reminiscent of the *condottieri* he admired. Rummaging among the spoils he plunders here a poet, there a painter—the pirate from the New World is re-dressing and re-painting the Old. Make it New! It is all done with a racy exuberance and, much more important, a singleness of heart and a generosity of mind, which are without parallel in modern times.

It may possibly be objected that in all this I have emphasised many of the stale and profitless criticisms of Pound that have helped in the past to obscure his merits. If so, there can be found in Hugh Kenner's study an answer to every censure. He has, with remarkable patience and erudition, surveyed the whole of Pound's poetry and carefully related it to Pound's critical dicta. He is well-grounded in his subject and can cite instances at all points to support his main thesis, which is that the Cantos are the culmination of Pound's work and form an ordered whole. He begins by saying that Pound is a far more important figure than Browning or Landor and that Donne's experiments in rhythm are 'kindergarten material beside the strategic audacities of the later Cantos.' Later he states that 'much of Pound's poetic organisation . . . . is essentially similar to Wordsworth's.' We begin to be suspicious. It would be equally unhelpful, and not less true, to say that much of Pound's poetic organisation was essentially similar to Byron's. Soon it is clear that Kenner is speaking to a brief and that the brief is to defend every line that Pound has written and every sentiment that he has uttered. Briefly, he sees the Cantos as a 'timeless bas-relief' in which 'a complex intellectual drama is enacted'. They are a 'multi-dimensional construction' going back behind the Cartesian philosophy to purify language and assert the importance of the work or the thing against the idea. The tension of the writing is provided by typographical signs; the principal technique is the 'ideogrammic method,' which enables 'rare accesses of insight and emotion' to be apprehended in the same way as the 'invisible fields of force surrounding the magnet can be apprehended through the behaviour of multitudinous particles of iron.' We become more suspicious. We finally gather that in the Cantos Pound is seeking to establish 'a hierarchy of values,' though 'everything may be said to be as important as everything else.' This is another way of saying that nothing in them is important.

Pound has a dangerous attraction for the young critic; he is the field of force that draws the susceptible iron filings. It is very tempting to try to prove that he is always right. But let us examine two or three of Kenner's remarks. At one point he talks of the three last pages of Canto LXXX as providing 'an ideogram of specifically English culture;' at another he states that one need not know the languages that Pound quotes—'even when we can't read them, their very inscrutability performs half their poetic function'—and that 'anyone can feel the play of silent cryptic finality in a Chinese ideogram . . . . without knowing what the ideogram means.' Anyone can see that the second and third remarks are pretentious nonsense, but the first is little better. Pound's acquaintance with Chinese literature, Kenner and others maintain, has enabled him to evolve a new technique of expression, the 'ideogrammic form.' What is an ideogram? It is a character symbolising the idea of a thing, in contrast to the word that names it; it is a graphic symbol. Pound's poetry is full of images, so is that of Keats; but both poets express their images in words, not in hieroglyphics. How then can three pages of words form an ideogram of a culture?

Pound is careless and it does not do to have an answer ready every time. In 1933 I noticed that in Canto XVIII Pound spelt Khan as 'Kahn' and (rather convincingly, I thought) I wrote that this 'spelling . . . . links Kubla with the family of bankers and the Morgan firm.' Imagine my chagrin on noticing at a recent re-reading that in the new Faber edition of the Cantos the mis-spelling had vanished. This kind of thing makes a good deal of Hugh Kenner's ingenuity pointless. In a letter to Carlo Izzo in 1938, Pound wrote: ' "Praedis." I don't care how you spell your wop painters, and I don't know whether A.P. was from Predi, Predo or Predis. Never been to his home town.' I too had been puzzled by the continual error of Ambrogio de Praedis in the Cantos. Now I understand. Pound didn't care.

After this niggling interlude, I must sum up Pound's positive achievements as impresario, teacher, critic and poet. He discovered T. S. Eliot and arranged for the first publication of his verse. It was through his influence that Joyce's *Portrait of the Artist* and parts of *Ulysses* were published. His example in verse and his critical precepts were crucial in the formation of Eliot's style and that of the later Yeats. His exploration of history and his experiments in rhythm have left a permanent mark on English poetry. 'Hugh Selwyn Mauberley' is one of the greatest poems of our time. Last, and perhaps most important, he is a man who has disinterestedly and selfishly devoted his life to poetry and the art of writing.

LITERARY ESSAYS

edited by T. S. Eliot

London, 22 January 1954
New York, 26 February 1954

126. Charles Tomlinson, review, *Spectator*

19 February 1954, cxcii, 212

Mr Tomlinson no longer approves of this review, and has requested that a statement containing his present attitude towards
Pound's criticism, and to this review, be included as a postscript.

Tomlinson (b. 1927), English poet, was educated at Queens'
College, Cambridge.

Our debt to the greatness and generosity of Ezra Pound is a vast one and
in the essays on his contemporaries in this volume we are reminded of
it most forcibly. Eliot, Joyce, Yeats—here we see Pound staking his
reputation and proving solidly right. This is the Pound one admires, the
Pound who underlines the relation of language with 'the health of the
very matter of thought itself,' the Pound quick to see the virtues of
Robert Frost and to dispose of the critical pretensions of Housman. But
having assented to Pound's valuation of three major writers and having
accepted his general dictums on good writing and on language in its
relation to thought, one remains painfully aware that this is only half
the matter, if quite that. What of the Pound of the reading lists, Pound
the teacher, for whom Gautier is of more use than Baudelaire and
Confucius than Shakespeare, and for whom the relative value of Donne
and Herrick is a question of 'some purely personal sympathy'? This
Pound is also represented in *Literary Essays*. One might say that it is the
Pound who comes to dominate them.

In 'The Teacher's Mission' Pound writes most trenchantly on the disease of abstraction, yet abstraction in the teaching of literary criticism is Pound's main failing. The sheer externality of his Melopoeia, Phanopoeia, Logopoeia and their uselessness as critical aids, and the inadequacy of his account of literature as the product of inventors, masters, diluters, add up to an incomplete account of poetic technique, of literary tradition and of the relations between the two.

Of Lionel Johnson Pound writes: 'You could have discussed with him any and every serious problem of technique . . .' and one realises here, in the light of Lionel Johnson's dilute achievement, how narrow a meaning technique so often has for Pound. The kind of technique implied is an abstraction, a manipulation of surfaces, a concept without due regard to the richness of sensibility which informs any technique worth the name. The externality of a technique so conceived appears in the idea of Melopoeia which is divorced from meaning and 'can be appreciated by a foreigner with a sensitive ear.' It appears in the idea of Phanopoeia ('a casting of images upon the visual imagination') and its misleading stress on the visual content of poetic imagery. Technique as seen from the outside is the idea at work when Pound is admiring 'the clean-cut ivory finish' of Joyce's poetry or Ford Madox Hueffer's 'The Three-Ten,' and far more seriously when he allows himself to remark, 'a sane man knows that a prose story can't be much better than the short stories of Maupassant . . .', and again in the absence of an organic outlook and of all critical relevance in: '*Ulysses* has more form than any novel of Flaubert's.' It is significant that Pound in his review (reprinted here) of *Love Poems and Others* can be fair to Lawrence where the discussion is one that resolves itself into a question of technique in a fairly narrow sense—significant that he should stick there with his estimate of Lawrence as a dialect poet and that the 'technique' of *The Rainbow* and of *Women in Love* should have bored him (see *The Letters of Ezra Pound*, page 394).

'Henry James,' writes Pound, 'was the first person to add anything to the art of the nineteenth century novel not already known to the French.' George Eliot's is the name which springs to mind and it was, after all, James himself who realised Flaubert's loss in not having read *Daniel Deronda*. Pound's remark is characteristic of his treatment of his literary tradition. We are given a Henry James without antecedents, without the fructifying, psychological originality of Hawthorne and of George Eliot behind him.

In the section of the present book labelled 'The Tradition' we have the Troubadours, Arnaut Daniel, the Cavalcanti essay, Dante, notes on

Elizabethan classicists, early translators of Homer, four pages on Crabbe, Laforgue almost rubbing shoulders with Swinburne (whose 'music' and rhythms receive Pound's approval), and finally Henry James and Rémy de Gourmont. Whatever else we may derive from these essays—and Pound's comments are often of the greatest interest—the lack of central-ity and the lack of any complete conception of tradition cannot but point us to the absence of the discipline of an organic literary-critical approach. One reflects that Pound's own approach results in judgements like that on Wyndham Lewis as 'the only English writer who can be compared with Dostoievsky,' and in his inability to see what a negative thing 'intellect' is in the connotation Wyndham Lewis gives it. One reflects also that one of the products of Pound's approach was *The Active Anthology*, where the presence of Eliot, Pound and Marianne Moore was insufficient to prevent the balance falling not merely on the side of the phony but of the plain dead. *That* was the result of thirty years of Pound's eclecticism. One is not surprised to hear at this date that Pound, as Mr. Eliot writes in the introduction, 'regrets he has not yet written a study of the work of Jean Cocteau.' A study of Cocteau, purveyor of the chic and the arty, would seem a sad misdirection of effort for a man who began in greatness and with a passionate concern for the direction of European culture.

In 1969 Mr Tomlinson wrote:
Looking back to a review like that above, one is dismayed that one's ignorance, safeguarded by the certainties of Cambridge English, did not recognize itself for such. It would be comforting to think that the con-ditions of weekly reviewing cramped one's style, but with more space at hand how self-exposed one might have stood *then*. How was it pos-sible not to see in a more lucid perspective such essays as 'The Serious Artist', 'Cavalcanti', 'The Renaissance', 'Henry James', 'Dr. Williams' Position'? Certainly there are oddities in Pound's criticism (even now I find his judgement of Wordsworth reprehensible) but, in the final analysis, it is the sense of our debt to him that should surely prevail.

127. Donald Davie, 'Instigations to Procedures', *New Statesman and Nation*

27 March 1954, xlvii, 410, 412

Davie (b. 1922), English poet and critic, is now Professor of English Literature at Stanford. See the Introduction, pp. 28–9, on Davie's important book on Pound.

'Heaven save us,' Pound protested, 'procedures are already erected into Rules!' That was in 1934. Faced with Binyon's translation of the Inferno, Pound realised that his own earlier polemics would lead the earnest Poundian of that day to dismiss Binyon just because he used inversions. Now the Poundians are more numerous and influential, and the erection of procedure into rule has gone on ever since. Because of this one reflects gloomily that this re-issue of many of Pound's critical articles will do more harm than good. For Pound was right when he called one of his critical volumes, *Instigations*. Instigations to experiment with, or at any rate to examine, some novel or neglected procedure— that is the most accurate as it is the most charitable description of most of the things reprinted here. Pound hardly ever even offers to give considered literary judgments. Give the Poundians some credit—some of them have done what the master directed and read, perhaps, Gavin Douglas's *Aeneid*; and it is they presumably who have reprinted Ernest Fenollosa's treatise of poetics. But far more often they have erected procedure into rule, until now there is a Poundian canon as there is a Leavisite canon, of authors made sacrosanct by the master's approval and so no longer questioned. How many of Pound's admirers, for instance, really *read* Landor, who reappears so continually in their pantheon? Yet no one can deny that Pound is fallible—Lewis is consistent by his lights, but Pound is quite unreliable, not just in matters of fact, but precisely in matters of judgment. There are here judgments, on Shelley in the otherwise just and still timely essay, 'The Serious Artist', and on Wordsworth in some scrappy pages on Crabbe, at which one can only boggle, open-mouthed.

The question arises whether in 1917 the situation was so desperate as to justify such questionable tactics. For to dismiss Wordsworth in a couple of sentences presumably without reading him is, it must be admitted, rather steep. Yet perhaps by 1917 the battle was already half won—Mr. Eliot puts the blackest hour some years earlier, when he writes with a shudder, 'the situation of poetry in 1909 or 1910 was stagnant to a degree difficult for any young poet of today to imagine.' And even more remarkable, perhaps, than the stagnation inside poetry itself, was the blankness of the stare which British and American society directed upon its poetry and its poets. Perhaps it really was a situation in which no holds could be barred. From this point of view the most interesting thing in this volume, as also one of the most carefully written, is an essay, new to me, called 'The Renaissance'. The renaissance of the title is the American renaissance that Pound looks forward to; and it prompts the unfamiliar sensation of counting one's many blessings. For it is remarkable how many matters of sheer social engineering that Pound desiderates if there is to be real cultural awakening, have, in the years since 1914, been settled more or less in the way he asks for. Heaven knows there is no room for complacency, but one cannot blink the fact, for instance, that in the U.S. certainly and to some degree in Britain, there has been since Pound wrote a radical change in respect of patronage, official and semi-official, and a recognition that, for instance, poets, young scholars, and literary magazines have a right to such patronage. Nobody needs to be told that the institution of schemes of patronage raises new and urgent problems and dangers. Still the gain is a real one, we owe it to Pound as much as to anyone, and we owe it to him, when we review his past polemics, to remember the different and worse situation in which he conducted his early momentous and some-what disreputable campaigns.

If I give the impression of making excuses for Pound, I cannot help it. He really needs all the allowances that can be made for him; and I'm not sure that he deserves them all, that the essay on 'Swinburne versus his Biographers', for instance, can be excused on any terms. On the other hand there are of course more substantial and ambitious pieces such as the essays on Cavalcanti and on Henry James, which are a different matter altogether. The Cavalcanti essay is very important. As for the scholarship in it, I am in no position to judge; and I dearly wish some specialist in medieval Italian would give me a ruling on it. For a great deal hinges on it—and not just for Pound. The early pages of this essay are as carefully written as anything in Pound; they are earnest and eloquent, and they attempt to define a mode of experience now lost. The parallel is with Eliot's essays on the metaphysical poets, and I find it odd that 'dissociation of sensibility' has been argued over so much and on the whole accepted so enthusiastically, while the more radical dissociation that Pound claims to find some centuries earlier is never seriously considered. Chaucerians ought to have something to say about this too. Instead, all we get by way of comment on the Cavalcanti essay, which appears to represent more sustained effort by Pound than any other single item of his prose criticism, is the occasional weaving together by young poets of diffuse and mellifluous 'canzones.'

And this brings us to another of the disquieting things about Pound's criticism and its influence. 'Procedure' is his word for what interests him most in poetry of the past; but that begs some questions. For sometimes 'procedure' in Pound's writing seems to mean what is still sometimes referred to as 'technique' where an interest in poetic technique means knowing the different rhyme-schemes of the true Petrarchan, the Spenserian and the Shakespearian sonnet. Sometimes 'procedure' seems to mean for Pound something every bit as mechanical as that, as external, and as remote from any questions of poetic meaning.

It is easy to rig the evidence. It is not hard to find judgments (*e.g.*, on the choice between *vers libre* and regularity) which deserve to hang as framed texts over any poet's bed. And in return for services rendered, it would be graceful to concentrate on these. But how far should one go in giving the benefit of the doubt?

128. W. W. Robson, review, *Blackfriars*

April 1954, xxxv, 184–5

Professor Robson has requested that a postscript follow this review.

Robson (b. 1923) is Professor of English Literature at the University of Sussex. He was educated at New College, Oxford, and is the author of *Critical Essays* (Routledge & Kegan Paul, 1966) and *Modern English Literature* (1970).

'Whatever Dante's symboligating propensities', we read on page 181 of this selection, 'he was a positivist in his craft, in this he was a *fabbro*, and one respecting the craft and the worker.' For 'Dante' we might fairly read 'Pound': his interest in other men's work (as T. S. Eliot explains in the Introduction) is always, when he is at his typical best, that of the contemporary 'craftsman'. 'Criticism', he observes (p. 4), 'is not a circumscription or set of prohibitions. It provides fixed points of departure. It may startle a dull reader into alertness. That little of it which is good is mostly in stray phrases, or if it be an older writer helping a younger it is in great measure but rules of thumb, cautions gained by experience.' Behind the eccentric dilettantism, the pervasive manner of Continental *grand maître* crossed with American professor, there is seriousness and devotion; they are very evident in the fine early piece 'The Serious Artist' (1913), reprinted here.

Pound's 'symboligating propensities', which notoriously bring out the less attractive aspects of his personality, are not to the fore in this selection, which is designed rather to represent the scale and range of his achievement in literary criticism; perhaps it does so even too generously, for some of the minor items, such as the early review of D. H. Lawrence's poems, were not worth reprinting. Doubtless to remark that all the essays are very 'dated' is, in a way, to pay an incidental tribute to Pound; it could be a means of saying that what good work they could do has been done, their contribution is assimilated. But on that account alone it is not possible to agree with Mr Eliot (p. xiii) that they form 'the *least dispensable* body of critical writing in our time'; not in the sense in which he means it; their importance is historical only. And there are other, graver, reasons for dissenting. Is not Ezra Pound largely disqualified as a critic? Not so much by his irresponsibility; still less by his famous howlers; but by a failure at the centre, his conception of 'technique' in literature—external, and at times painfully naive, as it is.

A Yeats or an Eliot perhaps could learn, and did learn, from Pound's criticism. But its influence on the humbler student of poetry, whether poet or not, might well only serve to confirm and consolidate misconceptions about 'form', 'style', 'content', etc.—which are quite active and mischievous enough already. Mr Eliot, defending Pound as a great critic, the compeer of Johnson and Coleridge, favourably contrasts his approach with the academic; but the academic approach at its worst could find much warrant and backing in the volume Mr Eliot is introducing: not least in the tolerance of charlatanism which we see so often, and so significantly, extended in its pages.

However, those who agree with Mr Hugh Kenner that the Cantos is a great modern epic will not be convinced by this, nor will those (if they make up a different class) who agree with Pound that the only alternative to his method is the earnest pondering of 'Jojo's opinion of Jimjim's explanation of Shakespeare' (p. 66), to the neglect of poetry.

In 1970 Mr Robson wrote:
This piece was clearly written in a mood of irritation at some 'perversity' of Pound's (but which, I cannot remember). It does not represent my present views, and I would like to dissociate myself from the opinions expressed in the last three paragraphs. If I were writing now, I would lay much more stress on Pound's generous and disinterested devotion to the art of poetry—of a kind rare in the academic or literary worlds— and pay tribute to his power of making us see good poems which we had missed, or had not properly appreciated; also to his ability to get himself out of the way and allow us to decide about them for ourselves. But as it stands the review may perhaps perform a small service, as a reminder of the kind of adverse comment which much of Pound's critical writings have provoked from the more conventionally-minded.

129. Roy Fuller, review, *London Magazine*

May 1954, i, 94, 96, 99, 100

Fuller (b. 1912), English poet and Professor of Poetry at Oxford, was educated at Blackpool High School. He is solicitor to the Woolwich Equitable Building Society. His *Collected Poems* appeared in 1962.

This large volume has been compiled from four of Pound's critical books—*Pavannes and Divisions* (1918), *Instigations* (1920), *Make It New* (1934), *Polite Essays* (1937)—and a number of his uncollected essays and reviews. It is very well arranged in three sections, entitled 'The Art of Poetry', 'The Tradition', and 'Contemporaries', and thus presents the familiar and not unsatisfactory appearance which critics usually give their assembled miscellaneous writings in an attempt to impose on them a *post hoc* uniformity or comprehensiveness. First comes the announcement of general principles, and then the examination, in historical order, of individual talents. But it would be an injustice to Pound to expect this conventional ordering to result in his case in the balanced and diverse book which might be made from the more or less casual criticism of a don or a critic of the weekly Press. Indeed, it is important to realize at the outset just what kind of a critic Pound is *not*. He is not systematic or solid or 'sensitive' or psychological or social or textual— he is not like Mr Eliot or Bagehot or Virginia Woolf or Mr Wilson or Caudwell or Mr Empson. His criticism is entirely a product of his efforts to develop his own poetry and his concern for the health of the literature of his time. It is therefore repetitive, narrow, often annoying, ill-considered and rude, sometimes parochially dated, egotistic.

And, above all, Pound is an American. His interest in literature, in certain writers he particularly values, is sometimes a proprietory interest—as, say, Hemingway's in drink and sex—which cannot concede an equal appreciation from any one else. But all these characteristics, which would be fatal to another critic, are inextricably mingled with Pound's strength, indeed, are frequently a source of it. His Americanism, especially, permits him to value the past without being overawed by it; it may irritate the English reader of Pound to come across 'Johnnie' Dryden and 'Willie' Blake, but the absurd familiarity is symptomatic of something worthwhile. More important is that Pound was an American at the end of the first decade of this century.

It is from Pound (and Wyndham Lewis, one must, in justice, add) that the hard, sharp critical view has stemmed during the last thirty years, a view that in England has been obscured by a native and historically-motivated fuzziness, respect and sentimentality. On the whole America has learnt from Pound far better than England how 'to exercise an antiseptic intolerance of all inaccurate reports about letters'. Old age, early death, or other adventitious reasons, make our advanced writers accepted, our advanced critics tame. It is ironical that some such process is now being attempted with Pound (the present volume, the Letters, the Translations, the Pound cult), but fortunately Pound himself has never been respectable nor can any part of his literary output be found to compromise him. These critical pieces stand up as sturdily and awkwardly as they did when they were first published; unequal in value, but always the working notes of a sincere, unvenal, uncanting, creative artist.

The book's first section hangs together best. Here Pound enunciates the principles of the 'modern movement' in poetry—principles which today are not perhaps very startling but which are still valid and are always in danger of being betrayed. Poetry must be exact—'true to human consciousness and to the nature of man'. It must be concrete—'I believe that the proper and perfect symbol is the natural object'. Its technique must be mastered—'poetry is an art and not a pastime'. Mastery of technique means mastery of traditional forms and of *vers libre*—and 'one should write *vers libre* only when one "must", that is to say, only when the "thing" builds up a rhythm more beautiful than that of set metres, or more real, more a part of the emotion of the "thing", more germane, intimate, interpretative than the measure of regular accentual verse'. Poetry must be sought that will be without 'flummery' and 'fustian'—'twentieth century poetry . . . will, I think, move against poppy-cock, it will be harder and saner . . . nearer the bone . . . its force will lie in its truth'.

Some of these, and similar, ideas were of very early date, and the brilliance of Pound's insight (and the force of his influence) can clearly be seen when he adduces examples of the 'new poetry' to support his theories—among them Padraic Colum, Joyce, and early Yeats! Indeed, not the least importance of the book is its incidental revelation of the mechanics of a change in literary taste. Pound's poetic revolution, like Wordsworth's—perhaps like all revolutions—started with bold theories but comparatively timid practice. One has to make the same effort of historical imagination to see how early Pound differs from the verse of the period as one has to distinguish early Wordsworth from the typical poetic product of the late eighteenth century. Pound's language in *Personae* and *Exultations*, the volumes of 1909, is still the language of the Rossetti translations, of Browning, of the 'nineties poets:

> Because I think not ever to return,
>   Ballad, to Tuscany,—
> Go therefore there for me
>   Straight to my lady's face,
>   Who, of her noble grace,
> Shall show thee courtesy.
>
>   *Rossetti*

> Beyond sea be thou sped, my song,
> And, by God, to my lady say
> That in desirous, grief-filled way
> My nights and my days are full long.
> And command thou William the Long-Seer
> To tell thee to my Lady dear,
> That comfort be her thoughts among.
>
>   *Pound*

It was Pound's rhythms, not his diction, which inaugurated the revolution—the rhythms even of those two early books, as their first reviewers half recognized. *The Daily News*, for example, talked about 'these curious metres' with a 'law and order of their own', and Pound's use of spondee and dactyl which 'comes in strangely and, as we first read it, with the appearance of discord, but afterwards seems to gain a curious and distinctive vigour'. Mr Auden has recently pointed out how Pound's translations of Cavalcanti, his reproduction in English of the cadence of the Italian hendecasyllabic, brought again to English poetry the possibility of other than iambic rhythms. The *Literary Essays* includes the long paper on Cavalcanti, and similar pieces: they are in Pound's worst critical manner—turgid, cocky, possessive, absurd in their erudition, but nevertheless embedded in them are several acute comments on the practice of poetry (I pick at random: 'I do not think rhyme-aesthetic, *any* rhyme-aesthetic, can ever do as much damage to English verse as that done by latinization in Milton's time and before') and, of course, some of the vital translations:

> I am blind to others, and their retort
> I hear not. In her alone, I see, move,
> Wonder. . . . And jest not. And the words dilate
> Not truth; but mouth speaks not the heart outright . . .

Later, Pound, like Hopkins, became intolerant of archaisms and inversions, and insisted on the necessary connection between the language of poetry and common speech—though he was sufficiently indulgent to sympathize, in an interesting review reprinted here, with Binyon's translation of Dante.

Mr Wyndham Lewis has said that Pound 'is not only *himself* a great poet, but has been of the most amazing use to other people'. Many of the pieces on his contemporaries included in the present volume were written long before their subjects found either their mature manner or proper recognition, but Pound is always quite fearlessly propagandizing for them and trying to find in their work not only the confirmation of his own principles but also their own true talents. A review in 1913 of Lawrence's *Love Poems and Others*, for instance, discovers the virtues of the dialect poems and discards the 'sort of pre-raphaelite slush' of the erotic verse—a view which, if not quite fair, enabled Pound to see even then that the source of Lawrence's strength was his 'realism' and his roots in 'low-life'. And, needless to say, the third section of the *Literary Essays* makes abundantly plain Pound's understanding appreciation of middle-Joyce and later-Yeats at the very earliest emergence of these two styles.

Possibly as a critic Pound would come out best in a severely selected volume such as Mr Hayward has made of Mr Eliot's prose [1953]. Certainly the sympathetic reviewer of the *Literary Essays* will be left with a number of aphoristic jottings on his hands which demand to be quoted—unless, Pound-like, he lumps them in as 'notes' at the end:

What, in the long run, makes the poet is a sort of persistence of the emotional nature, and, joined with this, a peculiar sort of control.

Even literature and poetry pay, for where there is enough intelligence to produce and maintain good writing, there society is pleasant and real estate values increase.

Poets of the worse sort seem seldom to have any reading.

Poets who are not interested in music are, or become, bad poets.

Art does not avoid universals, it strikes at them all the harder in that it strikes through particulars.

And so on. It is sometimes not particularly clever, not particularly original: it is often the voice of gran'fer Ezra from Idaho, rocking in his chair, spitting on the stove, and repeating the homespun philosophy of his forebears. 'I think that only after a long struggle will poetry attain such a degree of development, or, if you will, modernity, that it will vitally concern people who are accustomed, in prose, to Henry James and Anatole France, in music to Debussy', Pound wrote in 1911. The struggle is still going on, and it can best be conducted, and the gains of the Pound era defended, in terms similar to those Pound himself has used—terms consistently clear, forceful, intellectual and, on the whole, simple.

SECTION: ROCK-DRILL

New York, 30 March 1956
London, 15 February 1957

---

130. Noel Stock, review, *Meanjin*

March 1956, xv, 112–4

Stock (b. 1929) is an Australian critic. He is the editor of *Impact* (1960); a symposium in honour of Pound's eightieth birthday, *Ezra Pound Perspectives* (1965); and is the author of *Poet in Exile: Ezra Pound* (1964), and *Reading the Cantos* (Routledge & Kegan Paul, 1967). His *The Life of Ezra Pound* (Routledge & Kegan Paul, 1970) is the standard biography.

Most contemporary critics are conspicuous by their inability to cope with Pound's Cantos. A recent Yale broadcast, for instance, included comments by W. H. Auden, Archibald Macleish, Stephen Spender, and Robert Penn Warren.* Praise flowed for the *Personae* poems, *Cathay*, 'Mauberley', 'Propertius', but nothing worthwhile was said about the Cantos.

Pound has written: 'For 40 years I have schooled myself . . . to write an epic which begins "In the Dark Forest", crosses the Purgatory of human error, and ends in the light, "fra i maestri di color che sanno".' And, 'The sum of human wisdom is not contained in any one language, and no single language is CAPABLE of expressing all forms and degrees of human comprehension. This is a very unpalatable and bitter doctrine.'

Dr. Carlos Williams wrote, in 1934; 'He has taken, laudably, the speech of the men he treats of and, by clipping to essentials, revealed its closest nature—its pace, its "meaning".'

* *A Tribute to Ezra Pound* was broadcast on December 5, 1955, by the Yale Broadcasting Co. in honour of the poet's 70th birthday. Ernest Hemingway spoke of the Nobel Prize: 'I would have been very happy if the prize had been awarded to Mr. Pound, either last year when it was awarded to me or this year, and I would be very pleased if it was awarded to him next year.'

These latest cantos are labelled Rock-Drill. The poet takes samples from Time Past and maps the significant strata:

> All there by the time of Y Yin   (Canto 85)

> Galileo index'd 1616   (Canto 85)

> Alexander paid the debts of his troops   (Canto 85)

'Europe' said Picabia
    'exhausted by the conquest of Alsace-Lorraine'.   (Canto 87)

I dare say nobody will expect to understand these new cantos who has not already some knowledge of the direction of the other eighty and therefore some knowledge of Flaubert, Imagism, Vorticism, the 'ideogrammic method' and the spade-work done by Pound as long ago as *The Spirit of Romance* (1910). Pound has no equal in his ability to fix a tone of voice or the 'tonality' of a person:

> 'The irish are devout, moral, industrious'
> he even said: sober.   (Canto 89)

> For me nothing. But that the child walk in
>   peace in her basilica,
> The light there almost solid.   (Canto 93)

> And honour?
>   Fitzgerald: 'I was.'
> When he freed a man
>   who had not been at the Post Office
> (Oireland 1916)   (Canto 92)

The poet's mind moves from Manis the Sumerian who in the third millenium B.C. did not confiscate land but paid for it according to a strict measure, to Hutchins of the Ford Foundation and his accomplice, Maritain. Pound arranges anew, with more skill even than before, the essential gritty thoughts and definitions of his contributors to culture—John Adams, St. Ambrose, C. H. Douglas, Orage, Randolph, Antoninus Pius. Agassiz, who 'tracked' the Divine Intelligence through Nature; Kung the Anthologist who saw that it was 'All there by the time of Y Yin'; Apollonius of Tyana, on Demeter's side, who worked for the abolition of blood sacrifices; and Dante whose map of the spirit is for Pound still valid. The reader of the Cantos should turn—not so much to the problem of where all these components come from, as to how they go, and what holds them, together.

The principal source for Cantos 88 and 89 is Thomas Hart Benton's *Thirty Years' View* (1856), a forgotten book—or rather, lost in the historic blackout—which can stand with Blackstone's *Commentaries*. Here is Randolph of Roanoke whose thought went into action, down into details—

[quotes *Cantos*, pp. 614–15 'The teller' to 'a cart, Mr. Randolph?']

Pound's ideas are not written into the Cantos as abstract statements. He moves from the thing to the grouped things and his ideas grow in, or out of, the facts.

> 'You damn sadist!' said mr. cummings,
> 'you try to make people think'.   (Canto 89)

One thing that stands out is Pound's constructivity. Joyce built a Cloaca Maxima for the age of Capitalist Plunder; the ferocious Lewis blasted the dead minds; Eliot and Cocteau have been inclined to accept trends set by other (lesser) men. Pound, however, concerned with foundations, with justice and measure and with volition and intelligence has made distinctions and definitions for the young to build on—distinctions and definitions which are unpalatable to political, economic and philological theorists, as, for instance, these out of *ABC of Economics* (1933): 'People with no sense of responsibility fall under despotism.' 'The science of economics will not get far until it grants the existence of will as a component; i.e. will toward order, will toward "justice" or fairness, desire for civilization, amenities included.' 'A free private company may administer a nation's credit as justly and with as little graft as a board nominally of government officials, bribed or "influenced" by cliques of friends and acquaintances.' Or this, from *ABC of Reading* (1934): 'The "statesman cannot govern, the scientist cannot participate his discoveries, men cannot agree on wise actions without language," and all their deeds and conditions are affected by the defects or virtues of idiom.' Or *Carta da Visita* (Rome, 1942): 'Towards order in the state: the definition of the word.' Good cloth, good poetry, good distribution.

Pound is concerned with the establishment of clean values and his poem is a tremendous effort of clarification in and among millions of events, feelings, ideas which, to be intelligible, must be rendered whole, as it were; which require for their integrity that notice be taken, not only of themselves, but of complicating factors which cross or overlap them. The Tale of the Tribe has required a mind capable of leaping from details such as interest rates in the times of the Medici to the 'Divine Mind abundant' which binds together all the fabrics:

> In nature are signatures
> needing no verbal tradition,
> oak leaf never plane leaf.   (Canto 87)

which is in harmony with the opening lines of the *Paradiso*. And beyond is the power which 'causes' all this activity:

> You have stirred my mind out of dust.   (Canto 93)

Beyond civic order:

> l'AMOR.

131. Randall Jarrell on the extraordinary misuse of extraordinary powers

September 1956

From 'Five Poets', *Yale Review* (September 1956), xlvi, 103–6.

A few passages of Pound's new Cantos have a pure and characteristic beauty: 'The waves rise, and the waves fall / But you are like the moonlight: always there!'; 'Had Crab such crystal, winter were as a day'; 'The viper stirs in the dust, / the blue serpent / glides from the rock pool / and they take lights now down to the water / the lamps float from the rowers / the sea's claw drawing them outwards.' Some lines have an easy elegance, a matter-of-fact reality; the bare look and motion of the words, sometimes, is a delight. A great deal of the book is interesting in the way an original soul's indiscriminate notes on books and people, countries and centuries, are interesting; all these fragmentary citations and allusions remind you that if you had read exactly the books Pound has read, known exactly the people Pound has known, and felt about it exactly as Pound has felt, you could understand the Cantos pretty well. Gertrude Stein was most unjust to Pound when she called that ecumenical alluder a village explainer: he can hardly even tell you anything (unless you know it already), much less explain it. He makes notes on the margin of the universe; to tell how just or unjust a note is, you must know that portion of the text yourself.

Meaning seems to him—as morality seemed to Freud—self-evident, something the family naturally knows; and he makes family jokes about it, witty or ingeniously far-fetched allusions that are a delight to us insiders, a puzzle to the barbarians outside. (Pound does not want readers, really, but disciples, since he has the Greek feeling that wisdom is a way of life that disciples can share, and that reading is not a short cut to. As a result he has more disciples, almost, than readers.)

For instance, Pound says all at once—he has been talking about San Bertrand and Montrejau—'Elder Lightfoot is not downhearted, / Elder Lightfoot is cert'nly / not / downhearted, / He observes a design in the Process'; and that is the end of Elder Lightfoot, the poem deserts him for 'Miss Ida by the bars in the jail house' and 'Carrière show in Paris.' Here Pound is making fun, in what seems to me an amusing way, of Eliot and part of the 'Four Quartets'. How do I know? I just know—as more often, I just don't know, when the languages or ideographs or hieroglyphics (yes, these Cantos have hieroglyphics; next year Minoan B) or historical periods are ones I know nothing or little about. But here I'm better off, and smile, and say to explain the smile: Eliot is a deacon, and *Elder* is Pound's Br'er Rabbit Version of that; *Lightfoot* resembles Possum and pussyfooting, and goes well with all the Original Chameleon in Eliot, the part that seeks safety in conformity, apparent identity; *process* and *design* and *pattern* are used over and over in the 'Four Quartets' —to *observe* a design *in* the Process is as solemnly ludicrous as is the parody of the troops' *Are we downhearted? No*; the tone is Pound's regular tone for making fun of Eliot; and so on.

But when I read passages like 'pou éul cheu / pu erh[4] / 'O nombreux officiers / Imperator ait. / Iterum dico / T'AI MEOUI637 / 1562 / OU TING 1324 / 1265 / cognovit aerumnas / TSOU KIA reigned 33 years / wei / tcheng / tcheu / XV:II koung / naught about just contribution / invicem docentes siu M.2835 / hsü, in the first tone / kia6, chiao,[1-4]'—the Chinese words are accompanied by twelve ideographs—I bring little knowledge to the reading and carry away little knowledge from the reading. Yet, finishing, I seem to know—how I don't know—that all the Latin, Chinese and Ancient History in the world wouldn't make me think such a passage good poetry, good organization, or standing firm in the middle. Form, Kenneth Burke says, is a satisfied expectation; here, as in so much of the Cantos, it is only our uneasy expectation of disorder, of an idiosyncratic hodgepodge, that is satisfied.

If we pick an average passage, one neither at a height of lyricism nor a depth of carbon-copying, we get something like

[quotes *Cantos*, pp. 618–19 'Marse Adams done' to 'Macon, Guilford'.]

We cannot help noticing that this, like so much of the Cantos, doesn't have the connections and omissions, the concentration, that a work of art has: Pound throws in everything—the numbers of the pages, even. Pound has said that poetry ought to be as well written as prose; is this? Aren't good notes, even, more organized than *this*? When we finish reading it we have the approximate understanding that such a passage invites, but we have none of the aesthetic enjoyment we get from a poem, a story, a well-written passage of exposition. We do feel a pale pleasure at encountering so unexpectedly, back among the library stacks, this minstrel-show shrewdness, and think with a smile: 'Uncle Ezra done tol' 'em.' But here it is information, not lack of information, that gets in the way of the reader: if I had never read Tocqueville I might enjoy Pound's putting him in his place—as it is, I think, 'You may not understand Tocqueville, but Tocqueville would have understood *you*.'

Many writers have felt, like Pound: Why not invent an art-form that will permit me to put all my life, all my thoughts and feelings about the universe, directly into a work of art? But the trouble is, when they've invented it it isn't an art-form. The Cantos are a 'form' that permits Pound not even to try to write poetry; but since he is a poet, a wonderful one, he sometimes still writes it. The Cantos are less a 'poem containing history' than a heap containing poetry, history, recollections, free associations, obsessions. Some of the poetry is clearly beautiful, some of the history live: Pound can pick out, make up, a sentence or action that resurrects a man or a time. Many of Pound's recollections are as engaging as he is; his warmth, delight, disinterestedness, honest indignation help to make up for his extraordinary misuse of extraordinary powers, for everything that makes the Cantos a kind of *reductio ad absurdum*. His obsessions, at their worst, are a moral and intellectual disaster, and make us ashamed for him:

> Democracies electing their sewage
> till there is no clear thought about holiness
> a dung flow from 1913

and, in this, their kikery functioned, Marx, Freud
    and the american beaneries
Filth under filth. . . .

What is worst in Pound and what is worst in the age have conspired to ruin the Cantos, and have not quite succeeded. I can not imagine any future that will think it a good poem; but, then as now, scholars will process it, anthologies present one or two of its beauties, readers dig through all that blue clay for more than a few diamonds.

132. A. Alvarez, review, *Observer*

3 March 1957, 15

Alvarez (b. 1929), English critic, was educated at Corpus Christi College, Oxford. He is author of a study of modern poetry, *The Shaping Spirit* (1958), which contains a chapter on Pound.

Pound began writing his Cantos towards the end of the First World War. He continued writing them even after the Second World War, when he was held in the condemned-cages outside Pisa. Now, after eleven years in a lunatic asylum in Washington, he has brought out another instalment of the poem.

Like all the later Cantos, the new *Section: Rock-Drill*, Cantos 85–95, is difficult and uneven. The whole poem, in fact, has been more or less difficult from the start. Pound designed it on a mythic scale. Its subject was to be the flowering and decay of the major civilisations, and they were to be treated not patiently and diagnostically, one after the other, but with a growing, simultaneous complexity, like an elaborate fugue. And then the language was to have the solidity and concentration of the Chinese ideograms. So Pound wrote his huge poem without plot and with scarcely any comment of his own. He juxtaposed scene with scene, fact with fact, and left it to the reader to make the connections.

There are certain figures, themes and theories which recur through-out the Cantos. But as the work has grown, the references to these ciphers have become more and more condensed and oblique. In the beginning Pound used the method of the ideograms as a shorthand to save himself a great deal of tedious explanation. By the time he reached *The Pisan Cantos* the shorthand had become a code; the ideograms had broken down into heaps of fragmentary half-references. Now, in the opening cantos of *Rock-Drill*, the obliqueness has led him to the dis-appearing-point of poetry. A large proportion of the work is no longer *like* ideograms, it actually *is* ideograms. There are pages of Chinese characters and even some Egyptian hieroglyphics. Granted some are transliterated and a few translated—though as often into Latin or Greek as into English; granted, too, it is certainly strange and imposing: still, with the best will in the world, it is hardly comprehensible. The effect is of an enormous and elaborate failure to communicate, like someone shouting with great urgency, but just out of ear-shot.

Yet Pound is one of the great masters of English verse. If he has in places abandoned his art for code messages in foreign languages, the blame lies as much with his circumstances as with his powers. He could hardly write of what goes on around him. So perhaps Ancient Greece and China are the best way of escaping the public ward of St. Eliza-beth's Hospital. It is the remoteness of these civilisations that enables him to live so intensely through them. But Pound has reached the point where he can no longer see that the values he has *got to* believe in are not automatically and powerfully those of his audience.

Yet this claustrophobic shuffling of semi-private references occurs only when he is dealing with general values. When he turns to his own experience and writes the Cantos on love, 90–95, he is still capable of producing some of the most perfect poetry of this century:—

[quotes *Cantos*, pp. 640–1 'not arrogant from habit' to 'drawing them outward'.]

The plan of the Cantos, if they ever seriously had a plan, has run to earth long ago; the hectoring theories have broken down in confusion. But in *Rock-Drill*, as in parts of *The Pisan Cantos*, Pound is writing personal verse better than anything he has done since the early twenties. That work of such subtle control and lucidity should come from a poet over seventy is extraordinary enough; that it should come from one who has been locked away longer than most of the Nazi war criminals is hardly credible. One may not admire Pound's politics—I certainly don't—but his integrity and courage as an artist is unequalled. He is still *il miglior fabbro*.

133. Donald Davie, 'Bed-Rock', *New Statesman and Nation*

9 March 1957, liii, 316–17

Those many readers who wrote off Pound in the Thirties and were persuaded to give him a second chance, because of some poignant and direct passages in the *Pisan Cantos*, can now write him off again. For much of the new sequence of eleven cantos presents Pound at his most forbidding, stringing together 'gists' from unfamiliar works that he thinks wrongly neglected. Specifically, he draws here on three such sources: in Cantos 85 and 86, the Chinese history-classic, the Chou King; in Cantos 88 and 89, Benton's *Thirty Years' View*, a primary source for American history at the time of the Bank War; in Canto 94, the Bohn translation of the Life of Apollonius of Tyana, by Philostratus. Canto 85 will tax the patience of even a devout Poundian, since it can be read only with the Chinese source in one's lap. What with the Chinese characters, Couvreur's French version of these, and his Latin version, Canto 85 can hardly be called a poem in English at all. If, as Hugh MacDiarmid maintains, poetry must move 'Towards a World Language,' well, this is it. Cantos 90 and 91 seem to be Pound's Paradiso: they evoke what he calls 'The Great Crystal,' meaning by that the image of an ideal clarity which man of affairs and man of action, no less than poet and sage, have to keep before themselves. The paradisal flavour is in Pound's confidence, which he has expressed before ('it is not man Made courage, or made order, or made grace'), that this clarity, and the traditions of embodying it in thought, action and artifact, cannot be lost even when they go unhonoured. It's in the last few Cantos, where Pound guards against any hint of complacency, that we come nearest to the Pisan note:

443

But in the great love, bewildered
    farfalla in tempesta
under rain in the dark:
                Many wings fragile
Nymphalidæ, basilarch, and lycæna,
Ausonides, euchloe, and erynnis
And from far
                il tremolar della marina.

'Farfalla' is a real though rare and archaic word for 'moth'; with its
beautiful hint of 'farfallen' it expresses, tersely but as movingly as anything in *The Pisan Cantos*, Pound's compassion for those who cannot
stand the pace.

In short, the great gamble continues. The method is being pressed to
its logical conclusion. Either this is the waste of a prodigious talent, or
else it is the poetry of the future.

134. Philip Larkin, notice, *Manchester Guardian*

26 March 1957, 4

Larkin (b. 1922) is an English poet and novelist. He is probably the
most important contemporary English poet who has not been influenced by Pound.

Mr. Pound's latest eleven Cantos seem similar in method and perhaps
material to what has gone before: a tesselation of languages and civilisations and periods streaked by a kind of Josh Billings[1] humour and a
preoccupation with international finance. Comprehension and apprecia-

---

[1] Billings (1818–85), American humourist, mined a rich vein of paradox, popular cracker-
box philosophy, malapropisms and ridiculous spellings in his annual *Allminax* and other
publications.

tion will depend on the reader's knowledge and liking of what Mr. Pound is doing in this long twentieth-century poetic curiosity, the ultimate (and immediate) value of which I personally think very small. However, the numerous splinters of rhetoric, the sardonic asides, and the evocative images of this historical kaleidoscope are sufficiently fascinating to suggest that those who think otherwise may well be right.

135. Yvor Winters on the Cantos

1956

From 'Problems for the Modern Critic of Literature', *The Function of Criticism: Problems and Exercises* (Denver: Allen Swallow, 1967), p. 47.

Donald Davie, *Ezra Pound: Poet as Sculptor* (New York: 1964; London: Routledge & Kegan Paul 1965, p. 217) refers to this passage: 'Yvor Winters has challenged the basic assumptions of Pound's method perhaps more justly and searchingly than any other . . . .'

In our time we have had the Cantos of Ezra Pound, which may be an epic or not, according to your definition. The work has no narrative structure, such as that of *The Iliad*; it has no expository structure, such as that of *The Divine Comedy*. It thus avoids a variety of difficulties. There are a few loosely related themes running through the work, or at least there sometimes appear to be. The structure appears to be that of more or less free association, or progression through reverie. Sensory perception replaces idea. Pound, early in his career, adopted the inversion derived from Locke by the associationists: since all ideas arise from sensory impressions, all ideas can be expressed in terms of sensory impressions. But of course they cannot be: when we attempt this method, what we get is sensory impressions alone, and we have no way of knowing whether we have had any ideas or not.

The details, especially in the early Cantos, are frequently very lovely, but since there is neither structure nor very much in the way of meaning, the details are details and nothing more, and what we have is the ghost of poetry, though I am willing to admit that it is often the ghost of great poetry. The images are for the most part derived from Pound's reading, which has been wide, and, one might add, scattered; and the references to the reading are commonly so tangential as to be difficult. A number of young scholars at the University of California and at Northwestern University are now engaged in running these references down, and the voluminous notes which they have provided for a few of the Cantos are very helpful; but the notes are almost as voluminous as the Cantos and can scarcely be held in the head—in fact, when the work is completed, it may well be impossible to hold them in the hand —so that we shall eventually have to read the Cantos with a guide more awkward than anything required by Spenser or Dante.

THRONES
96-109 DE LOS CANTARES

New York, 7 December 1959
London, 4 March 1960

136. Delmore Schwartz, 'Ezra Pound and History', *New Republic*

8 February 1960, cxlii, 17–19

As one reads these thirteen new Cantos of Ezra Pound's long poem and then re-reads the ninety-five which have preceded it, one's first strong impression is that little change or genuine development of theme and attitude have occurred throughout the entire work. Through the years Pound has remembered a great deal, but he has learned nothing— nothing that could be called a new insight into the attitudes with which he began to write. Thus Canto 100 begins with

> Has packed the Supreme Court
> so they declare anything he does
> constitutional.
> *—Senator Wheeler, 1936*

Here in this denunciatory reference to Franklin D. Roosevelt and the New Deal, as elsewhere in these Cantos, it is clear that Pound's view of the New Deal and the Second World War have not been altered since the lamentable attempt to pack the Supreme Court. And this is but one instance of the fact that Pound has not reviewed, in the light of recent experience and recent knowledge, his attitude toward the Second World War: he has not asked himself what would have happened to Western civilization, America, modern literature and his own poetry, if Germany had won the Second World War. And yet Pound must know—in some sense—that to the Nazis his own kind of work and the creative work he admired and helped to bring into being was regarded as an intolerable

447

and barbaric manifestation of *Kulturbolscheivismus* and decadent cosmopolitanism.

Since the Cantos as a whole aspire to be a kind of philosophy of history, it is necessary to point out how, despite their frequent passages of great beauty, learning, metrical invention and prophetic significance, they are often no more than Pound's discursive monologue about his own *personal* experience of history, particularly 20th Century history, and particularly in relation to his own understandable obsession with the relationship of the creative artist and the statesman. This is perhaps the chief reason that he writes so often about economics and politics.

As a poet whose theme is the nature of history, Pound is inadequate in two important ways: he has an intense tendency to overinterpret and overgeneralize experience from a purely personal point of view or from the point of view very often of the assumed supremacy of the creative artist (as if other human beings were not necessary to the existence of creativity); and this inadequacy is made worse, time and again, by Pound's undisciplined and very often uninformed abstractions.

Here is a somewhat elaborate example: if the Cantos had been concerned with the fall of the Roman Empire as they are concerned again and again with the rise and fall of other great civilizations, Pound clearly would have blamed the fall of Rome upon the weakness and stupidity of a Caesar, or the personal strength of a Barbarian general, or perhaps upon the rise of debt and usury in Rome and the corruption of the aristocracy. What actually happened to cause the fall of Rome, according to J. B. Bury, was something seemingly trivial and implausable: the extraordinary advent of historical *coincidence* or historical *luck*. For centuries, the Barbarians had attacked Rome in great strength: it was only when the unique moment of Barbarian attack and Roman weakness occurred *at the same time* that the huge event of Rome's fall occurred and a great civilization perished. It can be argued that sooner or later this unique historical coincidence was bound to occur unless a great and wise Caesar extirpated the deeply-rooted causes of Roman weakness, and thus that political leadership is very important. But nowhere in this long poem about the nature of history is a sustained effort made to rise to the level of generality necessary to the extreme ambition of the poem; nor is there very much evidence of the intellectual awareness necessary to deal with the questions Pound raises about the nature of history.

The new Cantos have many interesting passages, some passages of unique lyrical beauty, and too many passages when inspiration and excited self-indulgence have been confused with one another.

Thus, at one point, in a passage dealing, I think, with the Byzantine Empire, Pound writes

> Some sort of embargo, Theodora died in the 19th Justinian.
> And the money sellers Ablavius and Marcellus
> Thought they would just bump off Justinian.
> A flood of fads swelled over Europe.
> But there could have been two Abduls
> And it would not have annoyed one.
> That is something to note. I mean as personality, when
> one says 'oriental.' The third bahai
> Said nothing remarkable. Edgar Wallace had his kind of modesty.

Here Edgar Wallace, a detective story writer once as well-known as Agatha Christie and Erle Stanley Gardner, suddenly emerges, and as suddenly departs from the 20th Century and appears in Byzantium as part of a discussion of the virtues and defects of an obscure historical regime's political luminaries. The relevance of a popular mystery story writer to a political discussion of a distant and for the most part very obscure historical period is, I think, tenuous but real. Edgar Wallace, of whose mystery fiction Pound avowed himself to be very fond in a book published more than twenty years ago, probably was *modest*, and it is probably true that Pound believes in and likes modesty—in other human beings. But the entire passage which is fairly characteristic of Pound's political discourses in the Cantos, is a good example of how easy it is to confuse inspiration and self-indulgence, and childishness.

The reference to Edgar Wallace's personal modesty in a passage dealing with Byzantine politicos is not bad in itself, but it is, in addition, quite self-indulgent and personal in the worst way. It does not matter that Pound takes a childish pride in being fond of Wallace and knowing him and bringing his character into an epic poem; and the passage is not bad because of the sudden transition to Wallace's modesty or because of the obscurity of Byzantine history. It is bad because some other and better embodiment or touchstone of modesty would have made the poetic point less tangential and lessened the strain upon the reader who not only has to find out or know who the third bahai and the two Abduls are, and in what way Edgar Wallace possessed the same kind of modesty as his predecessors. To be self-indulgent myself for a moment, I am willing to entertain the possibility that the third bahai was a really important personage, but I don't see what Wallace had to be modest *about*, although I am sure he did the best he could and received adequate compensation.

Nevertheless it must immediately be added that what is bad and self-indulgent in this passage is inseparable from Pound's poetic genius at its best: in other passages, the suddenness of transition and apparent randomness of historical juxtaposition and range are necessary to create the historical perspective of the Cantos, the sense that all history is relevant to any moment of history, and the profound belief that the entire past, at any moment and in any place, is capable of illuminating the present and the whole nature of historical experience.

The prose of the book jacket of *Thrones de los Contares* can serve as a summary of what is good and what is bad in this new section of the Cantos. As a description of the new Cantos, it is neither better nor worse than most book jacket prose. This is how the preceding section of the Cantos, *Rock-Drill*, is described:

'The human soul is not love, but love flows from it . . . it cannot, ergo, delight in itself, but only in the love flowing from it'. This is the major theme as the Cantos move into their final phase: 'The domination of benevolence'. Now the great poem has progressed into the realms of the 'permanent'; the poet has passed through 'the casual' and 'the recurrent' and come to values that endure like the sea.

The Cantos are a poem containing history; it is their purpose to give the true meaning of history as one man has found it: in the annals of China, in the Italian Renaissance, in the letters and diaries of Jefferson, the Adamses and Van Buren, in the personalities and currents of his own time. The truth must be hammered home by reiteration, with the insistence of a rock drill 'Drilling it into their heads . . . much in the way that a composer does in music'.

As a description of Cantos 85–95 and the new Cantos this is not only adequate, it has a good deal of the obscurity of unavoidable truth and the immense confusion of reality. And it participates in the barbarous contempt for most human beings—unless they are creative artists or patrons of the arts—which recurs throughout Pound's great poem. For it should be clear, by inspection, that the domination of benevolence, is a bad and impractical description of both love and statesmanship. It was, I think, Talleyrand who said to Napoleon, pointlessly enough: 'Sire, you cannot sit on bayonets.' And it should not be necessary to say, at this late date, that power which is maintained through domination of any kind—benevolent paternalism, for example—is worthless because it is temporary and must be sustained by tyranny. It should be a truism by now that genuine power depends upon consent, just as genuine love requires requited love. Finally to say that the truth must be hammered home by reiteration, with the insistence of a rock drill is revealing in ways which the author of the jacket did not intend: revealing and novel. This must be the first time that the acetylene torch has been advocated as a method of teaching the truth to human beings or writing poetry. One might just as well try out the surgeon's scalpel, psychoacoustical bombing, brainwashing and all the other forms of psychological warfare. And to compare the insistence of a rock drill with the repetition of musical phrases is to reveal a complete ignorance of music and to show how metaphor may be a means of justifying anything, if one is also eager to deceive oneself. If the insistence of a rock drill and the repetition of musical phrases resembled each other in any whatever, the interest in good music, which is small enough as it is, would not exist at all.

I have dwelt at length on the book jacket for several reasons. One is that it is a good summary of Pound's intention and what is wrong with it. But there is a more important reason. In recent years, for extra-literary reasons of all sorts, Pound's work has been praised too often and for the wrong reasons, without qualification or reservation, by ardent admirers and friends, in such a way as to antagonize readers who are not very well acquainted with his work. Indeed Pound has been praised by his friends—sometimes, perhaps, out of sympathy for his personal plight, rather than his poetry—in so lavish and uncritical a way as to have exactly the reverse of the effect which was intended. The mixed feelings of the reading public toward complicated new poetry are such that uncritical praise is at best merely bewildering. Indeed, the effort and ardor of most of Pound's friends is unfortunate enough to make one think, again: any human being who has friends of this kind has no need of enemies.

There is also an unfortunate and unnecessary antagonism to Pound's work which takes a variety of forms and which, whatever its form, is unjustified. Sometimes the antagonism is purely personal; sometimes the antagonism is political; sometimes it is literary; sometimes it is literary and asserts itself as political liberalism and sometimes it is political and literary, as in the critics who dislike modern poetry and Pound's kind of modern poetry and his political views which Pound makes explicit, from time to time in his poetry. The reference to Roosevelt and the New Deal which I have already quoted is but one of a good many in the present volume. Here is another explicit passage concerning Hitler:

> Adolf furious from perception.
> But there is a blindness comes from inside—
> they try to explain themselves out of nullity.

This is enough to make the uninformed reader—or the reader who has been told that Pound is a Fascist and an anti-Semite—dismiss Pound as a bad poet, or dismiss that which is valuable and beautiful in Pound's writing as trivial when the basic attitude of his work is anti-human. But here is another passage from an early Canto which should illustrate, among other things, the way in which Pound became a great poet:

> And that year I went up to Freiburg,
> And Rennert had said: 'Nobody, no, nobody
> Knows anything about Provençal, or if there is anybody
> It's old Levy.'
>
> And so I went up to Freiburg,
> And the vacation was just beginning,
> The students getting off for the summer,
> Freiburg in Breisgau
> And everything clean, seeming clean, after Italy.

There is a great deal more to be said about Pound's work and about the passages which disfigure it. For example there are several other passages —the description of a synagogue in Italy and its religious ceremonies and Cantos which contain the passionate denunciations of modern war which show that if Pound is, at times, anti-Semitic, he is also, at other times, philo-Semitic; and if he is anti-human, it is, at least, in part, partly through a disappointed and embittered love of mankind. Certainly no one who was wholly misanthropic could be so avidly interested in what happens to human beings and to so many forms of human art and culture. But this is a complicated subject which cannot be discussed with brevity. The first and most important thing to say about Pound's Cantos is that they ought to be read again and again by anyone interested in any form of literature.

137. John Wain, 'The Shadow of an Epic', *Spectator*

11 March 1960, cciv, 360

Wain (b. 1925), English poet, novelist and critic, is the author of an essay on 'The Reputation of Ezra Pound' collected in his *Preliminary Essays* (1957).

Here is a new instalment of Ezra Pound's Cantos bringing the total up to 109. The Cantos are sometimes declared to be unreadable, but I do not think this is so. They are very easy to read, surely, as long as you adopt the proper technique. Most poetry demands a slow and careful approach, with the reader's mind at a high pitch of concentration; in fact, the commonest fault among readers of poetry is failure to concentrate hard enough, so that there is always a pact between the bad poet and the lazy reader. (Poetry-and-jazz, for instance, is largely a device for protecting *ersatz* verse from close attention.) But in the Cantos Pound has produced something unique: verse which doesn't need—is actually better without—close attention, and yet is anything but perfunctory or spurious.

Nothing is simpler than to read the Cantos in such a way as to enjoy and admire them. You settle down by the fireside, make sure you are quite comfortable, and then go into a trance with the book open before you. Don't skip—that is the prime rule; your eyes must travel over every line that is on the page, including the ideograms. If, in this fashion, you sit there until the whole book has been read, you will find, when the last page is turned, that the experience was meaningful and even moving. It is merely that close concentration destroys the effect. The usual way of reading the Cantos is to open the book warily and leaf through it in search of 'good bits.' This, as C. S. Lewis[1] insisted in his book on Milton, is always a mistake in reading long poems, whose effects may take pages to develop and which cannot afford to provide quotable little gems to snag the reader's attention. The long poem is never meant to be read at the same high pressure of attention as the short

[1] *A Preface to Paradise Lost* (Oxford, 1942).

lyric. Traditionally, epic poets made use of stock phrases, invariable epithets, and other devices for allowing the reader or hearer to slacken off and so stay awake to the end. Modern poetry cannot afford these devices because one of its first principles is that language must be fresh and natural-sounding; however elliptical, it must have the ring of living speech—'the rest is literature,' and 'literature' is not a polite word. Stock phrases, recurrent adjectives, and the rest, are 'literature.' When they go out, we are face to face with Poe's declaration that the long poem is a contradiction in terms.

Ezra Pound has always been interested in the possibility of a modern epic poem, and it is typical of the man that he has devoted years of single-minded effort to the task of forming a modern epic style. To call the Cantos a long poem is perhaps stretching the word 'poem' slightly, for of course a good deal of the Cantos, as one leafs through them page by page, consists of notebook jottings and other material which bears no relationship to verse, epic or otherwise. Still, the dominant impression of the Cantos is majestic; the mind one feels behind it is a poetic mind, able to send gleams of imagination, or sudden piercing jabs of poignancy, darting through the mass of untreated material at any moment, and able to give us, when the strategy of the poem calls for it, sustained passages of high rhetoric.

I intend, therefore, no disrespect to the Cantos or their author when I say that the best state to get into before reading them is a state of trance. If one simply goes ahead, understanding perhaps one line in ten (in the clearer passages, this can rise as high as two lines in three), and letting the succession of thoughts and images flow into one's mind, the thing *works*. It is like listening through the keyhole to some grand old scholar, working on a vast theory of history, muttering to himself as he moves about his study, trying to put his hand on the right book, repeating dates and quotations to himself, suddenly bursting into oratory as he curses one character in the story or blesses another.

[quotes *Cantos*, p. 688 'down the church' to 'over Euphrates']

This kind of thing is not new in literature: one gets much the same effect from Sir Thomas Browne.

Much less whether the house of *Diogenes* were a Tub framed of wood, and after the manner of ours, or rather made of earth, as learned men conceive, and so more clearly make out that expression of *Juvenal*. We should be too critical to question the letter Y, or bicornous element of Pythagoras, that is, the making of the horns equal: or the left less than the right, and so destroying the Symbolic intent of the figure, confounding the narrow line of virtue; with the larger road of vice; answerable unto the narrow door of heaven, and the ample gates of hell, expressed by our Saviour, and not forgotten by *Homer*, in that Epithete of *Pluto's* house.

It is true that Browne makes it easier for the reader than Pound, by accompanying the text with a ribbon of footnotes in which such things as 'that expression of *Juvenal*' and 'that Epithete of *Pluto's* house' are quoted. But this is no great difference; Browne's notebook is in better order, perhaps.

Browne, of course, is a late Renaissance figure, a last inheritor of the glorious old rag-bag tradition. Pound, like Joyce, is deeply attracted to this tradition and may be said to have revived it; certainly, Joyce and Pound between them have made it much easier to write the kind of rambling, unclassifiable pantechnicon of a book, dominated by a central idea but free to embellish, meander, make raids on neighbouring territory, at the writer's whim. (The line would go on through Wyndham Lewis, David Jones, Hugh MacDiarmid: but are there any younger writers joining in? I can't think of any, though Norman Mailer's new book [*Advertisements for Myself*], not yet published here, sounds like a candidate.) Browne's work isn't 'poetry', but it could be said of him, as of Rabelais, that it contains much that is nearer to poetry, according to our modern ideas, than to prose. I would say the same of the Cantos; if this makes them the only interesting long poem of our time, as Mr. Eliot thinks, then one of the conclusions to be drawn is that Poe was right.

There is one other point about the Cantos which we cannot, if we are to be honest, shrink from making. Pound was confined for a number of years in an insane asylum, having been found unfit to plead his own cause when charged with treason to his country. During those years, as we all know, it was a widespread belief in Europe that Pound was not mad at all, but was merely being kept in custody for political reasons. I thought so myself, until I visited him in St. Elizabeth's Hospital, Washington, DC, in August, 1957. That visit left me with an impression of Pound's grandeur and dignity, but also, inescapably of his mental derangement. As he sat in a deckchair on the lawn, shirtless, revealing the muscular upper torso of a man twenty years his junior, and with his strange, sad little band of disciples listening carefully to every word, I felt like Edgar in the presence of Lear. 'Conversation,' in the ordinary sense, was not possible; Pound talked on and on, in connected sentences and with perfect logic and persuasiveness; but if anyone interrupted him with a question it simply threw the needle out of the groove, and he fell silent for a moment, passed his hand wearily over his eyes, and then went on talking, starting from a different point, as if the needle had been dropped back at random. He seemed unconscious of the question except as an interruption.

This bears on the Cantos to some extent, because there can be no denying that they do show signs of paranoia and monomania; their cloudy grandeur is very far from ordinary reasonableness, and if anyone wanted to call them 'mad' I would not argue with him. The real mistake, in my opinion, is made by those critics who see the Cantos as a logical, lucid, carefully worked-out problem in literary engineering. Years ago, Pound was in the habit of saying (he said it to Yeats, for instance) that when the hundredth Canto was published, the whole work would be seen to have a unity like that of a Bach fugue. And if he had indeed stopped at No. 100, the Tribe of Ezra would have got to work and justified the structure as a whole. But surely even they are disconcerted by the sight of the Master blandly sailing on past the hundred mark? I prefer, myself, to sacrifice the cloak of rationality; if the Cantos are 'mad,' fixated, obsessive, they are also magnificent and of a sombre fascination.

For these reasons I cannot agree with Mr. Robert Graves when he writes:

It is an extraordinary paradox that Pound's sprawling, ignorant, indecent, unmelodious, seldom metrical Cantos, embellished with esoteric Chinese ideographs—for all I know, they may have been traced from the nearest tea-chest—and with illiterate Greek, Latin, Spanish and Provençal snippets . . . are now compulsory reading in many ancient centres of learning.[1]

One of the things those 'centres of learning' may profitably do for us is to study the difference between the early, middle and late Cantos. The new ones have fewer lyrical passages and more doodling, and to that extent strike me as a falling-off. But for a riper judgment, balancing the new against the familiar, we shall need more time.

[1] Robert Graves, *The Crowning Privilege* (Penguin ed., 1959), p. 144.

138. Donald Hall, 'The Cantos in England', *New Statesman and Nation*

12 March 1960, lix, 368

D. J. Enright mentions this review in *Conspirators and Poets* (1966), p. 57: 'It is symptomatic that a recent reviewer in the *New Statesman*, a young man, should attack the world of letters for supposedly no longer paying enough attention to Pound. His implication was that the British were returning to their native element: a sort of eternal Georgianism.'

Hall (b. 1928) is an American poet and anthologist.

Ezra Pound is the poet who, a thousand times more than any other man, has made modern poetry possible in English. If anyone is tempted to grant Eliot this position, let him compare Eliot's critical ideas, which are germinal to his poetry, with Pound's earlier dicta in *The Spirit of Romance* and in the literary reviews. Eliot has developed and argued Pound's insights so that they are believed by critics and professors; it was Pound who originated them for poets. Let him compare most of Eliot's poetic styles to Pound's originals; even the documentary passages of the Cantos receive their homage in 'Coriolan'. To get the order straight is not to dismiss the achievement of Eliot—the Wright brothers made the first airplane, not the best one—but the order is worth knowing and if Pound is not the better craftsman (and I suspect that Eliot's ascription is precise) he is the man who invented the tools.

The paragraph above is not an apology. Pound is not only the cause of poetry in other men. He is a great poet, and the Cantos are his master work. There is a certain critical cosiness which settles for 'Mauberley'. There is considerably less than cosiness among critics who will settle only for a vague bow in favour of an 'influence' on T. S. Eliot. In a better world, literary men would queue all night to get their copies of *Thrones*, Pound's new section of the Cantos, to discover for themselves the latest utterances of a great poet now in his seventy-fifth year. But we know, don't we, that the critics and the reviewers will do nothing of the kind. In America, where Pound has been petrified into an industry by the academics, the first reviews have been either condescending or ignorantly respectful. In England they will copy everything but the respect, for England revels in a massive provincialism which must reject all evidence of the European mind. The common market isn't the only benefit from which England abstracts itself.

One would like to think that England was in a period of reaction ('consolidation', as some critics like to call it) yet really England has never abandoned the Georgian mood. Only the immense prestige of T. S. Eliot has kept modern art faintly respectable here. 'In a country in love with amateurs, where the incompetent have such charming manners, and personalities so fragile and charming that one cannot bear to injure their feelings by the introduction of competent criticism, it is well that one man should have a vision of perfection . . .' Pound wrote these words in 1914, while he was still in London, but he could write them as easily today—though perhaps without emphasising manners. Of course, as Wyndham Lewis wrote, 'a great incompatibility existed, first and last, between Pound and the Englishman'. (Lewis quoted an intemperate letter from Rapallo: 'There's only one thing to do with an Englishman—kick him in the teeth'.) But the incompatibility was not trivial; Pound made the social error of taking art seriously, of applying tough standards to what had become a polite accomplishment. For at least two hundred years, English society has confused social and intellectual achievement. In Pound's London, he offended the editors and critics by his commitment to art and intelligence. Now he offends against an opposite social rule. He writes poems about foreign cities. He uses languages a chap doesn't know.

I wonder if there is another country which is so tangled in its own class structure that its leading poetry reviewer could castigate Wallace Stevens as a 'cultural show-off'. Maybe if Wallace Stevens had been an English insurance lawyer, his French and his metaphysics would have been devices of advancement. I don't know or care. But it is a measure of English provinciality that foreign writers are confidently categorised in terms of the English class system. Call Pound vulgar because he is professional; call him pretentious because of his cosmopolitanism—you are a victim of your own class structure.

Cosmopolitanism is the type of the American writer. America is a country without a past; without parents, it has chosen to adopt the world. *Moby Dick* and *The Scarlet Letter*, no less than *The Ambassadors* and 'The Waste Land', are works of the international intelligence. No country but America could have produced, in Faulkner, a major novelist who has based *two* of his stories on the life of Christ. American authors have always borrowed from a variety of cultures; the American tradition is to scavenge among traditions.

His cosmopolitanism is not the only American trait of Pound. His politics, for all his attachment to Mussolini, remind me of an America which is visible now only in old men and in the history books, an America of political parties founded on monetary issues, strongly anti-colonial, devoted to local self-determination, and ferociously individual. The capitalist collectivism of the current American orthodoxy is as far from Jefferson as Idaho from Rapallo. Pound's appeal, when he was accused of treason, was to 'the Constitution'; this phrase used to be popular among Fourth of July orators, but to Richard Nixon's speech-writers it would be 'embarrassing,' 'naive,' 'old-fashioned.'

But this is only to characterise Pound and to damn the English literary scene, two endeavours only partly to the point. *Thrones* is a very good book. The Cantos have reached their Paradiso, which is a collection of virtuous men, actions and laws. Near the end of *Rock-Drill* —the last section of the Cantos, which was largely economic and re-capitulatory—the new series was announced:

> That it is of thrones,
>> and above them: Justice.

Thrones contains less of Chinese and American economics than *Rock-Drill*, though its economic burden is the same; it is concerned more with the legal limbs by which the values of good government operate. A strong figure in this paradise, towards the end of this section, is Sir Edward Coke, the Elizabethan and Jacobean lawyer who fought James's prerogative: 'the clearest mind ever in England'.

Pound's method juxtaposes laws and incidents and actions, and its references often lead back to other parts of the Cantos. Key citations will be incomprehensible to those who do not know earlier sections— much as a movie is obscure if you walk in when it's three quarters over. But to anyone who has had the sense to read the poem, *Thrones* brings new material into combination with the familiar, and continues the job of defining. The style remains that of most of the later Cantos. Fragments are built into wholes. The effectiveness of a juxtaposition (I avoid the word ideogram) is a function of the number of parts and the volume of each; it is simple enough to follow the effect of a sub and main plot in a novel, since there are only two factors, but when there are five or ten, they must be small, in order to be efficient. It is Pound's method in the later Cantos exclusive of some passages of lyric and narrative, to associate a variety of concrete references and dates, so that the comparison will make the 'new word' of a poem. But such passages do not quote; they will only frighten the timid. In Canto 106 there is a passage of lyric, from which one can choose these lines, if only to show that *il miglior fabbro* can still do this sort of thing when he wants to:

[quotes *Cantos*, pp. 778–9 'Circe, Persephone' to 'from sunset'.]

In all, Canto 106 is one of the finest achievements of the Cantos, at least to a reader who cares more for Pound's own persona, the speaking voice of the poet, than for his brilliant mosaic of other voices. One begins to sense here the drive and the exaltation of language which will carry the poet beyond his Beatrice, to the heights of his Paradise.

I have a depressing sense that few readers will be able to read even these lines with pleasure, In the first of the Cantos, Tiresias warned Ulysses: 'Shall return through spiteful Neptune, over dark seas/Lose all companions'. In the world we inhabit, the taste for verse has become rare, and so has disinterested intelligence. Pound is finishing his great poem in an amphitheatre without an audience.

139. W. D. Snodgrass, review, *Hudson Review*

Spring 1960, xiii, 120–2

Snodgrass (b. 1926), American poet, is the author of *Heart's Needle* (Pulitzer Prize, 1960) and *After Experience* (1968).

Reading the latest installment of Ezra Pound's Cantos, I feel a little as if I had married a romantical, schoolgirl poetess, only to discover (the honeymoon safely over) that she has turned into a lady executive, much determined to save souls, mine in particular. No doubt her long-term blueprint for my life will work to my own benefit; surely I will be slimmer, healthier, happier, when I learn to conform to her schedule; no doubt I will be wittier, more convincing, more fun at parties, when I have, finally, memorized all those phrases which she has written on flash cards for me. Yet, at the moment, I can think of the moment's loss of instinctual satisfactions: doctrine instead of passion, heat instead of warmth, vitamin pills instead of meals.

If Homer's use of epithets can be called (by Gerald Else) 'mail-sorter's verse'; if Empson's use of puns can be called (by himself) 'crossword-puzzle verse'; then this may be called 'flash-card verse.' And life with Ezra has come more and more to be a daily mid-semester test. I must spend hours each day watching him flash (a little faster each day) note cards containing significant phrases (a little shorter each day) past my nose. For each snippet of phrase I must produce a full historical context together with the received interpretation. Should I pass this test I prove my love so strong that I have laid aside my own vision to memorize his.

Of course, Pound has always had these inclinations. Yet some of his Cantos have also sung; there *have* been long, sustained passages, many with a heavy musical or ritual content, to carry us through. I need only mention the splendid hell Cantos, the usura Cantos, or such superb passages from the Pisan sequence as the famous 'vanity' passage from Canto 81 and the morning incantation of Canto 79:

[quotes *Cantos*, p. 521 'The moon has' to 'field of lynxes'.]

In the new section of Cantos, the only such passage occurs in Canto 106:

[quotes *Cantos*, p. 779 'Athene Pronoia' to 'that blossom'.]

Even this will turn up enough difficulties for those inclined to write scholarly articles; yet the lyric thrust tends to carry one past them. In most of the remaining cantos, however, one is bounced about from place to place and era to era in a way that I find completely mind-scattering. For instance, reading the beginning of Canto 98, all my schoolboy instincts rise: my hand goes up—I can do the 'Agada . . .' line; I *have* looked up my Frobenius (and very much enjoyed it, sir) and know where the Fasa heroes stopped in their reincarnation of Wagudu. *Very good, young man; now, what of Leucothea?* Well, I think I USED to know, sir. *How interesting; and Ocellus?* But sir, but sir, I can translate the Greek . . . please? . . . *I see. Then will you show us how the Greek phrases relate to the passage as a whole and to the Chinese character?*

I cannot. I know that I have disgraced myself. When the super-intendents, Mr. [Peter] Russell and Mr. Kenner, come through, I will be held up as a bad example. Surely I will be sent to bed early, alone and supperless, to sit up hours in the hope of doing better tomorrow.

Life by examination loses, eventually, some of its glamour. It is not just that one does not wish to learn; one hates to learn always for the purposes of others. If one wishes to know about Sir Edward Coke (and I should think most people would benefit by that knowledge), one would rather go to Catherine Drinker Bowen or to one of the standard historical treatments; however doctrinaire such treatments might be-come, they would at least give us (merely by giving us an extended handling of the subject) the opportunity to think about that subject and so to reach conclusions of our own. Pound's phrase-flash technique, however, never permits us to have thoughts—only to memorize a cer-tain number of incidents as examples of a pre-fixed meaning. It is like having one's meat pre-chewed by a solicitous mother, then passed down the table until it reaches us. Much like the Bible (cf. Auerbach's discus-sion of its paucity of detail),[1] the Cantos demand our complete spiritual subjection. It would be proper to call it, not a 'poem containing history' as its blurbs ambiguously claim, but rather 'a poem using history.'

The jacket blurb for the preceding section of Cantos, *Rock-Drill*, describes Pound's theme as 'the domination of benevolence.' No doubt that is what Pound intends. Yet, I think we are right to view that

[1] Discussed in the first chapter of Auerbach's *Mimesis: The Representation of Reality in Western Literature* (1953).

benevolence with some reserve. As Simone Weil points out, those who find themselves without political power are always, for the moment, 'on the side of justice, the general good, and things of that kind, that is to say, among the beautiful things which don't exist.' When they achieve power, they must face facts once again—including the facts of their own intention. And if I am to judge from that area where Pound *has* power— poetry—his insistent domination of my mind grows finally very binding and distressing.

I think we do well to suspect that domination regardless of stated intentions. I find the urge to enlist under any benevolent Throne or State (existent or nonexistent), thoroughly resistible; I am continually reminded that it was the Army indoctrination course which most suc- cessfully used the flash-card, teaching us to select those we would kill with a minimum of thought beforehand.

140. John Holloway, review, *London Magazine*

June 1960, vii, 81–2

Holloway (b. 1920), English critic and poet, is Professor of English Literature at Cambridge.

Pound's name is too often invoked as a war-cry by those absorbed in literary polemics and label-pasting. An effort has to be made if the real interest of *Thrones*, the latest instalment of the Cantos, is to be located. It does not lie in Pound's specific ideas for social policy (taken by them- selves these are sometimes trite and sometimes faddish), nor in his bare juxtaposition of ideas, omitting connecting links (this is ancient history); nor of course does it lie in the conventionally beautiful passages (aston- ishing as these are) which occur in this enigmatic work from time to time. But by now the Cantos can be seen to express a comprehensive vision, almost a mystical one, of human life as a part of total reality. As the poem has gone on, Pound's key ideas have been coming more and more substantially ('clearly' is hardly the word) into relation. No doubt what I say here is very much subject to error, but it seems to me that Pound is preoccupied with gold in currency matters (and hence with credit) because he sees gold as also the key substance in the work of the craftsman and artist, and again as the counterpart, in both these fields, to light and to the sun itself in life as a whole: finally, the link is then possible with light as intellectual clarity, the Chinese *ming* as he likes to call it. As for physical light, it is moving stone; and stone the embodiment in matter of a rule of law in men's affairs which is no set of mere rules, but a total mode of life. Thus the stone temple, the integrity of the mason (and with him every other manifestation of *techne* and genuine labour, of which Pound's sense is wonderfully authentic), the work of the good ruler, and the pulsating light-filled radiance of the natural world, all come together. The vision takes shape:

> The sages of Han had a saying
> Manners are from earth and from water . . .
> . . . the peoples
> Different each, different customs
> but one root in the equities,
> One in acumen,
> with the sun (chih)
> under it all

This is from Canto 99, one of those in *Thrones*. A full discussion would take one far back through the poem (at least to Canto 17): but this latest instalment does much to clarify the basic vision of the Cantos, and as such it has an outstanding claim to attention.

141. Louis Simpson, 'A Swift Kick in the Rhetoric', *Book Week*

2 January 1966, iii, 5, 15

This is a review of *Cantos (1–95)* and *Ezra Pound Perspectives*, edited by Noel Stock (Chicago: Regnery, 1965).

Simpson (b. 1923), American poet, teaches at the State University of New York, Stony Brook. His *Selected Poems* appeared in 1966.

In 1908, when Pound arrived in London, there had been no serious thinking about poetry in English for a hundred years. Symons had introduced Yeats to the French symbolists, but that was all. Those who published and reviewed poetry used Palgrave's *Golden Treasury* as the touchstone of verse. There was no criticism, only a genteel agreement between such men as Walter Raleigh at Oxford and J. C. Squire in Fleet Street that rhymed lines about Nature in the home counties were poetic. For deep thinkers there was A. E. Housman. The Romantic tradition in England had sunk to banalities from which it has not fully recovered.

Then Pound with his red hair began haunting the environs of the British Museum, carrying Imagist poems and the manuscripts of foreign poets in translation. He proceeded to insult the 'tradition':

Here are a list of facts on which I and 9,000,000 other poets have spieled endlessly: 1. Spring is a pleasant season. 2. The flowers, etc. etc. sprout, bloom, etc. etc. 3. Love, a delightsome tickling. Indefinable etc. . . . . 4. Trees, hills etc. are by a provident nature arranged diversely, in diverse places. . . .

To anyone who would listen, unknown beginning writers such as Hemingway, and authors of reputation such as Yeats, he explained what writing was:

Poetry must be *as well written as prose*. Its language must be a fine language, departing in no way from speech save by a heightened intensity (i.e. simplicity). There must be no book words, no periphrases, no inversions. . . . There must be no interjections. No words flying off to nothing. . . . Rhythm *must* have meaning. . . . There must be no cliches, set phrases, stereotyped journalese. The only escape from such is by precision, a result of concentrated attention to what is writing. . . .

Pound's ideas are responsible for most of the good writing in verse in the 20th century, and for a good deal of the prose too. But at the time, they were not ingratiating. As he went about London, cajoling or bullying people into writing better, showing his manuscripts from the Provençal or Chinese and poems by his friends, including a ridiculous American thing about someone named Prufrock, Pound made himself hated. He was attacking the 'tradition.' Now as we look back, it is easy to see that it was Pound who was the traditionalist: his enemies were merely ignorant.

As the public that does not read poetry but reads newspapers knows, Pound made some radio broadcasts during World War II under the auspices of Mussolini. After the war he was arrested for treason, found insane, and confined for years in an American hospital. And, while his indiscretions were still fresh, he was given a Bollingen award for 'American' poetry.

This was a scandal. At that time I attended a dinner of some society poets, at which the master of ceremonies impugned the motives of the Bollingen judges. Another speaker compared Pound's Cantos to the ravings of a maniac. In those circles, it seemed, Pound could be vilified. They didn't mind his political ideas, but they still hated him for what he had done to the 'tradition,' their kind of junk. If Pound has had enemies, however, he has also had friends. In the next moment a young poet took the microphone, said that he was ashamed to be present, and walked off the platform. Then a very famous poet indeed, who was sitting at the end of the guest table, had a coughing fit in his handkerchief and slipped away behind a screen, not to reappear. Sensation! At the table where I was, a gentleman-poet rose to his feet in anguish and exclaimed, 'And with Mrs. —— here! What will she say!' Mrs. —— was one of the rich people who supported poetry in America, or rather, retarded it.

Whenever I am tempted to criticize Pound harshly, as I am whenever I have to read the Cantos, I think of that dinner and what poetry would be like today if Pound had not existed.

Above all, he gave us a language to write in. Poetry contains ideas, but unless the language of verse has a relation to the language in which men really think in their own time, then the best ideas are still-born.

Pound made poets look at things as they were, and say what they truly saw and felt. He gave us 'something to read in normal circumstances.' He revitalized poetry as Wordsworth had a hundred years before. And his teaching is still urgent, for the ignoramuses, society-poets and mis-users of language always come creeping back. And some of them take strange shapes, for they have read the Cantos and wear the costume of the avant-garde—1910. But you can be sure that if Pound were a young man today, he would not write like his imitators. Pound was not a great poet. The success of his ideas is due to Eliot, who was.

In the Cantos you can see most clearly what Pound lacked—an identity. He had ideas, he had an excellent gift of mimicry—at one moment he has caught the voice of Browning, at another, that of a condottiere—but he never had a center of his own. And he was oddly naive, unable to think beyond appearances. He could not see that his famous Usury was not a cause, but a symptom. He thought that men go to war because of a conspiracy of arms-manufacturers. The so-called difficulties of the Cantos are all on the surface, in the refer-ences; underneath there is emptiness. Here and there, especially in the anthology-piece on Vanity, perhaps because Pound himself was vain, he experiences an idea:

[quotes *Cantos*, pp. 556–7 'What thou lovest' to 'outdone your eleg-ance.']

Pound is now 80 years old. In *Ezra Pound: Perspectives*, a number of poets and critics bear witness to his influence and their loyalty. Collec-tions like this can be embarrassing, but this collection is refreshingly honest. There is, for example, Herbert Read's remark:

A man who sets out (1908) with the idea that 'no art ever yet grew by looking into the eyes of the public' is bound to find himself increasingly isolated from the social matrix that ensures 'sanity' (which admittedly may be no more than an accepted code of conduct).

This has been Pound's tragedy, and the tragedy of all serious writers in the modern world. One does not want to hate society, but society being what it is, how can one stomach it? So the artist—Eliot, Joyce, Hemingway—the list goes on—creates a world of his own. It may be a very fine world indeed—as Proust's or Yeats' is—but it is invisible to the public at large, and the cost to the creator, in isolation, is terriffic.

As you might expect, the contributions to *Perspectives* by A. Alvarez and Hugh Kenner are careful examinations of Pound's method. Allen

Tate has an essay that discourses in a dignified manner, but as is the case with most of Mr. Tate's writings, I am not sure what the dignity consists of. And there is a tribute by Hugh MacDiarmid, the poet of Scotland, who happens to be a Communist. I do not know which to admire more, the teaching of Pound or the agreement of these disciples.

A LUME SPENTO AND OTHER EARLY POEMS

New York, 30 October 1965
London, 6 January 1966

---

142. Peter Levi, S.J., on the earliest Pound, *Jubilee*

February 1966

Levi (b. 1931) is an English poet and Fellow of Campion Hall, Oxford.

Ezra Pound, the only poet of the modern movement still alive, is eighty years old. In English poetry his achievement and influence have been dazzling and are still uncalculated. Pound started to write among the influences of the nineties and published his first book in 1908, when the mature powers of Eliot and even the strength of Pound's own talent were hardly a dream; now that the modern movement has passed its climax and before its work can be disentangled from a general atmosphere of excitement it is a useful, interesting, pleasant thing to have Pound's earliest poems, *A Lume Spento* with an appendix of other early work, reprinted in a fine new edition. Rereading these poems with hindsight we shall find in them a surprising degree of Pound's most characteristic virtues of language and most typical interests. They are in a sense a very ninetyish collection and one can see how the dandy self-consciousness of the nineties determined the revolutionary mannerism of modern poetry.

This beautiful book is in fact the first complete reprint of *A Lume Spento* since the original edition of 1908, and as that edition was of only a hundred copies this re-publication has genuine and considerable importance. Pound has apparently been reluctant to let such early work reappear, and has contributed a magnificent prefatory growl beginning 'A collection of stale cream puffs. Chocolate creams who hath forgotten you? . . . No lessons to be learned save the depth of ignorance or rather the superficiality of non-perception.' The strictures are justified but comparatively unimportant. The nineties literary movement, the heavy fragrance of which hangs like a mist over Pound's early poems, had a disorienting and in the end a releasing effect on educated taste, which, through a few poets of great genius, first opened the possibilities of the modern movement. In this process the work of Pound and of Yeats was central. These soft, rhythmic phrases and this breath of too many hothouse flowers were the adolescence of the modern Muse. She is now old and for the first time able to feel tolerant of those years: the Muse has forgiven Dowson and Lionel Johnson; she can leaf with indulgent interest through the early poems of Pound.

Looking back at the promise of genius when it was only promise is always in a way vertiginous: when the mists of sentiment clear, one asks oneself (confronted by nothing but youth, talent, uncertainty) whether one could really have forecast the wonderful future, and whether in fact future poems had any reality at that time? Pound's first book was on its own terms delightful—the vitality, sweetness, harshness and wit of this young poet were like a robust body bursting through make-believe clothes. In any terms he was already in 1909 a young poet with a fundamental strength and some odd and interesting aspects. But one is reminded of F. Scott Fitzgerald's metaphor about a young novel-ist: one is not interested in a soldier who is only partly brave, and in the life of a good writer all that talent represents is the physical qualifications for entry to West Point. Pound became a great poet only in writing his great poems.

143. Colin Falck, review, *Encounter*

August 1966, xxvii, 82

Falck (b. 1934), English poet and critic, was educated at Magdalen College, Oxford. He is now teaching at a technical college in London.

Precision, that great basic principle of Imagism (not that they were the first to discover it) was the basis on which Eliot's whole articulation of personal emotion into poetry was built. ('The exact curve of the thing', said T. E. Hulme.) The American 'projective verse' theorists who have rejected Imagism as too static—and who have disowned Eliot altogether —have only succeeded in finding yet another way of replacing imagination with talk. Few of their poems contain any images at all, and the way that they have followed Ezra Pound and William Carlos Williams in their anti-symbolist war on the shaping spirit suggests that they are really more interested in America than they are in poetry. That *il miglior fabbro* has many virtues as a poet has long been clear, but we are reminded by the diffuse, medievalised lyricism of the early poems republished in *A Lume Spento* that the ability to make significant forms out of his own emotions was never one of them. If one can somehow ignore what they actually say, there are lines in these poems where Pound's superb later free verse can be heard faintly twitching inside the iambics:

> Or come as faint blown wind across the strings
> Of this old lute of mine imaginings
> And make it whisper me quaint runes and high.

But Pound's pre-Imagist lute is so old that for the most part the interest of this collection is about as antiquarian as the subjects of most of its runes. (Stale creampuffs, says E. P. in his own disparaging foreword of 1964.)

144. Hayden Carruth, 'On a Picture of Ezra Pound', *Poetry*

May 1967, cx, 103-5

Carruth (b. 1921), American poet, was educated at the University of North Carolina and the University of Chicago. An earlier essay, 'The Poetry of Ezra Pound', appeared in *Perspectives* (1956), No. 16, 129-59.

It is an ordinary half-tone reproduction snipped from a magazine, pinned with silver thumbtacks to the rough-wood wall. I no longer remember the photographer's name, unfortunately. But it is a wonderful portrait of the poet as elder, as prophet, and most people who care anything about Ezra Pound must know it: the flashing white hair and beard, the dark, deep, almost blind-looking eyes, the attitude of stubborn concern; and then the other objects in the picture, arranged, perhaps accidentally, in shapes of meaning: an out-of-focus, black swirl of foliage behind the poet's head, figuring the tragedy of all our minds, a wide and lucid sky, 'the light there almost solid', and in the distance a campanile, I don't know which, showing the strong lines and planes of the great age of Italian architecture. Pound does not like symbols—

> In nature are signatures
> needing no verbal tradition

—and neither do I, but these 'signatures' are unmistakable. Even the silver-headed tacks and the hemlock grain of my wall make parts of the composition.

Not long ago when I mentioned casually, thinking it nothing exceptional, to a distinguished poet and editor of the 'anti-academic' school—and I use quotation marks because I have no more taste than anyone for these tags, though we all must use them:—when I mentioned to him that Pound had been one of the great influences upon my own writing, he was incredulous. 'You?' he replied. 'Why, you've got John Crowe Ransom written all over you'—or words to that effect. In truth I do think some of Mr. Ransom's poems are minor masterpieces. I have read them with care. But the poetry of Ezra Pound came to me earlier and much more strongly. In point of fact the first book of modern American poetry I bought was the 1938 edition of Williams's *Collected Poems*, and the second was the 1926 edition of Pound's *Personae*.

Not that it matters for me directly; at least not much. But it matters for Pound, and hence for me indirectly as one of his . . . well, one of his thousands upon thousands of disciples: the word is exact, for he has given us our discipline. American civilization, we all know, is excessive, and so doubtless we must look for excess from its literary movements. But when I see Ezra Pound's example appropriated exclusively by one or another group of poets, it seems to me that this is a diminution of his place in our world and that I must do what I can to correct it; for in respect to Pound several possibilities should be borne in mind. First, the possibility of preferring—and preference is not dogma—the poems of *Lustra, Cathay*, 'Propertius', and 'Mauberley', which Pound wrote at the same time as his influential prose statements of theory and criticism, to much of the Cantos, which he wrote at a considerably later period. Second, the possibility that Pound by himself re-invented the poetic line as the unit of poetry, variable and end-stopped, that his concept of modern verse measure was clearer and more workable than anyone else's, and that he came to it long before Williams conceived his notion of the variable foot. Third, the possibility—indeed, it is much more— that Pound was as closely associated with Eliot as with Williams *throughout their lives*, that on the other hand he damned London as heartily as he did Concord, and that his immense influence has descended *equally*, though no doubt differently, through the entire conspectus of Anglo-American writing to the present day; for example, if I do not know it as a fact, being unacquainted with Mr. Ransom personally, I am still certain that the best of his poetic practice, as in his use of the line-measure, was learned from Pound. Fourth and my last, although the points could be extended a long way, the possibility that Pound had the first and clearest view of the inter-objective relationship between poetry and nature, as distinct from Eliot and the Symbolists, and that he has maintained this view for sixty years while at the same time affirming, not rejecting, the values of international thought and culture *in se*, whether established or disestablished.

Pound is the leader, at the very forefront. Yet because of that, para-doxically he is at the center too: so much—one is inclined to say every-thing—comes from him. We at the center have a difficult time, often enough; always defining and redefining our position, entering correctives to the debonair pronouncements of the extremes. *Not* rationalism, we say somewhat acidly, but let us at least be reasonable; not positivism, but not enigma either; and in the matter of fashion, yes, we are friends with Robert Lowell, but we are friends with Robert Creeley too. It is a difficult work. But we take comfort from knowing that Pound is one of us, a man of the center, and that the love of proportion and justice requires, not a baser passion, as some assert, but on the contrary, as in his writing, the strongest and purest passion of all.

DRAFTS AND FRAGMENTS OF
CANTOS CX–CXVII

New York, 31 December 1968
London, 23 February 1970

145. Herbert Leibowitz, from 'The Muse and the News', *Hudson Review*

Autumn 1969, xxii, 501–2

Leibowitz (b. 1935), American literary critic, was educated at Brooklyn College, Brown University and Columbia, where he now teaches. He is the author of a book about Hart Crane, editor of a collection of Paul Rosenfeld's music criticism, and editor of *Salmagundi*.

Ezra Pound, the last survivor of the great generation of modernist poets, has issued some further *Drafts and Fragments of Cantos CX–CXVII*. If they do not clarify and round off that strangest and knottiest of long poems—at this late date that would be futile to hope—they are not simply the exhuming of literary remains, additions to an antiquarian's collection of curiosities like Isaac D'Israeli's, or harangues on economics. Like some visionary architect still perfecting the grand plan of his life, Pound cannot let go of this petted child. Passages of private ruminations, ideograms, and references are as obscure as those of a scrivener scratching mandarin lines on cuneiform, but the poems, fragmented as they may be, constitute an act of public contrition, a poetic last will and testament, that is very moving. The poet, for Pound, is the sun, 'God's eye,' and in old age he recalls his service to Artemis the goddess of beauty, and the times when 'came Neptunus/ his mind *leaping*/ like dolphins,/ The concepts the human mind has attained./ To make Cosmos—/ To achieve the possible—'. Like a Chekhovian character standing in his 'ruined orchard,' he admits his failure to enlarge the mind's space and let the 'unstill' river of time flow through it, 'to make gods out of beauty' in his encyclopedic poem.:

> Can you enter the great acorn of light?
>   But the beauty is not the madness
> Tho' my errors and wrecks lie about me. . . .
> I cannot make it cohere.
> If love be not in the house there is nothing.

'A little light / in great darkness,' 'like a rushlight / to lead back to splendour': the plight of poetry in a barbaric age and Pound's pittance of comfort in understanding late that unless justice derives from magnanimity, men will be destroyers. There are phrases and lines in these cantos that in limpidity and color and stately music match the phrases of *A Lume Spento* and *Pavannes and Divisions*.

146. Derwent May, review, *Observer*

15 March, 1970, 38

May (b. 1930), English critic, novelist, and literary editor of the *Listener*, was educated at Lincoln College, Oxford. He was co-editor of *Oxford Poetry 1952*.

The new set of scraps from Ezra Pound is more strictly for devotees. Even the fullest of these drafts for further Cantos are not so much mutterings as mumblings. But what one does hear often sounds remorseful and gentle:

> When one's friends hate each other
>   how can there be peace in the world?
> Their asperities diverted me in my green time.

The 'light' imagery so common in the later Cantos is also more modest. Canto CXVI here ends with the thought of

A little light, like a rushlight
To lead back to splendour.

But Pound's old preoccupation with the sin of usury persists, and here gets qualification; 104 per cent is 'usura', but 12 per cent is apparently acceptable to Pound as 'interest'. Which should give comfort in some quarters.

APPENDIX
The Printing of Pound's Works 1908–60

A selected list

The publications listed are those for which printing figures are available. See Donald Gallup, *A Bibliography of Ezra Pound* (second impression, corrected, London, 1969).

TITLE	PLACE OF PUBLICATION	DATE	QUANTITY	PRICE
A Lume Spento	Venice	1908	100	$1.00
A Quinzaine for This Yule	London	1909	100	1s. 6d.
Personae	London	1909	1,000 sheets printed, not more than 500 issued	2s. 6d.
Exultations	London	1909	1,000 sheets printed, not more than 500 issued	2s. 6d.
The Spirit of Romance	London and New York	1910	1,250 sheets printed, 300 for U.S.A.	6s. $2.50
Canzoni	London	1911	1,000 sheets printed, not more than 500 issued	3s. 6d.
Canzoni and Ripostes	London	1913	not more than 500	3s. 6d.
Cathay	London	1915	1,000	1s.
Catholic Anthology	London	1915	500	3s. 6d.
Ripostes (re-issue)	London	1915	400	1s.
Gaudier-Brzeska	London and New York	1916	1,000 sheets printed, not more than 450 used, about 200 for U.S.A.	12s. 6d. $3.50
Lustra	London	1916	800 trade, 200 unabridged	5s.
Certain Noble Plays of Japan	Churchtown	1916	350	11s.

TITLE	PLACE OF PUBLICATION	DATE	QUANTITY	PRICE
'Noh' or Accomplishment	London	1917	1,250 sheets printed	7s. 6d.
Dialogues of Fontenelle	London	1917	500	1s. 3d.
Quia Pauper Amavi	London	1919	500	6s.
Hugh Selwyn Mauberley	London	1920	200	15s.
Umbra	London	1920	probably 1,000	8s.
Indiscretions	Paris	1923	300	45 F.
Antheil and The Treatise on Harmony	Paris	1924	600	10 F.
A Draft of XVI Cantos	Paris	1925	90	400 F.
A Draft of the Cantos 17–27	London	1928	101	5 gns
Selected Poems	London	1928	1,000	7s. 6d.
A Draft of XXX Cantos	Paris	1930	220	40s. and 10 gns
Guido Cavalcanti Rime	Genoa	1932	about 500	L. 75
Profile	Milan	1932	250	$3.00
A Draft of XXX Cantos	New York and London	1933	1,500 in U.S.A., 1,000 in London	$2.50 7s. 6d.
ABC of Economics	London	1933	2,031 sheets printed, 300 for U.S.A., 720 destroyed during Second World War	3s. 6d.
Active Anthology	London	1933	1,516 sheets printed, 750 destroyed during Second World War	7s. 6d.
ABC of Reading	London and New York	1934	2,000 in London, 1,016 in U.S.A.	4s. 6d. $2.00
Make It New	London	1934	1,600	12s. 6d.
Eleven New Cantos XXXI–XLI	New York	1934	1,500, 500 used in second issue in 1940	$1.50
Homage to Sextus Propertius	London	1934	1,000	2s. 6d.
A Draft of Cantos XXXI–XLI	London	1935	1,500	6s.
Make It New	New Haven	1935	1,000	$3.75
Social Credit	London	1935	4,000	6d.
Chinese Written Character	London	1936	2,000	5s.

TITLE	PLACE OF PUBLICATION	DATE	QUANTITY	PRICE
Fifth Decad of Cantos	London and New York	1937	1,012 in London, 750 in U.S.A.	6s. $1.50
Guide to Kulchur	London	1938	1,487 sheets printed, 520 for U.S.A., 230 destroyed during Second World War	10s. 6d.
Cantos LII–LXXI	London and Norfolk, Conn.	1940	1,000 in London, 1,000 in U.S.A.	10s. 6d. $2.50
A Selection of Poems	London	1940	7,100	2s. 6d.
ABC of Economics	Norfolk, Conn.	1940	300	$2.00
The Pisan Cantos	Norfolk, Conn. and London	1948, 1949	1,527 in U.S.A., 1,976 in London	$9.75 12s. 6d.
The Cantos	New York	1948	2,897	$5.00
Selected Poems	New York	1948	3,400	$1.50
Seventy Cantos	London	1950	1,633	25s.
Letters	New York and London	1950, 1951	4,000 in U.S.A., 2,990 in London	$5.00 25s.
Translations	London and New York	1953	1,398 in London, 4,863 in U.S.A.	30s. $6.00
Literary Essays	London and New York	1954	1,745 in London, 5,000 in U.S.A.	30s. $6.00
Selected Poems	New York	1957	9,993	$1.15
Section: Rock-Drill	New York and London	1956, 1957	2,081 in U.S.A., 2,000 in London	$3.00 12s. 6d.
Sophokles: Women of Trachis	London and New York	1956, 1957	1,000 in London, 3,000 in U.S.A.	10s. 6d. $3.00
Pavannes and Divagations	New York and London	1958, 1960	4,000 in U.S.A., 1,000 in London	$4.75 25s.
Thrones	New York and London	1959, 1960	3,000 in U.S.A., 2,290 in London	$3.50 18s.

Bibliography

I CHECKLISTS

There is a useful preliminary compilation of reviews and criticism in the *Pound Newsletter* (1954-6), and a bibliography on Pound's trial after the war, and on the Bollingen controversy, in *A Casebook on Ezra Pound*, edited by William Van O'Connor and Edward Stone (1959). Marie Hénault has compiled *The Merrill Checklist of Ezra Pound* (1970). This is the closest approach to a comprehensive list of comment on Pound, though it is not complete.

II SECONDARY MATERIAL

MEMOIRS

One after another of Pound's contemporaries wrote accounts of how he seemed to them.

AIKEN, CONRAD, *Ushant: An Essay* (1952).

ALDINGTON, RICHARD, *Life for Life's Sake* (1941).

ANDERSON, MARGARET, *My Thirty Years' War* (1930).

BARRY, IRIS, 'The Ezra Pound Period', *Bookman* (October 1931).

BEACH, SYLVIA, *Shakespeare and Company* (1959).

BRYHER [ANNIE WINIFRED ELLERMAN], *The Heart to Artemis: A Writer's Memoirs* (1963).

CARNEVALI, EMANUEL, *Autobiography*, compiled and prefaced by Kay Boyle (1967).

COURNOS, JOHN, *Autobiography* (1935).

COWLEY, MALCOLM, *Exile's Return* (1934).

CROSBY, CARESSE, *The Passionate Years* (1955).

CUNARD, NANCY, *These Were the Hours* (1971).

DE RACHEWILTZ, MARY, *Discretions* (1971), an autobiographical memoir by Pound's daughter.

FLETCHER, JOHN GOULD, *Life is My Song* (1937).

FLINT, F. S., 'History of Imagism', *Egoist* (1 May 1915).

GOLDRING, DOUGLAS, *South Lodge* (1943).

HEMINGWAY, ERNEST, *A Moveable Feast* (1964).

KREYMBORG, ALFRED, *Troubadour* (1925).

MCALMON, ROBERT, *Being Geniuses Together* (1938), revised with supplementary chapters by Kay Boyle in 1968.

MONROE, HARRIET, *A Poet's Life* (1938).

PATMORE, BRIGIT, *My Friends When Young* (1968).

PUTNAM, SAMUEL, *Paris Was Our Mistress* (1947).

STEIN, GERTRUDE, *The Autobiography of Alice B. Toklas* (1932).

WILLIAMS, W. C., *Autobiography* (1951).

BIOGRAPHICAL AND HISTORICAL STUDIES

BULLOUGH, GEOFFREY, *The Trend of Modern Poetry* (1934).

COFFMAN, STANLEY K., *Imagism: A Chapter for the History of Modern Poetry* (1951).

FRASER, G. S., *The Modern Writer and His World* (1953).

GILMER, WALKER, *Horace Liveright: Publisher of the Twenties* (1970).

GOLDRING, DOUGLAS, *The Last Pre-Raphaelite: A Record of the Life and Writings of Ford Madox Ford* (1948).

GRANT, JOY, *Harold Monro and the Poetry Bookshop* (1967).

GREENBAUM, LEONARD, *The Hound & Horn: The History of a Literary Quarterly* (1966).

GREGORY, HORACE, and ZATURENSKA, MARYA, *A History of American Poetry 1900–1940* (1946).

HALPERT, STEPHEN, with JOHNS, RICHARD eds, *A Return to Pagany: The History, Correspondence, and Selections from a Little Magazine 1929–1932* (1969).

HAMBURGER, MICHAEL, *The Truth of Poetry: Tensions in Modern Poetry from Baudelaire to the 1960s* (1969).

HASSALL, CHRISTOPHER, *Edward Marsh* (1959).

HOUGH, GRAHAM, *Image and Experience: Studies in a Literary Revolution* (1960).

HUGHES, GLENN, *Imagism and the Imagists* (1931).

HUTCHINS, PATRICIA, *Ezra Pound's Kensington: An Exploration, 1885–1913* (1965).

HYNES, SAMUEL, *The Edwardian Turn of Mind* (1968).

JONES, A. R., *The Life and Opinions of T. E. Hulme* (1960).

LIDDERDALE, JANE, and NICHOLSON, MARY, *Dear Miss Weaver: Harriet Shaw Weaver 1876–1961* (1970).

MACSHANE, FRANK, *The Life and Work of Ford Madox Ford* (Routledge & Kegan Paul, 1965).

MACSHANE, FRANK, ed., *Ford Madox Ford: The Critical Heritage* (Routledge & Kegan Paul, 1972).

MARTIN, WALLACE, *The 'New Age' Under Orage* (1967).

MINER, EARL, *The Japanese Tradition in British and American Literature* (1958).

MIZENER, ARTHUR, *The Saddest Story* (1971).

PEARCE, ROY HARVEY, *The Continuity of American Poetry* (1965).

PRESS, JOHN, *A Map of Modern Verse* (1969), a critical anthology.

REID, B. L., *The Man From New York: John Quinn and His Friends* (1968).

ROSE, W. K., 'Ezra Pound and Wyndham Lewis: The Crucial Years', *Southern Review* (winter 1968).

ROSS, ROBERT H., *The Georgian Revolt* (1965).

SPEARS, MONROE K., *Dionysus and the City: Modernism in Twentieth-Century Poetry* (1970).

STEAD, C. K., *The New Poetic* (1964).

TAUPIN, RENE, *L'Influence de symbolisme français sur la poèsie américaine (de 1910 à 1920)* (1929).

WASSERSTROM, WILLIAM, *The Time of 'The Dial'* (1963).

LETTERS

Relevant collections include those of D. H. Lawrence (1932), Florence Ayscough and Amy Lowell (1945), Hart Crane (1952), Gertrude Stein (1953), W. B. Yeats (1954), T. E. Lawrence (1954), W. C. Williams (1957), James Joyce (1957, 1966), H. L. Mencken (1961), Wyndham Lewis (1963), Robert Frost (1964), Ford Madox Ford (1965), Edward Thomas (1968), Carl Sandburg (1968), and E. E. Cummings (1970).

CRITICISM

Among the most interesting critical comment not included here:

AIKEN, CONRAD, review of *Personae* (*New Republic*, 22 June 1927) (i.e. not No. 149) is collected in *A Reviewer's ABC* (1961)

BLACKMUR, R. P. 'The Masks of Ezra Pound' (*Hound and Horn*, January–March 1934) is reprinted in *Ezra Pound: A Critical Anthology*, edited by J. P. Sullivan (1970). Blackmur's 'An Adjunct to the Muses' Diadem' is reprinted in *American Critical Essays: Twentieth Century*, edited by Harold Beaver (1959). Both essays are collected in Blackmur's *Language as Gesture* (1952).

CONNOLLY, CYRIL, review of *Literary Essays* (*Sunday Times*, 14 February 1954), voicing his doubts at the 'very tiny trail' blazed by Pound, is collected in *Previous Convictions* (1963).

DAVIE, DONALD, *Ezra Pound: Poet as Sculptor* (1964, Routledge & Kegan Paul, 1965); the chapter on *Rock-Drill* is reprinted in *Modern Poetry: Essays in Criticism*, edited by John Hollander (1968) and an excerpt is included in *New Approaches to Ezra Pound*, edited by Eva Hesse. Davie first suggested the importance of Adrian Stokes in an essay in *Twentieth Century* (November 1956) and he contributed a detailed analysis of 'Mauberley' to *The Pelican Guide to English Literature: VII, The Modern Age*, edited by Boris Ford (1961). His *Articulate Energy* (Routledge & Kegan Paul, 1955) includes important chapters on Hulme and Fenollosa.

ELIOT, T. S.: A collected edition of his work is planned, and it was not possible to include any of the following:
Review of '*Noh*', or *Accomplishment* in *Egoist* (August 1917).
Ezra Pound: His Metric and Poetry (1917). reprinted in *To Criticize the Critic and Other Writings* (1965), and in *Modern Poetry: Essays in Criticism*, edited by John Hollander (1968).
'A Note on Ezra Pound', *To-day* (September 1918).
Review of *Quia Pauper Amavi* in *Athenaeum* (24 October 1919).
Review of *Personae* in *Dial* (January 1928).
'Introduction', *Ezra Pound: Selected Poems* (1928).
A passage in *After Strange Gods* (1934).
'On a Recent Piece of Criticism', *Purpose* (April–June 1938).
'Ezra Pound', *Poetry* (September 1946); reprinted in *Ezra Pound: A Collection of Critical Essays*, edited by Walter Sutton (1963).

KENNER, HUGH: It was not possible to come to a satisfactory agreement with Professor Kenner to include any of his numerous writings about Pound. A selected list includes:
Review of *The Pisan Cantos* in *Hudson Review* (Winter 1949).
Review of *Patria Mia* in *Hudson Review* (Autumn 1950).
The Poetry of Ezra Pound (1951); the chapter on 'Mauberley' is reprinted in *Ezra Pound: A Collection of Critical Essays*, edited by Walter Sutton (1963).
Review of *Letters* in *Kenyon Review* (Spring 1951).
Review of *Confucius: Great Digest and Unwobbling Pivot* in *Poetry* (October 1952).
'Introduction', *The Translations of Ezra Pound* (1953).

Review of *The Spirit of Romance* and *Kulchur* in *Poetry* (October 1953).

'The Broken Mirrors and the Mirror of Memory' in *Motive and Method in the 'Cantos' of Ezra Pound*, edited by Lewis Leary (1954).

Review of *Classic Anthology* in *Poetry* (December 1954).

Review of *Section: Rock-Drill* in *Hudson Review* (Autumn 1956); reprinted in Hugh Kenner, *Gnomon* (1958).

Review of *Women of Trachis* in *Poetry*, July 1957.

'Ezra Pound and the Light of France' in Hugh Kenner, *Gnomon* (1958).

'Ezra Pound and the Chinese', *Agenda* (October–November 1965).

'Leucothea's Bikini: Mimetic Homage' in *Ezra Pound Perspectives*, edited by Noel Stock (1965).

'Dante à travers Pound et Eliot', translated by Pierre Alien, *L'Herne: Ezra Pound*, edited by Dominique de Roux (1965).

'The Invention of China', *Spectrum*, Spring 1967.

Review of *Pound/Joyce* in *New York Times Book Review*, 7 January 1968.

'The Muse in Tatters', *Agenda*, Spring 1968.

'Blood For the Ghosts' in *New Approaches to Ezra Pound*, edited by Eva Hesse (1969).

The Pound Era (1972).

LEAVIS, F. R., chapter on Pound in *New Bearings in English Poetry* (1932) is reprinted in *Ezra Pound: A Collection of Critical Essays*, edited by Walter Sutton (1963). His review of *Active Anthology* (*Scrutiny*, December 1933) is reprinted in *A Selection from Scrutiny* (1968), and that of *Letters* (*Scrutiny*, June 1951) is collected in his own '*Anna Karenina*' and Other Essays (1967).

MOORE, MARIANNE, review of *XXX Cantos* (*Poetry*, October 1931) is collected in *A Marianne Moore Reader* (1965); there is 'A Tribute' in *Ezra Pound Perspectives*, edited by Noel Stock (1965), and 'A Note' in *Agenda* (October–November 1965).

TATE, ALLEN, review of *XXX Cantos* (*Nation*, 10 June 1931) was collected in *Reactionary Essays on Poetry and Ideas* (1936), and in *Collected Essays* (1959); Tate's 'Ezra Pound and the Bollingen Prize' is in *Collected Essays* and in *Ezra Pound Perspectives*, edited by Noel Stock (1965).

WILLIAMS, W. C., review of *XXX Cantos* (*Symposium*, April 1931) is collected in his *Selected Essays* (1954), in *Ezra Pound: A Collection of Critical Essays*, edited by Walter Sutton (1963), in *L'Herne: Ezra*

Pound, edited by Dominique de Roux (1965), and in *Ezra Pound: A Critical Anthology*, edited by J. P. Sullivan (1970).

WILSON, EDMUND, review of *Poems 1918–21* (*New Republic*, 19 April 1922) is collected in his *The Shores of Light* (1952).

YEATS, W. B., 'A Packet for Ezra Pound' (1927) is available in *A Vision* (revised edition 1937; frequently reprinted); the relevant passage is reprinted in *Ezra Pound: A Critical Anthology*, edited by J. P. Sullivan (1970). Yeats's Introduction to *The Oxford Book of Modern Verse* (1936), containing a trenchant, brief criticism of Pound, is reprinted in *Ezra Pound: A Collection of Critical Essays*, edited by Walter Sutton (1963), and in *Modern Poetry: Essays in Criticism*, edited by John Hollander (1968).

ZUKOFSKY, LOUIS, review of *XXX Cantos* (*Criterion*, April 1931) is collected in his *Prepositions* (1967). His 'American Poetry 1920–1930', with its interesting comparison of Pound with Robert Frost, and then to Robinson Jeffers, in *Symposium* (January 1931), is in the same volume.

POUND IN EUROPE

Save in Italy, where he lived and published extensively, Pound's European reputation is primarily a post-Bollingen Prize phenomenon. His work only became available in translation, other than in anthologies such as Eugene Jolas's *Anthologie de la Nouvelle Poésie Américaine* (1928) and Carlo Linati's *Scrittori Anglo-Americani d'Oggi* (1932), in the fifties. In Germany Eva Hesse translated *The Pisan Cantos* (1956), *ABC of Reading* (1957), *Women of Trachis* (1958), and *Personae* (1969), as well as editing and translating an anthology, *Dichtung und Prosa* (1953). She has also edited the most substantial volume of criticism in German, *Ezra Pound: 22 Versuche über einen Dichter* (1967). An English version appeared as *New Approaches to Ezra Pound* in 1969.

In France the situation has been basically similar, the majority of translations appearing in the fifties. Of particular interest in French criticism of Pound is Raymond Queneau's review of *Kulchur* in the *Nouvelle Revue Française* (October 1939), and Michel Butor's essay, 'La tentative poétique d'Ezra Pound', *Critique* (1956), xv, pp. 306–19, reprinted in Butor's *Répertoire: Etudes et Conférences 1948–1959* (1960). Dominique de Roux edited *Les Cahiers de l'Herne: Ezra Pound*, a lavish two-volume collection of translations of Pound's work, and a wide range of critical essays and *témoignages*.

Princess Mary de Rachewiltz, Pound's daughter, has translated *Gaudier-Brzeska* and *A Draft of XXX Cantos* into Italian. There is a useful survey of Italian criticism of Pound by A. M. Leonide Hornung, 'Pound et la critique italienne', in *L'Herne: Ezra Pound*.

No attempt has been made to represent European criticism of Pound here. The pressure of Anglo-American material was very great, and the reception they describe sufficiently complex, to warrant the exclusion of this material in the hope that a study, or an anthology, would do it justice in its own right.

Index

The index is divided into three sections: I. Ezra Pound's works; II. Characteristics and topics; III. General (including critics, periodicals, etc.).

I. EZRA POUND'S WORKS

ABC of Economics, 341, 437
ABC of Reading, 294, 324, 437
Active Anthology, 424
'Alba', 160, 175, 222
'Alba Innominata', 173
'Albatre', 124, 125
A Lume Spento, 2, 4, 42, 53, 60, 84, 476
A Lume Spento and Other Early Poems, 469–71
'An Immorality', 210
'Ancient Wisdom, Rather Cosmic', 115, 122, 124
'Ancora', 136, 210
'And Thus in Nineveh', 52, 54
Antheil and the Treatise on Harmony, 246
'Apparuit', 96, 179, 234
'Arides', 127, 129
'Aux Belles de Londres', 65, 175

'Ballad for Gloom', 3, 9, 53, 54, 56, 130
'Ballad of Life', 96
'Ballad of the Goodly Fere', 7, 19, 63, 64, 65, 66, 72, 74, 115, 173, 212, 218, 222
'The Beautiful Toilet', 108, 125
'Li Bel Chasteus', 80, 84
' "Blandula, Tenulla, Vagula" ', 82, 207

'Camaraderie', 59
'Cantico del Sole', 191
Cantos, 13, 15, 19, 20, 128, 202, 206, 214–17, 228, 237–8, 241, 246–72, 280, 292–9, 309–20, 324, 326–7, 335, 338–53, 359–87, 401–4, 416–21, 435–

45, 445–6, 447–64, 473; epic., 216, 253, 340–1, 364, 382, 403, 416–17, 445–6, 454; structure, 217, 241, 246, 259–61, 317, 339, 343–4, 352, 364–6, 378, 384, 397, 404, 417, 440, 441, 445, 456; subject, 241, 258, 269, 293, 314, 341, 348, 355, 363, 401–2 *see also* 'Three Cantos'
Cantos LII–LXXI, 22, 338–53
'Canzon: The Spear', 82
'Canzon: The Yearly Slain', 82, 179
Canzoni, 7, 8, 9, 10, 77–85, 96, 142, 164, 179, 390, 395
Carta da Visita, 437
Cathay, 11, 13, 19, 23, 108–11, 114, 124, 129, 134, 146, 147, 172, 173, 176, 181, 221, 234, 235, 351, 394, 396, 435, 473
Catholic Anthology, 4, 137
'Causa', 125
Certain Noble Plays of Japan, 12
'Cino', 51, 53, 71, 175, 392, 395
'Coitus', 121, 124
'The Coming of War: Actaeon', 129
'Commission', 121, 123, 129
'The Condolence', 101
The Confucian Analects, 412–14
'Contemporania', 9, 10, 11, 70, 107

'Dance Figure', 212
'De Aegypto', 80
'Defiance', 173
Des Imagistes, 11, 390
Dialogues of Fontenelle, 12, 136, 144
'Δώρια', 19, 96, 175

488

'Dr. Williams' Position', 424
A Draft of Cantos 1 7–27, 229
A Draft of XVI Cantos, 215–17, 229
A Draft of XXX Cantos, 20, 35, 246–72, 300, 418
Drafts and Fragments of Cantos CX–CXVII, 475–7

'Effects of Music upon a Company of People', 94, 96, 210–11
Eleven New Cantos XXXI–XLI, 292–9
'The Encounter', 129
'Epilogue', 10
'Epitaph', 123
'Era Mea', 80
'Erat Hora', 80
'Exile's Letter', 134
Exultations, 6, 36, 40, 41, 61–6, 82, 84, 97, 132, 171, 172, 174, 175, 179, 185, 196, 231, 390, 393, 395, 432

'Famam Librosque Cano', 36, 53, 395
'Fan-Piece for Her Imperial Lord', 129
'A Few Don'ts', 390
Fifth Decad of Cantos, 309–20
'Fish and the Shadow', 129, 210, 212
'For E.McC.', 53
'Formianus' Young Lady Friend', 210
'La Fraisne', 3, 53, 175, 176, 179, 211
'Francesca', 115, 173
'From Syria', 52
'From the Saddle', 52
'Further Instructions', 121, 123, 210, 212, 213

'The Garrett', 212
Gaudier-Brzeska: A Memoir, 118, 119–20, 324
'Grace Before Song', 41
Guide to Kulchur, 31, 35, 273, 332–7, 403
Guido Cavalcanti Rime, 273–9, 323–4

'Heather', 135
'Historical Survey', 191
'Histrion', 64, 66, 132–3, 395
'Homage to Sextus Propertius', 4, 14, 155–64, 166–7, 169–71, 173, 183–4,

204, 208, 223, 235–7; separate publication in 1934, 300–8, 320–9, 335, 393, 394, 395, 396, 416, 435, 473
'L'Homme Moyen Sensuel', 143, 146, 149
How to Read, 20
'Hugh Selwyn Mauberley', 16, 17, 20, 26, 194–5, 205–6, 208, 234–5, 245, 280–4, 300, 302, 307, 393, 395, 396, 397, 398, 402, 409, 416, 421, 435, 457, 473

'An Idyl for Glaucus', 52, 54, 62
'Impressions of François-Marie Arouet (de Voltaire)', 222
'In a Station of the Metro', 129, 135
Indiscretions, 403
'In Durance', 54, 395
'In Praise of Ysolt', 47, 52, 54, 175, 392
Instigations, 15, 16, 186–93, 207, 425, 430
'In Tempore Senectutis', 51, 54
'Ité', 128, 135

Jefferson and/or Mussolini, 31, 324, 353
'Jodindranath Mawhwor's Occupation', 144

'The Lake Isle', 123
'Lament of the Frontier Guard', 109, 181
'Langue d'Oc', 14, 160, 165, 183, 204
'Laudantes (decem pulchritudinis Johannae Templi)', 65
'Li Po', 115
Literary Essays of Ezra Pound, 422–34
'Liu Ch'e', 182
Lustra, 4, 11, 12, 14, 121–31, 143, 172, 181, 207, 212, 234, 396, 473

Make It New, 285–91, 319, 430
'Marvoil', 175
'Masks', 395
'Meditatio', 121, 123
'Mesmerism', 198
'Les Millwin', 222
'Mr. Housman's Message', 84
'Moeurs Contemporaines', 4, 14, 161, 165, 183, 204–5, 208

'Murder by Capital', 31

'Na Audiart', 47, 175
'Near Perigord', 173, 212, 394, 396
'Nel Biancheggiar', 65
'The New Cake of Soap', 121, 123, 129
'New York', 128, 129, 175, 212, 396
'Night Litany', 63, 64, 71, 114, 198, 211–12
'Nils Lykke', 173
Noh or Accomplishment, 12, 134

'Occidit', 53
'On His Own Face in a Glass', 115, 173
'Ortus', 212

'A Pact', 121, 135, 176, 212
'Papyrus', 121, 129, 403
'Paracelsus in Excelsus', 82, 84
Passages from the Letters of John Butler Yeats (ed. Ezra Pound), 76
Pavannes and Divisions, 15, 142–7, 240, 261, 263, 430, 476
Personae, 5, 7, 20, 24, 26, 36, 40, 41, 43–59, 63, 65, 73, 82, 84, 96, 130, 132, 172, 174, 175, 178, 179, 185, 196, 231, 233, 311, 325, 390, 392, 395, 432, 435
Personae: The Collected Poems of Ezra Pound, 19, 35, 218–28, 473
'Phasellus Ille', 2, 129, 234
'Phyllidula', 123
'Piere Vidal Old', 61, 63, 130, 173
Pisan Cantos, The, 25–6, 27, 359–87, 399, 402, 404, 405–10, 417
'Planh', 65, 114, 175
'Plotinus', 65
'Plunge', 96
'Poem by the Bridge at Ten Shin', 221
Poems 1918–21, 16, 17, 203–8, 214
Polite Essays, 430
'Portrait', 9, 63
'Portrait d'une Femme', 96, 129, 198, 234
'Preference', 212
Profile: An Anthology, 239
Provença, 7, 70–4, 142, 143, 354, 356
'Psyche of Eros', 84

Quia Pauper Amavi, 4, 14, 155, 172, 180, 182, 262
A Quinzaine for This Yule, 5, 60, 84

'The Renaissance', 424, 426
'The Rest', 211, 212
'The Return', 96, 125, 133, 175, 185, 210, 212, 234, 401
'Revolt Against the Crepuscular Spirit in Modern Poetry', 45, 46, 53, 71, 391
Ripostes, 9, 94–8, 133, 172, 173, 175, 179, 180, 181, 196, 234, 390, 396, 401
'The River-Merchant's Wife: A Letter', 111, 221

'Salutation', 99, 129, 212, 213
'Salutation the Second', 100, 123
'Salvationists', 121, 212
'Salve Pontifex', 95, 129
'Scriptor Ignotus', 51, 395
'Seafarer, The', 9, 95, 96, 110, 111, 199, 212, 234, 235, 356, 379
Section: Rock Drill, 27, 435–45, 459
'Seeing Eye, The', 121, 123
Selected Poems (ed. T. S. Eliot), 20, 229–38, 263
'Serious Artist, The', 15, 424, 425
'Sestina: Altaforte', 63, 64–5, 71, 74, 114, 173, 175, 395, 400; read to Poets Club, 97, 390
'Sestina for Ysolt', 173
Social Credit: An Impact, 341
'The Social Order', 129
'Song of The Bowmen of Shu', 108, 111
'A Song of The Degrees', 403
Sonnets and Ballate of Guido Cavalcanti, 86–93, 172, 179, 432
Spirit of Romance, 5, 67–9, 96, 116, 132, 174, 187, 436, 457
'Stark Realism', 144
'A Stray Document', 290
'Study of French Poets', 189
'Sub Mare', 96

'The Teacher's Mission', 422–3
'Temperaments, The', 121, 123

'Tenzone', 99, 100, 134, 212
'Three Cantos', 14, 133, 160, 165, 166, 173, 182, 262
'Threnos', 3, 84
Thrones: 96–109 de los Cantares, 27, 28, 445–64
'To a Friend Writing on Cabaret Dancers', 124
'To Whistler-American', 98
'The Tomb at Akr Çaar', 96, 179
'Tree, The', 231
'Troubadours: Their sorts and conditions', 289

Umbra, 5, 16, 175, 196–9

'Victorian Eclogues', 82
'Villanelle: The Psychological Hour', 212, 398
'A Villonaud: Ballad of the Gibbet', 51, 58
'Villonaud for this Yule', 175
'A Virginal', 197, 234
'Vision, The', 179

'White Stag, The', 48

II. CHARACTERISTICS AND TOPICS

affectation, 7, 35, 43, 54, 58, 81
anti-Semitism, 23, 31, 386, 396, 406, 410, 452
archaisms, fondness for, 5, 48, 49, 58, 167, 176
audience, attitude towards, 16, 132, 135, 144, 149, 176, 194–5, 267–8, 336, 357–8, 439, 442

beauty, 5, 8, 15, 38, 41, 44, 45, 46, 52, 59, 65, 95, 99, 108, 109, 136, 172, 179, 228, 241, 309, 318, 438
bookishness, 8, 13, 63, 84, 173, 214, 258

carelessness, 81, 115, 174, 267, 420
craftsmanship, 8, 115, 141, 255, 374, 393, 400, 428

development, 13, 15, 20, 95–6, 131–6, 171–3, 179–85

erudition, 17, 129, 144, 157, 166, 189, 203, 208, 209, 216, 221, 222, 251, 252; defective erudition, 283, 286; 'not as learned as he seems to be', 319, 339, 432

Fascism, 342, 353–4, 357–8, 406, 452
form, 8, 48, 66, 70, 74, 79, 80, 85, 96, 100, 111, 182, 196, 260, 377, 471

individuality, 44, 55, 58, 125, 196, 392,

393; 'too egotistic and not individual enough', 81
influence, Pound's, 21, 127, 145, 175, 209, 240, 242, 261, 280, 283, 286, 312, 347, 374, 389, 391, 409, 415, 418, 419, 472; 'wide and pernicious influence', 30
influences on Pound, 47, 72, 174, 231, 341; *see also* Whitman; Browning; Yeats
intensity, 48, 52, 66, 109, 125

objectivity, 21, 133, 377, 378, 384
obscurity, 27, 42, 58, 61, 62, 176, 182, 194, 257, 258, 274, 280, 300, 319, 352
originality, 20, 94, 103, 104, 140, 152, 178, 232, 233, 393–4

passion, 63, 73, 100, 127, 185, 397; lack of, 180
persona, use of, 15, 58, 228, 254, 395, 402, 416, 460
personality, 6, 8, 10, 41, 46, 51, 68, 69, 102, 130, 133, 142, 167, 190, 265, 318, 357, 367, 392–3, 399, 400, 402–3, 409; 'we must also forget his disagreeable personality', 373

rhythm, use of, 50, 61, 66, 91, 102, 117, 240, 373

sales, 6, 16, 21

technique, mastery of, 13, 22, 114, 140, 141, 202, 231, 234, 237, 240, 257–8, 263, 423, 427, 429, 431

translations, use of, 12, 13, 14–15, 22, 67, 69, 79, 85, 86–93, 97, 114, 122, 124, 132, 136, 155–64, 166–7, 169–71, 179, 183, 204, 213, 228, 235, 261, 280, 300–8, 320–9, 343, 393, 394

vers libre, use of, 16, 58, 96, 103, 111, 126, 140, 153, 161, 173, 175, 209, 210, 427, 431

III. GENERAL

Abercrombie, Lascelles, 58, 220

Accent, 351

Adams, Brooks, 23

Adams, Henry, 396

Adams, John, 23, 341, 350, 352, 362, 366, 403, 436

Adams, John Quincy, 340, 342, 350

Adams, Leonie, 26

Adelphi, 23, 415

Aeschylus, 230, 287, 404

Agassiz, Louis, 436

Agenda, 388

Aiken, Conrad, 15, 25, 26, 40, 145–8, 150, 171

Alden, R. M., 100–1

Aldington, Richard, 10, 19, 130, 172–3, 390

Allen, Walter, 177

Alvarez, A., 441–3, 467

Ambrose, St, 436

American Literature, 30

American Mercury, 18, 353

Anderson, Sherwood, 355

Antoninus Pius, 436

Antheil, George, 246

Apollinaire, Guillaume, 391

Apollonius of Tyana, 436, 443

Apuleius, 68

Aquinas, St Thomas, 275, 276–7

Archer, William, 141

Aristotle, 230, 243, 269, 276, 333–4, 337, 360, 379, 381, 382, 383

Arlen, Michael, 287

Arnold, Matthew, 369

Athenaeum, 14, 15

Atlantic Monthly, 11, 30, 75, 330

Auden, W. H., 26, 316, 390, 398, 410, 415, 432, 435

Auerbach, Erich, 462

Avicenna, 276

Babbitt, Irving, 243

Bach, J. S., 241, 259, 270, 364, 456

Bagehot, Walter, 430

Bailey, John, 89–92

Balzac, Honoré de, 333

Barker, George, 297–9

Barrett, William, 27, 406

Barrie, Sir James, 16

Baudelaire, Charles, 221, 391, 422

Beardsley, Aubrey, 3

Beddoes, Thomas Lovell, 381, 387

Beethoven, Ludwig van, 212, 376, 404

Belloc, Hilaire, 5

Benda, Julien, 23

Benton, Thomas Hart, 437, 443

Bergson, Henri, 237

Berryman, John, 388–404

Billings, Josh, 444

Binyon, Laurence, 32, 120, 425, 433

Birrell, Augustine, 123

Bishop, John Peale, 207–8, 312

Blackfriars, 428

Blackmur, R. P., 18, 19–20, 22, 227–8, 303–4, 321, 344, 377, 381, 391; *The Double Agent*, 25, 344

Blackstone, Sir William, 437

Blake, William, 128, 152, 153, 230, 234, 424, 431

Blast, 10, 116, 118, 177, 180, 184, 189, 390

Bodenheim, Maxwell, 130, 137–8, 203–6

Bogan, Louise, 26

Boni and Liveright, 15, 19

Book of the Rhymers' Club, 3

The Bookman (London), 5, 6, 54, 60

The Bookman (New York), 8

Book News Monthly, 42
Book Week, 465
Boston Evening Transcript, 75, 124
Bottomley, Gordon, 30, 36, 54
Bottrall, Ronald, 264, 415–21
Bourne, Randolph, 15
Bowen, Catherine Drinker, 462
Bowles, William, 230
Boyle, Kay, 148
Brahms, Johannes, 322
Braithwaite, W. S., 75
Braque, Georges, 260
Brecht, Bertolt, 398
Bridges, Robert, 346
Bridson, D. G., 264–8
Brodzky, Horace, 187
Brooke, Rupert, 5, 58–9
Brooks, Van Wyck, 15, 16, 31, 40, 186–9
Browne, Sir Thomas, 454–5
Browning, Elizabeth Barrett, 185
Browning, Robert, 9, 43, 45, 47, 50, 51, 54, 56, 58, 62, 72, 81, 111, 130, 144, 149, 157, 160, 163, 176, 182, 198, 226, 231, 232, 237, 240, 253, 287, 295, 349, 354, 389, 392, 394, 398, 400, 418, 419, 432; 'Bishop Blougram's Apology', 111; 'Sordello', 157, 160, 163, 216, 231, 253, 295, 319
Bunting, Basil, 386
Burke, Kenneth, 439
Burns, Robert, 90
Bury, J. B., 448
Buss, Kate, 4, 124–5
Butler, H. E., 300
Butler, Samuel, 295
Bynner, Witter, 38
Byron, 44, 230, 357, 419

Cambridge Magazine, 31
Cambridge Review, 5, 8, 58
Campbell, Joseph, 66
Campbell, Thomas, 230
Campion, Thomas, 167
Canby, Henry Seidel, 25
The Cantos of Ezra Pound: Some Testimonials, 21

Carman, Bliss, 3
Carnevali, Emanuel, 148–54
Carruth, Hayden, 472–4
Casement, Sir Roger, 398
Catullus, 90, 166, 176, 209, 234, 283, 289, 322, 326, 327, 402
Caudwell, Christopher, 430
Century, 2
Cézanne, Paul, 259, 298
Chapbook: A Monthly Miscellany, 171
Chapin, K. G., 26
Chapman, George, 400, 412
Chaucer, Geoffrey, 168, 207, 295, 427
Chekhov, Anton, 475–6
Chesterton, G. K., 287–8
Chicago Daily News, 153
Chicago Evening Post, 7, 70, 98
Chicago Tribune, 30, 99
Child, Harold, 9, 94–5
Christie, Agatha, 449
Churchill, Sir Winston, 171
Cicero, 89
Cimabue, 83
Clare, John, 232
Clutton Brock, Arthur, 11
Cocteau, Jean, 224, 252, 263, 424, 437
Coke, Sir Edward, 459, 462
Cole, G. D. H., 82
Coleridge, S. T., 214, 230, 233–4, 345, 346, 402, 414, 429
Collins, Adrian, 160
Collins, John Churton, 105
Colum, Padraic, 431
Colvin, Sir Sidney, 168
Confucius, 250, 333–4, 349, 369, 412–14, 417, 422, 436
Connolly, Cyril, 209
Conquest, Robert, 14
Conrad, Joseph, 6, 7, 139
Copland, Aaron, 18
Corbière, Tristan, 393
Courtney, W. L., 5, 44–5
Cousins, Norman, 406
Coward, Noel, 287
Cowley, Malcolm, 30, 405–11
Cowper, William, 232
Crabbe, George, 144, 153, 232, 424, 425

Craig, Edward Gordon, 131
Crane, Hart, 258, 316, 475
Crane, Stephen, 104, 222
Creeley, Robert, 474
Crevel, René, 387
Criterion, 19, 21, 31, 110, 174, 229, 243, 288, 297, 309, 332
Cronin, G. W., 126
Cubism/Cubists, 99, 119, 226
Cummings, E. E., 25, 27, 248, 386, 409

Daily News, 432
Daily Post (Birmingham), 7
Daily Telegraph, 5, 44
D'Annunzio, Gabriele, 404
Dante, 10, 32, 46, 66, 71, 83, 85, 87–8, 89, 90, 171, 224, 232, 254, 258, 261, 263, 273, 317, 339, 340, 355, 366, 380, 384, 398, 404, 423, 428, 433, 436, 446
Davie, Donald, 28–9, 425–7, 443–4, 445
Davis, Richard Harding, 311
Day Lewis, Cecil, 415
Debussy, Claude, 41, 56, 247, 434
de la Mare, Walter, 185
Del Re, Arundel, 86–8
Dell, Floyd, 7, 30, 70–2, 98–9
Della Robbia, Luca, 118
Descartes, René, 274, 419
Deutsch, Babette, 131–6
Dial, 10, 15, 19, 30, 101, 106, 119, 145, 209, 269, 404, 415
D'Israeli, Isaac, 475
Dobrée, Bonamy, 288–91
Dolmetsch, Arnold, 144, 146, 148
Donne, John, 295, 339, 384, 415, 419, 422
Donoghue, Denis, 32
Doolittle, Hilda (H.D.), 130, 138, 203, 390
Dostoievsky, Fyodor, 148, 424
Doughty, C. M., 166
Douglas, Major C. H., 9, 23, 31, 268, 293, 335, 341, 357, 436
Douglas, Gavin, 295, 425
Dowden, Edward, 5
Dowson, Ernest, 3, 231, 396, 470
Dreiser, Theodore, 142
Drinkwater, John, 185

Dryden, John, 228, 384, 393, 394, 412, 416, 431
Du Bellay, Joachim, 82
Duncan, Ronald, 243–5

Eastman, Max, 15
Eberhart, Richard, 25, 375–87
Eddy, Mrs Mary Baker, 104
Edwards, John Hamilton, 28
Egoist, 10, 13, 137, 171, 177, 285
Eichmann, Adolph, 24
Eliot, George, 423
Eliot, T. S., 4, 5, 12–14, 16, 17, 19, 20, 21, 22, 25, 26, 27, 30, 31, 40, 130, 137, 138, 140, 153, 174, 178, 187, 188, 208, 230, 231, 233, 242, 245, 252, 256, 257, 258, 262, 263, 267, 280–1, 283, 295, 302, 304, 306, 308, 311, 312, 315, 321, 323, 327, 346, 349, 350, 367, 373, 374, 376–7, 380, 381, 385, 386, 387, 389, 390–1, 398, 399, 406, 407, 409, 410, 411, 412, 415, 417, 418, 419, 420, 421, 422, 424, 426, 427, 428, 429, 430, 433, 437, 439, 455, 457, 458, 467, 469, 471, 473; *After Strange Gods*, 40; *Ezra Pound: His Metric and Poetry*, 12, 29, 140–1; *Four Quartets*, 376, 439; *Homage to John Dryden*, 22, 302; *Poems 1909–1925*, 22; *Prufrock and Other Observations*, 4, 177, 395; *The Sacred Wood*, 25; *Selected Essays*, 22; *To Criticize the Critic*, 29; 'The Waste Land', 14, 29, 30, 252, 261, 266, 280, 312, 316, 389, 390–1, 459
Emerson, R. W., 224
Empson, William, 415, 430, 461
Encounter, 19, 300, 351
English Review, 6, 7, 50, 218; tries to cheat Pound, 12
Enright, D. J., 457
Epstein, Sir Jacob, 97
Evans, B. Ifor, 400
Evans, Donald, 239
Evening Standard and St. James's Gazette, 2, 43
Ewart, Gavin, 280
Exile, 18–19, 324

Fabre, J. H., 113
Falck, Colin, 471
Farr, Florence, 39, 97
Faulkner, William, 459
Fenollosa, Ernest, 11, 16, 110, 129, 133, 172, 181, 343, 351, 365, 366, 384, 396, 400, 403, 425
Feuchtwanger, Lion, 25
Figgis, Darrell, 57
Fitts, Dudley, 21, 246–55, 335–6
FitzGerald, Edward, 221, 237, 389
Fitzgerald, F. Scott, 470
Fitzgerald, Robert, 19, 26, 351–3, 359–63
FitzGerald, T. D., 97
Flaubert, Gustave, 11, 198, 217, 423, 436
Flecker, James Elroy, 209
Fletcher, John Gould, 130, 171–4, 187, 229–38
Flint, F. S., 5, 13, 46–7, 63, 84–5, 95–8, 174, 390
Ford, Ford Madox, 5, 7, 11, 12, 15, 19, 21, 31, 153, 174, 210, 218–23, 237, 357, 362, 383, 387, 389–90, 423
Forgue, Guy J., 142
Fortnightly Review, 44
France, Anatole, 434
Freeman, 186
Freewoman, 77
Freud, Sigmund, 329, 339
Frost, Robert, 171, 203, 311, 312, 389, 422
Fuller, Roy, 430–4
Furioso, 26
Future, 13

Gallup, Donald, 18, 30
Galsworthy, John, 6, 7
Garbo, 278–9
Gardner, Erle Stanley, 449
Gaudier-Brzeska, 12, 178, 188, 390
Gautier, Théophile, 193, 391, 422
Geddes, Vergil, 17
George, Henry, 23
Georgian Poetry, 7, 174
Gesell, Silvio, 341
Gilkes, Martin, 30
Gilmer, Walker, 30

Gilson, Etienne, 273–9
Giovanitti, Arturo, 126, 127
Glidden, Carlton, 76
Goethe, J. W. von, 224, 399
Golden Treasury, 237, 465
Golding, Arthur, 261, 295
Goldring, Douglas, 38
Golffing, Francis, 26
Gosse, Edmund, 170, 290
Gould, Joe, 386
Gourmont, Rémy de, 15, 137, 144, 148, 151, 188, 189, 230, 285, 289, 290, 424; Pound's translation of *Physique de l'Amour*, 324
Gower, John, 267
Graham, R. B. Cunningham, 7, 30
Granta, 7
Granville, Charles, 77–80
Graves, Robert, 248, 456
Green, Paul, 26, 406
Greenbaum, Leonard, 246
Greenburg, Clement, 27
Gregor, A. James, 32
Gregory, Horace, 25
Gregory, Lady Isabella Augusta, 30, 39
Grierson, H. J. C., 243
Grigson, Geoffrey, 20, 259–64
Gunn, Thom, 27
Gurdjieff, 110

Hale, W. G., 14, 27, 155–7, 169, 214
Hall, Donald, 28, 457–60
Handel, 322
Hardy, Thomas, 3, 6, 16, 26, 232, 363, 381, 392
Harrison, John R., 32
Harvard Advocate, 40, 391
Hassall, Christopher, 29, 58
Hawthorne, Nathaniel, 423, 458
Hayward, John 433
Heine, Heinrich, 79–80, 85, 129, 176
Hemingway, Ernest, 18, 21, 27, 219, 312, 409, 418, 430, 467
Henderson, A. C., 100, 112
Henley, W. E., 72
Henn, T. R., 243
Heppenstall, Rayner, 23
Herrick, Robert, 232, 422

Hewlett, Maurice, 5, 50, 383
Hillyer, Robert, 26, 406, 407, 411
Hitler, Adolph, 342, 348, 451
Hobson, J. A., 101
Holloway, John, 463–4
Homer, 90, 193, 258, 259, 261, 313, 340, 400, 424
Hopkins, G. M., 297, 298, 346, 378, 384, 415, 433
Horace, 126, 164, 228, 326
Housman, A. E., 209, 232, 422, 465
Hovey, Richard, 387
Howard, Brian, 209–11
Howells, W. D., 188, 311
Hubbard, Elbert, 294
Hudson Review, 475
Hudson, W. H., 6, 7
Hueffer, *see* Ford
Hulme, T. E., 12, 97–8, 241, 313, 367, 390, 471
Hunt, Violet, 38
Hutchins, Robert Maynard, 436

Ibsen, Henrik, 186
Image, Selwyn, 3
Imagi, 371
Imagism/Imagists, 30, 117, 118, 128, 130, 140, 143, 144, 150, 177, 181, 205, 239, 240, 241, 242, 345, 355, 370, 389, 416, 436, 471
Impressionism, 150, 365
Independent, 7
Iriquois, Frank Robert, 252
Isis, 392

James, Henry, 6, 7, 116, 178, 188, 189, 191, 192, 238, 244, 249, 285, 286, 290, 311, 319, 391, 398, 423, 424, 426, 434, 458
Janssens, G. A. M., 353
Jarrell, Randall, 348–50, 438–41
Jeffares, A. N., 30
Jefferson, Thomas, 313, 317, 341, 342, 345, 403, 459
Johnson, Lionel, 3, 4, 231, 232, 423, 470
Johnson, Samuel, 429
Johnston, Mary, 221
Jones, David, 455

Jonson, Ben, 168
Joyce, James, 3, 11, 12, 15, 21, 137, 150, 153, 178, 189, 256, 257, 298, 311, 312, 319, 325, 339, 354, 355, 362, 378, 389, 391, 398, 417, 420, 422, 423, 431, 433, 437, 455, 467; *Chamber Music*, 3; *Dubliners*, 400; *Finnegans Wake*, 354, 401; *Portrait of the Artist as a Young Man*, 4, 420; *Ulysses*, 259, 312, 319, 403, 417, 420, 423
Jubilee, 469
Jung, C. G., 406, 407

Kahn, Gustave, 96, 151
Kant, Immanuel, 313
Keats, John, 47, 112, 399–400, 420
Keble, John, 95
Kenner, Hugh, 14, 28, 415, 416, 419–20, 429, 462, 467
Kenyon Review, 292, 294
Keynes, J. M., 31
Kipling, Rudyard, 16, 74
Kirstein, Lincoln, 246, 353
Knopf, Alfred A., 12, 14
Konody, P. G., 5
Kreymborg, Alfred, 171

Laforgue, Jules, 146, 149, 151, 153, 183, 192, 331, 391, 424
Lancaster, Marie-Jacqueline, 209
Landor, W. S., 144, 168, 199, 230, 291, 295, 389, 419, 425
Lane, John, 3
Larkin, Philip, 27, 444–5
Laughlin, James, 25, 320–9, 338–45
Lawrence, D. H., 4, 11, 38, 185, 245, 325, 423, 428, 433
Lawrence, T. E., 7, 10
Lawrence, W. G., 10, 30
Leavis, F. R., 20, 243–5, 266, 281–4, 291, 303, 307, 415
Left Review, 309
Leibniz, G. W. von, 334
Leibowitz, Herbert, 475–6
Leopardi, Giacomo, 85
Levi, Peter, 469–70
Levy, Professor, 313, 452
Lewis, C. S., 453

Lewis, John, 31
Lewis, Wyndham, 12, 16, 116, 168–9, 178, 189, 237, 311, 367, 390, 424, 425, 431, 433, 437, 455, 458
Liberator, 70
Lindsay, Vachel, 106, 107
Listener, 287, 476
Literary Digest, 6
Little Review, 15, 137, 177, 178, 184, 191, 209, 321
Locke, John, 445
London Magazine, 430, 463
London Mercury, 83, 210
Longfellow, H. W., 60, 76, 346
Lowell, Amy, 171, 203, 390
Lowell, Robert, 25, 26, 31, 32, 474
Ludwig, Richard M., 31
Lyrical Ballads, 240

Mabie, Hamilton Wright, 311
McAlmon, Robert, 148
MacDiarmid, Hugh, 443, 455, 468
Macdonald, Dwight, 406
Mackail, J. W., 14, 163, 169, 171
MacLeish, Archibald, 258, 330–1, 338, 410, 411, 435
Macleod, Fiona, 231
MacNeice, Louis, 335
Maeterlinck, Maurice, 104
Mailer, Norman, 455
Mairet, Philip, 332–4
Mallarmé, Stéphane, 166, 188
Maltz, Albert, 25
Manchester Guardian, 444
Mann, Thomas, 398
Marinetti, F. T., 237
Maritain, Jacques, 436
Marlowe, Christopher, 295
Marmontel, Jean-François, 95
Marsden, Dora, 77
Marsh, Edward, 7, 170, 171
Marston, John, 234
Martial, 234
Martz, Louis L., 364–8
Marvell, Andrew, 384
Masefield, John, 185, 207
Masses, 70
Masses and Mainstream, 32

Masters, Edgar Lee, 118, 127, 171
Mathews, Elkin, 3–5, 6, 11, 40, 41, 121, 123, 389, 390
Matisse, 95
Matthiessen, F. O., 25
Maupassant, Guy de, 11, 423
May, Derwent, 476
Mellon, Paul, 406, 407, 411
Melville, Herman, 458
Mencken, H. L., 8, 16, 18, 73–4, 142, 143, 190
Meredith, George, 3, 81
Michelson, Max, 138
Miller, Arthur, 25
Milton, John, 144, 220, 244, 291, 326, 346, 393, 397, 399, 432, 453; 'Lycidas', 393; *Paradise Lost*, 260, 284, 340
Mitgang, Herbert, 32
Mockel, Albert, 104
Molière, 166, 224
Monet, Claude, 71
Monro, Harold, 12, 174–6
Monroe, Harriet, 9, 10, 18, 24, 30, 41, 58, 100, 105–6, 106–7, 117, 138, 211–14, 215
Montale, Eugenio, 418
Moody, William Vaughn, 75, 105, 106, 107
Moore, George, 7, 16
Moore, Henry, 261
Moore, Marianne, 138, 269–72, 311, 392, 424
Moore, T. Sturge, 5, 37
Moore, Tom, 230
Morison, Mary, 90
Morning Post, 21, 68, 284
Morris, William, 231
Mozart, 313, 361
Muir, Edwin, 16, 194–5, 196–9, 309–10, 347–8
Munson, Gorham B., 24, 293
Mussolini, 24, 31–2, 326, 334, 337, 353, 409, 414, 459, 466

Napoleon, 450
Nation (London), 5, 24, 55, 66
Nation (New York), 7, 10, 22, 67, 100, 292

The New Age, 6, 12, 14, 46, 64, 83, 110, 140, 155, 160, 163, 194, 196, 199
Newbolt, Sir Henry, 5
New Directions Publishing Corp., 25, 32, 320, 350, 359, 388
New English Weekly, 40, 239, 264
New Freewoman, 171
New Masses, 25
New Republic, 15, 17, 142, 336, 351, 359, 405, 412, 447
New Statesman and Nation, 373, 425, 443, 457
New Verse, 259, 280, 283
New Weekly, 30
New York Call Magazine, 126
New York Evening Post Literary Review, 19, 224
New York Herald Tribune Books, 19
New York Times, 26
New York Times Book Review, 256
Nichols, Robert, 14, 27, 165–7, 170–1
Nietzsche, Friedrich, 114, 152, 153, 160, 310
Nixon, Richard, 459
Nolte, William H., 73
Norman, Charles, 25
Noyes, Alfred, 100

An Objectivist's Anthology, 239, 241
Observer, 14, 53, 165, 168, 169, 285, 441
Olson, Charles, 29
Orage, A. R., 11, 14, 23, 110–11, 140–1, 155, 158–9, 163, 199–202, 293, 328, 341, 387
Ossian (Macpherson), 51, 68, 103, 230
Others, 137
Outlook, 108
Ovid, 68, 109, 258, 259, 261, 263, 289, 295, 317, 398, 402
Owen, Wilfred, 415
Oxford Book of Victorian Verse, 9
Oxford Poetry 1914, 82
Oxford Poetry 1952, 476

Paige, D. D., 415
Palestrina, 212
Palgrave, F. T., 465
Partisan Review, 22, 27, 388, 406

Pater, Walter, 103, 163, 170, 171, 237
Perles, Alfred, 344
Petrarch, 427
Pinker, J. B., 123
Pissarro, Camille, 367
Plato, 333
PM, 24
Podhoretz, Norman, 31
Poe, Edgar Allan, 116, 221, 224, 455
Poetry: A Magazine of Verse, 8, 10, 14, 17, 19, 41, 98–9, 100, 112, 137, 138, 148, 155, 180, 211, 212, 213, 312, 317, 369, 391
Poetry and Drama, 95, 174
Poetry Australia, 30
Poetry Review, 58, 84, 174
Pope, Alexander, 228, 234, 295, 394, 400
Porteous, Hugh Gordon, 323
Porter, Katherine Anne, 26
Poussin, Nicholas, 259, 261
Proust, Marcel, 467
Puccini, 354
Punch, 6, 10
Purpose, 347

Quarterly Review of Literature, 375
Quiller-Couch, Sir Arthur, 9, 243, 244
Quinn, John, 3, 12, 15, 30, 76, 139, 320

Rabelais, 455
Radcliffe, Mrs Ann, 230
Raine, Kathleen, 412–14
Rakosi, Carl, 19
Raleigh, Walter, 465
Ramsey, F. P., 31
Randolph of Roanoke, 436, 437
Ransom, John Crowe, 25, 294–6, 472
Rascoe, Burton, 14, 30
Read, Sir Herbert, 5, 29, 467
Reed, John, 106, 107
Reedy's Mirror, 117, 131
Reedy, William Marion, 117–18
Reid, B. L., 30, 139
Rennert, Hugo, 452
Renoir, Pierre, 399
Rexroth, Kenneth, 239, 241
Rhys, Ernest, 5, 7
Richardson, Dorothy, 177

Rice, Philip Blair, 292–3
Rice, Wallace, 101–6
Richards, I. A., 243, 244, 314
Riding, Laura, 415
Rilke, R. M., 384
Rimbaud, Arthur, 149, 151, 339
Robbins, J. A., 128
Robinson, Edwin Arlington, 75, 171
Robson, W. W., 28, 428–9
Rodin, Auguste, 118
Rogers, Samuel, 230
Ronsard, Pierre de, 51, 82,
Roosevelt, F. D., 330, 447, 451
Roosevelt, Theodore, 104
Rosenfeld, Paul, 18, 24, 31, 353–8, 475
Rossetti, Dante Gabriel, 62, 89, 90–1,
    163. 170, 171, 231, 287, 432
Rosten, Norman, 25
Russell, Peter, 462
Rylands, George, 244

Salmagundi, 475
Sandburg, Carl, 18, 39, 112–17, 127,
    138, 153, 171, 213
Santayana, George, 311
Sappho, 289
Sassoon, Siegfried, 185
Saturday Review (London), 20, 30
Saturday Review of Literature, 25, 26,
    227, 294, 335, 406, 407, 410, 411
Schelling, Felix, 225
Schneider, Isidor, 25
Schönberg, Arnold, 247, 271
Schopenhauer, Arthur, 334
Schubert, Franz, 212
Schwartz, Delmore, 22, 25, 311–20,
    345–7, 447–52
Scott-James, R. A., 392
Scribner's, 2
Scrutiny, 243, 302
Seferis, George, 417
Seldes, Gilbert, 30
Selver, Paul, 160
Shakespeare, Olivia, 356
Shakespeare, William, 51, 224, 225,
    229, 252, 295, 317, 318, 355, 381, 399,
    422, 427
Shapiro, Karl, 25, 26, 406

Shaw, Bernard, 5, 16, 220, 225, 287
Shelley, P. B., 143, 153, 212, 230, 240
Sillen, Samuel, 32
Simpson, Louis, 465–8
Sinclair, May, 5, 75, 177–85, 218
Sitwell, Dame Edith, 21, 324, 373
Smart Set, 8, 16, 73, 190
Smith, Harrison, 406
Smith, Lewis Worthington, 30
Snodgrass, W. D., 461–3
Southey, Robert, 230, 291
Soutine, Chaim, 381
Sparrow, John, 280–4
Spectator, 62, 300, 453
Speirs, John, 15, 302–8
Spencer, Theodore, 25, 26
Spender, Stephen, 300–1, 309, 415, 435
Spenser, Edmund, 427, 446
Sprague, Claire, 186
Squire, J. C., 8, 13, 83–4, 465
Steffens, Lincoln, 387
Stein, Gertrude, 438
Stendhal, 11
Stevens, Wallace, 138, 171, 398, 458
Stickney, Trumbull, 387
Stock, Noel, 287, 435–8, 465
Storer, Edward, 97, 390
Strachey, Lytton, 189
Strater, Henry, 216
Strauss, Richard, 56
Stravinsky, Igor, 252, 271
Sullivan, J. P., 14
Sunday, Billy, 149
Swift, Jonathan, 418
Swinburne, Algernon, 3, 81, 95, 105,
    129, 187, 212, 231, 240, 289, 346, 370,
    389, 398, 424, 426
Symbolism/Symbolists, 126, 242, 295,
    355, 390, 465, 473
Symons, Arthur, 3, 127, 465

Tagore, Rabindranath, 106, 107
Tailhade, Laurent, 177, 183
Talleyrand, 450
Tancred, F. W., 97
Tanselle, G. Thomas, 30, 70
Tate, Allen, 21, 22, 25, 295, 345, 415,
    468

Taylor, Bert Lester, 99
Tennyson, Alfred Lord, 50, 111, 170, 171, 251, 377
Thayer, Scofield, 191
Thirlwall, John C., 35
This Quarter, 18
Thomas, Edward, 6, 11, 30, 36–7, 48–53, 54, 61–2, 68–9, 218–19, 392
Thompson, Francis, 47
Thomson, James, 394
Thorp, Willard, 26
Tietjens, Eunice, 24
Tillyard, E. M. W., 244
Times Literary Supplement, 9, 11, 19, 21, 89, 94, 194, 220, 409
Tinckom-Fernandez, W. G., 40
Tocqueville, Alexis de, 440
To-day, 13
Tomlinson, Charles, 28, 422–4
Torrence, Ridgely, 75

Uccello, Paolo, 383
Untermeyer, Jean Starr, 128
Untermeyer, Louis, 15, 128–31, 142–4

Vanity Fair, 16, 18
Verhaeren, Emile, 151
Viereck, Peter, 410
Villon, François, 49, 51, 66, 69, 73, 173, 212, 305, 321, 392, 398
Virgil, 254, 258, 287, 295, 324, 327, 340, 412
Vorticism/Vorticists, 118, 120, 130, 133, 136, 146, 180, 181, 220, 390, 436

Wade, Allan, 30, 39
Wagner, Richard, 212
Wain, John, 453–6
Waley, Arthur, 412, 418
Wallace, Edgar, 449
Wallace, Emily Mitchell, 35
Walpole, Horace, 89
Walpole, Hugh, 21, 31
Walsh, Ernest, 18
Walton, Eda Lou, 25, 256–9
Warren, Robert Penn, 435
Watson, Dr J. S., 191–3
Watts, G. F., 187

Weaver, Harriet Shaw, 4, 77
Webster, John, 381, 384, 391
Weil, Simone, 463
Welby, T. Earle, 20
Wells, H. G., 6, 287
Westminster Gazette, 8, 80
Wheeler, Senator Burton K., 447
Whistler, James McNeil, 71, 117, 120, 144, 152, 187, 188, 357
Whitman, Walt, 5, 42, 45, 51, 56, 59, 62, 69, 72, 81, 96, 103, 104, 116, 126, 135, 148, 151, 176, 212, 224, 232
Whittemore, Reed, 369–71
Wilcox, Ella Wheeler, 2–3
Wilde, Oscar, 102–3, 151, 357
Willey, Basil, 243
Williams, William Carlos, 4, 19, 24, 25, 26, 31, 35–6, 83, 138, 224–7, 239, 241, 311, 336–7, 371, 399, 404, 410, 435, 471, 473; *Autobiography*, 35; *Collected Poems*, 473; *Paterson*, 29, 410; *The Tempers*, 4
Wilson, Edmund, 17, 30, 31, 430
Winters, Yvor, 215, 391, 445–6
Woodberry, George, 311
Woodward, Daniel H., 30
Woolf, Virginia, 430
Wordsworth, William, 144, 168, 230, 232, 281–2, 345, 394, 397, 419, 424, 425, 426, 432, 467
Wright, James and Orville, 457

Yale Review, 27, 438
Yeats, J. B., 12, 76, 139
Yeats, William Butler, 3, 5, 7, 10, 18, 20, 30, 38, 47, 51, 62, 76, 104, 105, 106, 107, 115, 168, 174, 179, 207, 208, 212, 231, 259–60, 308, 310, 311, 318, 327, 343, 362, 364, 365, 373, 383, 389, 392, 394, 395, 398, 399, 409, 412, 418, 419, 421, 422, 429, 431, 433, 456, 465, 467, 469
The Yellow Book, 3, 355
Young, G. M., 285–6

Zaharoff, Sir Basil, 326
Zukofsky, Louis, 19, 21, 239, 241, 249, 298

MUSKINGUM COLLEGE LIBRARY

PS 3531   Bomberger
082
Z647   Ezra Pound

DATE DUE

11 May 79			
AP 17 '83			

GAYLORD   PRINTED IN U.S.A.

THE CRITICAL HERITAGE SERIES

GENERAL EDITOR: B. C. SOUTHAM

Volumes published and forthcoming

JANE AUSTEN	B. C. Southam
BROWNING	Boyd Litzinger and Donald Smalley
BURNS	Donald A. Low
BYRON	Andrew Rutherford
THOMAS CARLYLE	Jules Paul Seigel
CLOUGH	Michael Thorpe
COLERIDGE	J. R. de J. Jackson
CONRAD	Norman Sherry
CRABBE	Arthur Pollard
DEFOE	J. P. W. Rogers
DICKENS	Philip Collins
DRYDEN	James and Helen Kinsley
GEORGE ELIOT	David Carroll
HENRY FIELDING	Ronald Paulson and Thomas Lockwood
FORD MADOX FORD	Frank MacShane
GEORGE GISSING	Pierre Coustillas and Colin Partridge
THOMAS HARDY	R. G. Cox
HAWTHORNE	J. Donald Crowley
IBSEN	Michael Egan
HENRY JAMES	Roger Gard
JOHNSON	James T. Boulton
JAMES JOYCE (in 2 vols)	Robert H. Deming
KEATS	G. M. Matthews
KIPLING	Roger Lancelyn Green
D. H. LAWRENCE	R. P. Draper
MEREDITH	Ioan Williams
MILTON (in 2 vols)	John T. Shawcross
WILLIAM MORRIS	Peter Faulkner

Continued